W9-AAE-510

MUSSOLINI AND HITLER

MUSSOLINI AND HITLER

THE FORGING OF THE FASCIST ALLIANCE

CHRISTIAN GOESCHEL

YALE UNIVERSITY PRESS
NEW HAVEN AND LONDON

For information about this and other Yale University Press publications, please contact:
U.S. Office: sales.press@yale.edu yalebooks.com
Europe Office: sales@yaleup.co.uk yalebooks.co.uk

Set in Adobe Garamond Pro by IDSUK (DataConnection) Ltd
Printed in Great Britain by Gomer Press Ltd, Llandysul, Ceredigion, Wales

Library of Congress Control Number: 2018935621

ISBN 978-0-300-17883-8 (hbk)

A catalogue record for this book is available from the British Library.

10 9 8 7 6 5 4 3 2 1

CONTENTS

	List of Plates	*vi*
	Acknowledgements	*viii*
	Introduction	1
1	In Mussolini's Shadow, 1922–33	17
2	First Date, June 1934	37
3	Second Time Around, September 1937	60
4	Springtime for Hitler, May 1938	93
5	On the Road to War, 1938–9	128
6	Point of No Return, 1939–41	164
7	Into the Abyss, 1941–3	206
8	Endgame, 1943–5	254
	Conclusion	291
	Endnotes	*297*
	Bibliography	*348*
	Index	*370*

PLATES

1. Hitler in front of the Grand Hotel on Canal Grande on his way to his first conversation with Mussolini, June 1934. ullstein bild Dtl. / Getty Images.
2. Hitler and Mussolini in the gardens of Villa Pisani near Venice, June 1934. Picture by Heinrich Hoffmann. Bavarian State Library, Munich / Picture archive.
3. Constructing pillars along Unter den Linden for Mussolini's state visit to Germany, 25–29 September 1937. akg-images.
4. Hitler bidding farewell to Mussolini at Lehrter Bahnhof, 29 September 1937. akg-images.
5. Hitler and King Victor Emmanuel III at Roma-Ostiense station, 3 May 1938. Picture by Heinrich Hoffmann. Bavarian State Library, Munich / Picture archive.
6. Mussolini, Hitler and Galeazzo Ciano at the Villa Borghese during Hitler's state visit to Italy, 6 May 1938. Bavarian State Library, Munich / Picture archive.
7. Assembly at the Mussolini Forum on the occasion of Hitler's visit to Italy, 8 May 1938. akg-images / Luce Institute. Alinari Archives Management, Florence.
8. The Munich conference, 29–30 September 1938. Bavarian State Library, Munich / Picture archive.

9. A meeting between Mussolini and Hitler in the Duce's saloon car at the Brenner Pass, 18 March 1940. Bavarian State Library, Munich / Picture archive.
10. Mussolini and Hitler in Obersalzberg, 19–20 January 1941. Bavarian State Library, Munich / Picture archive.
11. Mussolini piloting Hitler's aeroplane during a visit to the eastern front, 28 August 1941. Bavarian State Library, Munich / Picture archive.
12. Banners and pictures of Hitler and Mussolini on an Italian troop train to the eastern front, *c.* 1942. George (Jürgen) Wittenstein / akg-images.
13. 'Ave Caesar! Morituri te salutant', a satirical picture by the Political Intelligence Department of the Foreign Office dropped over Italy during the Second World War. © British Library Board. All Rights Reserved / Bridgeman Images.
14. Mussolini and Hitler at the station during the Duce's visit to Schloss Klessheim, 7–10 April 1943. Bavarian State Library, Munich / Picture archive.
15. Mussolini and Hitler at Wolf's Lair after Mussolini's liberation, September 1943. ullstein bild Dtl. / Getty Images.
16. Mussolini and Hitler inspecting the bomb-damaged conference hut at Wolf's Lair, 20 July 1944. Bundesarchiv Bild 146-1969-071A-03.
17. The body of Mussolini (second from left) next to Clara Petacci (middle) and other executed Fascists, Piazzale Loreto, Milan, April 1945. akg-images / WHA / World History Archive.

ACKNOWLEDGEMENTS

Without the support of my colleagues, friends and family I would never have finished this book. To start with, I would like to thank the librarians and archivists in Italy (especially at the Biblioteca di storia moderna e contemporanea in Rome, the Biblioteca nazionale centrale in Florence, the library of the Deutsches Historisches Institut in Rome, the library of the European University Institute in Florence, the Istituto storico della resistenza in Toscana in Florence, the Archivio storico del Comune di Firenze, the Archivio storico capitolino in Rome, the Archivio centrale dello Stato in Rome, and the Archivio storico diplomatico del Ministero degli affari esteri in Rome), in Germany (especially at the Bundesarchiv in Koblenz, Freiburg and Berlin, the Politisches Archiv des Auswärtigen Amts in Berlin, the Bayerische Staatsbibliothek and the Institut für Zeitgeschichte in Munich), in Britain (especially at the British Library's Humanities Reading Room 2, the National Archives, the German Historical Institute in London and Manchester University Library) and Australia (especially at the ANU Chifley Library and the splendid Petherick Room of the National Library of Australia in Canberra) for supplying me with the material.

One of the main inspirations for this book was the work of the German historian Wolfgang Schieder, among the first scholars to examine in depth the relationship between Fascist Italy and Nazi Germany. His German monograph on Hitler's views on Mussolini appeared only after the completion of the present book. A paper at a workshop on the history of transnational fascism in May 2010 in London was my first foray into Italian history, and I must thank the audience for their encouragement. Richard Bosworth generously invited me to speak in Australia in September 2010. Ever since, historians of modern Italy have kindly accepted me into their ranks, including Paul Corner, the late Christopher Duggan, John Foot, Paul Ginsborg, Stephen Gundle, David Laven and Lucy Riall. At various stages of my project, conversations with Giulia Albanese, Pam Ballinger, Martin Baumeister, Patrick Bernhard, Ralph Dobler, Bianca Gaudenzi, Lutz Klinkhammer, Andrea Mammone, Benjamin Martin, Alessandra Tarquini and especially with Oliver Janz were extremely instructive.

Conversations with Jan Rüger, Sean Brady, Naoko Shimazu, Serafina Cuomo and my former students at Birkbeck College, where a Leverhulme Early Career Fellowship, although awarded for a different project, gave me the time to read and think, helped me get the project started, as did exchanges with Daniel H. Magilow, Dejan Djokić, Geoff Eley, Brendan Simms, Christopher Wheeler, Giuseppe Laterza and especially Sir Richard Evans. Kilian Bartikowski generously shared some documents with me. In Australia, I benefited enormously from conversations with my students and colleagues at the Australian National University, which funded two research trips to Europe, including Gemma Betros, Frank Bongiorno, Alex Cook, Tom Griffiths, Pat Jalland and Carolyn Strange. Elsewhere in the Antipodes, Andrew Bonnell, Aedeen Cremin, Hubertus Klink and Glenda Sluga supported my work. At Manchester I have enjoyed many fruitful conversations with students and colleagues, including Stuart Jones, Thomas Tunstall Allcock and Frank Mort of Manchester's Political Cultures group, Georg Christ and Alexia Yates.

I owe a particular debt to colleagues and students at the Department of History and Civilization at the European University Institute in Florence who have helped me advance my work, especially Lucy Riall, Pieter Judson, Marla Stone, Regina Grafe, Gabriel Piterberg, Dirk Moses, Gaël Sánchez Cano, Natasha Wheatley, Laura Lee Downs and Tara Zahra. A visiting fellowship at the same institution, hosted by Lucy Riall, in the spring of 2017 during my sabbatical semester at Manchester University gave me time to complete the book. I should also like to thank lecture and seminar audiences at the Australian National University, the Freiburg Institute for Advanced Studies, the University of Queensland, the University of Sydney, the University of Genoa, the University of Cambridge and the University of Western Australia for valuable suggestions.

Several friends and colleagues, including Hatsuki Aishima, Gemma Betros, Andrew Bonnell, Paul Corner, Moritz Föllmer, Sir Ian Kershaw, Molly Loberg, Mark Offord, Naoko Shimazu, Marla Stone and David Laven have commented on draft chapters. Sir Richard Evans's advice and encouragement was particularly generous and helpful. As I was finishing the book, discussions with Hannah Malone, Anirudha Dhanawade, Catherine Brice, Carmen Belmonte, Sir Ian Kershaw and, above all, David Laven, Dejan Djokić and Naoko Shimazu were most helpful. At Yale University Press, Heather McCallum, Rachael Lonsdale and Marika Lysandrou have been brilliant, supportive and patient. Jonathan Wadman ably copy-edited the manuscript, and Douglas Matthews compiled the index. I should also like to acknowledge the anonymous readers for making some valuable suggestions. Particularly special thanks are due to Georgina Capel and her team for their unflinching support of my project.

Earlier versions of some of the material used in chapters 1 and 3 have appeared as my preface to Renzo De Felice, *Mussolini e Hitler: I rapporti segreti, 1922–1933, con documenti inediti*, Bari/Rome, 2013, pp. v–xxiii, and as my article 'Staging Friendship: Mussolini and Hitler in Germany in 1937', *Historical Journal*, 60 (2017), pp. 149–72.

My final thanks go to my friends in Italy – Elena Pezzini, Valentina Pezzini and Marcello Adam, Cristina Rognoni, Giancarlo Raddi and Katja Rosenhagen, Walter Baroni and Gabriella Petti, and Caterina Sinibaldi – for their tremendous kindness and generosity, as well as to my parents, my brother and Francesco Filangeri. Without the support, encouragement and friendship of Lucy Riall, who read the entire manuscript, it is unlikely that I would have ventured into the field of Italian history.

The greatest thanks go to Hatsuki Aishima, who constantly reminds me of the joys of life.

Manchester, June 2017

INTRODUCTION

I

At lunchtime on 20 July 1944, a bomb exploded in Wolf's Lair, Adolf Hitler's headquarters in East Prussia. The Nazi leader escaped with only slight injuries. That afternoon, the first guest to be received by Hitler was Benito Mussolini. In the course of the previous year, the Duce had fallen from power, gone to prison and been liberated by the Nazis. He was at present head of the Italian Social Republic, a formally independent, but effectively German-controlled, state in central and northern Italy. A year earlier, in July 1943, the Allies had landed in Sicily. Now – only a month since the Normandy landings – Nazi victory seemed ever more unlikely.

Both leaders inspected the ruin of the wooden hut in which the bomb had exploded. Even though he had just survived an attempted assassination, Hitler seemed in total control of German politics, and he enjoyed the full support of his Italian friend, ally and ideological fellow traveller. This was the last of the seventeen encounters between the two dictators. They had met more often and with much greater fanfare than any other pair of leading Western statesmen during the inter-war years and the Second World War.[1]

What drew Hitler and Mussolini together? Was it purely the requirements of a critical military alliance? Was it the exceptional ideological affinity between two fascist dictators and the movements they headed, emerging in the aftermath of the First World War and intent on revising the Versailles Treaty and achieving territorial conquest?[2] Or was it friendship, a deep personal rapport based upon parallel biographies? Interpretations of this relationship are to this day overshadowed by its depiction in American popular culture, above all in Charlie Chaplin's *The Great Dictator* (1940), a film which ridicules Mussolini and Hitler as vain, pompous and jealous rivals and pokes fun at bombastic Fascist and Nazi propaganda. There were other contemporary manifestations of this relationship, such as Carson Robison's country-music hits 'Mussolini's Letter to Hitler' and 'Hitler's Reply to Mussolini', released in the US in 1942 when it seemed that the Axis was going to win the war. The lyrics present Mussolini as an idiot and opportunist, if nonetheless useful to Hitler, an image that has endured until now in popular culture and history.

In this book, I shall examine a relationship that at the time and since has been judged decisive in destroying the inter-war Wilsonian order and in causing the Second World War. I will address some of the central interpretative problems involved in studying the personal relationship of political leaders and in considering the role of the dictator in diplomacy. The story of the relationship between Mussolini and Hitler is in part a story of a friendship – albeit one that was fabricated, comprised stresses and inequalities, and which was characterised by a mixture of admiration and envy on both sides. It is also a story that reveals a tension between myth and reality. And it is a story that had profound consequences for European history in the 1930s and 1940s.[3]

This book is not a biography or a study of the 'parallel lives' of the dictators, but an exploration of their relationship, its representation and its overall political significance. Through my focus on the representation of their relationship, I reconsider the power – imagined, constructed and real – of Mussolini and Hitler to shape and run foreign policy. However, I do not subscribe to the traditional interpretation that the dictators' intentions dominated policy. Hitler rarely had to give direct orders within the Nazi political system in which party and state officials were 'working towards the Führer'. Mussolini's position as a dictator was much weaker than Hitler's, as the Duce had to consider the monarchy dominated by the long-serving King Victor Emmanuel III as well as the Vatican and the 'infallible' pope, even though both institutions broadly supported the Fascist regime for much of its existence.[4]

At first glance, the two leaders shared many similarities. Both came from relatively humble and provincial backgrounds. Both were charismatic. Both rose to power using a blend of political violence and seemingly legal methods to dominate their nations in an atmosphere that resembled a civil war. Both constantly emphasised their masculinity and militarism.[5] Both promised to unite the masses and turn their nations into world powers. Both also tried, to varying degrees, to maintain a balance between repression and the manufacturing of a consensus of the masses. Both were ruthless and determined to establish, through war and conquest, what they saw as a New Order. Both pursued domestic and foreign policies geared towards war, with fundamentally different results, given the sharply divergent economic performances of their nations and their distinct political cultures. And yet their relationship was not only fraught with tensions, some ideological contradictions and personal rivalry, but also shaped by the very different national contexts in which both men operated. Hitler had a much more explicitly focused ideology, centring on anti-Semitism and the conquest of living space in eastern Europe, than Mussolini did.[6] It is clear that for Hitler and the Nazis anti-Semitism was central and led to the Holocaust, while in Italy domestic racism that built upon racial exclusion practised in Italy's colonies only became more pronounced as Fascist–Nazi relations solidified in the mid- to late 1930s.

At the same time, theirs was also an unlikely relationship, which disguised the fact that both men were friendless and mistrustful. Mussolini posed as a family man, while Hitler stylised himself as someone completely devoted to the German nation. Both leaders had fought on opposite sides in the Great War, which Germany had lost. Italy, at least officially, had won the war, but there was dissatisfaction about its alleged 'mutilated victory' (*vittoria mutilata*): the Allies agreed to the handover of some, not all, of the territories Italy had been promised when it had entered the war on the Allied side after its exit from the Triple Alliance with Germany and Austria-Hungary. In both Italy and Germany, powerful national stereotypes loomed large against the other nation, amplified by the Italian–German antagonism in the Great War which prompted many Germans to see Italians as traitors.

The story of Mussolini and Hitler is best understood as an instrumental union and politically constructed relationship rather than an ideologically inevitable pact or real friendship, although there was undoubtedly some ideological affinity, such as the quest for the New Order, the belief in political violence and the transformative quality of war, and disdain for liberal democracy. For both leaders and their regimes, the relationship was functional and concerned the enhancement of their own power – an insight that is by no means antithetical to the idea that there were ideological parallels. At a time when the interpretation of the Second World War is sometimes skewed towards eastern Europe's 'bloodlands' – an interpretation that potentially erases crucial differences between Stalin's and Hitler's regimes – this book should serve as a reminder that, as a fatal result of the Italo-German entanglement, Italy became a theatre of war in 1943, and experienced what some have called a civil war.[7]

Mussolini's dictatorship was not a comedy show run by a bumbling buffoon. Rather, he and his regime served, in the 1920s and early 1930s, as a strategic model for the rise of Hitler and Nazism, as Wolfgang Schieder has suggested. Italy was at war almost continuously at least from the 1935 invasion of Ethiopia until the end of the Second World War in 1945 and made full use of a repertory of violence, including extremely brutal warfare in the Balkans and Africa. Another historian has even suggested that Fascist practices of racism in Italy's African colonies had a profound influence on the Nazis' brutal racial order in eastern Europe during the Second World War. While this interpretation reinforces the need to explore Fascist–Nazi entanglements in detail, it also runs the risk of omitting the wider context of European imperialism more generally and its role in shaping the unprecedented brutality and scale of the Nazi war of racial conquest and extermination.[8]

Initially, it was Hitler who sought out Mussolini, not the other way around, because the Duce was the original driving force behind the attempt to reshape inter-war politics and diplomacy. Hitler saw Mussolini as a strong, steely and determined leader who had rescued Italy and its purportedly weak and degenerate people from the left and transformed it into a powerful dictatorship. This idealistic view was strongly influenced by the Fascist cult of Mussolini.[9] After Hitler's appointment as Reich chancellor on 30 January 1933, Italo-German relations remained tense. This was not least because Hitler wanted to extend his control over Austria, the sovereignty of which was guaranteed by Fascist Italy. But the relationship between the two leaders soon changed dramatically. Hitler's rapid consolidation of the Third Reich and a series of stunning foreign policy successes, most notably the remilitarisation of the Rhineland in March 1936, elevated him to the position of the doyen of European fascism and demoted Mussolini to the second rank. In the wake of Italy's occupation of Ethiopia, the subsequent League of Nations sanctions against Italy, and the Spanish Civil War, the politics of Italy and Germany became increasingly entangled with each other. For Mussolini, who insisted, like his Liberal predecessors, that Italy must be a great power in Europe, an alliance with the now more powerful Germany was a way to enhance his country's prestige and a strategy to underwrite the Fascist project to transform Italy into a totalitarian nation.[10] The stronger Hitler became, the more Mussolini, an intensely vain man, felt flattered by his admiration.[11] Overall, Mussolini's goal was to establish Italy, a geopolitically weak nation, as the dominating power in the Mediterranean and to conquer living space (*spazio vitale*). Mussolini's proclamation of the Rome–Berlin Axis in November 1936 signalled this change, although the Duce, seemingly just as concerned with Italy's prestige as with an ideologically justified and desirable bond with the Third Reich, tried to maintain, until the late 1930s, that Italy was the 'determining weight' (*peso determinante*) between France and Britain on the one hand and Germany on the other.

An alliance with Mussolini's Italy and with Britain had been Hitler's goal since the early 1920s, as he hoped that it would weaken the French arch-enemy. Unlike Mussolini, who behaved like an elder statesman and wanted to retain his diplomatic flexibility, Hitler was much keener on such an alliance, but his requests fell on deaf ears in Italy until the crucial turning points of the Ethiopian war and the Spanish Civil War. Beginning with Mussolini's visit to Germany in 1937, a powerful performance of unity and friendship in Italian and German propaganda reinforced the Mussolini–Hitler relationship as the strongest emblem of the nascent Italian–German alliance.

Many commentators have written off this relationship as a failure from the outset, due to mutual suspicion, the readiness of the leaders, their advisers and the wider population to entertain national stereotypes, the lack of wartime strategic coordination and Italy's disastrous military performance in the Second World War. Yet Italo-German political, economic and cultural networks intensified from the late 1930s. The notion that the dictators' friendship was mirrored by their nations soon became such a successful performance that it made many domestic and international audiences, and the leaders themselves, believe that the bonds between Italy and Germany, and the idea of a New Order based on conquest and subjugation, were far more solid than in reality they were.[12]

In this book, the Mussolini–Hitler relationship stands as a potent example of how performance and representation, both central features of the exercise of Fascist and Nazi politics, can create a political momentum – a broader question also relevant to other historical contexts. In particular, I take seriously the Fascist–Nazi displays of unity and friendship, made manifest in meetings, correspondence and other actions, which took on such a direct political significance. The purpose of the Duce's 1937 visit to Germany and of Hitler's triumphant visit to Italy in 1938 was to create just such a display of unity and friendship; this would be an expression of the Fascist and Nazi quest for a New Order in Europe that would replace the post-1919 liberal-internationalist order represented by the League of Nations. Yet tensions behind the scenes always accompanied the powerful displays of propaganda. It was no coincidence that a formal military alliance, the Pact of Steel, was only signed in May 1939, and that Italy did not enter the Second World War on Germany's side until June 1940. After Italian military failures dashed Mussolini's hopes for a 'parallel war' in the Mediterranean, dependence on Hitler increasingly restricted the Duce's room for manoeuvre until his fall from power in July 1943, followed by the disastrous defeats of both countries and the deaths of both leaders in April 1945. Nevertheless, the potent performances of unity, albeit toned down after 1940, usually succeeded in obscuring tensions. In this way, the meetings of Mussolini and Hitler were more than 'just' propaganda shows. Instead, I argue, drawing upon the cultural sociologist Jeffrey C. Alexander's concept of 'social performance', that the displays of friendship created a powerful political dynamic which had a direct impact on European politics. The perception of a purportedly deep ideological affinity between Mussolini and Hitler as one that would reshape the world order determined their relations and international reactions. Thus, while there were some considerable ideological differences between the two regimes and their leaders, many contemporaries, in Italy and Germany but also abroad, regarded this relationship as a menacing one as they believed it was held together by a common ideology.[13]

Against this background, my study of the Mussolini–Hitler relationship, placed in the wider context of Italo-German relations and diplomatic culture, has two principal aims. First, I contend that the history of the alliance between Fascist Italy and Nazi Germany was much more complex than has been suggested in recent work arguing that the alliance was more or less motivated by a shared ideology and successful cooperation.[14] Contingency, strategic tensions and national stereotypes shaped this relationship throughout its existence. A strange mix of reciprocity and hostility, of ambivalence and adoration, characterised both the personal relationship between Mussolini and Hitler and the one between Fascist Italy and Nazi Germany.

Second, I argue that we cannot begin to understand what fascism was unless we study the political relationship of the two principal fascist statesmen in its wider context. The history of the relationship between Mussolini and Hitler helps to reveal the mass of inner contradictions that existed within fascism.[15] Rather than pursuing a theoretical project along the lines of the theories of scholars such as Roger Griffin and Roger Eatwell concerning the 'fascist minimum' or a 'consensus in fascist studies', which would risk distorting the complexities, ambiguities and tensions within the archetypal fascist bond between Mussolini and Hitler, I shall take a different approach.[16]

Inspired by historians such as Naoko Shimazu and Johannes Paulmann, whose work has focused on the rituals, ceremonies, emotions, gestures and other socio-cultural aspects of diplomacy that help to effect political outcomes, I approach the Mussolini–Hitler relationship through the dialectics of national interests, emotions and ideology. Itineraries, correspondence and seemingly trivial aspects of politics, such as dress codes, salutations and meeting venues, matter for our understanding of the Mussolini–Hitler relationship. In this way, the broader significance of this bond will become clear.[17]

Mussolini and Hitler's relationship was a prototype of fascist diplomacy. This term might strike the reader at first glance as an oxymoron: here were two leaders who tried to step outside formal diplomacy and establish their own fascist networks of international political negotiation and representation. But by taking cues from recent work on the cultural history of diplomacy the significance of the representational aspects of the Mussolini–Hitler relationship becomes clear. I depart from the work of historians such as David Reynolds who have recently explored face-to-face meetings of other twentieth-century politicians, focusing heavily on the political decision-making processes at such summits, and instead emphasise, as far as the sources permit, the representational dimensions of these meetings that were crucial instruments of Fascist and Nazi rule and soon became politically significant.[18]

While the dictators were served, to varying degrees, by expert diplomats throughout, Mussolini and Hitler's relationship was based on a different idea and practice of diplomacy in which the dictators took executive decisions, often without consulting diplomatic experts – a style of policymaking that may ring some bells for readers today. This non-bureaucratic and non-expert conduct of diplomacy developed a dangerous dynamism and brought Europe to war in 1939. Hitler and Mussolini's style of diplomacy, which relied heavily on publicly staged personal meetings and mingling with the crowds, reflected the regimes' determination to shake up the Versailles settlement and replace it with a New Order. Outside Italy, in the 1920s southern Latin Europe saw the emergence of anti-Communist dictatorships in Spain and Portugal, and it is not a coincidence that other leaders on the European far right, such as the Portuguese and Spanish dictators António de Oliveira Salazar and Francisco Franco, also relied heavily on face-to-face meetings.[19] The personal coming together of leaders was, of course, not an entirely new style of diplomatic practice. A protocol for state visits had gradually emerged over centuries and had been further refined over the course of the long nineteenth century, but the point of them was still very much representation, not the conduct of substantive political debate.[20]

The meetings between Mussolini and Hitler were robust projections of an aggressive challenge to the Wilsonian post-war order. The Fascist and Nazi regimes defied lurking tensions to promote a powerful image of unity, a unity symbolised by the dictatorial friends meeting amidst their peoples – in marked contrast to Western statesmen, who, according to Fascist and Nazi propaganda, preferred secret alliances, furtive negotiations and quiet diplomacy – a way of conducting international relations that, many believed at the time, had helped cause the First World War.[21] Although in reality hardly any significant strategic or political decisions were taken at the meetings, the Fascist and Nazi regimes, together with their diplomatic staffs, staged them as bellicose floutings of the purportedly rational political culture of liberal internationalism that had supposedly dominated the 1920s (and which has recently received renewed scholarly attention).[22]

Mussolini and Hitler increasingly seemed to take back control of diplomacy, at least in public, posing at face-to-face meetings staged by the regimes' propaganda machines and amplified by mass media. The style of the meetings, particularly in the early stages, was characterised by a mix of traditional forms of diplomacy with new forms of representation, negotiation and performance that included the masses as key participants. Four crucial characteristics of this fascist pageantry stand out.

First are the political ramifications of the emotive politics of the Mussolini–Hitler relationship, as well as the various strategies in which German and Italian officials, journalists, politicians and, of course, the leaders themselves constructed and represented their purported friendship. Their gestures of friendship, such as greetings, the awarding of medals and the writing of friendly letters, were part of this spectacular construction, and depicted by their propaganda apparatuses from the late 1930s onwards as emblematic of the friendship of the German and Italian peoples. The image of the camaraderie between the two ex-corporals who had risen from humble origins to the top of government was above all a Fascist and Nazi strategy to appeal to the masses and make the Italo-German alliance appear distinct from the Franco-British coalition, which was made out to be held together by the machinations of secretive and elitist diplomats. The Fascist and Nazi representation and construction of the Mussolini–Hitler relationship as a friendship provided a personal, emotive form of diplomacy that challenged the supposedly rational order established at the Paris Peace Conference. Yet such a reading of the post-1919 order was a simplification for propagandistic effect: big personalities and personal relations had also shaped the post-war era, above all the Big Four at the Paris Peace Conference: the British prime minister David Lloyd George, the French prime minister Georges Clemenceau, the US president Woodrow Wilson and the Italian prime minister Vittorio Orlando.[23]

Italy and Germany had strong connections with other states, and an Italo-German alliance was by no means inevitable. Therefore, Italian and German propaganda projected the strong ties of a dictatorial friendship that extended across the Italian and German peoples. These stagings altered over time in terms of their size and intensity, reflecting the changing relations between Italy and Germany. A crucial aspect of the Mussolini–Hitler meetings was that both dictators believed that they were making history, a message reinforced by their propaganda.

Second, Mussolini and Hitler posed as friends united by a common ideology and the shared goal of challenging the purported hegemony of the 'plutocratic democracies', Britain and France – countries which, Mussolini believed, prevented Italy's territorial expansion. But Nazi and Fascist commentators did not offer a detailed explanation of the common ideology because ideological parallels remained largely superficial, although both regimes were united by the desire to conquer territories and smash the Wilsonian order. Their attempt to redraw the rules of modern diplomacy in an age of mass politics and propaganda was a symbolic reflection of their aggressive and bellicose nature. While there was a gradual shift towards personal meetings among other leaders – especially Churchill and Roosevelt, who soon became the principal rival pair of statesmen – the Mussolini–Hitler alliance was not only the chief alternative to the 'special relationship' of Britain and the United States but arguably also pioneered this kind of leaderly relationship as an expression of a joint geopolitical enterprise and as an extension of each regime's construction of leadership cults.[24] A new culture of face-to-face meetings of assertive fascist leaders who, reflecting their allegedly omnipotent power, could dispense with traditional diplomacy was supposed to replace the culture of inter-war diplomacy, above all the internationalism of the post-1919 period, manifested by the League of Nations and similarly despised by Hitler and Mussolini. In this way, the Mussolini–Hitler meetings symbolised the attempt of the two principal fascist regimes to cooperate with one another in order to create a New Order in Europe. This cooperation was of far greater political significance than that of other, more minor European fascist movements or institutions that have recently come under renewed historiographical scrutiny. While Italy's war was hardly successful, it seemed to many at the time that the Axis might create a New Order – until 1942/3 when the Allies clearly achieved a position of superiority. Yet, despite the apparent cooperation between Italy and Germany, the shape of the New Order remained contested as the two regimes continued to jockey for dominance and influence.[25]

This was a relationship between dictators based on a broadly similar ideology of territorial conquest, uniting the masses and, in contrast to the Soviet dictator Joseph Stalin, appealing to the old elites. Throughout its existence, it was a relationship that reflected differing strategic approaches. Indeed, it is difficult, though not impossible, to unpick the nature of the relationship between Mussolini and Hitler, since both leaders, especially the Duce, were inclined to change their opinion of the other depending on circumstances.

Third, this insight invites a consideration of the significance of personal factors in the making and maintaining of transnational associations. Except for the (often tense) relations between Churchill and Roosevelt that emerged as a liberal-democratic counterfoil to the already established rapport between Mussolini and Hitler, no other relationship between two political leaders was as politically significant as the dictatorial pact of Mussolini and Hitler in Europe in the first half of the twentieth century.[26]

Fourth, I will explore the Fascist and Nazi regimes' spectacular construction of the Mussolini–Hitler relationship. An important question in this regard is who was making the decisions about how the relationship should be constructed. Certainly the dictators, who by no means always saw eye to eye and, significantly, kept changing their views of what the relationship was and should be, made choices in this regard; but so did their staffs. Their relationship relied heavily on show and the representation of domestic and international power, above all on the ceremonies and rituals performed during their seventeen meetings. It was largely through propaganda and ritual that the relationship became known to the peoples of Italy and Germany and an international audience, and it is also how it was remembered after the Second World War. Thus, in this book I examine the organisation of the seventeen meetings and explore how the staging of these events changed over time. For example, after a string of Italian military setbacks in 1940/1, Germany had to provide Italy with military assistance. Reflecting this changing hierarchy, Hitler travelled to Italy only twice during the war, while Mussolini and his entourage travelled to Germany for almost all of the remaining meetings, including those at Hitler's East Prussian headquarters.

Beyond the levels of performance and high politics, I also look at political and popular responses to these meetings. Powerful propaganda images showing Mussolini and Hitler mingling with the people seem to suggest that there was popular support for the alliance amongst the vast majority of Italians and Germans, at least until the outbreak of the Second World War. Both regimes relied heavily on the participation of the masses in these spectacles as expressions of a common will of the nations, united behind their leaders.[27] Fascist and Nazi propaganda staged some of the dictators' meetings as symbols of the affective bonds of the dictators as well as the

Italian and German peoples who had fought each other in the First World War. In reality, the images of enthusiastic masses celebrating their leaders were crafted by both regimes using coercion and terror, but also some degree of bribery, for instance by giving people a day off to participate in the spectacles.[28] In this respect, the book closely analyses the tension between the propagandistic depictions of consensus for the Italo-German alliance and the more complex reality of prevailing and strengthening national stereotypes, which placed a heavy burden on the Mussolini–Hitler relationship.[29] Despite all the spectacle, which transformed the relationship between Mussolini and Hitler into a highly politically effective self-perpetuating myth for local and global audiences alike, it was riven throughout its existence by misunderstandings, some ridiculous scenes and mounting tension.

II

Surprisingly, no serious historian has fully investigated the relationship between Mussolini and Hitler, despite a recent upsurge in research on other aspects of the Italian–German alliance and a spate of new work on the two dictators themselves.[30] A milestone in the interpretation of Mussolini and Hitler's relationship was the 1962 study of their 'brutal friendship' by F.W. Deakin, who highlighted the centrality of this relationship in determining the political and military decisions of the German and Italian regimes during the war. Deakin's study was based on original Italian and German documents captured by the Allies, but, reflecting his interest in military history, the focus was on the final period of the war, from 1943 until 1945, so his coverage of the crucial build-up of the Mussolini–Hitler relationship was sparse.[31] Challenging the notion that the Axis was an outright failure, a rich and diverse literature, written under the impact of transnational history, has recently begun to emerge, emphasising that Italo-German political, economic and cultural networks intensified from the late 1930s and created a strong bilateral relationship between the two fascist dictatorships.[32]

Some significant historiographical and political issues have held back scholars since Deakin from exploring this relationship, as the principal focus of historians shifted from political and diplomatic history to social history in the 1970s and then to cultural history in the 1990s. Above all, since the 1990s and the emergence of the Holocaust as the focal point of public memories of the Third Reich, some have argued that Nazi Germany was a unique racial state held together by Hitler's charismatic rule, which cannot be usefully compared with other dictatorships, including Fascist Italy or the Soviet Union under Stalin.[33]

If many historians of Nazi Germany are generally reluctant to study the Third Reich in a broader European context, their counterparts working on Fascist Italy are even less enthusiastic about comparing other dictatorships with the Fascist *ventennio*. One reason is that a significant strand of public memory of Fascism in Italy is that Mussolini's rule was a relatively benign dictatorship, especially when compared with the brutality of the Third Reich. Although long dismissed by many Italian historians, this problematic yet characteristic view still generally holds sway among the general public in Italy. It was first articulated at the end of the war by Italian political and intellectual elites in order to distance Italy from any association with the Third Reich. Renzo De Felice, author of the most exhaustive biography of the Duce and perhaps post-war Italy's most controversial historian, also sharply rejected any meaningful parallels between Mussolini's Italy and Hitler's Germany. De Felice argued that Nazi Germany was a racial dictatorship, responsible for the Holocaust; Fascist Italy was not. In so doing, De Felice ignored or severely diminished the extent of Italian atrocities in the Balkans and Africa.[34]

Closely connected to the interpretation of Fascist Italy as a relatively 'benign' regime is the stereotype of the 'good Italian' versus the 'evil German'. After Mussolini's fall from power, as Filippo Focardi has demonstrated, this concept became part of Italian diplomatic and official politcal strategy to dissociate Italy from Nazi Germany and to deny Italy's culpability for the war; this not least because of the continual presence of political elites in Italy who had served the Fascist regime. The victorious allies also fostered such views. This was in part because the British and the Americans wanted to keep Italy out of the hands of the Communists, but also because the Soviet Union wanted to give legitimacy to the Italian Communist Party within the Italian electoral system. The common denominator of this version of history was that the Axis between Italy and Germany had been the product of machinations between a power-hungry Mussolini and the bully Hitler. Thus, the overwhelming majority of the Italians supposedly opposed – even if they did not resist – Fascism, particularly between 1943 and 1945, in sharp contrast to the masses of Germans who blindly followed Hitler until 1945.[35] Such views, while extremely partisan, colour a good deal of what has been written in Italy on Fascist–Nazi relations, although many historians, including Davide Rodogno, have pointed out that Fascist Italy also fought an extremely brutal and ruthless war, and often, as with the use of poison gas in Africa, with a genocidal dimension – but never to the same extent as the Germans.[36]

III

Telling the history of the Mussolini–Hitler relationship only on the basis of Italian and German sources is like looking at a valley from one side only. For the Mussolini–Hitler relationship, the most powerful symbol of Italo-German relations, resulted from the tensions of inter-war foreign policy, not simply from ideological parallels between Fascism and Nazism. I consider diplomatic and media sources from the Western great powers – that is, France, Britain and the US – to help situate my story of the relationship between Mussolini and Hitler within a broader international context.[37]

Reflecting the political, social and cultural perspectives I adopt in this book, I use a wide range of sources. The recent completion of the relevant official edition of Italian diplomatic documents from the Fascist period has considerably facilitated my work, although I am aware of the potential political biases in the compilation of these and other source editions, including Mussolini's *Opera Omnia*, edited after 1945 by the ex-Fascist Susmel brothers.[38] This is why I have also spent considerable time in the archives of the German, British and Italian governments and foreign ministries to fill in gaps, supplementing the official editions with records of embassies in Rome and Berlin, diplomats' memoirs and other material. I equally consider sources that in terms of my focus have not been fully exploited so far, such as documents from the propaganda ministries, pamphlets, photographs and the recently published diaries of Reich Propaganda Minister Joseph Goebbels, which give a unique perspective on Hitler's changing attitudes towards Mussolini.[39] In the absence of a satisfactory critical edition of the diaries of Galeazzo Ciano, Mussolini's son-in-law and foreign minister from 1936 until 1943, I have drawn on the Italian version that comes closest to the original diaries.[40] I have also investigated the correspondence between Mussolini and Hitler, which, although a crucial part of the display of unity and friendship, has never been published together and in full, reflecting perhaps the indifference of diplomatic historians towards the seemingly trivial personal aspects of the men's relationship. For example, birthday telegrams from one leader to the other and Hitler's regular telegrams to Mussolini on the anniversary of the March on Rome were not irrelevant jottings but highly symbolic exchanges that demonstrate how much both leaders took care to make a visible display of valuing each other.

This book tells the story of the Mussolini–Hitler relationship from its beginnings in the aftermath of the First World War until the downfall and death of both leaders in 1945. Strategic reasons led Mussolini to offer tactical support to Hitler after the Nazi party's 1930 breakthrough in the Reichstag elections. Once in power, Hitler had long been craving a meeting with the Duce and flew to Venice in 1934 on his first journey abroad as chancellor. Tensions rankled between both countries, not least with regard to Nazi claims over Austria, the independence of which was supported by Italy.

In the context of the Ethiopian crisis of 1935 and 1936 and the Spanish Civil War, the Mussolini–Hitler relationship grew stronger. Despite the Duce's proclamation of the Axis in November 1936 as a rival front to the alleged hegemony of France and Britain, neither Italy nor Germany was fully invested in the relationship; this raises questions regarding the centrality of ideology in binding both countries together. Mussolini's visit to Germany in September 1937 and Hitler's visit to Italy in 1938 were strong displays of unity and friendship, yet diplomatic tensions were lurking behind the scenes. In the months preceding the outbreak of the Second World War, the Mussolini–Hitler relationship was put to the test. At the Munich conference of 1938, the two men for the first time presented themselves as the dictatorial couple who were successfully challenging the European order. Nevertheless, and to Hitler's fury, Mussolini and the Italian political elite refused to enter the war on Germany's side in September 1939. Soon, Germany had to bail out Italy in the Balkans and north Africa. The Mussolini–Hitler meetings became routine to keep the performance of Axis unity and friendship going. As Italy became more and more dependent on Germany, both Italian political elites and ordinary people began to question Mussolini's authority. Indeed, in July 1943, after a string of military defeats, a coalition of Fascists and national conservatives removed him from power. In the Duce's wake, Italo-German relations deteriorated dramatically and led to the German occupation of the north and centre of the peninsula.

It was the relationship between the two dictators, operating on interpersonal, popular and international levels, that was instrumental in forging the fateful Fascist–Nazi alliance during the Second World War. The entanglements and exchanges between Fascist Italy and Nazi Germany changed the course of twentieth-century European history. The two men's alliance led to unprecedented destruction and total warfare. The extraordinary means by which that relationship emerged, operated and eventually collapsed is the subject of the pages that follow.

1

IN MUSSOLINI'S SHADOW
1922–33

I

After the German revolution of November 1918 and the establishment of the Weimar Republic, Munich had been a hotbed of political extremism. Here, in the early 1920s, Hitler and the Nazis, a small fringe amongst many on the far right, wanted to conquer power in Germany. Their aim was to cleanse Germany of the Jews and create 'living space' in eastern Europe. In order to increase their international and domestic reputation, the Nazis put out their feelers to the Italian Fascists, formally established in March 1919 by Mussolini as a national movement that was determined to avenge Italy's alleged *vittoria mutilata* in the First World War and to turn Italy into a great power. It is noteworthy that the initiative came from the Nazis, not from the Fascists, highlighting the Nazis' obscurity and the fact that the Italian Fascists were the world's first fascist group. In September 1922, as Mussolini was preparing to reach power, Hitler sent Kurt Lüdecke, a shady character, to meet the Fascist leader in Milan. Mussolini wanted to cultivate good relations with the European right more generally in order to boost the influence of Italy, and thus received Lüdecke, who had a letter of recommendation from Hitler's most famous ally, General Erich Ludendorff, considered a war hero in Germany.[1] It was then that Mussolini probably heard Hitler's name for the first time. Mussolini had visited Germany in March 1922, as he reckoned that Germany would soon emerge again as a great European power, but Hitler had been far too obscure then for him. Instead, Mussolini cultivated good relations with a range of more politically promising groups and factions, especially the German Army and the far-right *Stahlhelm*, a paramilitary veterans' association. Given Mussolini's prominence as a rising star in Italian politics, leading politicians, including the liberal German foreign minister Walther Rathenau, the leader of the national liberal DVP Gustav Stresemann, and even Chancellor Joseph Wirth of the Catholic Centre Party, received him.[2]

After taking office as Italian prime minister in late October 1922 in the wake of the Fascist March on Rome, Mussolini, also in charge of the Foreign Ministry, no longer received Lüdecke because this would have undermined official relations with the German government, although the German Foreign Ministry had dismissed Lüdecke as an insignificant figure in an exchange with the Bavarian authorities, who were keeping an eye on the nascent Nazi party. Significantly, contrary to the Fascist myth, the demonstration of Fascist strength during the March on Rome alone did not bring Mussolini into power. Rather, it was King Victor Emmanuel III who appointed Mussolini. The combination of Fascist violence with a seemingly orderly and constitutional transfer of power was noteworthy. Mussolini could rightly claim the title of Europe's first fascist head of government, and it would be some time until he learnt more about the Nazi leader.[3]

It is worth considering Hitler's views of the nascent Fascist government in Italy. A few days after Mussolini's appointment, Hitler told a German right-wing activist: 'One calls us German fascists. I do not want to examine to what extent this comparison is right. But we have in common with the fascists the uncompromising love for the fatherland, the will to rip the working class from the claws of the International and the fresh, comradely frontline spirit.'[4]

Hitler here tried to legitimise and publicise the Nazis by pointing to the apparent political success of the Italian Fascists, who had been gaining notoriety amongst some and admiration amongst others throughout Europe for their brutal violence against the Italian left. Hitler's jumping on the Fascist bandwagon was remarkable, since prejudices against the former enemy from the Great War were common in Germany. There was a widespread view of Italians as unreliable, treacherous and undisciplined. Thus, Hitler avoided any direct association with Italy which may have put off potential Nazi supporters. He implied that the Nazis, a German ultra-nationalist group, were not mere copycats of the Italian Fascists. Rather than simply a similar ideology, it was strategic considerations that prompted Hitler to point to the Italian Fascists and liken himself to Mussolini. For Hitler, the cultivation of links to Mussolini's Italy was a means to legitimise and promote the Nazis in Germany, while for Mussolini, contacts with Hitler and the Nazis were a way to assert his role as doyen of European fascism and extend Italy's power.[5]

On many other occasions, the Nazi leader articulated his adoration for the Duce. But Hitler was not the only far-right German politician making these references to Mussolini.[6] After the March on Rome, Bavarian newspapers used the new political terminology introduced by the Italian Fascists. They ran reports on 'the Bavarian Fascists' and their leader Hitler, 'the German Mussolini'.[7] Significantly, not only the German far right but also British diplomats and newspapers soon saw Hitler as the 'German Mussolini'. Dismissing such references as superficial misses the point, as they reflected the widespread appeal of Mussolini's nascent regime for the German right. Here seemed to be an ideal pact between the anti-Communist Fascists and traditional institutions, above all the Italian state and monarchy, a political configuration that would bring order and stability to the purported post-war social and political chaos. A year after the March on Rome, on 2 October 1923, Adolf Hitler echoed this sentiment in an interview with the conservative *Daily Mail.* He declared: 'If a German Mussolini is given to Germany . . . people would fall down on their knees and worship him more than Mussolini has ever been worshipped.'[8]

Amidst the unprecedented national crises of 1923, the hyperinflation and the Franco-Belgian occupation of the Ruhr, Hitler implicitly adhered to the belief that Germans were superior to Italians. He suggested that the German people would be even more receptive to a dictator who would be even stronger than the Duce. Hitler aimed for an anti-French alliance with Italy, thereby driving a wedge between these countries, former allies (both were permanent members of the Council of the League of Nations) who had defeated Germany in the Great War.[9]

Yet Hitler did not fully understand that Mussolini's rule in Italy was far from total. Contrary to Hitler's impression, nurtured by Fascist propaganda, Mussolini was not a strong dictator. In reality, at least until the signing of the Lateran Treaties with the Catholic Church in 1929, the

Duce was consolidating his power and trying to balance it through constant negotiations between the conservative monarchy and state bureaucracy on the one hand and radical elements within the Fascist party who were demanding to bring the Italian state under the party's control on the other.[10] Hitler's references to Fascist Italy and Mussolini gradually helped legitimise the Nazis amongst wide sections of society beyond the Nazis themselves. To many in Germany and elsewhere in Europe, the nascent Fascist regime appeared as a compromise between the new far right and traditional elites, above all the monarchy, and thereby appeared as a powerful weapon against the left after the Bolshevik and other left-wing revolutions had caused a considerable sense of unease and fear amongst the European bourgeoisie.

Other right-wing German commentators stressed that the March on Rome was a model for Germany. Arthur Moeller van den Bruck, the intellectual who coined the term 'the Third Reich', had opined in his 1922 essay 'Italia docet' that the coming to power of Fascism, a movement of the young, was only a matter of time in Germany. Contrary to most Germans, Moeller van den Bruck thus praised Italy as a role model for Germany, just as it had been in the nineteenth century when Germany followed Italy in achieving national unification. However, a few months later, he changed his mind and dismissed Italian Fascism as reactionary, reflecting ambivalent views on Italy that were typical of most Germans. It should be added here that not all of those on the German right who took an active interest in Italian Fascism embraced Nazism.[11]

II

Turning to Mussolini's perceptions of Hitler and the Nazis, a strong relationship was all but inevitable. On 17 November 1922, weeks after Mussolini's appointment as Prime Minister, Adolfo Tedaldi, the Italian delegate at the Inter-Allied Rhineland High Commission, established in the wake of the Versailles Treaty to supervise the Allied occupation of the Rhineland (Italy had been incapable of sending troops), reported to Mussolini about separatist forces in Bavaria. These separatist tendencies concerned the Italian government, determined to keep the nearby South Tyrol under control. Known in Italy as Alto Adige, this was a territory near the Austrian border with a German-speaking majority whose annexation had long been on the agenda of Italian irredentists intent on reclaiming lands deemed to belong to Italy. As part of the post-war settlement, the South Tyrol had come under Italian control, prompting massive protests from the local population and German nationalists. In his lengthy report, Tedaldi devoted ample space to 'Hittler'. The misspelling of Hitler's name revealed the Nazi leader's obscurity. Hitler had no interest in bringing the South Tyrol under German control, so Tedaldi singled him out in his report to the Duce. Tedaldi left the Duce in no doubt that Hitler was a great speaker, with a manifesto lifted from the Fascists: to restore order and crush the left. Hitler was keen to enter in direct contact with the Italian Fascists and obtain 'directives and advice on which method to follow'.[12]

Tedaldi's report should not be overestimated, because Mussolini, as Europe's first fascist head of government, cultivated good relations with other far-right and/or fascist groups from across Europe that were more significant at that time. A much more important admirer of Mussolini was Miguel Primo de Rivera, who had risen to power in Spain in September 1923 through a coup d'état. Two months later, Primo de Rivera and King Alfonso XIII visited Rome where Alfonso told King Victor Emmanuel III that Primo de Rivera was 'his' Mussolini. Primo de Rivera even spoke of Spain's following in the footsteps of Italy, and Spain, a Mediterranean country with what appeared as an ideologically related regime, seemed a more suitable ally for Italy.[13]

Neither the Nazis nor Germany were the focus of Mussolini's attention in the autumn of 1923, as Mussolini, backed by nationalists, was pulling off his first aggressive foreign policy act. Italy occupied the strategically important Greek island of Corfu. Although Italy eventually had to withdraw, the Corfu incident was a major victory for Mussolini as it enhanced his international and domestic prestige. Furthermore, since it was the Conference of Ambassadors, rather than the League's formal bodies, that resolved the crisis, the League was exposed as ineffectual. Despite Italy's prominent role as a permanent member of the League's Council, the belligerent Mussolini despised the League, as one of its core aims was to maintain the post-1919 order and peace through international negotiation. Nevertheless, Italy remained a member of the League for prestige reasons and to boost its international influence. In the other major international incident of 1923, the occupation of the Ruhr valley, Germany's industrial centre, in retaliation for missed reparations payments, Mussolini played the register of European diplomacy. He did not send Italian troops, as he was concerned about Italy's need for coal from the Ruhr. The aim of Mussolini's skilful manoeuvring was to enhance Italy's status. This was a continuation of the foreign policy of Liberal Italy, and, indeed, most of Italy's diplomats had served under the Liberal governments. But Mussolini's foreign policy was not simply about bluff and manoeuvring, but also about attacking the Wilsonian order of liberal internationalism, as the Corfu incident revealed.[14]

Hitler continued with his strategy to gain legitimacy through stressing his proximity to Italian Fascism. His references to Fascism remained vague, suggesting that it was not Fascist ideology as such but the Fascist method of seizing and consolidating power that attracted Hitler.[15] An October 1923 interview by the Fascist journalist Leo Negrelli of Hitler was a tacit acknowledgement of Hitler's increasing significance within the German far right. Hitler, probably hoping that Mussolini would read the article, declared that the day of a German revolution would come soon and praised Mussolini's decisive political strategy of overcoming the purported political chaos in Italy.[16] A few days later, Hitler spoke to a journalist from the pro-Fascist *L'Epoca*. He renewed his pledge that the South Tyrol issue should not stand in the way of good relations between Italy and Germany. This statement was highly controversial amongst the German right because Hitler thereby sacrificed the South Tyrol to a good relationship with Mussolini's Italy. Having Mussolini's support would, in a short-term perspective, help the Nazis become famous and reach power and, in a long-term view, lead to a military alliance with Fascist Italy.[17]

Hitler's attitude towards the South Tyrol issue highlighted tensions within the Nazi movement about his pro-Italian strategy. In 1926, Hans Frank, a Nazi lawyer, resigned from the party in protest against Hitler's surrender of German claims for the South Tyrol.[18] But Hitler's views on the South Tyrol were uncompromising, and he repeatedly defended this point, even in public, which shows that he was willing to sacrifice nationalist principles, a core part of Nazi ideology, to strategic considerations. Hitler gave reasons for this decision: in his *Second Book*, written in 1928 but not published during his lifetime, he identified Italy as Germany's natural ally against France, as Italy was also determined to revise Versailles and expand its territories. Thus, this particular case confirms that Hitler's courting of Mussolini was not only about ideology, but also about strategy.[19]

III

If there was any direct Fascist influence on the nascent Nazi movement at that time, it was Hitler's admiration for the simplification of Fascist strategy projected by Fascist propaganda.[20] On 9 November 1923, five years after the proclamation of the German republic and in the midst of hyperinflation, Hitler and the Nazis, alongside national conservatives, tried to seize power in Munich in the Beer Hall Putsch. According to the Nazis, the putsch took some inspiration from the March on Rome, but in reality the similarities were rather limited: the Fascists were already a mass movement by the time of the March on Rome, while the Nazis were at this point still largely a Bavarian, rather than a national, force. For the Nazis, the March on Rome served as a foundational myth, and it became shorthand for the successful conquest of power, following the Italian elevation of this event into a powerful legend. Indeed, the Nazi party's historical archive is full of newspaper clippings and other publications on the March on Rome and Italian Fascism. Even in the Nazi party's official memory, therefore, Italian Fascism and the March on Rome appeared as a model for the Nazis.[21]

During the same period, the Nazis also tried to gain legitimacy through select references to other contemporary dictatorships, above all Turkey under Atatürk. The point about Hitler's references to charismatic foreign leaders is that the Nazis were not simply imitating the political strategy of these foreign regimes. Rather, such references were attempts to promote and legitimise Nazi claims for power. While the Beer Hall Putsch failed and ended with Hitler's imprisonment, it made him and the Nazis notorious throughout Germany and Europe. Fascism, then, inspired the Nazis, not just in their way of seizing power, but also as a means of attracting publicity, even in the event of failure.[22]

Mussolini's newspaper *Il Popolo d'Italia* was not slow in ridiculing Hitler's putsch as a 'caricature of Italian Fascism'. Nevertheless, here was a semi-official Fascist recognition of the Nazis.[23] After the failed putsch, Hitler was put on trial. He used it as a propaganda platform, turning the putsch into a considerable success that helped raise him and the Nazis from obscurity to political prominence. The Nazi party's re-establishment in 1925, following Hitler's early release from prison, coincided with Mussolini's proclamation of dictatorship in January of that year and the increasing crackdown on political opposition, above all on the left. In this way, the nascent Mussolini myth became even more attractive to the German right. Here was a charismatic and ruthless leader who ruled the unruly Italians with an iron rod, while at the same time seeming to respect the authority of the Italian state and monarchy. This cult of the Duce, promoted through books, articles and images, began to serve the Nazis' advantage, as it helped make them attractive to conservative voters.[24]

Hitler himself articulated this Nazi cult of Mussolini in the second volume of his autobiographical account *Mein Kampf*, written during his spell in prison and published in 1926. In it, Hitler acknowledged Mussolini as a tough, anti-Marxist and patriotic leader who combated internationalism, a reference to their shared low opinion of the League of Nations.[25]

Almost immediately after his release from prison in late 1924, Hitler is said to have requested a meeting with Mussolini. Mussolini's attitude towards Hitler remained lukewarm: on the one hand, some leading Nazis, including Hermann Göring, a flying ace in the world war with good connections to the German nobility, were granted effective asylum in Italy, creating the basis for cordial relations with the Nazis in the event they would grow into a major party; on the other hand, Mussolini, the statesman, kept his distance from the Nazis, a movement aiming to destroy the German government with which Italy had official relations. He first accepted but then postponed a meeting with Hitler.[26]

Mussolini's wavering only intensified Hitler's admiration for him. Hitler requested signed photographs of the Duce which, exhibited in the Nazi party's office, would, he felt, be a visible reminder of the purported alliance between Fascist Italy and Nazism, and further legitimise the Nazis. Mussolini refused even to acknowledge these requests, as he did not want to jeopardise official relations with the German government. Not even this diminished Hitler's enthusiasm for the Duce.[27]

Yet, in spite of all this inspiration and admiration, the ideological impact of Fascism on Nazism was in reality quite minor. Nazi ideology had already been formulated in the Nazi party manifesto in 1920, focusing on anti-Semitism, before Hitler and the Nazis had heard of Mussolini and his Fascists. Some Nazi leaders even criticised Fascism. For example, in 1924, the leading Nazi ideologue Alfred Rosenberg wrote admiringly about the ultra-nationalism of Italian Fascism, but lamented its lack of anti-Semitism. Rosenberg thus highlighted some tensions within the Nazi movement on how to view Fascism.[28] In contrast to Rosenberg, other Nazis were keen to draw close ideological parallels between Nazism and Fascism. Göring wrote a series of articles in 1926 from his Italian exile for the Nazi party daily *Völkischer Beobachter*. Göring, seeking legitimacy for the Nazis, compared them to the Fascists and underlined ideological parallels, such as the reliance on political violence and hatred of the Versailles Treaty and parliamentary democracy. Göring also claimed that the Nazis and Fascists were both anti-Semitic. This was a stretch of the imagination: strong anti-Semitic tendencies within the Fascist regime only emerged much later, and anti-Semitism did not play as central a role in Fascist ideology as it did in Nazi doctrine.[29]

IV

The more fragile the Weimar Republic appeared, the more explicitly did the German right portray Mussolini's rule as an alternative for Germany. Crucially, Mussolini's appeal went beyond Nazi sympathisers. Led by the masculine, authoritarian and tough Duce, whose propaganda machinery developed him into a powerful cult that reverberated beyond Italy, his regime seemed to be fully integrated with traditional Italian elites, such as the monarchy and army, and the Catholic Church. While this representation was heavily influenced by Fascist propaganda and bore little resemblance to the complex and fraught nature of Fascist rule in Italy, Mussolini's Fascist regime became increasingly attractive as a bulwark against the left to the German right more generally, not just the Nazis, such as the paramilitary Steel Helmets or figures such as Konrad Adenauer, member of the Catholic Centre Party and lord mayor of Cologne.[30] Fascist support for the Nazis was therefore far from inevitable, and Mussolini's attitude towards Hitler remained unclear.[31] Furthermore, the significance of Fascist support, financial and otherwise, for the Nazis in the 1920s was not as great as some observers later claimed, and the Nazi party remained a fringe group in terms of parliamentary seats on a national level.[32]

Let us consider in more detail how the Fascist template of securing power inspired Hitler and the Nazis in the increasingly fragile context of the Weimar Republic. The Nazis were particularly influenced by the Fascists' twofold strategy of seizing power. First, there was extreme political violence stirred up by the Fascists against the left; second, there was a quest for conquering power through apparently legal political activity. The second aspect, gaining power by seemingly adhering to the law, was particularly important for Hitler after the Nazi party's re-establishment in 1925, following Hitler's release from prison. Playing by the rules appeared as a viable tactic to secure the support of the middle classes, concerned with law and order amidst the perceived threat from the left.[33]

In spite of all the references to what they saw as Mussolini's strategy, the Nazis scored badly in the May 1928 Reichstag elections. For diplomatic reasons, Mussolini still rejected Hitler's requests for a meeting. In order to maintain contact, other Fascist representatives met the Nazi leader outside official channels. In late 1928, for instance, Hitler encountered Senator Ettore Tolomei who, like many Italian nationalists, had since before the world war advocated the Italianisation of the South Tyrol, and who was now responsible for the imposition of Italian on the German-speaking majority in the South Tyrol, vehemently opposed by most Germans. Hitler and Tolomei met clandestinely in the house of an Italian businessman in the leafy Nymphenburg suburb of Munich. In a report to the Duce, Tolomei praised Hitler as a talented politician who unconditionally accepted that the South Tyrol was Italian. Hitler's remarks about the status of Austria, which many Germans and Austrians wanted to unite with the Reich, were more cautious, as the Nazi leader knew that Mussolini saw the Alpine republic as a buffer state between Italy and Germany. Hitler also renewed his request to meet Mussolini, but politely added that such a meeting might be inopportune at the current time. Mussolini's reaction to Tolomei's report is not known, but it is clear that Hitler was keen to ingratiate himself with Mussolini.[34]

Hitler's flirtations with Fascism led to much controversy amongst the German right, and more specifically to two trials in 1929 and 1930.[35] Hitler, defended by Hans Frank, who had rejoined the Nazi party in the meantime, sued the right-wing politician Albrecht von Graefe for claiming in a newspaper article that the Nazi leader had sacrificed German claims to the South Tyrol 'in his Mussolini intoxication' in return for secret funds from Mussolini. Graefe thus denounced Hitler as a traitor who had been bought off by the Italian government.[36] This article, made in heaven for anti-Nazi journalists, infuriated Hitler. The accusation of secret Italian funding for the Nazi party concerned him because of powerful anti-Italian stereotypes in Germany. But the defendants were unable to prove their allegations. They were fined by the court, as they could not demonstrate that the Nazis had received money from Italy. Still this was not the end of the story. In February 1930 the defendants presented a new witness: the journalist Werner Abel. Hitler, competing with other right-wing parties over the leadership of the German right, again vehemently denied claims that he had received Italian funding. The trial dragged on through the various instances of the court system until June 1932, when Abel was given a prison sentence. The German Foreign Ministry, alarmed at Italy's support of the Nazis, and Italian Fascist journalists followed the trial very closely. At the same time, Italian reports presented the increasingly influential Hitler as the coming leader in Germany and drew parallels to the rapid rise of Mussolini, so the trial and the publicity it generated worked in Hitler's favour.[37]

In the meantime, the Weimar Republic became more and more frayed amidst the Great Depression. From late March 1930, after the fall of the grand coalition government, there was no more parliamentary-based government. Instead, Heinrich Brüning's cabinet ruled on the basis of Article 48 of the Weimar constitution, which gave the Reich president emergency powers. Mussolini sensed the chance for a pro-fascist German government, although he publicly denied his strategy to expand Fascism abroad, above all a tactic since the consolidation of his rule to increase Italy's influence.[38] Since he wanted to maintain good relations with the German government, he reaffirmed in a May 1930 interview with the liberal German-Jewish journalist Theodor Wolff that Fascism was not 'an article for export.'[39] At the same time, Mussolini instructed the Italian consul-general in Munich, the aristocrat Giovanni Capasso Torre di Caprara, to sound Hitler out. On 20 June 1930, Capasso reported to Mussolini about his secret meeting with the Nazi leader. Apart from praising Mussolini, Hitler restated his policy on the South Tyrol. Furthermore, he had prophesied that the Nazis would come to power in Germany soon.[40]

V

The first major turning point in the Mussolini–Hitler relationship was the September 1930 Reichstag elections, when the Nazis scored a stunning success that brought them closer to power. They increased their parliamentary seats from 12 to 107 and became the second largest party. Mussolini saw the collapse of German democracy and the drift of German politics towards the right as a good opportunity for Italy to increase its influence on German politics.[41] The Fascist flagship journal *Gerarchia* ('Hierarchy') commented on the September 1930 Nazi electoral breakthrough: 'The fascist idea is moving ahead in the world,' thus crediting Mussolini for the Nazi success. The Nazi paper *Völkischer Beobachter* too highlighted Mussolini's alleged personal endorsement of the Nazi success at the polls in order to legitimise the Nazis by pointing to the Italian Fascist model.[42]

It was no coincidence that in the wake of the Nazis' electoral success, Mussolini began to increase his support for them. At the same time, he retained an ambivalent attitude towards Hitler. Significantly, his support was through intermediaries outside diplomatic channels, as direct support of the Nazis would have triggered a diplomatic row with the German government and may have alienated France and Britain. Mussolini's ambivalence towards Hitler was typical of his foreign policy, in which Italy, a nation craving great-power status since national unification, officially maintained a policy of equidistance vis-à-vis France, Britain and Germany, and pursued alliances which would then determine power relations in Europe. In this way, Mussolini's indirect flirting with Hitler and other far-right leaders across Europe was part of Italy's strategy to increase its international influence. Key contacts included Prince Philip of Hesse, son-in-law of King Victor Emmanuel III, and like many members of the German high nobility a Nazi party member since 1930, and above all the enigmatic Major Giuseppe Renzetti, director of the Italian Chamber of Commerce in Germany. Renzetti was well networked in Berlin's political and social elite and became Mussolini's direct liaison to Hitler outside diplomatic channels. After the 1930 Reichstag elections, Renzetti, who had initially cultivated good relations with the pro-monarchist *Stahlhelm*, began to support Hitler and the Nazis. It was then that Mussolini began to accept that a Nazi seizure of power could be in Italy's interest.[43]

In a reflection of Mussolini's increasing support for the Nazis, Italian newspapers printed more and more interviews with Hitler, helping him raise his international profile and suggesting to their readers that Fascist Italy endorsed a Nazi government that stood in Mussolini's debt. As leader of a mass movement, Hitler, like other modern political leaders, used newspaper interviews to communicate his political opinions. Yet, unlike Mussolini, Hitler lacked access to official diplomatic networks, so he made more frequent use of newspaper interviews as a communication strategy to boost his international status. Let us look in more detail at Hitler's interview with Pietro Solari for the Turinese *Gazzetta del Popolo* on 29 September 1930, a fortnight after the Nazis' election success. In it, Hitler again praised the Duce and reiterated that the fate of the German-speaking majority in the South Tyrol must not stand in the way of good Italo-German relations.[44] Yet Hitler also used these interviews to highlight differences between Fascism and Nazism. In a spring 1931 interview with Mussolini's *Il Popolo d'Italia*, for instance, Hitler insisted that the Nazis had made more sacrifices than the Fascists on their way to power, a hint that a Nazi government would not be an easy negotiation partner for Italy.[45]

Despite Hitler's intense praise and lobbying of the Italian dictator, a correspondence between both leaders only began in April 1931. An exchange of photographs and letters was the highly symbolic beginning of this direct communication: Mussolini gave Göring a signed photograph for Hitler. Hitler had long been craving an autographed image of the Duce, but Mussolini withheld granting his first official acknowledgement of Hitler until the moment when Nazi success was being consolidated.[46] In June 1931, Hitler thanked the Duce for the signed portrait with an autographed photograph of himself in Nazi uniform. He clumsily wrote: 'The in many points existing spiritual relations between the basic ideas and principles of Fascism and the National Socialist movement led by me make me hope vividly that, after the victory of National Socialism, in which I fundamentally believe, there will be similar relations between Fascist Italy and Nazi Germany for the good of these two great nations.'[47] This exchange had a symbolic significance in that it made Hitler believe that the Duce was taking him seriously.

A clear indication of growing Fascist interest in Hitler was another interview with Solari for the *Gazzetta del Popolo* on 6 December 1931. Solari was pleased to report that Hitler had finished the interview with the 'Roman greeting', copied from the Fascists. Yet the history of the Nazi appropriation of the Roman greeting, turned, with a slight variation of the physical movement of the right arm, into a personal glorification of Hitler as the *Heil Hitler* salute, reveals that not all Nazis shared Hitler's fascination for Mussolini and Italian Fascism. For instance, Hans Frank, upon quitting the Nazi party in 1926, had lamented the Nazi use of the Roman greeting because it was un-German. Similar complaints prompted Rudolf Hess, Hitler's private secretary, to backdate the origins of the

Nazi greeting to 1921, allegedly a time before the Nazis had heard of Italian Fascism.[48]

Needless to say, there were also Italian stereotypes of the Nazis as brutal, unsophisticated thugs, reflecting Italians' attitude towards the Germans that was characterised by a mix of admiration and envy for German punctuality and efficiency and a dismissal for the Germans' purported lack of sophistication and refinement. While the Roman Empire had been a beacon of civilisation, went the story, the Germans lacked this long history. Hitler, ingratiating himself, knew that the cult of *romanità* was an increasingly important propagandistic tool for Mussolini. The Nazi leader thus showed respect towards Italy when he expressed the view in a 1931 conversation with the Italian consul-general that Italy, unlike Germany, could rightly claim a history of 2,000 years.[49]

Fascist–Nazi relations thus remained unclear. The Italian government made some concessions to the Nazis, allowing the gradual opening of branches of the Nazi party's foreign organisation for the German expatriate community in Italy.[50] Nevertheless, Mussolini insisted in a series of conversations with Emil Ludwig, the German-Jewish author of bestselling biographies and interviews with other celebrities including Stalin, that Fascism was not for export. Ludwig's book appeared in 1932 at the height of the Great Depression and the increasing political deadlock of the Weimar Republic. In this context, many in Germany, not only those on the far right, saw a dictatorship modelled on Mussolini's regime as a potential solution for Germany. Significantly, Mussolini, a master of staging interviews and audiences, disguised his clandestine support for Hitler. In Ludwig's book, the Nazi leader was not explicitly mentioned, and Mussolini denied that Fascism was anti-Semitic. Mussolini, once again, reassured his German audience that Fascism was unique to Italy, although, in reality, the Duce was influencing German politics at this time as part of his strategy to enhance Italy's power in Europe.[51]

Although the Nazis appropriated Fascist methods, they were keen to obfuscate some aspects of their debt to Fascism, partly a result of the German left's ridiculing of the Nazis as copycats of the Italian Fascists and partly because of anti-Italian prejudices looming large in Germany. The paradox of an ultra-nationalist movement owing some of its central strategies to another one had to be toned down. This ambivalent attitude to the Fascist 'heritage' needs to be recognised if we are to understand the complex relationship between the two movements and their leaders.

Typical of this ambiguity was a preface Hitler contributed to the German translation of a book on Fascism's nature by the primary school teacher Vincenzo Meletti which appeared in 1931 with the Nazi party's Eher publishing house. In his preface, Hitler highlighted basic parallels between Fascism and Nazism, such as their common origins in the Great War and their allegedly genuine popularity. However, he insisted that Nazi ideology had emerged 'completely independently of Italy' and, significantly, did not use the term 'fascist' to refer to the Nazis.[52] Although the Eher Verlag sent copies of Meletti's book to Mussolini in May 1931, he apparently ignored them.[53] This inconsistency, coupled with unpredictability, was an integral part of Mussolini's political repertoire and enabled him to change his position according to his interests, while at the same time reminding his audience, in this case Hitler, of his power and superiority.[54]

Mussolini's mixed responses made Hitler crave a strong relationship with the Duce even more. Soon, in October 1931, the *Stahlhelm* and the German national conservatives joined ranks with the Nazis in the Harzburg Front. When Renzetti reported this news to Mussolini, the Duce awarded him a high monthly salary of 4,000 lire.[55] It is unlikely that this alliance between the national-conservative right and the Nazis was principally the result of Renzetti's meetings with Hitler and other Nazi leaders. Nevertheless, the Harzburg Front made a Nazi takeover of power more acceptable to wide sections of society, similar to the Fascists' coalition with Luigi Federzoni's Nationalists in the 1920s.

In the light of all this contact and influence, including the frequent meetings between Renzetti and Hitler, it is tempting to overestimate both Renzetti's significance and Mussolini's direct impact on Hitler's rise to power.[56] It would be absurd, for example, to claim that Renzetti's advice was a principal factor that brought Hitler into power. Popular and electoral support for the Nazis was crucial – to a much larger extent than it had been for the Fascists in 1922. Nevertheless, Renzetti's influence on Hitler's political strategy is hard to deny. It was Renzetti, amongst others, who encouraged Hitler to seek power through seemingly lawful activities and to turn down invitations to join a national-conservative government as a junior partner. Hitler stressed this strategy of legality in October 1932 (a strategy with which some Nazis disagreed), a month before the Reichstag elections, in an interview with *Il Tevere*, edited by the notorious Fascist anti-Semite Telesio Interlandi, who was close to Mussolini. Hitler's interviewer may have been impressed by the life-size bust of Mussolini which adorned the Führer's office in the Nazi party's Munich headquarters.[57]

In December 1931, Hitler was still eagerly waiting for an audience with his political idol in Rome. According to Renzetti, Hitler was 'extremely happy to be able to come to Rome to pay homage to the Duce'. The respectful wording suggested that Hitler acknowledged Mussolini's role as senior statesman.[58] The prospect of Hitler's visit to Italy greatly alarmed the German government. The German ambassador to Italy therefore provided the German Foreign Ministry with details of Hitler's visit. The Nazi leader was due to stay at the luxurious Grand Hotel as a guest of the Fascist party, rather than the state. This arrangement was a clever calculation by Mussolini, seeking ostensibly to reflect diplomatic sensitivities. For the same reason, Mussolini instructed the Italian press to keep quiet about Hitler's visit. Yet, according to the German ambassador, not only the Duce but also the king was prepared to receive Hitler, a clear acknowledgement that, for the Italian state, it was likely that Hitler would soon come to power in Germany. At the same time, after the German ambassador objected that the official reception of Hitler would be an obstacle to Italo-German relations, Mussolini cancelled the visit, not least since, a week previously, Nazi plans for a coup d'état had been discovered. These placed heavy doubts on the Nazi party's official strategy of legality.[59]

As much as Hitler's flirting with Mussolini was not universally popular amongst the Nazis, Mussolini's cultivation of Hitler met some opposition from Fascists. Thus, in his book on the coup d'état, published in French in 1931 and a year later in German translation, the maverick author Curzio Malaparte, a member of the Fascist party, ridiculed Hitler as 'a dictator who won't become [one]' and dismissed him as a poor imitation of Mussolini. This was a theme frequently highlighted by German anti-Nazis, and, for Malaparte, Hitler lacked the courage to seize power by violent means, unlike the Fascists.[60] However, Renzetti intervened in Rome on the Nazi leader's behalf: Mussolini, concerned that Malaparte's savage criticism would undermine his influence on Hitler, instructed the Italian embassy in Berlin to tell Hitler that Malaparte had no influence in Fascist Italy. Indeed, the book did not appear in Fascist Italy. Nevertheless, the damage had been done, as many Nazis wrongly saw Malaparte as a leading representative of Fascism. The *Giornale d'Italia* published a sharp critique of Malaparte's ideas, and Renzetti forwarded the article to Hitler with an apology.[61]

As the Nazi party became a serious contender for power in Germany, Hitler made another attempt at direct communication with the Duce. The occasion was the death in December 1931 of Mussolini's brother Arnaldo, who had been in effective charge of the Fascist flagship newspaper *Il Popolo d'Italia*. Hitler sent his condolences in a letter delivered by Renzetti. Mussolini thanked Hitler with some polite but standard formulations. It is noteworthy that the Duce put off his reply until mid-January 1932, reflecting his senior position and the previous diplomatic issues around Hitler's planned visit.[62]

Encouraged by this exchange with Mussolini, Hitler told Renzetti that he wanted to meet the Duce, adding that he fully understood why Mussolini had cancelled the 1931 meeting.[63] In the gloomy atmosphere of the Great Depression and the increasing polarisation of German politics, Hitler, in June 1932, weeks before the Reichstag elections, politely requested another audience with Mussolini via Renzetti, as he hoped that his visit would legitimise Nazi rule amongst even wider sections of society and help secure more votes for the Nazis. Renzetti lobbied Mussolini to receive Hitler, who had 'the dying wish to meet the Duce', as an obsequious Hitler would be ready to receive Mussolini's advice. Thus, a meeting with Hitler would be a powerful opportunity for the Duce to influence German politics. Hitler, like a typical German admirer of Italian culture, even requested to visit Florence, Rome and Naples. He suggested he should fly from Munich to Milan, thereby avoiding Austria, where he was *persona non grata*.[64]

Renzetti, keen to make himself indispensable as power broker between the two leaders, had already planned the itinerary. As in the failed 1931 visit, it was the Fascist party, rather than the state, that would host Hitler in order to avoid a diplomatic row with the German government. Security had to be tight. Furthermore, Renzetti reminded Hitler's hosts that the Nazi leader was a vegetarian and a teetotaller. In order to please Hitler, tours of the monuments and some of the museums of Rome had to be planned.[65]

Despite Renzetti's preparations for Hitler's journey to Italy,[66] Mussolini ordered the postponement of the visit until the conclusion of the Lausanne conference on German reparations and the ongoing Geneva disarmaments talks. Mussolini was concerned that France and Britain would view Hitler's visit to Rome as an illegitimate meddling with German affairs and international negotiations. Thus, diplomatic considerations overshadowed the relationship between Mussolini and Hitler.[67]

As Renzetti gave increasingly detailed strategic advice to Hitler, visits of Fascist functionaries to Germany and Nazi delegations to Rome increased. In November 1932, when the second Reichstag elections of the year were held, in which the Nazis made considerable losses, Göring and Alfred Rosenberg, accompanied by the *Stahlhelm* leader, Franz Seldte, visited a congress organised by the Royal Italian Academy. Mussolini immediately arranged for a special plane for Göring to take him back to Berlin to enable the Nazis to take the reins in Germany.[68]

VI

At this time, the Duce increasingly believed that a Nazi government, allied with the German national conservatives (DNVP), was in Italy's interest. Through Renzetti, Mussolini even knew the names of some of the key members of Hitler's 'new cabinet' – days before Hitler's appointment as chancellor of a Nazi–DNVP coalition government, which seemed similar to Mussolini's first coalition government.[69] In fact, on the night of his appointment as Reich chancellor on 30 January 1933, Hitler invited Renzetti to the Reich Chancellery to watch the Nazi victory parade through Berlin. In his report to Mussolini, Renzetti boasted that 'Hitler ha[d] wanted me next to him throughout the entire march-past', but Renzetti had refused, perhaps because his visible presence would have given rise to speculations about Fascist Italy's role in bringing Hitler into power.[70]

After his appointment as chancellor, Hitler continued to court Mussolini. Significantly, Hitler, in one of his first official acts as Reich chancellor, received Renzetti on 31 January 1933 to convey a message to the Duce. Hitler insisted 'that from my place I will pursue with all my force that policy of friendship towards Italy which I have till now supported enthusiastically'. The new chancellor acknowledged that 'I have arrived at this point surely because of Fascism.' This compliment must have pleased Mussolini, just like Hitler's insistence that Mussolini had created the ideology which united the Fascist and Nazi movements, a bland remark that remained unspecific because Hitler, as leader of an ultra-nationalist movement, was unable to acknowledge the influence of a foreign political leader on him. For this reason, Hitler refrained from similar hyperbolic remarks in public, as many

Germans, including Nazi supporters, remained sceptical of an alliance with Italy. Undoubtedly, Hitler's flattery reflected his genuine admiration for Mussolini, but it was also a diplomatic calculation. Renzetti's reply was not less inflated when he stated that Mussolini had always supported the Nazis 'with the greatest sympathy'. The flattery and hyperbole of both Renzetti and Hitler anticipated tense Italo-German relations which were and would be characterised in the years ahead by a constantly changing balance of ideological and diplomatic factors.[71]

Hitler and the Nazis soon began to consolidate their rule in a much more violent and rapid manner than the Fascists had managed to do in Italy. In the 5 March 1933 Reichstag elections, held after the dissolution of parliament in an atmosphere of Nazi terror and intimidation, Hitler's coalition government was confirmed with a slight majority, although the Nazi party itself failed to win an absolute majority, with the Social Democrats and the Communists still scoring well despite their massive persecution, which had intensified after the Reichstag Fire Decree of 28 February. Mussolini continued to look down on Hitler, a tendency also reflected in the Fascist press and in a lukewarm declaration by the Fascist Grand Council on 10 March 1933.[72]

During the election campaign, the Nazis had received some financial support from Fascist Italy. At the request of the Nazi party's Eher Verlag, trying to generate cash for the party, the Duce funded an Italian edition of Hitler's *Mein Kampf* with 250,000 lire, the equivalent of more than 50,000 Reichsmark. This was a substantial amount for foreign rights, but, in reality, a small sum for a political subsidy. The request, made via Renzetti, was in line with the general pattern of the relationship between Mussolini and Hitler: contacts were initiated by the Nazis, not the Italians. Moreover, the significance of this gesture was in reality quite small, as Mussolini subsidised many other right-wing regimes in Europe. For instance, just ten days after the acquisition of the Italian rights of *Mein Kampf*, Mussolini donated five million lire to the Austrian chancellor, Engelbert Dollfuss, in order to defend Austria against the rise of the Nazis. Thus, Mussolini's purchase of the Italian rights, which could be interpreted as a pro-Nazi gesture, did not necessarily mean that he was an enthusiastic supporter of the Nazis.[73]

Mussolini's ambivalent policy towards Hitler continued: the Duce postponed a visit by the new Reich chancellor, now keener than ever before to meet his idol in Rome. Mussolini was reluctant to give the new German government too much prestige by receiving its leader, as an open endorsement of Hitler would have committed Italy too much to Germany, potentially damaging relations with France and Britain.[74] De Felice has even interpreted Mussolini's reserve towards Hitler as a reflection of the Duce's suspicion and fear. In reality, Mussolini underestimated Hitler and had no idea that Hitler's rapid consolidation of Nazi power in Germany would change Europe's fate so dramatically and soon transform the relationship between the two leaders.[75]

It had taken the Nazis almost ten years from their first rise to international prominence in the 1923 Beer Hall Putsch to come to power, while Mussolini and the Fascists had entered the Italian government just three years after the foundation of the *Fasci italiani di combattimento* in March 1919. It was Hitler who took the initiative to contact Mussolini and who desperately sought his attention and strategic advice. However, sooner than Mussolini expected, Hitler and the Nazis would turn Germany into a dictatorship in a much faster, more ruthless and more effective way than Mussolini had done in Italy. Over time, the relationship between the two aggressive and warmongering leaders – the internationally inexperienced Hitler, desperately seeking Mussolini's attention, and the aloof Mussolini, ignoring these requests – would change dramatically, with profound consequences for the European geopolitical order.

2

FIRST DATE
June 1934

I

In March 1933, weeks after Hitler's appointment as Reich chancellor, Mussolini suggested a four-power pact between France, Britain, Italy and Germany. In the Duce's draft treaty, the four signatories committed themselves to continue disarmament negotiations at Geneva. The pact was a way to undermine the League of Nations. Mussolini, alongside Italian nationalists, believed that the post-war order was preventing Italy from becoming a great power, while Hitler, followed by the majority of Germans, thought that it had crippled Germany and deprived it of major territories. Despite some reservations within the German Foreign Ministry, the Nazis exploited Mussolini's draft treaty as a means to emphasise their alleged commitment to peace. For Mussolini, harbouring the desire for an aggressive foreign policy whereby Italy would come to dominate the Mediterranean, the pact's purpose was to have Italy recognised as a great power. Mussolini knew that Hitler's ascendancy had an enormous potential to destabilise Europe, and he seized the pact as a chance to play the senior statesman and as a way to increase Italy's influence on the international stage.[1] The basic idea, shared by many Italian statesmen before Mussolini and articulated most clearly by Dino Grandi, foreign minister between 1929 and 1932 and ambassador to London from 1932 until 1939, was that Italy's role was that of the 'determining weight' between

Germany on the one hand and France and Britain on the other.[2] While Mussolini was formally in charge of Italian foreign policy as foreign minister, he had to rely on the Italian diplomatic service, which was far from fully Fascist. Within the Foreign Ministry, many officials, while supporting Italy's revisionist policy, preferred a close relationship with Britain over one with Germany. An alliance of Fascist Italy with Nazi Germany, so keenly desired by Hitler, was unlikely.[3]

A few weeks after Mussolini's initiative, the Nazi regime announced the boycott of Jewish businesses, thereby demonstrating the centrality of anti-Semitism to the Nazi project. Scheduled for 1 April 1933, the aim of the boycott was to contain the waves of grassroots-level Nazi violence against Jews. As soon as the Duce heard about the boycott, he instructed the Italian ambassador, Vittorio Cerruti, to intervene with Hitler. Mussolini was concerned that Hitler might damage his international reputation quickly and thereby undermine the Duce's diplomatic endeavours to increase Italy's power. Thus, Mussolini sent Hitler a personal message via Cerruti. Mussolini, acting as the senior statesman, advised his inexperienced colleague to cancel the boycot as it would do irreparable damage to Germany's reputation and '[would] increase the moral pressure and the economic reprisals of world Jewry'. Hitler was irritated when Cerruti presented him with the Duce's advice, even though Mussolini had flaunted his anti-Semitic belief in a Jewish world conspiracy. Yet Hitler did not want to offend Mussolini. After a polite opening in which he acknowledged that Mussolini had greatly inspired the Nazi rise to power, Hitler asked Cerruti to tell Mussolini that he, the Nazi leader, knew better about the dangers of 'Judaeo-Bolshevism'. Hitler even insinuated that he would be remembered in a few hundred years for having exterminated Jewry, a frequent theme in his violently anti-Semitic rhetoric. On his way out of Hitler's office, Cerruti ran into the national-conservative foreign minister, Konstantin von Neurath, who begged him to ask Rome to issue an official statement condemning the foreseeable anti-German propaganda abroad following the anti-Jewish boycott. Mussolini agreed with this request because he wanted to maintain basic relations with Hitler.[4] The centrality of anti-Semitism for the Nazis highlighted the ideological differences between Fascism and Nazism at this time, and Hitler would not compromise on anti-Semitic policy.[5] Now that he had reached power, he had no reason to be obsequious towards Mussolini.

However, Mussolini continued to capitalise on Hitler's affinities towards him and exerted personal pressure on the Reich chancellor to accept the four-power pact. In a direct message to Hitler, Mussolini emphasised that he had always been supportive of the new German government – a clear exaggeration – and that Hitler's reluctance to sign the pact was undermining Mussolini's position. Eventually, Hitler agreed to sign the treaty. But, due to French opposition, it was never ratified.[6]

Mussolini's strategy to exploit Hitler's personal sympathies for him thus seemed to work, and Hitler congratulated the Duce on his fiftieth birthday on 29 July 1933 in a telegram, published in the German press, in which he commended Mussolini for his 'admirable work for the consolidation of European peace', a reference to the four-power pact.[7] In reality, rivalry over which country would be the leading fascist power in Europe would soon characterise Italo-German relations. Many issues were at stake between both nations, above all the question of whether Austria, Hitler's home country, should be incorporated into the Reich. At the Geneva disarmaments conference, negotiations over Germany's demands for rearmament escalated in October 1933. The German delegation, spurred on by Reich war minister General Werner von Blomberg, demanded that France and Britain must give up their insistence on limiting Germany's rearmament. On 12 October 1933, Mussolini, presenting himself as the champion of European diplomacy and again underlining his seniority, tried to appease Hitler and instructed Cerruti to suggest to the chancellor a gradual German rearmament over a number of years. According to the American consul-general in Berlin, George Messersmith, who claimed to have been told this by a 'most reliable source', a furious Hitler shouted at Cerruti that Mussolini 'was deserting him, that he was jealous because Fascism had never had world influence and that National Socialism was the real fascism'. On his way out, Cerruti allegedly told the people outside the chancellor's office that their boss was 'unbalanced'.[8] Here was an early reflection of Hitler's superiority complex over Fascist Italy.

In order to leave nobody in any doubt about Nazi Germany's rejection of the post-Versailles order, the German delegation walked out from both the disarmaments conference and the League of Nations in October 1933, after Blomberg's and Neurath's lobbying of Hitler. This step was a massive reassertion that Nazi Germany would not accept anything but parity with the great powers. It was a huge domestic victory for Hitler, as his strongly revisionist policies resonated with many Germans. Although Hitler had tried to warn Mussolini of his exit from the conference the night before, this unilateral step was a blow for Mussolini, as it effectively undermined a potential Italian–German revisionist alliance within the framework of the League.[9]

Significantly, despite his extreme self-confidence, Hitler felt it necessary to explain his move to the Duce. He politely addressed Mussolini as 'Your Excellency', and, to add weight to the missive, had it hand delivered by the Prussian minister president, Hermann Göring, on 6 November 1933. As on previous occasions, Hitler remained vague about ideological parallels between Fascism and Nazism, underlining his 'desire for cooperation of our two nations, fulfilled by the spirit of true friendship, which [are] ideologically related and can, through a practical pursuit of [their] same interests, contribute an incredible amount to the pacification of Europe'. Because of their common experience in the trenches, Hitler insisted that he and Mussolini must preserve peace in Europe. He thanked Mussolini for supporting Germany, before blaming France and Britain for disregarding Germany's legitimate pursuit of rearmament.[10] Days later, on 12 November 1933, Reichstag elections were held, coupled with a referendum over the German exit from Geneva. Unsurprisingly, the Nazis won the rigged election with a huge majority which gave a tremendous boost to Nazism's domestic and international standing.[11]

Apart from Hitler's obsequious advances to Mussolini, Italian and German newspapers, both subject to censorship, carried many hostile articles on the other country. Reports were so inimical that Cerruti complained in late February 1934 to Neurath that Italo-German relations were 'as bad as [they had not been] for many years'.[12] Typical in this respect was the exchange of aggressive reports on the occasion of the passing of the German Law for the Order of National Labour in January 1934: the law had been praised by the German press as far superior to the 1927 Italian Labour Charter (*carta del lavoro*), which had enshrined corporatism in the Italian economy. Maintaining private enterprise and capitalism, while suppressing free trade unions, the corporatist order was seen by many in Europe as a way to overcome class conflict, especially during the worldwide depression. Karl Busch, a journalist who had travelled through Italy, published his experiences in March 1934 in *Der Deutsche*, official organ of the German Labour Front, the Nazi organisation of employers and employees, modelled partly on the corporatist framework pioneered by the Fascists. His article was peppered with dismissive remarks such as 'Fascism has not permeated the entire Italian people.' Busch played on typical anti-Italian stereotypes and insisted: 'The German people is in its entirety racially superior.' For Nazi Germany, Busch boasted, 'there was not much more to be learnt' from Fascist Italy. Clearly, the Nazis had consolidated their rule much faster than the Fascists, and Busch articulated this insight very aggressively. But this was not all. Busch also personally attacked Mussolini: 'One says that the Duce has recently aged.'[13]

Renzetti complained to Hitler about the 'offensive' claims, and penned a riposte to the editor of *Der Deutsche*.[14] It was not published, as anti-Italian prejudices featured prominently within Nazi circles and German society at large. Hitler, keen not to offend Mussolini, feigned concern over this article to Renzetti. Hitler could have easily instructed the editor to publish Renzetti's riposte, but he failed to do so. This reveals a paradox in Hitler's view on Italy and Mussolini: while he admired Mussolini as a person and as a political model, he, alongside many Germans, saw the Italians as lazy, treacherous and unreliable.[15] Eventually, in May 1934, the dispute was settled when Busch apologised to Renzetti.[16]

Within Fascist circles, too, many sharply criticised Nazism. The target was no less a figure than the Nazi leader himself on the occasion of the publication of the Italian edition of *Mein Kampf* in the spring of 1934. Hitler had written a new preface in early March 1934 for the Italian edition. In it, he echoed a typical view of superficial ideological parallels. He declared: 'Fascism and Nazism, which are intimately akin to each other in their basic ideals, are called upon to show new paths for fruitful international cooperation.'[17] Even before the official publication date, *Il Popolo d'Italia* carried a lukewarm review of Hitler's book by 'Farinata', the Fascist journalist Ottavio Dinale, who had been received twice by Mussolini days before the review appeared. While there is no clear evidence that Mussolini had instructed Dinale to write a nasty review of *Mein Kampf*, it must remain a possibility. Dinale, like many other Fascists hostile to Nazi Germany, insisted that Italy, the first fascist regime, would lead the path, not Germany, which was obsessed with the ideal of the Germanic race. Mussolini must have heartily approved of these views, as they confirmed his superior role over Hitler, whose meteoric rise to power unseated him from his position as doyen of the European right.[18]

II

In this context, German officials took the initiative in spring 1934 to organise a meeting between Mussolini and Hitler. Hitler and the Nazis were still in the process of balancing their power against other institutions, including the army and the stormtroopers. In formal terms, the encounter was not a state visit, as neither leader was head of state.[19]

Franz von Papen, deputy Reich chancellor, and Ulrich von Hassell, German ambassador to Italy, sounded out Mussolini on whether he would be prepared to meet Hitler. Significantly, other bureaucrats of the German Foreign Ministry were excluded from the preparations, since they had cautioned against a risky meeting of the diplomatically inexperienced Hitler with Mussolini, the elder statesman. Italian diplomats worried that the rather haphazard preparations would lead to some embarrassing gaffes. A few weeks later, on 3 April 1934, Hitler gave a hint about his meeting with Mussolini in an interview with the American journalist Louis P. Lochner. Without referring specifically to Mussolini, Hitler insisted that he preferred 'man-to-man diplomacy' over the allegedly secretive diplomacy of other past and present leaders. Here was a significant indication of Hitler's favoured style of diplomatic negotiation, which allegedly dispensed with bureaucrats and put the fate of the German nation into his own hands, boosting his ego and reinforcing his leadership cult. Hitler also insisted that he wanted to discuss foreign policy, on an equal footing, with other leaders. This was an articulation of his ideas about diplomatic culture which would shape his encounters with the Duce.[20]

Despite these allusions, Hitler insisted that the meeting with the Duce should not be announced, given the diplomatic tensions between Italy and Germany over Austria where nationalists, and above all Nazi groups, pushing for an incorporation of Austria into the Reich, were undermining the government. The Italian government initially agreed with this request to keep quiet about the meeting.[21] Mussolini, on the other hand, wanted to reassert his authority as elder statesman. He thus arranged for a leak of the news of Hitler's visit. On 11 June 1934, the international press, including the *New York Times*, announced the encounter. It cited Italian 'semi-official circles' and recorded that no Italian newspaper had yet written about the meeting.[22]

Renzetti, the principal contact between Mussolini and Hitler outside diplomatic channels since 1930, briefed Hitler before his departure and reported on 7 June 1934 to Mussolini that the Nazi leader was greatly looking forward to his meeting 'with the Head of Fascism and the leader of Italy'. Hitler had asked Renzetti whether he needed an interpreter to communicate with Mussolini. Renzetti insisted that this was unnecessary because of the Duce's excellent German (in reality, contrary to claims by Mussolini and, later, by German sycophants, his German was just fair and would often cause misunderstandings).[23] Renzetti even gave rather hyperbolic advice on Hitler's dietary preferences, hoping that it would ease tensions. The vegetarian Hitler particularly enjoyed 'spaghetti and tagliatelle with butter, cut in small pieces'. Renzetti mentioned Hitler's alleged love for Italian food to reassure Mussolini of the superiority of Italian culture, but failed to detail whether Hitler, a frequent visitor to Osteria Bavaria, one of Munich's finest Italian restaurants, was able to eat this long pasta without making a mess.[24]

Even the location of the meeting in Italy reflected the hierarchy of the leaders. Hitler had not been abroad since the Great War, and this first official foreign journey suggested that he would be paying homage to the more senior Mussolini. Hitler was not keen to go to Rome this time, though, as Mussolini had not reacted to his offer to visit Rome almost immediately upon coming to power in 1933. Therefore, the meeting was to be held in northern Italy, halfway for both dictators, an arrangement suggesting some basic parity between Mussolini and Hitler. Acknowledging Mussolini's role as the more senior statesman, Hitler left the choice of the date to the Italian dictator.[25]

Eventually, both sides agreed to meet in Venice on 14 June 1934. The Italian government, for which politics was a communal spectacle that symbolised the unanimous support of Italians for Mussolini and Fascism, had suggested the location. Venice was an ideal site to showcase Fascist Italy's grounding in culture and Italy's glorious past, present and future as a power dominating the Adriatic and the Mediterreanean more generally. Furthermore, Mussolini's visit to Venice, like his frequent visits to Italy's regions, would provide him with the opportunity to connect his regime with the Venetian people and enhance popular support for Fascism.[26] The preliminary programme scheduled two extended conversations between Mussolini and Hitler.[27] Hitler would travel by aeroplane – his preferred mode of transport, which projected an image of technological modernity – not least because he could not cross Austrian territory by train or car due to the unresolved Austrian question.[28] The Italian government even asked the German government to ensure that the Austrian Nazis who were undermining the Dollfuss regime, supported by Mussolini, would be keeping a low profile during the meeting.[29] As the one-to-one meeting of the two leaders was supposed to be informal, Mussolini suggested they dispense with 'tails and medals', the usual paraphernalia of official diplomatic visits; Hitler agreed. His small German delegation was joined by a few SS men and police detectives, suggesting German distrust of the Italian security arrangements. Rumours of a bomb plot against Hitler reinforced this distrust.[30] Security in Venice was tight, and the *Wall Street Journal* reported that the Italian government had deployed eighty secret policemen.[31]

Hitler did not have a fully developed plan for a military alliance with Italy in his luggage. Before Hitler's departure for Italy, Renzetti reported to Rome: '[Hitler] will fall for the Duce's charm [and] Hitler wants to reach an Italo-German understanding. The chancellor realises the problem of Europe and of the white race: Italo-German and Fascist–Nazi solidarity could lead to a common effort to convince other nations of Fascism and then achieve a great agreement between various Fascist countries.'[32] This was a lofty vision for a European fascist alliance that would, Renzetti expected, be dominated by Italy. But, first of all, Italian–German relations had to be improved. This was the tenor of a confidential report by Renzetti about conversations he had had with leading Nazis, including Göring, who was anxious that the Austrian question, if raised too directly by Hitler, would seriously impede the relationship between Mussolini and Hitler. Most significantly, Göring worried that Hitler might come too much under Mussolini's influence because of the Führer's affection for the Duce: a foreign policy guided by Hitler's emotional bond for Mussolini might jeopardise Germany's interests. Not all within the Nazi leadership thus agreed with Hitler's flirting with Mussolini. Renzetti concluded that those Germans still sceptical of or opposed to the Nazis hoped that Mussolini would have a moderating influence on Hitler and advise him to remove the most fanatical elements from the Nazi party, such as SA leader Ernst Röhm. At the very least, Renzetti added sarcastically at the end of his report, the Venice meeting would increase the number of German tourists going to Italy. The most important tourist, Hitler, was about to leave Germany for Italy when Renzetti sent off his report.[33]

III

On 14 June 1934, a sunny morning, Lufthansa's Ju-52 registered D-2600, named *Immelmann* after the German flying ace of the Great War, took off from Munich's Oberwiesenfeld airfield carrying Hitler on board. An embellished account of Hitler's flight can be found on the front page of the *Völkischer Beobachter*, the Nazi newspaper with a readership that went beyond party members. Hitler's air travel had been a familiar propaganda theme for most Germans since the election campaigns in the early 1930s. Crossing the Alps into Italy was another familiar trope for most German audiences, conjuring up images of German invaders, pilgrims and tourists. According to the Nazi newspaper, the Tyrol was covered by thick cloud while Hitler flew over it, an implicit reference to the tense Austro-German relations. After flying over the Brenner Pass into Italy, the sky allegedly cleared. Hitler joined his pilot in the cockpit to admire the Dolomites. The report did not mention that large parts of the Dolomites were in the South Tyrol; for Hitler this was no longer an issue, as he believed that this renunciation was the price for an alliance with Italy.[34] The plane flew over the lagoon and the Adriatic twice, an implicit acknowledgement that Italy was the unquestioned power in the Adriatic and the Mediterranean. There was a more mundane reason for this circling: an early arrival would have upset diplomatic protocol. Finally, the plane landed on the San Nicolò airfield on time, as could be expected from the Germans.[35]

The *Völkischer Beobachter* also covered the Duce's trip to Venice, suggesting that both leaders were equals. Mussolini, accompanied by his dandyish son-in-law Galeazzo Ciano, in charge of the head of government's press office, and Fulvio Suvich, the anti-German undersecretary of state in the Italian Foreign Ministry, had travelled from his holiday home in Riccione on the Adriatic to the Villa Pisani in Stra, a villa adorned with frescoes by the Baroque artist Tiepolo. The site was historically significant as Napoleon had previously stayed there when he had dominated most of Europe. Now, it was the turn of Mussolini, determined to turn Italy into a great power, to receive Hitler, the junior statesman. Mussolini's *Il Popolo d'Italia* emphasised that on the journey to Venice the Duce himself had been behind the wheel of his car, a metaphor suggesting that he was in control not just of Italy's but also of Europe's fate.[36]

For the Fascist press, Mussolini was naturally superior to Hitler. Typical was a report by the Fascist journalist Filippo Bojano. He wrote condescendingly that the journey to Venice was Hitler's first trip abroad and declared that 'Mussolini and Hitler lead two strong peoples, [both having an] ancient and firm tradition, a glorious past, who bear lots of hope and trust for the future.'[37] But this was not the full story of Fascist press coverage of Hitler's visit: in order to appeal to anti-German Italian audiences *Il Popolo d'Italia* also ran a report on the visit to Munich of a delegation from the Dante Alighieri Cultural Association, with strong links to Fascism. The article predictably highlighted that Munich's beautiful architecture had been inspired by Italy, thereby emphasising Italy's cultural superiority over Germany. Yet it also claimed that each Bavarian drank eight litres of beer per day, a gross exaggeration, which suggested that all Bavarians, and, by implication, the Nazis, were uncivilised drunkards.[38]

It is worth spending more time on the choreography of Hitler's arrival, which reflected the power relations between the Italian host and his German guest.[39] International newspapers were not slow in noticing this. For instance, the Italo-American Arnaldo Cortesi, the *New York Times* correspondent in Rome, a man with some Fascist sympathies, stressed Mussolini's seniority over Hitler.[40] Some small but noteworthy details revealed Mussolini's feeling of superiority. For instance, contrary to the agreement with the German Foreign Ministry to keep the meeting informal, Mussolini was dressed in a showy uniform and riding boots. In contrast, Hitler wore a belted beige trenchcoat, striped trousers, a white shirt and a tie. He was carrying a rumpled fedora, as he awkwardly climbed off the aeroplane. At the time and in subsequent accounts, Hitler's dress was ridiculed, as it made him look like an office worker or 'a peasant who wears his best clothes to go into town', as André François-Poncet, the French ambassador to Germany at the time, later sarcastically put it.[41] It is a moot point whether Hitler's civilian suit made him look like a fool compared with the uniformed Mussolini. Hitler, still in the process of consolidating the Third Reich, wore a suit because it presented him as someone civil who, despite pursuing a revisionist foreign policy and presiding over a brutal regime, followed international conventions. His dress was thus a symbol to reassure conservative German audiences, including the frail Reich president Paul von Hindenburg, that he was reasonable and not a belligerent carpet-biter bent on waging a world war.

Furthermore, his civilian attire communicated his civility to international audiences, including in Italy.[42]

While Hitler greeted Mussolini with the Nazi greeting, Mussolini simply shook his hand. Mussolini's refusal to salute Hitler with the Fascist greeting could be seen as a distancing act, suggesting that the Duce did not consider Hitler as a fascist leader on an equal footing.[43] The two leaders stood to attention to listen to a military band playing the German anthem, followed by the *Giovinezza,* the Fascist anthem. An embarrassed and insecure Hitler kept smiling throughout: Mussolini had clearly stolen the show. According to the anti-German Suvich, Hitler had tears in his eyes upon seeing his Italian idol for the time.[44]

After the welcoming ceremony, Mussolini walked with his guest to a motorboat that was waiting to take them to Venice. Hitler, in deference to Mussolini, the more senior statesman, stepped aside to allow Mussolini to get on the boat first, but Mussolini, placing his arm on Hitler's shoulder, insisted in a gesture of polite superiority that Hitler must get on the boat first.[45]

The organisation of the meeting followed diplomatic protocol closely. For instance, a telegram was sent on Hitler's behalf to Victor Emmanuel III, King of Italy since his father's assassination in 1900, as soon as Hitler's plane had landed. This diplomatic gesture reflected the tradition of monarchs paying tribute to their peers while visiting other countries. In his obsequious telegram, published a few days later in the *Völkischer Beobachter*, addressed to 'Your Majesty', Hitler expressed the hope that his visit would 'contribute to the wellbeing of both friendly countries and to world peace'. Here was a typical example of Hitler's peace propaganda and his genuine enthusiasm for an Italo-German alliance for which the king, who had led Italy in the First World War against Germany and Austria-Hungary, did not care much.[46]

Seemingly enthusiastic crowds – an integral part of any Fascist ceremony – had been mobilised by the regime, and lined the shores as Mussolini and Hitler sped across the water into Venice. A flotilla of Italian torpedo boats, with their officers and sailors on deck, greeted their motorboat, in order to leave nobody in doubt that Italy was a great naval power, determined to dominate the Mediterranean. Hitler and the German delegation got off at the Grand Hotel,[47] owned by the businessman Giuseppe Volpi, who had served as Mussolini's finance minister from 1925 until 1928.[48]

Behind the scenes of the welcoming ceremony, tensions were lurking. For example, Elisabetta Cerruti, the wife of Ambassador Cerruti, had been approached by the manager of the Grand Hotel for advice on Hitler's dietary preferences. She recommended the chef to serve puddings to Hitler, who had a fatal weakness for sweets. Suddenly, it turned out that the Grand Hotel's chef was Jewish. Concerned about the political consequences if Hitler upset his stomach with food prepared by a Jew, the manager reassigned the cook to the Excelsior Hotel on the Lido, also owned by Volpi, for the duration of Hitler's visit.[49]

On the way from Venice to Stra, Italian flags and 'Duce, Duce' posters were put up to impress Hitler with the powerful Mussolini cult. Venice prompted the *Völkischer Beobachter* to publish some historical musings: it was an ideal venue for Hitler's first meeting with the Duce because Venice and her seaborne empire had supposedly always maintained good relations with Germany, but not with Austria, which had allegedly suppressed the Veneto until its incorporation into the Kingdom of Italy in 1866. For the Nazi paper, it was therefore a historical inevitability that Germany and Italy would eventually become allies.[50] On his way to Stra, Hitler sailed past the Palazzo Vendramin, where the composer Richard Wagner, Hitler's greatest idol except for Mussolini, had died in 1883. Once the motorboats arrived at the new road connecting Venice with the mainland, the delegation changed into cars and travelled 'through long villages where one feels the satisfaction and order of the Fascist state', as the *Völkischer Beobachter* insisted. Needless to say, Fascist propaganda had staged the trip to show off Italians' acclaim for the Duce. After about twenty minutes, the cars arrived in Stra. Mussolini was already expecting his guest on the steps in front of the villa.[51]

Lunch at the Villa Pisani must have been excruciating for everyone involved, as Stra was plagued by a heat wave which brought out huge mosquitoes.[52] The subsequent conversations between Mussolini and Hitler took place without interpreters or other staff, so as to create an intimate atmosphere between the two leaders. Furthermore, Mussolini took pride in showing off his German.[53] Neurath later compiled minutes of these two encounters, based on what Hitler had told him. The lack of minute takers was meant to suggest that the conversations were personal ones that did not follow the stiff conventions of bureaucratic diplomacy to which the German and Italian foreign ministries subscribed.[54]

Let us consider the substance of the first Mussolini–Hitler conversation in more detail. Held in an excruciating atmosphere, it lasted two and a half hours and mainly focused on the Austrian question. An angry Hitler demanded Nazi participation in the Austrian government, but declared that 'the question of the Anschluss did not interest him' at present. Finally, Hitler asked Mussolini 'to remove his backing of Austria[n] [independence]'. Mussolini did not comment. For Hitler, an enormous gap opened between his idealised image of Mussolini and the mundane reality that the Duce was pursuing Italy's interests, rather than an ideological alliance with Fascism's purported Nazi relatives.[55]

A huge parade attended by 70,000 in Piazza San Marco, symbol of Venice's seaborne empire and Mussolini's claims for the *mare nostrum*, on the following day again emphasised Mussolini's superiority. The parade involved the Fascist militia, young Fascists and war veterans, including those who had been wounded. The presence of the wounded was a stark reminder of the long shadow of the Great War, but it could also be read as a symbol that the wounds of the war were healed. Again, Mussolini was dressed in uniform and Hitler in a civilian suit. Hitler's adjutant Fritz Wiedemann, who thought little of Italian military achievements, later claimed that the parade was disorganised. Two formations of the militia overran the military band, as they were all hoping to get a glimpse of the two leaders. According to Wiedemann, Hitler dismissed the Fascist militia as inefficient, just as he was looking at an Italian battleship through the window of his hotel room. The sailors had hung up their underwear to dry on the masts, thus reinforcing the low German opinion of the Italian armed forces.[56]

Hitler's mood did not improve. After the parade, he visited the Modern Art Biennale, one of the showcases of the modernity of the Fascist regime.[57] The German leader, extremely hostile towards modern art, spent most of his time in the German pavilion where he admired officially sanctioned Nazi art, but was disgusted by rooms full of what he saw as 'degenerate art'.[58]

More tensions overshadowed the subsequent lunch in the grounds of the Venice Golf Club on the Lido. This was an unlikely location for a meeting of the leaders, who had always stressed their humble origins. The club, founded in the late 1920s, catered to the Anglophilia of many well-off Italians, including Ciano.[59] Signora Cerruti, who sat next to Hitler, later remembered that someone had put salt into the coffee and that the food was disgusting. Was this perhaps a silent protest from the Jewish cook of the Grand Hotel against Hitler's anti-Semitic policies? After an awkwardly silent lunch, the two dictators walked off together to the golf course and sat down on a bench close to the clubhouse for their second conversation, which lasted for one and a half hours and was watched by the lunch guests.[60] It seemed as if common strategic interest provided Mussolini and Hitler with some basis for understanding. According to Neurath's summary, Hitler believed that he and the Duce found 'a significant rapprochement of [their] views', as both voiced strong criticism of France and the League of Nations. Towards the end of the conversation, both statesmen agreed that closer Italo-German relations were essential and that 'the Austrian question' must not stand in their way.[61]

A photo essay by Hitler's personal photographer Heinrich Hoffmann appeared in the Nazi glossy magazine *Illustrierter Beobachter* after Hitler's return to Germany. Hoffmann's picture of the talks presented the two dictators in animated conversation together; not a coincidence, as photographs of both leaders together suggested that they had something in common and represented a New Order.[62]

In Hitler's presence, the diplomatically experienced Mussolini hid his frustration about the Reich chancellor and did not contradict him. Behind the scenes, Mussolini reported his low opinion of Hitler to Cesare Maria De Vecchi, one of the *quadrumviri* who had helped organise the Fascist March on Rome and Italy's ambassador to the Holy See.[63] In the end, Hitler invited Mussolini to Germany.[64]

Predictably, the Nazi press celebrated Hitler's first visit abroad as a huge success. At a press conference on 15 June 1934 in Venice, Reich press chief Otto Dietrich declared that the historically significant meeting was dominated by the 'spirit of friendship' and an 'ideological bond'. Yet he insisted that 'Fascism is Italian, National Socialism is German'.[65] This emphasis of national differences was crucial for the Nazis, an ultra-nationalist movement, and suggests that ideological parallels alone made an Italo-German alliance unlikely.

After the build-up of parades and meetings, the highlight of the visit was a speech in the evening by Mussolini in the packed Piazza San Marco, full of enthusiastic people who had apparently been told by the authorities to attend. Addressing the 'people of Venice', Mussolini, interrupted by enthusiastic applause that was typical of Fascist rallies, mentioned the

Battle of Vittorio Veneto, Italy's greatest military triumph over Austria-Hungary at the end of the First World War, to remind Hitler that Italy, not Germany, had won the war. Mussolini showed off his rhetorical skills and boasted about Fascism's political achievements to Hitler before he eventually mentioned his German guest with some vague statements about common German and Italian efforts to maintain peace in Europe.[66] Crowds had been shipped into Venice on special trains, part of the regime's staging of a Fascist spectacle, suggesting unanimity between the leader and his followers. They were cheering the uniformed Mussolini, not the Nazi leader, still in his suit. The speech was a lesson for Hitler and once again reflected Mussolini's superiority as the doyen of the European far right. Significantly, while Mussolini was at the centre of attention, speaking from the balcony of the Palazzo Reale, Hitler had to look on from the balcony of the Procuratie Nuove. Hitler did not speak and was thus marginalised. Mussolini's paper *Il Popolo d'Italia* identified the speech as an 'unforgettable demonstration of the people for the Duce' and minimised Hitler's role.[67]

According to the diaries of Alfred Rosenberg, in charge of the Nazi party's foreign political office (*Außenpolitisches Amt*), a keen rival of the Foreign Ministry, Hitler's admiration for Mussolini and the Fascist spectacle was genuine. In reality, Hitler had not much choice to tell leading Nazis otherwise, since he had, for more than a decade, articulated his admiration for the Fascist leader, sometimes meeting opposition from other Nazi leaders. Fascist performance thus created political meaning. Hitler told Rosenberg that the Italians loved and respected the Duce as much as they liked the pope. Mussolini had posed like Caesar, Hitler added, suggesting a belief in the importance of spectacle.[68]

According to another source, however, Hitler's feelings towards Mussolini were more ambiguous. On his last evening in Venice, the Nazi leader had told Hassell that his idea of Mussolini had been fundamentally different from the real Mussolini. Hitler had reportedly said to Hassell: 'Now I look forward to being back again in Berlin tomorrow night, in Dr Goebbels' circles, where I feel comfortable.'[69] An official memorandum circulated to all German diplomatic missions highlighted the friendly atmosphere and the allegedly cordial relations between Mussolini and Hitler. Neurath, perhaps typically for a career diplomat, did not mention the term 'fascism' at all and did not dwell upon ideological similarities between Fascism and Nazism.[70] An official communiqué, issued by the Italian and German governments, remained vaguer and stated that talks would continue, based upon the personal contact of Mussolini and Hitler, an admission that the relationship between them remained tense.[71]

Hitler's final morning in Venice on 16 June 1934 started off with a tourist visit to the Basilica of San Marco. At the crack of dawn, the piazza was completely deserted, except for the pigeons. Suddenly, some German boys appeared and cheered Hitler with shouts of 'Heil Hitler!' The famous pigeons of Piazza San Marco were scared and flew away, hardly a good omen for a rapprochement between Italy and Germany. Thus, Hitler's visit ended on a hilarious note.[72]

IV

For the official farewell Mussolini escorted Hitler to his aeroplane, accompanied by a military band playing the German anthem followed by the Nazi and Fascist party songs. After take-off, in honour of Mussolini, the planes flew a circuit over the airfield and then turned north. While on the way towards Italy the Alps had been overcast, the *Völkischer Beobachter* suggested in its embellished coverage of Hitler's departure that, after the successful Venice meeting, the sky was now clear. The report mentioned that Hitler flew over the South Tyrol, another reference to the unresolved conflict over that region. As Hitler flew over the Austrian Tyrol, crowds were allegedly cheering him, suggesting that a German annexation of Austria was on the Nazis' agenda.[73]

Hitler's plan to create a solid bond with Mussolini in the context of a new diplomatic style had not succeeded. This point did not escape the attention of British diplomats. For instance, the British ambassador to Italy, Sir Eric Drummond, reported to the Foreign Office, concerned about a potential rapprochement between Italy and Germany, that Mussolini had dismissed Hitler's emotional and sentimental behaviour towards him. Drummond's information was based on a conversation with Suvich, and his report downplayed the significance of the Mussolini–Hitler meeting.[74]

And what of Hitler's verdict on the meeting? Renzetti's papers give us a rare insight into the Führer's views on his first encounter with the Duce.

Hitler invited Renzetti to a lunch shortly after his return from Italy, which was attended by leading Nazi officials such as Rudolf Hess, Hitler's deputy, Hans Frank, the Nazi lawyer, Reich press chief Otto Dietrich and Theodor Habicht, who would in due course play a notorious role in Austria. In a confidential report, probably seen by Mussolini, Renzetti paraphrased Hitler's remarks. Hitler had raved: 'Men like Mussolini are born only once every thousand years . . . I, and that's natural, found myself rather awkward with the Duce, but I am happy to have been able to talk to him for a long time [and] to have heard his ideas . . . What a great orator Mussolini is . . . ! And what great authority over the people!'

Hitler's flattery of the Duce and his display of enthusiasm about the Venice meeting would, he hoped, reach the Duce via Renzetti. Hitler's strategy here was to downplay Mussolini's reserved attitude towards him. (Indeed, according to the unrepentantly pro-Fascist ghosted post-war memoirs of Mussolini's widow, Mussolini had not warmed to Hitler at all in Venice.)[75]

Hitler had raved about the Venice meeting on various other occasions, according to Ambassador Cerruti's reports to Mussolini. Several Nazis were puzzled as Hitler was normally quite reserved. Yet all was not what it seemed. After a German tabloid had leaked news of an imminent Mussolini visit to Germany, the German Foreign Ministry postponed the visit indefinitely and Reich Press Chief Dietrich, in his daily guidelines to the German press, told editors to suppress reports about any such potential trip.[76]

V

After his return, domestic politics were increasingly on Hitler's mind. On 17 June 1934, Vice-Chancellor Franz von Papen delivered a lecture at Marburg University, written by his conservative aide Edgar Ernst Jung. In his speech, Papen, deeply complicit in bringing Hitler into power, criticised Nazi terror and the continuing Nazi undermining of the German state.[77] Still, Papen sent Hitler an obsequious telegram from Marburg, offering his heartfelt congratulations on the 'brilliant course of the Venice encounter which has shown how much the new Germany has the ear and the interest of the entire political world'. For the German national-conservative right, Mussolini embodied German hopes for a restoration and the integration of the party into the state's bureaucracy. Such hopes were quickly dashed.[78] Hitler and the Nazis were furious about Papen's speech and censored it. Mussolini, on the other hand, requested the full text from Ambassador Cerruti because it was 'an eloquent sign of the spiritual confusion and the feeling of unease [that was] coming to light in Germany'.[79] Mussolini was probably not displeased about the inner tensions within the Third Reich, as he hoped that they would shift the Nazis' attention from foreign policy, especially their aggressive policy on Austria.

On 21 June 1934, Hitler visited the ailing Reich President Hindenburg on his estate in Neudeck in East Prussia, formally to report to him the outcome of the Venice meeting. Like many leading German officials, Hindenburg had a low opinion of Italy. He had previously declared: 'Mr Mussolini may be an excellent politician and [a] good head of government, but one thing he will never achieve: to turn Italians into good soldiers and [to turn] Italy into a loyal ally.'[80] In reality, Hitler called on the president to obtain his permission to act against the SA, which was pushing for a second wave of the Nazi revolution and threatening to undermine the stability of the Third Reich and the power of the army. A few days later, on 30 June 1934, Hitler and the SS eliminated the SA as a political force and murdered its leaders, using false charges of treason against the SA leader, Ernst Röhm. Conservative opponents of the Nazis, including the ex-chancellor General von Schleicher and his wife, alongside 150 to 200 men, including Jung, were shot. Papen was effectively put under house arrest.[81]

International opinion reacted with shock to the so-called Night of the Long Knives, with its blatant political murders that were later legally sanctioned. In Italy, though, the press relied on official German material, without commenting on it, a clear gesture of sympathy for the Nazis. Thus Mussolini's *Il Popolo d'Italia* justified the brutal crackdown.[82] It is noteworthy that only the *Osservatore Romano*, the Vatican's official organ, openly condemned the murders. Cerruti even reported to Mussolini on 3 July 1934 that, according to rumours, Hitler had received advice from Mussolini in Venice about reasserting his authority 'and tak[ing] over the reins of the totalitarian leadership of Germany'. In reality, the Röhm purge demonstrated Hitler's ruthlessness, which greatly exceeded that of Mussolini; he did not murder his Fascist critics or rivals such as Roberto Farinacci, the radical ex-secretary of the Fascist party.[83]

Hitler had not acted on Mussolini's purported suggestion, but these rumours must have pleased the Duce because they implied that Hitler was still his disciple. Renzetti, reporting to Mussolini after Hitler's justification of the murder spree before the Reichstag in mid-July 1934, doubted that Röhm had planned a revolution, but still justified the violence.[84] According to the post-war memoirs of Mussolini's sister, keen to downplay her brother's role, the Duce had been completely shocked by Hitler's ruthlessness against Röhm and the SA.[85] The Night of the Long Knives confirmed the Nazis' brutality and their readiness to use violence whenever necessary, and Hitler's ruthless actions put Mussolini more and more into the shadow. It had taken Mussolini and the Fascists several years after Mussolini's appointment as prime minister to secure their power; Hitler asserted his position much more quickly and ruthlessly.

At the same time, Mussolini was increasingly aware of Hitler's determination to take over Austria, and he did warn the Austrian government via the Italian chargé d'affaires in Vienna to remain vigilant against the Nazis, as Hitler wanted to unite his home country with the Reich.[86] Mussolini rejected German claims as he saw the Alpine republic as a buffer state between Germany and Italy. Moreover, German–Italian strategic and economic interests in south-eastern Europe, in the successor states of the Habsburg monarchy, were an ongoing issue between both countries. Most Austrians wanted to be united with Germany, but the Allies had rejected this after the Great War. In an extremely polarised political climate the Socialists and the Christian Social party fought each other in a civil-war-like atmosphere from the late 1920s onwards. In 1933, the Christian Social chancellor, Engelbert Dollfuss, created an authoritarian regime that displayed an affinity with Mussolini. Hitler's appointment as Reich chancellor prompted the Austrian Nazi party to push for the Anschluss of the Alpine Republic with Germany with violence and terror that led to their banning. At the same, the Socialists also put pressure on Dollfuss's regime. Their uprising in February 1934 was suppressed by the Austrian army.[87]

In the wake of the Socialist uprising, Dollfuss tried to reinforce his power and displayed his affinity to Mussolini in order to protect Austrian sovereignty. Thus, a few days after the Venice meeting, he thanked the Italian government for its firm position on Austria during his Venice conversations with Hitler.[88] Indeed, Dollfuss enjoyed cordial relations with Mussolini, and his wife and children even stayed at the Duce's house on the Adriatic in the summer of 1934. Their holiday was brutally interrupted: on 25 July, Austrian SS members killed Dollfuss in Vienna. The putsch was quickly put down by the Austrian government and became an international embarrassment for Nazi Germany.[89]

A furious Mussolini saw Dollfuss's assassination as a personal affront, as he had to tell Mrs Dollfuss that she was now a widow. Mussolini immediately sent four Italian divisions to the Austrian border, a clear signal to Hitler that Italy would guarantee Austria's sovereignty.[90] The Duce squarely laid the blame on Hitler. Italian diplomats mustered support in France, Britain and the United States for a formal protest against Germany which appeared to be isolated on the European diplomatic stage.[91]

At the time of the Nazi coup in Austria, Hitler was enjoying himself at the Wagner festival in Bayreuth. He was embarrassed about the amateur putsch, and Mussolini's reaction had completely taken him by surprise. Clearly, Hitler had misread Mussolini's silence during their Venice discussions as tacit approval of Nazi claims for Austria.[92] He appointed the Catholic Franz von Papen as ambassador to Vienna,[93] a signal to Mussolini that Germany would pursue a more moderate policy towards Austria. The German Foreign Ministry, reflecting its concern over the deterioration of Italian–German relations, created a special file on Italian reactions to the Nazi putsch. In it, an alarming article from *Il Popolo d'Italia* is preserved which condemned Nazism as a dangerous folly, despised everywhere in the world. Other Fascist papers were even more aggressive. For instance, *Il Popolo di Roma* opined that the term 'Nazi' was synonymous with murder and pederasty. This prompted formal German diplomatic protests.[94] What is more, on 30 July 1934, the Italian border police sent a telegram to Rome, claiming that Hitler had survived an assassination attempt at the Bayreuth festival. While this rumour was false, the border police official who sent this telegram must have calculated that news of an attempt on Hitler's life would be well received by the Italian government.[95]

Many German officials in positions of authority such as Ulrich von Hassell believed that the assassination of Dollfuss had caused irreparable damage. Mussolini, until recently a staunch advocate of an agreement with Germany, increasingly gave in to the pro-French faction in the Italian Foreign Ministry, which advocated an agreement with France, to create a front against German revisionism.[96] He publicly condemned Nazi Germany in the months after the Nazi putsch in Austria. An angry

Mussolini, envious of Hitler's conclusion of the Nazi seizure of power in August 1934, did not restrain himself. Consider the Duce's speech in Bari on 6 September 1934: in it, he ridiculed Nazi race theories and dismissed the Germans as uncivilised compared to the ancient Roman civilisation, a familiar Italian trope. He railed: 'Thirty centuries of history allow us to look with sovereign pity at some doctrines from the other side of the Alps, sustained by the descendants of people who did not know how to write . . . at the [time] when Rome had Caesar, Vergil and Augustus.'[97] In response to these anti-German rants, Hitler dismissed Italy. For example, at a dinner on 17 August 1934, according to Hamburg's mayor, Carl Vincent Krogmann, he identified the Italian army as unreliable and the Italian people as racially inferior.[98]

Despite these tensions, the Italian and German governments did not break off diplomatic relations, as they still saw each other as useful potential allies in revising the post-1919 order. By late 1934, the relationship between Mussolini and Hitler was tense, bordering on the hostile. Although Mussolini had to accept grudgingly that Austria would eventually be united with Germany, he tried to delay the Anschluss for as long as possible and even cancelled the delivery of Italian aeroplanes to Germany. He thus began negotiations with the French and British governments to contain Germany. This was not because he was principally opposed to Hitler's revisionism, but rather because he wanted to ensure that he would be able to implement his plans to extend Italy's possessions in Africa, more specifically in Ethiopia, where the Italians had suffered one of their most traumatic defeats at Adowa in 1896.[99]

It is noteworthy that even in this tense atmosphere, beyond official contacts, non-official links continued between Mussolini and his followers in Germany, intent on improving Italian–German relations. For example, on 15 November 1934, the Duce received Louise Diel, a German journalist who had promoted the Mussolini cult in Germany. She had ingratiated herself with Hitler to help improve Italian–German relations, overestimating her own role like so many of the other self-appointed non-official contacts between the dictators, including Renzetti. During her audience with the Duce, Diel asked him to sign a copy of her recent hagiographic book on him, to which he had contributed a preface. The autograph was not for herself, but for Hitler, she added. Mussolini, trying to keep his options open in improving his relations with Hitler, wrote a dedication to 'Reich Chancellor Hitler'. Mussolini condescendingly did not address Hitler as 'Führer', as he was jealous of Hitler's superior status. Diel eventually presented an overjoyed Hitler with this copy on 20 December 1934, an early Christmas present from his Italian idol. Hitler finally thanked Mussolini on 1 February 1935 with a telegram, signed by the status-conscious Hitler as 'Führer and Reich chancellor'.[100]

Despite missions such as Diel's, official relations between Italy and Germany remained tense. In an audience with the Duce on 5 December 1934, Hassell was subjected to violent criticism of Germany. The Duce loudly complained that Poland, for many Germany's natural enemy after obtaining sizeable chunks of German territory in the wake of Versailles, was showered in the German press with compliments, while Italy only received opprobrium. (Poland had signed a non-aggression pact with Germany in January 1934, one of Hitler's first diplomatic achievements.) Mussolini even accused Germany of preparing a war against Italy. The chief of a delegation sent by the German army which visited Italy in early December 1934 offered a plausible interpretation of Mussolini's extremely hostile attitude: the Duce knew, of course, that Germany was not preparing a war against Italy, but this sharp accusation served as a warning that he would not support German rearmament. Mussolini's ability to change his behaviour and his display of emotions, such as fury, anger and kindness, was masterful. In this particular situation, his calculated fury was a hint that Italy need not rely on Germany, but could instead reach an agreement with France over disarmament at Germany's loss. Mussolini's overall concern in this situation was to maximise Italy's diplomatic standing in the run-up to the planned invasion of Ethiopia.[101]

But there were other reasons for the Duce's display of his anti-German attitude in late 1934. Mussolini envied Hitler, who was increasingly stealing the show from him on the diplomatic stage. Furthermore, the anti-Italian statements on display in Germany that portrayed it as an inefficient, weak and inferior nation had offended the Duce, bent on turning Italy into a land of warriors. The German ambassador correctly diagnosed that Mussolini was suffering from a 'constant nervous condition' because he feared that the rise of the Third Reich would marginalise Italy and thereby derail Italian plans for the invasion of Ethiopia, a long-standing ambition of Italian imperialists and a project taken up by Mussolini and the Fascists with particular determination and ruthlessness.[102]

Italy's future seemed to lie with France, rather than Germany. Thus, in January 1935, Italy signed an agreement with France. France, represented by foreign minister Pierre Laval, effectively left Italy a free hand in Ethiopia, a country that had long been on Italy's wish list. Laval hoped that these concessions would turn Mussolini away from Hitler and secure a western front against the Third Reich. Mussolini, determined to maximise his room for manoeuvre in the run-up to the invasion of Ethiopia, thus told the French ambassador to Italy that Fascism and Nazism were only loosely united by their rejection of communism. Geopolitical considerations thus continued to shape the relationship between Fascist Italy and Nazi Germany.[103]

Mussolini soon pursued a strategy of collective Western security, trying to bring together France, Britain and Italy as a bulwark against the Third Reich. Yet his ambitions in Ethiopia rapidly derailed any hopes for a Western anti-Hitler alliance and, over the course of 1935 and 1936, laid the foundations for what had long seemed highly unlikely from a diplomatic perspective: a rapprochement between him and Hitler.

Throughout 1933 and 1934, Hitler's first two years in power, rivalry between the Nazi leader and Mussolini increased, as Hitler and the Nazis consolidated their power more ruthlessly and profoundly than Mussolini's Fascists had ever managed to do. If Hitler had borrowed strategic aspects of gaining power from his idealised reading of Mussolini's Italy, by the end of 1934 he no longer had any need to follow Mussolini's advice. Both regimes shared not so much a common ideology as a shared strategic objective, namely destroying the post-1919 order and replacing it with a new expansionist order. Yet, despite Mussolini and Hitler's first date in Venice, tensions were running so high after the Nazi putsch in Austria that Italy and Germany were nearing the brink of war. This was an unlikely alliance, as the Fascist staging of the Mussolini–Hitler meeting in Venice, with its constant emphases of Mussolini's power, had revealed. Yet, over the course of a few years, the expansionist geopolitical aims of Mussolini and Hitler would begin to coalesce to the extent that more amicable relations between both countries became possible.

3

SECOND TIME AROUND
September 1937

I

After the rapid consolidation of Nazi power, Hitler increasingly focused on foreign policy and self-confidently pursued the revision of the Versailles Treaty. In March 1935, Germany reintroduced conscription and announced that it had an air force: both in blatant breach of the Versailles Treaty. Mussolini's reaction was not slow in coming. He invited Pierre Laval and the British prime minister, Ramsay MacDonald, to Stresa, a small town on the shores of Lake Maggiore in northern Italy. The location of the meeting was significant, as it gave prestige to Mussolini, who liked to see himself as the arbiter of war and peace in Europe. Mussolini exploited Anglo-French concerns over German rearmament and presented himself as the champion of an anti-Nazi alliance. His overarching calculation at Stresa was that an alliance with the two Western powers against Hitler would give him a free hand in Ethiopia.[1]

Like Hitler, Mussolini wanted to revise Versailles and conquer territories. Since the beginning of his premiership, the Duce had pursued an aggressive foreign policy, since for him and many other Italian statesmen past and present, war, military service and blood sacrifice would turn Italy into a great power and a nation of warriors, while also redeeming past crushing military defeats. Mussolini reinforced this sentiment by emphasising Italy's lineage to the Roman Empire with the cult of *romanità*.

Mussolini was a brilliant showman who often used aggressive warmongering language even when he knew that Italy lacked the military resources to fight a long war. Yet his emphasis on show and rhetoric on the diplomatic stage does not make him a buffoon, as some commentators, including the historian Denis Mack Smith, have suggested. Rather, his often keenly effective rhetoric was a means to deal with Italy's limited military power.[2]

At the April 1935 Stresa meeting, Mussolini ensured that the final declaration focused on the maintaining of peace in Europe, diverting attention from East Africa. Mussolini misunderstood this as France and Britain's tacit approval for his planned invasion of Ethiopia.[3] A successful conquest of the east African state, next to the Italian colonies of Somaliland and Eritrea, established before the Great War, would allow Mussolini to avenge the 1896 Italian defeat at Adowa, assert Italy's status as a great power vis-à-vis the nascent Third Reich, and provide Italy with *spazio vitale* (living space). Furthermore, victory in Ethiopia would give a new boost to the Fascist regime, uniting Italians behind the rallying cry of foreign expansion.[4]

Nothing seemed more unlikely than an alliance of Fascist Italy and Nazi Germany, as the Stresa front isolated the Third Reich. The May 1935 conclusion of the Franco-Soviet Treaty of Mutual Assistance and, the same month, the Czechoslovak–Soviet Treaty of Alliance, as well as the June 1935 announcement of Franco-Italian military accords reinforced a sense of German isolation and encirclement. This had the convenient side-effect for Italy that French troops were moved from the Italian border and from north Africa to the German border, which allowed Italy to move its own troops from the French border to East Africa.[5]

Before long, the Stresa front disintegrated, as Mussolini began to realise that his planned conquest of Ethiopia did not meet with the unreserved support of France and Britain. Instead, Mussolini, over the course of 1935 and 1936, began to put out feelers to Hitler. Some historians later claimed that Mussolini was uncertain whether Italy should side with Nazi Germany or with France and Britain, Italy's allies during the First World War, in order to create an Italian Mediterranean empire. Some commentators, above all the historian Rosaria Quartararo, have identified his apparent wavering as strategic uncertainty and claim that Rome kept at an equal distance to Paris and London on the one hand and Berlin on the other.

According to this school of thought, a number of Britain's politicians were impressed by Mussolini's domestic achievements and his suppression of the left, but they were annoyed by Italy's challenge to British supremacy in the Mediterranean and East Africa. Thus, they did not allow Mussolini to go ahead in Ethiopia, calling for the League of Nations to place Italy under trade sanctions. For commentators like Quartararo, then, it was British unwillingness to grant Italy its fair share of a colonial empire, ironically at a time when other European imperial powers were beginning to consider decolonisation, that brought Mussolini into the arms of Hitler. Yet this view confuses cause and effect and downplays Mussolini's responsibility for going to war in Ethiopia. At the same time, this flawed interpretation nevertheless shows that, first and foremost, power considerations and not simply a common ideology would determine Mussolini's attitude towards Hitler, as much as they did Hitler's views on Mussolini.[6]

What is clear is that there was no strategic uncertainty for the Duce. The conquest of Ethiopia had priority, and he cleverly played the register of European diplomacy, which brought him eventually into Hitler's arms. Italian propaganda, using colonial tropes familiar since before the rise of Fascism, accused the British, after all the world's leading colonial power, of hypocrisy, since Italy, a young and 'proletarian' nation, deserved its small slice of Africa. It was not the British, but Mussolini, soon followed by Hitler, who destroyed the post-1919 liberal-internationalist order with their revisionist and increasingly aggressive foreign policies. An important precedent to their aggression had been set by the 1931 Japanese invasion of Manchuria, which had exposed the League of Nations as powerless in maintaining its vision of a peaceful international order.[7]

Another reason for Stresa's failure was that the three signatories were unwilling to go to war against Hitler. Within less than two months, in June 1935, the Stresa declaration was obsolete, as Britain, without consulting Italy and France, signed a naval agreement with Germany which allowed the Third Reich to rearm its navy up to a size of 35 per cent of the Royal Navy, clearly in excess of the provisions of Versailles. This was a clear British acknowledgement that Nazi Germany's rearmament was legitimate and that the Western Allies had been too harsh on the Germans at Versailles.[8] Italy's claim for Ethiopia, on the other hand, was seen as pure aggression in Britain, a view advocated particularly forcefully by Robert Vansittart, permanent under-secretary at the Foreign Office.[9]

As he was planning the invasion of Ethiopia, Mussolini put out his feelers to Hitler to prepare for the eventuality that Italy would find itself isolated on the international stage. Both dictators communicated indirectly with each other, via diplomats and especially via the established unofficial channels. As a significant goodwill gesture, Mussolini accepted Hitler's request, communicated by Renzetti, to replace Ambassador Cerruti, whom Hitler had accused of undermining an Italo-German rapprochement by deliberately misrepresenting Hitler's policies in his reports to Mussolini. At the same time, however, in a direct snub to Hitler, Mussolini immediately appointed Cerruti ambassador to Paris, where the diplomat openly expressed his negative views of the Third Reich.[10]

A number of visitors from outside the Italian and German governments' state bureaucracies in 1935 and 1936 helped improve Italian–German relations. A July 1935 audience of the Hamburg editor Sven von Müller with Mussolini illustrates how the Duce's relationship with Hitler was changing dramatically. During the audience, the urbane Fascist leader was in his element, as he used audiences as representations of his power. Mussolini politely welcomed his guest at the door of his huge office in the *Sala del Mappamondo* of Rome's Palazzo Venezia. Mussolini knew, of course, that Müller would report to Hitler, and, indeed, Müller's notes have survived in the files of Hitler's Reich Chancellery. Mussolini lectured Müller about the planned invasion of Ethiopia, and railed against the Jews, who could not be proper Fascists. These statements reflected Mussolini's desire to present himself as ideologically close to Hitler. While Mussolini liked to tell his audiences what they wanted to hear, his remarks coincided with a gradual shift towards the development of an Italian racial ideology, as Italy was preparing for colonial warfare in Africa. In a significant volte-face, Mussolini again showed his keenness on developing closer bonds with Hitler when he admitted that 'Austria, as a second German country, could *not in perpetuity pursue a policy directed against the Reich*'. This was an implicit concession that Italy would accept German supremacy over Austria as long as Hitler firmly supported Italy during the Ethiopian campaign. In contrast to his previous statements, Mussolini emphasised the 'common basic ideas of Fascism and National Socialism' (a year previously, after the Nazi putsch in Austria, he had ridiculed Nazism). His remarks were, in typical fashion, deliberately vague and could easily be misunderstood by senior German officials, including Hitler, as a turning point in Italian–German relations.[11]

Further meetings outside diplomatic channels helped improve the Italian–German relationship. In order to sound out Germany's position on the planned Ethiopian campaign, Mussolini sent Professor Guido Manacorda (a noted Italian Germanist with close connections to the Vatican and Mussolini) to Berlin. Hitler spoke to the scholar for more than one and a half hours. Such a long audience with the Nazi leader was a significant honour. After his return to Italy, Mussolini received Manacorda twice. Apparently, Hitler had reassured Manacorda that Germany would not join in any potential League sanctions against Italy. This in turn reassured Mussolini that Germany would support Italy in the Ethiopian war.[12] After a long build-up of Italian materiel and troops and days after Manacorda's audience with the Nazi leader, Italy invaded Ethiopia on 3 October 1935, meeting fierce resistance. Yet despite their bravery the Ethiopian forces could do little against the Italians' extremely brutal methods, which included, with Mussolini's authorisation, the use of poison gas.[13]

The British government, Italy's principal critic in the Ethiopian campaign, perceived the emergent Italo-German entanglement with concern. For instance, on 15 October 1935, the British ambassador to Germany, Sir Eric Phipps, reported to Foreign Secretary Sir Samuel Hoare that anti-Italian views were widespread amongst the German people during the Ethiopian campaign. Phipps declared that 'the Italians themselves are disliked in Germany and are despised for their unreliability and lack of military virtues. The Italian tutelage of Austria is resented and the betrayal of the Triple Alliance in 1914 is still remembered.' But Phipps's hopes that popular German anti-Italian feelings would stand in the way of a growing Italian–German relationship were soon dashed.[14]

Hitler and the Nazis were also aware of the persistent anti-Italian popular sentiment in Germany. This is one of the reasons why Hitler's strategy towards Italy was Janus-faced during the Ethiopian campaign. While Germany did not join the League of Nations' sanctions against Italy that were imposed soon after the invasion, the Third Reich simultaneously delivered weapons to the Ethiopian government to prolong the war. This tactic deepened divisions between Italy and the Western powers, whose attention was focused on the Italian campaign in Ethiopia, rather than on Germany's revisionist designs. Isolated by the Western powers, Mussolini had little option but to cultivate better relations with Nazi Germany. He even compromised on Austrian independence. In January

1936, the Duce thus told Hassell that Italy would be prepared to accept Austria as a German satellite state, as long as Austrian independence was formally maintained. Mussolini confirmed that the Stresa front was dead. Hitler and other German officials in positions of authority initially did not trust Mussolini's promises as Italy's deployment of troops at the Austrian border after the failed 1934 Nazi putsch was still on their minds.[15]

Mussolini wanted to overcome Italy's isolation and continued his advances towards the Third Reich. Another meeting outside diplomatic channels is worth exploring in more detail to understand Mussolini's strategy towards Germany. On 31 January 1936, Mussolini received the journalist and SS officer Roland Strunk in Rome. The Duce's guest was a colourful man who had covered parts of the Ethiopian campaign for the *Völkischer Beobachter* and would later die in a duel. Mussolini appeared even more gregarious than at Müller's audience and insisted that Italy and Germany had a common anti-Bolshevik ideology. Typically, he refused to detail it. Significantly, for the first time, Mussolini stated that he had always been a friend of Hitler, 'a great man, a genius and genuine leader'. This calculated use of emotional language was a clever tactic to flatter Hitler, who had been longing for Mussolini's recognition since the early 1920s. A year previously, such friendly overtones would have been unthinkable.[16]

These friendly statements reinforced Hitler's conviction that Italy would not intervene if Germany remilitarised the Rhineland. In March 1936, German troops crossed the Rhine. The German remilitarisation of the Rhineland, blatantly illegal under the provisions of the Locarno Treaty, rendered any hopes for an anti-Nazi western front obsolete, as Mussolini had anticipated, and was a major coup for Hitler that raised his popularity in Germany and boosted his international position.[17]

At this point, there was still was nothing inevitable about closer cooperation. Below the level of high politics, Italian–German networks began to emerge. For example, as Benjamin G. Martin has recently shown, Italian and German intellectuals and artists were beginning to cement closer ties with one another in an attempt to challenge the purported cultural hegemony of the Western democracies, decried as decadent, with a new Fascist–Nazi European cultural order. Such contacts, like those of academic experts, undoubtedly helped create closer Italian–German bonds. But these 'soft power' networks did not make a political alliance of Fascist and Nazi Germany inevitable.[18]

Hitler's strategy towards Italy remained mixed. Thus, he did not inform the Italian government of Germany's February 1936 offer to rejoin the League of Nations. The Third Reich was never serious about rejoining the League; rumours about a return to Geneva were attempts to calm the British and were cleverly spread at a time when Mussolini was threatening Italy's exit from the League because the international organisation was considering oil sanctions against Italy. Eventually, there were no oil sanctions, as France and Britain did not want to alienate Italy further. Mussolini was furious about Hitler's unilateral action, which had made Hitler look more reasonable than himself.[19]

Hitler's march into the Rhineland and the effective surrender of the Italian guarantee of Austrian independence in exchange for German support in the Ethiopian campaign marked a turning point in the relationship between the two dictators. From this moment, Mussolini would pursue closer cooperation with Germany, without severing entirely his links with Britain. Mussolini's skilful indirect communications with Hitler via intermediaries made the Nazi leader believe that the Duce was becoming friendly towards Germany and himself. Mussolini also played an emotive register to appeal to Hitler. On 20 April 1936, for example, he sent a telegram to Hitler on the occasion of the Nazi leader's birthday. This was reciprocated on 28 July 1936 with Hitler's telegraphic birthday 'best wishes' to the Duce. Whether or not the friendly feelings expressed in these telegrams were genuine is a moot point. What matters is that they were duly archived and thus took on an official meaning. Such exchanges helped cement the notion, initially within the Italian and German state bureaucracies, that Mussolini and Hitler were about to become friends.[20]

Undeniably, both leaders wanted to revise Versailles and expand their territories, but this alone was not a strong enough basis for a solid alliance. The relationship between Mussolini and Hitler remained contingent on the strategic interests of both sides, rather than being predetermined by a shared ideology. Although Hitler continued to crave Mussolini's friendship and recognition, both leaders prioritised territorial expansion over an ideologically motivated alliance. As a symbol of rapprochement, Germany was the first nation to recognise the Italian Empire, proclaimed after the

May 1936 fall of Addis Ababa. League sanctions were lifted in July 1936. All this was a massive victory that gave a tremendous boost to Fascism and above all to Mussolini's cult, and he now reached the climax of his popularity.[21]

Mussolini's claim about the common anti-Bolshevik denominator of Italy and Germany was soon put to the test when, in May 1936, the Popular Front won the elections in France, following the election victory of their Spanish counterparts in February. After the nationalist coup of General Francisco Franco against the Spanish Popular Front government in July 1936, Italy and Germany intervened on Franco's behalf. Italy would soon be the largest foreign participant in the war, with up to 50,000 troops in action by February 1937, including about 29,000 from the Fascist militia. Germany mainly provided air transport. Mussolini's commitment of Italian troops to Spain further weakened Italy's capacity to stop Nazi advances in Austria. Indeed, in July 1936, Austria formally agreed that it was a German state, as Mussolini had sacrificed his guarantee of Austrian independence to improving Italo-German relations.[22] Not all in positions of authority in Italy agreed with these policies, and a stream of anti-German articles was still appearing in the Italian press.[23]

Despite this ambiguity, a clear indicator of improving Italo-German relations was the increasing visits of Nazi officials to Italy. Visitors included Prince Philip of Hesse. In August 1936, the prince on Hitler's behalf explored with Mussolini the possibility of a joint Italo-German intervention in Spain. But such missions were not as significant as some historians later claimed. Likewise, the importance of the German–Italian Police Accords of March–April 1936, which saw increasing cooperation between the Italian and German police forces, should not be exaggerated. They were above all an instrument for both revisionist regimes to signal to the international community, especially France and Britain, that they were becoming closer to each other under the guise of fighting Bolshevism, rather than a straightforward reflection of an ideological alliance between Germany and Italy. It should be added that, at that time, Italian–Soviet relations were friendly, if hardly close, and Mussolini's anti-Bolshevism lacked the intensity and passion of Hitler's.[24]

In the summer of 1936 Mussolini began to project his growing pro-German sentiment more clearly. In June, as a symbol of the Italo-German rapprochement, Ciano, the deeply opportunistic son-in-law of the Duce with pro-German leanings, was made foreign minister. At the same time, the Austrophile Suvich was demoted. But this was not all. In September 1936, Hans Frank, president of the German Academy of Law, visited Mussolini in Rome. Frank invited the Duce to Germany on Hitler's behalf, effectively a renewal of Hitler's 1934 invitation. Frank's visit was another example of Hitler and Mussolini communicating outside diplomatic channels via personal envoys. Mussolini accepted Hitler's invitation. Significantly, the Duce insisted that this meeting would have to be more than a traditional state visit and instead a powerful symbol of the new comradely relations between both nations and their peoples.[25] Here was an articulation of what Mussolini saw as a joint Fascist–Nazi front against the alleged dominance of the decadent Western democracies. Nevertheless, despite the Fascist and Nazi attempts to present this relationship as a new form of diplomacy, the visit did not happen in a historical vacuum. Aspects of the performance were borrowed from the rituals of state visits that had emerged over the centuries, so both regimes were struggling to present the Mussolini–Hitler relationship as distinct in style and substance.[26]

II

Mussolini's acceptance of the invitation was significant, as he was normally unwilling to step beyond Italy's frontiers, concerned that he would not be in control outside Italy and risked exposure to anti-Fascist protests, or that he would look ridiculous, as he had at the 1925 Locarno conference.[27] Furthermore, his general refusal to travel abroad was an assertion of symbolic power for Mussolini, as he calculated that Italy was such an important nation that other statesmen and diplomats must call on him in Rome. Through his acceptance of Hitler's invitation, Mussolini projected the message that his relationship with Hitler and Germany was special.[28] Given Hitler's admiration, Mussolini calculated that he would be accorded a triumphant reception which would boost his cult and his self-confidence, both in Italy and abroad. His insistence on a face-to-face meeting was also a reflection of his determination to challenge the post-war order and above all of the fact that he was only head of government and therefore not entitled to a state visit. As a clever tactician, Mussolini, again using emotional language, had told Hans Frank that he 'admire[d] [Hitler] with all [his] heart'. Mussolini even declared that the 'Führer ha[d] always been an ideal' for him, even before 1933. This was a gross distortion of his then-negative attitudes towards the Nazis.[29]

The real reasons for Hitler's pro-Mussolini enthusiasm in 1936 deserve closer examination. At this time, Hitler was geared to go to war at any cost to fulfil his plan to conquer living space in the East, as evidenced by his August 1936 memorandum on the Four-Year Plan, which stipulated that the German war economy must be ready for war within four years.[30] Despite his courting of the Duce, Hitler used plans for an Italian alliance as an instrument to put pressure on the British. In October 1936, the snobbish Joachim von Ribbentrop, formerly a salesman of German sparkling wine, took up his ambassadorship in London. Ribbentrop's mission, to cultivate an alliance with Britain, failed, but the Nazi courting of the British suggests that the Fascist–Nazi alliance was not ideologically inevitable, as Mussolini realised at the time. In the same month, Ciano, on his first official visit abroad as foreign minister, visited Hitler in his Bavarian mountain retreat. This was a great honour granted to the Italian foreign minister. Hitler showed Ciano the panoramic view of the Austrian mountains, a scenic illustration of German claims for Austria. Ciano knew how to use Hitler's seemingly unbounded personal affection for Mussolini and conveyed the Duce's greetings, not without adding hyperbolically that Mussolini had always been sympathetic towards Hitler.[31]

The concrete result of Ciano's mission to the Reich was a confidential German–Italian protocol, signed on 23 October 1936. Far from entering into a military alliance, both powers identified Bolshevism as a threat. In return for Germany's recognition of the Italian Empire, Italy expressly welcomed the normalisation of Austro-German relations, a euphemistic renewal of the formulation that Italy would no longer stand in the way of an eventual German annexation of Austria.[32]

A closer examination of Nazi press reports on Ciano's visit reveals the strategic rationale behind the German strategy for the Italian–German rapprochement. For instance, the *Völkischer Beobachter* did not dwell upon a common Fascist and Nazi ideology. The Nazi paper emphasised instead that the organisation of Ciano's visit went beyond outdated diplomatic protocol, as Ciano had spoken to 20,000 Hitler Youth members and talked to Nazi leaders face to face.[33] This style of mingling with a mass political organisation was a powerful statement of the special relationship between

Italy and Germany, a threatening gesture suggesting that Italo-German rapprochement was in the making in order to challenge the purported hegemony of the Western powers. In reality, Italo-German cooperation remained localised in the Spanish Civil War. Two days later, Ribbentrop and the Japanese ambassador to Berlin signed the Anti-Comintern Pact, implicitly directed against the Soviet Union. Italy did not join it initially. Still, in a speech on 1 November 1936 in the Cathedral Square in Milan, Mussolini declared: 'The Berlin encounters have resulted in an agreement between both countries on specific problems which are particularly acute these days. But this agreement . . . this vertical axis Berlin–Rome is not a diaphragm, but rather an Axis with which all European States animated by the will to collaborate and to peace can collaborate.'[34]

Milan was a significant location, as Fascism had been founded in that city. But it was also the place where, in 1848, the people had risen against the Austrians, then often called *tedeschi*, or Germans. While Mussolini praised Germany's recognition of the Italian Empire, he said little about ideological parallels between Fascism and Nazism, reflecting the paradox of fascism, an ultra-national movement that could not acknowledge debts to or similarities with foreigners. Moreover, this vagueness reflected the strategic nature of the Italian–German relationship. This was not a full-fledged alliance, and using the vague term 'Axis', a metaphor previously used by the Hungarian prime minister, Gyula Gömbös, and mentioning the possibility of other European states joining it, allowed Mussolini considerable room for pursuing other alliances, although the Ethiopian war had made a pact with France and Britain seem unlikely. Yet the fact that Mussolini mentioned Berlin before Rome was an implicit acknowledgement that Germany would dominate this union, since the Third Reich had proved to be the more dynamic and radical regime. Probing Mussolini's reasons to announce a vague cooperation with Nazi Germany, Schieder has recently suggested that Nazi Germany became the focus and ideological backbone of Mussolini's foreign policy. On a domestic level, Mussolini's public proclamation of the Axis meant that his dictatorial rule was underwritten by Hitler. This would give a radical impetus to Italians on their road to a totalitarian society.[35]

While perceptive about the domestic ramifications of Mussolini's speech, Schieder's interpretation glosses over the many remaining dissonances between Italy and Germany, above all that Mussolini refused fully to commit himself to the Third Reich and was keen to avoid severing links with Britain.

For Mussolini, the Axis was not just about Italo-German cooperation, but rather a metaphor for revisionist European powers to oppose Bolshevism.[36] The historian D.C. Watt has characterised this relationship as existing both as a myth and a reality which was stronger on a rhetorical or propagandistic level than on a political-diplomatic one. Yet the rhetoric and propaganda soon made the main protagonists of the relationship – that is, Mussolini, Hitler and their officials, but also domestic and international audiences – believe that a strong Italian–German relationship existed. The myth of the alliance thus gradually became translated into politics.[37]

This was a relationship of two uneven sides. Germany did not only surpass Italy politically, but also economically. Especially in the wake of the League of Nations' sanctions against Italy, Italy had become more and more economically dependent on Germany. By 1936, 20 per cent of Italy's exports went to Germany, a huge increase from the 11 per cent of 1932. German imports, especially coal and other raw materials, to Italy also rose dramatically, from 14 per cent in 1932 to 27 per cent in 1936–8, increasing to 40 per cent in 1940.[38] In the wake of the October 1936 announcement of the Four-Year Plan, Italy began to deploy its workers to the Reich. After negotiations in 1937, more than 30,000 Italian agricultural labourers, most of them jobless at a time of high unemployment in Italy, were sent north. This was a humiliating practice illustrating Italy's poverty, in sharp contrast to Fascist rhetoric about stopping Italian emigration. Pragmatic considerations, such as the reduction of Italian unemployment and the improvement of the Italian trade balance with Germany through the Italian workers' wages, and, above all, the symbolical value of sending workers to Germany, overruled Mussolini's ideological rejection of Italian migration. Fascist propaganda celebrated the deployment of the workers as symbols of the Italian–German rapprochement. Several thousand workers followed in 1938 and helped build the Volkswagen plant in Wolfsburg. Despite propaganda celebrating this worker exchange as a tangible symbol of the Axis, life was not easy for the Italian workers in Germany. The German authorities discouraged contacts with Germans, and the Italian labourers were housed in separate camps. They were subjected to strong anti-Italian prejudices, often bordering on the racist, like the many Italians who had migrated to Germany since before the First World War.[39]

Mussolini's strategy to let Hitler wait for a formal alliance only increased Nazi desires. At the same time, Germany's refusal to send ground troops to

Spain disappointed Mussolini, who had seized upon the idea that ensuring Franco's victory would be a way for Italy to prove itself as a great power. After the failure to reach an alliance with Britain, leading Nazis intensified their courting of Mussolini. Thus, in mid-January 1937, Göring visited Italy. The Italian government put on an opulent programme for the air force general and his wife, which included audiences with the king and Mussolini, banquets, a hunt and a holiday in Capri. The Italian government was such a good host that it even provided four packs of the morphine-based Eucodal for Göring, a drug addict, although Mussolini's secretariat later explained that the drugs had, in fact, been for Mrs Göring. For the Axis to turn into a real military alliance, Göring insisted that Germany would be prepared to recognise the Brenner border and recognise the South Tyrol as a part of Italy. At the same time, he insisted that Austria would sooner or later have to be reunited with Germany.[40]

Hitler continued his advances to Mussolini in his Reichstag speech on 30 January 1937, the fourth anniversary of his appointment as Reich chancellor. The speech was couched in peaceful language but littered with demands for German parity in Europe and anti-Bolshevik propaganda. Hitler also expressed his hope for closer relations with Italy. Mussolini instructed the Italian ambassador to tell Hitler how much he had enjoyed the speech while listening to it on the radio. Here was a manifestation of Mussolini showing off his diplomatic skills of seduction.[41]

Hitler soon replied, after the failed assassination attempt on the Italian viceroy of Ethiopia, Marshal Rodolfo Graziani. Italian troops had retaliated with unprecedented violence, wiping out entire villages and torturing and slaughtering up to 20,000 people, although some records suggest an even higher death toll. As soon as he heard of the assassination attempt, on 20 February 1937, Hitler sent a telegram to Mussolini, expressing his 'deep outrage' at the attempt and relief that Graziani, one of the chief representatives of Fascism's colonial flagship project, had survived. Mussolini immediately thanked Hitler for this telegram.[42]

By 1937, the stream of German delegations to Italy had increased so dramatically that Hitler ordered that only those personally authorised by him would be allowed to travel there.[43] As the Italian troops in Spain were suffering a heavy defeat at the hand of the Republicans in March 1937, seen at the time as a personal blow to Mussolini, Ambassador Attolico too complained to Ciano about the rising number of Italian delegations to

Berlin he had to host.[44] The intensifying contacts of officials from both regimes, while often little more than free holidays with tourist itineraries, nevertheless helped perpetuate the idea that Italy and Germany had a common future, shaping Europe's New Order.[45]

Yet the Italian–German relationship remained peculiar. Its main protagonists, Mussolini and Hitler, had only met once so far, in 1934. Leading Fascists were not slow in commenting on this unusual arrangement. In an April 1937 letter to Ciano, Grandi, the Italian ambassador to Britain, succinctly characterised the Axis. He hoped that the Axis would force Britain, anxious that Nazi Germany would become too powerful, to side with Italy. He insisted that 'Italy and Germany are engaged but not yet married. It depends on you whether this wedding will happen or not.' Grandi's significance has been exaggerated by historians like De Felice, who more or less minimised Italy's responsibility for the alliance with Germany and put the blame on Britain for the subsequent pact with the Third Reich. After the war, Grandi fiddled with the texts of some of his speeches in his private papers to put across his favourite idea that Italy was the 'determining weight' between the Western powers and the Third Reich, an apologetic view that became popular in Italy after 1945. In reality, an Italian alliance with Britain was becoming increasingly unlikely, as Mussolini was turning more belligerent and gradually being driven to march alongside the Third Reich.[46]

Indeed, in a speech in Palermo in front of several hundred thousand people on 20 August 1937, Mussolini emphasised solidarity between both Axis countries. He told his Sicilian audience, standing in the scorching heat: 'One does not arrive in Rome by ignoring Berlin or against Berlin, and one does not arrive in Berlin by ignoring Rome or against Rome.'[47] Mussolini's imminent visit to Germany, in the context of growing imagined and real pro-Axis declarations, would be the biggest imaginable propaganda show to reinforce the notion of the Axis, both for audiences at home in Italy and Germany, sceptical of such an alliance given persistent national stereotypes, but also for other powers, above all France and Britain.

III

Mussolini's acceptance of Hitler's invitation was also exceptional for Germany, as there had not been many significant state visits to the country in the recent past, given its relative international isolation for many years after the end of the Great War.[48] The Italian and German regimes designed Mussolini's September 1937 visit as an assertive symbol of the growing Italo-German alliance, no doubt in order to make the vain Duce happy, but also in order to present the Fascist and Nazi regimes as a united front against the alleged hegemony of the 'plutocratic' democracies. Propaganda rendered the leaders not as a traditional alliance of statesmen, but as one of the Italian and German peoples, led by Mussolini and Hitler. Thus, Nazi propaganda described Mussolini's visit as the apotheosis of the will of the Italian and German peoples and a 'popular peace demonstration', familiar tropes at a time when most people, still remembering the First World War, did not want another major conflict. Mussolini was clearly impressed by the arrangements and later told his lover Clara Petacci that 'they have not given a similar welcome to kings or emperors, to nobody'.[49]

A massive performance was staged to cement the relationship between the Duce and Hitler. Since Mussolini vainly insisted on being acknowledged as 'the creator of a new Italy', Goebbels was determined to flatter the Duce through a spectacular show.[50] This would show to the world, particularly to the Western allies, that Italy and Germany were firmly united. In fact, the visit was one of the biggest and most expensive propaganda events in the Third Reich's short history.[51]

Tensions remained which the itinerary completely underplayed: Hitler was still hoping for an Anglo-German alliance and Mussolini was still not prepared to enter into a formal alliance with the Nazis. For Hitler, the visit was a stellar opportunity to show off Germany's military might, while Mussolini expected to be celebrated, which would give a huge boost to his ego and his regime. As François-Poncet reported to Paris, both Italy and Germany wanted to avoid alienating Britain, which is why the general tone of the meeting was focused on peace propaganda.[52]

Both the Italian and the German press gave broad coverage to the Duce's visit and projected an image of unity. Gone were the days of the recent Italo-German press wars.[53] German papers flattered Mussolini, to the delight of Italian consular officials.[54] For the *Völkischer Beobachter*'s Wilhelm Weiß, Mussolini's visit was far more significant than ordinary state visits because of their 'common political destiny and ideological ideas of the state'. Such propaganda created political meaning in that it reinforced the central message of the Nazi show: unity and friendship between Mussolini and Hitler, Italy and Germany, and the Italian and German peoples, all in sharp contrast to the liberal democracies that had failed. Particularly noteworthy is Weiß's remark about Italy's and Germany's 'common political will and ideological aims', which had 'always proved to be stronger and more decisive in history than the paragraphs of any possible alliance decisions'.[55]

However, the Nazi paper found it hard to explain away the fact that for Fascism, at least at that time, the racial question (*Volkstumsfrage*) was not as central as racism was to the Nazi project. The Nazi author therefore had to insist that Fascism and Nazism, despite their shared anti-Bolshevism and anti-liberalism, were not the same. Nevertheless, the article culminated in the words 'When Adolf Hitler and Benito Mussolini shake hands with each other today, this new order of the continents [will have] found a symbolical expression.'[56] The theme of the friendship of the two dictators thus overshadowed the political tensions between Italy and Germany and a vaguely articulated ideological proximity between Fascism and Nazism. While such articles remained superficial, the Nazi strategy to highlight parallels between Fascism and Nazism such as the 'commonality of the political will and the ideological goal' fulfilled the visit's objective to portray Mussolini and Hitler as leaders of a New Order.[57]

Other projections of a union with Italy also emphasised its uniqueness by pointing to its allegedly deep historical roots, with Italy and Germany having been friends since the Middle Ages. For example, in a commemorative book, Fred Willis, a Nazi propaganda official, stressed the historical inevitability of the dictators' meeting. Personalising the Italian–German relationship, Willis declared that Mussolini and Hitler's bond continued the alleged friendship between the Italian prime minister Francesco Crispi and the German chancellor Otto von Bismarck, who had presided over the making of the Italian and German nation states, pushed for their imperial expansions, and sealed the Triple Alliance between their nations and Austria-Hungary. For Willis, it was therefore not a coincidence that, almost exactly fifty years after Crispi's visit to Berlin to see Bismarck, 'Bismarck and Crispi [saw] their work confirmed by their grandsons', a reference to the familiar trope at the time to envisage Crispi and Bismarck as the predecessors of the Duce and Hitler. At the same time, Willis emphasised an important difference in style: in 1887, the encounter of the heads of government had been 'a ministerial visit', but the meeting of Mussolini and Hitler was more substantive, namely 'the commitment of two great peoples to a new spirit!' In order to maintain his spin about the historical inevitability of Italo-German friendship, Willis had to omit inconvenient facts such as Italy's exit from the Triple Alliance during the Great War and the many wars between Germans and Italians since the days of the Roman Empire.[58]

For the Nazis, the purpose of this unique show of unity and friendship, rooted in the past, was to threaten the post-1919 European old order with a New Order of territorial conquest. This aggressive challenge required a new style of diplomacy. Thus, Reich press chief Otto Dietrich, in a commemorative photographic book of Mussolini's visit to Hitler, dismissed the old-style 'visits of political officials with diplomatic phrases and polite gestures, with gala dinners . . . with irrelevant communiqués and promising, but non-committal sayings'. Instead, the Duce's meeting with Hitler was characterised by emotive bonds between the leaders and 'peoples coming together . . . in a mission of hearts'.[59]

Italian propaganda struck a similar chord and insisted that the second Mussolini–Hitler meeting would be a 'decisive event in the history of Europe' and much more than a traditional state visit, namely an 'encounter of two nations'. *Il Popolo d'Italia* prepared its readers for Mussolini's journey and described the meticulous German preparations for him, such as the lavish renovation works on his accommodation in Munich, hoping to create a sense of excitement amongst its readers, presumed to be sceptical of an alliance with Germany.[60]

Loudspeakers were set up to broadcast the highlights of Mussolini's visit to the *piazze* of Italy. On 24 September 1937, a huge rally of handpicked Fascist supporters at Rome's Termini station saw off Mussolini and his retinue, which included Ciano, Fascist party secretary Achille Starace, minister of popular culture Dino Alfieri and Mussolini's secretary Osvaldo Sebastiani. Mussolini's officials had meticulously planned the Duce's departure and sent out invitations to state, army and party officials, with specific instructions that Fascist officials had to wear their black shirts, suggesting images of Fascist determination and belligerence. As Mussolini's train passed through Italy towards the Austrian border, masses of Italians cheered their leader at stations en route, as his train slowed down. The Fascist party had organised these purportedly popular demonstrations to convey an image of unanimous popular support for Fascism and the Axis with Germany.[61]

Propaganda thus constructed and defined, but did not constrain, the relationship between Mussolini and Hitler.[62] Therefore, the itinerary was packed with parades, banquets and tours, leaving almost no time for serious political discussions between the two leaders.[63] This arrangement did not go unnoticed by the British. George Ogilvie-Forbes, a leading diplomat at the British embassy in Berlin, later reported to the foreign secretary, Anthony Eden: 'Whatever the subordinate staffs may have done, it is doubtful whether Herr Hitler and Signor Mussolini can have had time to discuss their common problems in more than the most cursory manner.' Nonetheless, leading British diplomats viewed the Duce's posing with Hitler as a threatening symbol.[64]

IV

Behind the scenes, some aspects of the Duce's journey were bordering on the ridiculous, and not everyone in Mussolini's delegation was completely serious about the spectacle. On the long train journey to Germany, Mussolini was accompanied by his riding and fencing instructor. One of the instructor's principal tasks was to assist the Duce in the difficult task of pulling on and kicking off his riding boots. Apart from Mussolini, diplomats, Fascist officials and some hand-picked journalists, a group of pot-bellied, grey-haired railway officials were on the train. They spent most of their time eating spaghetti and even took off their uniforms and boots to feel more comfortable on the long journey.[65]

While the Ministry of Popular Culture, striving for a perfect choreography of the visit, ordered print and radio journalists to wear Fascist or army uniforms and bring along some formal evening wear,[66] a closer examination of Fascist propaganda strategies reveals further cracks in the facade of the Axis. Mario Appelius, a special correspondent for *Il Popolo d'Italia*, gave readers an account of Mussolini's journey, but did not dwell on the fact that the train travelled through the South Tyrol with its German-speaking majority in the very early morning while it was still dark outside. This timing was a clever calculation which prevented Mussolini from having to witness an embarrassing silence from the South Tyrolese, who were craving a unification with Germany, even though Hitler had publicly renounced German claims over the South Tyrol in the 1920s. At 6.20 a.m., the train stopped at the Italo-Austrian border. Three years earlier,

Hitler had been unable to cross this border, the most tangible symbol of tense Italo-German relations, and thus had to fly to Italy. Despite his 1936 declaration that Italy would eventually accept a German annexation of the Alpine state, Italy still formally guaranteed Austria's independence, which Mussolini emphasised by stopping at Innsbruck station. Here, dressed in Fascist uniform, he shook hands with the Austrian foreign minister, representing an increasingly fascist regime, before greeting the Austrian flag with the Fascist salute. The *New York Times* reported that a letter by Dollfuss's widow had been handed over to the Duce. Mussolini's gesture was a clever tactic towards Italians in positions of authority who were critical of an alliance with the Third Reich.[67]

Most German papers did not mention Mussolini's stop in Austria. The editor of a Berlin newspaper who did was scolded by a Nazi propaganda official for this unwelcome reminder of Italo-German discord. *Il Popolo d'Italia* carried a report of Mussolini's stop at Innsbruck in its 26 September 1937 edition, but inside, rather than on the front page, to avoid offending the Germans. Mussolini's train continued to the Austro-German border, hotly contested by Germany, at Kufstein/Kiefersfelden. Here, Mussolini was welcomed by Rudolf Hess, Hitler's deputy, alongside members of the Italian embassy in Berlin, German diplomats, including the protocol chief of the Foreign Ministry, and the Wehrmacht. The train then sped off to Munich, birthplace of the Nazi party and capital of the Nazi movement (*Hauptstadt der Bewegung*). Jubilant crowds, waving swastika and Italian flags, lined the railway to the Bavarian capital. Many people, most of them members of one Nazi party organisation or another, had been drafted to cheer the Italian leader.[68] The regime had massively stepped up security at any place visited by Mussolini. British newspapers, later filed by German diplomats, dwelt upon the tight security arrangements of the SS. According to the *Daily Telegraph*, Mussolini was travelling in a 'bullet-proof train', with thousands of SS guards lining the railway to Munich. Here was a strong implication that the Mussolini–Hitler alliance was hollow and that most Germans had low views of the Italians and Mussolini, which is why so much repression was necessary.[69] Indeed, the regime had specifically confined political suspects in the Dachau concentration camp before Mussolini's arrival. Munich was full of plain-clothes policemen as the Nazis were concerned about the safety of Mussolini and Hitler within Germany.[70]

Many Germans remained reserved towards Mussolini and Italians, as far as the limited evidence on popular opinion suggests. Agents of the exiled Social Democratic Party (*Sopade*) had overheard conversations at Munich railway station a few days before Mussolini's arrival. The stage set for Mussolini's arrival was so huge that the ticket offices had to be relocated. When a peasant who had missed his train because he could not find the ticket office complained loudly, he was immediately arrested, as the regime was keen to portray all Germans as enthusiastic supporters of an Italo-German alliance. Another passenger had said, 'I think that they [the Italians] aren't different today; we'll see' – another reference to Italy's supposed betrayal of Germany in the Great War. Even the massive and concerted Nazi propaganda could not transform this deep-seated resentment.[71] In order to suppress such dissenting voices, Nazi officials and employers forced ordinary people, including war veterans and women, to line the streets to display enthusiasm for Mussolini and the Axis, otherwise risking dismissal from their jobs or worse.[72]

Tensions were rife behind the scenes not only on a popular level. Tight and wide-ranging security was necessary, according to the SS newspaper *Das Schwarze Korps*, to prevent overexcited crowds from crushing Mussolini and Hitler because they were so popular. The SS paper could not hold back from showing off German superiority over Italy and boasted that the Italian officers in Mussolini's retinue deeply admired the disciplined nature of the SS and the German army. Building on a powerful stereotype, the report suggested that the Germans were far better soldiers than the Italians.[73]

V

As during Hitler's journey to Italy in 1934, Nazi propaganda densely documented the dictators' movements, this time focusing on Mussolini as the guest of honour. After two days of heavy rain the sky had cleared up for Mussolini's arrival, declared the German press. Soldiers, alongside SS, Reich Labour Service and SA troops, surrounded by members of the Hitler Youth and the German Girls' League (BDM), were waiting for the Duce outside Munich's central station. Hundreds of thousands of Munich people, alongside local Italian Fascists in their black shirts, were out in eager anticipation of the Duce, waving Italian tricolours, which the regime had distributed. Half an hour before Mussolini's scheduled arrival, Nazi party grandees, including SS Reich leader Heinrich Himmler and Goebbels, began to appear on the scene. Following the choreography of Nazi party rallies, Hitler was the last to arrive, heightening the suspense. The audience turned silent in anticipation of the Duce's arrival. Finally, Mussolini's train pulled in on schedule. Appropriately, the platform had been turned into a stage set adorned with laurel trees, Roman sculptures, German and Italian flags, and an enormously long red carpet, stretching from the point of the platform where Mussolini was supposed to alight to the square outside the station. A military band played the 'Hymn to Rome' (*Inno a Roma*), composed by Giacomo Puccini in 1919 and often used by the Fascists to celebrate their *romanità*. According to Nicolaus von Below, Hitler's air force adjutant, who stood two metres away from the two leaders on the platform, both seemed happy about their first encounter in more than three years. Unlike in 1934, the two leaders greeted each other with their outstretched right arms, symbolising fascist unity, and then shook hands, before walking down the red carpet outside the station. After gun salutes in Mussolini's honour, the leaders inspected the troops of honour while a band played the Fascist *Giovinezza* anthem and the German national anthem. Mussolini and Hitler were then driven through a triumphal arch, adorned with an 'M', specifically built for the visit, followed by other cars, each shared by a Nazi and a Fascist leader to suggest that the alliance was between not just Mussolini and Hitler, but also other high-ranking officials, not to mention the German and Italian peoples. The route was adorned with pylons, wooden lictor rods and flags, all creating the atmosphere of a spectacular performance.[74]

Yet, despite the meticulous preparations for the parade, the welcoming ceremony was marred by a hilarious blunder. Hitler was furious that the ceremony had failed to create the desired effect that the German people unanimously supported the Axis alliance. The reason was that the SS had overzealously cordoned off the streets so tightly that the people could not get anywhere near the leaders' cars. Hitler later rebuked Himmler for the overall poor organisation. In a sardonic report, the Italian Ministry of Popular Culture also lamented the poor crowd management of the Nazis, implying Italian superiority.[75]

All items on the itinerary symbolised the friendship of the two dictators and their nations. For instance, Mussolini and Hitler had an hour's conversation over tea and cakes in Hitler's Munich apartment, their first private talk since their meeting at Venice. No official record of their conversation has survived. Paul Schmidt, the Foreign Ministry's interpreter, was present, although his services were not required because the two dictators were conversing in German. Schmidt later remembered how disappointing and dull Hitler seemed in comparison to the vivid, brilliant and witty Mussolini. Rather than discuss a future strategy, their conversation remained superficial.[76] Wider strategic concerns were subsumed to the pomp and circumstance of the performance.

A further glimpse at the substance of Mussolini's talks with the Nazi dictator can be gleaned from what the Duce subsequently told Vicco von Bülow-Schwante, the German Foreign Ministry's protocol chief. Mussolini knew that the German diplomat would report back to the Nazi leader. He thus claimed that he and Hitler had laid firm foundations for an Italian–German alliance. Only a Fascist–Nazi pact would be able to defeat Bolshevism, and the Spanish Civil War was a test case for this alliance. Mussolini's remarks, including his racist ones, were calculated to leave Hitler and the Nazis with the impression that Italy would be a firm ally. Significantly, in his conversations with Bülow-Schwante, Mussolini expanded on his racist views and claimed that he did not have any problems with the Jews. He insisted, though, that the racial question was a high priority for him. Here, the Duce was trying to impress the Nazis and was reflecting the increasing racism of the Fascist regime.[77]

No pact was signed during the visit. Ernst von Weizsäcker, director of the political department of the German Foreign Ministry, later noted that the visit had been a pompous display with almost everyone showing off their uniforms. He joked that 'for the many medals the Italians have awarded here one could easily have a Thanksgiving feast today'. At the same time, he expressed his doubts over whether ordinary people were really deeply enthusiastic about an Italo-German alliance, given their strong anti-Italian resentment.[78] Yet Weizsäcker's remarks misses the point if we consider the centrality of propaganda and pomp and circumstance in creating the Axis.

As a gesture of friendship and in line with the protocol of royal state visits, the Duce bestowed an honour on Hitler: the rank of honorary corporal of the Fascist militia. This symbolised the humble origins of Mussolini and Hitler as truly popular leaders who had both served their countries as corporals in the war on opposite sides. The question whether the honorary corporalship was the most tactful gesture was raised by an official from the Italian Ministry of Popular Culture who noted that Hitler had been known in the Weimar Republic's conservative circles rather dismissively as the 'Bohemian corporal'.[79] In any case, Goebbels, undoubtedly carried away by the pomp and circumstance, was relieved that, after the Venice meeting, Mussolini and Hitler had finally found a personal line to each other.[80]

The performance continued with its strong display of unity between Mussolini, Hitler and their nations. At an official lunch in the Nazi party headquarters, Hitler and Mussolini were joined by leading diplomats and Nazi officials, including Himmler, Rosenberg, Goebbels and Hess, and Italian representatives, including Ciano and Starace. Renzetti, now consul-general in Berlin, was there too, as was Prince Philip of Hesse. This arrangement suggested that the Axis, while dominated by Mussolini and Hitler, was also supposed to close the ranks between members of the traditional Italian and German bureaucracies alongside the newer Fascist and Nazi party elites. Given the formal setting and language problems, it is unlikely that an animated conversation ensued amongst the Italian and German guests. Heinrich Hoffmann's pictures show the two leaders relaxing like two friends, on a sofa.[81] After lunch, SS and party formations goose-stepped for an hour, according to an elaborate choreography which Himmler and his men had developed for some weeks, this time showcasing German military discipline and strength.[82] Mussolini was so impressed by the goose-step that he later introduced it to Italy as the *passo romano*. Here was an Italian appropriation of a German tradition, just as the Nazi introduction of the *Heil Hitler* greeting had, in fact, been a copy of the Fascist Roman greeting. Nazi Germany was now clearly a model for Italy.

Expectations that the meeting would follow a distinctly new style of diplomacy were not met entirely. For instance, after the parade, in line with diplomatic protocol, Hitler paid his guest a brief return visit and awarded Mussolini an order, the Great Cross of the German Eagle with diamonds, a new honour which was much more prestigious than the honorary corporalship Hitler had just received from Mussolini. Furthermore, the Führer bestowed another distinction upon the Duce: a golden Nazi party lapel pin, an even more special show of appreciation. The claim, articulated throughout the visit and afterwards by Fascist and Nazi propaganda, that the Mussolini–Hitler relationship was so special and different from the post-Versailles diplomatic order that it could dispense with traditional diplomatic protocol was thus wrong. Instead, like fascism more generally, the visit's itinerary combined the old and the new, highlighting that fascism was a compromise of traditional elites with newer forms of radically right-wing politics.[83]

Behind the scenes of the show, further rivalry and tension between the two leaders and their regimes appeared. For example, Hitler, the amateur artist, walked with his guest to the new House of German Art where the regime showed off its 'blood and soil' art, in contrast to the modernism that Hitler had seen at the 1934 Venice Biennale. Mussolini, not a great art lover, must have found this visit excruciating and sighed with relief when the tour ended after less than an hour. This was followed by the departure of the two leaders in separate trains to the Wehrmacht's autumn manoeuvres at Mecklenburg, where the Nazis showed off their armed forces to their potential Italian ally. Hitler, the caring host, took his guest in a motorcade to the station from where both leaders departed on separate trains.[84] This arrangement revealed that, below the surface of unity, the central theme of the visit, both leaders preferred to be amongst their own retinues.

VI

The Nazis' central aim was to show off German strength and popular unity to Mussolini in order to win him over into a military alliance. This point did not get lost on François-Poncet, who stressed the powerful military manoeuvres in his report to the French foreign minister, concerned about an Italo-German alliance.[85] In Mecklenburg, the two ex-corporals, as representatives of the millions of Europeans who had fought in the First World War, admired the German army. A mock battle, involving tanks, aeroplanes and artillery, greatly impressed Mussolini. To give weight to the military cooperation between both states, Hitler received high-ranking Italian officers on his train, while Mussolini met German military leaders. Ironically, many of the Italian officers Hitler met had fought against Germany in the Great War, including the chief of the general staff, Marshal Pietro Badoglio, one of the officers responsible for the crushing Italian defeat at Caporetto in 1917. All this made a military alliance unlikely. In order to brush over such tensions, Giorgio Pini of *Il Popolo d'Italia* boasted that the Axis was fundamentally different and more profound than the Triple Alliance, culminating in the statement that Hitler's Germany 'is not the Germany of Wilhelm II'.[86] Together with Italy, Germany could reshape Europe. From Mecklenburg, both leaders travelled, again on separate trains, to Essen, the 'Reich's armoury'. Nazi propaganda highlighted the allegedly unanimous enthusiasm of the Krupp factory workers for the dictators, suggesting that the German working class was fully behind an alliance with the leader of the Italian ex-enemy.[87]

From Essen, the leaders travelled on separate trains to Berlin. The regime had ensured that the railways were lined by enthusiastic crowds. For the journey's last fifteen minutes, the leaders' two trains ran exactly alongside each other on parallel tracks, a powerful metaphor for the strong parallels between the leaders, their regimes and their peoples and, of course, a powerful display of German engineering and efficiency. A few minutes before the trains' scheduled arrival at a station near the Olympic stadium, Hitler's train overtook Mussolini's and arrived exactly one minute earlier, allowing Hitler to receive his guest on the platform. This gesture of overtaking symbolised that Hitler and the Nazis had overtaken Mussolini and the Fascists as the world's leading right-wing regime. From the station, the two leaders drove in an open car down the East–West Axis, a pompous street recently designed by Albert Speer and decorated with thousands of Italian and German flags, towards the Unter den Linden boulevard and the Wilhelmstrasse government district where Ogilvie-Forbes saw 'four rows of illuminated white pylons bearing golden eagles' and 'gigantic German and Italian flags', for which 55,000 square metres of fabric had been woven.[88]

Hitler had instructed Reich stage designer Benno von Arent to design the decorations for a massive parade. All in all the Berlin celebrations of Mussolini cost more than a million Reichsmarks.[89] For Erich Ebermayer, a screenwriter and thus an expert at performance, the Nazi show had been effective: 'Everything was gigantic: the sea of flags, the pilasters, the cheers, the weather, the barriers, the fear of an assassination attempt.'[90] Performance was central to the creation of the Italo-German alliance, which still had not been formalised.

An essential part of the performance was the enthusiastic crowds lining the streets. They were not merely spectators, but crucial participants. The regime had ferried in almost a million spectators from Germany's regions to cheer Mussolini, many more than the Fascist regime had assembled in Venice in 1934. Workers and schoolchildren had been given the day off so that they could attend the parades (and to ensure that the city's public transport system could cope with the crowds expected to attend the events).[91]

Yet behind the facade of popular enthusiasm were several layers of Nazi repression and control, according to *Sopade* agents, keen on identifying workers' dissatisfaction with the regime. For example, the German Labour Front had forced its members – German workers and employers – to attend the ceremonies. And the employees of a large Berlin bank had received a letter a few days before Mussolini's arrival, ordering them to participate in the celebrations with 'absolute discipline'. Workers who refused to attend were disciplined and had their pay docked for the day. Each group of workers was given detailed instructions where to stand and cheer Mussolini. Many people grumbled as they could not get a glimpse of Mussolini because three to four lines of SS men, altogether 60,000, as Ogilvie-Forbes estimated, were protecting the dictators from the crowds, highlighting security concerns.[92] Still, Nazi propaganda was not entirely unsuccessful. Even the critical *Sopade* agents conceded: 'The philistine is today prepared to recognise that Mussolini is Germany's friend. At the same time, there is still enough resentment left over from the last war.'[93]

Ambiguity, rather than outright enthusiasm, characterised the views of ordinary people towards Mussolini and Italy. Ogilvie-Forbes noticed that the crowds were not overenthusiastic for Mussolini, but rather 'in a happy holiday mood, anxious to see the show'. Moreover, he added perceptively, 'the man in the street viewed the Italian entente with no enthusiasm and with some misgiving'. Nevertheless, the massive propaganda left some positive impression on Germans and made them more receptive to an alliance with Italy as 'the fear of Mediterranean entanglements largely gave way to a feeling of self-esteem at the spectacle of the union of two powerful States extending from the Baltic to the Eastern Mediterranean'. François-Poncet, worried, like Ogilvie-Forbes, about the effects of the performance in creating a strong Italian–German Axis. For him, the significance of the visit lay in the symbolic reunion of Mussolini and Hitler, which, for Italy and Germany, was more than a usual diplomatic encounter, but rather representative of the bond between the Italian and German people.[94]

At an official dinner in the Reich Chancellery attended by German and Italian political officials and guests from high society, both leaders gave toasts, a central aspect of state banquets, although Hitler was teetotal and Mussolini hardly drank. Hitler flattered Mussolini as 'the genius creator of Italy' and emphasised that their encounters were different from usual diplomatic meetings, as their nations were united by the 'real interests of life' (*realen Lebensinteressen*), a veiled threat that both nations were determined to expand their territory. Mussolini reinforced Hitler's remarks.[95] The vagueness of the toasts reflected the unclear nature of Italo-German relations, with no pact having been signed and no in-depth political discussions held during the visit.

VII

Mussolini's visit culminated in a mass rally on 28 September 1937 attended by around 650,000 people, although Hitler, exaggerating the popularity of his union with the Duce, claimed that there had been at least a million. The location was the Maifeld, just outside the stadium built for the 1936 Berlin Olympics. Hitler praised the 'demonstration joined by 115 million members of two peoples in greatest sentiment and followed by hundreds of millions more or less interested listeners all over the world! . . . From the common Fascist and National Socialist revolution not only a common view, but also a common action has emerged today.'[96] After Hitler's powerful but ultimately vague speech, the Duce spoke in German, showing off his vanity but also his bond with his host nation. Mussolini thanked Germany for its refusal to support the League of Nations' sanctions against Italy. For Mussolini, the Axis had emerged in the autumn of 1935. He also insisted that the Axis between the two countries 'against Bolshevism, the modern form of the darkest, byzantine rule of terror' and their peoples was firm. 'No government, in any part of the world, has the acclaim of the people to such an extent as the governments of Germany and Italy.' Italy and Germany would create a New Order in Europe. Spectators on the Maifeld were impressed by Mussolini's clear German accent. Ogilvie-Forbes implied that Mussolini's German speech was a symbol of closer Italo-German bonds. In truth, it was hardly intelligible to radio listeners as he bellowed into the microphone.[97]

A hilarious scene occurred: the Duce's histrionics and his powerful rhetoric took place in a downpour of heavy rain. This prompted the audience to worry about the weather rather than listen to Mussolini's elaborations on the Axis. Never short of good jokes, Berliners began to parody the popular exclamation 'Duce! Duce!' as '*Dusche! Dusche!*', the German word for shower. The speeches were followed by a military tattoo, illuminated by a 'dome of light', a typical part of Nazi rituals, and the playing of the Italian and German state and party anthems. The event ended in a huge stampede as the crowds hurried to the exits to escape the rain as soon as the parade was over. So many people tried to enter the U-Bahn stop next to the Olympic stadium that some were reportedly trampled to death, an inconvenient fact that was kept secret by the regime.[98]

Far from being the tough Fascist warrior, Mussolini caught a serious cold on the Maifeld. Hitler recommended the Duce take a hot bath. But there was no hot water in Mussolini's apartment, which made him cast into doubt German efficiency. As it turned out, a dutiful technician had shut down the hot water supply, following a Reich government regulation that it must be stopped in all public buildings in the late afternoon. Eventually, Mussolini had his bath at the luxurious Hotel Adlon nearby.[99]

All the strength-in-unity propaganda was picked up with some concern by British diplomats. Below the surface of Italo-German friendship, Ogilvie-Forbes diagnosed tensions between Italy and Germany. Carried away by the propaganda performance, he argued that basic ideological similarities rather than common political and strategic interests drove both regimes together, but wondered whether these ideological parallels were sufficient for a military alliance. Furthermore, recent conflicts between Italy and Germany were still on everyone's mind, such as the Stresa front and the breakdown in Italo-German relations after the failed Nazi putsch in Austria. For Ogilvie-Forbes, it was clear that after this enormously successful visit, neither the Germans nor the Italians could afford to allow their new friendship as well as the amicable relationship between the two fascist dictators to cool. Ogilvie-Forbes ended on a gloomy note. The peace rhetoric deployed by Mussolini and Hitler was simply propaganda.[100] Indeed, to remind everyone of the real Nazi objective for a union with Italy, there was a massive and well-organised military parade to impress Mussolini.[101]

When the Nazi delegation saw off Mussolini and the Fascists at Berlin's Lehrter station, Heinrich Hoffmann took a photograph of a happy Duce talking through an open train window to a pensive Hitler. This picture was a tribute to Mussolini's vanity, as Hitler, standing on the platform, had to talk up to the Duce. Yet the Führer had the last shot. Another picture by Hoffmann shows him waving goodbye to Mussolini's train as it is departing.[102] Goebbels, flattered by Mussolini giving him a signed Duce portrait, claimed that Mussolini was crying when Hitler saw him off at the station. 'These two men belong together,' Goebbels insisted.[103] Hitler was sentimental when his Italian guests departed. In his diary, Goebbels gave the Axis a human touch that would bond Italy and Germany together. No formal military alliance had been concluded, but for Goebbels the Italo-German relationship manifested itself through an emotional image of the friendship of the two dictators and their peoples.[104] Germans lined the railway from Berlin to the Austrian border, cheering the Duce as his train progressed through the Reich.[105]

Although both leaders claimed that their encounter had gone beyond traditional diplomatic rules, Mussolini still followed the protocol when he sent Hitler a telegram upon crossing the Austro-German border, which was still an obstacle to better Italo-German relations. The Duce insisted that his stay in Germany had convinced him of the 'indissolubility of . . . friendship'. His visit, a charming but calculating Mussolini wrote, had greatly increased his admiration for Hitler's achievements and his friendship with the Nazi leader. Mussolini used this opportunity to invite Hitler to Italy. Since the telegram was published in the Italian and German press, Mussolini's remarks reinforced the meeting's message of closer Italo-German cooperation.[106]

Mussolini knew that his ostensible pro-German attitude was not without its critics, even from amongst Fascist supporters. On his return journey to Rome, the Duce stopped at Verona to meet the poet Gabriele D'Annunzio, the hero of Fiume who had, in some ways, pioneered the road for the Fascist seizure of power, and who was a known opponent of an Italian alliance with Germany. Their meeting, covered in *Il Popolo d'Italia*, sent out the message to Fascist supporters that the future of Italian foreign policy was still open.[107]

As Mussolini arrived back in Rome, a huge spectacle awaited him. State and party workers were given the day off so that they could welcome the Duce. Public buildings were illuminated and adorned with flags. The ceremony reinforced Mussolini's sense of having experienced a triumph on his visit, which made him more convinced of an alliance with Germany.

Mussolini addressed the Italian people, boasting that Italo-German friendship was now at the heart of the two nations. Although he stressed the solidarity between 'the two revolutions', he remained unspecific about plans for a formal Italo-German collaboration. No pact had been signed in Germany. But the stunning show in Germany gradually became a self-fulfilling prophecy for Mussolini, who was so deeply impressed by Hitler and the Reich that he told Italians that a deep friendship between Fascist Italy and Nazi Germany had developed in the hearts of their peoples and would remain strong.[108] A report on popular opinion, kept in the files of the Ministry of Popular Culture, boasted that the masses of the Italians had been delirious about Mussolini's visit to Germany and had received him with enthusiasm. This was a realistic description of the Duce's popular reception in Rome, clearly the result of the careful Fascist staging and managing of the masses which included pressure and coercion.[109] Reflecting the new friendship between Italy and Germany, the radio broadcast of the welcoming ceremony for Mussolini in Rome was transmitted by all German radio stations.[110]

Soon after Mussolini's return to Rome, Ciano confirmed in a conversation with the German ambassador that Mussolini had greatly enjoyed his stay in Rome and that he was keen to deepen the Axis.[111] In his own diary, Ciano was more sceptical and wondered whether the alliance between the two regimes was sufficient 'to unite in a meaningful way two peoples on opposite poles in terms of race, culture, religion, and tastes?' Nevertheless, for Ciano, the Axis was not just a political manoeuvre but a pursuit of a common ideology, reinforced by Mussolini's political views.[112]

While some of his pro-Hitler and pro-German remarks were tactical calculations, Mussolini was genuinely impressed by his reception in Germany. On 4 October 1937, he wrote to the king that his journey had 'had the intended demonstrative character'. The Duce tried to convince the king of an alliance with Germany, and told him that 'the German people had [had] a very likeable demeanour'.[113] Mussolini clearly believed that his bonds with Hitler, leader of the most powerful right-wing dictatorship, would boost his ego and his regime. A month after his return from Berlin, Mussolini confided to Clara Petacci that he had felt genuine German admiration, suggesting that the Nazi performance had been successful in seducing the Duce. He boasted to Petacci that Italy and Germany could conquer the world together and insisted:

> They are loyal, and they have felt the power of the [fascist] regime. They understand that if one falls, both fall: we are too closely united. And they have realised that Italy is serious. They are a fine people. They know how to do things on a big scale. Imagine, they are still talking about me . . . The ordinary people are completely conquered. They have felt my force.[114]

Mussolini was thoroughly satisfied that Hitler and the Germans had recognised Italy as a great power and told Petacci that 'Italy is no longer with France and England'. The Nazi performance of unity had been so effective that it even made the Duce believe that he was more popular in Germany than Hitler.[115]

Here was Mussolini's recognition of Nazi Germany as a desirable ally which, by implication, was more powerful than Italy, a significant change in Mussolini's thinking. In sharp contrast to the 1934 Venice encounter, Mussolini could no longer look down on Hitler. Nevertheless, in an article for *Il Popolo d'Italia*, published anonymously in early October after his return from Germany, the Duce implied that Fascism was spiritually superior to Nazism, as Fascism had been the first doctrine and movement to rise to power. Despite his emphasis of the common fate of Italy and Germany, Mussolini categorically insisted that each nation would have its own fascist movement, dampening hopes that Italy would ally itself with the Third Reich for purely ideological reasons.[116] For both Mussolini and Hitler, the visit opened a new chapter in their foreign policy and clearly revealed to the world the growing links between both regimes. For Goebbels and Hitler, after Ethiopia, Mussolini had almost inevitably been driven into an alliance with Germany. Mussolini thus had no choice but to ally himself with the Third Reich, which for Goebbels was the best basis for a friendship. The Nazis would be in charge of this friendship, so from its very beginning, the Fascist–Nazi alliance was dominated by the Germans.[117]

Still, the Fascist press gave the illusion that both countries, indeed both leaders, were on an equal footing. On 1 October 1937, Mussolini's *Popolo d'Italia* announced that Hitler would come to Italy soon. Here was a reversal of the roles of both dictators. In the 1920s and early 1930s, Hitler had been desperate for an audience in Rome with Mussolini, which the Duce postponed until 1934. Just three years later, it was Mussolini who invited Hitler to Italy. Yet German propaganda officials in charge of directing newspaper content discouraged editors from discussing Hitler's visit to Italy, as tensions beneath the glittering surface of Nazi propaganda remained. Anticipating questions as to why no formal treaty had been signed and why there was no official communiqué, a propaganda official reminded editors that Mussolini's and Hitler's speeches on the Maifeld contained all the important points. The strong display of unity between Germany and Italy rendered a formal treaty unnecessary, the official insisted. Thus diplomatic spectacle took over from formal declarations, adding weight to the propagandistic claim that the Mussolini–Hitler relationship ushered in a new style of diplomacy. The real reason why no concrete agreement was signed was that Mussolini, while attracted by the idea of an alliance with Hitler, avoided severing ties with Britain. He believed this tactic would enhance Italy's diplomatic status.[118]

Leading Nazis, including Goebbels, remained sceptical whether the Italians would honour the Axis. When, after his return to Italy, the Duce sent Hitler a signed portrait, dedicated 'in sincere friendship', Goebbels commented sarcastically: 'Hopefully, also in loyal [friendship]. Well, let's wait and see.'[119] Leading Nazis admired Mussolini and his regime, without fully understanding its complexities and inner contradictions, but remained hostile towards the Italian people, sometimes even seeing them as racially inferior.

However, the concerted efforts of the Nazis to cultivate an Italo-German alliance were not entirely without an impact on Germans. While it is notoriously difficult to evaluate popular opinion in the Third Reich, it is noteworthy that hundreds of thousands of Germans had participated in the celebrations during Mussolini's visit out of curiosity or enthusiasm or because of Nazi pressure. Their complaints about the massive costs of the visit were accompanied by tremendous respect for the Nazis' perfect organisation skills. Paradoxically, while many Germans rejected the Nazis' courting of the Italians, Mussolini's visit helped consolidate people's attitudes towards the Nazi regime, even amongst those who were critical of specific Nazi policies. *Sopade* agents quoted a Munich homeowner who found Mussolini dislikeable and untrustworthy. He grumbled constantly about the Nazis' lavish spending on Mussolini's visit, but at the same time greatly admired their military and ceremonial pomp. The man said: 'Mussolini will have to look around; the Italians wouldn't be capable of [organising] something like this. There, Hitler's showing them [the way] . . . He knows exactly what to think of the Italian; he wants to show to him that we Germans are a power.' It was spectacularly clear that Germany was now a great military power, less than five years after Hitler's appointment as Reich chancellor. Mussolini had no more right to look down on Hitler.[120]

In Italy, the regime's propaganda advocated a closer cooperation with Nazi Germany and issued a commemorative book, *Il Duce in Germania*, which reprinted some of the pictures Hoffmann had taken of the two leaders. Gherardo Casini, the general director of the Italian press, provided a preface in which he insisted that Italians were following their Duce's enthusiasm for the Italo-German friendship, which was 'at the heart of both peoples'. In reality, despite increasing Italian pro-German propaganda, most Italians remained reserved towards such an alliance.[121]

Despite its ambiguous popular reception, Mussolini's visit to Germany struck a chord with foreign observers, suggesting that the principal objective of the visit, to portray Italy and Germany as staunch allies, held together by a common ideology and the close bonds of the dictators, had succeeded. Here was a face-to-face meeting of two dictators in charge of two regimes challenging the post-war settlement. The choreography of the meeting projected a powerful and menacing image of two dictators, enjoying the unanimous support of their peoples, leading Europe towards a New Order of conquest and domination. Mussolini increasingly believed that fate had bound him together with Hitler, a feeling long held by Hitler himself. All this created a potent image, in an age of mass propaganda, of Italo-German strength and unity. But misunderstandings, tensions and mutual suspicion were deeply ingrained in the union of Mussolini and Hitler, as they were in the relationship between both regimes, and would be a liability in the years ahead.[122]

4

SPRINGTIME FOR HITLER

May 1938

I

On 5 October 1937, weeks after Mussolini's return from Germany, US president Franklin D. Roosevelt gave his 'quarantine speech'. In it, he warned Fascist Italy and Nazi Germany, but also Japan, that the international community would not tolerate aggression. Although the German Foreign Ministry believed that Roosevelt's warning had been mainly directed against Japan, international concern about the rapprochement between Mussolini and Hitler was palpable.[1]

Mussolini's visit to Germany had coincided with a broader shift in German foreign policy from revisionism to open expansionism. In the wake of the Duce's departure, on 5 November 1937, Hitler told the commanders-in-chief of the armed forces that Germany must annex Austria and Czechoslovakia in 1938 and prepare for a large-scale war to conquer a living space by 1943–5. Hitler's elaborations, summarised by Colonel Friedrich Hoßbach, later became the subject of much controversy. Hitler, concerned about a throat polyp which he feared might be cancer, felt that that his time was running out. However, for the Wehrmacht leadership, who were broadly in agreement with Hitler's objectives, the Leader's schedule was far too risky. Indeed, many German generals believed that France and Britain would intervene and defeat Germany, not yet ready for a large-scale war. During the Hoßbach meeting, Hitler said little about

Italy, which suggests that Mussolini's dictatorship did not play a central part in his strategy. Furthermore, he knew that his military audience thought little of the Italian army. One historian suggests that, for Hitler, the principal objective of his flirting with Mussolini was to pressure Britain into an alliance with Germany. However, this objective had proved unrealistic, and the friendship with Mussolini had already developed its own political momentum during and after the Duce's visit to Germany.[2]

The radicalisation of German foreign policy was accompanied by increasing repression of Jews and social outsiders such as the homeless and alleged 'habitual' criminals within Germany. Amidst preparations for war, Hitler removed key army officials General Werner von Fritsch and Field Marshal Werner von Blomberg, who were potentially too cautious regarding Hitler's aggressive foreign policy. Thus, in early 1938, Hitler became supreme commander of the army. In a telegram to Hitler, Mussolini declared that his taking over of the supreme command was an event 'destined to reinforce the comradely relations between our armed forces and our regimes'. The telegram reflected Mussolini's respect, and also his envy that Hitler could take such radical steps, for, in Italy, the king remained commander-in-chief of the Italian armed forces and the figurehead for many officers. Hitler responded enthusiastically and declared that he considered it his 'task to consolidate the political and ideological relations that already exist between Germany and Italy'. The point of these telegrams, which were published in the Italian and German press and couched in a vague and formulaic language, was to keep the momentum of the Axis going.[3]

Mirroring his reshuffle of the military leadership, Hitler replaced Neurath, a career diplomat, with the sycophantic Ribbentrop. This appointment, despite the creeping Nazification of the Foreign Ministry since 1933, was an important gesture which suggested that the time was ripe for a new, aggressive and non-bureaucratic diplomacy that would blindly follow and implement Hitler's wishes.[4] Hitler also used the reshuffle to affirm the special relationship with Mussolini, similar to Mussolini's replacement of Ambassador Cerruti in 1935. Thus, Ambassador Hassell was replaced by Hans Georg von Mackensen, well networked in military and diplomatic circles, being the son of a field marshal and the son-in-law of Neurath. Although Ciano and Ribbentrop could not stand each other, hardly a good basis for closer Italo-German cooperation, both

Mussolini and Ciano welcomed the reshuffle, echoing the views of leading Nazis who had long accused Hassell of undermining an Italo-German alliance.[5]

It is noteworthy that the Fascist regime in Italy too became more radical in the wake of Mussolini's German journey. This trip had boosted his leadership cult. The Duce believed that he had found the most appropriate ally in Nazi Germany, with whom Italy had a common destiny, namely war with France and Britain that would bring Italy *spazio vitale*. Fascist expansionism was balanced at home by an increasing drive towards the 'totalitarianisation' and militarisation of domestic life as well as a stronger push for autarky.[6] One of the first tangible diplomatic indications of this radical dynamic was Italy's accession to the Anti-Comintern Pact with Germany and Japan. This treaty was implicitly directed against the Soviet Union and, in a secret clause, committed Germany and Japan to neutrality if one of them found itself at war with the Soviet Union. That was an unlikely prospect for Fascist Italy. Here was the final blow to French and British hopes that the Stresa front against Germany could be revived. Nevertheless, the Italian Ministry of Propaganda and Culture instructed newspaper editors to avoid emphasising Italy's joining the pact, still reflecting Mussolini's inconsistent and increasingly impracticable policy of keeping Italy as a 'determining weight'.[7]

But this was not all. In a further attack on the Versailles order, Italy walked out of the League of Nations in December 1937. Unsurprisingly, the German press gave broad coverage to this event, which seemed to confirm Italy's adherence to the Third Reich. At the same time, a small but nevertheless significant gesture emphasised Italian–German cooperation towards a New Order. Keeping up with the performative nature of the Italian–German friendship, Mussolini, in the same week that Italy quit the League, received a generous present from the lord mayor of Hanover: a Hanoverian gelding, from the famous Hanover Cavalry Academy, along with a pair of silver spurs. Mussolini, who was a keen but not particularly competent rider, was delighted, and his acceptance of a German cavalry horse just days after Italy left the League implied that Italy's future would be on Germany's side.[8]

In a further drive towards creating a totalitarian state in the Third Reich's shadow, the party, led by Achille Starace, launched an anti-bourgeois campaign that soon took on a racist, anti-Semitic twist. For example, the regime instructed Italians to avoid the formal second-person address '*lei*' and use the colloquial '*voi*' in public. But the Fascist drive to reshape the lives of Italians did not stop here. Handshakes, thought to be unhygienic, were to be replaced with the Roman salute. Many Italians, including those from Mussolini's inner circle, such as Ciano and his wife, but also Clara Petacci and her family, continued to live a bourgeois lifestyle and did not always follow these rules which some saw as silly attempts to imitate the Nazis. Yet the party, as in its justification of the adoption of the *passo romano*, insisted that these practices had emerged from ancient Rome.[9]

Despite all these pro-German manifestations, Mussolini and Ciano continued to operate a Janus-faced foreign policy in public in order to increase Italy's prestige, although this policy was increasingly unrealistic after the closing of ranks during the Duce's visit to Germany. In January 1937, Italy had signed the so-called Gentleman's Agreement with Britain, a mutual recognition of the status quo in the Mediterranean. Italian propaganda officials instructed newspaper editors to comment in a 'sober and dignified' way and, rather paradoxically, ordered them to portray the agreement as a stroke of Mussolini's genius that would reinforce the Axis with Nazi Germany and bring stability to Europe.[10]

Beyond this rhetoric, Mussolini, like Hitler, ultimately wanted to go to war. For the Duce, echoing a widely held Italian nationalist sentiment, war had a transformative quality that would make Italians a stronger and more cohesive people. War would fulfil the aims of the Risorgimento and turn Italy into a great power.[11] However, Mussolini hesitated to commit Italy to a military alliance with Germany, although not because of a lack of willingness. Rather, he wavered because Italy, bound up in the Spanish Civil War with a large troop contingent, lacked the military and economic resources to take on the Western powers. This is why Mussolini had to continue with his diplomatic manoeuvring. But this approach became more and more unfeasible because of Italy's growing economic dependency on Germany and Mussolini's ideological attachment to Hitler.[12] It was in this context of a growing ideological attachment, which remained highly ambiguous and confusing, that the preparations for Hitler's second journey to Italy began in earnest. Unlike in 1934, this was an official state visit hosted by Victor Emmanuel III, not Mussolini. This setup would lead to confusion, tension and absurd scenes during Hitler's journey.

II

In late November 1937, Ciano, acting upon Mussolini's orders, set up a commission of high-ranking party, propaganda, state and police officials to plan Hitler's visit. The commission's aim was to outdo the German staging of Mussolini's stay in the Third Reich so as to convince Italian and German domestic audiences, as well as international ones, especially in France and Britain, that Italy was a great power, tied to the Third Reich.[13] The various agencies involved were obsessed with creating an even more powerful picture of unanimous popular support for the Axis than the Nazis had projected in 1937. In order to document their efforts and justify the high costs of the event, they left a vast number of documents which permit a much closer exploration of Hitler's visit to Italy than of Mussolini's 1937 visit to Germany.[14]

One of the first tasks of the commission was the compilation of a long list of repair works to be carried out on houses facing the railway line from Rome to Naples which Hitler would be using, as the regime wanted to project the image of a powerful, efficient and prosperous Italy. Many facades looked so battered that their owners had to repaint them or cover them up with flags. The gap between propaganda and the more mundane reality used here in the creation of Potemkin villages would run through the Fascist choreography of Hitler's visit like a red thread. For example, no fewer than 11,671 Italian and 11,264 German flags would be shown along the railway, the almost identical numbers suggesting that Italy and Germany were equals. The only place where Italian flags were to outnumber German was Bolzano in the South Tyrol, where the authorities feared too much enthusiasm from the local German-speaking population for Hitler.[15]

Various state and party institutions tried to outdo one another in their zealous preparations for the Hitler visit, with occasionally laughable results. As if the almost equal quantity of flags was not sufficient number-crunching evidence for the efforts of the Italian government to display Fascist–Nazi unity, the regime was set to distribute a further 1,910,000 Italian and German banners in the provinces which Hitler's train would cross. Nevertheless, despite all this enthusiasm, the Finance Ministry, in an angry but altogether hilarious letter, complained to the prime minister's office on 29 March 1938 that many prefect's offices had ordered flags in the wrong sizes, creating some unnecessary expense and casting into doubt the efficiency of the Fascist state.[16]

Reflecting unity propaganda, the Italian and German press began to announce the visit with great fanfare in late February 1938 and reinforced the message projected during Mussolini's visit that both countries would eventually become allies.[17] For Hitler, the visit to Italy went beyond the conventions of a state visit and was supposed to demonstrate and reinforce his special relationship with Mussolini. Significantly, he thus told Ribbentrop that he would not accept invitations to any other state visits. Accordingly, Ribbentrop and his new undersecretary of state Ernst von Weizsäcker instructed the German Foreign Ministry to plan the trip as a unique event. Special protocol arrangements would reflect this uniqueness, part of the new spin of Nazi diplomacy that closely mirrored the shift of Nazi foreign policy from revisionism to open aggression.[18]

Reflecting tense relations with the Holy See, it was decided that Hitler would not visit the Vatican. Pius XI, whose stance towards Nazi racism and Nazi attacks on Catholic doctrine had been expressed in the 1937 encyclical *Mit brennender Sorge*, did not want to meet Hitler either.[19] In a clear gesture, the pope would leave Rome for his residence at Castel Gandolfo, in the Alban Hills, before Hitler's arrival in Rome. He also ordered the closure of the Vatican Museums, as he did not want Hitler to visit. The Vatican's *Osservatore Romano*, a newspaper with a mass circulation in Italy, declared that Pius's withdrawal to Castel Gandolfo had nothing to do with 'petty diplomacy', but was 'because the air of Castel Gandolfo makes him feel good, whereas the [air in Rome] makes him feel bad'. This was a barely disguised dismissal of Hitler's visit, couched in a bare minimum of diplomatic politeness.[20] In Italy, only a few years after the conclusion of the 1929 Lateran Treaties, the pope's rejection of an alliance between Italy and the Third Reich carried significant political weight. Indeed, Ciano was so concerned about the Vatican's opposition to the Axis that he instructed the Italian embassy in Berlin to suggest that Hitler make a statement to placate the Church's irritation with the Third Reich. Hitler refused. In early April 1938, Mussolini thus adopted an anti-Hitler stance with the Jesuit Pietro Tacchi-Venturi, his unofficial contact with the Vatican, and suggested that Hitler should be excommunicated. Mussolini's objective here was to maintain good relations with the Vatican, which had, despite some conflicts, underwritten the Fascist regime since 1929.[21] Eventually, in order to soften tensions with the Vatican, Ciano issued a secret order in late March 1938 that churches and buildings owned by the

Vatican must not be illuminated or adorned with flags during Hitler's visit. In fact, Hitler avoided visiting churches while in Italy.[22]

III

Despite Hitler's order to Ribbentrop to make the visit stand out from state visits, the nitty-gritty details of preparations were left to the German Foreign Ministry's protocol department, which was used to a more traditional style than the one desired by Hitler. Some of the formal planning thus built on existing precedents of royal and imperial state visits, not least because the king, not Mussolini, was the official host. Behind the scenes, there lurked some unresolved tensions between monarchical and Fascist rituals.[23] Unlike during Hitler's 1934 visit to Italy, the German delegation was massive, reflecting the special character of the visit. As the king's guest, the Nazi leader would have to stay at the Quirinal Palace, the official Roman residence of the king.[24]

Despite the meticulous Italian preparations, the German Foreign Ministry informed the Italian side of Hitler's peculiar requirements for his accommodation and diet in a secret memorandum that bordered on the pedantic. Hot chocolate and cakes were to be served to the German dictator for breakfast. Vegetarian food was to be provided, with the occasional Italian dish. Sparkling water and dark bread were to be supplied from Germany. Hitler's room had to be quiet. His bed had to be comfortable, with a camelhair blanket and a wedge-shaped bolster. A nightstand with a lamp had to be placed to the right of the bed. As if this list was not exhaustive enough, the memorandum also recommended decorating Hitler's room with fresh flowers and providing him with illustrated books on the buildings of ancient Rome. The point about these requests, not entirely unusual in the run-up to state visits, is that, by 1938, the German government felt confident enough to dictate to the Italian Foreign Ministry how they should treat Hitler. The hierarchy between the two dictators had changed: Hitler was at the vanguard of the European right, not Mussolini. The history of the preparations of Hitler's state visit is thus not one that suggests a dichotomy between style and substance. Instead, style reflected and constructed political substance.[25]

Other details too reflected political matters. For example, unlike in 1934, when he had still been consolidating Nazi power, Hitler would be wearing a uniform throughout the visit. The diplomatic members of the official German delegation were fitted with special uniforms, designed for the occasion by Reich stage designer Benno von Arent, who had created the street ornaments during Mussolini's 1937 visit to Berlin. That a stage designer devised the uniforms was not a coincidence, suggesting the centrality of performance to create an image of unity. However, the uniforms gave much rise to ridicule, and some members of the German delegation thought that they looked like costumes for a fancy dress party. Hitler, desperate to leave a better impression than on his previous visit to Italy, took the dress code seriously, eventually ordering that nobody should wear white uniforms in order to avoid the impression that the Germans were behaving like colonisers towards Italy. Hitler's order reflected feelings of German superiority, but also displayed his and other Nazi leaders' awkwardness on their first large-scale visit to Italy. The fear of offending Mussolini and the Italian regime was palpable throughout the visit.[26]

IV

We must interrupt our story here, as events in Austria overshadowed preparations for Hitler's visit to Italy. Despite Mussolini's 1936 reassurance that Italy recognised Austria as part of the Nazi sphere of influence, Italy still officially guaranteed Austrian independence. However, as Hitler was gearing for war, he wanted to bring Austria under full German control, thereby completing the Nazi seizure of power in Greater Germany. Thus, in February 1938, after severe bullying by Hitler, the Austrian chancellor, Kurt von Schuschnigg, Dollfuss's successor, legalised the Austrian Nazi party and made the Nazi Arthur Seyß-Inquart interior minister. Schuschnigg then called a referendum on Austrian independence, in which Hitler feared that the Austrians might vote in favour. After escalating Nazi violence in Austria the referendum was cancelled. On 11 March 1938, following a request from the Austrian Nazi party, German troops reached Vienna on the pretext of pacifying the country.[27]

Hitler knew that Italy was still heavily involved in the Spanish Civil War and thus unlikely to resist German advances into Austria. Still, on the night of 11 March 1938, he had the Prince of Hesse deliver a personal letter to Mussolini. This gesture was supposed to suggest that Hitler genuinely cared for Mussolini's approval for the invasion, in complete contrast to his attitude towards the failed 1934 Nazi putsch in Austria.[28] In his letter to the Duce, Hitler apologised to Mussolini for informing him late about a decision that had 'already become irrevocable'. He then explained why Germany had no choice but to invade Austria, couched in a way that made the German invasion look beneficial to Italy. Above all, Germany would recognise the Brenner border in perpetuity, thereby reassuring Mussolini of the surrender of German territorial claims for the South Tyrol. Towards the end of his letter, Hitler expressed his regret that he could not discuss these matters with Mussolini personally and signed the letter with 'always in friendship'. An Italian communiqué subsequently reported the delivery of Hitler's letter to Mussolini. The missive was also published after the Anschluss in Germany. Both reports aimed to create the impression that Hitler had consulted Mussolini and reaffirmed Fascist–Italian unity. In reality, Hitler did not wait for Mussolini's reply; he ordered the invasion long before hearing back from the prince, briefed to report Mussolini's reaction immediately to Berlin. The prince only rang Hitler after the Nazi leader had already given his orders.[29] In the telephone conversation between the prince and Hitler, recorded by Göring's wiretapping agency, the prince reported that Mussolini had 'taken the entire matter in a very friendly manner' and had conveyed 'very friendly greetings' to Hitler. 'Austria was a done deal,' Mussolini had said. Hitler rejoiced and instructed Hesse to 'tell Mussolini that I will never forget it' and that he was prepared 'to go through thick and thin' with Mussolini. These statements became set phrases of the Mussolini–Hitler relationship. Hitler wanted Mussolini to believe that he felt genuinely indebted to the Duce, since he knew that Mussolini had been furious about his exposure of Italian weakness during the Anschluss.[30]

To reinforce his gratitude to Mussolini, Hitler repeated the phrase 'Mussolini, I will never forget you for this' in a telegram to the Duce on 13 March 1938, which was widely published in Germany and Italy.[31] Mussolini had the telegram archived in his personal files, an indication that he would hold Hitler to his word, which casts into doubt that he believed in Hitler's steadfast loyalty.[32] Mussolini only replied the following day, curtly stating that his position was determined by the friendship of both countries. While Hitler had politely addressed his thank-you telegram to 'His Excellency', an angry Mussolini, who, in order to save face, had no option but to accept the Anschluss and be polite to Hitler, sent his to 'Hitler-Vienna'. His reply was published in the Italian press, but also in German newspapers, because the Nazis mistook it as his approval of Germany's unilateral action.[33]

Hitler never forgot Mussolini's non-intervention in March 1938 and subsequently used it to dismiss any criticism of Mussolini amongst his officials. Hitler, while enjoying his triumph in Vienna, told the correspondent of *Il Popolo d'Italia*: 'Our friendship is beyond all formalities . . . We are ready to show our friendship and gratitude, if Italy will need it one day.'[34] In reality, the relationship, even at the moment of Hitler's public gratitude and reinforcement of the special Italo-German friendship that could dispense with diplomatic formalities, was clouded by private misunderstanding. Mussolini was in fact furious about Hitler's success and his own failure to act unilaterally. An envious Duce confided to Clara Petacci that 'the scenes of fanaticism for Hitler [in Austria] have been really disconcerting. Not even we Southerners go that far.' Thus Mussolini believed in the strength of Germany. It should be added that Mussolini, amidst the Austrian crisis, found the time to have sex with Petacci.[35] Reflecting Mussolini's ambivalent view, oscillating between private anger and jealousy and public support of Hitler, the Italian Ministry of Culture and propaganda instructed the Italian press to downplay the dramatic events of the Anschluss and to avoid references to Hitler's 11 March 1938 letter to Mussolini.[36]

French and British diplomats interpreted Mussolini's passivity with some concern, as they believed that an Italian–German alliance was in the making and had just launched an attack on the post-1919 liberal-internationalist order. Reports left no one in doubt over Italy's subservient position in this alliance. For instance, Nevile Henderson, the British ambassador in Berlin, told his American colleague on 12 March 1938 that Mussolini was 'the final loser among the big powers of Europe'. Henderson added sarcastically that 'if the Axis remained Italy would be the tail of the dog'. For François-Poncet, Mussolini was a fool 'now condemned to subservience to Germany'.[37]

Mussolini's pro-Hitler policies were not popular amongst all Fascist leaders. Within the Italian government and the top ranks of Fascism, tensions behind the public displays of accord were discernible. In order to present Italy's more or less forced support of the Anschluss as the logical outcome of Fascist foreign policy, the Fascist Grand Council, an advisory assembly of Fascist notables, approved Mussolini's pro-Hitler policy. In the meeting, Italo Balbo, one of the *quadrumviri* of Fascism and governor-general of Libya, attacked Germany. Mussolini rebuked him and insisted that Italy would have also annexed a territory with an Italian-speaking majority if it were able to do so, a reference to Italian irredentism.[38] The minutes of the meeting concluded that the German annexation reflected the desire of the majority of Austrians. Via the Prince of Hesse, Mussolini and Ciano, keen to maintain their reputation, also sought Hitler's approval for publication of an edited version of his letter to the Duce, which the Führer happily granted. The protocol of the meeting was published the following day, together with Hitler's 'historic letter' to Mussolini, in *Il Popolo d'Italia*.[39]

As German troops marched into Austria on 12 March 1938, meeting no resistance, Mussolini had no option but to swallow the news – in complete contradiction to his earlier promises to guarantee Austrian sovereignty. Thus, in his speech to the Chamber of Deputies a few days later, the Duce presented the Anschluss as historically inevitable. The Brenner border was inviolable, he declared, a clear message to Germany that Italy would defend the South Tyrol. Mussolini declared that he was set for closer collaboration with Germany and repeated that the Axis was far more than a diplomatic alliance, but the expression of the will of millions of Germans and Italians, inevitably brought together by their parallel histories.[40] Behind the scenes, Mussolini ordered the intensification of construction works on the *Vallo del Littorio*, a fortification of Italy's alpine borders with France and Germany. This was another reflection of Mussolini's ambiguous attitude towards Germany, which constantly fluctuated between enthusiasm and hostility, as did his personal attitude towards Hitler, oscillating between admiration and envy. A perceptive interpretation of Mussolini's speech was provided by William Phillips, the American ambassador to Italy, who reported to Washington, DC, that the objective of Mussolini's speech had been to reassure Fascist officials and intellectuals, who increasingly resented that Italy, the first fascist country, was now playing second fiddle to Germany.[41]

Yet Fascist propaganda promoted an alliance with Germany in newspapers, on newsreel and on the radio in the run-up to Hitler's visit and in order to overshadow these tensions. Most Italians, as far as the limited evidence suggests, were still under the impact of powerful anti-German propaganda from the First World War, and rightly associated the alliance with Germany with warmongering and its adverse effects on living standards.[42] Indeed, both the political police and Fascist party informers picked up hostile views towards an alliance with Germany. Many people believed that such an alliance would mean war. For example, on 1 April 1938 the political police reported that anti-German leaflets had been distributed in Naples, just when Hitler's visit to the city had been announced.[43]

Mussolini knew that the Axis was unpopular with the majority of Italians, which is one of the reasons why he frequently talked about changing sides and continued to maintain relations with Britain. What he thought in private is more difficult to discern, for his views towards Germany and Hitler oscillated, as we have seen. His preference was an alliance with Hitler, but envy for Hitler's greater power, together with the need to balance his own admiration for the Führer with the more cautious attitudes of Fascist and state officials, often made him articulate anti-German views. In late April 1938, for instance, he told Ciano that Italy '[would] destroy Germany for at least two centuries' if the Germans dared to invade the South Tyrol. This remark suggests that Mussolini did not believe Hitler's renunciation of claims for this territory. But this was pure rhetoric. Italy neither had the intention nor the capacity to crush Germany.[44]

Nevertheless, Mussolini's public cultivation of the alliance with Hitler continued. For instance, on 18 March 1938, he received a delegation of German war veterans, led by Carl-Eduard, Duke of Saxe-Coburg-Gotha, a Nazi party member and grandson of Queen Victoria. Ciano ridiculed the duke's 'really unfortunate physique' and concluded that not all Germans were 'the giants described by Tacitus'. Mussolini gave a speech that drew strong parallels between Italy and Germany and finished with a salute to Hitler and the great German nation.[45] Unlike Germany, Italy could not celebrate bloodless foreign policy triumphs. Italian contingents were still fighting in Spain and suffering high numbers of casualties, including at the March 1937 Battle of Guadalajara against the People's Republican Army. In total, Italy lost more men in the Spanish Civil War than in the war in Ethiopia, with 3,819 dead and 11,000–12,000 wounded, according to official figures – although these should be read with caution, as the Fascist regime glorified death in battle as a way to transform Italy into a nation of warriors.[46] Mussolini continued with his belligerent rhetoric in a speech to the Senate on 30 March 1938, boasting that Italy was ready for war, carefully avoiding a formal commitment to either Germany or Britain. If Italy went to war again, he would personally command the army, Mussolini said. Thus, Mussolini and the king were both made Marshals of the Empire, a gesture which pleased the vain Mussolini, jealous of Hitler's status as supreme commander of the Wehrmacht.[47]

In order to reinforce his tactic to play off Britain and Germany against each other in public, Mussolini renewed the Gentlemen's Agreement with Britain in April 1938, as Chamberlain's government hoped to contain the Third Reich via a closer alliance with Italy, a controversial policy within the British cabinet at the time. Still, Britain insisted that Italian troops would have to leave Spain before the agreement could be ratified. Mussolini refused, so the treaty was little more than an example of his showmanship. Mussolini was geared towards war on Germany's side and, at the same time, tried to maximise Italy's position by invoking the 'determining weight' rhetoric. In contrast to the interpretation later forwarded by some historians, it was through his own choosing that Mussolini, supported by some but not all leading Fascists, pushed Italy into an alliance with Hitler's Germany.[48] After his triumphant visit to Germany and his pro-German behaviour during the Anschluss, his room for manoeuvre on the international stage, considerably reduced after Italy's attack on Ethiopia, narrowed even more.

V

Notwithstanding disagreement behind the scenes, both regimes cooperated when it came to suppressing dissent during Hitler's visit to Italy. Long before the Anschluss, the Italian police, led since 1926 by Arturo Bocchini, had given a number of instructions about maintaining public security during Hitler's visit in order to protect the dictators against potential assassination attempts and to create a sense of order at the mass rallies.[49] These instructions were based on earlier police regulations on maintaining security at mass events, a key instrument of Fascist rule. Several thousand troops were to be deployed to Rome and Naples and placed at the disposal of the police authorities. More detailed instructions were made. Rail passengers had their identity documents and their luggage checked at stations.[50]

As we have seen, the Nazi and Fascist agencies of repression had started collaborating, initially against Communists, in 1936, in the wake of the

Police Treaty. Already in early October 1937, weeks after Mussolini's departure from Germany, a secret circular from the General Directorate of Public Security instructed Italy's prefects to keep a close eye on all Germans in Italy. Lists had to be prepared of Germans, indicating whether they were Nazi supporters, anti-Nazis or Jews.[51]

This increasing cooperation soon created its own dynamism and made officials on both sides believe that an alliance would be beneficial to both nations. In late autumn 1937, Heinrich Müller, the leading Gestapo official, met Guido Leto, the Italian police official in charge of cooperation with the German police and soon to become director of the public security division of the political police.[52] Following the Gestapo's suggestion, they agreed to examine the political reliability of all German expatriates in Italy. The Italian police compiled a first draft of a list of German citizens in Italy, assisted by members of the Nazi party's foreign organisation in Italy, seconded to the provincial police headquarters (*questura*). Displaying typical Nazi paranoia, the Gestapo believed that emigrants from Germany, including political exiles and up to 8,000 Jews, would pose a potential threat during Hitler's visit. Despite the increasing anti-Semitism of many leading Fascists and Mussolini himself, Italy, appearing as a more humane country than the Third Reich, harboured Jewish refugees from Germany as long as they were not involved in open anti-Nazi activities.[53]

The German police increasingly passed on information to the Italians about anti-fascist German Jews in Italy, which resulted in the widespread stigmatisation of German Jews by the Italian authorities. High-ranking Nazi police officials, including Himmler, a personal friend of Bocchini's, and Reinhard Heydrich, chief of the Security Police (*Sicherheitspolizei*), helped coordinate the arrests. On 2 December 1937, the German embassy in Rome ordered German consulates in Italy to prepare detailed reports about suspicious Germans resident in their consular districts. But this was not all. During Hitler's visit, the Italian police arrested around 500 German Jews and took them into 'preventive custody', at the request of the German police. Detailed plans for the arrests had met Mussolini's approval, as a document from the Province of Florence, filed by Mussolini's secretariat in late 1938, reveals. According to Prefect Ruggiero Palmeri, a German police delegation had requested that a total of 122 suspect male German and Austrian Jews were to be arrested on 1 May in the Province of Florence. Like the Nazis during Mussolini's visit, Italian authorities thus used preventive arrests in order to create an image of order, unity and unanimous popular support.[54]

Police cooperation worked relatively smoothly, despite all the tensions in other policy areas. On 30 March 1938, for instance, the German consul in Leghorn reported to the embassy in Rome that one Ekkehard W., a stage painter, was politically unreliable. He had come to Italy after the Great War and did not have a permanent address. It is not clear whether W. was arrested during Hitler's visit, but it must remain a possibility. On top of the 500 German Jews, an unknown number of non-Jewish Germans were arrested during Hitler's visit by the Italian authorities. Desperate pleas to the authorities for the release of the Jews, such as one from the chief rabbi of Merano, filed by Mussolini's secretariat, were ignored.[55] The regime, anxious of being seen as anti-Semitic and thus too close to the Germans by the international press, hotly denied that the round-up was specifically targeted at German Jews.[56]

Italian anti-Fascists too felt the full force of state repression, as the Italian police, alarmed by rumours about planned anti-Fascist attempts on Hitler's life, stepped up their surveillance. On 3 May 1938, after Hitler's arrival in Italy, the Bolzano border police sent an urgent telegram to Police Chief Bocchini with details about the arrest of Gherardo M., allegedly from the Sudetenland, source of increasing diplomatic friction between Germany and the European powers. He had been carrying two revolvers and bullets. Even though the telegram did not explicitly state that he had been trying to kill Hitler, the Italian police handed him over to the German police.[57]

An anti-Semitic panic shaped the reports of Italian officials in the months before Hitler's visit. This reflected the regime's growing anti-Semitism at a time of improving bilateral relations with Germany (this is not to say that one should view the Fascist regime's increasingly anti-Semitic policies as a direct result of closer contacts with Nazi Germany, a theme that will be explored in more detail in the next chapter). For instance, the prefect of Modena claimed that 'the Jews Masons Communists', a reference to the Fascist belief in a world conspiracy of Jews, Bolsheviks and freemasons, had paid two Jews the considerable sum of 10,000 lire, more than the price of a Fiat Topolino, for an attack on Hitler's train. Especially after the Anschluss, some anti-Fascists communicated their dissatisfaction with Mussolini's pro-German policy and Hitler's visit in anonymous letters to Fascist institutions and the Duce. Take the case of a correspondent who called himself Alfa, 'the boss of the Death Squad', a young unemployed university graduate: on 28 March 1938, he posted a threatening letter to the Duce from Naples which was duly received by Mussolini's special secretariat. The correspondent accused Mussolini of living in pomp and circumstance, while the Italian people were suffering in economic misery (not an altogether unfounded accusation given the declining living standards in Italy). He advised Mussolini to avoid coming to Naples with his friend Hitler, 'the murderer of the little great Austrian chancellor', a reference to the Nazi assassination of Dollfuss in 1934. The authorities were alarmed and started an investigation, although there is no evidence that they ever found the correspondent.[58]

VI

Below the surface of the Fascist display of unity with Nazi Germany, many – including members of Italian society's upper echelons, even the monarchy, parts of the armed forces, the Vatican and also Fascist party members – remained sceptical of Mussolini's courting of Hitler. Let us consider an incident from late March 1938 that was brought to the attention of the prefect of Florence. He reported to the Interior Ministry that anti-German leaflets had been discovered in the city. After lengthy investigations, the author of the leaflets was identified on 27 April 1938 as Giacomo L., a 40-year-old who had been cashiered from the Fascist party in 1923 for his failure to adhere to party discipline, lest he wanted, like many of the Fascist squadrists, to take the revolution further along the lines of a more violent, uncompromising and 'original' Fascism. The authorities arrested him carrying anti-German leaflets. Even some core supporters of Fascism thus saw the rapprochement with Nazi Germany, after all the enemy in the First World War, as a betrayal of Fascism.[59]

To drown such critical voices, both regimes made significant propaganda efforts. Alfieri's Ministry of Popular Culture tried to outdo Goebbels' planning for Mussolini's visit to Germany, reflecting rivalry between the regimes. In a memorandum of April 1938, a propaganda official prescribed the close monitoring of Italian and foreign correspondents. Foreign correspondents would be issued daily communiqués to guide their reports. The German correspondents were given especially kind treatment by the

Italians and subsequently wrote glowing reports.[60] But some complained to Alfieri about the inferiority of the Italian preparations in contrast to the German ones the previous year. For instance, one correspondent lamented that the facades of important buildings in Rome were illuminated in such bright colours that it was impossible for camera crews to film them.[61]

As could have been expected, national rivalry coloured much of the preparations for Hitler's visit. In early March 1938, Ciano heard that schoolchildren in Florence were being taught to sing the German national anthem. Following Ciano's furious reaction, Guido Buffarini Guidi, undersecretary of state in the Interior Ministry, was anxious that Hitler's visit would be a triumph for Germany, but not for Italy. Therefore, he passed a decree on 24 March 1938, just after the Anschluss, which banned the singing of German songs in Italy during the official events of Hitler's visit.[62] Ciano's commission meticulously planned each stop on Hitler's itinerary, representing Italians as firmly united behind Mussolini and Fascism in their support for an alliance with Germany. In line with the visual politics of the regime, memorabilia of the visit, such as pamphlets and books, had to be approved by the Ministry of Popular Culture, trying to control the visual representation of the Mussolini–Hitler encounter.[63]

Disagreement and tension lurked throughout the preparations, and soon some Nazi officials began to annoy Italian functionaries with bossy requests that could be interpreted as German arrogance. Consider an episode that was emblematic in this respect. On 27 April 1938, Erwin Ettel, the leader of the Nazi party branch for German expatriates in Italy, demanded that the City of Rome clean the litter-strewn street near the Nazi party offices in Via Salaria, as Hitler might pass through during his visit. Rome's city council only replied after Hitler's arrival in Italy and curtly stated that the street was in good order and thus required no work.[64]

Mirroring the press strategies employed during Mussolini's visit to Germany, German and Italian newspapers excited their readers about Hitler's approaching arrival. This occasion would give the Fascist regime the opportunity to stage an even grander spectacle than during Mussolini's trip to Germany. For instance, on 29 April 1938, following propaganda officials' directives, *Il Popolo d'Italia* dedicated its cover to Hitler's visit and provided readers with a dramatis personae of his huge retinue. The German delegation was considerably bigger than Mussolini's a year earlier and included, amongst others, Himmler and Goebbels.[65] The Fascist regime exercised tight control over newspaper reports and photographs of the visit to create a sense of the unanimous support of Italians for an alliance with Germany. Thus, the Ministry of Popular Culture forbade Italian journalists from publishing unauthorised pictures.[66] Following a royal decree, 3 May 1938, the day of Hitler's arrival in Italy, and 5 and 9 May were declared national holidays for the regions visited by Hitler. As during Mussolini's visit to Germany, these public holidays gave a festive character to the visit and drew out spectators, even if they were not ardent Fascist supporters.[67] Nevertheless, not all were as enthusiastic about Hitler's visit as Fascist officials had hoped, prompting the Ministry of Propaganda and Culture to instruct newspaper editors to publish stories that hotel rooms were still available in Rome during the visit.[68]

Italian journalists, following the regime's guidelines, published articles waxing lyrical about an Italo-German alliance. Filippo Bojano, for instance, declared that 'Italy and Germany [are] guarantors of world peace', while other journalists published histories of Nazism. On 2 May 1938, the day of Hitler's departure from Berlin, *Il Popolo d'Italia* offered its readers a powerful metaphor of the Axis when it suggested that the railway from Berlin to Rome was covered in 'a sea of Italian and German flags along the way between the two capitals', an expression of the 'unalterable solidity of the Axis'. Readers were also presented with photographs of the two previous Mussolini–Hitler meetings, showing both leaders together as a human symbol of their friendship and the Axis. Read differently, the image of the two leaders meeting amidst their peoples was the menacing symbol of a New Order in Europe, and Hitler's visit, massive in size, went far beyond the usual preparations of other state visits at the time.[69]

The German media covered the visit step by step too. A special issue of the *Italien-Beobachter*, the magazine of the Italian Nazi party branch for German expatriates, cited lofty pro-Axis declarations by Hitler and Mussolini and other Fascist and Nazi grandees. It coupled Nazi and Fascist leaders, a media strategy highlighting the historically inevitable unanimity between Italy and Germany.[70]

As a result of these grand press announcements, ordinary people swamped the German embassy with requests for tickets for some of the planned events. On 12 April 1938, for example, Cesare S., from Calabria, wrote an obsequious letter, insisting that he had always wanted to see the two leaders. While some correspondents were enthusiastic about the alliance with Germany, others emphasised the pomp and circumstance. German tourists in Italy too applied for tickets. Consider the case of Paul H., an ex-hussar who had been blinded in the First World War. He wrote to the German embassy and asked for tickets to witness the visit of Hitler to Rome and Naples. His request was granted, while most other applicants were sent a standard reply, which asked them to report to the embassy's chancery to apply for tickets in person.[71]

Others used Hitler's visit to extract favours from the authorities. Such practices reflected a long-standing tradition of requesting favours from monarchs on special occasions, rather than any deep-seated emotional bonds of Italians with Mussolini. For example, days before Hitler's visit, a young German woman, married to an Italian porter, had given birth to a son. She had called him 'Adolfo Benito' and immediately, via the German embassy, asked Hitler to become the baby's godfather. Since the boy was an Italian citizen, the embassy refused to pass on the request to him. Instead, it opened a savings account with 2,000 lire, considerably more than the average monthly wage of a worker, and claimed that the money had come directly from Hitler. Whether or not the young German woman was an ardent supporter of the Axis is unclear. Nor is it clear that the teachers of children in an Apulian orphanage who were awarded 500 lire by the embassy upon sending a pro-Hitler letter were pro-Nazi. They all knew that Hitler's visit was a splendid occasion on which to send him begging letters.[72]

VII

With the Austrian question resolved, Hitler was able to travel to Italy by train, unlike in 1934. His predictably punctual departure on 2 May at 4.44 p.m. was carefully choreographed. Berlin's Anhalter station was adorned with swastikas and Italian flags. Tens of thousands of Berliners were out on the streets. Before Hitler boarded the train, he exchanged a few words with members of the Italian Fascist party's branch in Berlin.[73] Crowds greeted his train on its way to the Brenner Pass. On 3 May 1938, the Duke of Pistoia, representing the House of Savoy, and Starace, as a delegate of the Fascist party, officially welcomed Hitler to Italy. This arrangement showcased the fact that Mussolini's regime was a compromise of the old elites with Fascism. It also reflected the ambivalent style, including traditional elements of a state visit alongside newer elements projecting the aggressive challenge of Mussolini and Hitler to create a New Order, that would dominate the itinerary of Hitler's visit.[74] In a similar vein, the huge size of the German delegation reflected Hitler's insistence that his visit to Italy was more substantive than a traditional state visit. The delegation included the wives of Nazi grandees, including Frau Ribbentrop, Frau Hess and Frau Frank, in lieu of an official German first lady. Altogether, three special trains were required to carry the huge delegation to Italy.[75]

It is significant that German newspaper reports remained awkwardly silent about the response of the population of the South Tyrol as Hitler's train passed through. As part of a clever Italian choreography, Hitler got off the train for a brief walk on the platform at Bologna, rather than Bolzano, the capital of the South Tyrol. While Bologna was a city that boasted a long socialist tradition, the authorities hoped that they would be able to control the masses more efficiently here than at Bolzano, where the regime feared a pro-Nazi demonstration of the German-speaking population. Indeed, the Italian authorities in the South Tyrol were so anxious about waves of pro-German demonstrations that Prefect Giuseppe Mastromattei banned the distribution of posters with the slogan 'Heil Hitler' specifically printed for Hitler's visit. But such attempts to suppress expressions of support for Hitler were largely ineffective, as a telegram from Trento reveals, sent shortly after Hitler's special train had passed through. According to the telegram, people had remained restrained as Hitler's train went through the South Tyrol's railway stations as they had been under close surveillance and pressure to comply. In contrast, alongside the railway lines, peasants had shouted supportive slogans as the train sped past. The farther south the train travelled, the more enthusiastic the masses became, according to Fascist propaganda. In Verona, for instance, the local Fascist party claimed that 30,000 people had saluted Hitler in a huge assembly (*grandiosa adunata*).[76] According to Goebbels, Hitler, wearing the insignia of an honorary corporal of the Fascist militia, was impressed by the brilliant reception.[77]

While there were, of course, Fascist supporters amongst the crowds, there has been a ferocious debate amongst historians about the nature of consent for Fascism. Rather than posit a black-and-white dichotomy between coercion and consent, most historians now agree that Fascism, through various means of coercion, terror and control, created a propaganda image of consensus. Similar observations can be made about Nazism. Whether or not the masses were genuinely enthusiastic is hard to say, but they became essential participants, not simply passive spectators, in the grandiose spectacle that was Hitler's visit to Italy.[78]

Whether expressions of anti-German sentiment were representative or not is a moot point. What matters is that Mussolini's special secretariat filed a number of protests against Hitler's visit that had been sent in by ordinary Italians. These protests were therefore known to the authorities and probably to Mussolini himself. Correspondents built on a central aspect of the Mussolini cult, according to which the Duce was available to listen to and act on such petitions.[79] Most letters were anonymous, highlighting correspondents' fear of potential reprisals for criticising Mussolini's flagship propaganda project of an alliance with Hitler. A man who had been travelling around the country in the weeks after Hitler's visit wrote to Mussolini on 20 May and shared his concerns about the unpopularity of an alliance with Germany. The correspondent claimed that there had been absolutely no enthusiasm in Rome for Hitler. A graffito near the Piazza Venezia, seen by the correspondent at 11 p.m. on the night before Hitler's arrival, read: 'Rome receives from the Reich the scum with flagpoles, tripods and the cops [*sbirraglia*].' Unsurprisingly, this rude text made everyone who walked past laugh. The regime's security measures had been ineffective if such statements could be scrawled on the walls near Mussolini's office. This suggested that Fascism's project to transform Italians into ardent believers had failed and, more generally, that the regime lacked control over Italian society.[80]

Such incidents were not isolated. In a bar in Catania, people even talked openly against Germany, and most war veterans across Italy were said to be particularly opposed to the Germans. One such correspondent offered a truthful conclusion of Hitler's visit. He later wrote to Mussolini that the result of the visit had been 'costs, costs and costs at the expense of the people. A setting that has not showcased the real view of Italy and Rome.' The correspondent lamented that many people had been arrested during the visit of Hitler, a German and anti-Catholic heretic.[81]

Hitler arrived in Rome in the magical atmosphere of a late spring night. The station building at Ostiense had been revamped for him. The king, rather than Mussolini, was the first to welcome him with the military, not the Roman, salute. Despite propaganda claims to the contrary, Hitler's journey was a state visit to be met by the head of state. This organisation also demonstrated that Mussolini's domestic power was far weaker than Hitler's. In a picture in Mussolini's *Il Popolo d'Italia*, Victor Emmanuel is hidden behind another official, perhaps a reflection of Mussolini's envy that he was not the head of state.[82] Inside the same issue, the Fascist newspaper reprinted a letter to the editor of *The Times* from G.M. Trevelyan, the Italophile Whig historian. In his letter, Trevelyan praised the Easter Treaty with Britain. The reprinting of the letter was an implicit reminder to an Italian readership dissatisfied with Mussolini's pro-German policies, and to international observers, above all in Britain, that Mussolini was not yet prepared to enter into a formal alliance with Germany. Mussolini was maintaining the illusion that Italy's options were still open, also dropping a hint to the German delegation who were keen to sign a treaty with Italy.[83]

During Hitler's carefully choreographed arrival, another conflict immediately appeared, this time one of images and protocol. Hitler was unhappy as he had to board a horse-drawn carriage with the monarch rather than with the Duce. He was tense in Victor Emmanuel's presence, and subsequently let Mussolini know how uncomfortable he had felt, as the king had insisted on conversing with him in French, a language which Hitler did not speak and detested.[84] Victor Emmanuel's horse-drawn carriage was an old-fashioned mode of transport – unlike Hitler's fast Mercedes cars or Mussolini's aeroplanes. Furthermore, Hitler was opposed to monarchy, which he saw as an outdated form of government, exacerbated by the alleged interbreeding of royalty. He even told the Duce to abolish the monarchy. Mussolini was apparently irritated by this unsolicited advice, as it made him jealous of Hitler's stronger political position. Unsurprisingly, Victor Emmanuel did not warm to Hitler and later told Ciano and Mussolini that Hitler had asked for a woman during his first night in Rome, causing much consternation amongst the courtiers, who believed that he wanted a prostitute; allegedly, Hitler had requested a woman to turn his bed, for otherwise he could not sleep. Ciano doubted whether these rumours were true and blamed the king's anti-German feelings.[85]

Other members of the Nazi delegation did not endear themselves to the Italian court either. Himmler and Hess rudely dismissed the old-fashioned court etiquette, which made them feel socially insecure, while praising the 'atmosphere of revolution' at the Palazzo Venezia.[86] Goebbels went even further and demanded to have 'this entire pack of courtiers' shot. Hitler's reaction to his discomfort in the king's company was to develop an obsession with the Italian monarchy. After his return to Germany, he told one of his military adjutants that the Italian court and most of the Italian officer corps were a pack of degenerates. Even almost four years later, in January 1942, Hitler still railed to his entourage about the Italian monarchy and Fascism's failure to destroy it. The Duke of Pistoia, who had received him at the Brenner Pass, was 'a real sausage'. Hitler pitied 'the poor Duce', whose revolution had come too early: it would have been far better for the Fascists if, like in Germany in 1918, a socialist revolution had abolished the monarchy. The Nazis' deep suspicion of the Italian monarchy and army, core parts of the Fascist state, hardly formed a good basis for closer cooperation with Italy. The idealised image of Mussolini as the strong man of Italy, a powerful Nazi myth since the 1920s, had thus been shattered by the king's prominent role. In this way, at least, Hitler's visit was counterproductive as it clearly revealed to him and other Nazi leaders the structural weaknesses of Mussolini's regime.[87]

Despite such dismissive views of the House of Savoy, the Nazi leaders' wives wanted to be received at court by Queen Elena. This request caused consternation amongst snobbish German diplomats who feared that the Nazi wives did not know how to curtsy and asked the German ambassador's wife, Winifred von Mackensen, to teach them court etiquette. Unfortunately, most of the Nazi wives were too fat to curtsy, and some refused to do so in front of the queen, to whom they condescended, as she had been born in Montenegro. Frau von Ribbentrop, keen on being the first wife of the delegation, wanted to sit on the queen's right in the seat of honour, but the queen, visibly irritated by the imposition to receive the wives, just gestured towards Frau von Mackensen to join her and then ignored the Nazi women.[88] Eva Braun, Hitler's mistress, who came with him to Italy, was not at the reception. Hitler did not want to have an official partner, in order to maintain the myth that he devoted all of his energy to Germany, and she had to stay at a hotel in Rome. Apart from filming her impressions of Italy, which she later showed to Hitler, she spent most of her time shopping.[89]

On the route from the station to the Quirinal Palace, a carefully scripted spectacle presented itself and highlighted Fascism's alleged roots in ancient Rome, a long pedigree which Nazism could not claim. The *Italien-Beobachter* printed Hitler's route to illustrate an essay by the director of the

German Archaeological Institute in Rome on the 'festive street . . . which cannot be found elsewhere in the world'.[90] Hitler entered Rome as a triumphant leader through the Porta San Paolo. The streets were adorned with Italian and swastika flags. The cortege rumbled past the Obelisk of Axum, a symbol of the new Italian Empire looted as war booty in Ethiopia, the Palatine and the Arch of Constantine. Here, the Via dell'Impero, a Fascist project, began, and Hitler was driven past the Colosseum and the Roman forum. All of these sights were illuminated, following extensive preparations with state-of-the-art projectors. The objective was to emphasise Fascism's Roman heritage so as to set it apart as superior to the new Nazism, which lacked such a profound heritage. Once past the forum, the cortege passed the monument to King Victor Emmanuel II, symbol of Italy's recent history as a young nation, similar to Germany, and the Palazzo Venezia, Mussolini's residence. To Hitler's dismay, the cortege did not stop here and turned instead towards the Quirinal Palace. A historian writing for the city of Rome's official journal placed Hitler's triumphal arrival into a longer history of entries into the Eternal City. He likened it to Emperor Charles V's triumphant 1536 entry after his victory at the Battle of Tunis. The author glossed over the more immediate association most Romans had with Charles V: the 1527 Sack of Rome by Charles's German mercenaries, who had wrecked and plundered the city. In this way, Hitler's entry into Rome could also be read as a bad omen for an Italian–German alliance.[91]

While the visit's choreography focused on Mussolini and Hitler, the cortege from the station to the Quirinal Palace included pairs of party and state officials such as Ribbentrop and Ciano, and Goebbels and Alfieri, who followed Hitler and the king in separate carriages. As in Berlin in 1937, this arrangement was designed to reinforce the Axis by pairing Fascist leaders with their Nazi colleagues. According to Goebbels, the king was extremely reserved and stiff, unlike the 'courageous and wise' Mussolini. And Goebbels doubted the reliability of the Italians 'in a serious emergency'; he envied the great history of ancient Rome for which Germany could only compensate with great victories. Goebbels was annoyed that the army and the Fascist militia, concerned about security, tightly cordoned off the streets from the crowds, preventing close contact between Hitler and the Romans, as the SS and police had done in Munich a year earlier.[92]

Hitler's mood improved greatly as soon as he could talk to Mussolini, who, in line with diplomatic protocol, paid Hitler a brief visit at the

Quirinal Palace. A second conversation with Hitler took place at Mussolini's office in the Palazzo Venezia on the same day, although it lasted merely half an hour. This arrangement was typical because the overall purpose of Hitler's visit was not the discussion of political substance, but the reinforcement of the display of unity and friendship between himself and Mussolini, alongside their nations. At the end, Hitler handed over a telescope and a certificate to the Duce, committing Germany to fund a huge observatory in Italy. This symbolic gift would help Mussolini see into the future of a strong Fascist–Nazi alliance. Despite the subsequent German investment of more than one million Reichsmarks, the observatory, a prestige project whose progress Hitler monitored himself, was never finished. Its fate became a symbol of the vicissitudes of Italo-German relations.[93]

Neither side was prepared to commit itself to a treaty which would bind it to support the other in military adventures. But this does not mean that the visit was mere propaganda or show. Rather, the visit created a powerful image of friendship and unity that soon gained its political dynamic. Minutes of Mussolini's conversations with Hitler have not survived: most of the Italian documents of the Mussolini–Hitler conversations were destroyed by mould at the end of the war.[94] But Goebbels' diaries reveal that Hitler was happy about Mussolini's willingness to cooperate with Germany.[95] However, the Italian government refused to sign a military alliance with Germany, planned by Hitler since at least the Anschluss and after the failure to reach an agreement with Britain. Ciano presented Ribbentrop with a counter-treaty which, according to Weizsäcker, was a 'peace treaty with an enemy [rather] than a pact of loyalty with a friend'. In particular, the Italian government wanted to keep out of the conflict that was emerging between Germany and Czechoslovakia over the German-speaking territories of the multinational state, as Italy needed time to prepare for a large-scale war.[96] The German delegation refused to sign. After the Mussolini–Hitler encounter, Goebbels and other Nazi grandees were invited to join the dictators in Mussolini's grand office, which left them with a lasting impression of the Duce's power and determination, just as it did with Mussolini's other visitors.[97]

Beyond the pomp and circumstance lurked the ridiculous and hostile. For example, Goebbels noted in his diary that at the ceremonies the Fascist militia and the Italian army did not perform well, which prompted Mussolini to chide their leaders in front of his Nazi guests.[98] A display of unity and friendship, rather than intimate or in-depth political discussions, thus dominated Hitler's visit, following the pattern set during Mussolini's trip to Germany in September 1937. Show overshadowed the itinerary, which combined the protocol of state visits with new elements of fascist diplomacy. In line with protocol, Hitler thus visited the graves of kings Victor Emmanuel II and Umberto I at the Pantheon, and the monument for Victor Emmanuel II, which included the tomb of the unknown soldier. According to the itinerary prepared by the German military attaché, both ceremonies took place within fifteen minutes of each other, suggesting that they were a mere formality.[99]

Overall, the Fascist organisation greatly impressed Hitler and the Nazis, such as the huge parade by the Ballila, the Fascist youth organisation. At night, paying heed to a new diplomatic style that boasted about organising the masses, Hitler spoke near the Roman forum, a venue chosen to give the Italo-German alliance historical legitimacy. Hitler's audience consisted of up to 6,500 Germans living in Italy who had been invited by the Italian branch of the Nazi party. Mussolini joined this ceremony, underlining some supposed historical lineage between Fascism and Nazism, although Hitler did not refer to the alliance with Italy in his speech. Instead, he presented the German expatriates in Italy as steadfastly National Socialist. Hitler thus boasted to the Duce that he enjoyed the support of all Germans, even those living abroad.[100]

The densely packed programme left Hitler and the Nazi delegation exhausted, and the ambiguous nature of Italo-German relations shaped the wording of toasts exchanged between Hitler and the king at the gala dinner at the Quirinal Palace. While both leaders mentioned Italo-German friendship in diplomatic courtesies, they did not specify the contours of Italo-German collaboration.[101] After the state dinner, the delegations left on overnight trains for Naples, where the king welcomed Hitler at the station. Around 10,000 uniformed officials were deployed to maintain security and make the Camorra crime syndicates maintain a low profile, reflecting Fascism's concern with crime repression.[102] The king accompanied the delegation to the harbour, where they boarded the battleship *Cavour*, a symbol of Italy's power in the Mediterranean. *Il Popolo d'Italia* boasted about the power of the Italian navy, manifested by a simultaneous diving manoeuvre of Italian submarines which met with German admiration (*ammirazione tedesca*). Indeed, since the late 1920s, German naval leaders, unlike their counterparts in the army, had been admiring the Italian navy as a symbol of a new and dynamic Italy. Admiral Erich Raeder, supreme commander of the navy, even believed that Italy's navy would soon be capable of dominating the Mediterranean.[103]

Despite all the efforts invested into organising Hitler's visit, some events bordered on the hilarious. Consider the end of the Naples visit. Here, a gala performance was put on at the Teatro San Carlo of two acts of Verdi's *Aida*, originally composed for the opening of the Cairo Opera House. The officials who scheduled this orientalist opera, two years after the Italian conquest of Ethiopia, must have found it an appropriate illustration of Italy's colonial empire. As with other events on the itinerary, the seat allocation created a lengthy correspondence amongst the Italian authorities, as members of the court claimed the best seats, while the prefect insisted that policemen had to be given priority, highlighting security concerns.[104]

Other glitches revealed the ridiculous aspects of the show: Hitler, wearing white tie for the opera performance, was told that he had to inspect troops, without having time to change into his uniform. A photograph shows Hitler greeting troops with his outstretched right arm, his left hand on his white waistcoat, standing next to the fully uniformed king. This image created unwanted memories of Hitler's dress in Venice in 1934. Whether or not this blip was the result of a deliberate plan by the court to ridicule Hitler is a moot point. Hitler's ire fell on the chief of protocol of the German foreign ministry, who was forced to resign. Clearly, the meticulous dress regulations prepared by German diplomats, which had prescribed five different sets of dress for each member of the German delegation, had not been followed entirely.[105]

An essential part of the show was to boast about the strength of the Italian armed forces. Thus, apart from the naval and air force manoeuvres, a lengthy military parade on Rome's Via dell'Impero took place. The covers of *Il Popolo d'Italia* and the *Völkischer Beobachter* showed Hitler, Mussolini, the king and the queen reviewing the parade of 50,000 troops marching in the *passo romano*. The photograph highlighted tensions: Mussolini and Hitler greeted the troops with their outstretched right arms, while the king gave a military salute. Nevertheless, the parade met with Hitler's approval, although some German officers lamented the fact that the Italians were still using artillery guns from the First World War, a confirmation of the powerful anti-Italian sentiment amongst the German army and of concerns over Italian military efficiency. Hitler's air force adjutant later claimed that Hitler was not at all impressed with the performance of the Italian army during his visit. At the same time, Göring and other Luftwaffe leaders had long admired the Italian air force for its great technological advances and believed that it would be able to fight effectively. Hitler even admitted that an alliance with Italy was unpopular in Germany. The only basis of Italo-German friendship was his good rapport with Mussolini, as the events in the run-up to the Anschluss had shown, the Nazi leader insisted. But an alliance with Italy was Hitler's only choice as Britain was not prepared to give in to his demands for German parity of rearmament, a dubious but probably true account of Hitler's feelings for Mussolini and Italy.[106]

Emphases of Italian strength were paralleled by strong representations of Italian cultural superiority over Germany. For instance, Mussolini and Hitler visited the *Mostra Augustea della Romanità*. This was a key Fascist exhibition held on the 2,000th birthday of Emperor Augustus, designed to legitimise the rule of Mussolini, the founder of the Third Rome. Guided by a curator who was fluent in German, Hitler admired reproductions of Roman victory columns that had been discovered in Germany. Hitler was desperately keen to underline the common history of the ancient Germanic tribes and the Romans and visited the exhibition again on the next morning, as rain had led to a postponement of military manoeuvres. The wars between the Germanic tribes and the Romans were conveniently ignored in the manifestation of Italian–German unity.[107]

More demonstrations of Italian cultural superiority were offered up to the culture-hungry Hitler as he continued on a tour of Rome, guided by Ranuccio Bianchi Bandinelli, a leading archaeologist, also fluent in German. Sights included the Baths of Diocletian, the reconstructed tomb of Augustus and the Galleria Borghese, which boasted many of the Renaissance paintings favoured by Hitler and the Nazis.[108] According to Bianchi Bandinelli's post-war account, the two leaders did not like each other: Mussolini, speaking in fluent German but with a heavy accent, treated Hitler offhandedly, while the Nazi leader was deferential but never really friendly to the Duce. Mussolini was annoyed, as Hitler's attention was entirely focused on Bianchi Bandinelli's explanations, rather than on him.[109] The city of Rome's official journal condescendingly praised Nazi Germany's sponsorship of archaeological fieldwork in ancient Rome as a major contribution to the 'salvation of European civilisation'. However, this compliment could also be interpreted differently in the sense that Mussolini's Italy was unable to finance the 'salvation' of the monuments of ancient Rome and had to rely instead on the increasingly powerful Germany.[110]

Like many other tourists to Italy, the Nazi delegation was completely exhausted by Rome's artistic treasures and made to feel socially insecure. In this regard, the reception held in Hitler's honour on the Capitol was emblematic. Here, the Fascist *governatore*, Prince Piero Colonna, welcomed Hitler with words approved by Ciano, who tried to control the choreography of Hitler's visit. In his speech, Colonna reminded Hitler of Rome's ancient history which attracted 'the great minds of Germany' and then gave Hitler a bronze replica of the famous Romulus and Remus statue.[111] Hitler did not feel comfortable at the Capitol, as Colonna had assembled members of the Roman nobility.[112]

Still, overwhelmed by the massive propaganda efforts, Hitler told Goebbels over dinner that he had sealed his friendship with Mussolini. The Duce once again agreed with the German annexation of Austria and promised to support German claims for the Sudetenland, which reinforced Hitler's determination to invade Czechoslovakia.[113]

Official Italian accounts of Hitler's visit delivered historical legitimisations of the Axis, based on a selective interpretation of Italo-German history. Prominent examples of this genre include a special issue of the Fascist flagship periodical *Gerarchia* and Paolo Orano's *L'Asse nel pensiero dei due popoli*, published in both Italian and German. In a similar tenor to the photo essays published on the occasion of Mussolini's visit to Germany, Orano claimed that Italy and Germany had been friendly since the Risorgimento. He quoted the popular hero Giuseppe Garibaldi, who had, in reality, had an ambiguous attitude towards Germany: 'The brotherhood of these two peoples will result in great benefits for humanity.'[114] While an interesting attempt at rewriting the past, the use of select quotations from Garibaldi to legitimise the Axis remained ineffectual at eliminating tensions between both nations.

Mussolini's and Hitler's toasts at a dinner hosted by the Duce at Palazzo Venezia also attempted to give the Axis and their friendship some historical substance. In this collective ritual of the toast, both leaders remained vague, not least because the Italian government had refused to sign up to a formal alliance with Germany. The speeches were broadcast on Italian and German radio so that domestic audiences could witness this allegedly historical moment. Foreign diplomats followed the speeches with concern. Jules Blondel, the French chargé d'affaires, found Mussolini's speech cold, perhaps a reflection of Mussolini's anger at Hitler's unilateral actions during the Anschluss. Hitler's toast, on the other hand, was more emotional. Blondel also duly noted the threatening undertones of Mussolini's toast, as the Duce had likened the Axis to the rise of the Italian and German peoples against Napoleon. This was an unveiled threat to France.[115] Significantly, Hitler, in his toast, confirmed that the South Tyrol would belong to Italy for good and pledged that Italy and Germany would never go to war again.[116] Nazi officials too were disappointed by Mussolini's lukewarm toast about the 'unchangeable friendship of our two peoples', which is why officials in charge of directing newspaper content instructed editors that they must not comment on the speeches. Instead, in lieu of tangible political results and a communiqué, editors were told to stress the uniqueness of the Italo-German friendship.[117]

As if this fanfare was not enough, the performance continued on the next day, showing off once more Italy's military power in air force and army manoeuvres. Italian fighter aeroplanes flew in swastika formation, and, at the Mussolini Forum, 100,000 participants paraded. German propaganda, determined to convince German newspaper readers of the alliance with Italy, commended the manoeuvres. In reality, though, too many tickets had been distributed, resulting in a run for seats, as an angry spectator who preferred to remain anonymous later reported to Mussolini, expressing his concern that the poor organisation would reflect badly on Italy.[118]

As an implicit acknowledgement of Italy's relative military and political weakness compared to the Third Reich, an essential aspect of the show was to highlight Italian cultural superiority and refinement over Germany.[119] This sentiment also dominated the staging of the final part of Hitler's Italian journey: a packed eight hours in Florence on 9 May 1938 ended Hitler's visit. After a triumphant welcoming ceremony, Mussolini escorted Hitler to the Palazzo Pitti. Florence, an ideal venue for the 'artistic' Hitler, had been spruced up with banners, flags and decorations for the visit, following months of preparations by the Florentine Office of Public Works and Urbanism to convey the message to a domestic and international audience that Fascism stood in a line of continuity with Florence's glorious Renaissance past. A copy of Donatello's *St George*, representing the power, stamina and readiness of the Renaissance man, a model for the Fascist 'New Man', and above all a symbol of the cultural superiority of Italy over Germany, was placed near the Palazzo Pitti where, it was expected, Hitler and others would be able to see it from their motorcades. The Florentine authorities spent the staggering sum of nineteen million lire on Hitler's visit, of which only one million was covered by the central government. Two years after Hitler's short visit to the Tuscan capital, government offices were still sorting out the budget and even asked homeowners to contribute to the costs of restoring their facades for the visit.[120]

Mirroring their visit to the Nazi shrine of fallen martyrs in Munich, the leaders visited the crypt of the fallen of the war and the Fascist Revolution martyrs 'in the sacred temple of Italian glory' in the basement of Santa Croce.[121] With the king absent, Fascist propaganda could highlight the encounter between 'the two leaders'. Hitler indulged in his passion for Renaissance art at the Uffizi, accompanied by a bored Mussolini who was apparently visiting the museum for the first time.[122] A rally in the Piazza Signoria cheered the two leaders, standing on the balcony of the Palazzo Vecchio from where previous rulers had taken the ovations of the people of Florence. During his visit to Florence, Hitler gave a statement to the official Italian Agenzia Stefani, distributed to the world press. He said that he genuinely admired Italy, its people and its regime. His visit had been organised perfectly. The Italian armed forces were efficient. What is more, the popular enthusiasm (though obviously orchestrated by the regime) had touched him. He implicitly admitted that the Italo-German friendship and that between Mussolini and himself had been constructed: 'It has been very beautiful . . . Believe me, ours is a friendship which one cannot construct artificially.' The staging of the visit had thus fulfilled one of its principal objectives: to show off Fascist Italy as a powerful ally for Nazi Germany. The official German news agency also reprinted Hitler's remarks, leaving German readers in no doubt about their leader's genuine love of Italy. Behind this propaganda of unity and friendship, however, lurked political and strategic tensions, misunderstandings and conflicts.[123]

Even more than during Mussolini's visit to Germany, the festivities and propaganda, with an almost total emphasis on unity and prestige, both of Mussolini and Hitler and of their nations, created a powerful image of close bonds between the two leaders, their states and their peoples which overshadowed the elements of tension beneath, especially the mutual popular ill-feeling of Germans and Italians towards each other. The show of unity and friendship had a strong political effect as it helped erase tensions, at least superficially, and made the Axis a self-fulfilling prophecy. Propagandistic ritual thus did not only reflect a political agenda but also shaped its own political reality. The pomp and circumstance of the Fascist propaganda performance, despite the strangely squalid elements of the visit, made Hitler believe that Italy would be a capable military ally. For Mussolini, Hitler's visit allowed him to present his regime as a worthy and reliable potential ally, linked because of a purportedly common political agenda and ideology.[124]

VIII

A tired German delegation crossed the South Tyrol at night to avoid pro-German demonstrations from the local population.[125] Goebbels and Hess agreed that this territory was the price of an alliance with Italy.[126] Yet Goebbels, like other Nazi leaders, remained sceptical of an alliance, which is why he claimed in his diary that had had seen some German-speaking South Tyrolese people crying as the train crossed the Brenner Pass in the morning. Along these lines, propaganda officials prohibited German newspaper editors even to mention the status of the South Tyrol in their coverage of Hitler's Italian journey.[127] This instruction followed an earlier pattern. Until 1938, the Third Reich had tried to silence the German speakers of the South Tyrol, as their status was an obstacle to better Italo-German relations. It is doubtful whether Hitler and Mussolini had discussed a resettlement of the South Tyrolese. Their fate remained unresolved and continued to reflect the vicissitudes of Italo-German relations.[128]

Like Mussolini in 1937, Hitler sent telegrams upon crossing the border. Other Nazi leaders such as Goebbels did the same and wrote to their Italian counterparts to reinforce the message that the Axis was not just a pact between Mussolini and Hitler, but also between other officials, and above all between the Italian and German peoples.[129] While the king received a dry note from Hitler, the Duce got a more enthusiastic telegram, written in an emotive language. Hitler waxed lyrically:

> The days which I could spend together with you in your beautiful country have left me with indelible impressions. I admire your work of

> the creation of the Empire. I have seen the Italy renewed by you in the spirit of Fascism in the glory of the armed services aware of their power . . . Above all, these days have enabled me, Duce, to get to know your people . . . The spiritual community of the Fascist and Nazi movements are a safeguard that the comradeship which links us will also be transferred to our peoples.[130]

Despite all his praise for Mussolini's achievements in creating the Empire and Italy's military prowess, Hitler's statement about the ideological relationship between Fascism and Nazism remained typically vague. The fact that both leaders and their propaganda machineries reinforced the symbolism of friendship suggests that they knew themselves about the lack of widespread popular support for the Axis. Hence the claim in the *Völkischer Beobachter* that all Germans had been to Italy, as they had been following the Hitler journey step by step through the media.[131] Through constant repetition by Fascist and Nazi propaganda, the Mussolini–Hitler friendship as well as the Axis turned into a powerful political dynamic. Increasingly, this myth became a constituent part of Fascist and Nazi policy, so that to distinguish between the Axis as a myth and as a reality is, in effect, misleading.[132]

Once back in Greater Germany, Hitler received an unsurprisingly enthusiastic welcome as his train progressed to Berlin. He had ordered that the welcoming ceremony be at least as enthusiastic as his reception in Italy. For otherwise, many Germans would have started to doubt that Hitler and Nazi Germany were more powerful than Mussolini and Italy.[133] According to Goebbels, Mussolini had told Hitler at the farewell ceremony: 'And no power in the world shall ever separate us.' This was a rhetorical master stroke which Hitler apparently took seriously, as he had started to cry, according to Ciano.[134] Mussolini was pleased too, as he boasted to Clara Petacci. He was convinced that Hitler and the German military leadership had been thoroughly impressed by the Italian armed forces and his regime, which even prompted him to tell Petacci that 'these Germans are likeable, and Hitler is a big guy like me'. Hitler had even told him, the Duce claimed, that 'these have been the most beautiful days of my life, and I will never forget them'.[135] Again, the performance had assuaged most doubts and reinforced Mussolini's sense that an alliance with the Third Reich was Italy's destiny.

However, despite the display of Axis unity during Hitler's visit, Mussolini did not completely surrender himself to an alliance with Nazi Germany. The *Manchester Guardian*'s diplomatic correspondent noted that Mussolini had been rather 'reticent' towards Hitler, while the Nazi leader had been much more enthusiastic.[136] Indeed, the *Manchester Guardian*'s claim, based on inside information presumably from the British Foreign Office, was confirmed by Mussolini's actions after Hitler's departure from Florence. Mussolini returned to Rome, from where he travelled to Genoa via the port of Gaeta on the *Cavour*, in an attempt to highlight Italy's claim over the Mediterranean. On 14 May 1938, he spoke in Genoa's Piazza della Vittoria, followed closely by the international press. After his volte-face legitimisation of the Anschluss, Mussolini insisted that 'friendship with Germany' would endure. Yet, significantly, he reminded his audience of the recent Gentlemen's Agreement with Britain. Thus, the Axis between Italy and Germany was not Italy's only option, a hint to Hitler and Italians not in favour of an alliance with Germany. The German Foreign Ministry understood this point and concluded that Hitler's visit to Rome had failed to clear the path for an alliance with Italy.[137]

At an international level, reservations about the solidity of the Axis remained. In the eyes of Jules Blondel, for example, the Axis was more of a necessity for the Italians and the Germans, rather than a relationship based on love. François-Poncet's report to the French foreign minister was even more critical. He wrote that Hitler had not managed to win over Mussolini. Yet despite his cool evaluation of the Mussolini–Hitler rapport, François-Poncet concluded that their representation as friends was a threat to peace in Europe.[138]

Reactions in Germany and Italy were mixed too, notwithstanding the huge amounts of propaganda. Some Nazi institutions remained critical. For example, the SS newspaper *Das Schwarze Korps* reminded its readers of Italy's role in the First World War, but concluded, paying lip service to Axis propaganda, that it was time to draw a line under all these tensions. The Italo-German relationship rested on rather shaky ground if even members of the SS intellectual elite remained so critical.[139]

In Italy, many Fascist supporters remained ambivalent, if not opposed, to an alliance with Germany. According to a conversation between a German diplomat and an informer from within the Fascist regime, Italian popular opinion had been hostile towards Hitler before his visit, which had happened soon after the Anschluss. The tight police surveillance had not helped improve this mood. Yet the author of the memorandum, keen on ingratiating himself with his superiors, insisted that Hitler's toast at the Palazzo Venezia in which he rescinded German claims for the South Tyrol had won over Italians for an alliance with Germany. The author highlighted an important aspect of the visit's choreography. As in 1937, given the special character of Italo-German relations, no official communiqué was issued, contrary to diplomatic custom. Here was another articulation of Hitler's and Mussolini's claim for a New Order that, however vague, tried, not always successfully, to ignore the conventions of diplomatic protocol and instead construct a new protocol.[140]

Fascist party reports on popular opinion filed after Hitler's return to Germany suggest that the nascent alliance with Nazi Germany remained unpopular. For instance, according to a 25 May 1938 report in the Province of Milan, people were worried that Hitler was set to go to war with Czechoslovakia. Indeed, the show in Italy had emboldened Hitler to escalate his foreign policy from revision to aggression.[141]

Thus, the propaganda, with its almost total emphasis on unity and prestige, both of the dictators and their nations, was a success in creating a menacing display of Italo-German solidarity. It was not simply perplexity and fear that characterised Italian attitudes to Germany. Hostile popular attitudes owed a lot to Pius XI's opposition to Nazi policies towards the Church and the Fascist regime's inability to penetrate deeply into Italians' minds. Yet, as we have seen, the Fascist staging of Hitler's visit as the apotheosis of a Fascist–Nazi alliance mobilised millions of Italians on the streets, in rallies and in other manifestations, and was thus central to the creation of an Italo-German alliance.[142] Hitler and Mussolini's growing partnership would soon bring Europe to the brink of war.

5

ON THE ROAD TO WAR
1938–9

I

In the months after Hitler's return from Italy the dynamism generated by the 1937 and 1938 meetings of Hitler and Mussolini developed the Axis to a point from which neither leader could retreat without losing face. Broad ideological agreement stood in tension with strategic differences and, of course, the unpopularity of an Italian–German alliance amongst large parts of both nations. The relationship between Mussolini and Hitler was soon put to a test in the summer and autumn of 1938, after Hitler's visit to Italy had reinforced the Nazi leader's determination to shift his foreign policy from revisionism to aggression. Fascism's massive display of power and unity during Hitler's visit had made the Nazi leader overestimate Italy's military capabilities. In contrast, high-ranking German military officials such as the military attaché at the German embassy in Rome, Enno von Rintelen, offered a more realistic assessment and emphasised the weakness of the Italian armed forces. Such views infuriated Hitler, who had internalised the position that an alliance with Italy was in Germany's interest. When, in the winter of 1938/9, German military intelligence compiled a memorandum on the strengths and weaknesses of the Italian armed services, he ordered that all copies must be pulped.[1]

Notwithstanding the ambiguity of Fascist–Nazi relations, Mussolini and Hitler increasingly began to believe that their fates were linked. In late

1938, the Axis, which at that point was not a military alliance but a display of Italian–German unity and friendship, served for the first time as a decisive instrument against the 'plutocratic democracies' in Europe. It was Hitler who set the agenda, not Mussolini.

Reflecting the momentum of what had become a self-fulfilling prophecy, networks of Axis functionaries, going beyond the 1936 Police Treaty, began to grow. Such contacts included mutual visits by Fascist and Nazi youth organisations and academic and cultural exchanges, but no formal contacts amongst the armies. A clear illustration of these growing contacts is an agreement of late 1938 between the German and Italian authorities on restricting the awarding of medals to representatives of the other country, as the number of gongs awarded had reached excessive levels.[2] Increasing Italian–German links can also be gleaned from the rising number of air passengers on Lufthansa, the German airline, between Berlin and Rome. Figures more than doubled, albeit from a low basis, between 1933 and 1937. Given the high expense of air travel, most of these passengers were rich tourists, businessmen or political officials.[3]

In Italy, the regime pushed forward with its determination to create a totalitarian society.[4] Axis rhetoric became the order of the day. For instance, when an Italo-German congress of law was held in Rome in June 1938, even Giuseppe Bottai, minister of national education, editor of *Critica Fascista* and critical of an alliance with Germany, applauded the speech of Hans Frank. Ciano sardonically commented in his diary that even Fascist officials critical of Nazi Germany recognised the change of direction in foreign policy, an admission that some Fascist officials were merely paying lip service to the alliance with Germany. The point of this episode is that the alliance with Germany was contingent and problematic, but that Mussolini and Hitler, alongside some, but not all, Fascist and Nazi leaders, increasingly internalised it.[5]

It was amidst this intensification of Axis contacts that Hitler provoked a severe diplomatic crisis in central Europe, making territorial demands on Czechoslovakia, a multinational state created in the wake of 1918. More than three million Germans, the Sudeten Germans, lived there in areas close to the German border. They felt increasingly oppressed by the Czechoslovak government, despite a number of concessions. After the Anschluss, they had hoped for annexation by the Reich, and the Nazis soon began to support the Sudeten German party, led by Konrad Henlein. In a speech in Karlsbad in late April 1938, Henlein had demanded autonomy for the Sudeten Germans, an implicit request for an incorporation of their region into the Reich.[6] Hitler was determined to seize the Sudetenland, which boasted a significant armaments industry, and cited the Sudeten Germans' right to national self-determination, a Wilsonian principle enshrined into the post-1919 peace settlement. Many high-ranking German military officers, while broadly agreeing with Hitler's expansionist plans, were concerned about their timing and their potential to unleash a war, given that Czechoslovakia was formally allied with France. A British intervention was likely, despite the strong anti-war mood in Britain.[7]

Mussolini's role in the Sudeten crisis has been the subject of a heated debate. Clearly, he sensed the crisis as an opportunity to raise Italy's power status, which is why he declared his unflinching support of Germany on several occasions. He had little choice after the crucial watershed of his earlier reversal of his position on the Anschluss. Even if he, like his Liberal predecessors, liked to play the independent statesman vis-à-vis other powers for as long as he could, Mussolini had cast his lot as an ally of Hitler. It is not true, as De Felice claims, that Mussolini initially avoided any commitment during the Czechoslovak crisis and that he only became involved in mid-September 1938, after Hitler's aggressive speech at the Nuremberg party rally in which the Nazi leader insisted on the annexation of the Sudetenland. According to this tendentious interpretation Mussolini only intervened when a European war was likely.[8]

In reality, Mussolini was geared towards war, but his aggression, as we have seen, was hampered by Italy's geographical location, its relative military weakness and its lack of natural resources. While in favour of an alliance with Germany, he therefore continued to play the diplomatic register to act as the 'determining weight' between the Western powers and Germany. Some historians see Mussolini's flirting with Germany as evidence of his opportunism, while others dismiss any mention of his lack of commitment as an apologetic downplaying of his undeniable aggressiveness and his desire to ally himself with Nazi Germany. What is clear is that Mussolini was bellicose and at the same time an expert in manoeuvring the vicissitudes of international politics.[9]

Mussolini's intention to go to war with the Western powers had crystallised much earlier. Mussolini knew that Italy had no power to fight a long war against France and Britain, as Italy was exhausted by the Ethiopian campaign and the ongoing Italian involvement in the Spanish Civil War. Moreover, the Duce knew that many Italians were hostile towards war on Germany's side. Mussolini's actions during the Czechoslovak crisis were aggressively pro-German and reflected his preference to fight a war alongside Hitler. At the same time, he hoped that this belligerence would further radicalise the Fascist regime at home and ensure that Italy would not fall behind Germany in the mobilisation of the masses.[10] Fundamentally, Mussolini's room for manoeuvre was severely hampered by Italy's growing economic dependence on Germany. Italy had imported most of its coal from Britain until the implementation of League of Nations sanctions during the Ethiopian war, but soon began to rely on German coal, with imports from Germany having risen to 60.7 per cent by 1937.[11]

Thus, the three principal interpretations of Fascist foreign policy, namely the prioritisation of the 'determining weight' policy, the emphasis on Mussolini's showmanship and the accentuating of his aggressive intentions, are not mutually exclusive to each other.[12] First, like other Italian leaders before him, Mussolini believed in the transformative quality of war, which would make Italians stronger and more masculine. The gap between the propaganda that war would purify the Italian nation and the dire reality of geopolitical weakness created an aggressive dynamic, increasingly pushing Mussolini to war. Second, the Duce thought that an alliance with Hitler's Germany against the 'decadent' Western powers, infringing Italy's position in the Mediterranean, was inevitable. Third, Mussolini thought little of the multinational and liberal-democratic Czechoslovakia, created as a result of the hated post-war settlement. For Mussolini, an absorption of French-allied Czechoslovakia by Germany would diminish French influence in the Danube basin and increase Italy's influence in south-eastern Europe, bringing Czechoslovakia, Romania and Yugoslavia (known as the Little Entente countries, backed by France) into the Italian sphere. Mussolini's main objectives were the positioning of Italy as the hegemonic power in the Mediterranean and the consolidation of the African empire. But Mussolini received contradictory advice from diplomats, ministers and military officers, who in turn were trying to guess what he wanted to hear. Moreover, he often wavered from full-fledged support for the Germans to some more seemingly reasonable pro-British statements.

However, the Duce, impressed by Hitler, increasingly believed that his aims were best reached alongside the Germans and thus escalated the

Czech crisis by declaring repeatedly his unwavering support for Germany. This was also a strategy to threaten Britain and France, for whom an alliance of the two revisionist-aggressive countries run by Mussolini and Hitler was an increasing concern. To keep the momentum of his warmongering rhetoric going and serve the vain Fascist belief that Italy was a great power, Mussolini joined Hitler in anti-Czechoslovak propaganda and defended Nazi claims over the Sudetenland, supplied with information solicited from Hitler. In August 1938, as the Czechoslovak crisis escalated, whipped up by Nazi propaganda, the Italian ambassador, Bernardo Attolico, acting on Mussolini's instructions, told Ribbentrop that Italy would fight alongside Germany if France intervened militarily in the Czech crisis (although Mussolini did not really expect at the time that France and Britain would go to war). Attolico even told Ribbentrop that Germany and Italy were basically allies who would sooner or later sign a formal military treaty. The Axis relationship was developing a dangerous dynamism. Mussolini's role in the Sudeten crisis was that of an aggressor, not a moderator.[13]

As the crisis escalated in September 1938, Mussolini's role in backing Hitler to push forward with German aggression was essential, and a closer examination of their exchanges tells a different story of the origins of the Second World War, which often remains focused on France's and Britain's failure to appease Hitler. However, Italo-German coordination of foreign policy and propaganda did not always operate smoothly. Although the Italian government sought information from the Third Reich about its strategy in the Sudeten crisis, this was not always forthcoming, because of German distrust and suspicion. For instance, in early September 1938, Mussolini complained to Ciano that the German government had not provided concrete information about plans for an attack on Czechoslovakia.[14]

Britain's prime minister, Neville Chamberlain, attempted in September 1938 to reach a peaceful solution of the Czech crisis with Hitler. Like other British officials, Chamberlain had an ambiguous attitude towards Hitler and Mussolini. While the British conservative political establishment was broadly attracted by the anti-Communist stance of Berlin and Rome, the threat of a common Italo-German front, which crystallised during the Sudeten crisis, was deeply disturbing. Rather than risk a war with the two revisionist powers, Chamberlain preferred to negotiate Czechoslovakia's fate and appease Hitler. After all, Chamberlain and the

British government were guided by the belief that the British public would not be prepared to go to war over the territorial integrity of a distant state of which most people knew little, and which played almost no strategic role in British interests.[15]

II

As the clouds gathered over Europe, more and more Germans, according to the SS security service (SD), were becoming anxious about a war, suggesting that five years of Nazi warmongering propaganda had not succeeded in preparing them for conflict.[16] Social Democratic agents even diagnosed a war psychosis in Germany.[17] In this context, Hitler approached Mussolini, who would, Hitler hoped, help create a joint front and thereby strengthen the German position. The Nazi leader thus sent the Prince of Hesse with a memorandum to Mussolini on 7 September 1938.[18] German military action against Czechoslovakia was inevitable, Hitler insisted in his communication to the Duce, because of the growing repression of the Sudeten Germans. Faced with a similar situation, Mussolini would act in the same way. Despite this consultation, Hitler was determined to go to war, with or without Italy. This decision had been facilitated by Italian declarations of support as early as May 1938 when Mussolini had implicitly assured Hitler of his backing in the Czechoslovak crisis.[19] By reminding Mussolini of Germany's support during the Ethiopian war, Hitler restated his expectation of Mussolini's help.[20] This created a situation in which neither leader could sever his ties with his opposite number without losing face.

Nevertheless, some Italians in positions of influence or authority articulated reservations about an alliance with Nazi Germany. Let us consider a conversation between an unnamed Italian diplomat and the German chargé d'affaires in Washington, DC, on 2 September 1938, when a European war was becoming increasingly likely. The Italian official insisted that Italy could not possibly intervene militarily alongside the Germans. If it were to do so, France and Britain, joined by the USA, would fight an ideological war against the 'totalitarian states', which would end in all likelihood in an Italian defeat. Ideally, the war would have to be short, with a swift German victory over Czechoslovakia. France and Britain would not be able to defeat Germany because of excellent German preparations. This view was unrealistic, as even high-ranking German officers, while in principle backing Hitler's objective of invading Czechoslovakia, remained sceptical of Germany's readiness for war. The German chargé d'affaires believed that the Italian diplomat's remarks closely reflected official Italian policy, and forwarded a report to the German Foreign Ministry. Indeed, the diplomat implied the dilemmas of Italian foreign policy. Exacerbated by the economic downturn that had hit the country in the late 1930s, Italy's military and economic resources were increasingly exhausted because of the Ethiopian war and the ongoing Italian involvement in Spain. Thus, some German officials doubted Mussolini's proclamations about fighting a war alongside the Axis partner, highlighting the ambiguity of German views on an alliance with Italy.[21]

Yet Mussolini's sophisticated playing of the diplomatic register and his displays of wavering between steadfast solidarity with the Germans and a more reasonable attitude towards Britain did not go unnoticed by British diplomats. They still hoped that a formal alliance between Italy and Germany could be prevented. On 15 September 1938, for instance, a senior British diplomat reported to the foreign secretary, Lord Halifax, that Ciano had expressed his desire 'to exercise a moderating influence' and had denounced the radically pro-Nazi statements made by Mussolini's rival Roberto Farinacci, the extreme Fascist and anti-Semite, at the September 1938 Nazi party rally at Nuremberg. His appearance was a powerful symbol of the ever closer Axis. While matters were more complex, the Western perception of ever closer Italian–German ties demonstrated the potency of Axis propaganda.[22] A typical manifestation of this display unit was *Il Popolo d'Italia*'s claim on 10 September of 'the reconfirmation of the indestructability of the Rome–Berlin Axis'.[23] The image of Mussolini and Hitler as a dictatorial couple thus became a menacing instrument of foreign policy.

Few articulated their fears of a Mussolini–Hitler alliance more pronouncedly than Winston Churchill, the well-known Conservative MP, who was sharply opposed to appeasement. In an article in the American weekly *Collier's*, published on 3 September 1938, Churchill expressed his long-standing admiration for Mussolini as someone who had saved Italy from the left. He insisted that an alliance between the Duce and Hitler would have dreadful consequences and must be stopped, if necessary through military means. He added that Hitler was a much greater threat to peace than Mussolini, after all leader of the weak Italy. While Churchill's statement reflected a typical British view of the Italians, seen with a mix of condescension and contempt, he noted strategic tensions between Italy and Germany, such as over the undecided fate of the South Tyrolese, who were looking to Germany 'for deliverance from the Italian yoke'. Mussolini's impotence vis-à-vis the Germans had been brutally exposed during the Anschluss, Churchill opined, before drawing attention to the low opinion most Germans held of Italy.[24]

Yet, as British concerns over war in Europe increased, Mussolini and Hitler, as well as their staffs, intensified the display of a common Axis front. In this menacing atmosphere, Chamberlain sent Viscount Runciman to Czechoslovakia in order to solve the mounting crisis. Runciman's idea of giving the Sudetenland autonomous status within Czechoslovakia was predictably rejected by Hitler. At this crucial juncture, Chamberlain offered to meet Hitler to prevent a European war. For reasons of prestige, Hitler received Chamberlain at his mountain retreat in Berchtesgaden, whither the prime minister travelled by aeroplane, for the first time in his life. Hitler's position was greatly enhanced by Mussolini's support. For on 15 September 1938, the day of the meeting between Hitler and Chamberlain, the German press published a translation of an article by Mussolini from *Il Popolo d'Italia*. In it, Mussolini, the journalist with a keen eye for effective headlines, restated Hitler's views almost exactly, as delighted German diplomats noted. Couched in terms of an open letter to Runciman, the Duce aggressively dismissed Czechoslovakia as an unviable multinational state, a 'crocodile state or sausage state', which brutally violated the Sudeten Germans' right to national self-determination. Hitler did not plan an invasion, Mussolini declared, but justly insisted on a plebiscite amongst the Sudeten Germans. Furthermore, Mussolini asserted that the 'game [was] really not worth the candle'.[25] Here was again the image of the two dictators side by side, posing a menacing front against Britain and France.

During their meeting, Hitler reassured Chamberlain that German claims were restricted to the Sudetenland, not to Czechoslovakia as such, and that a gradual handover of the Sudeten territories to Germany would be acceptable to Germany. Chamberlain agreed.[26] A sense of relief was palpable across Europe that war had been avoided. Senior Italian army officers shared this view, as they knew that Italy was incapable of going to war, as the British embassy in Rome reported to Lord Halifax on 16 September 1938.[27]

A closer examination of the available evidence suggests that Mussolini stepped up his pro-German rhetoric as Hitler increased his territorial demands. Before a speech in Trieste scheduled for 18 September 1938, Mussolini requested more details from Hitler about his strategy for the Sudetenland so that he could incorporate them into his speech. The German reply was not slow in coming. Hitler thanked the Duce profusely for backing the German position and demanded 'an immediate radical solution' of the Sudeten crisis. For otherwise, like in Spain before the Italian and German intervention on Franco's side, 'the Bolshevik element would gain ground'.[28] In his Trieste speech, Mussolini echoed the German position and appealed to Britain to facilitate a peaceful solution to the Sudeten crisis. The Duce peppered his speech with a heavy dose of anti-Semitic rhetoric against 'the Jewish problem', reflecting the gradual development of official racial legislation in Italy which many saw as a manifestation of the Axis with Germany. Hitler had previously expressed satisfaction at the announcement of anti-Semitic legislation, initially concerned with the exclusion of Jews from state education. Crucially, contrary to subsequent apologetical claims, Italian racial legislation, which grew out of the July 1938 Manifesto of Racial Scientists, was not a response to Nazi pressure. At the same time, it was a powerful symbol of Italy's growing alignment with the Third Reich as a bulwark against the 'plutocratic' Western democracies and as a power bloc with plans for a new European order. Speaking in front of several thousand, mobilised by the regime, the Duce reinforced the Axis with a veiled threat to the Western powers that 'Italy's position is already chosen'.[29]

Mussolini's message did not go unnoticed by Western diplomats. Particularly incisive was the interpretation provided by Jules Blondel: Mussolini's speech had remained vague enough so as not to commit him to an alliance with Hitler, let alone war on Germany's side. Furthermore, the Duce's references to peace had reflected the fact that his belligerent intentions lacked public support in Italy. In Germany, according to a report by François-Poncet, Mussolini's speech had had its desired effect of pleasing Hitler, who interpreted it as an expression of Mussolini's unflinching support for the German position in the Sudeten crisis.[30]

It was no coincidence that Mussolini gave similar speeches as the Sudeten crisis escalated. In Verona, he stated that the crisis yielded the opportunity to create a New Order in Europe. Neither was it by chance that the Duce's speeches took place in the Italian regions that had previously belonged to Austria-Hungary. The location served as a reminder to Hitler, as he was pushing into central Europe, that these regions were integral parts of Italy.[31] Like the Trieste speech, these events were organised as Fascist mass rallies and broadcast on the wireless. Despite concerted efforts to display Axis unity and glorify war, Mussolini's speeches failed to mobilise Italian enthusiasm for war, as Blondel noted astutely.[32] While there were no major military preparations in Italy, Mussolini's belligerent rhetoric continued. On 25 September 1938, after seeing Ciano and the Prince of Hesse, who had conveyed Hitler's gratitude towards the Duce, Mussolini told Ciano that he was prepared to go to war on Germany's side, but only if Britain intervened, as such an intervention would have given the Sudeten crisis a clearly ideological twist, which would force him to honour his promises to Nazi Germany. In reality, of course, war against Britain was out of Italy's reach.[33]

It was Mussolini's display of Italo-German solidarity that helped to encourage Hitler to increase his demands. Chamberlain soon found this out when he met Hitler for the second time, on 22 September 1938, in Bad Godesberg. Hitler insisted that the Sudetenland must be handed over to Germany by 1 October 1938. Chamberlain rejected this plan, as he thought he had already made sufficient compromises to Hitler.[34]

As the Sudeten crisis escalated further, the Italian government stepped up its belligerent rhetoric. For example, Ciano told the British ambassador to Rome, Lord Perth, that the crisis needed to be resolved in a 'totalitarian fashion', a veiled threat to Britain and France.[35] Nevertheless, despite all this warmongering, some Germans in positions of authority, including Göring, believed that Hitler had made a fatal mistake when he rejected the agreement with Chamberlain which prescribed the surrender of the Sudetenland and its armaments industry to Germany. For Göring, the risk of a war with France and Britain which Germany would be unable to win was too great.[36]

Yet Hitler brushed aside such caution. As Europe was on the brink of war, he reminded Goebbels on 28 September 1938 that the Duce had successfully stood up to France and Britain in 1935–6. Surely he, Hitler, could do the same. Goebbels boasted: 'Two such men – how can England and France counter this?'[37] Later that day, a Wehrmacht division paraded through Berlin's government district, where many embassies were located. The menacing sound of the soldiers marching in jackboots was not aimed at whipping up public support for war, but was a display of Germany's readiness to go to war.[38] On the same day, Perth asked Ciano to prompt Mussolini 'to make use of the proven friendly relations of the Duce with the Führer' and to help prevent war through a mediation of the conflict. Perth's reference to the 'proven' friendship of Mussolini and Hitler is significant, as it demonstrates the effectiveness of the Axis displays.

Mussolini's intervention with Hitler was decisive. Spurred on by Göring, the calculating Duce encouraged Hitler to accept the British proposal for a settlement of the conflict by international negotiation. Hitler backed down at the final hour, and accepted the idea of a four-power conference, which Mussolini enthusiastically embraced. For this setup of four powers, already proposed by Mussolini in 1933, officially recognised Italy as the fourth great power in Europe, next to Britain, France and Germany. Representatives of the Czechoslovak government were not invited to the conference. The attack on Czechoslovakia, scheduled for 1 October, was to be delayed.[39]

Contrary to Mussolini's intentions to turn Italy into a nation of warriors, however, many Italians, according to the French chargé d'affaires in Rome, credited Mussolini for engineering the last-minute conference to avert war, and expressed hope that he would exercise a moderating influence on Hitler.[40] Mussolini wanted war, but was not at ease with simply plunging in alongside Hitler. While often not informed of the disastrous state of the Italian war machine, he was not so stupid as to be unaware of its serious shortcomings. He knew that Italy's long coastline was vulnerable to attack and that the country could easily be blockaded. Much Italian materiel was still tied up in Spain. Clearly, Italy lacked resources and could only fight alongside a powerful ally. The sense of sharing a common mission undeniably inclined the Duce towards Hitler, as did the Nazi leader's aggressiveness. For Mussolini, war was the way through which Italians were to be remade from a nation of mandolin-playing waiters into a nation of warriors. But the Duce was realistic and therefore hesitant about going to war in 1938, flitting from position to position. Altogether, Mussolini's foreign policy in 1938 was ambivalent, characterised by a strong ideological and aggressive drive on the one hand, and a powerful sense of realism on the other.[41]

III

France's and Britain's agreement to a meeting in Munich, the birthplace of Nazism, added prestige to the Third Reich. The Duce, accompanied by Ciano, left Rome on the night of 28 September 1938. The Italian Ministry of Popular Culture instructed newspaper editors to emphasise the conference as the Duce's 'personal triumph', suggesting that it had been Mussolini who had suggested the conference. Alfieri expressly forbade editors to cover the demonstrations accompanying the Duce's departure, for these could be misread as a sign of pacifism. On a symbolic level, the fact that Mussolini went to Germany for a second time within one year suggested that Germany's power was in the ascendant and that Italy's position was increasingly entangled with it.[42]

Still, closer examination of Italian popular opinion reveals that there was broad opposition to the Duce's pro-German exclamations. On 29 September 1938, for instance, Starace expressed his concern to the Milan party's secretary about a public opinion report that had recently been received. The informer had been mingling with the Milanese working class, whose attitude towards the regime was ambiguous at best. His report lamented: 'The people do not believe in the friendship with Germany.' He added that the working class did not understand the ideological underpinnings of the Fascist friendship with the Third Reich.[43]

Despite the build-up to Munich, which had seen a strong display of Axis unity, tensions between Italy and Germany continued to exist behind the scenes. A clear indication of these tensions is that, like during his 1937 journey to Germany, the Duce crossed the South Tyrol by night, thereby avoiding any inconvenient encounters with the German-speaking population. Mussolini's train arrived at the Brenner Pass in the early hours of 29 September 1938, where Hitler's deputy, Rudolf Hess, welcomed the Duce. The train continued via Innsbruck to Kufstein, at the former border with Austria. It was here, rather than on formerly Austrian territory, that Hitler greeted the Duce, as the Nazi leader was keen to avoid hurting Mussolini's sensitivities just six months after the Anschluss. A small detail of Mussolini's uniform did not escape the attention of close observers: instead of his Fascist cap, Mussolini had donned a peaked cap, similar to Hitler's. The different headgear suggested his closer proximity to Hitler.[44] The Duce and Ciano then joined Hitler on his train to Munich. The journey gave the dictators time to coordinate their conference strategy. Unlike in 1937 when the Italian delegation had travelled on its own train, Mussolini's journey on Hitler's train revealed the changing power dynamics between the dictators and their countries. It also presented the dictators as united versus the British and French. This was a menacing display, suggesting that both leaders would fight together, should France and Britain fail to meet Hitler's demands. In the Nazi leader's saloon car, maps with the territories claimed by the Germans were already spread out.[45] People were lining the railways, decorated with swastika flags and banners with the slogan 'Duce!' on the way to Munich, as they had done a year previously when Mussolini had first visited Hitler in Germany. Now, in September 1938, the climate was geared towards war, although many Germans genuinely hoped that war could be prevented.[46]

The Nazi welcoming ceremony at Munich station followed the choreography of Mussolini's visit in 1937: schoolchildren were given the morning off and cheered the dictators with Italian and swastika flags. Thousands of SS guards were deployed to protect the leaders, a reflection, as in the previous year, of security concerns. Significantly, unlike the pomp and circumstance put on for the Duce's arrival, the French and British prime ministers, Édouard Daladier and Neville Chamberlain, were only greeted by Hitler at the conference venue. However, as *The Times*'s correspondent noted, the crowds cheered Chamberlain as he was driven through the streets of Munich, reflecting their hopes for peace.[47]

The location of the conference in the Nazi party headquarters added to Hitler's prestige: the French and British leaders had agreed to enter the German lion's den. Huge Tricolour and Union Jack banners adorned one entrance of the building, while swastikas and Italian flags were flying from another, a visual reminder of the two opposing fronts at the conference. SS sentries with shouldered rifles guarded the venue.[48]

Power in Europe seemed to have shifted from the Western democracies towards the two European Axis states, and Munich was yet another exposure of the inability of the League of Nations to resolve conflicts in Europe and elsewhere. The attire of the principal casts in the performance illustrates this point: Daladier and Chamberlain appeared in civilian dress, which seemed to represent the bygone age of liberal parliamentarianism, while Mussolini and Hitler wore uniforms, giving them a military and masculine look. At the conference's opening, Hitler credited the Duce for proposing the conference. Yet Mussolini disliked the atmosphere, which, to him, resembled redundant parliamentary negotiations. Nevertheless, the multilingual Duce made *bella figura* and politely conversed with Chamberlain in English. This did not fail to have an effect on some of the German delegates, who immediately recalled the Anglo-Italian Easter Treaties and the possibility of closer Anglo-Italian cooperation.

Eventually, all four powers agreed that Germany would occupy the Sudetenland by early October. While Göring and other German officials, including the former foreign minister von Neurath and Weizsäcker, had prepared this agreement, Mussolini presented it as his idea, which greatly annoyed Ribbentrop. The presentation of the compromise as his own project was a brilliant success for the Duce, as it raised Italy's international reputation and made Hitler appear as moderate, given that the plan to dismantle Czechoslovakia had officially been put forward by the Duce, not by the Nazi leader.[49]

Mussolini's performance was so convincing that François-Poncet and leading historians later believed that Italy was still pursuing the policy of the 'determining weight'.[50] Nevertheless, Mussolini did not arrange for a special meeting with Chamberlain, as he did not want to offend Hitler. The conference resulted in the dismantling of Czechoslovakia, without consulting the Czechoslovak government. The Nazi leader signed an Anglo-German declaration, prepared by Chamberlain, which committed both sides 'never to go to war with one another again'. In reality, Hitler fumed that Chamberlain had made him sign an international treaty, a form of diplomacy he despised, and thereby spoiled his military triumph against Czechoslovakia.[51]

It was at this point that the idea that the two dictators were friends seemed to have gained momentum. François-Poncet later remembered how Hitler had proudly been showing off his friendship with the Duce. Mussolini, by far the more experienced statesman, had made Hitler feel inferior. Hitler, carried away by Mussolini's presence, had even started mimicking the Duce's gestures and had tried to scowl like him. According to François-Poncet, this was not a real friendship.[52]

Mussolini's return journey to Italy was accompanied by the rapturous applause of Germans and Italians who credited him with saving peace. The itinerary of the journey has survived in the files of the Ministry of Popular

Culture. During stops at Verona, Bologna and Florence, local Fascist officials organised popular rallies for the Duce.[53] Except for his triumph after the Italian invasion of Ethiopia, Mussolini's prestige was probably never as great in Italy as after Munich. The king, displaying his agreement with Mussolini's strategy, even travelled to Florence to welcome the Duce. Boosted by this wave of popular acclaim, Mussolini told a massive crowd from the balcony of the Palazzo Venezia that he had worked hard for peace at Munich, although, in reality, he wanted to be seen as a warrior, not as a saviour of peace.[54]

Munich reinforced Mussolini's belief in his own mission, which would be on Hitler's side. As he boasted to Clara Petacci, Hitler, 'a sentimentalist', had had tears in his eyes when he met him. Still, in order to make up for his feeling of inferiority towards Hitler's power, he laughed that Hitler 'does not have a wife'. Undoubtedly, Mussolini was boasting when he took credit for the Munich conference, as he was trying to compensate for the fact that it was Hitler and not him who was dominating European politics. His belief in the New Order overlapped with Hitler's for now, which is why he told Petacci that 'at this point the democracies must surrender to the dictatorships'.[55] Mussolini even claimed in a speech to the national council of the Fascist party on 25 October 1938 that Italy 'had a preponderant and decisive part' in European politics for the first time since national unification. This was a dubious claim, for Munich was a diplomatic triumph, not a military one, as Italy's army and economy remained unprepared for war.[56]

Italian popular opinion towards an alliance with Germany remained hostile, as far as the scarce evidence suggests. A brochure by the underground Italian Communist party, dated 16 November 1938, that was duly archived by the police gives a good insight into how anti-Fascist Italians saw the growing entanglement between Italy and Germany. The pamphlet insisted that even Fascist supporters had been opposed to Mussolini's passivity during the Anschluss and bitterly lamented the fact that Mussolini was modelling Italy on Nazi Germany:

> Each time Mussolini bows to Hitler and prostitutes Italy for Germany we have to signal to the Fascists whether, at this rate, one does not reach the complete submission of our country . . . After that, Hitler . . . becomes increasingly the boss of Mussolini, who, in any case, pushes our

> country into modelling itself on the oppressive German characteristics; the *passo romano* is the imitation of the German goose-step, as the new theories on race are the servile copy of German racism.[57]

Reports compiled by the Fascist party in Italy's provinces for the attention of the party's leadership, determined to maintain popular support, discerned an ever more critical attitude of many Italians towards the Fascist regime and an alliance with Germany, which it was widely believed would lead to war. In the late 1930s, Fascism's aggressive and warmongering rhetoric found itself more and more at odds with popular opinion, disillusioned with Fascism's unfulfilled promises to reform the state, improve living standards and make society more equal through the corporate state.[58] Popular enthusiasm for Mussolini's purported peace efforts suggested that Fascist policy to remake Italians into warriors had failed. It furthermore suggested that most Italians knew that the country was not ready for another war. Still, Mussolini's achievement to have Italy recognised as a great power in Europe met with widespread approval.[59]

Popular reactions to Mussolini's pro-German strategy deserve further attention. Even before Munich, hundreds of Italians had written to the Duce, imploring him to make Hitler adopt a more moderate stance. An engineer from Rome, a member of the Fascist party, had even advised the Duce to tell Hitler that the Sudeten territories should be occupied by Italian forces until a plebiscite could be held, and that he should then fly on to Chamberlain and make him accept this offer. The engineer, reflecting Fascist propaganda, had expressed his hope that 'Hitler will perhaps accept [this], since he considers you a good friend . . . for the formal promise you have given him to be on his side in the case of a conflagration.'[60] After Munich, the Duce's secretariat received even more congratulatory notes from Italians of all classes and generations. Several hundred adulatory letters and telegrams were archived by the secretariat. Mussolini did not have the time to read them, but he was informed of the general tenor of the correspondence, which praised him as a man of Providence and saviour of peace, a reputation he resented. The letter of a schoolgirl from the Province of Varese in northern Italy was emblematic in this respect: 'Dear Duce, Piccola Italia, daughter of an old Ardito with a firm heart, I thank you, Your Excellency Head of Government, because you have sealed the peace. I believe that all children will be happy if they have a father like me . . .'[61] Widespread relief that war had been avoided suggests that Fascism had failed in its central aim to transform Italians into a nation of tough warriors.[62]

Like its Italian counterpart, Nazi propaganda had not succeeded in transforming Germans into enthusiastic backers of a European war or staunch supporters of the alliance with Italy. A *Sopade* report from south-western Germany cited widespread relief: 'Thank God, there is no war.' Some Germans even stated that Hitler should have better solved the plight of the South Tyrolese living under Mussolini's yoke, rather than concentrate his efforts on the Sudeten Germans.[63] Another report was submitted by *Sopade* agents from Danzig, the free city under a League of Nations mandate whose government was pushing for its incorporation into the Reich. Here, in a restaurant, three lower-middle-class men chatted about the Munich conference. They dismissed Mussolini as an opportunist who was so keen to maintain peace because Italy was simply not ready for war.[64]

Despite the powerful display of unity at Munich, the increasing cultural and academic exchanges, police cooperation and the growing trade between both countries, Italo-German relations remained tense on both official and popular levels. There was no military alliance.[65] At the same time, the alliance of Mussolini and Hitler had become menacing. At Munich, they had jointly forced France and Britain to make territorial concessions to Germany. In this respect, Munich marked a turning point in the relationship between the two dictators. Their collaboration and its propagandistic elevation to a friendship had enabled Hitler to dismantle Czechoslovakia. From that point onwards, it became difficult, if not impossible, for either side to leave the Axis.[66]

Politicians such as Chamberlain believed that Hitler would not make further territorial claims after Munich, a view that was widely shared in Britain, as Chamberlain's triumphant reception at home and his 'peace for our time' speech suggest. Other influential British politicians, above all Churchill, fundamentally disagreed and continued to warn about an Italo-German alliance.[67] The violent nature of Nazism soon came to the fore when, in order to implement the results of Munich, German troops quickly seized the Sudetenland, accompanied by a wave of Nazi terror that included the arrest of 10,000 opponents of Nazism.[68]

IV

For Mussolini, the momentum of Munich further unleashed his aggression. Days after his return to Italy, he had his foreign policy, with its focus on the relationship with Nazi Germany, approved by the Fascist Grand Council. Warmongering rhetoric was accompanied by a drive towards the totalitarianisation of the state. For instance, in early 1939, the Chamber of Deputies became the Chamber of *Fasci* and Corporations, effectively a body to rubber-stamp Mussolini's decisions. Attacks on Jews intensified. Thus, in October 1938, the Grand Council announced the racial laws, based on the July 1938 Racial Manifesto, according to which the Italians were Aryans. Mussolini had endorsed the manifesto, written by racial scientists.[69] Already, on 7 September 1938, a law had been passed that expelled all foreign Jews and stripped those Jews who had been naturalised after 1 January 1919 of their Italian citizenship. But this was not all. Another September 1938 law stipulated the eviction of all Jewish teachers and pupils from Italian schools and universities.[70]

Many later claimed that these tough racist laws were a more or less straightforward imitation of Nazi anti-Semitic legislation, if not an imposition by the Nazis. Such an interpretation implicitly supports the view that Fascist Italy was a relatively harmless dictatorship if compared to the Third Reich. Clearly, the racial laws reflected Mussolini's desire to demonstrate Italy's ideological proximity to Hitler.[71] Thus, the laws were approved by the Council of Ministers under Mussolini's chairmanship on 10 November 1938, the day after the Nazis had launched their most brutal attack to date on the Jews: *Kristallnacht*. In the November pogrom, Nazi activists had murdered more than a thousand Jews and had set Jewish houses, businesses and synagogues on fire. Up to 30,000 Jewish men had been taken to concentration camps, on Hitler's direct orders. The brutal message of *Kristallnacht* was that Jews were no longer desired in Nazi Germany. Undoubtedly, the timing of the Italian anti-Semitic legislation suggests that Mussolini wanted to appear as Hitler's ideological ally and show to France and Britain that he was serious about pursuing an alliance with the Third Reich. But these insights do not mean that the Italian racial laws were a mere show.[72]

Mussolini wholeheartedly approved of the pogrom and told Ciano that he would have acted even more radically against the Jews than the Nazis had. On the next day, however, Mussolini slightly restrained his anti-Semitic remarks and expressed his concern that, after this outburst of Nazi violence against the Jews, the Catholics might be next in the Third Reich's firing line, undermining Axis support in Italy. In fact, protests by Pius XI at the discrimination against baptised Jews did not help promote the popularity of the Italo-German alliance. While the Nazis did not target Catholics in a systematic way, Mussolini's statement reveals that he knew that the Axis was quite unpopular in Italy.[73]

A closer examination of the genesis of the racial laws reveals that there was no German pressure on Fascist Italy to adopt legislation for the *difesa della razza*. The laws came into force on 17 November 1938, after the king had signed them. The king's signature suggests that the racial legislation was supported not only by diehard Fascists but also by conservative forces, motivated, in part, at least, by centuries of Catholic Jew-hatred. The law stipulated the dismissal of Jews from the army and the public service as well as from banks and insurance companies. Furthermore, the law banned marriages between 'Aryan' Italians and those from other races and offered a clearly racist definition of a Jew.[74]

Moreover, while broadly supportive, Nazi propaganda officials instructed German newspaper editors not to portray the Italian racial laws as an imitation of the Nuremberg laws to avoid the impression of Nazi condescension. Yet, at the same time, many Nazi officials believed that the Italian laws had not gone far enough.[75] Thus, there can be no doubt that crucial differences existed between Nazi anti-Semitism and the creeping Fascist anti-Jewish discrimination. Mussolini was a racist, and the legislation against Jews was racist, going well beyond Catholic hatred of the Jews. Yet the Italian anti-Semitic laws had emerged from colonial racism towards Muslim and black populations in the Italian colonies in Africa, and were part of a broader trajectory of imperialist racism. Despite the incontestable significance of anti-Semitism under Fascism, however, it was never as central to Mussolini's regime as it was to the Third Reich. In Italy, anti-Semitism was a particular strategy of racial exclusion, but not the central part of an agenda of racial extermination. The Fascist regime used the racial laws to whip up support, with devastating consequences for the Jews of Italy. Yet – unlike in Nazi Germany – racism was never the regime's defining feature.[76]

In spite of these strong displays of an apparent ideological proximity to Nazi Germany, Mussolini held back from signing a formal alliance with

Germany.[77] Instead, reflecting his brinkmanship and opportunism, amidst Britain's desperate attempts to disentangle Italy from the Third Reich an Anglo-Italian declaration was signed on 16 November 1938 which reaffirmed the spirit of détente. According to Ciano, Mussolini had insisted that this declaration would not change his attitude towards Nazi Germany, part of his strategy in mainland Europe, while his policy towards Britain was part of his Mediterranean strategy. While the Duce wanted eventually to go to war with Britain over control of the Mediterranean, Italy was unable to risk such a conflict. A détente with Britain would also give the Duce more negotiating power with the Germans. Here, he was playing the diplomatic register, with his 'determining weight' rhetoric. Thus, Mussolini agreed to an official visit by Chamberlain to Rome in January 1939. When the German ambassador, curious about the announcement of the visit, questioned Ciano about this invitation, the foreign minister replied enigmatically that the 'Italian programme was not to pursue a programme'. This was a tongue-in-cheek characterisation of Fascist Italy's desire to use the myth of its diplomatic versatility to increase its power, although, after Munich, Italy's proximity to Nazi Germany had become so strong that there was no realistic way back for Mussolini.[78]

Since Italy lacked the power to provoke a war with Britain over dominance in the Mediterranean, France came increasingly into Mussolini's firing line. He believed that Italy would easily win a war against France, a degenerate nation, further weakened by the Popular Front government. Ciano's aggressively anti-French speech in the Chamber on 30 November 1938 was emblematic of Italy's stance against France. Foreign diplomats attended, including the new French ambassador, François-Poncet, who had recently been transferred from Berlin in the hope that he could exercise a moderating influence on the Duce and place a wedge between him and Hitler. Organised tumultuous applause interrupted the speech several times, and choruses demanded the reacquisition of Corsica, Savoy and Nice, territories long claimed by Italian nationalists, including Giuseppe Garibaldi, who had been born in Nice.[79] But Ciano's speech, which reinforced Italy's ties with Germany, did not deliver the desired effect, as the French government did not take these threats seriously.[80]

It was in this climate of growing Italian and German belligerence that Chamberlain visited Italy in January 1939. For reasons of prestige,

Mussolini had asked the British to request this meeting. Accompanied by Lord Halifax, the prime minister visited Rome under the watchful eyes of German diplomats. Significantly, en route, Chamberlain and his delegation conferred with the French government in Paris, a powerful message to Mussolini that the British would not abandon their alliance with France, despite Italy's increasingly anti-French propaganda.[81]

Unlike Hitler's 1938 journey, the Italian government organised Chamberlain's visit on a significantly smaller scale. The itinerary followed the protocol of a traditional diplomatic visit and included audiences with the king and the pope, along with the laying of wreaths at the Pantheon and on the tomb of the unknown soldier at the monument for Victor Emmanuel II. Not much emphasis was given to mingling with the crowds, a central aspect of the programme of Hitler's visit. Another detail set Chamberlain's visit apart from Hitler's: Fascist officials were instructed to wear civilian dress. Mussolini even put on white tie and tails for a reception and a visit to the opera. It is noteworthy that the Ministry of Popular Culture instructed the Italian press to treat Chamberlain with sympathy, but also to emphasise the solidity and efficiency of the Axis. Thus, for the Italian government, the purpose of Chamberlain's visit was to assert Italy's status as a great power.[82]

Ciano and Mussolini, alongside troops and a relatively small number of civilians, welcomed Chamberlain and Halifax with an 'enthusiastic reception' at the railway station.[83] Both British and German diplomats noted that ordinary people were happy to see Chamberlain and Halifax. The reports implied that most Italians would prefer an alliance with Britain to one with Germany. This popular sympathy for the British was noteworthy. Unlike Germany and Italy, Britain and Italy had never been at war with each other; in fact, Britain had supported the national unification of Italy, and had been an ally in the First World War.[84]

Foreign Office minutes give us an insight into Mussolini's versatility as a statesman. In his conversations with Chamberlain, held in the Duce's office in the Palazzo Venezia, he seemed reasonable and polite. Yet the British were also struck by Mussolini's repeated claims that Hitler was an honourable man with peaceful intentions.[85] And, in his toast to Chamberlain at a state banquet, Mussolini called Britain 'a great friendly nation' and spoke about 'the friendship between our two countries'.[86] But, despite these friendly words, Chamberlain realised that he ought to intensify military negotiations with France.[87] Although Mussolini put out feelers to the French through unofficial channels for a détente, his attempt to drive a wedge between France and Britain had failed.[88] Chamberlain's visit had the effect intended by Mussolini of making the German government suspicious, and the German ambassador promptly expressed his concern about Anglo-Italian collaboration to Ciano. A bureaucratic detail suggests that the Axis was solid: Ciano forwarded copies of the Italian minutes of the Mussolini–Chamberlain conversations to Hitler. But this gesture could also have added pressure on Hitler to take Italy more seriously in his plans for further territorial expansion.[89]

V

Territorial expansion was Hitler's priority, and he needed Mussolini's support. On 30 January 1939, marking the sixth anniversary of his appointment as Reich chancellor, he delivered a lengthy speech to the Reichstag. In a frequently quoted part of the speech, Hitler threatened the extermination of the Jews if there were ever another world war. Hitler's remark set the agenda for the regime's anti-Semitism, which became more and more violent, subject to competing ideas from different parts of the Third Reich's political institutions. He also sought to increase pressure on other countries to accept Jewish refugees from Germany. At the time, British diplomats found that the alliance with Italy had been the central subject of Hitler's speech. Indeed, days after Mussolini's flirting with Chamberlain, the Nazi leader devoted ample time in his speech to his views on Mussolini. Hitler invoked the usual references to the historically inevitable friendship between Germany and Italy. Together with Mussolini, he would rescue 'Europe from the threatening Bolshevik extermination'. Hitler even praised the Italian army in order to increase pressure on Italy to enter into an alliance with Germany. After all, Italy was Germany's only potential ally after Britain's rejection of German advances. Goebbels confirmed this view in his diary: 'Carte blanche for Italy: in a war regardless of what kind on Mussolini's side. We have no other choice.' Thus, Hitler had no option but to cultivate an alliance with Mussolini, especially after Nazi propaganda about Mussolini and Fascism had taken on a strong dynamic.[90]

Unsurprisingly, Mussolini and Ciano greatly enjoyed Hitler's speech, as the Nazi leader had publicly acknowledged Italy's central political role in

Nazi strategy. In a telegram to Hitler, sent on 31 January 1939, the Duce extended his 'most cordial and comradely congratulations, inspired by the loyal profound friendship which, through the Axis, unites our two peoples in the present and the future in a firm bond.' The Fascist Grand Council officially sanctioned Hitler's speech on 3 February 1939, echoing Italy's increasing alignment with the Third Reich.[91]

Despite the pro-Nazi statements by Mussolini and other Fascist leaders, Hitler had no qualms about acting unilaterally when Nazi Germany marched into Czechoslovakia on 15 March 1939. Hitler had not even consulted Mussolini, who bitterly complained to Ciano that he would soon be the laughing stock of the Italian people: 'Every time Hitler occupies a state he sends me a message.' As he had done on the eve of the Anschluss, Hitler sent the Prince of Hesse to present the Duce with a fait accompli. Mussolini had no option but to swallow the news. Germany's push into central Europe was a further blow to the Italian strategy to dominate the Danube basin. Behind the scenes, Mussolini, desperate to save face, confided to Clara Petacci that 'in Hitler's situation, I would have done the same'. Ciano found Mussolini annoyed and depressed, and, to compensate for his frustration, the Duce railed that Italy would destroy France without German assistance. Mussolini knew that he was playing second fiddle to Hitler and did not pass on the news of Hesse's visit to the press, as he feared that the Italian people, largely hostile towards an alliance with Germany, would ridicule him as Hitler's lackey. Indeed, a Fascist party report on popular opinion in the Province of Rome, dated 30 March 1939, highlighted concerns about Italy's turning into a 'lieutenancy of Hitler' (*luogotenenza di Hitler*). Hitler, aware of Mussolini's anger, placated the Duce via Hesse and later via diplomats, reiterating his unconditional support for Italy.[92]

Apart from his fury at being sidelined by Hitler, Mussolini worried that Hitler's breach of the Munich Agreement would prompt a French and British intervention and provoke a war for which, everyone in Paris and London knew, Italy was unprepared. As a result of his staggering brinkmanship, Mussolini had to remain silent. This passive attitude began to attract severe criticism from Italians in positions of power: according to Ciano, the king had humiliated Mussolini after Hitler's march into Prague when he shared the rumour that the Duce was known in Munich as the Italian *Gauleiter*. An angry Duce told Ciano in a rare moment of comparative political analysis that he could be as successful as Hitler if he did not have to report to the king. But Mussolini also knew that he did not have the power to take on the monarchy.[93] In his frustration, Mussolini ordered troops to the Italo-German borderlands in the Veneto. Construction of the *Vallo del Littorio* intensified.[94]

Given Mussolini's jealousy and irritation and Hitler's triumphant territorial conquests of Austria and large parts of Czechoslovakia, it is tempting to argue that Mussolini's policy towards Hitler was shaped by his perennial fear of Nazi Germany. Undeniably, ideological motives played some role in Mussolini's increasing entanglement with Germany.[95] What really united both leaders and their regimes was a drive for expansionism and war, and this despite the unpopularity of war amongst the vast majorities of the German and Italian people. Mussolini's aggressive pro-Axis statements which committed Italy to supporting Nazi Germany gave him the opportunity to push for war, which would rally the Italian people behind him. A renunciation of this pro-German policy would have undermined his credibility. Thus, on 21 March 1939, the Fascist Grand Council met in an atmosphere of growing anti-German sentiment and war-weariness which the popular opinion reports of the Fascist party had registered across Italy. The published minutes emphasised Italy's unflinching commitment to the Axis. Some Fascist *gerarchi*, such as Giuseppe Bottai, disagreed with Mussolini's pro-Axis stance, as they believed that Germany had deprived Italy of its international influence.[96]

Hitler, guided by his admiration for Mussolini but also by the lack of other suitable allies, knew how to flatter Mussolini and used emotion in order to put pressure on him to commit to a military alliance with the Third Reich. He thus continued to shower Mussolini with friendly missives.[97] A long letter which Hitler sent to Mussolini on the occasion of the twentieth anniversary of the establishment of the *Fasci italiani di combattimento* on 23 March 1939 reveals this use of emotional diplomacy. In his letter, signed 'with unbreakable friendship', Hitler emphasised the Duce's pioneering role in creating Fascism and rebuilding the Roman Empire. This was an implicit acknowledgement to the vain Mussolini that Fascism had predated Nazism. Using a trope that had become familiar in Axis rhetoric, Hitler insisted that there is 'moreover a lot of affinity in the evolution of our two ideologies and our two revolutions'. This characteristically vague formulation of ideological parallels between Fascism and

Nazism masked the strategic tensions lurking behind the lofty Axis rhetoric. Indeed, the initiative for a formal alliance came from the Germans, and Mussolini played hard to get in an attempt to increase his negotiating powers.[98]

As Hitler had no other suitable ally, the same was true of Mussolini. Above all, neither leader could afford to renounce Axis rhetoric and stop pursuing a Fascist–Nazi alliance without losing his credibility. In this way, a dangerous dynamic emerged.[99] Thus, in an aggressive speech at a Fascist party rally on 26 March 1939 at Rome's Mussolini Forum, the Duce stressed the ideological affinity between the regimes, declaring: 'The Axis is not just a relationship between two states; it is an encounter of two revolutions which present themselves as the clear antithesis to all the other concepts of modern civilisation.' As General Franco's forces were about to take Madrid, the last bastion of the Popular Front government, Mussolini coupled anti-French rhetoric with veiled threats to the British, insisting that the Mediterranean was 'a living space' for Italy.[100]

As large-scale war was too risky, Italy began to focus its attention on Albania, a strategically important country and long a target of Italian territorial ambitions. War-weariness in Italy remained strong. When the king opened the Chamber of *Fasci* and Corporations on 29 March 1939, he talked about peace, rather than war, adding to Mussolini's irritation towards the monarchy.[101] A Fascist party report on popular opinion showed that many Italians had received the king's speech favourably. Ordinary people in Rome were said to complain about 'Germany's behaviour and the excessive power which she has acquired and will continue to acquire'. The report continued: 'There are those who grumble that Italy is already on her way to becoming one of Hitler's client states because she is no longer in a position to break the Axis alliance even if she wanted to. The public, meanwhile, believes that Germany's attitude will be the indirect cause of war and loses no opportunity to express its hostility.' An alliance with Germany would only bring Italy war and misfortune. Fascist pro-German propaganda had not entirely succeeded, according to German diplomats' cables to Berlin.[102]

Despite unresolved tensions, a clear indication that the war rhetoric had put the Italian and German governments on the spot was the meeting in Innsbruck on 5 April 1939 of generals Alberto Pariani, chief of the general staff (*Stato Maggiore dell'Esercito*), and undersecretary of war, and Wilhelm

Keitel, chief of the Wehrmacht's Supreme Command (*Oberkommando der Wehrmacht*), in order to discuss details of a military alliance. These were, in fact, the first formal Italian–German staff talks, and neither side played with open cards. Pariani did not mention plans for the invasion of Albania, and Keitel remained silent about Poland, the next target of German aggression. Hitler feared that some Italian generals would leak details to the Western powers and therefore prohibited Keitel from disclosing any details to the Italians.[103]

Two days later, on 7 April, the Duce ordered the invasion of Albania. Italian troops marched into the country on Good Friday 1939. Some contemporary observers such as François-Poncet but also some historians later interpreted the invasion as a copycat act of revenge by the jealous Mussolini against Hitler's unilateral invasions of Austria and Czechoslovakia.[104] But such interpretations overlook the fact that the invasion of Albania was not just about jealousy and rivalry. It was above all a clear demonstration of the aggression of Fascism and its core belief that war was necessary to strengthen the Italian nation. In fact, it had been Ciano who had pushed for the annexation in March 1938, as he hoped to profit financially and boost his political profile through the invasion.[105] However, if Mussolini had intended to impress Hitler with the Albanian war, his strategy had failed. Goebbels drily acknowledged that the Duce had learnt a lot from Nazi strategy: 'Mussolini takes drastic measures in Albania. He has learnt a lot from us for his argumentation. The world's conscience is raging in Paris and London. But nobody considers counter-actions.'[106] The Albanian campaign was ill prepared and took much longer than Mussolini had anticipated. It uncovered the wide gap between Mussolini's boastful rhetoric and poor Italian military performance. Furthermore, the Albanian adventure alarmed the British and French, who declared their solidarity with Greece and Turkey, concerned that Italy would soon make claims over these countries.[107]

In mid-April 1939, as a European war seemed increasingly likely, US president Franklin D. Roosevelt appealed again to Mussolini and Hitler to maintain peace in Europe. But this fell on deaf ears. Instead, Göring's visit to Rome reinforced the sense that there was a powerful Italo-German front.[108] Despite Nazi distrust of Italy, highlighted in a report from Heydrich to Ribbentrop, Mussolini and Hitler continued to use their purported friendship to intensify their menacing reputation as a dictatorial couple. Consider the cordial telegram exchange on the occasion of Hitler's fiftieth birthday. Mussolini, the king, Ciano and Italian military leaders all sent telegrams to the Nazi leader. Hitler's replies to Mussolini and the king were published in the German press. While his telegram to the king was dry, his glowing reply to the Duce ended with 'the assurance of the unshakeable bonds with you and the Fascist Italy created by you'.[109]

The use of such repetitive rhetoric of friendship was typical of the Mussolini–Hitler relationship and reinforced the dictators' belief that they were marching together towards creating the New Order. This pattern created a dynamic that made it impossible for either leader to change tactic.[110] Similar rhetoric guided Hitler's Reichstag speech of 28 April 1939, which included a sarcastic reply to a note by President Roosevelt and an outline of Hitler's demands for Poland. Hitler's remark that closer relations with Japan and Italy were 'the permanent aim of the German state's leadership' was a broad hint to Mussolini that the time was ripe for a formal alliance, as well as a reminder of the potential threat of an alliance of all revisionist powers, together determined to create their own respective New Orders.[111]

VI

Before negotiations for a formal alliance commenced, Mussolini had insisted that Italy needed at least three years of peace to prepare for a general war. For the time being, Mussolini's Italy maintained friendship with Britain, as he hoped that this would strengthen the Italian negotiating position vis-à-vis Germany.[112] Unresolved tensions remained between Italy and Germany, above all over the South Tyrol.[113] At the same time, in early May 1939, the new pope, Pius XII, suggested a conference of the four Munich powers and Poland to discuss the fate of Danzig and Italian territorial claims on France. As during the Sudeten crisis, Mussolini and Hitler coordinated their strategies. Hitler refused the multilateral conference and let the Vatican know that he had to consult with Mussolini first, a further reinforcement of the Axis.[114]

Ciano and Ribbentrop met in Milan on 6 and 7 May 1939 to discuss a military alliance. Mussolini and Hitler, leaders who claimed to be in charge of their nations' foreign policies, left the detailed negotiations to their foreign ministers, a strategy which confirmed their special positions aloof from bureaucracy. This alliance was to be the third Italo-German pact in modern history after the Prussian–Italian pact in the Austro-Prussian war of 1866, and the Triple Alliance, which Italy had exited in 1915. Ribbentrop had originally planned a tripartite pact with Japan and Italy, but the treaty did not materialise after inconclusive negotiations with the Japanese.[115] Unlike other military treaties, the Italo-German treaty was offensive, not defensive, reflecting the aggressive nature of both regimes. Both countries had different objectives. For Ribbentrop, the existing Anti-Comintern Pact with Japan and the isolation of the Soviet Union were the principal aims of a formal alliance with Italy. For Italy, a pact with the Reich would guarantee peace for the next few years in order to facilitate rearmament.[116]

As on previous occasions, the location was significant. Originally, the meeting had been scheduled at Como, on the shores of the eponymous picturesque lake. But Mussolini soon decided to move it to Milan in order to send a strong message that Fascism was popular amongst all Italians, including the working class. The relocation was a reaction to claims in the French press that the largely working-class population of the Lombard capital was opposing Fascism. A report by the Milanese Fascist party of 4 May 1939 confirmed Mussolini's suspicion. The report gave details of popular dissatisfaction with the regime's economic and foreign policies. Fascism's glorification of war and the constant stream of pro-German propaganda had thus failed to resonate. In this adverse climate, the increasing scarcity of coffee, an Italian staple, did not help raise the regime's reputation, prompting the Ministry of Popular Culture to start a press campaign to explain, hilariously, the necessity for the abolition of coffee-drinking.[117]

In order to downplay the extent of popular opposition to the Axis and in order to display a common Italian–German front, Mussolini wrote a diplomatic bulletin, circulated to foreign diplomats and journalists. He emphasised 'the exceptionally warm receptions' by the Milanese for Ribbentrop, who had been welcomed by 'a crowd of several hundreds of thousands of persons'. Mussolini's claim that the Axis was geared towards peace, not war, was a bitter acknowledgement of his popular standing in Italy after Munich as the saviour of peace in Europe. Officials of the Ministry of Popular Culture instructed newspaper editors to emphasise the power of the Axis, as it was now based on the unanimous support of the Italian and German peoples. The latter point was meant to project the image that the Italian–German alliance was new and different in substance and style from other military alliances, as it had the friendship of Mussolini and Hitler and the Italian and German peoples as a foundational factor.[118]

In Milan, the Fascist regime had mobilised cheering crowds, according to the SS officer Eugen Dollmann, a dashing womaniser and, on this occasion, Ciano's interpreter. Ribbentrop thus received a triumphant welcome. According to Ciano, the Italian and German delegations were negotiating in a friendly and relaxed atmosphere. So cordial was the atmosphere that some younger German diplomats even stopped clicking their heels. According to the German minutes of the negotiations, Ciano sarcastically paraphrased the Duce's mantra that the Axis must 'always talk about peace and prepare for war'. This suggests that Ciano had internalised the Duce's performative diplomacy. The reckless mix of brinkmanship, opportunism and pro-Axis rhetoric further intensified the political momentum of the Axis and committed Italy to Nazi Germany in a display of friendship and unity that was hard, if not impossible, for the British and French to disentangle.[119]

As the Ribbentrop–Ciano talks were continuing, Mussolini, in a public pro-Axis display, visited the German book fair in Rome on 7 May 1939. This exhibition had been organised by Goebbels' Ministry of Popular Enlightenment and Propaganda and was held in Trajan's Market, a symbolic reference to *romanità*. The Fascist and Nazi press gave the Duce's visit broad coverage and emphasised the historically inevitable intellectual and cultural bonds between both nations which had been formalised in the November 1938 Cultural Treaty. Except for a single display of German books on Dante, however, the exhibits consisted overwhelmingly of Nazi literature. This raised Italian complaints that the Germans did not sufficiently appreciate Italian culture and highlighted the cultural and political rivalry of both nations.[120]

There were further signs of tension. A week after the conclusion of the Ribbentrop–Ciano talks, on 15 May 1939, workers displayed signs of dissent at a rally that featured a speech by the Duce in Turin. The Piedmontese capital was a hotbed of royalism as well as of working-class discontent. Despite tough security preparations, which included the arrests of suspected enemies of the regime, workers at Fiat's Mirafiori plant gave the Duce an extremely frosty reception, voicing their dissatisfaction with their deteriorating livelihoods and foreign policy. A report by the political police, written days before Mussolini's visit, had warned of the workers' anti-German attitude. Furthermore, according to the report, workers had voiced their concern that Italy would become a Nazi satellite state if Mussolini continued with his warmongering and pro-German foreign policy.[121]

But these dissonant voices did not stop the conclusion of a formal alliance. Ciano, upon receiving the German draft treaty, wrote in his diary: 'I have never read a similar pact: it is true and real dynamite' – later seen as an indication of his distancing himself from Mussolini.[122] After a fortnight, Ciano and Ribbentrop signed the treaty in Hitler's presence on 22 May 1939 in the Reich Chancellery. Mussolini was absent, as another trip to Germany within a short time would have further undermined his domestic reputation. In fact, the location of the signing ceremony reinforced the view that Germany, not Italy, was the senior power. The name of the alliance, Pact of Steel, displayed the aggressive and supposedly robust foundations of the alliance, which was implicitly unlike the pre-1914 secretive alliances. (Mussolini had initially preferred the term 'Pact of Blood', reflecting his belief in the transformative quality of war.) A propaganda pamphlet issued by the Ministry of Popular Culture insisted that this was an alliance that departed from earlier pacts. The pamphlet located the history of the pact in 1935–6, when Germany had supported Italy in the Ethiopian campaign, and presented it as historically inevitable. Documents, including Hitler's and Mussolini's various pro-Axis declarations, alongside bulletins from the Stefani news agency, were used to illustrate this point. Crucially, the pamphlet reprinted the king's endorsement of the pact and included his telegrams to Hitler and Ciano in which he had congratulated them on the occasion of the signing of the pact. This was a strategy to represent the pact as the fulfilment of the desires of the Italian nation as a whole and not just of the Fascists. Hitler and Mussolini were given ample space in the pamphlet. Hitler had emphasised the 'unbreakable commonality of Fascist Italy and National Socialist Germany consecrated in a solemn treaty', while Mussolini, echoing a similar sentiment, had insisted that there was 'the unbreakable union of our will'. As usual, these declarations remained vague and lofty.[123] Other propaganda messages went even further. For example, the *Italien-Beobachter* titled a cover story 'Linked for Life and Death!', giving the pact an existential meaning. The cover story of *Il Popolo d'Italia* emphasised the military strength of the Italian Empire and menacingly insisted that 'against the power of the Axis, there is nothing to do'. Goebbels, still doubtful whether the Italians would honour the treaty, observed Hitler's joy at having sealed the alliance with Italy.[124]

If the style of the propaganda on the pact had emphasised unity, so did the substance of the treaty. The pact prescribed mutual consultation of foreign and military policies. This was wishful thinking, given the mistrust that characterised the relationship between both countries and their leaders, who had failed to consult each other on several previous occasions such as the Anschluss and the invasion of Albania. At Mussolini's behest, this clause was superseded by a paragraph which committed both allies go to war if either of the signatories found itself involved in war-like conditions. This clause went way beyond other defensive military treaties and reflected the aggressive nature of the Axis.[125]

Through a combination of Mussolini's boasting and Ciano's incompetence at the negotiations, Italy had effectively given carte blanche to the Third Reich.[126] For Hitler, the pact gave him backing for the planned invasion of Poland. Although Mussolini and Ciano later claimed that they had not known about Nazi plans for an attack on Poland, Ribbentrop's briefing notes for his conversation clearly discuss a possibility of war with that country.[127] Yet, days after the signing of the pact, Mussolini panicked. After seventeen years of Fascist rule, Italy was not ready for a modern war, not least because of its lack of equipment and insufficiently trained troops and officers. The Duce thus sent General Ugo Cavallero to Germany, with a memorandum stipulating that Italy needed peace for at least three years. The myths of a peace-minded Duce and a secret clause to the Pact of Steel committing Italy and Germany to a period of three or four years of peace became part of the Italian political and diplomatic elites' wider strategy after 1945 to dissociate Italy from responsibility for the Axis alliance and the Second World War.[128]

VII

With the Pact of Steel under their belt, Hitler and his staff prepared the attack on Poland. Mussolini hesitated. He turned down Hitler's request for a meeting in June 1939, and proposed instead another international conference to boost Italian prestige. Still, he reassured Hitler in late July 1939 that

Italy would be ready for war, if Germany found that the moment had come.[129] But Mussolini knew that a German invasion of Poland would prompt a French and British attack on Germany and cause a European war for which Italy was not sufficiently prepared. Despite all strategic dissonance, Hitler sent Mussolini a cordial birthday telegram 'in loyal confidence' on 29 July 1939, as Europe was at the brink of another war.[130]

At this point, a nervous Duce sent Ciano to meet Ribbentrop to communicate his view that a war with Italian involvement had to be postponed by at least four years. Ribbentrop replied to Ciano that Italy could seize territory in the Balkans and that a major war with British and Soviet involvement was unlikely. Ciano's diaries and his minutes of his encounter with Ribbentrop and Hitler at the Berghof on 12 and 13 August 1939 illustrate his growing disillusionment with the Third Reich, which made him return to Rome 'disgusted by Germany'.[131] Ciano's minutes were published in 1953 in the Italian diplomatic documents, edited under the auspices of the Italian Foreign Ministry, amidst a general Italian sentiment to deny blame for the Second World War. Nazi Germany's dominant position in the military alliance and Italy's military weakness allowed Italian political elites after 1945 to escape responsibility for their ambiguous foreign policy, part of a long-standing diplomatic strategy to turn Italy into a great power, which had brought Europe to the brink of war. While, according to the German minutes too, Ciano had insisted that Mussolini needed a period of two to three years of preparations for a showdown with France and Britain, such a delay had not been agreed during the negotiations of the Pact of Steel.[132] Italy's wavering did little to enhance its reputation with Hitler. He believed that it was as unreliable and disloyal an ally now as it had been in 1914. Goebbels even accused Italy of 'complete betrayal'. Nevertheless, both leaders and their countries were now stuck with each other, and were unable to distance themselves from the Axis after the Pact of Steel had been signed.[133]

A string of letters exchanged between Mussolini and Hitler, written with the input of their military and diplomatic staffs, did not convince the Duce to support the Nazi attack on Poland. The publication of these letters in the relevant 1953 volume of the official edition of Italian diplomatic documents, edited by the prominent historian Mario Toscano, formed another part of the concerted effort by Italian political and academic elites, many of whom had been complicit with the Fascist regime, to dissociate Italy from the warmongering Germany. Read outside the context of the build-up of the Axis, the letters suggest that Mussolini was still wavering between Britain and Germany, trying to support the winning side. But this portrayal of Mussolini as a mere opportunist who tried to prevent a European war, rather than as an ideologically driven aggressor interested in enhancing Italian power, is wrong.[134] In reality, Mussolini's expression of his commitment to the Axis in his letters to the Nazi leader had further encouraged Hitler to go to war.[135]

Despite some broad ideological congruence between Mussolini and Hitler, national self-interest guided Hitler's policy in the build-up to the attack on Poland. The Molotov–Ribbentrop Pact, a non-aggression treaty between Germany and the Soviet Union, reveals that strategic considerations with Nazism's arch-enemy, Bolshevik Russia, were at the time just as important for Hitler as his alliance with Italy. Despite being in a formal alliance with Mussolini, Hitler had failed to consult the Duce beforehand and presented the non-aggression pact with the Soviet Union to him as another fait accompli on 25 August 1939.[136] Mussolini, nervous about Italy being dragged into war, had no option but to commend the German–Soviet pact as a good strategy to neutralise France and Britain. He repeated to Hitler that Italy would be unable to help Germany if it attacked Poland.[137]

Hitler was disappointed by what he saw as an unexpected backtracking and immediately implored Mussolini in a brief note to tell him about Italian requirements for entering the war on Germany's side.[138] The long list of demands for German deliveries of war materials sent by the Duce to Hitler on 26 August 1939 was apparently written after consultation with the chiefs of staff. The demands, including a request for six million tonnes of coal and two million tonnes of steel, were set so high that Germany could not possibly fulfil them. This gave Mussolini a convenient excuse to remain outside the war.[139]

Mussolini's refusal to enter the war annoyed Hitler, but his letters to Mussolini had to be couched in polite rhetoric that employed the familiar trope of Axis propaganda that both countries were fighting for a common cause.[140] Given the years of pro-Axis rhetoric which had become a central aspect of Nazi propaganda, Hitler had no choice but to maintain a superficially cordial rapport with Mussolini. Anything else would have undermined the credibility of the Nazi regime, which is also why Hitler insisted that his correspondence with Mussolini in the run-up to the German invasion of Poland must remain secret.[141]

The correspondence of the dictators with each other reads like an exchange of niceties in which neither side openly expresses its views and plans. For instance, on 27 August 1939, Hitler expressed his hope that Italy would enter the war soon. The least the Duce could do, according to Hitler, was to send more Italian workers to Germany. Hitler implored Mussolini to keep Italy's neutrality secret, but Ciano, with Mussolini's backing, playing the diplomatic game to maintain Italy's status, assured the French and British of Italian neutrality.[142] What is also striking about this correspondence is that Mussolini and Hitler exchanged more letters than ever before in late August 1939, with Europe being at the brink of war. Despite the frequent references to the Axis, the letters illustrated the wide gap between an ideologically justified alliance and strategic divergence that was characteristic of the Mussolini–Hitler pact. Despite all manifestations of friendship between the two states and their leaders, relations remained unclear. In fact, Hitler blamed senior Italian officers and the royal family for driving a wedge between Italy and Germany. He even believed that the signing of the Anglo-Polish Agreement of Mutual Assistance of 25 August 1939 had been prompted by Italy's open reluctance to join Germany in the war. Hitler's belief in an Italian conspiracy against him and Mussolini thus put a heavy burden on Italo-German relations.[143] In the end national interest prevailed in the Axis, held together by the belief in the displays of unity, friendship and a common ideology.

Mussolini's demand for yet another peace conference fell on deaf ears in the Reich Chancellery and in London, illustrating the marginal position Italy occupied in reality, contrary to the Duce's boastful 'determining weight' rhetoric.[144] Hitler was set to go to war, either with or without Italy, which shows that concerns over the Italian alliance were never at the centre of his foreign policy. As German troops crossed the Polish border in the early hours of 1 September 1939, Hitler wrote again to Mussolini. In a gesture that allowed Mussolini to save face, he thanked the Duce for his diplomatic efforts, but insisted that Germany could manage without Italy's help. His letter ended with an appeal to future collaboration between Fascism and Nazism. Mussolini had the letter published in the press and read out over the radio, as it seemed like an acknowledgement of Italy's support for Germany.[145] But in another letter, sent on the same day, Hitler, irritated by the Italian declaration that they would not enter the war, outlined his reasons why he had rejected Mussolini's idea for an international peace conference.[146]

Some German officials held such a low opinion of their Italian allies that Ribbentrop circulated a telegram to all members of the German diplomatic service on 2 September, insisting lamely that Italo-German policy was based on a 'total and clear agreement between the Führer and the Duce', and threatening any critics with severe penalties.[147]

When France and Britain declared war on Germany on 3 September, following the German refusal to evacuate Poland, Italy did not intervene, despite the provisions of the Pact of Steel. Twenty-one years after the end of the First World War, another European war had started, bringing to the fore Nazism's main aim: a war for the conquest of living space in the East and the creation of a new racial order in Europe. Before departing for his military headquarters, Hitler wrote to Mussolini, insisting that the war was 'a struggle for life and death', echoing his remarks to the Reichstag on 1 September 1939. There was to be either total victory or total defeat. Hitler reminded Mussolini that 'destiny will still bind us together', implying that Italy was increasingly dependent on Germany. He warned that 'if National Socialist Germany were destroyed by the Western democracies, Fascist Italy would face a very difficult future'. Here was a reminder that Italy had blatantly violated the provisions of the Pact of Steel. The terminology used by Hitler furthermore reflected the glaring repetition of Italy's refusal to honour its alliance with Germany in 1914.[148]

In this embarrassing situation, which had exposed Italian weakness, Mussolini instructed that the term 'non-belligerency' (*non belligerenza*) must be used instead of 'neutrality'. This terminology reflected the centrality of war for Fascism.[149] Reports on popular opinion, compiled by the political police, diagnosed a widespread desire amongst the population that Italy would maintain peace, and equally an increasing criticism of Germany.[150] Contrary to the apologetic claim that Mussolini wanted to preserve peace, the Duce was geared towards war, but Italy was not ready to intervene. Belligerent rhetoric and boasting about Italy's military power continued.[151] The lack of coordination, mutual support and joint military action in the autumn of 1939 reveals that the Axis was, despite all its ideological and propagandistic appeal, tense, ambiguous and full of inner contradictions.

While Mussolini was genuinely drawn to the alliance with Hitler, he had naively tried carefully to play off London against Berlin, but, ultimately, the British saw through his manoeuvring. Blame for the Italian alliance with Hitler lies with Mussolini and his coterie, not with the British. At the same time, Mussolini was constantly wavering and pursued a policy in which he reacted to events, such as the Sudeten crisis, as they emerged, which makes it hard to diagnose a consistent pattern in his policy. The result of this contradictory and often amateurish policy was a highly ambiguous alliance with no common strategy, let alone common war aims. All this mess, created by dictators with little experience of diplomacy and facilitated by their sycophantic staffs, would have dire consequences for Europe in the years to come.[152]

6

POINT OF NO RETURN
1939–41

I

Within four weeks, Nazi Germany took Warsaw and, days later, defeated Poland, whose territories were divided up between the Third Reich and the Soviet Union. Mussolini wavered between respect and envy for Hitler, who had, he thought, put him into an embarrassing situation by triggering a European war for which Italy was not prepared.[1] On the western front, despite the French and British declarations of war on Germany, there were no major military operations. In contrast to Hitler, who had withdrawn from public social life, the Duce continued with his everyday activities, which included playing tennis and seeing Clara Petacci. At the same time, Mussolini considerably increased public spending on armaments, which, by 1941, reached 23 per cent of the gross national product; this was almost a doubling from the previous year.[2] While he continued with his pro-German rhetoric, Mussolini told Petacci: 'Let us first see how Hitler keeps his promises', reminding her that Hitler had broken his earlier promise not to invade what had remained of the Czech lands after the Munich conference.[3]

Spurred on by the swift German advances in Poland that were accompanied by German violence against Poland's Jews, Mussolini told Ciano on 24 September 1939 that Italy would enter the war before long. Mussolini's attitudes towards Hitler ranged from enthusiasm for a German victory to jealous hopes that France and Britain would defeat the Third Reich, since he was concerned that no booty would be left for Italy if Germany continued with its swift victories. As Hitler celebrated the German triumph in Poland in his Reichstag speech on 6 October 1939, Mussolini rejoiced, since he wrongly believed that Italy could negotiate between Germany and the Allies after France and Britain had predictably rejected Hitler's not very serious offer of peace negotiations.[4] At the same time, the Ministry of Popular Culture continued to invoke the implausible 'determining weight' rhetoric in Italy and instructed newspaper editors to write sympathetically about the Third Reich, while simultaneously adopting a moderate tone towards Britain and France, whose Maginot line Mussolini and his generals thought impossible for Germany to cross.[5]

In the context of Italian non-belligerency, Germans in positions of authority remained sceptical of the alliance with Italy, as it reminded them of Italy's refusal to enter the First World War in 1914 and raised strong doubts over the reliability of the Italian ally. Noteworthy in this regard was an aggressively anti-Italian remark by the Saxon *Gauleiter* Martin Mutschmann in November 1939 that was subsequently brought to Ciano's attention. At a hunting party, Mutschmann had warned that Germany's disloyal friends were far more dangerous than its enemies. This was an implicit reference to Italy. While Mutschmann had no influence on German foreign policy, his undiplomatic remarks reflected a typical view of the disloyal and treacherous Italian.[6] Hitler's admiration for Mussolini, though battered by 'non-belligerency,' thus stood in contrast to the Italophobic views of other leading Nazi and state officials, alongside those of ordinary Germans.[7]

As the Fascist regime wanted to maintain ideological solidarity with Nazi Germany, the Fascist Grand Council approved Mussolini's phrase 'non-belligerency' (*non belligerenza*) in December 1939.[8] Yet some Fascist leaders openly articulated anti-German views. For instance, in his 16 December 1939 speech in the Chamber of *Fasci* and Corporations, Ciano made some implicitly anti-German remarks and blamed Germany for causing the European war. Mussolini tolerated, if not encouraged, Ciano's anti-German statements to maintain the illusion that Italy was still the 'determining weight' in Europe between the Western democracies and Nazi Germany, even though the Duce was set to enter the war as Germany's ally. This message did not go unnoticed by the Nazi leadership, as Goebbels' diaries reveal.[9]

Yet it would be mistaken to place Mussolini alone at the centre of this analysis of Italy's position at the beginning of the Second World War. It was not only he who hesitated to go to war. Ciano, the king, and a number of Fascist and military leaders too were reluctant, as they thought that Italy was simply not ready to engage in a major conflict. Despite years of Fascist sabre-rattling, rearmament and belligerent rhetoric, Italy remained in a relatively weak military position.[10]

German officials were not slow in commenting on Italy's weakness. Let us consider in detail a memorandum by Johannes von Plessen, a councillor at the German embassy in Rome, penned on 3 January 1940. The text is a candid analysis of Italian–German relations since 1935, written by a diplomat concerned with the long-term diplomatic relations of his country. For Plessen, Italy and Germany were historical adversaries. Relations had improved after the Ethiopian war and the German occupation of the Rhineland only 'for reasons resulting from a difficult situation concerning both countries' rather than because of a 'similarity of Fascism and National Socialism'. Germany's territorial acquisitions since the Anschluss had seriously upset the Duce, while Germans in positions of influence and authority feared another 1915, that is, Italy's changing sides. In both countries, the alliance lacked popular support, Plessen added, offering a realistic assessment. Some Italians, he warned, even feared that Germany would soon make claims on Italian territories. National interest alone, not loyalty to Nazi Germany, would determine Mussolini's decision on whether to enter the war. Plessen concluded that the alliance with Germany was Mussolini's only realistic option. There is no evidence that the German embassy ever sent off this critical report to Berlin, since Plessen's sombre and candid diagnosis of Italo-German relations suggests that the substance of the alliance remained on shaky grounds – in sharp contrast to propaganda.[11]

Turning to the question how Italians viewed the alliance with Germany during the period of *non belligerenza*, it becomes clear that many sections of Italian society remained sceptical, if not hostile, towards war on Germany's side. For instance, a Fascist party report on popular opinion in Udine Province, dated 7 February 1940, left little doubt about the hostility of the population towards going to war on Germany's side.[12] German consular officials, who were in closer touch with ordinary people than diplomats, assessed Italian popular opinion in a similar way. In late February

1940, for example, the German consul in Palermo reported to the German embassy on a conversation he had had with a high-ranking Fascist from the Sicilian capital. For the local Fascist, the regime, even after eighteen years of Mussolini's takeover of the premiership, had failed to bring Sicily under control. When the Italian government had declared *non belligerenza* in September 1939, the informer added, the Ministry of the Interior had asked the prefect of Palermo three times how the local population had reacted, highlighting the regime's concerns about popular war-weariness.[13]

In this situation, Mussolini sacked senior army and party leaders, notably Starace. With these dismissals, the Duce shifted the blame for the failure to prepare the country for war – which had become clear after the partial mobilisation in September 1939 – onto army and party leaders.[14] Unlike Hitler, Mussolini knew little about military strategy and failed to realise that the Italian armed forces had long been suffering from serious structural problems, including poor leadership and an antiquated military culture inadequate for fighting a modern war. While Mussolini was minister of each of the three armed services and had therefore been able to dismiss General Alberto Pariani, the army chief of staff, and General Giuseppe Valle, the air force chief of staff, in 1939, the armed forces remained closely connected to the monarchy. The king, not Mussolini, retained the right to declare war, and he only reluctantly handed over his supreme command partially to Mussolini in the early summer of 1940. This was in stark contrast to Hitler's powerful position as supreme commander of the Wehrmacht.[15]

As the tumultuous 1939 came to a close and 1940 began, Mussolini and Hitler resumed direct communication through a written exchange. In their formulaic telegrams and letters, which became part of the display of unity and friendship, both leaders highlighted Axis solidarity. Significantly, Hitler, still sentimentally attached to the Duce despite his disappointment at Mussolini's refusal to enter the war, had taken the initiative to write.[16] For Mussolini had felt embarrassed about Italy's inability to join hostilities. It took him until early January 1940 to write a substantive letter to the Nazi leader. Mussolini was in a defensive position and felt that he had to justify *non belligerenza* to the Nazi leader, maintaining that, after a 'waiting period', Italy would join the war. This was an acknowledgement that Mussolini knew that his refusal to enter the war in September 1939 had seriously annoyed Hitler. In order to downplay his defensive position and accentuate his irritation with the German non-aggression pact with the Soviet Union, Mussolini adopted an aggressive and condescending tone, reminding Hitler of his 'forty years of political experience'. The Duce continued: 'I am a born revolutionary and have not changed my mentality, and I am telling you that you cannot permanently sacrifice the principles of your revolution to the tactical needs of a decisive political moment.'[17]

More was at stake between the two leaders than *non belligerenza*, however. Mussolini had written to Hitler in the context of the Finnish–Soviet War, also known as the Winter War. Italian volunteers were supporting the Finns against the Soviets, who had attacked Finland in late November 1939. Following the August 1939 non-aggression pact between the Third Reich and the Soviet Union, Germany backed the Soviet Union, its ideological nemesis, while Fascist Italy, not least because of Pope Pius XII's condemnation of the Soviet attack, supported Finland and even tried to send fighter planes and volunteers. This war, like the Nazi–Soviet non-aggression pact, was undermining one of the central claims of the Axis alliance to fight Bolshevism together, and was putting considerable strain on the Italian–German alliance. For Ciano, siding with the Finns and taking an anti-Soviet position was also a way to distance himself from the alliance with Nazi Germany. After some wavering, Mussolini supported Ciano's anti-Soviet campaign because the Duce was concerned that the Nazi–Soviet non-aggression pact would devalue the Axis and therefore further dent the status of Italy, stuck in the awkward position of non-belligerency. Ultimately, however, Italy had no realistic alternative to pursuing the alliance with the Third Reich which, demonstrating its superiority over Italy, blocked the sending of Italian aircraft to the Finns.[18]

Hitler, preoccupied with the preparation of further German campaigns, did not immediately reply to the Duce. This made Mussolini nervous. Senior German diplomats believed that Mussolini's letter had done little to raise his reputation as a loyal ally; instead, there was a widespread belief within the German foreign ministry that Mussolini, despite his veneer of pro-German solidarity, was still keeping his options open.[19]

Some have taken Mussolini's letter to Hitler as clear evidence that the Duce tried to keep his distance from the Third Reich. But this interpretation misses the point. For Mussolini, the French and British, not the Germans, were his enemies. In reality, then, Mussolini's letter was an inconclusive attempt to delay the German attack on France and Britain, not because he was interested in peace, but because he knew that Italy was not ready yet to intervene. An immediate German attack on France and Britain would leave Italy without any booty, the Duce believed, and therefore undermine the long-standing aim of Fascists and Italian nationalists alike: to turn Italy into the leading Mediterranean power.[20]

Hitler, instead of replying directly to Mussolini's letter, resorted to the often-tried method of indirect communication, partly in order to let Mussolini knew how busy he was, partly to express his displeasure at Mussolini's policy of *non belligerenza*. Thus, in February, he sent the Prince of Hesse to Rome. The prince's mission was to organise a meeting of both dictators that would reinforce the friendship and unity display of their pre-war meetings. Another Mussolini–Hitler meeting would also project the powerful image of the dictators' special relationship that was working for a New Order in Europe and could therefore dispense with the grinding mills of diplomatic routine. In the meantime, Italy ceased armament exports to the British, who, in turn, soon implemented a naval blockade of German deliveries to Italy.[21]

Amidst growing pressure on Italy to intervene, in late February 1940, just as an Italo-German trade agreement was being concluded, President Roosevelt sent Benjamin Sumner Welles, the under secretary of state, to Europe. Roosevelt hoped that this peace mission might persuade Mussolini to stay out of the war or significantly delay Italy's entry into it. While Ciano, increasingly concerned that war on Germany's side would be too risky for Italy, was receptive to Welles' proposal to disentangle Italy from its German alliance, Mussolini, in a display of his plan eventually to go to war on Germany's side, was rude to the American diplomat. Welles' subsequent consultations in Berlin did not succeed either, as Hitler saw no reason to stop the war while the German campaign was going so well.[22]

As Germany was preparing its attack on Denmark and Norway in order to anticipate an Allied occupation of these strategically important countries, with Norway being crucial for German access to Swedish iron ore through the port of Narvik, the British naval blockade began to affect essential deliveries to Italy by sea, above all of coal. Hitler's long-awaited reply to Mussolini's January letter was delivered by hand to Rome by Ribbentrop, who was given a frosty reception by Ciano at the railway station. The fact that Hitler's letter was even longer than Mussolini's January missive reflected his belief in his superiority. He suggested meeting the Duce and put pressure on him. Hitler threatened: 'The result of the war also determines Italy's future.' Unless Italy was content with being 'a modest European state', it should go to war soon. The formulaic nature of this letter, with references to the 'fate of our two countries, our peoples, our revolutions' that were 'indissolubly tied together', is striking. The two dictators and their staffs involved in drafting these letters had internalised the propaganda of unity and friendship and used it as a veneer to downplay tensions. Mussolini's response to Hitler's letter was reserved, although he left him with the impression that he was prepared to go to war soon, not least because he knew that Italy depended on German coal deliveries after the start of the British naval blockade.[23]

Mussolini, increasingly under pressure owing to his expressions of Axis solidarity, was more and more set to march with Germany, hoping to gain some booty in France, at least, and have his long-awaited war against the British in the Mediterranean.[24] He thus agreed to meet Hitler at the Brenner Pass.[25] The location, half way between Rome and Berlin, reflected Mussolini's belief that he was still Hitler's equal.

Behind the scenes, Mussolini's continuing concerns over an all-too-powerful Germany prompted the intensification of the construction of the *Vallo del Littorio*. More money was spent on fortifying the border with Germany than with France. Although Italian propaganda officials prohibited newspaper editors from mentioning the ongoing works on the fortifications, they did not escape the attention of German political and military leaders, creating further tensions behind the facade of the Italian–German alliance.[26]

II

The meeting of Mussolini and Hitler on 18 March 1940 at the Brenner Pass, the Italo-German border since the Anschluss, served as a show of Axis unity. A small detail added prestige to Mussolini's Italy: the meeting took place on the Italian side of the border.[27] Tensions over the future of the South Tyrol, adjacent to the Brenner Pass, remained unresolved, despite Hitler's official renunciation of German claims on this territory and subsequent Nazi schemes, under the auspices of Reich Leader SS Heinrich Himmler, to organise the resettlement of the South Tyrolese. Following the Italo-German accords of June 1939, these schemes included a so-called 'option' for the South Tyrolese to decide by the end of the year to remain in Italy or be relocated to Germany within the next three years. The latter was the Nazis' preferred option and the vast majority of the South Tyrolese chose it, although in the event fewer than a third actually left for Germany. The population transfer began to stall by the summer of 1940, as the Third Reich focused increasingly on the war.[28]

What is striking about the scheduling of the Brenner meeting is that the German government had been able to call it at short notice, a reflection of German arrogance and superiority, but also of concerns about the potential undermining of the Axis by Welles' mission. At the same time, the lack of advance warning and the fact that Hitler had let it be known that he only had ninety minutes to spare made Mussolini believe that Germany was determined to attack France and Britain sooner rather than later. This realisation put him under even more pressure to fulfil his promise to enter the war, lest he risk losing what was left of the regime's credibility, at home and abroad.[29]

When Mussolini and Ciano left Rome on 17 March 1940 by train, there was no pomp and circumstance, unlike during the Duce's previous visits to Germany. This arrangement reflected Mussolini's wavering and his awareness that the alliance with Germany was unpopular. Before leaving for the Brenner Pass, he had told Petacci: 'I don't have much trust in the outcome of my journey.'[30] The Italian and German governments only issued press releases at short notice to create suspense amongst domestic and international audiences.[31] Various Italian authorities, including the police, meticulously documented Mussolini's train journey. His train arrived at the Brenner Pass forty minutes before Hitler's.[32] Heavy snowfall greeted the delegations. For security reasons, the busy railway was closed for all other trains. Even freight trains carrying the essential German coal deliveries to Italy were not allowed through. Performance thus took precedence over everything else.[33]

While waiting for Hitler's train in the freezing cold, the Duce worked himself into a pro-Hitler mood and professed his adoration of the Führer to Ciano.[34] In reality, strategic interest mattered more to Mussolini than Axis solidarity. This did not go unnoticed by Germans in positions of authority; for instance, Weizsäcker sarcastically characterised Mussolini's attitude towards Germany as follows: 'It has been said by experts that Mussolini has two halves of his brain that work separately [from each other]: a Latin-rational one and a Fascist-inspired one.'[35]

A communiqué issued by the German news agency (Deutsches Nachrichtenbüro) gives a vivid description of the Brenner meeting, veiled by Nazi propaganda. According to the report, the meeting was held in a more low-key atmosphere than the previous triumphant meetings between Mussolini and Hitler, owing to the war, although German propaganda gave weight to the dictators' relationship, insisting that this was their fifth meeting, which was being followed by the world 'with breathless tension' (*in atemloser Spannung*). That an official communiqué was released, unlike after the 1937 and 1938 meeting, suggests that the Brenner meeting was a business-like negotiation, rather than a repeat performance of the new style of diplomacy premiered in Germany in 1937 and reperformed in Italy in 1938, owing to the pressures of war. For similar reasons, large crowds were absent. A guard of honour greeted the Nazi leader at the station on the Brenner Pass, adorned with German and Italian flags. When Hitler alighted from his train, he shook hands with Mussolini. A military band played the German national anthem and the *Giovinezza*, while the dictators inspected the guard of honour, before boarding Mussolini's train, which was standing at the opposite platform. The meeting on the Duce's train was a gesture of deference, not least because Hitler had last hosted Mussolini at the Munich conference, so his visit to the Italian side of the border once again reinforced the sense that both leaders were equals. Talks began immediately between the two leaders, who were accompanied by their foreign ministers. The official report was deliberately vague about the substance of the talks, using instead the usual rhetoric about a common Italo-German front against the 'plutocratic Western powers'. The communiqué added that the meeting had been prepared 'with that fast decisiveness and at the same time absolute discretion' characteristic of the Axis. This dubious remark was an implicit reference to the fact that Ciano, apparently acting on the orders of an envious Mussolini, had warned the Belgian ambassador about the planned German attack on his country. While this information had not significantly undermined the German attack, Ciano's tip-off had confirmed Nazi suspicions about Italy's lack of loyalty.[36]

Goebbels was ultimately in charge of the propagandistic reporting of the meeting and dispelled rumours that it might lead to peace negotiations with the Allies. He therefore instructed the German press to keep reports of the meeting brief.[37] For the propaganda minister, the meeting had demonstrated Mussolini's loyalty. Goebbels subsequently instructed the

German press to intensify Axis propaganda, which had been scaled back after Italy's decision to be a non-belligerent.[38] Coverage in the German press predictably blew the trumpet of the Axis. An article in the best-selling *Berliner Morgenpost*, for instance, repeated the message of the Mussolini–Hitler meeting as an attack on 'those idiots in western European countries who have recently been waffling about the estrangement of the Axis powers'.[39]

A similar tenor was maintained by the Italian press. *Il Popolo d'Italia* portrayed the meeting as 'the historical Italo-German conference', printing a photograph showing Mussolini and Hitler inspecting a guard of honour. The Ministry of Popular Culture later instructed the Italian press to avoid any references to peace and to highlight how Italy was increasingly orienting itself towards Germany.[40] Nevertheless, *Il Popolo d'Italia* remained vague about popular reactions to the Axis in Italy, as the Fascist leadership was aware of the unpopularity of war on Germany's side. The paper briefly mentioned Mussolini's arrival in Rome on the night of 18 March 1940, stating that crowds had been waiting at Rome's station until 11.45 p.m. to give him a warm welcome with 'a vibrant demonstration'.[41] As during the 1937 and 1938 dictatorial encounters, albeit on a smaller scale, the meeting reinforced the sense that Mussolini and Hitler were marching side by side.

Yet what went on behind the scenes in the claustrophobic atmosphere of the saloon railway car was more complex. Mussolini later complained to Ciano about Hitler's dominant role that reflected Germany's strength and Italy's weakness.[42] Official Italian and German minutes summarised the conversation. These documents, circulated amongst diplomats and politicians, became part of the display of unity and friendship that characterised the Mussolini–Hitler relationship. Against expectations, the conversation lasted longer than anticipated because Hitler delivered a long lecture to the Duce about Germany's military supremacy and increased his pressure on Italy to enter the war, hitting a raw nerve with Mussolini's vanity and belligerence. Thus, according to the German minutes, Hitler did not even have to finish his sentence 'Were Germany to lose—' as Mussolini immediately interjected: 'Then Italy has also lost!' Hitler luridly tapped into the long-standing belief of Italian statesmen that Italy must become a great power, and repeated his earlier warning to the Duce: 'If Italy were to content itself with a second-rank position in the Mediterranean then it did not have to do anything, but if it wanted to be a first-rate Mediterranean power, England

and France would always be in its way.' Hitler, in a condescending manner, outlined Italy's two strategic alternatives. It could either postpone its intervention until the defeat of the Allies and content itself with a small amount of booty or, if the war between Germany and the Allies turned into a prolonged affair, it could strike and shift the balance towards a German victory. This was a curious reference to the Italian policy of the 'determining weight'. Mussolini had little option but to restate that Italy was unable to fight a long war but promised in turn that it would be ready to strike within months. Unlike in their previous conversations (of which no such detailed records exist), Hitler and Mussolini broached the substance of their alliance when they talked about the Nazi non-aggression pact with the Soviet Union, the mortal enemy of fascism and Nazism. Hitler bluntly confirmed that the Nazis' short-term pact with the Soviets was a political necessity and reassured Mussolini that 'for Germany, there is only one ally and one friend and that is exclusively Italy'. The Axis alliance was, even for its principal protagonists, as much about strategy as it was about ideology. Indeed, Mussolini did not have much choice but to enter the war on Germany's side because of Italy's growing economic dependency on Germany and the impact of his own belligerent, pro-German rhetoric. Finally, Mussolini admitted to Hitler that Italy had to go to war, because of 'the honour and interest' of the country.[43]

Needless to say, the meeting failed to eliminate the existing prejudices, both amongst Italian and German political elites, and amongst ordinary people. As Michele Lanza, a diplomat at the Italian embassy in Berlin, recorded in his diary, Germans in positions of authority continued to doubt Italy's ability to enter the war. This sentiment prompted Ribbentrop to issue an unconvincing language regime (*Sprachregelung*) to German diplomatic missions: 'The intensive and cordial conversation between the Führer and the Duce has again confirmed the clear and unchangeably positive attitude of Italy towards Germany in this war, and the complete agreement about the future position of both countries was noted.'[44] Yet, in contrast, Luca Pietromarchi, another Italian diplomat, concluded in his diary that 'the conversations remain[ed] general'.[45]

Hitler's doubts continued. Thus, after the conclusion of the talks, he refused to send Schmidt's minutes of the meeting to Mussolini. Hitler feared that distrustful elements within the Italian government might circulate them to the Allies. After Mussolini had demanded the minutes on several occasions from the German ambassador, Hitler compiled a redacted version, which omitted strategic details. At the same time, he accused the Italian royal family of informing the British royal family in the summer of 1939 that Italy would remain neutral in the event of a German attack on Poland. Hitler believed that this information had prompted the British to guarantee Polish sovereignty, thereby causing the European war in September 1939. Altogether, the Italian–German alliance remained unconsolidated.[46]

Mussolini's adherence to Nazi Germany was reinforced by his meeting with Hitler. This tendency was articulated with boastful headlines in *Il Popolo d'Italia* about 'the efficiency of the Italo-German alliance confirmed by the Brenner meeting', although such language was met with some criticism from Fascist and army leaders.[47] Upon his return to Rome from the Brenner Pass, the opportunistic Ciano boasted to Sumner Welles that the meeting had not changed anything about Italy's position towards Germany or the Allies.[48] Mussolini, by contrast, sent the king a telegram about his encounter with the Nazi leader. Then, on 31 March 1940, the Duce outlined his determination to go to war in a secret memorandum to the king, Ciano and the leaders of the armed services. Echoing the views of his Liberal predecessors, whose strategy had also been shaped by Italy's lack of natural resources, Mussolini insisted that Italy would only be able to fight a short war or a 'parallel war'. This would exploit Germany's military advances, allow Italy to seize territories in the Balkans and north Africa, and turn Italy into a great power. Fear that time was running out to gain territories if Italy did not intervene sooner rather than later was palpable. This concern was especially strong given the continuing military success of the Third Reich, which defeated Denmark in April 1940 and Norway in June the same year.[49] As with his previous military plans, Hitler did not inform Mussolini before the German attacks and presented him with a fait accompli.[50] Mussolini welcomed the German invasion as a further blow to the French and particularly the British, whom the Germans had successfully resisted at Narvik, the Norwegian port from where Swedish iron ore was shipped to Germany. Mussolini's enthusiasm about the German advance and the defeat of 'the great democracies' was echoed by *Il Popolo d'Italia*.[51]

III

Riding high on euphoria as Germany started to win the war in western and northern Europe, many in positions of authority in Italy, including the king, began to warm to the idea of a short war on Germany's side. This, they believed, was the moment for Italy finally to fulfil its ambition and become a great power. Pro-Axis propaganda increased markedly. Articles in the Fascist flagship journal *Gerarchia* boasted about the 'destiny of the Axis'.[52] At that time, Allied observers, such as the diplomatic correspondent of *The Times*, noticed an increasingly anti-Allied tone in the Italian press after the Brenner meeting following 'orders to boost Germany'.[53]

On 2 April 1940, at a meeting of the Council of Ministers, Mussolini talked enthusiastically about Hitler as 'a calm, perfectly calm man, sure of himself'.[54] For the opportunistic Ciano, who had begun to distance himself from Mussolini's pro-Hitler course, the Axis was shaped overall by Mussolini's belief in Hitler and, even though Ciano's diaries have to be read with a pinch of salt, it is clear that Mussolini had no option but to enter the war if he did not want to lose face, given the years of pro-Axis propaganda. Over the coming weeks, despite some wavering, Mussolini's determination to enter the war increased. On top of his envy and fascination for Hitler's conquests, reinforced during the Brenner talks, Mussolini feared that no territories would be left for Italy if it did not join the war soon; the latter view was shared at the time by many Italian political and military leaders.[55]

Growing domestic pressure on Mussolini's regime considerably narrowed his room for manoeuvre. In contrast to the sabre-rattling, a Fascist party popular opinion report from Milan suggested that some people, facing declining living standards, hoped that Mussolini would be the saviour of peace as he had been during the Sudeten crisis.[56] Discontent at the directionless regime was also rife in other parts of Italy, both rural and urban, and in all sections of society. Particular scorn was heaped upon the Fascist party and its officials, widely seen as corrupt and useless. Even party members voiced their doubts over the direction of the regime. For example, the 1940 celebrations for the anniversary of the establishment of the *Fasci di combattimento*, held five days after the Brenner meeting, were poorly attended. According to the Milanese political police, while people were in awe of Germany's victories, they opposed war on Germany's side.[57]

At the same time, the Fascist leadership associated the increasingly widespread manifestations of anti-German attitudes with pacifist and anti-Fascist viewpoints. This reflected the view that the Third Reich had boosted the radical and belligerent dynamic of Fascism since the late 1930s. Let us consider an April 1940 incident in a Milanese cinema. Here, a police informer witnessed a powerful display of anti-Fascism in the Odeon cinema, allegedly frequented by a well-heeled bourgeois audience. During the screening of *Sei mesi di guerra* (*Six Months of War*), a war documentary, members of the audience had started applauding when footage of Chamberlain appeared on screen. In contrast, some in the audience had started booing footage showing Hitler. The police arrested some protesters who represented groups viewed by the regimes with some suspicion, including 'some foreigners, a Jew, professionals, a student and no less than a Milanese patrician'. Reportedly, the same film had been received more favourably in a working-class area of Milan. This was a dubious claim, motivated by Fascist anti-bourgeois and anti-Semitic sentiment. This emblematic episode nevertheless reveals that the regime's ever closer association with Nazi Germany largely failed to resonate.[58]

Mussolini, under pressure to act due to his belligerent rhetoric, but held back by Italy's lack of preparation for war, railed against the situation in a conversation with Clara Petacci. On 11 April 1940, days after Germany's defeat of Denmark, she found the Duce in a foul mood. He immediately reprimanded her for being late and then launched into a tirade against the Italian people that was typical of his dismissive views of his own nation: 'I hate this riffraff of Italians! . . . This so-much-praised serenity of Italians is beginning to disgust me. They are cowards and weak, they are afraid: these bourgeois swine who quiver for their belly and their bed!'[59]

Even the cult of Mussolini, one of the most central integrative forces holding together the regime, became compromised. Rumours spread that the king would soon replace Mussolini as head of government, casting into doubt the degree to which Mussolini and Fascism had ever managed to penetrate the beliefs of Italians.[60] In this bleak context, as Paul Corner has suggested, Mussolini's push for war was probably the only viable solution for him to remain in power, as war gave him the opportunity to distract the Italian people from the regime's grave crisis. A successful war would allow him finally to establish the totalitarian state, get rid of the monarchy and cement his rule once and for all.[61]

After Germany's swift victories, more than ever before, Mussolini was in a marginal, subordinate position to Hitler. Following a radio silence, caused by both Hitler's resentment at Mussolini's failure to intervene in the war and Mussolini's envy for Hitler's successes, Hitler sent a battery of boastful letters to the Duce in April and May 1940. In these missives,

Hitler re-emphasised their common cause and friendship, a way of adding pressure on Mussolini to enter the war. As Germany went from one victory to another, Hitler used the letters to brag about Germany's superiority over the Allies, and, implicitly, over Italy.[62] Indeed, Italian war preparations were haphazard because of structural defects, amplified by Mussolini's unclear strategy. The Italian armed forces were unprepared for modern warfare and still relied heavily on artillery weapons from the First World War. A slow and inflated bureaucracy in the War Ministry too stood in the way of effective war preparations. For example, it took six months for the bureaucrats to approve a Molotov cocktail anti-tank weapon developed in July 1940. In the end, 73 divisions, rather than the higher figure of more than 120 divisions which the army leadership had anticipated, were mobilised in spring 1940.[63]

In order to increase the pressure on Mussolini, Hitler used emotive language. A good example in this respect is his letter of 18 April 1940:

> What these operations mean for us, and especially for me, is only understood in the world by one man apart from me, and that man is you, Duce. You once had the courage to conduct your action in Abyssinia under the English guns. My situation until today has not been that different; but I have also decided not to follow common sense during these most difficult hours but to appeal to the force of honour, to the sense of duty and finally to the heart.

Only the Italian version of this emotional missive, translated in typical Fascist style, with Hitler addressing Mussolini as '*voi*', instead of '*lei*', has survived in the German archives. A note on an adjacent file states that the original German draft had remained in Hitler's possession 'because this letter contains some private messages'. Through emotional language Hitler had expressed doubt and fear over whether Mussolini would back him in the war.[64]

Given Hitler's increasing emotional pressure on the Duce and, of course, Germany's stunning victories, Mussolini's determination to intervene in the war intensified even further. Nevertheless, his regime never managed fully to mobilise the Italian economy for war, not least because of structural weaknesses, including a lack of raw materials and insufficient production capacities, and because Mussolini feared that a push for armament would come at the expense of consumption and therefore put his legitimacy at risk. It is worth exploring this aspect in more detail. To start with questions of scale, the Italian economy was substantially smaller than Germany's, with Italy's GDP in 1940 at just $147 billion compared with Germany's $387 billion, Britain's $316 billion, the USSR's $417 billion and the USA's $943 billion in the same year. Other figures reveal that Italian war mobilisation remained limited throughout the war compared to the other major belligerents. In 1940, only 12 per cent of Italy's GDP was spent on arms, in sharp contrast to 40 per cent in Germany and 44 per cent in Britain. As we have seen before, Italy almost doubled this figure in 1941 to 23 per cent, but the Fascist regime never managed to exceed this proportion, which dropped to 22 per cent in 1942 and 21 per cent in 1943. In comparison, despite debates over whether these figures were exaggerated for effect by the Nazis, Germany radically increased its military spending to 52 per cent of GDP in 1941, 64 per cent in 1942 and 70 per cent in 1943. But the incomplete economic mobilisation was only one of the many problems facing Italy. The officer class had remained aloof from the population and had a stronger sense of loyalty to the monarchy than to Mussolini. Furthermore, in a country where personal connections matter, many well-connected conscripts managed to avoid being called up.[65]

Another potential obstacle to Mussolini's belligerency was the Catholic Church, which, at the time, opposed Italy's entry into the war. In an April 1940 article for the Vatican's *Osservatore Romano*, the anti-Fascist Guido Gonella criticised Germany's attack on Norway and Denmark, two neutral countries. Therefore, the Germans were brutal and not a suitable ally for Italy. The Vatican's negative stance towards an Italian intervention deeply concerned the regime, as the Church had a considerable hold over popular opinion.[66]

In this context, Mussolini moved in small steps towards war. A noteworthy reflection of Mussolini's increasing pro-German policy was his spring 1940 decision to replace Ambassador Attolico, whom the Nazis saw as insufficiently committed to the alliance. Before his departure from Berlin in May 1940, Attolico reportedly told a German diplomat: 'Everybody wants me to say Italy is strong. I think it is more honest and personally stronger to say she is weak. Don't you let Italy enter the war too soon, otherwise you will be sorry about it.' Attolico's replacement was a powerful signal to the international community that Mussolini was set to march on Hitler's side, since the replacement of ambassadors had been a central symbolic feature of the vicissitudes of the Italian–German relationship. As Attolico's successor, Hitler had favoured the Fascist hardliner Roberto Farinacci, but Ciano, anxious that the radically anti-Semitic and pro-German Farinacci would push for an immediate Italian intervention in the war, opted instead for Alfieri, a good-looking womaniser, ex-minister of popular culture, former ambassador to the Holy See, and associate of Ciano's.[67]

The pattern of the correspondence between Mussolini and Hitler in the spring of 1940 was that Hitler sent boastful letters to maintain the pressure on the Duce to enter the war, while Mussolini's promised an imminent Italian intervention. As Germany was preparing the next step of the war, the attack on western Europe, Germans in positions of influence continued to doubt the Italians' reliability and highlighted the growing dispute between Mussolini and Ciano over whether Italy should march with the Germans.[68]

On 19 May 1940, days after the German invasion of France, Luxembourg, Belgium and the Netherlands, which was progressing extremely swiftly, Mussolini boasted to Hitler that 'the Italian people . . . are by now convinced that the period of non-belligerency cannot last much longer'.[69] Mussolini's options had run out, as he had burned his bridges with the French and the British. All the years of Fascist warmongering rhetoric and Axis propaganda had put the Duce under considerable pressure to act. Mussolini's decision to intervene was also facilitated by reports from the political police and the Fascist party which claimed that the Italian population was finally seeing a brief intervention in the war as opportune. A report by the Fascist party from the Province of Rome of 17 May 1940 was typical in this respect. It insisted:

> One does not talk about anything but the imminence of the Italian intervention . . . The spirit of the people reveals itself most clearly everywhere in view of the intervention . . . The German victories make everyone shake with joy, with the people feeling by now close to the realisation of what initially seemed like an unreachable dream: the full liberation of and supremacy over the Mediterranean. Today, the people are all Francophobic and Anglophobic. One wants to run at

> once to war because anxious eyes rest on Nice, Savoy, Corsica, Malta, Cyprus and Corfu.[70]

Clearly, the authors of this and similar reports had internalised Fascist rhetoric about the imminence of the Italian intervention and pro-German propaganda. Whether the Italian people had genuinely accepted that a brief war was in Italy's interest, as one historian has claimed, is a moot point and unlikely, given the Church's anti-war stance. What matters more is that these reports likely reinforced Mussolini's decision to push for war, as he thought that he had the backing of the Italian people.[71]

Apart from police and party reports on popular opinion, Mussolini's decision to march with Germany may have been considerably strengthened by hundreds of letters in favour of an Italian intervention in the war, written by ordinary Italians under the spell of the Mussolini cult and duly filed by the Duce's secretariat. Whether or not the correspondents genuinely approved of war or were merely paying lip service to the regime is arguable. What matters more is that the letters served as evidence to Fascist bureaucrats and Mussolini that the Italian people wanted war. A typical letter was one by Arturo S. from Nola, a small town near Naples. In his letter to Mussolini, he articulated the central tenets of Fascist propaganda, anti-Bolshevism and the 'greedy hegemony of England and France'. Arturo reflected the long-standing tradition of viewing Italy as a proletarian nation that could only become a great power through war. He thus volunteered to be amongst the first to fight the British and French.[72]

But this was not all. On 19 May 1940, days after the surrender of the Netherlands, Mussolini's secretariat showed him a batch of letters with a pro-German tone, sent in by ordinary Italians, both men and women. Again, the filing of these pro-war letters by Mussolini's secretariat is noteworthy. One such letter was written by Rosa S. from Udine. She insisted that 'we cannot wait any more' for 'the war against the hated democracies'. Another letter, addressed to Mussolini by an Italian war veteran living in the United States, who wanted to remain anonymous as he feared reprisals in his new country, suggested that the Brenner meeting was directly linked to Italy's imminent war against France and Britain alongside 'Germany[,] our most loyal friend'. Even if, in reality, there was no direct link between the Brenner meeting and the Italian entry into the war, this letter suggests that Fascist propaganda had succeeded in making some believe that the personal encounter between Mussolini and Hitler had been the principal decision-making forum for this momentous decision.[73]

Mussolini's secretariat filed the letters in separate categories according to whether they were pro-German, for war or against war. This filing system suggests that Mussolini and his secretariat were aware of the divided nature of Italian popular opinion.[74] An anonymous letter, written by a group of Triestine irredentists, presumably anxious of potential German supremacy over the principal port city of the former Habsburg Empire, articulated disillusionment with Mussolini's pro-German course. The letter also blamed Mussolini's relationship with Hitler for the imminent Italian entry into the war. It warned: 'You have positioned yourself with Hitler, without God and outside the law, whom now everyone hates – we don't trust you any more!'[75]

Mussolini had to intervene, not least because the German campaign in France was progressing swiftly. The British evacuation of Dunkirk, which had begun on 26 May 1940, made a German victory over both France and Britain ever more likely. Hitler's boasting about Germany's stunning advances in France, 'days of a great historical content', put Mussolini under pressure to intervene still further. While his decision to intervene had already crystallised, Mussolini assured Hitler on 30 May, just after the surrender of Belgium, of his 'comradely friendship' and told him about 'the announcement of my decision to enter the war on . . . 5 June'. The Duce's fear that no booty would be left for Italy was palpable. Thus, entering the war on Nazi Germany's side reflected as much Mussolini's belligerent ideology as the long-standing aim of Italian political elites to ensure Italy was a Great Power.[76]

Following the set pattern of his correspondence with Mussolini as a display of friendship and unity, Hitler's reply was an emotional affirmation of his comradely rapport with the Duce, peppered with remarks such as 'moved most deeply'. Together, they would form 'the new face of Europe'. That Hitler did not need to explain the contours of the New Order was a concession to the formulaic nature of his relationship with Mussolini. Hitler's request to postpone the intervention by a few days reflected German concerns that an immediate Italian intervention might jeopardise a swift German victory over France. Thus, tensions between the two Axis powers remained. It is instructive in this respect to consider the war diary of the chief of the general staff of the German army (*Chef des Generalstabes*

1. Hitler, dressed in a trench coat, awkwardly climbs into a boat on his way to meet Mussolini near Venice in June 1934. The Führer's attire was later the subject of much ridicule, but, in reality, matters were more complex.

2. Mussolini and Hitler in animated conversation in the gardens of Villa Pisani in Stra. The leaders' outfits give a good idea of their different standing in June 1934.

3. The Nazis staged Mussolini's September 1937 visit to Germany as a performance of Fascist–Nazi unity. Here, workers, observed by crowds, are setting up decorations near Berlin's Brandenburg Gate.

4. Hitler bidding farewell to Mussolini at the end of the Duce's September 1937 visit to the Third Reich. The picture is a tribute to Mussolini's vanity in being the senior leader, as he is looking down on Hitler. Pictures like this helped to create an iconography of Italo-German unity and strength.

5. King Victor Emmanuel III and Hitler on their way from the station to Rome's Quirinal Palace after Hitler's arrival in Italy in May 1938. The awkward faces of both men reveal their intense dislike for each other.

6. Mussolini and Hitler in Rome's Galleria Borghese in front of Canova's statue of Pauline Bonaparte, May 1938. Contrast Hitler's admiring appreciation with Mussolini's grim and bored expression.

7. Propaganda images likes this one of a Fascist rally at the Mussolini Forum during Hitler's May 1938 visit made Hitler and the Nazis believe that Fascist Italy would be a strong ally.

8. Hitler stands front and centre in this Nazi propaganda picture of the Munich conference on 29–30 September 1938. In the first row, the pinstripe-suited representatives of liberal democracy Neville Chamberlain and Édouard Daladier, on the left, are outnumbered by the uniformed Hitler, Mussolini and Galeazzo Ciano, standing for the New Order.

9. This snapshot by Heinrich Hoffmann of Mussolini and Hitler conferring in the saloon car of the Duce's train at the Brenner Pass was taken on 18 March 1940, when Italy was a non-belligerent and Hitler wanted to secure Mussolini's intervention in the war.

10. Hitler scolded Mussolini at his mountain retreat in January 1941. This meeting marked a turning point in their relationship, which henceforth would gradually deteriorate.

11. Mussolini at the controls of Hitler's aeroplane during their visit to the eastern front in August 1941. In a striking illustration of the Duce's position, Mussolini is in the co-pilot's chair. Still, the image was not published in Germany.

12. An Italian troop train bound for the eastern front, probably in 1942. The decorations illustrate how the Duce–Führer relationship had entered everyday culture.

13. A leaflet dropped by Allied aircraft over Italy in 1942. Whilst Mussolini was certainly more than a puppet controlled by Hitler, the cartoon provides a perceptive interpretation of the Mussolini–Hitler relationship.

14. The dictators at Schloss Klessheim in April 1943, surrounded by photographers and film crews. The photograph suggests that the men's meetings had become routine and that the Mussolini–Hitler relationship was constantly being performed.

15. After his fall from power and subsequent liberation, Mussolini was flown to Germany to meet Hitler. Mussolini's civilian suit bespeaks his status as a fallen dictator.

16. Mussolini was the first guest to be received by Hitler following the failed attempt on the Führer's life after a bomb detonated at Wolf's Lair. This would be the last of their seventeen meetings.

17. Mussolini's inglorious end. The corpses of the Duce and his lover Clara Petacci are hanged upside down in Milan's Piazzale Loreto, 29 April 1945.

des Heeres), General Franz Halder: he laconically stated that Germany would not give any military support to Italy.[77]

IV

After much wavering and just before Nazi Germany had completely defeated France, Mussolini proclaimed war on France and Britain on 10 June 1940 from the balcony of the Palazzo Venezia. This was a major turning point. Ominously, this was the anniversary of the assassination of the Socialist Giacomo Matteotti by Fascist thugs in 1924, which had put Mussolini's nascent regime into a deep crisis.[78] Ciano had already declared the opening of hostilities to the British and French ambassadors. A depressed François-Poncet, who had tried, in vain, to dissociate Mussolini from Hitler, warned Ciano that the Germans would be 'hard masters'.[79]

Speaking to a seemingly enthusiastic crowd assembled outside the Palazzo Venezia, Mussolini presented the declaration of war as Italy and Germany's showdown with the 'plutocratic and reactionary democracies of the West', the inevitable result of their obstruction of the Italian nation's existence. It is significant that Mussolini tried to legitimise his decision to enter the war on Germany's side by constructing a historical trajectory to his 1937 speech in Berlin, insisting that 'when one has a friend one marches with him after all'. Needless to say, he did not mention the embarrassing period of *non belligerenza*. But he also tried to appeal to those Italians who were not in favour of the alliance with Germany when he mentioned the king. As Mussolini pronounced Hitler's name, the crowd predictably applauded. Here, finally, was the closing of ranks, announced at the 1937 and 1938 meetings, between both dictators and their nations, united in war.[80]

Despite this pro-war sentiment, it was clear that the Fascist regime had failed to prepare the army and the people for hostilities. On the day after the proclamation of war, Maria Carazzolo, a teenager from Montagnana, near Padua, saw soldiers who had been called up on the train to Padua. At five o'clock in the afternoon, air raid sirens started to sound before Mussolini's declaration of war was broadcast on the streets. Despite these bombastic manifestations, Maria found others quite incredulous. She overheard the following conversation on the train back to her small town: 'And now, where are we, eh?' 'At war?' 'Yes.'[81]

Hitler's reaction to the Italian declaration of war on France and Britain was ambivalent. He immediately congratulated Mussolini by telegram on the 'world historical decision' and assured the Duce of the 'indissoluble fighting community of the German people with the Italian people'. He also sent a telegram to the king to reinforce the bond between Italy and Germany. *Il Popolo d'Italia* published both telegrams on its front page to suggest the unanimity between Germany and Italy. Yet it remained doubtful whether the war would help overcome the tensions between the two countries.[82]

Hitler's real views on Mussolini were altogether different. In front of his army adjutant, Major Gerhard Engel, and Wehrmacht generals, he gave a stinging verdict on Mussolini's tactical and opportunistic manoeuvring: 'This is the worst declaration of war in this world . . . I would not have thought the Duce so primitive . . . Have been wondering latterly about his naivety . . . have to be even more careful vis-à-vis the Italians in political matters in future.' Engel reflected wider German disillusionment with the Italian allies. He commented: 'Actually an embarrassing matter: first, they are too cowardly to participate, and now they are rushing in order to partake of the war booty.'[83]

Such views were also picked up in official reports on popular opinion in Germany. The stunning successes of the German army in early 1940 had created a frenzy of national pride even amongst those who normally grumbled about certain policies of the regime.[84] However, support for Hitler did not necessarily mean support for the wartime alliance with Italy. On the day of the Italian declaration of war, a report by the SD on popular opinion was circulated amongst the Nazi leadership. According to the report, some Germans believed that the Italian *non belligerenza* had yielded some benefits for the Germans as the Allies had had to keep some of their troops in reserve for a potential Italian intervention, instead of deploying them against Germany. Others, however, were sarcastic and stated that chairs had had to be sent to Italy, as the Italian soldiers had been standing at order arms for too long in anticipation of war during the period of *non belligerenza*.[85]

Since Italy's armed forces were not sufficiently prepared for an invasion of France, the Italian campaign against France only began in earnest after the latter had requested an armistice with Germany. Italy wanted to gain as much French territory as possible before the Franco-German armistice came into effect on 25 June 1940. Against the advice of senior military staff, the Italian army was told to attack France directly across the Alps. Because of Mussolini's arrogance, the early Italian campaign was a disaster and foreshadowed in many ways the problems of the Italian armed forces during the war. Over five days of fighting, more than 600 Italian soldiers were killed, 2,500 were injured and 2,500 more suffered from frostbite, because they did not have winter uniforms. Italy only managed to occupy a small strip of southern France – to the derision of the German general staff, who found their prejudices about poor Italian military capabilities confirmed.[86]

A sense of inferiority and anxiety motivated Mussolini to offer Hitler *bersaglieri* elite troops to fight alongside Germany. Moreover, Mussolini, who believed in remaking Italians through war, thought the sacrifice of a few thousand men was necessary. Without Italian casualties, the Duce feared, Nazi Germany would not let him share the booty.[87] Despite his Janus-faced views on Mussolini's tactic, Hitler accepted immediately and gave the Duce advice on how to win the war: 'It is really only the spirit, Duce, and the will which form the man and which are at the same time his strongest weapons.'[88]

Ever since Italy's entry into the war, Mussolini's role in the lead-up to 10 June 1940 has been the subject of much controversy. One historian later claimed that Mussolini wanted 'to declare war, not to make it'.[89] For Churchill, British prime minister since May 1940, the answer was clearer. In his December 1940 broadcast to the Italian people Churchill insisted that war had broken out between the British and Italian nations, traditional friends since the Risorgimento, 'because of one man'. It was Mussolini who had dragged Italy into the war.[90] But, despite Churchill's rhetoric and reassertion of Anglo-Italian friendship, it was not just Mussolini who was to blame for Italy's entry into the war, although, after the war, Churchill's remarks served as an alibi for the millions of Italians who had been complicit with the Fascist regime and its warmongering politics, including the king and diplomatic, party and government officials. In reality, Italian war strategy was shaped by a combination of the aggressive aims of Mussolini, and the more cautious Badoglio, chief of the general staff, who also wanted war with the British and French given a good opportunity, but believed, similar perhaps to a number of leading German generals in the run-up to the Sudeten crisis, that the armed forces and the economy were not yet ready for war.[91] As Fascist propaganda had droned on about the imminent fall of France in May and early June 1940, many Italians began to see this moment as a golden opportunity for Italy to fight a short and decisive war. Even the Vatican, despite its earlier reservations, had begun to express support for a short war.[92] Altogether, then, by June 1940, many Italians in positions of authority, not just Mussolini, had thought that the time for a brief and decisive war had come.[93]

Military coordination of the Axis powers was lacking. Before Italy's entry into the war, there had only been a few meetings of high-ranking Italian and German generals. During the German attack on Belgium and the Netherlands, Hitler, alongside leading Nazis such as Göring, had insisted on a closer coordination between German and Italian military strategy, but the German general staff could not care less about Italian support, as the German campaign was going so well. This showed tensions within the German leadership. At this time, the German admiralty opposed the cooperation of the Italian navy.[94] Even after Italy's entry into the war, there was no effective coordination of military strategy with the German ally. Some German army officials had previously expressed contempt for Italians as racially inferior. According to a January 1940 memorandum by the German Army High Command, for instance, the Italians were bad soldiers, given 'racially caused weaknesses' and 'Southern mood swings'. Fascist attempts to turn the Italians into a 'people of soldiers' (*Soldatenvolk*) had failed. Only strong leadership would help, the memorandum stated and so implied that Mussolini was a weak dictator. Amidst these tensions, the propaganda display of Mussolini and Hitler's friendship served as an integrative force for the tense Italo-German alliance; hence Hitler's request for a personal meeting with Mussolini at Munich on 18 June 1940. The location demonstrated Germany's superiority once again.[95]

V

On their train journey to Germany, Ciano found Mussolini depressed because Hitler had defeated France without substantial Italian participation and was now set to take on Britain. The Duce's rant against soft Italians was an admission of failure: Fascism had failed to remake Italians into a nation of warriors.[96] As on Mussolini's previous visits to the Reich, the railway from the Brenner Pass towards Munich was lined by enthusiastic crowds. At 3 p.m., the train arrived on schedule at Munich, as *Il*

Popolo d'Italia boasted in typical Fascist rhetoric, suggesting that Italy was a loyal, efficient and reliable ally. To make up for his inferior status, Mussolini donned the uniform of the First Marshal of the Empire (Hitler wore his simple grey tunic). Still, the war had created a clear hierarchical difference between Hitler, set to dominate Europe, and Mussolini, whose troops had thus far not fought major battles against France and Britain.[97]

A massive rally welcomed Mussolini at the station. Unlike at the Brenner meeting, when Italy had been non-belligerent, both regimes invoked the familiar motive of the dictators' meeting amongst their nations to reinforce their supposedly common stand against France and Britain. Mario Roatta, deputy chief of staff of the Italian army, and the chief of the Wehrmacht Supreme Command, Wilhelm Keitel, were in attendance, suggesting to domestic and foreign observers that, contrary to reality, there was a common military front.[98] As during the previous Mussolini–Hitler meetings, the choreography was supposed to cast away these tensions. At the Nazi party headquarters, Hitler and Mussolini talked without an interpreter. No direct record exists of the conversation. According to Ciano, Mussolini was made to feel awkward (*impacciato*) because Hitler had given him a long lecture on Germany's stunning victories. This made a bitter and jealous Mussolini realise that Hitler would not back Italian territorial claims on France.[99]

Indeed, after two hours of lecturing Mussolini, Ribbentrop, Ciano, Roatta and Keitel were allowed into Hitler's study. The Nazi leader flatly refused to allow Italy to attend the German armistice negotiations with France. On top of Savoy, Mussolini, alongside other Italians in positions of authority subscribing to dreams of an imperial New Order, had expected to get hold of Djibouti, Tunis and Corsica, to take over the French fleet, and to increase Italy's presence in Africa. The reality was direr, as Hitler, keen to ensure that occupied France would cooperate with the Axis, refused to make such concessions to Italy. In the end, after the Italian armistice with France, Italy had to make do with a small demilitarised zone and an even smaller occupation area in the south of France.[100]

To help Mussolini save face and in line with the protocol they had established, Hitler accompanied the Duce to the train station and saw him off on the platform. They exchanged a long handshake through the train window. Hitler Youth members shouted '*Heil Duce*', suggesting that the Duce–Führer relationship expressed, like Fascism and Nazism more generally, the will of the young, as opposed to the bygone era of liberal democracy, represented by the French and British adversaries.[101] Unlike the broad coverage in the Fascist press, the *Völkischer Beobachter* focused on Germany's stunning success in the French campaign and only devoted one column on its front page to the encounter between Mussolini and Hitler. This editorial strategy implied that Italy's role in the Nazi war was marginal.[102]

Mussolini received a graphic reminder that war was real on his way back to Italy, as his train was held up in an air raid alarm. In a subsequent letter, Hitler expressed his worry that Mussolini might get killed in a bombing. This reflected his concern that Italy would not remain Germany's ally for long without the Duce at the helm. Hitler thus gave Mussolini two railway anti-aircraft guns as a 'personal gift'. At the same time, he declined Mussolini's offer to provide Italian troops and aeroplanes. To save Mussolini from embarrassment, Hitler assured him that they both faced Britain together.[103]

For Mussolini, Hitler's refusal to accept Italian military assistance was humiliating. It reinforced his obsession that Italy would be unable to obtain significant rewards from the war, let alone become a great power.[104] To save face and to placate popular opinion, Mussolini published a report on the Munich meeting in *Il Popolo d'Italia* in which he had little option but to claim that Hitler had treated him as an equal. In Munich, he averred, they had been walking back and forth in Hitler's office, occasionally looking at maps spread out on a huge table to designate their spheres of interest. But this was not childish play: it was the bitter reality of war. Mussolini reminded his readers that war on Germany's side was the only option for Italy and would soon yield benefits for Italy.[105]

Nevertheless, Mussolini, vis-à-vis Hitler, was obliged to maintain the friendship propaganda. Like a small boy jealous of another child's toys, Mussolini boasted that Italian preparations for an attack on the British in Egypt were almost complete. The imminent French armistice left him with no immediate possible war theatre, except for north Africa. References to their common cause or the 'revolution' were never explicitly articulated because of different Italian and German strategic objectives. The internalisation of an Axis rhetoric with its set phrases had become an integral aspect of the Mussolini–Hitler relationship in order to gloss over dissonances. It was therefore no coincidence that Mussolini described Hitler's gift of the anti-aircraft gun in *Il Popolo d'Italia* as 'another symbol of the indissoluble brotherhood of arms which binds Greater Germany and Imperial Italy together, during peace and war'.[106]

While Mussolini had little to show off, Hitler basked in what was perhaps the greatest triumph of his career. On 22 June 1940, France signed the armistice with Germany in a humiliating ceremony in Hitler's presence at Compiègne, in the very railway car where the Germans had been made to surrender in November 1918. The Nazi regime, which located its roots in the German defeat of 1918, allegedly brought upon by a coalition of Jews, Bolsheviks and Socialists who had stabbed the German army in the back, had finally erased the purported national disgrace of that year and restored Germany's honour.[107] Mussolini was deeply upset by the ceremony, which confirmed Italy's marginal role.[108] After the signing of a separate Italian armistice with France, some within the Italian military leadership, concerned about being further marginalised, advocated a more formal cooperation with the German armed forces, but the German army remained reluctant.[109]

German officials, such as the military attaché in Rome, Enno von Rintelen, continued to doubt the reliability of the Italians as good fighters. In a report of 3 July 1940 about Mussolini's visit to the Alpine front, Rintelen reprinted Mussolini's order of the day in which the Duce had boasted about allegedly swift Italian advances. Rintelen drily commented that 'the grand words of this decree bear no relation to what has been achieved'. For Rintelen, poor leadership, not ordinary Italian soldiers, was to blame for the abysmal Italian military performance, a realistic assessment of the situation.[110]

The Italian attack on the British in Malta did not yield much success either. Soon, the British Royal Air Force retaliated with bombings of northern Italian cities, including Milan and Turin, which revealed that the regime's preparations for the war had been a shambles. The British air raids enraged the Duce, who immediately requested anti-aircraft guns from Hitler.[111] Although the British raids were quite small they had a devastating effect on Italian morale, confirming the British view that Fascism did not have a strong grip on its population.[112]

VI

After the conquest of France, Hitler's attention turned towards Britain. In his Reichstag speech on 19 July 1940, attended by Ciano in order to emphasise the Italo-German alliance, Hitler made a final peace offer to the

British, insisting that he had always wanted friendship with Britain. Mussolini worried that the British might accept and deprive him of the chance to go to war. But the Duce need not have worried: the British immediately rejected Hitler's offer, which was so weak they did not take it seriously. Hitler knew that his German audience was hardly excited about the Italian ally, which is why he only made a vague mention of Italian support for Germany. At the same time, in order to please Mussolini, whom he called a 'genius', Hitler renewed his claims about the parallel history of Fascist Italy and Nazi Germany. In order to boost the alliance with Germany, the Italian Ministry of Popular Culture instructed editors to give broad coverage to the speech.[113]

After the beginning of the Battle of Britain in July 1940, enthusiasm for war in Italy was lacking. A Fascist party report on popular opinion in Milan, dated 14 August 1940, diagnosed that 'the condition of the population is quite depressed' and concluded that most people wanted to return to normal life again.[114] During the summer of 1940, when a German victory over Britain seemed likely, the Italian government gradually slowed down work on the fortifications of the Italo-German border, as they were keener than ever to avoid offending their powerful ally. One historian suggests that this resulted from Hitler's direct intervention with Mussolini, but there is no direct evidence to support this hypothesis.[115] The general expectation that Hitler would defeat Britain made Mussolini push forward with the Italian attack in north Africa. Here, in early September 1940, the Italians pushed their way towards British-controlled Egypt, raising high hopes that Italy would soon control the Suez Canal and thereby the Mediterranean and the British trade routes to India.[116]

Propaganda continued to keep the momentum of the Axis going. In this respect, the signing of the Tripartite Pact with Japan on 27 September 1940 considerably strengthened the image of the Axis. Here was a global manifesto for a New Order, led by Italy and Germany in Europe and by Japan in Asia. In reality, the genesis of the pact was considerably more complex, and the three powers did not share a concrete vision for the war and the future. For instance, some Japanese leaders feared that Germany, which they expected would soon dominate Europe, might extend its grip into Asia. The pact was thus not simply directed against the United States, but also presented a mechanism for the Japanese to designate their sphere of interest against potential German claims over French and Dutch possessions in south-east Asia.[117]

Soon, however, the Axis campaigns lost their momentum. By the autumn of 1940, the German campaign to conquer Britain, aided by some Italian fighter planes that Mussolini had imposed on Germany, stalled. There was still no real coordination of the Italian and German general staffs, reflecting the mundane reality of the Axis beneath the surface of the Mussolini–Hitler relationship.[118]

On 4 October 1940, Mussolini and Hitler met at the Brenner Pass after the soon-to-be Spanish foreign minister Ramón Serrano Suñer had visited Rome and Berlin. Amidst this Axis victory euphoria, it seemed likely that Franco, who had wanted to seize French colonies in north Africa, including Morocco and parts of Algeria, and Gibraltar, would soon join the Axis war against Britain. However, Hitler had rejected a Spanish intervention, as he did not want to put a swift German armistice with the French at risk.[119] This was the third meeting between Mussolini and Hitler within a year, a powerful display that Italy and Germany were now fighting the war together. Initially, plans of the meeting were kept secret, but the Italians leaked them to the international press, which confirmed Goebbels' doubts about the reliability of Italian officials.[120]

According to an article in the *New York Herald Tribune* written amidst American concerns about the direction of the war, the leaders' trains were armoured, implying that the dictators, like Italians and Germans at large, could be subject to British air attacks. The German foreign ministry, concerned about the international reception of the display of unity and friendship, filed the report. According to the American report, Sicilian grenadiers, alongside militia men and members of the Fascist *Ballila* youth organisation, were expecting the Duce on the platform. After Hitler's arrival, they exchanged the usual cordial greetings, followed by the playing of the national anthems and the reviewing of the guard of honour. The choreography of their meetings had become institutionalised. After ten minutes, Mussolini and Hitler, followed by Ribbentrop and Ciano, boarded the Duce's train and had the blinds pulled. Policemen prevented anyone from getting too close to the train. Three hours later, Mussolini and Hitler were seen eating together in the dining car after the blinds had been opened. Hitler, according to an American correspondent, seemed impatient, while Mussolini kept smiling. All these rituals had become an integral part of the Mussolini–Hitler relationship and were supposed to help ease the strategic tensions between Italy and Germany. Significantly, apart from the two dictators, Ciano, Keitel and Roatta were present, giving the meeting the atmosphere of an Axis war cabinet. A record of Mussolini and Hitler's private lunchtime conversation does not exist. But for their official conversation minutes have survived. As usual, a boastful Hitler dominated the talks, although he had to admit, for the first time in the war, that the invasion of Britain had stalled. This delighted the jealous Mussolini, who showed off about Italy's attack on the British in north Africa, which had begun in early September 1940. German help was not required, declared the Duce, although he added the caveat that German tanks might come in handy at a later stage.[121]

The point of this meeting, as of the previous dictatorial encounters, was not to discuss political substance. Rather, the meetings themselves, together with their choreography, resulted in a performance for German, Italian and international audiences that reinforced the Italian–German alliance on three levels: that of Mussolini and Hitler; that of the Italian and German bureaucracies; and that of the Allies. The Ministry of Popular Culture later instructed editors to emphasise Italo-German solidarity and stress the international echo of the encounter. While not articulated at the meeting, tensions on both sides ran too high for a more specific declaration. Gone were the days of public face-to-face meetings of Mussolini and Hitler. Despite Axis propaganda about the historic meeting of the two leaders, there had been little harmony. *Il Popolo d'Italia* boasted that the dictators had agreed on an 'implacable war' against Britain.[122]

VII

These ritualised performances of friendship and unity did not necessarily eliminate tensions, let alone facilitate strategic cooperation, as the case of Italy's autumn 1940 attack on Greece reveals. Various interpretations of the genesis of this attack exist. The most prominent one sees the Italian attack on Greece as Mussolini's pay-back to Hitler. In late September 1940, the Italian government discovered that Germany was to deploy a military mission to oil-rich Romania, in spite of the August 1940 Second Vienna Award, brokered by Italy and Germany to settle territorial disputes between Romania and Hungary. Germany was planning to secure the oil fields with a view to coordinating a joint Romanian-German intervention against the Soviet Union. Here was a clash between Italy and Germany over hegemony in the Danube–Balkan basin – for Italy, the only directly reachable area with essential raw materials.[123] Ciano claims in his diaries that the news of German troops crossing into Romania from early October 1940 onwards was yet another of Hitler's notorious faits accomplis. According to Ciano, whose view is seconded by some historians, it was this incident which prompted a jealous Mussolini to order the Italian attack on Greece. The attack would demonstrate that the Duce was able to stand up to Hitler.[124]

There are two problems with this interpretation. First, Ribbentrop had informed Mussolini and Ciano during his September 1940 visit to Rome about German designs on Romania's oil fields.[125] As the German ambassador reported at the time, the Italian government was extremely disgruntled about this graphic illustration of German superiority. Furthermore, Germany's push into Romania, thought to be in Italy's sphere of influence, reinforced Mussolini's feeling that it was high time for Italy to press forward with its war, lest Germany might otherwise bag all the booty.[126] Second, Mussolini had long planned to attack Greece, bribing Greek generals in the hope that they would be amenable to an Italian invasion. Plans for an invasion had been developed for the spring of 1940. Hitler had asked the Duce to postpone the attack, as the Nazi leader had been concerned with massing the Axis forces on the western front, rather than opening another war theatre. This was short shrift, suggesting that Germany would not get involved in the Balkans until after the defeat of Britain. Furthermore, the Italian attack on the British in north Africa had delayed the invasion of Greece, causing a messy and risky Italian military strategy.[127] Ciano, after falling out with his father-in-law in 1943, redacted the passages from his diary concerning his own responsibility for the attack on Greece and put the blame on the Duce.[128] Like Churchill's 'one man alone' rhetoric, this view became a convenient alibi for the Italian military leadership, who, after 1943, could wash their hands and put all the blame for the attack on Greece on Mussolini. Nevertheless, other contemporary observers, such as the American chargé d'affaires in Vichy France, reporting to Secretary of State Cordell Hull in early November 1940, believed that Mussolini had ordered the attack on Greece to affirm Italian prestige when Hitler was negotiating for closer Franco-German collaboration.[129]

Given the strange nature of his relationship with Mussolini, Hitler tried to muster support from other far-right European leaders for the war against

Britain. Thus, he was touring southern Europe in late October 1940, trying to win over Francoist Spain and Vichy France, regimes he thought sufficiently keen on joining in the war against Britain in return for territories, to fight alongside Germany. On 22 October 1940, Hitler met the vice president of the Council of Ministers of Vichy France, Pierre Laval, who in the mid-1930s had tried in vain to contain Nazi Germany in the Stresa front with Britain and Italy. Laval wanted to retain France's African colonies and tried to avoid the payment of heavy reparations to Germany, so he was open to military cooperation with the Germans. Hitler then went to the Spanish border at Hendaye to meet Franco, whom he and Mussolini had helped to win the Spanish Civil War. Contrary to post-war Francoist mythology, Franco was greatly tempted to fight alongside the Germans, but Spain was not in a position to do so after the Civil War. Hitler found Franco's demands for French territories and Gibraltar excessive, especially given the German leader's aim to bring the French on side. Both dictators intensely disliked each other. Hitler was so annoyed by Franco's behaviour that he later told Mussolini that he 'would prefer to have three or four teeth taken out' rather than have another round of negotiations with the Caudillo, 'not a man who was up to the job of the political and material construction of his country'. This criticism of Franco was probably also a strategy for Hitler to reassure the Duce that their relationship was special.[130]

On his return to Germany, Hitler stopped at Montoire to meet Marshal Philippe Pétain, the ageing president of Vichy France, in order to involve France in the war against Britain. Despite his fascination for the hero of the Great War, Hitler failed to obtain any formal commitment for French cooperation with the Axis. On the long return trip, Hitler told his generals that he would invade the Soviet Union in 1941. As the Führer's train was speeding through Europe on 25 October, Hitler, in a bad mood given the inconclusive results of his exhausting journey, was told about the contents of a letter Mussolini had written to him on 19 October from his holiday home at Rocca delle Caminate. This time, it was Mussolini who presented Hitler with the fait accompli of the Italian invasion of Greece, a major turning point in Italy's war and in the Italian–German relationship. Mussolini had already set the date of the attack on Greece for 28 October, the anniversary of the 1922 March on Rome. Hitler, furious about Mussolini's lack of coordination and concerned about the disastrous effects of this risky war for the German campaign, decided, instead of returning to Berlin, to take a detour via the snow-covered Alps to meet the Duce in Florence. The Tuscan capital was Hitler's favourite Italian city and the choice of this location projected images of Axis harmony. While Hitler knew that he could not halt the Italian invasion of Greece, he wanted to tie Italy into closer cooperation with France. Mussolini was reserved, as he feared that such cooperation would annul Italy's claims for French territories. Above all, another meeting with Mussolini was a powerful symbol of Axis solidarity vis-à-vis Britain and the United States where President Roosevelt, increasingly set to intervene in the war, was standing for his third re-election on 5 November 1940. Hitler's abrupt decision, if not order, to meet the Duce left the Italian government little time to prepare the meeting.[131]

VIII

On 28 October 1940, Hitler's train crossed the Brenner Pass in the early morning, again avoiding direct contact with the German-speaking population of the South Tyrol. The Nazi-controlled press reminisced about Hitler's triumphant 1938 visit to Italy, projecting images of the cordial friendship of the leaders and their nations. The anniversary of the March on Rome brought out some historical musings of a Nazi journalist, firmly subscribing to the centrality of the Duce–Führer relationship: 'Everyone has the feeling that Italy at war will celebrate this anniversary of its revolution with new deeds of both men in whose hand lies today the fate of Europe and that new decisive events have to follow the political encounters of the past weeks.'[132]

In contrast, in Milan, the anti-Fascist poet Magda Ceccarelli De Grada saw 'poor flags at the windows' and characterised the Fascist holiday as 'a lukewarm party', pointing to the lack of enthusiasm of the Milanese for the regime.[133] Despite the short notice, the Fascist regime had organised an enthusiastic crowd at Bologna station, which Hitler's train passed in the morning. Shouts of 'Hitler! Hitler!' and 'Duce! Duce!' reminded domestic and international audiences of Hitler's triumphant 1938 visit to Italy.[134]

Hitler arrived in the late morning at Santa Maria Novella station, decked out with Italian and swastika flags, two hours after receiving the news of the Italian invasion of Greece. Mussolini and Ciano were waiting for their German guests on the platform. The usual cordial greetings were exchanged, and Mussolini immediately told Hitler that Italian troops had just crossed the Greek border. Hitler, despite his fury, remained calm. This was the eighth meeting of the two dictators. On top of their two meetings at the Brenner Pass, Mussolini had been to Germany three times, while this was Hitler's third visit to Italy. Here was a powerful suggestion that both leaders were equals. The *New York Times*'s correspondent reported that Italian air force planes were purring above the city, a display of Italian airpower, but implicitly also an illustration of the potential of British air strikes.[135]

Although it was pouring with rain, Mussolini and Hitler travelled in an open car to the Palazzo Vecchio to evoke the spirit of their meeting in Florence in 1938. In the Piazza Signoria, crowds mobilised by the Fascist regime demanded from Mussolini and Hitler an appearance on the balcony. The meeting in Florence evoked the power, splendour and glory of the Renaissance and was supposed to bestow a sense of historical legitimacy on Mussolini and Hitler.[136] Fascist propaganda stressed the popular enthusiasm for the 'two leaders', and insisted, in typical fashion, that there had been 'complete agreement about the current questions'.[137] In order to overshadow the tensions Axis propaganda became more pronounced.[138]

A closer examination of Mussolini and Hitler's conversation, held in the presence of their foreign ministers and the interpreter Paul Schmidt, reveals that it followed the set pattern of previous encounters. Hitler, as usual, monopolised the conversation, but did not broach the invasion of Greece. Altogether, the talks, like previous ones, remained inconclusive. Mussolini's main concern was to obtain as big a slice as possible of France and its empire, but Hitler refused to make concessions. Although the German and Italian minutes, compiled by Schmidt and Ciano respectively, exude an air of harmony, they also reveal some tension. For example, while the German minutes do not mention Hitler's views on the Italian campaign in Greece at all, Ciano's minutes briefly refer to his expression of solidarity with Italy in the Greek campaign and his offer of divisions of paratroopers to occupy Crete.[139] A harmonious façade disguised strategic disagreement. Indeed, the war diary of the Wehrmacht's Supreme Command stated laconically that no representatives of the Italian army had been present at the Florence meeting.[140]

Italy's campaign in Greece was disastrous. Ill-conceived, the Italian offensive soon came to a halt. Greece, led by the dictator General Ioannis

Metaxas, soon began to push the Italians out. The abysmal overall Italian military performance in the Greek campaign did little to raise its reputation with its Axis partner. Hitler was furious about Italy's invasion and told General Halder that the 'Italians can do [this] on their own'.[141]

Thus Germany, in violation of the Pact of Steel, did not immediately declare war on Greece. The German frustration about Italy did not go unnoticed by American diplomats. For instance, Leland B. Morris, the American chargé d'affaires in Berlin, reported to Secretary of State Hull that Germany was still maintaining diplomatic relations with Greece. Morris wondered whether Germany deliberately did not intervene on Italy's side to teach Mussolini a lesson by exposing Italy's military weakness.[142] This interpretation was astute. Hitler even declared in front of the Wehrmacht's Supreme Command that he had lost 'any inclination to a close military collaboration with Italy', a statement which the overwhelmingly anti-Italian officers must have found appealing.[143] Ordinary people too, according to a November 1940 SD report on popular opinion, blamed poor Italian performance for the German failure to win the war. This effective scapegoating of Italy for Germany's war fortunes built on the anti-Italian stereotypes prevalent within large sections of German society.[144]

After years of pro-Mussolini propaganda, Hitler had no option but to continue his public admiration for the Duce and told Goebbels: 'Only Mussolini is a real man.' For the Nazi leadership, well informed about the crumbling of popular support for Mussolini's regime, the danger was real that Italy might leave the alliance with Germany if Mussolini lost his power. It is important, however, to emphasise that, for Hitler, Mussolini stood apart from what he regarded as lazy, cowardly and inefficient Italians.[145]

Mussolini's reputation with the Nazis did not rise, however. In mid-November 1940, the Greek counter-offensive, supported by the British Royal Air Force, pushed the Italians back into Albania. Without German assistance, Italy was unable to defeat Greece. Numbers of casualties give an idea of the alarming magnitude of poor Italian planning and leadership. During the Greek campaign, which lasted until April 1941, Italy had deployed about 500,000 officers and men. Of these, 38,832 soldiers were killed or went missing, 50,874 were injured, 12,368 developed frostbite and 52,108 were temporarily out of action.[146] Another disaster, the British sinking of significant ships of the Italian navy in Taranto, further confirmed Italy's military ineptitude. Reflecting their military supremacy, German military and political officials now adopted an officious tone in their dealings with Italians, which Badoglio was made to feel in his meeting with Keitel in Innsbruck on 14 and 15 November 1940, the first wartime meeting of the chief of the Wehrmacht's Supreme Command and his Italian counterpart from the *Comando Supremo*.[147]

Hitler's decision, taken before these Italian military disasters, that Germany would fight north of the Alps and Italy south was rendered obsolete by these events.[148] Hitler's views on Mussolini seemed unchanged when he talked to Italian officials, but the behaviour of the Nazi leader and his military officials towards Italy became more assertive amidst the disastrous Italian campaign in Greece. While exaggerated for effect, Ciano's depiction of his meeting with Hitler on 20 November 1940 in Vienna, on the occasion of Hungary's joining the Tripartite Pact (alongside Slovakia and Romania), captures the essence of Hitler's feelings for the Duce. According to Ciano, Hitler had tears in his eyes when he reminded the foreign minister that he had sent Mussolini his famous telegram on the day of Anschluss from Vienna, promising that he would never forget the Duce's support. Hitler's display of affection for Mussolini was coupled with a rational calculation to help the dictators save face. After years of Axis propaganda, no other strategy was viable but to persevere with the Italo-German alliance.[149]

In reality, there could be no doubt that Hitler dominated the relationship and could more or less issue orders to Mussolini. Let us consider the letter to the Duce which Hitler gave to Ciano in Vienna's luxurious Hotel Imperial. It was couched in the now standard emotive language of friendship. Hitler promised to help Italy in the Balkans. Yet his fury with Mussolini was palpable; he wrote about 'very grave psychological and military implications'. His letter reads like an order to the Italians to consolidate the Axis position in the Mediterranean before commencing with any other campaign. That Hitler felt the confidence to give short shrift to Mussolini was a reflection of Germany's superior military position and Italy's growing strategic and economic dependence on the Third Reich. When Mussolini read the letter, he initially feigned indifference to Ciano in an attempt to save face, before admitting that Hitler had rebuked him.[150]

Mussolini had no choice but to reply defensively to Hitler's letter and admitted that he had 'had . . . my black week, but my spirit is calm', like a naughty schoolboy's admission of guilt to his teacher. At the same time, he vacuously reassured Hitler that Italy was facing a difficult military situation but insisted that the Italian people, spurred on by the unsuccessful beginning of the campaign, were prepared to make sacrifices to win the war. The replacement of Badoglio with the more pro-German General Ugo Cavallero reflected the Duce's determination to appear as a staunch and loyal ally.[151] Amidst these military humiliations, Mussolini spoke to the provincial leaders of the Fascist party on 18 November 1940. In familiar, yet unconvincing rhetoric, he insisted that Italy and Germany formed an inseparable bloc, led by himself and Hitler.[152]

Italy's poor military performance in Greece brought the country into further disrepute with ordinary people in Germany, according to SD public opinion reports from late 1940. Typical in this respect was a report of 21 November 1940 which stated that Germans had had mixed feelings towards Mussolini's speech, widely seen as kowtowing to Hitler. The report cited a widespread sentiment about the Italians: 'They shouldn't talk so much but rather fight.' Furthermore, Mussolini's promise to call up more Italian men into the army raised critical eyebrows amongst many Germans, as the Duce admitted that only a small fraction of those men eligible for military service had been called up. For the Italophobic authors of the SD report, this lack of wartime mobilisation was unacceptable. Here was an image of the brave, masculine German soldier who sacrificed himself while the cowardly and effeminate Italian soldier shirked his patriotic duty.[153] Another central tenor of the reports was that many people believed, not entirely without reason, that Germany had had to clear up the mess created by Italy's abysmal military performance. Many Germans also dismissed the performance of the Italian forces and lamented the boastful declarations of Mussolini, which were not paralleled by the soldiers' military achievements. The authors of these SD reports had internalised anti-Italian stereotypes and knew that their readers within the Nazi leadership would be receptive to such views.[154]

Nevertheless, for reasons of prestige, Mussolini had been reluctant to accept the offer of German troops to bail out Italy in the Mediterranean, which he saw as being in Italy's sphere of interest. Only in late 1940 did the Italians accept German cargo planes which helped transport Italian troops to the Greek front.[155] Significantly, the Luftwaffe refused to put their aeroplanes under Italian command because they insisted that Germany was not at war with Greece. Despite his earlier reservations about

German troops, Mussolini eventually had to admit indirectly that the Mediterranean was after all not *mare nostrum*.[156]

As if this were not enough, in late December 1940, another Italian request for assistance reached Germany; this time for a tank division and just under 7,850 lorries, 800 tanks and 2,640 anti-aircraft guns. Italy was unable to fight the war on its own.[157] Even while their limited resources were heavily engaged in Greece, in north Africa the Italians had been trying to invade British-controlled Egypt since September but were crushingly defeated by a relatively small Anglo-Indian army near Sidi Barrani. This campaign diverted troops and material from the Balkans.[158] Italy did not fare much better in Ethiopia where in April 1941 a small contingent of African troops under British command humiliatingly defeated the Italians. The remaining Italian colonies in Eritrea and Somaliland were also occupied by the British, destroying the long-standing Italian prestige project of an East African Empire.[159]

Mussolini's strategy of a parallel war had failed spectacularly. The very idea had been flawed from the beginning. As the historian Giorgio Rochat has argued, there were two necessary conditions for a parallel war: first, a swift German victory over Britain, and second, the ability of the Italian armed forces to seize territories in other locations and to use those territorial gains as the basis for negotiations with the Allies. Neither objective was met by Mussolini's Italy, not least because the Italian military and political leadership had failed to prioritise and clarify its targets and strategies.[160]

Behind the scenes, following the Italian setbacks, some German officials demanded an effective subordination of the Italian armed forces under German command. For example, after Christmas 1940, Otto von Bismarck, a German envoy in Rome who was living the high life in Rome's diplomatic circles with his Swedish wife, suggested closer Italo-German military cooperation in which the stronger Germans would effectively control the weaker Italians. Bismarck, grandson of the eponymous Iron Chancellor, cautioned, however, that such a move must be done discreetly to avoid offending the Italians and undermining the Duce's prestige, anticipating Hitler's concerns about maintaining a good rapport with Mussolini. Likewise, in a report of 2 January 1941, Enno von Rintelen drew a gloomy picture of the Italian armed forces to justify his suggestion of exerting a stronger German influence on the Italian armed services. The Italian army suffered from poor leadership, insufficient strategy and the 'low resilience of the Italian soldier'. While patriotic and capable of fighting heroically, Italian soldiers lacked the will 'to persevere alone at a difficult duty post and also to defend [themselves] until the last bullet'. Aside from these typical anti-Italian stereotypes, such remarks showed that the Axis had been compromised from the start.[161]

But this was not all. Counter-Admiral Kurt Fricke in January 1941 bluntly suggested putting the Italian armed forces under German command. Hitler rejected such requests because of his personal affection for Mussolini, whom he rightly saw as the crucial link between the Axis partners. Hitler thus forbade any German military or political official 'to undertake anything that could offend the Duce and thereby lead to the loss of the most valuable link of the Axis, namely the mutual trust of both heads of state'. This order was noteworthy, as it revealed that, for Hitler, it was his relationship with Mussolini that held the Axis together. Without the Duce, he feared that the alliance with Italy would collapse, an implicit admission that it lacked a solid grounding. Hitler's order would guide the attitude of Nazi officials towards Italy for the years to come, at least on an official level. Needless to say, it failed to eliminate latent anti-Italian sentiments within the German leadership and the German people more generally.[162]

There was another factor behind Hitler's order. Any ostensible display of German military superiority could potentially make Mussolini change his mind and return to the negotiating table with the British. While this was an extremely unrealistic scenario, it reveals that Hitler knew that his alliance with Mussolini had been resting on shaky foundations since the beginning. In this context, Nazi Germany thus had no option but to provide military assistance.[163]

Along the lines of Hitler's order, Nazi propaganda officials instructed the German press to support the Italian campaign and hold back with any criticism, as this would have added to the domestic crisis of the Fascist regime. To discuss the future of Axis strategy, especially the disastrous state of the Italian campaign in the Balkans, Hitler suggested on several occasions a meeting with Mussolini. An embarrassed Mussolini hesitated to accept, since his promise to turn Italy into a global power with a Mediterranean empire had failed miserably. General Cavallero, in a letter to his son, even compared the disaster to Caporetto. The Duce feared another rebuke by Hitler which would have been an admission of his failure as a political and military leader. Naively, he hoped that Italy's military performance would soon improve, which would make German military assistance unnecessary.[164]

IX

Contrary to his previous order to avoid offending the Duce, Hitler made no secret of his disappointment with Mussolini. Thus, in December 1940, Alfieri duly noted that Hitler had failed to ask about Mussolini, against his usual custom. The Führer subjected Alfieri to a barrage of aggressive criticism of the Italian campaign, before offering German military support and insisting that the Duce had to come and see him at the Berghof, allegedly because he kept all of the necessary maps there. However, Hitler was keen to avoid the impression that he was, in fact, ordering Mussolini to the Berghof and offered to meet instead at the Brenner Pass. This gesture allowed Mussolini to save face, as Hitler had little option but to maintain the alliance with Italy.[165]

Hitler and Mussolini had reached a point of no return from the Axis. They continued with Axis rhetoric and insisted that they were friends. They had both internalised the Axis and believed that without them, it would disintegrate. Principal decisions about military strategy were thus the domain of the two leaders. Mussolini, in charge of a country increasingly dissatisfied with his regime, was tied to Hitler for better or for worse, and Hitler had the upper hand. All these unity and friendship displays had put them in a difficult situation. Not only would the Axis disintegrate without them, but with it so would the idea of a New Order. Both had fully committed to each other and lacked other allies. Hitler's letter to the Duce on the occasion of New Year's Eve 1940 is instructive in this regard. Hitler declared that he felt 'much warmer feelings of friendship, as I can imagine that the last events have made you lonelier vis-à-vis actually insignificant people, but also more receptive to the honest comradeship of a man who feels connected to you in good and bad days for better or worse'.

Hitler's attempt to soothe Mussolini's sense of inferiority did not go down well, as the Nazi leader's patronising references to the perseverance of famous German leaders such as Frederick the Great added insult to injury. Hitler, articulating his awareness of the domestic crisis of Fascism, renewed his offer to meet Mussolini.[166] Needless to say, Mussolini was reluctant, as he feared being chided for the Greek disaster. Alfieri advised him that Hitler would become angry if Mussolini did not meet him soon.

Wavering any longer would have disastrous consequences for Italy, as it was unable to fight the war without German help.[167]

A few months after Italy's entry into the war, Mussolini had become a shadow of his former dictatorial self. Eventually, the dictators' meeting was scheduled for 19 January 1941 at the Berghof. The location was a loss of prestige for the Duce. Mussolini insisted on secrecy, as he did not want to come across as inferior and weak. He even sounded out the German ambassador as to whether it would be possible for him to arrive in Berchtesgaden at night so that his arrival would go unnoticed by the public. Owing to Italy's disastrous military situation, this was a remarkable contrast to their pre-war meetings, which had been staged as the apotheosis of the friendship of the dictators and their nations.[168] As during his previous journeys to Germany, Mussolini's train, carrying a large delegation of leading military and political officials, crossed the border at night to avoid direct contact with the South Tyrolese.[169] Given the desolate status of the Italian–German alliance, in contrast with their previous encounters there was no grand welcoming ceremony, and Hitler collected the Duce from a small railway station near Salzburg. The Gestapo had cleared the station and its surroundings of any outsiders. Mussolini tried hard to keep smiling but he clearly felt uncomfortable about asking Hitler for military assistance, as Alfieri later remembered. Mussolini and Hitler then travelled in Hitler's car to the Berghof where they spent two hours talking on their own. As on previous occasions, German and Italian officials were coupled in other cars to facilitate conversation and to represent Italo-German friendship.[170]

Afterwards, in a private conversation with Alfieri, Mussolini said that Hitler had been hysterical since he had had tears in his eyes when Mussolini told him, during their face-to-face conversation, about Italy's adverse military situation. Mussolini, offended by Hitler's patronising behaviour, told Alfieri: 'He was too eager to make me feel and appreciate his kindness, his generosity, his strength and superiority. By the sincerity, the deliberate earnestness of his effort to save me from embarrassment he has only succeeded in offending me. He'd better not shout too soon. We still don't know the ultimate intentions of the Gods of battles.'[171]

After a tedious lunch, Hitler asked Mussolini to use his influence with Franco to bring Spain into the war, a request which did not materialise. Mussolini and Hitler's talks were matched by others between Ciano and Ribbentrop, and between Keitel and General Alfredo Guzzoni, undersecretary of war and deputy chief of the Supreme Command. As always, during the two days of Mussolini's stay, Hitler did most of the talking, so that the meeting was more of a Hitler monologue than a genuine conversation between allies. For the first time, however, the leaders had a detailed discussion of military strategy, a discussion that was unsurprisingly dominated by Hitler, yet the Nazi leader did not inform Mussolini about his plan to invade the Soviet Union. Hitler, as per his usual routine at the Berghof, subjected his Italian guests to a lengthy dinner, where he dominated the conservation, and the screening of a Leni Riefenstahl film alongside war documentaries displaying German military superiority. Hitler greatly enjoyed these films; Mussolini was half asleep. While at their previous encounters Mussolini and Hitler had treated each other as equal, the Berghof meeting represented a turning point in their relationship. Both leaders tried to continue posing as friends, but it was clear that Mussolini, although Ciano had found him 'elated', was definitely playing second fiddle.[172]

Mussolini had no choice but to continue his alliance with Hitler. Days after his return from Germany, on 22 January 1941 the British and the Australians took the port of Tobruk in Libya from the Italians. Some 25,000 Italian men were taken prisoner of war. This and other disastrous Italian defeats in north Africa prompted Hitler, aware that he could not invade Britain, to take on the British in the Mediterranean. German troops were thus deployed to north Africa in February 1941.[173]

The Berghof meeting marked the failure of Mussolini's strategy, which was swiftly to conquer *spazio vitale* in the Mediterranean while Germany was fighting the Allies elsewhere. The encounter exposed the new and clear hierarchy between the two dictators.[174] Italy had effectively become Germany's dependant. To maintain the illusion of Italo-German parity, Italian propaganda officials instructed newspaper editors to cover the meeting as a 'normal encounter'.[175] Therefore, in contrast to the boastful coverage of the previous Mussolini–Hitler meetings, Italian and German newspapers gave bland reports, using formulaic Axis propaganda.

Gone were the days when these meetings represented a new face-to-face diplomacy of two regimes making a New Order in Europe. According to a 23 January 1941 SD report on public opinion, Germans did not care much about the latest Mussolini–Hitler meeting.[176] The myth of the dictatorial couple began to fade. Mussolini's Italy had lost its momentum because of a fateful combination of military incompetence, Mussolini's callow attitude towards Hitler, and Italy's lack of military resources.

Germans in positions of authority such as Goebbels were aware of the increasingly difficult position of the Fascist regime. On 29 January 1941, he wrote in his diary: 'The situation in Italy gives rise to some concerns . . . Fascism is really on the losing side . . . Heavy signs of corruption . . . All hopes directed towards the Reich. Mussolini has lost a lot of [his] reputation.' Goebbels' views of Italy were shared by ordinary people, according to the SD: Germans began to describe Italian war bulletins as 'spaghetti reports', as they were long and thin.[177] A more sober diagnosis of Italo-German relations was provided by Weizsäcker, who noted that, ever since Hitler's first visit to Italy in 1934, the initiative for an alliance had come from Germany, while Italy had often reacted reservedly towards German advances. Mussolini's indecisive wavering meant that the Italians were increasingly being led by the Germans. Indeed, the Italian parallel war had turned into a subaltern war (*guerra subalterna*).[178]

Italy's crushing defeats in 1940 prompted a profound change in the Mussolini–Hitler relationship between a weak Italy and a strong Germany that was set to become Europe's leading power, having conquered much of northern and western Europe in swift campaigns. While the Axis had failed to defeat Britain, its victory, dominated by Germany, seemed likely. All this had exposed the display of friendship and unity with Italy as a sham, but both leaders and their regimes kept promoting it to save face. The maelstrom of destruction that followed in the wake of the Italian–German alliance, spearheaded by Mussolini and Hitler, was devastating.

7

INTO THE ABYSS
1941–3

I

On 30 January 1941, soon after the fateful Berghof meeting that had marked the end of Italy's 'parallel war', Hitler spoke in Berlin's Sportpalast on the anniversary of his appointment as Reich chancellor. He declared: 'The Duce and I, the two of us are neither Jews nor profit seekers. When we shake hands with each other, then this is the handshake of men who have honour!' In order to assuage doubts over the alliance with Italy, Hitler reinforced the special nature of his relationship with Mussolini and contrasted it implicitly to that of Churchill and Roosevelt, seen by the Nazi leader as part of a Jewish world conspiracy.[1] According to an SD report, the 'German people' welcomed Hitler's speech, as his frank remarks about Italy's string of defeats and his simultaneous declaration of loyalty towards Italy suggested that its poor military performance was not central to the German campaign.[2]

Despite Italy's military failures, Mussolini continued to express a strong belief in an Axis victory. Changing his rhetoric would have entirely undermined his regime. Let us consider the speech he gave on 23 February 1941 to an audience of Roman Fascists in the Teatro Adriano, weeks after the fall of Tobruk. This speech was an annual ritual to legitimise Fascist rule with its alleged roots in the Roman Empire. Like Hitler in his Sportpalast speech, Mussolini railed against Italy's enemies, 'the Masonic, democratic, capitalist world'. Had Italy been ready to go war, he declared, it would have done so in September 1939 on Nazi Germany's side. Mussolini even claimed that Italy's non-belligerency had facilitated the triumphant German victories of 1939 and 1940. This was an implicit justification of his strategy of the parallel war, which had failed spectacularly. Mussolini's desperate attempts to legitimise the war with references to Garibaldi and Mazzini were unconvincing because the heroes of the Risorgimento had, of course, been supported by Britain in their efforts to create a united Italy. Predictably, tumultuous applause followed the Duce's remarks and suggested that the Fascist regime was on the right course.[3] According to the SD's analysis of the reception of the Duce's speech in Germany, Germans had noted that Mussolini had finally articulated Italy's poor military performance and acknowledged Germany's leadership of Europe.[4]

Hitler's concern about Italian conduct in the war was palpable. On 5 February 1941, he sent Mussolini a condescending letter, written 'with the feeling of worry to do the right thing to help you, Duce, overcome a situation which must be having permanent psychologically adverse implications not only for the rest of the world but also for your own people'. Hitler feared that Italy would leave the Axis if Mussolini's regime were toppled. Mussolini, who wanted to prove the value of Italy by committing more men to the war effort, forwarded the letter to the king and insisted that Hitler's concerns about the Italian campaign were right. Here was further evidence that the Italo-German alliance was compromised and an increasing liability for Germany.[5]

In spite of that, German and Italian military officials had internalised the significance of Mussolini and Hitler as the dictatorial couple reshaping Europe through the Axis. Important matters would eventually be resolved by the dictators, diplomatic and military officials believed. To give an example, Alfieri claimed in his post-war memoirs, part of a wider strategy to exculpate himself from the war and put the blame on the dictators, that he had encouraged Mussolini in June 1941 to use his relationship with Hitler as a lever to improve Italy's position in the alliance with Germany.[6]

Italy's military situation deteriorated further. Germany increasingly feared a defeat of its principal ally and was compelled to assist Italy in north Africa and also prepared plans for an intervention in Greece. On 12 February 1941, General Erwin Rommel, acting on Hitler's instructions, arrived in

Tripoli with his German Africa Corps. Rommel's views on Italy were largely negative, as he had fought against Italy in the First World War, distinguishing himself in 1917 at the Battle of Caporetto. That an ex-enemy was called in to help save Italy's Empire was a great irony. Significantly, before his departure to Libya, Rommel had reported to Mussolini in Rome, as he was officially under Italian command, a concession to Mussolini's sensitivities.[7]

Coinciding with Rommel's arrival in Africa, Hitler issued a directive to the Wehrmacht about the 'conduct of German troops in Italian war theatres'. German troops towards must not display any 'offensive arrogance' towards Italians, he warned. Hitler confirmed the suspicions of German soldiers that Italy was poorly equipped because of the 'limited war-economic performance' and that Italian troops were fighting against 'a strong superiority of the enemy'. Hitler's concern to avoid further humiliating Mussolini was palpable. Thus, all German troops in Libya were to be placed under the tactical command of the Italians, while they formally remained subordinated to the German army's High Command. Hitler's decree was a desperate attempt to enforce good relations with the Italian allies.[8] Needless to say, German soldiers continued to make dismissive remarks about their Italian allies, as deep-seated anti-Italian stereotypes within the German army were exacerbated by the perception that Germany was having to bail out Italy.[9]

In the event, Rommel and his men could not have cared less about Italian orders. He even disregarded German orders and advanced towards Egypt where he hoped to crush the British. Rommel's troops, in whose wake the Jews of Axis-dominated north Africa and other ethnic groups became subject to racial persecution, almost reached the Suez Canal, raising hopes that Germany might gain access to the oil fields of the Middle East.[10] But it would be inaccurate to portray Rommel, later celebrated in British and German popular culture, as the hero who sorted out the mess created by the cowardly and clueless Italians. In reality, Italian troops, while poorly led, often fought bravely in the north African campaign.[11]

As Italy had already been sliding from defeat to disaster, Hitler keenly avoided public statements about its military failure. Secret reports on declining support for the Fascist regime crossed the desks of people in positions of authority. For example, on 31 March 1941, Rintelen diagnosed a 'feeling of mourning and shame' amongst wide sections of Italian society, following the string of military setbacks. The military attaché had discerned a complete breakdown in popular opinion.[12] Around the same time, German diplomatic missions in Italy received a batch of anti-German letters avoiding diplomatic niceties. For instance, an anonymous correspondent insisted: 'Cursed is Hitler and cursed are all the Germans.'[13]

Soon, the alliance was put to another test. On 25 March 1941, the Yugoslav government and Prince Regent Paul had given in to German pressure and signed an accession to the Tripartite Pact. Yugoslavia's adherence to the pact was essential to the German plan for the invasion of Greece. But, a few days later, a coup d'état by Serb officers of the Yugoslav army opposed to an alliance with Germany ousted Paul. A furious Hitler immediately ordered the invasion of Yugoslavia. At midnight, he sent a telegram to Mussolini, explaining the inevitability of the German attack. As on previous occasions, Hitler presented Mussolini with a fait accompli when he asked the Duce to suspend the Italian offensive against Greece and instead to deploy troops to secure the Yugoslav–Albanian border. Lacking another option, Mussolini had to resort to the usual formulaic claim that 'the current crisis will lead to a total and decisive success of the Axis'. Echoing his belief in the New Order despite military failure, he told the German ambassador that it was high time 'to clean up this last artificial state edifice created at Versailles under Wilson's sponsorship'. Before long, Yugoslavia was dismantled. The Croatian ultra-nationalist Ante Pavelić, then in Italy, and his Ustaše soon created a regime of terror in Croatia, persecuting and murdering tens of thousands of Jews and several hundred thousand Serbs. His regime was propped up by the Germans and Italians, who soon found themselves attacked by partisans and responded with the utmost brutality, deporting suspected partisans to concentration camps. In Slovenia, where the south and the west were annexed by Italy, more than 100,000 people were deported to Italian camps. On the island of Rab, for instance, the mortality rate was at 19 per cent.[14]

Despite all the violence, Italy had failed abjectly in its aim to dominate the Mediterranean. Even worse, German assistance was required, which amplified frictions between both allies. The Mediterranean was clearly no longer the domain of Mussolini's Italy, but was instead set to become dominated by Nazi Germany. In early April 1941, the Germans invaded

Greece and soon created a terror regime in their zone of occupation that included economic exploitation, starvation and a fierce crackdown on the Greek resistance. By late April, after heavy fighting, the British, stationed in mainland Greece, had to evacuate almost 60,000 troops. Finally, in May 1941, the British and their allies suffered a crushing defeat in Crete, which the Germans had invaded in an airborne operation.[15]

Instead of open criticism of Mussolini, who had been effectively forced to bury his imperial dream of *spazio vitale*, Hitler condescended. A good indication of this tendency is Hitler's 4 May 1941 Reichstag speech, a celebration of German triumphs in the Balkans. Hitler had to serve two key audiences: Mussolini and the Italian leadership on the one hand and, more importantly, the German people on the other. In order to boost Mussolini's morale, he credited the Italian contribution to the war in the Balkans, acknowledging Italy's 'exceedingly high casualties' (*die überaus große Blutlast*) since the attack on Greece in October 1940. Hitler implausibly added that 'the deployment of the German forces was therefore not aid for Italy against Greece', but a preventive attack against the British.[16]

Mussolini, who had listened to Hitler's speech on the wireless, was not impressed. But it was not just the speech that had annoyed him. The day before, he had heard that Rommel had been threatening Italian soldiers in Libya with 'referral to military tribunals'. Mussolini asked Farinacci, perhaps the most pro-Nazi Fascist leader, to draft a letter to Hitler to protest against the behaviour of German troops. In the end, the letter was not sent, not least because Mussolini was partly satisfied by Hitler's lukewarm pro-Italian declarations in his speech. Another reason why Farinacci's letter was not sent was that, in the end, Mussolini jealously wanted to guard his exclusive access to Hitler from other Fascist leaders.[17]

As Italy came increasingly to depend on German military support and raw materials, Germans in positions of authority began to demand an Italian quid pro quo. Since Italy and Germany were both short of hard currency, trade between the nations had been carried out since the 1930s by clearing. As we have seen, a number of Italian workers had been sent to the Reich since 1937. By June 1940, when Italy had entered the war, 80,000 Italians were working in Germany. Numbers would soon rise dramatically. In January 1941, the Italian authorities received a German request for 54,000 Italian construction and mining workers. Under considerable

German pressure, the Italian authorities offered 150,000 workers. But, on 19 June 1941, the German authorities, reflecting their superiority, demanded another 100,000. Given the Italian reliance on German military and economic support, the Italian authorities had little choice but to fulfil these requests.

Across Italy, the regime recruited labourers and sent them to Germany. Workers were promised that they would be treated well there. In reality, the labourers often faced extremely harsh conditions, not surprising given the hardships of the war and the anti-Italian attitudes of many Germans. They soon complained about their poor treatment, inadequate housing and, above all, bad food. In response, the Italian and German authorities planned to import Italian provisions for the workers which would be prepared by Italian chefs. However, given the huge numbers of Italian workers, this ambitious scheme could not be realised, and the labourers had to make do with potatoes rather than pasta. But this was not all. German allegations that many Italian workers were having sex with German women soon escalated into a major political conflict.[18]

Particularly noteworthy was a September 1941 incident in Recklinghausen in the Ruhr valley. Here, a German woman accused of having sex with an Italian worker had her hair shaved and her face smeared with asphalt. This public humiliation, according to the Italian government, had been caused not least by the anti-Italian circular of the local Nazi party *Kreisleiter* issued beforehand. In the circular, the Nazi official had insisted: 'A mixing is not desirable at all, but the mixing of blood of a German girl with a foreigner of related blood and workers from occupied territories (Norwegians, Danes, etc.) and even enemy peoples (English) is more desirable than the mixing with foreigners of alien blood (Italians are to be regarded as that).'[19]

But this incident was just the tip of the iceberg. The harsh and often completely arbitrary punishment of Italian workers by the German police, including detention in Gestapo-run work education camps (*Arbeitserziehungslager*), prompted Ciano to protest to the German ambassador in September 1941. Mussolini was furious about the ill-treatment of Italian workers, as this further revealed Italy's vassal status. After lengthy negotiations and an intervention by Hitler, both sides agreed to hand over workers to be punished or disciplined at the Brenner Pass, where they would then be dealt with by the Italian authorities. The system whereby the Italian state effectively implemented punishments given out by Nazi Germany led to massive disgruntlement in Italy, as it further emphasised Italy's subordinate position. Despite many protests to the German government, Mussolini and the Italian leadership did not have the power to improve the plight of the Italian workers.[20] In November 1941, after Hitler's intervention, Ribbentrop had to reassure Alfieri of the generally positive attitude of the German people towards Italy, a dubious claim. In direct denial of official Nazi reports on popular opinion, he declared that most Germans believed in the alliance with Italy and dubiously claimed that only 'incorrigible elements who cannot follow the politics of the Führer' held anti-Italian views. This correspondence, seen by Mussolini, was emblematic of growing distrust, unease and hostility within the Italo-German alliance, both on a popular and on an official level.[21]

II

In May 1941, Hitler had more pressing concerns on his mind than the fate of the Italian workers in Germany, as preparations for the German attack on the Soviet Union intensified. When on the night of 10 May Rudolf Hess, Hitler's deputy, concerned about a war on two fronts, flew to Scotland, Hitler and the Nazi elite were shocked. Rumours of possible German peace negotiations with Britain risked severely undermining the Third Reich's alliance with Italy and the other Axis states. Hess had naively hoped that he could negotiate a separate peace with Britain.[22] As a result, Hitler sent Ribbentrop to Rome to confer with Mussolini. The Duce reacted with schadenfreude, as the escape of Hitler's deputy to Scotland was a heavy blow to the Third Reich's domestic and international reputation. Nevertheless, to avoid offending the German government, the Ministry of Popular Culture banned the Italian press from publishing details of Hess's flight.[23]

In his talks with Ribbentrop, Mussolini broached the subject of the planned invasion of the Soviet Union, but Ribbentrop did not give away any details, since Italy did not play a prominent role in Nazi Germany's flagship campaign of a racial war to create living space. Yet Mussolini had long known about the German plan to attack the Soviet Union and was keen to participate.[24] In order to reaffirm the display of unity with Italy which would reinforce Germany's military might, Ribbentrop scheduled a meeting of the dictators on Hitler's behalf at the Brenner Pass. It was to be held as soon as the Hess affair had disappeared from the news.[25] Once again, Hitler summoned Mussolini to a meeting at short notice without telling him of the agenda. This infuriated the Duce, who had no option but to swallow this humiliation.[26] Bureaucratic diplomacy was not working at all in this context, and the haphazard organisation of the meeting stood in the way of substantial talks.

On 2 June 1941, traffic on the busy Brenner railway came to a standstill. During their journey to the border, Mussolini and Ciano exchanged trade gossip about the Nazi leadership with Bismarck. Ciano later recorded that 'Göring has lost much of his influence with Hitler because he cautions him too much and the dictators don't like this'. Mussolini was 'in a rather good mood but does not now see the reason for this hasty talk'.[27] As during previous journeys, Mussolini's train had departed from Rome at night and had crossed the South Tyrol in the early morning to avoid any bristles with the South Tyrolese. Mussolini's principal concern was that Germany, in order to muster French support for the planned invasion of the Soviet Union, wanted to rush through a peace treaty with France without giving Italy a sufficient share of French territories – with potentially devastating consequences for the domestic reputation of his regime. Thus, the meeting with Hitler was held in a secretive atmosphere in response to the overwhelmingly hostile public responses in both Italy and Germany towards the Axis alliance. An SD report on popular opinion later conceded that the German people had shown little interest in the Brenner meeting. Perhaps as an excuse for this effective failure of Axis propaganda, the report insisted that the Mussolini–Hitler meetings had become routine.[28] In contrast to the usual pattern of the Duce's trips to and from Germany, *Il Popolo d'Italia* reported that, on his way back to Rome, Mussolini had been greeted with rapturous applause at Bolzano station, orchestrated by the regime, as his train had made an allegedly unplanned stop. This was a stark reminder that the South Tyrol would be Italian for good amidst the ongoing resettlement schemes for the German-speaking population.[29]

Given the well-rehearsed choreography of Hitler–Mussolini meetings, Italian and German officials in charge of planning the encounter had little to prepare. A report in the *New York Times* reflected American concerns over the outcome of the meeting, as previous Duce–Führer meetings had always allegedly prompted major events in the war. In this instance, the *New York*

Times had internalised Fascist and Nazi propaganda which suggested that the two dictators took all major decisions about Axis strategy.[30]

Mussolini and Hitler spoke on their own for just under two hours. According to Mussolini, Hitler 'above all talked about the Hess case'. Ciano, Ribbentrop and Paul Schmidt joined them, as Hitler was lecturing Mussolini. As ever, Hitler dominated the talks and gave a lengthy account of German strategy, occasionally interrupted by the Duce. Mussolini later told Ciano that the Nazi leader had wept when talking about Hess's flight, suggesting that Hitler saw him as a close friend.[31] Unsurprisingly, no in-depth strategic plans were discussed at the Brenner Pass, and the choreography of the Mussolini–Hitler meetings remained a veneer for the fraught Italo-German alliance.[32]

According to the official minutes, a distrustful Hitler had left his Italian allies in the dark about his plans for the attack on the Soviet Union, although he did mention German plans for purging Europe of the Jews. Hitler stated that the Jews would perhaps be sent to Madagascar after the war, a plan that would have led to the death of thousands on the way there. But this project had already been shelved by the Nazi leadership. The Nazi persecution of the Jews had escalated significantly after the outbreak of the war, with increasing marginalisation of those who remained in Germany, including deportations, and the ghettoisation and murder of Polish Jews. Hitler's failure to discuss the conquest of the Soviet Union with Mussolini, his purported principal ally, confirms the view that he did not consider the Duce a key associate in the Nazis' central project of creating a racially homogeneous living space in eastern Europe. In reality, according to Goebbels' diaries, Hitler had provided Mussolini with general information about the planned invasion, though not with strategic details.[33]

After the meeting, German plans for the invasion of the Soviet Union, code-named 'Barbarossa', intensified. Here was a campaign, planned from the outset as one of racial conquest, annihilation and domination, to destroy 'Judaeo-Bolshevism'. This was a war of genocidal violence, directed against Soviet civilians and Jews, following Hitler's notorious Commissar Order of 6 June 1941. The Nazi aim was the conquest of living space and the enslavement of the Slavs, part of a design to create a New Order in Europe.[34] While Nazi and Fascist propaganda had claimed that Italy and Germany were marching towards a New Order, the future New Order was, in reality, contested ground between both countries. Prominent figures such as Bottai, the minister of national education, believed that Italy, as a beacon of Western civilisation, had more legitimate claims to bring a New Order to Europe than Germany, a new country, ruled by barbarians until the arrival of the Romans. But Germany undoubtedly had more power to implement its visions than Italy.[35]

When German troops invaded the Soviet Union in the early hours of 22 June 1941 in an attack that took Stalin and the Red Army by surprise, Mussolini was asleep in his holiday home on the Adriatic. Suddenly, the telephone rang: Ciano was on the line with urgent news. He had received a long letter from Hitler addressed to Mussolini and read it out to the sleepy Duce, translating it simultaneously with the help of Bismarck, the German diplomat. Signing the letter 'with cordial and comradely greetings', Hitler feigned that he had not consulted Mussolini previously 'because the final decision will only be taken tonight at 7 o'clock'. In the letter, Hitler broached Mussolini's previous offer of military assistance and declined it for the time being, as he preferred Italy to fight Britain on the other fronts. Eventually, Italy was allowed to fight against the Soviet Union on the southern section of the new eastern front, alongside Romania and Hungary. Mussolini had insisted on Italy's military participation above all for reasons of prestige, but here Hitler implied that Italy was not a central ally in the Barbarossa campaign. In reality, Mussolini had no option but to express his agreement with Hitler's strategy, not least because Bismarck was listening in to the telephone conversation.[36]

Il Popolo d'Italia boasted about the 'immediate Italian solidarity'. But there needed to be more than a shared anti-Bolshevik ideology for Italy to join in the attack against the Soviet Union, as Fascist Italy had previously enjoyed good relations with Moscow.[37] Mussolini, seconded by his army leaders, believed in a German victory and expected that a significant Italian participation in the war against the Soviet Union would, after the devastating and humiliating failure of the 'parallel war', rehabilitate Italy as a great power and allow it to rebuild its empire. Whether or not all this and his promise to Hitler 'to march with the German people until the end' was delusion is a moot point.[38] Mussolini had no option but to march on Germany's side, whatever the cost. Envy of Germany's success in the war was matched by Mussolini's realisation that Italy could fulfil its territorial ambitions only as Germany's ally. Furthermore, the Duce hoped that an Italo-German victory against the Soviet Union would lead to the defeat of

Britain, as the Axis powers would eventually be able to attack Britain and its allies in the Middle East from the Caucasus.[39]

Amidst news of the swift German advance in the Soviet Union, a jealous Mussolini could only look back to the shambles of the flagship project of an Italian Empire. Even in the South Tyrol, Fascist imperial dreams could not be fulfilled, as the German resettlement programme had almost completely stopped. Himmler's office in charge of repatriating the Germans, the Reich Commissar for the Strengthening of German Volkstum (*Reichskommissar für die Festigung Deutschen Volkstums*), was now focused on the Soviet Union. Mussolini was so envious of German successes that he railed against Hitler and even told Ciano that he was prepared to defend the South Tyrol militarily against the Germans. Frustrated at his subordinate position to Hitler, he told Ciano that he hoped either for a compromise peace or for a long war, as these two scenarios would help Italy regain its status in Europe.[40]

Beyond the level of the dictators and their political and military entourages, the German invasion of the Soviet Union came as a surprise to many ordinary Italians and Germans.[41] But bulletins of rapid Axis advances soon gave way to hopes for a quick victory. When news of Italian assistance in the Barbarossa campaign reached Germany, the SD picked up typically hostile views: 'If the Italians do parades for much longer the war against Russia will be over! In Germany, one only does parades after the victory.'[42]

In Italy, the campaign against Bolshevism met the support of the Catholic Church and thus helped mobilise many Italians, even those reserved or opposed to the regime.[43] It is worth considering in this respect that Mussolini's secretariat received a cache of letters from ordinary Italians in support of the Soviet campaign. One of the letters was sent by a Capuchin monk from Termini Imerese, in Sicily. On 22 June 1941, he wrote to Mussolini to congratulate him on the 'holy war' and 'the defence of Christian civilisation and the destruction of the Bolshevik world'. Since the Axis had won its first attack on Bolshevism in the Spanish Civil War, the monk insisted, it would prove itself in the Soviet campaign.[44] The war against the Soviet Union gave a brief boost to the Fascist dictatorship which had been disintegrating since the beginning of the war.[45] In this vein, the German military attaché in Italy reported on 25 June 1941 that Italians had received the news of Barbarossa well, as he wanted to reinforce the notion of closed ranks between the Italian people and the regime.[46]

Yet Italy's subordinate status was clear to German propaganda officials, who denied that the country played a central role in the Barbarossa campaign. An article in the July 1941 issue of *La Svastica*, a German propaganda journal targeted at Italian readers, insisted that Barbarossa was a war of 'Europe in arms against Bolshevism'. Another article highlighted the contribution of other Nazi allies such as Finland and Romania, rather than of Italy. Still, the report ended with the formulaic mention of Mussolini and Hitler as the spearheads 'of European civilisation and freedom'.[47]

Nevertheless, views within the Italian leadership on the alliance with Germany remained divided. In mid-July 1941, Mussolini rebuked Alessandro Pavolini, who had succeeded Alfieri as minister of popular culture, for an article that had been published by Giovanni Ansaldo, a journalist close to Ciano. Ansaldo had written that Hitler was directing the war in the Soviet Union. This obvious fact infuriated Mussolini, as it confirmed his secondary role.[48] He once again railed against the Germans, amidst news of German successes in the Soviet Union. He ranted: 'I forecast an inevitable crisis between both countries.' His rage intensified into delusion, and he even declared that the Veneto must be fortified as the Germans might soon be attacking Italy there.[49]

Despite Mussolini's mood swings, following military plans from spring 1941, Italy soon deployed the Italian Expedition Corps in Russia (*Corpo di spedizione italiano in Russia*, CSIR). It was placed under strategic German command and largely relied on German supply lines. In total, the Italian forces consisted of 62,000 men and made up a small contingent of the 690,000 troops from other Axis states, including Romania. Altogether, the number of Italian soldiers, even though they were subsequently increased to 230,000 to form the Italian Army in Russia (*Armata italiana in Russia*, AMIR), was dwarfed by the more than three million Wehrmacht soldiers who fought on the eastern front.[50] Contrary to the powerful myth that the behaviour of Italian troops on the eastern front was characterised by a compassionate attitude towards the civilian population and suspicion of the Germans engaged in a racial war, some Italian soldiers were involved in war crimes, including the execution of prisoners of war. A racist attitude towards the Soviet population was prevalent, not least because of a widely shared belief that this war was a crusade against Bolshevism praised by many Catholic organisations, although the Vatican remained neutral. The advances of Italian troops in the Soviet Union thus for a short while increased the Fascist regime's domestic reputation, especially because it coincided with Axis victories in north Africa.[51] Yet Germans in positions of authority continued to doubt the reliability and stability of Mussolini's Italy. The SD picked up rumours that the deployment of the troops had been accompanied by protests against the Duce and his regime in Rome and Naples.[52]

Amidst the German victory euphoria, Hitler, in a generous mood, accepted the Italian offer of troops, as this would be 'a symbol of the liberation war pursued by you, Duce, and me'. For Hitler, the deployment of Italian troops only had a propagandistic purpose, symbolising the closing of ranks between Germany and Italy. Hitler asked Mussolini 'if it were not psychologically right if the two of us met up at some point somewhere on the frontline'. While Hitler had little interest in making any concessions to Italy, a meeting with the Duce would reinforce the powerful display of unity, as Europe seemed to be dominated by the Axis. Mussolini agreed with this performative strategy, as the meeting 'from a political and moral point of view would have a great repercussion for our two peoples and for the rest of the world'.[53]

III

In public, both leaders thus maintained their closed ranks to project the Axis. This did not go unnoticed by the international press. On 7 August 1941, Mussolini's son Bruno died when his bomber plane crashed on a test flight. Hitler immediately sent the Duce a telegram to offer his condolences, which the *New York Times* reported as a sign of Italo-German solidarity.[54] Yet Roosevelt and Churchill soon took over the headlines as an alternative couple of friends, embracing liberal democracy against the Axis threat. On 14 August, on a naval ship in Placentia Bay off the coast of Newfoundland, they signed the Atlantic Charter, a strong display of Britain's and America's common war goals and of American material and financial support of Britain via 'lend-lease' agreements. Behind the scenes, their alliance, one of necessity, was not without friction either but Churchill and Roosevelt discussed military strategy and seemed to like each other, unlike Hitler and Mussolini.[55]

On 23 August 1941 Mussolini boarded a train to Germany. As usual, the Duce's train crossed South Tyrol by night. It stopped at the Brenner

Pass, where Mussolini and the Italian delegation were greeted with military and diplomatic honours. The German government had kept Mussolini's visit secret to create a diplomatic sensation with this apotheosis of the New Order.[56] From the Brenner Pass, the train crossed Germany and continued towards East Prussia, arriving in the morning of 25 August at a small station near Hitler's headquarters outside Rastenburg, also known as Wolf's Lair. Hitler, accompanied by a phalanx of military leaders and high-ranking Nazi officials, was expecting the Duce, who got off the train dressed in a marshal's uniform, as *Il Popolo d'Italia* later reported. His showy dress was a marked contrast to the Nazi leader's simple tunic.[57]

Hitler's sparsely furnished and gloomy bunker, where the dictators met in private, provided a stark contrast to Mussolini's bourgeois residences. After his usual boastful 'detailed presentation of the military events', the Führer praised Italy's contribution to the Soviet campaign only in passing and instead 'repeated praise for the Finnish troops who [were] fighting in an admirable way'. Mussolini was left speechless and later expressed 'his serious desire that the Italian armed forces participate in greater measure to the operations against the Soviets'. But Hitler left no one in doubt that he was the master and refused to give in to Italian demands for the incorporation of more French territories. The signing of the Atlantic Charter had put additional pressure on the Axis, as both leaders expected an American entry into the war before long. In their personalised view of history, Hitler and Mussolini, aspiring to 'the construction of the New European Order', served as the far-right alternative to Churchill and Roosevelt. Despite these strategic, military and personal tensions, both dictators remained friendly to each other in order to maintain the Axis facade.[58]

As during the dictators' September 1937 and May 1938 encounters, the itinerary was densely packed, leaving little time for Hitler, Mussolini and their military staffs, including Cavallero and Keitel, to discuss strategy. The schedule reveals the real nature of these meetings as performative events designed to maintain the appearance of a close Axis alliance, projecting this image at home and to the Allies. Along these lines, *Il Popolo d'Italia* boasted that there were no other statesmen, an implicit reference to Churchill and Roosevelt, who could talk so openly with each other as the two dictators did.[59] As on previous occasions, the German choreography of the encounter placed the Italian and German delegations together on some occasions to project the image of a common stance by Italy and Germany, fighting alongside each other for a New Order.[60] Otherwise, the delegations remained separate.[61]

Two conclusions can be drawn from this arrangement. First, contrary to the popular notion that Mussolini and Hitler were friends, Hitler's feeling of superiority and Mussolini's sense of envy were hardly reconcilable. At the same time, Hitler had little option but to express his admiration for Mussolini, yet he wanted to maintain his credibility. Just a month previously, in a night-time monologue in front of his entourage, Hitler had praised the Duce and Fascism as a strategic model for Nazism, waxing lyrical, though with an element of desperation, about Italy's beauty, while acknowledging his dissatisfaction with the Italian monarchy.[62] Second, tensions about military strategy had increased, and the Italian delegation was not in a position to determine the itinerary. But the Italian and German leadership had to maintain the momentum of their alliance to avoid losing their credibility at home and suffering a heavy blow to their international reputation, especially vis-à-vis the British and the Americans. What is more, the choreography, with its minute planning of trips, required a great deal of manpower and technical equipment such as trains which could have been better used at the front. Efforts to maintain the display of unity and friendship thus took precedence over the military requirements of the war.[63]

Hitler and Mussolini flew to the eastern front, admiring German and Italian troops allegedly fighting harmoniously together. This was a powerful symbol of the purported technological and military superiority of the Axis, but could also be seen as loftily looking down on the soldiers who were doing the fighting. In reality, the German and especially the Italian troops on the eastern front relied to a large extent on horsepower.[64] On the flight back from Ukraine, where the dictators had inspected Italian troops, an annoyed Mussolini, who had endured lectures by a boastful Hitler in front of Italian troops, decided to put the Nazi leader in his place. After take-off, he announced that he wanted to pilot Hitler's huge Condor plane and soon took a seat in the cockpit next to the captain. As soon as the Duce took over the controls, the plane started shaking. The passengers, including Hitler, began to fear for their lives, as Mussolini, despite Fascist rhetoric about his aviation skills, was not a particularly competent pilot. In the event of a real emergency, the German pilot would have seized the controls, which reflected the nature of Italo-German relations. A photograph of Mussolini in the cockpit was published by *La Svastica*. To leave no one in doubt that Germany, not Italy, was the leading power, the picture showed Mussolini in the co-pilot's chair.[65]

A closer look at the ways in which the visit was reported in the press uncovers further tensions and rivalries. For instance, the Italian news agency Stefani proudly reported Mussolini's piloting Hitler's plane in order to emphasise the Duce's prestige. This suggests that he was after all the more senior statesman who literally held Hitler's fate in his hands.[66] Goebbels banned German newspapers from reprinting the Italian reports, as he thought that the image of Mussolini piloting Hitler's plane would upset German newspaper readers. Accordingly, the report in the *Völkischer Beobachter* was extremely curt.[67]

Mussolini and Hitler ate and chatted with their soldiers in a field mess. This suggested that they were brave military leaders who joined their troops at the frontline, unlike Roosevelt and Churchill, who had met in relatively peaceful surroundings off the coast of Newfoundland. The contradistinction between Mussolini and Hitler as representatives of the New Order at the height of Axis power and Churchill and Roosevelt as advocates of the nascent liberal-democratic alliance between Britain and the USA was made at the time by American newspapers. Thus, in its report of the Mussolini–Hitler meeting, the *New York Times*, relying on the official communiqué, interpreted the encounter as a response to the Churchill–Roosevelt meeting, a point also picked up by the Royal Institute of International Affairs, which regularly compiled a digest of the foreign press for the attention of the British government.[68]

For the Nazis too, the dictators' meeting served as a counterfoil to that of Churchill and Roosevelt. An SD report on the response of the German public towards the meeting picked up on the typical anti-Italian voices in Germany but lamented that 'only a part of the population puts the encounter of both statesmen with the meeting of Churchill and Roosevelt'. It can be concluded from this report that Nazi propaganda surrounding the meeting had not resonated particularly well with the German people.[69]

What went on beyond the official level revealed deep-seated tensions. During the dictators' visit to the eastern front, an Italian diplomat had overheard a German official calling Mussolini the *Gauleiter* of Italy. Mussolini was under no illusions and told Ciano that 'there are certain [gramophone] records in Germany'. On the first record, the sentimental Hitler waxed lyrical about Italy as a 'loyal ally'. On the second disc, which Hitler would play 'after the victories', Mussolini continued, 'Europe would be dominated by Germany'. If Germany's war did not succeed, Mussolini finished his conversation, Hitler would play the third disc and, in this scenario, 'our collaboration [would] be most useful'.[70]

Clearly, the Duce knew that, behind the facade of Axis propaganda, the relationship between Italy and Germany was above all based on strategic interest rather than on an ideological or personal bond. His frustration was palpable. He was presiding over a country in crisis, while Hitler's Germany was at the height of its power. Growing popular discontent undermined the Fascist regime. A particularly grave problem for ordinary Italians was the food supply after rationing had been introduced in 1941. The daily official ration in 1941 was a mere 1,010 calories, and many people, including Fascist party officials, resorted to the black market. The sense of the regime's having lost touch with the population was palpable, and the German leadership as well as the German public knew about the fragile state of the Fascist regime. An SD report of 6 November 1941, for instance, discerned growing tensions between the Fascist party and factions loyal to the king, alongside general war-weariness. Mussolini tried to shift the blame onto one of his favourite scapegoats: the bourgeoisie, whom he blamed for being selfish and unconcerned with the Italian nation.[71] Since the highly bureaucratic and inefficient Fascist party could not cope with this situation, the belligerent Duce, echoing his belief in the redemptive quality of war, insisted that more Italians had to die in the war against the Soviet Union.[72]

In the Soviet campaign in 1941–2, Italian troops achieved some military successes together with the much larger German troop contingents. Amidst such advances, relations between the Italian and German armies and their soldiers were often good, contrary to the subsequent myth that, on the eastern front and elsewhere, the Germans had always treated their Italian comrades badly. For the Italian army, such successes were bitterly needed after the many humiliating setbacks since Italy entered the war. Despite initial Italian successes on the eastern front, which cheered up Mussolini, the Italian involvement in the Barbarossa campaign was of secondary importance to Hitler.[73] For Hitler and the German military leadership Italy was part of a wider European crusade against Bolshevism, which included troops from countries such as Finland, Hungary and Romania. Hitler made no secret of this and, once again, only mentioned the Italian participation in the war in passing in a speech to a packed audience in the Sportpalast on 3 October 1941. Duly reported to Rome by the Italian ambassador, the Nazi leader praised instead the bravery of Romanian and Finnish troops. An SD report, picking up German views on the speech, registered that most radio listeners had interpreted Hitler's praise of the Finns and Romanians as a criticism of their Italian ally.[74]

Mussolini was irritated by Hitler's speech. His plan to raise Italy's reputation through its intervention in the Soviet Union had failed.[75] In late October 1941, he thus offered to send more troops to the eastern front to demonstrate Italy's willingness to sacrifice itself through war. Mussolini dismissed the reservations of his generals, thus highlighting his growing detachment from reality. At the same time, reflecting Mussolini's distrust of the Germans, work on the *Vallo del Littorio* continued. This prompted German protests because steel imported from Germany was being used for the construction works, rather than for producing guns. Construction works went on until Mussolini, in an even weaker position, ordered their cessation in October 1942.[76] To add to these tensions, Italy's dependency on German deliveries of food, oil and coal remained a bone of contention, even after the signing of the secret Italo-German economic accords in February 1941. German authorities in charge of these deliveries were divided over whether further shipments of raw materials, increasingly scarce given the massive extent of the German campaign, should be made to the unreliable Italians. Italian officials, in turn, grew impatient about growing German debts in the clearing process, which were putting the Italian economy under further pressure. Complaints about the insatiable German demands for Italian workers further reflected Italo-German tensions.[77] In this context, Mussolini sensed a chance to assert some power over Germany; he thus began to push for the withdrawal of Italian workers from Germany to reduce the German debts to Italy and to use this manpower for the war effort. In February 1943, Hitler permitted the workers' return after sharp disagreements within the Nazi leadership, many of whom wanted to continue to exploit Italian manpower for the German war effort. Still, by the autumn of 1943, about 120,000 Italian workers remained in the Reich.[78]

As the campaign in the Soviet Union reached its climax with the attack on Moscow, Hitler gave a speech in Munich on 8 November 1941, commemorating the 1923 Beer Hall Putsch. After railing against Churchill, a 'mad drinker', Hitler justified the German attack on the Soviet Union as a European crusade and, formulaically, highlighted Italy's and Germany's similar fates, insisting that the bond between him and Mussolini was unbreakable. This was a much-needed message of support for Mussolini.[79] Soon, on 18 November, the British started an offensive against the Axis powers in north Africa. Both Italy and Germany suffered heavy casualties. One of the Axis flagship projects, the campaign in north Africa, was thus at the brink of failure.[80]

As the harsh winter set in, the German campaign in Russia soon slowed down, and Germany's rapid advance suffered a setback outside the gates of Moscow. Ciano commented on it with schadenfreude.[81] The deployment of more Italian troop contingents on the eastern front, seen by the Germans as auxiliary troops, laid bare further tensions between pro-Axis factions within the Italian armed forces and those more sceptical ones who saw the king, not Mussolini, as the leading authority in Italy.[82] After the war, a German officer working for the US Army's Historical Division, subscribing to popular anti-Italian prejudices, declared that Italo-German military cooperation on the eastern front had been overshadowed by communication problems, Italian vanity and an Italian lack of comprehension of the 'sober German command voice'.[83]

IV

Hitler had realised that neither the Axis nor the Allies would be able to win the war soon, not least given the growing likelihood of an American intervention. Thus Germany organised the accession of a number of small states, including Romania, Finland, Denmark and Slovakia, to the Anti-Comintern Pact in November 1941 in order to keep the momentum going of the German-led crusade against Bolshevism and Britain. Italy's and Japan's roles as the Third Reich's principal allies were confirmed, but the fact that the meeting was in Berlin left no one in doubt that Germany, not Italy, was the leading Axis power.[84] After the Japanese attack on Pearl Harbor, Italy and Germany declared war on the United States.[85]

Here was the war on two fronts which Hitler had long expected. He believed that the USA would be so weakened by Pearl Harbor that the German attacks on American convoys in the Atlantic would soon lead to defeat for the United States before they had rearmed fully. Furthermore, for Hitler, this war would be the final reckoning with 'Judaeo-Bolshevism'.[86] Thus Hitler declared war against the United States on 11 December 1941, four days after the Japanese attack on Pearl Harbor. He announced a formal military alliance comprising Italy, Germany and Japan. But this was only directed against Britain and the USA, since, despite all anti-Communist rhetoric, the Japanese remained neutral in the war against the Soviet Union. As Hitler was announcing the German declaration of war against the USA in the Reichstag, Mussolini announced Italy's declaration from the balcony of the Palazzo Venezia. Although there had been no concerted cooperation of Italian and German foreign policy, the simultaneity of the dictators' speeches suggested their closed ranks. In Rome, applause was thin, as after all the military setbacks even supporters of the regime on the streets were beginning to lose faith, particularly now that Italy was at war with a country that had long been a destination for Italians seeking a better life.[87]

Soon after the declaration of war on the USA, Hitler took over the supreme command of the German army, as he blamed his generals for the slowing down of the Soviet campaign. Mussolini, though envious of the Nazi leader's ability to exercise his power over the army, greeted the news with admiration for the tough Hitler.[88] Hitler's belief in the 'Judaeo-Bolshevik' conspiracy behind Roosevelt made him push forward with his basic decision to kill Europe's Jews, taken in the victory euphoria of summer and autumn of 1941. The Nazis had been murdering Jews on a large scale since the beginning of the Barbarossa campaign, and Nazi coordination of mass killings was speeding up. Hitler firmly believed that war could not be won unless the Jews were annihilated. On 20 January 1942, the regime formalised the comprehensive policy of extermination at a conference in a villa on the Wannsee in Berlin. The Nazi war became ever more geared towards race and living space, pushing the alliance with Italy into the margins.[89]

As the Axis was running into more problems in north Africa, Germany's offensive in the East came to a standstill outside the gates of Moscow in December 1941. German propaganda targeted at Italian readers insisted that, unlike Napoleon in 1812, the Axis would soon win the war against Russia. An envious Mussolini welcomed news of German setbacks, but, because of belligerence and vanity, increased the number of Italian troops on the eastern front.[90] Rivalry and tension between both regimes and their leaders were not confined to military strategy alone, however. Italian authorities were unhappy about the effective stop to the resettlement of the South Tyrolese. Furthermore, in the Independent State of Croatia, set up in April 1941 and claimed by the Italians as being in their sphere of interest, conflict soon erupted between the Italians and the Germans, who had occupied the more prosperous northern part of the country. Mussolini even believed that the Germans wanted to bring Croatia under their control, further destroying what was left of Axis solidarity. The signing of a secret military convention of the Italian and German armed forces with the Japanese army and navy on 18 January 1942, delineating spheres of influence and operational zones for each power, did not solve these tensions.[91]

V

In the midst of the severe crisis of the regime and the party, Mussolini was keen to give the regime a new radical impetus. In late December 1941, he thus replaced the ineffective party secretary Adelchi Serena with Aldo Vidussoni, a young Fascist radical who had earned his spurs in the Spanish Civil War and the university militia. Mussolini expected Vidussoni to mobilise the Fascist party for the war effort. But this scheme failed, as German officials had expected.[92] As Italy's war fortunes deteriorated further, Mussolini, long suffering from an ulcer, battled with his health, which further undermined his reputation as a youthful and vigorous leader. Moreover, in late 1942, knowledge of his affair with Clara Petacci became widespread in Italy. The fact that Mussolini had effectively protected members of Petacci's family involved in corruption scandals from prosecution added further to the loss of his popular appeal.[93]

Hitler reacted to Fascist Italy's growing political and military problems with condescension and concern over whether Italy would turn into a greater liability, as the Axis was fighting on two fronts. For instance, in a long letter of 29 December 1941, Hitler pompously reinforced the sense of their shared fate: 'These are the greetings of a man whose personal and ethnic fate is so closely linked with yours and that of Fascist Italy.' But he could not hold back from giving Mussolini direct instructions about how to organise the supply lines for the north African front. While Hitler couched his instructions in flattery, praising the Duce as 'the creator of the New Roman State', the letter was effectively a dressing down. For Hitler, his relationship with Mussolini had lost its exclusive nature. Thus, unbeknownst to the Duce, the Führer was in a writing mood on that day and sent similarly warm letters to other allies such as Marshal Antonescu of Romania and the Hungarian leader, Admiral Horthy.[94]

Mussolini feigned that his regime had Italy under control and asked Hitler for a meeting.[95] According to Ciano, he had failed to realise that Hitler's respect for him was rapidly declining, although he also believed that Hitler had adopted a much friendlier tone towards him after the German setback outside the gates of Moscow.[96] Mussolini's insecurity and jealousy explain why he only penned a curt reply to Hitler in late January 1942, taking an imminent trip by Göring to Italy as an excuse not to engage fully with Hitler's letter.[97]

Amidst a German-led Axis recovery in the Mediterranean, Göring, like Ribbentrop keen to make a mark on the alliance with Italy, arrived in Rome on 28 January 1942 and was received by the Duce in the Palazzo Venezia. Hitler and Göring insisted on more Italian military involvement in north Africa. But the conversation soon turned to a discussion of Fascism's decline. Mussolini repeated his mantra that the Fascist party had the population under control. Because of German distrust Ciano found it difficult to obtain a copy of the German minutes of the meeting. Göring's pompous behaviour did not help improve the atmosphere.[98]

While Göring was living the high life in Italy (he and his entourage ran up the staggering bill of L124,692.30 for their stay, which included more than L100,000 at the luxurious Excelsior Hotel in Rome and in excess of L15,000 for a meal given in his honour),[99] Hitler waxed rhapsodically at Wolf's Lair about Mussolini. Reminiscing about his 1938 visit to Italy, he ranted against Italy's nobility and officer corps, describing one admiral as 'a real court toad' (*eine richtige Hofkröte*). Hitler droned on that the officers were decadent and had gourmet meals even on the frontline, while ordinary soldiers received little more than watery soup. In front of his entourage, Hitler pitied Mussolini, as the Duce had to respect the king and the court. These were condescending statements which further destroyed the Duce's reputation amongst the Nazi leadership. If only Fascism had come to power a year later, Hitler speculated, the Communists would have deposed the king, and Mussolini would have been able to push through his Fascist agenda without having to respect the monarchy. Here was a sentimental reaffirmation of Hitler's belief in Mussolini's personality, but his enthusiasm for the regime had long been on the wane, reflecting Italy's military misfortunes.[100]

Mussolini was increasingly deluded that Italy could still win the war. For Easter 1942, he received a huge amount of congratulatory letters: soldiers, civilians, men, women and children all wrote to the Duce to wish him a happy Easter and expressing their wish for an Italian victory, usually without referring to Mussolini's rapport with Hitler. For most correspondents, many of them members of one Fascist organisation or another, propaganda about the alliance with Germany had not taken root. Mussolini's secretariat received so many letters that they were placed in seven thick folders. A small detail is noteworthy about some of the letters from soldiers, as they were written on forms provided by the *Dopolavoro* branch of the armed forces (*Dopolavoro Forze Armate*) for letters home, embossed with a quotation by Mussolini. The quotation chosen suggested that the alliance with Germany was inevitable at a time of crisis: 'Whatever happens, Italy will march with Germany, side by side, until the end. Those who have tried to suppose something else forget that the alliance between Germany and Italy is not only one between two states or two armies, but between two peoples and two revolutions, destined to shape the century.' One correspondent who used this form was Ferruccio C. He wrote to the Duce on 29 March 1942, wishing him 'faith, hope, courage' until victory.[101] Even while Mussolini did not read these letters, news of this affirmative and adulatory correspondence, orchestrated by local Fascist groups, suggested to him that Italy could still win the war.

In the meantime, Rommel, bypassing the Italian *Comando supremo*, had begun an offensive in Libya, reconquering many territories previously lost in the war. His Africa Corps and the Italians subsequently retook Tobruk on 21 June 1942, as Roosevelt and Churchill were conferring at the White House. Tobruk was a sensational victory which made Mussolini hope that he would be able to enter Egypt triumphantly, as the ancient Romans had done. Ciano found the Duce 'in an excellent mood' (*di ottimo umore*). But then Hitler promoted Rommel to field marshal in a telegram in which Italian military contributions were not acknowledged. A furious and petty Mussolini soon promoted General Cavallero to field marshal as a quid pro quo.[102]

After Rommel's triumph at Tobruk, Mussolini flew to Libya in late June 1942. He piloted his own plane to show off his virility. A second plane with his chef and barber crashed. Just as the Duce arrived, the Axis offensive began to stall. Mussolini stayed in Libya for three weeks and toured war hospitals and Tobruk. Not once did he visit the frontline, however, which the German military attaché, Rintelen, who was travelling with the Duce, noted bitterly. On 20 July 1942, Mussolini returned to Rome, annoyed about the slow progress of the offensive. He left his luggage in Libya in the hope that he would soon return to celebrate an Italian victory. He did not collect his bags.[103]

VI

As the war on the eastern front met fierce resistance by the Soviets, German casualties were staggering. By March 1942, more than 1.1 million German soldiers, about a third of the forces deployed in 1941, had been killed or wounded or had gone missing in action on the eastern front.[104] These setbacks further intensified tensions with Italy, seen by Germans in positions of authority as an increasing liability. In this context, German and Italian diplomats suggested a meeting of the dictators to reinforce the Axis. But some officials remained sceptical of the outcome of another Mussolini–Hitler encounter. For instance, Alfieri wrote to Weizsäcker in late March 1942 that a meeting would not help resolve strategic tensions. Rather, it would be useful 'for generally psychological reasons'. Here was an astute diagnosis of the real significance of these wartime meetings. Their principal purpose was not the solution of political problems or the coordination of Italian and German military strategy, but rather the projection of a powerful image of the dictatorial couple determined to create a New Order.[105] An arrogant Ribbentrop instructed the German ambassador to impress on the Italians that such a meeting had to take place in Schloss Klessheim, the imposing Baroque palace near Salzburg, built in the eighteenth century for the Prince-Archbishops of Salzburg and lavishly spruced up for Mussolini and his retinue. This location would enable the Nazi leader to reach his military headquarters quickly. In reality, Hitler, exhausted from directing the war, needed a holiday at the Berghof.[106]

Mussolini, acting as the elder statesman, initially refused to obey Hitler's order to come to the Reich. But Hitler soon flattered Mussolini in what would be his final Reichstag speech. Here, he admitted that the German campaign in the East had suffered severe setbacks because of the harsh

Russian winter, allegedly even colder than in 1812 when Napoleon had failed to conquer Russia. Hitler called Mussolini 'also a uniquely blessed' man in their common battle against 'Judaeo-Bolshevism'. Eventually, the Duce agreed to the date proposed by the Germans.[107]

Before his departure to Salzburg, Mussolini assembled the prefects in Rome to discuss his concern that the regime was losing control because of the food crisis and news of defeats. Hitler's public admission that Germany would be unable to defeat the Soviet Union soon had shocked many Italians and added more pressure on the Fascist regime. In this gloomy atmosphere, the Duce left Rome with Ciano on 28 April 1942, once again without knowing the agenda for the meeting.[108]

Following the well-rehearsed routine of the dictators' encounters, Hitler welcomed Mussolini, Ciano and their delegation at a train station near Salzburg and then escorted them to Schloss Klessheim. Gone were the days of triumphant meetings involving the German and Italian publics. According to Goebbels the meeting was 'one of the regular contacts of the chiefs of government'. As usual, Hitler and Mussolini talked without an interpreter for two hours. Mussolini's summary of their conversation has survived in the Italian archives. He found this document so important that he kept it safe until his death, because the minutes suggest that he remained passive – implying that Hitler was the chief culprit for what had gone wrong in the war. Hitler gave the Duce an 'emotional and dramatic account' of the campaign in Russia.[109] After the tete-à-tete, the dictators were joined by their delegations, and Hitler delivered his usual tedious lecture. As on previous occasions, Mussolini had little to say, apart from conceding that Italy was in deep crisis, with a catastrophic food shortage. Emphases of unity overshadowed a discussion of serious strategic issues. Yet, for the first time in a conversation with the Duce, Hitler had to admit some German military shortcomings, as the campaign in the Soviet Union had stalled in the winter of 1941/2. Indeed, 'a courageous heart' was necessary.[110]

While the atmosphere at Klessheim was cordial, Ciano noted that 'the bonhomie of the Germans is always in an opposite relation to their fortune'. He also realised Hitler had 'much white hair', given the demands of the war on the Nazi leader.[111] In the meantime, Keitel and Cavallero held separate talks, similarly inconclusive. Like Mussolini and Hitler's meetings, such encounters served to maintain the facade of the Axis and yielded few substantive results.[112] Talks continued the following day at the

Berghof, scene of Mussolini's humiliation by Hitler a year previously. Hitler presented his plan to attack the British on Malta, but insisted that they had to be defeated in north Africa first. In the event, the Axis plan to invade Malta failed. According to the minutes compiled by the German army, Mussolini did not utter a single word. He got bored and looked at his watch. His passivity reflected Italy's weak position.[113]

Press coverage of the meeting was much more assertive than after the recent Mussolini–Hitler encounters and reinforced claims about the solidity of the Axis amidst mounting tensions.[114] Indeed, *The Times*, the voice of the British establishment emphasising tensions within the Axis alliance, commented on the official communiqué, couched in vague language about Italo-German friendship and 'brotherhood in arms', that this was Italian and German strategy to dispel rumours that Italy would quit the war.[115] German superiority over Italy was matched by a growing sense amongst Italians in positions of authority that Italy had to assert itself vis-à-vis the Axis partner. A reflection of these tensions was the continuing lack of an effective strategic and military coordination, in sharp contrast to the Allied Combined Chiefs of Staff, set up in 1942.[116]

VII

In late June 1942, a new German offensive started. Troops advanced towards the Caucasus, with its oil fields, the Crimea and Stalingrad. In September 1942, news of the progress at Stalingrad of the German Sixth Army, led by General Friedrich Paulus, reached Alfieri. He wrote a telegram to Hitler to congratulate him on the fall of Stalingrad. This telegram was premature, as the Soviets, who had massively increased armaments production and mobilised more than a million troops to take on the German Sixth Army, soon surrounded the Axis troops, including an Italian contingent.[117]

Nevertheless, the Axis offensive in the Soviet Union made some Fascist officials believe that the war could still be won. Particularly noteworthy in this regard was a report by Vidussoni on his visit to Germany and the eastern front in the autumn of 1942. In his report, written in the Fascist rhetoric of sacrifice on paper embossed with the Fascist slogan 'To Win' (*Vincere*) and addressed to Mussolini, Vidussoni boasted that the Italian troops on the eastern front had a great fighting spirit. He furthermore reported that the Jews were 'treated severely', which included their being shot. However, contrary to propaganda, relations of Italian soldiers with the Germans were not 'very cordial'. The highlight of Vidussoni's report was a visit to Hitler's headquarters. Hitler, Vidussoni declared, had praised the Italian contribution to the eastern campaign and forwarded his warmest wishes to the Duce. Undoubtedly, these were formulaic declarations. Vidussoni expressed admiration for the power of the Nazi party, which was much greater than that of the Fascist party. Mussolini must have welcomed the report, as it reinforced his delusion that the war could be won. But such hopes were unrealistic, given Italy's constitutional structure, with the king as head of state and the party being effectively merged with the organs of the state. Not least because of this fundamental difference between Fascist Italy and Nazi Germany, Mussolini was unable to fight a more effective war and mobilise society for the war effort.[118]

Although *spazio vitale* was beyond Italy's reach and Germany had come under increasing pressure on the eastern front, the display of unity continued, and the stream of German visitors to Rome and of Italian visitors to the Reich did not stop. Thus, on 11 October 1942, Mussolini received Himmler, one of the architects of the ongoing mass murder of the Jews. In a report to Ribbentrop, forwarded to Hitler, Himmler offered a detailed account of his audience with the Duce. He found the dictator in good health, reflecting the concern of leading Nazis over Mussolini's condition, itself a reflection of their belief that, without Mussolini, Italy would cease to be an ally. After some chitchat, the conversation turned to the Nazi campaign against the Jews. Fascist intellectuals such as Giovanni Preziosi had long been railing against the Jews, and the regime had recently intensified its anti-Semitic campaigns. (For example, in the September 1942 issue of his *Vita italiana*, Preziosi had advocated a complete solution of the 'Jewish problem'.) Himmler told Mussolini about the mass deportation of Jews from Germany and the occupied territories, but, in typically euphemistic Nazi language, did not mention the Nazi mass extermination of the Jews, insisting instead that the Jews were dying because they were not used to hard physical labour, although Himmler did admit that many Jews, including women and children, had been shot because of their alleged partisan activity. Mussolini completely agreed with this strategy.[119] In fact, he fully supported the Nazi extermination of the Jews. In May 1942, he had already ordered the purging of the Dalmatian coastlands, annexed by Italy, of Jews. Furthermore, in August 1942, he had agreed with the German request to intern the Croatian Jews in the Italian zone of occupation and hand them over to the Germans or the Ustaše, which meant deportation and death.[120]

From autumn 1942, the Allies were increasingly seizing the initiative. Some figures give an indication of scale. Even in 1941, the joint GDP of the Allied powers had been almost double of that of the Axis nations. Over 1942, this trend would continue, and by 1943 the disparity had grown to the extent that the Allies' joint GDP was two and a half times that of the Axis countries. In 1941, the combined forces of the Axis and the Allies (including the USA) had comprised around twelve million men each. Yet, by 1942, not least because of the massive mobilisation of the Red Army, the Allied armies had more than nineteen million men under arms compared to the fifteen million soldiers fighting for the Axis. The difference between the Axis and Allied forces further increased. Thus, by 1943, the Allies had mobilised more than twenty-five million men, compared to just under seventeen million for the Axis forces. Given these economic factors, it was extremely challenging for the Axis to win the war, and it is tempting to argue, without advocating a deterministic economic interpretation, that Mussolini and Hitler were increasingly biting off more than they could chew.[121]

Sensing Mussolini's declining political fortunes, Hitler became even more sentimental: anything other than lending moral support to and maintaining his bond with the Duce would have further undermined the Axis.[122] In his usual letter on the occasion of the anniversary of the March on Rome in October 1942, Hitler expressed his 'insoluble connection with you and the connection between the National Socialist movement and the Fascist [one]'. Hitler insisted that he had been a keen admirer and follower of Mussolini since the early 1920s and reiterated his belief that 'two men and two revolutions determine the face of the new era', insisting that the only difference between them was 'the circumstances of the races formed by blood and history and the geopolitically determined living spaces'. Despite all their differences and diverse strategic spheres of interest, Hitler declared that the allegedly parallel history of Italy and Germany would inevitably bring both countries together, led 'by the friendship of the two men which will one day be a historic one'. Here, Hitler reiterated his belief in the importance of his relationship with Mussolini, and wanted to give Mussolini the feeling of still being his equal, but in reality, as we have seen, the Duce had long lost momentum in Italy and in his rapport with Hitler. Still, the Nazi leader wanted to see Mussolini in Italy, but because of the war such a visit would be impossible, he warned, suggesting instead a meeting at the Brenner Pass in November. Hitler's implicit order to the Duce to meet him was yet another articulation of his superiority.[123]

Pressure on the Axis increased. On 23 October 1942, just two days after Hitler had sent off his letter to Mussolini, the British, led by Bernard Montgomery, launched an attack on Rommel's forces, leading to their victory at El Alamein. Rommel's forces had to retreat with heavy losses of 30,000 men. But this was not all: a few weeks later, the Allies landed with more than 60,000 men in French North Africa, which was a major turning point in the campaign in north Africa.[124]

As the Allies seized the initiative, they pushed back the Axis and raised hopes amongst the British government that Italy would soon be defeated. Churchill had already insisted in December 1941 that 'the heat should be turned on Italy'. Accordingly, British area bombing of Italy began in earnest in late 1942 after earlier raids on a smaller scale (in 1940 and 1941, there had only been 119 raids altogether on Italy; and from January until September 1942, there had only been 1 raid on civilians, in the Ligurian town of Savona, with 34 raids on harbours and bases of the Italian Royal Air Force).[125] The Italian Royal Air Force had failed to establish sufficient air defences, and the regime had not prepared enough welfare and civil defence services. Therefore, the effect of the large-scale bombings of late 1942 were devastating, including six area raids on Genoa, seven on Turin, and one against Milan, the main cities in Italy's industrial triangle. The bombings prompted even more popular discontent and further exposed the inefficiency of the regime.[126]

Some of the leaflets dropped by the Allies on towns directly blamed Mussolini's alliance with Hitler for the misery of the Italian population under Allied bombing. These leaflets came to the attention of the German Foreign Ministry, as German consuls forwarded them, reflecting their concern over a lack of Italian public support for the alliance with Germany. During an October 1942 raid on Genoa, for instance, the British dropped a leaflet with a cartoon showing Mussolini giving a speech on the balcony of the Palazzo Venezia to Italian troops marching towards 'Russia, Libya and Death'. In the cartoon, Mussolini is depicted as a marionette of Hitler, who is pulling the strings, a perceptive if exaggerated depiction of the nature of the Mussolini–Hitler rapport. Another leaflet, in a clever twist, claimed that in the Nazi New Order, the Italians would be on the bottom rung and receive lower rations than almost any other people in Europe. Italians were dying merely 'for the glory of Mussolini and the benefit of the Reich'. In short, according to the leaflet, an Allied victory was imminent, and ordinary Italians would suffer most.[127]

Tensions and the increasingly difficult military situation of both countries, with Germany also the subject of severe area bombings by the Allies, stood in the way of another encounter between the two dictators. Rumours of secret peace negotiations between the Italians and the Allies in Lisbon did not improve tensions, although leading Nazis such as Ribbentrop dismissed such rumours as concerted Anglo-American efforts to undermine the alliance with Italy. From 1942, there were indeed some Italian attempts, both from military leaders such as Badoglio and from Fascist leaders such as Grandi, then serving as minister of justice, to sound out the British for a separate peace. Yet, the British government, especially Foreign Secretary Anthony Eden, committed to Italy's unconditional surrender, did not take these overtures seriously, not least because the British hoped that Fascism would collapse from within.[128]

While Hitler and the Nazi regime were still firmly in control of German society, not least because of their use of a fine balance between various forms of direct and indirect coercion on the one hand and the maintaining of a superficial consensus on the other, the power of Mussolini and the bureaucratically paralysed Fascist party began to wane further. Declining support for the regime, growing tensions within the Italian ruling elites, and military failure seemed to seal Mussolini's fate. As pressure mounted on Mussolini's regime, the role of Victor Emmanuel III became more important as a guarantor of the Italian state. The Vatican, leading industrialists and the monarchy became increasingly receptive to the idea of ending Italy's involvement in the war. But this was a gradual process.[129]

In November 1942 Ciano travelled to Germany, just after the Allied landing in French North Africa, which had made an Allied invasion of Sicily ever more likely. Hitler received Ciano, taking the place of the sick and tired Mussolini, in his office in the Nazi party headquarters, adorned with a Mussolini bust. Ciano stated on several occasions during the talks that Mussolini had been unable to come, as his presence at the Italian headquarters was indispensable, a variation of Hitler's excuse to order Mussolini to come to Salzburg in April 1942. The meeting was held at Hitler's request to discuss the position of France together with Laval, just days after Mussolini had told the German ambassador that peace with the Soviet Union and a settlement with France had to be reached soon. To avoid an Allied landing on the coast of southern France, the Germans invaded Vichy France on 11 November 1942. Italy was finally able to occupy Corsica and Savoy.[130]

Yet, at the end of 1942, it was widely known that Italy was set to lose the war, as the Allies were encircling the Axis troops from both sides in north Africa and dropping more and more bombs on Italy and Germany. This view became clear in Bismarck's memorandum to the German Foreign Ministry. Bismarck had spoken with a high-ranking Italian political informer who preferred to remain anonymous. According to the informer, all sections of Italian society believed in an Axis defeat. The Vatican, he added, was hoping for an Anglo-American victory, while fearing a Bolshevik triumph. Still, the informer insisted, the king was supporting the Duce, although it remained unclear whether the court would continue to back Mussolini if the military situation deteriorated further. Strikingly, as a reminder to the Germans about the military alliance with Italy, the informer ominously predicted that Germany would lose the war if Italy were defeated.[131]

Connected to the likelihood of an Italian defeat, Mussolini's charismatic authority was on the wane, as was his health. In this situation, the Duce, suffering from stomach pain, resorted to his usual rhetoric about renewing the radical dynamism of Fascism. In a speech on 3 December 1942 to the new directorate of the Fascist party, he spoke quite openly about Italy's critical situation and likened it to the Matteotti crisis. But Mussolini's historical references and his appeals to unity failed to correct the impression that his regime had not succeeded in remaking Italians into a class of warriors.[132] Nevertheless, Goebbels claimed in his diary that he was impressed by Mussolini's candid speech, hoping desperately for more dynamic Italian fighting. After reading SD reports on the popular reception of Mussolini's speech in Germany, he concluded that the German people were still respecting the Duce, while continuing to be sceptical of the achievements of the Italian army. Here was a typical internalisation of the view of Mussolini as the indispensable link of the Axis.[133]

In this atmosphere of Italian war-weariness and growing German doubts about the reliability of its principal ally, Hitler more or less ordered Mussolini to his East Prussian headquarters. In December 1942, the sick Duce, who was unwilling to be humiliated by Hitler, sent Ciano, tasked with pressing the Germans to end the war with the Soviet Union in order to free up troops for the Balkans and north Africa. Ciano claimed that Hitler had not really wanted to enter 'into general political discussions' with the Duce. This was the clearest sign so far that the relationship between Mussolini and Hitler was fraught. Mussolini's idea of a peace with the Soviet Union was unrealistic, given German mass atrocities there and the centrality of the project of living space and racial conquest for the Nazis. Mussolini's frantic quest for a separate peace in the East suggests that, for Italy, the war against the Soviet Union had primarily been instrumental, rather than ideological, notwithstanding Italian atrocities against Soviet citizens. The atmosphere at Hitler's headquarters was depressing, and Ciano, used to luxury, was bothered by 'the sadness of this humid forest and the boredom of collective life in the Command barracks', not to mention 'the smell of cooking, of uniforms and of boots'.[134]

On the verge of military defeat, especially with regard to the tense situation at Stalingrad and mounting pressure on the Italian Eighth Army at the river Don, Italo-German talks were held for the first time in an openly hostile atmosphere. Thus, the Italian military delegation blamed poor German planning for the massive attack on the Eighth Army, while the German military delegation openly accused the Italians of undermining the war effort by deserting to the Soviets, thereby endangering the remaining German troops at Stalingrad. Hitler gave instructions directly to the Italian delegation. He told Ciano to ask the Duce to issue a decree that Italian soldiers must not withdraw. This was an order to a subordinate.[135] The sense of Italian subordination to the German effort was palpable also amongst ordinary Italian soldiers, according to popular opinion reports compiled by the political police. Typical was a report of 23 February 1943 which emphasised that the Italian troops in north Africa and Russia were sacrificing themselves 'to cover the German retreat'.[136]

Soon after the conclusion of the Ciano–Hitler talks, the Axis suffered more defeats. Tripoli, symbol of Italian colonialism, under both the Liberal and the Fascist states, was about to fall. This prompted Bottai to speculate in January 1943 that Mussolini was about to reach one of his goals. When he had been a leading socialist before the First World War, Mussolini had protested against Prime Minister Giovanni Giolitti's push into Libya in 1911. The bitterly sarcastic Bottai believed that Mussolini's 1911 slogan 'Away from Libya' (*Via della Libia*) was now being confirmed. Tripoli eventually fell on 23 January 1943.[137] And in early February, the German Sixth Army under General Paulus finally surrendered to the Soviets, although Hitler had expressly forbidden a retreat or a surrender. Paulus went into Soviet captivity together with fewer than 100,000 surviving German soldiers.[138]

Italy and Germany reacted differently to military disaster, having realised that the war could not be won soon. In Germany, the Nazis intensified the fighting, with Goebbels pronouncing 'total war' in February 1943. This war would have to be fought until total victory, and Germany must not surrender at any cost. Nazi repression against those deemed community aliens or social outsiders increased drastically. In Italy, the Fascist regime simply began to disintegrate further amidst this string of defeats, increased Allied bombings and popular discontent; by contrast, the ever more repressive Nazi regime, despite growing popular discontent in Germany too, remained in control of society. The Fiat strikes in Turin of March and April 1943, the first large-scale industrial action in Axis Europe, revealed that the Fascist regime had lost control over the population.[139] Whether or not the strikes really threatened the regime is a moot point. What matters in our context is that, for Hitler, the fact that the Fascist regime had failed to repress the strikes further revealed Mussolini's weakness.[140]

In this critical situation, Mussolini, in order to give his regime a radical impetus, stepped up his aggressive rhetoric and sacked the chief of police, Carmine Senise, and party secretary Vidussoni. But these were desperate gestures.[141] Furthermore, in order to maintain the impression of his infallibility and to project an image of a determined, steely Duce, Mussolini replaced Cavallero with Vittorio Ambrosio as chief of the general staff. On 6 February 1943, he dismissed prominent politicians deemed insufficiently pro-German, including Bottai, Grandi and Ciano, from the cabinet in another desperate act. German propaganda could do little but represent the reshuffle as a 'concentration of forces', as for example in *Rom Berlin Tokio*, the flagship journal of Axis propaganda, published in German, Italian and Japanese.[142] Ciano, long disliked by Hitler, was appointed ambassador to the Holy See. This appointment was seen as a powerful overture to peace negotiations with the Allies. For Hitler and Goebbels, the cabinet reshuffle, like the previous replacements of ambassadors that had been a central indicator of the vicissitudes of Italian–German relations, briefly gave them a false sense of security that Mussolini had taken the reins again.[143]

Nevertheless, as Fascist Italy was on the verge of defeat and under increasing domestic pressure, leading Nazis began to voice their hostile views on Mussolini more openly. Such views had been more or less silenced in the wake of Hitler's February 1941 order banning statements that could offend the Duce. Increasingly, Nazi leaders viewed the sick Mussolini as a liability. For instance, Goebbels threatened in his diary that if Italy negotiated a separate armistice with the Allies, Mussolini would not be able to expect any mercy. The concern that Italy would stop being a German ally without Mussolini was palpable, fuelled by more self-confident Italian demands to repatriate the workers based in Germany for the Italian war effort.[144]

VIII

Mussolini and Hitler had not seen each other since April 1942. In contrast, Roosevelt and Churchill met again at Casablanca in January 1943 where they discussed their plan to fight Germany until its unconditional surrender, although, in reality, the British and the Americans did not always agree on strategy. Even the acerbic Goebbels grudgingly acknowledged the tremendously powerful impact of the Roosevelt–Churchill meeting on international opinion.[145] Because of the lack of meetings amidst military setbacks, the Mussolini–Hitler relationship had lost most of its appeal. In March 1943, Bismarck offered an evaluation of the dictatorial relationship that squarely blamed Mussolini for its demise:

> He has also avoided in the past raising questions of principle during the various encounters with Hitler, and it is unlikely that he does it now. Hitler does not think and talk about anything but military matters, and this is not a favourable stage for Mussolini. One cannot say about Hitler that he has not made and [does not still make] mistakes, but he has ended up becoming competent in military matters. Mussolini has remained an amateur.[146]

Apart from his lack of expertise in military matters, the real reason for Mussolini's passivity at his meetings with Hitler was Italy's weak position and Hitler's unbound self-confidence, bordering on arrogance.[147]

While there were reassurances that Italy would remain a loyal ally, the wording of these statements is worth investigating more closely. For example, when Giuseppe Bastianini, the new undersecretary of state in the Foreign Ministry, reassured Ribbentrop in Rome in early March 1943 that Italy would continue its alliance with Germany, he implied that Italy was ready to consider other options. The Italian side also broached the idea of another Duce–Führer meeting, this time in a larger round with other Axis representatives as counter-propaganda to the Casablanca conference. Hitler refused, as such a meeting would have undermined the years of unity and friendship propaganda.[148]

As the tide turned further against the Axis, Hitler continued to indulge in historic reminiscences of the origins of Nazism in a letter to Mussolini on 16 February 1943, which Ribbentrop had annotated as 'private'. Hitler started on a personal note, voicing his concern over the Duce's poor health, 'because states are after all ruled and therefore preserved by men and not the other way round'. He warned the Duce that a repeat of 1918, when Germany had allegedly been stabbed in the back by Judaeo-Bolshevism, must be avoided at any cost. Nazi Germany would mobilise everyone in Germany for total war. Hitler pressed Mussolini to do the same in Italy to avoid the 'destruction and . . . annihilation' of 'European culture'. Hitler wanted to meet the Duce as soon as possible in Klessheim and, reflecting his superiority, did not even offer to come to Italy.[149] Mussolini reassured the Nazi leader that Italy was prepared to make further sacrifices, adopting typical Fascist rhetoric. Striking a personal chord, he thanked Hitler for his kind remarks about his health problems, but insisted that these ailments were minor ones, compared to the diseases caused by the plutocrats and the Jews. In typical fashion, having internalised the notion of his encounters with Hitler, he agreed that the military situation should be discussed at a personal meeting.[150]

Alongside these superficially friendly exchanges, the German government took a more aggressive stance towards its Italian ally, laying the foundations for a systematic scapegoating of Italy for Germany's military misfortunes. More precisely, here developed the myth that Germany's bailing out of Italy in the Mediterranean had used up German resources and manpower and therefore prevented a swift German victory over the Soviet Union in 1941. Thus Ribbentrop lamented to Alfieri on 8 March 1943 that the Italian officer corps, not obedient to the Duce, was to blame for Italy's poor military performance and, by extension, for the declining military fortunes of the Axis alliance.[151]

On the surface, the dictators' conferences continued to keep the unity and friendship propaganda going. Once again, the location of the summit confirmed Germany's superiority, and it is striking that Hitler had not been to Italy since it had lost momentum in the war. The gathering, symbolically scheduled for 24 March 1943, the day after the anniversary of the foundation of the *Fasci di combattimento*, had to be rescheduled at Mussolini's request because of the Anglo-American offensive in Tunisia.[152] A German diplomat rightly predicted that, unlike in the run-up to their previous reunions, Mussolini would not raise any principled questions this time, given Italy's profound military and political crisis.[153]

As with the previous wartime meetings of Mussolini and Hitler, except for their visit to the eastern front, this meeting was held in a more or less clandestine atmosphere, with no propagandistic announcements. Yet the German organisers maintained the display of friendship and unity. Observers were startled by Mussolini's and Hitler's poor physique. Both looked exhausted. In fact, Mussolini was so unwell that he was accompanied by his doctor and had to extend his stay at Klessheim by a day to rest.[154]

Reflecting Hitler's belief in Mussolini's irreplaceability, Hitler instructed his physician, Dr Theo Morell, to examine Mussolini for his ulcer, suggesting that the Duce's Italian doctors were incompetent. Goebbels, well informed about Hitler's movements, recorded in his diary that the atmosphere was good and that Hitler had told Mussolini 'everything . . . [t]hat he had intended to'.[155] Himmler should help the Duce establish special divisions to help suppress any dissent within Italy. Comprising militia members who had fought in the Soviet Union, these 'M' divisions were supposed to become the Italian equivalent to the SS. But even these plans failed to stabilise Mussolini's regime.[156]

In order to project the image that Italian–German relations were as stable as ever before, the scenery at Schloss Klessheim was even more imposing than in 1942. The palace had been redecorated ostentatiously with tapestries, marble floors and expensive carpets. SS guards of honour stood at every door and clicked their heels when members of the delegation walked through.[157] No direct record exists of the Mussolini–Hitler conversations. In his account of the Klessheim meeting, F.W. Deakin drew upon interviews with Bastianini and the latter's post-war memoirs. But these sources were overshadowed by Bastianini's post-war attempt to dissociate himself from the alliance with the Nazis.[158] Instead, evidence has survived from British intelligence intercepts of telegrams from the Japanese chargé d'affaires in Rome to Tokyo. According to these intercepts, Mussolini and Hitler 'held five conversations alone, lasting ten hours. They did not follow any formal programme.' The high number of personal conversations was unusual, owing to Italy's military crisis and the realisation on the part of both leaders that their fate was inextricably linked with each other. Indeed, the Japanese diplomat stated: 'For Italy there is no road other than that of fighting to the end along with Germany.'[159]

Even if the sickly Mussolini broached the subject of peace negotiations with the Soviet Union – the only way, he believed, to end the war on multiple fronts – he did not have the power openly to confront Hitler. Bastianini had developed a plan for a front of European states in a New Order, which, he hoped, would persuade Hitler to agree to peace negotiations with the Soviets. This plan would release Italian forces to take on the British and Americans in the Mediterranean. With this project, Bastianini hoped to unite the Axis states such as Bulgaria and Hungary behind Italy, after all the first Fascist nation, which could, amidst a likely defeat, at least claim authorship and thereby leadership of the New Order. In reality, the New Order, strongly rivalled by the Atlantic Charter and the Allies' Casablanca resolution to fight until the Axis's unconditional surrender, had long been a favourite subject of Fascist and Nazi intellectuals. Despite some basic agreement about the need to create a new geopolitical structure for Europe, the idea of the New Order failed to ease tensions between Italy and Germany. Hitler subsequently ridiculed Bastianini's ideas as 'completely flimsy' (*stinkfaul*) and yet another piece of evidence of Italian defeatism.[160]

Despite the tensions, the usual joint communiqué highlighted the 'total agreement of the Axis in the conduct of war'. Goebbels had edited the text, as he believed that the communiqués issued after the previous Hitler–Mussolini meetings had been too formulaic. Moreover, the Italian government had disagreed with the wording. At Bastianini's behest, the communiqué was toned down, as a forceful declaration about the New

Order was unlikely to impress Italian audiences living the war experience.[161] Furthermore, Allied observers highlighted the defensive tone of the communiqué and emphasised the waning fortunes of the Italian–German alliance. The British Royal Institute of International Affairs, in its digest of the Axis press, went even further and diagnosed a number of strategic dissonances between Italy and Germany over the future shape of Europe. The digest cited the disputes over the origins of the New Order: Italy as the older regime of the two claimed to have invented it.[162]

In a self-fulfilling prophecy, the Reich propaganda offices claimed that the German people had been impressed by Mussolini's visit. Even anti-Italian sentiment was allegedly on the wane. SD reports echoed their authors' anti-Italian attitudes: many Germans had been worried about the unusual length of the summit, as, to them, this reflected the grave military situation. The SD also cited typical anti-Italian views, including those who complained about the 'utter failure of the Axis partner'. Others were quoted as saying: 'The Führer once again had to give a dressing down to the Duce.'[163]

Despite increasing tensions, both regimes had little choice but to maintain the outward appearance of the Axis, for example with the usual telegram exchange between the king, Mussolini and Hitler on the latter's birthday.[164] In reality, the Mussolini–Hitler rapport had lost its special nature for the Nazi leader in the light of Italy's string of defeats, as he had also received leaders of other Axis countries including Hungary and Romania, reflecting German concerns about maintaining its military alliances.[165]

IX

Mussolini, in serious pain because of his stomach problems, gave an energetic speech on 5 May 1943, the anniversary of his announcement of victory over Ethiopia, from the balcony of the Palazzo Venezia and insisted that 'the bloody sacrifices of these hard times will be compensated by victory'. After hearing about the Duce's speech peppered with the usual rhetoric about the transformative quality of war, Goebbels, subscribing to his own propaganda, believed that the meeting with Hitler had reinvigorated Mussolini.[166] But Goebbels' hopes for a military recovery were soon dashed, as the crucial harbours of Tunis and Bizerta fell a few days later.

Even the deployment of German aeroplanes to help the Italians in north Africa, subject of a desperate plea by Mussolini in a telegram to Hitler on 30 April, failed to improve Italy's military situation.[167] The Axis's African adventure was over with the surrender on 13 May 1943. No fewer than 275,000 German and Italian soldiers were taken prisoner of war by the Allies. An Allied invasion of southern Italy became more and more likely. In this context, the Vatican sounded out the king, asking him to suggest a separate peace to Mussolini. The Duce refused, since peace was the total contradiction of Fascism.[168]

As the Fascist regime disintegrated, Italo-German relations became even more strained. For instance, on 18 May 1943, Ribbentrop instructed the German embassy to investigate the rumour that German soldiers had been banned from wearing their uniforms in Rome.[169] In fact, German military planning for the eventuality of a putsch against Mussolini had already begun after the fall of Tunis in mid-May, with Rommel being put in charge of an army group.[170]

Attempts to keep the momentum of the Axis going in public were overshadowed by hostility. An examination of Hitler's letter to Mussolini of 19 May 1943 reveals that the days of their overtly friendly correspondence, even at times of tension, were over. In the letter, Hitler ranted against the *Comando supremo*, 'which completely ignores the situation . . . now'. While Hitler finished his letter with the usual 'most cordial greetings', his barely disguised anger at the Italian generals was palpable. For Hitler, Mussolini was not the chief responsible for the military chaos. Instead, Hitler blamed the officer corps and the monarchy. Hitler's letter was so aggressive that Rintelen, who had been instructed to deliver it to the Duce, asked Berlin for confirmation whether he should really hand it over.[171]

Mussolini knew that his fate was closely linked to the military situation. Thus, in early July 1943, anticipating increasing political pressure and a possible attack on the Duce, a special police office attached to the Presidency of the Council of Ministers issued a secret memorandum with detailed plans on reinforcing the security arrangements for both Mussolini's office in the Palazzo Venezia and his private residence in the Villa Torlonia.[172] As if there were not enough mounting pressure on the Fascist regime, the Allied invasion of Sicily exposed most dramatically that the days of Fascist rule over Italy and Europe were numbered. On the night of 9 July, the Allies landed in Sicily with 1,800 artillery guns, 600 tanks and 181,000 men. The 28,000 German and 175,000 Italian soldiers, alongside 57,000 support troops, could do little to halt the Allied advance. Hitler himself ordered that the German army must take over military leadership in Sicily which increased tensions within the Italian–German alliance. The Allied landing prompted desperate Italian requests for further German military assistance. Hitler was furious and accused the Italian army's leadership of cowardice and disloyalty. While Hitler promised Mussolini that he would deploy further German troops to the island, he bluntly told him that the war would be lost if Italian forces did not fight harder. On 17 August, the Allies reached the Strait of Messina and were in easy reach of the Italian mainland and the European continent.[173]

Italy's imminent defeat was not surprising. The Fascist regime, with its stick-and-carrot policy of coercion and consensus, had never managed fully to mobilise the population and the economy for a long conflict. A good illustration of this point can be gleaned from armaments production. For instance, between 1940 and 1943, Italy produced a mere 11,000 aeroplanes, compared to the 25,000 produced in Germany, 26,000 in Britain, 35,000 in the Soviet Union and 86,000 in the United States in the year 1943 alone. In this regard, it is also striking that the Italian state did not fully mobilise men to fight in the armed forces. In 1940–3, there were approximately 4.5 million troops out of a population of 43 million Italians compared to the 5.2 million troops that had been mobilised in 1915–18 out of a total population of 36 million Italians.[174]

In the end, the German reinforcements were not sent, reflecting the concerns of Hitler and General Field Marshal Albert Kesselring, in charge of German troops in Italy (*Oberbefehlshaber Süd beim italienischen Oberkommando*), that the Allies would soon land on the peninsula itself. Furthermore, German troops were heavily engaged in the other war theatres. The days of friendship were long gone.[175]

Mussolini's rule in Italy was reaching its end. As the Allies increased the bombing campaign against Italy even further, Fascist propaganda drew a gloomy picture. *Il Popolo d'Italia* warned on its title page on 25 July 1943 that 'the English intend to exterminate the Italians'.[176] But such stories had no impact on most Italians, as it was too late to avert the Allied advance. Neither Mussolini nor the editors in charge could have foreseen that this would be the final edition of the Fascist flagship newspaper, as events dramatically unfolded.

As the military situation became desperate, leading Fascists had sounded out the king about dismissing Mussolini from his office as prime minister. Despite the fact that the private archives of the House of Savoy are still not open to historians, the diaries of Paolo Puntoni, the monarch's army adjutant, published after the war, suggest that the king had long been unwilling to sack the Duce. Victor Emmanuel's main concern was to safeguard the monarchy and to exit the war, but he did not seek to restore the Liberal state.[177] It is likely that the king only withdrew his support from Mussolini, even though an alternative cabinet led by Marshal Badoglio was waiting in the wings, when pressure increased on the Duce from within the Fascist elite.[178] Because of this mounting pressure Mussolini had little choice but to convene the Fascist Grand Council for the first time since 1939. Political and military leaders faced a stark dilemma. It was one thing to replace the Duce, but such a move and an Italian armistice with the Allies would lead to severe German reprisals.[179]

Before the meeting of the Grand Council, scheduled for 24 July 1943, Mussolini had to see Hitler. With a day's notice, as Alfieri later remembered, a meeting was set up for 19 July, leaving hardly any time for preparations. Alfieri himself had to rush from Berlin to upper Italy in a plane borrowed from the Italian air attaché.[180] The Nazi leader was not in the best of moods, as the German offensive against the Soviets near Kursk had failed after what was one of the largest tank battles of the war.[181] At Hitler's behest, the German military leadership had prepared for the eventuality of Fascism's downfall. Initially designed as operations to repel the Allies on the new southern front, these scenarios would allow the Germans to act decisively in the event.[182]

That Hitler came to Italy – the first time he had done so since his brief trip to Florence at the beginning of the disastrous Italian campaign in Greece – gave Mussolini prestige. One detail is noteworthy about the welcoming ceremony for Hitler at Treviso airport. Hitler's plane arrived some minutes early and therefore flew a holding pattern to ensure a punctual landing. Even during a severe crisis, diplomatic protocol had to be maintained. When the Italian delegation queried the German delegation about this, Ambassador Mackensen quipped that the plane was scheduled to land at nine o'clock, an implicit reminder of German reliability and efficiency versus Italian sloppiness.[183]

From Treviso, the delegations travelled by train to Belluno, making their final journey in the hot summer weather by car to the Villa Gaggia near San Fermo (not Feltre, as some accounts wrongly claim), a location selected for its beauty, but above all for its isolation and its safety from Allied air raids. Mussolini later summarised the atmosphere of the meeting in his self-exculpatory autobiographical notes. He complained that the diplomats, obsessed with protocol, had unnecessarily extended the meeting, which could have easily been held at Treviso airport. This suggests that Mussolini had lost control over his diplomats.[184]

Mussolini, Ambrosio and Bastianini were outnumbered by Hitler and his entourage, which included diplomats and military officials. This created an intimidating atmosphere. According to the German minutes, Hitler almost immediately launched into a lengthy monologue about the war, 'a struggle fought for the destiny of Europe'. Mussolini was sitting passively and cross-legged in an armchair, as Hitler embarked on a lecture about war strategy and the need for an 'energetic crackdown' on the home front. Finally, Hitler lamented: 'What has now happened in Sicily must not repeat itself!' He once again blamed poor Italian leadership for the invasion and reminded the Italian delegation that they had received considerable German support. He repeated that Italian soldiers must fight harder; otherwise, no more German troops would be deployed to Sicily. Mussolini did not have the courage to confront Hitler with his plans for a separate peace with the Soviet Union. This was a missed opportunity.[185] During Hitler's monologue, a messenger entered the conference room and delivered a note to Mussolini: Rome was being bombed by the Allies, a sensational triumph for them and a huge defeat for the Italian regime, not least for Mussolini, who had legitimised his rule with the cult of *romanità*.[186] A tactless Hitler continued with his lecture on the superiority of the German army as if nothing had happened. Protocol dictated lunch, which finally stopped Hitler's tirades. Alfieri claims in his post-war memoirs, putting all blame on Mussolini, that he and Bastianini had harangued the Duce to confront Hitler, a proposition which the exhausted Mussolini had rejected.[187]

As Mussolini and Hitler were conferring in San Fermo, Pope Pius XII visited the working-class San Lorenzo area of Rome, which had been bombed particularly heavily. His appearance, emphasised by tumultuous applause, revealed that Fascism had lost its power, marked further by the absent Duce. Initially, the delegations did not want to issue a communiqué, but Goebbels insisted that such a text would add some much-needed prestige to Mussolini. In the end, the Germans released a one-line communiqué, saying that Hitler and Mussolini had met in upper Italy to discuss the military situation. The Italian Ministry of Popular Culture issued a slightly longer statement about the meeting, and instructed editors at the same time to avoid reports of the pope's visit to the bombed areas of Rome.[188]

X

After his return from northern Italy, it seemed to be business as usual for Mussolini. He duly reported to the king on 22 July 1943. The monarch allegedly told him that he should resign: this is unlikely, though, as the king had always backed Mussolini, despite Italy's string of military defeats. But pressure from within the Fascist leadership would soon prove decisive for the Duce's position. Fascist grandees, above all Grandi, Bottai and Ciano, had been planning his removal from office, and had sounded out the king before the Fascist Grand Council met. Grandi had tabled a motion appealing to national unity and effectively calling for Mussolini's removal. Before the meeting, the German military attaché had reported to Berlin that most Italians had lost hope in an Italian victory. At the Grand Council meeting, Rintelen had anticipated, leading Fascists would be pushing for Mussolini to take a more decisive role. His prognosis could not have been more inaccurate.[189]

On the hot afternoon of 24 July, the Grand Council met in the Palazzo Venezia's Parrot Room (*Sala del Pappagallo*). The meeting began earlier than usual, as Mussolini expected a long discussion. Mussolini began with a lengthy speech in which he criticised the army's leaders for letting him down. Generals Emilio De Bono and Cesare Maria De Vecchi, two of the *quadrumviri* of Fascism's March on Rome, angrily defended the army against these accusations. In this heated atmosphere, Grandi blamed Mussolini's proximity to Hitler as a key reason for Italy's abysmal situation and the crisis of Fascism. Nineteen members of the Grand Council voted for Grandi's motion, which asked the king to resume his constitutional powers. This was an implicit call for Mussolini's dismissal. There were only eight no-votes from radical Fascists such as Farinacci, and one abstention.[190]

Since the Fascist Grand Council merely had advisory powers, the Duce did not believe that the vote would have serious consequences. He thus returned home for a short rest and went back to the Palazzo Venezia in the morning. In the afternoon, on 25 July, the king received Mussolini in a routine audience. Significantly, Mussolini was wearing a civilian suit on the advice of the king's staff. As if the dress code had deeper political connotations, the king dismissed Mussolini after almost twenty-one years in office as prime minister; he had already appointed Marshal Badoglio as Mussolini's successor. After the audience, Mussolini was arrested and taken to a barracks in an ambulance. Such was the unglamorous fall of a dictator who had used performance as a central instrument of his exercise of power. Late at night, Badoglio announced the regime change on the radio. He insisted that the war would go on. Badoglio's tactic reflected Italian concerns over German reprisals for the second Italian 'betrayal' in recent history, as Ernst von Weizsäcker, the new German ambassador to the Vatican, noted.[191]

The diaries of the Florentine anti-Fascist law professor Piero Calamandrei give a vivid account of the reception of Badoglio's announcement. Calamandrei was spending the evening with friends and family, enjoying cigarettes and liqueur, when he heard the news of Mussolini's downfall on the radio. Fear over how Hitler would react immediately dampened his joy at the end of Fascism: 'Hitler knows that his personal position will be weakened by the fall of the accomplice.'[192] On 26 July 1943, newspapers printed declarations by Badoglio and the king, the latter insisting that Mussolini had offered his resignation. A campaign to delegitimise the Duce commenced.[193]

Throughout Italy, some people released their built-up anger against Fascism and smashed Mussolini statues and ransacked Fascist party offices, while others vented their wrath against Germany. But this was not all. In Milan alone, according to a 1944 Fascist investigation, 10 suspected or real Fascists were killed, 100 wounded, 1,200 evicted from their homes and 4,765 sacked from their jobs. For Fascists, the sudden downfall of their regime, which had, at least to some extent, guided their values, norms and everyday lives, was a major blow and led to an identity crisis.[194]

But the vast majority of Italians waited for further news. Maria Carazzolo celebrated the news of Mussolini's downfall with her friends and family. Her uncle offered Marsala wine to celebrate the occasion. She had heard rumours that a crowd had looted a local bank branch and had smashed busts of the Duce. Maria, like many other Italians, also worried greatly about the consequences of the regime change: 'But tomorrow, what will be tomorrow?' Reflecting a similar sentiment, in Milan Magda Ceccarelli De Grada, while welcoming the news of Mussolini's fall from power, remained reserved and concerned, as it would be difficult for Badoglio to exit the war on Germany's side, she believed.[195] Badoglio's authoritarian regime was not slow in bringing in a curfew and repressing strike action. Badoglio's government wanted to bring the disastrous war to an end, but knew that this would lead to German reprisals and the occupation of Italy. Negotiations for peace with the Allies thus coincided with promises to the Germans that Italy would continue to fight the war as an Axis ally.[196]

Mussolini's shambolic downfall was a major blow for Hitler, who had insisted for years that his fate was inextricably linked to Mussolini's. Furthermore, the alliance with Italy, based on the personalised relationship with Mussolini, had been a Nazi flagship project, and Hitler expected that Italy would soon leave the Axis, making Germany vulnerable to an Allied attack from the south.[197] At this time, although it took the Nazi leadership several hours to ascertain what had really happened in Italy, articulations of anti-Italian stereotypes prevalent amongst the Nazi leadership increased. Hitler and Goebbels also feared that the news of the fall of their erstwhile idol, in power for almost twenty-one years, would encourage anti-Nazis in Germany to plot against the regime.[198]

To discuss the Italian crisis, Hitler, in a violently foul mood, assembled his entourage at his East Prussian headquarters. Mussolini's downfall was not the only crisis with which the Nazi leader had to cope. Apart from the Axis setbacks in Sicily and the Soviet Union, the British mass bombing of Hamburg, one of the most severe series of bombing raids on Germany of the war, which cost the lives of between 34,000 and 40,000 people, had further exposed German military vulnerability and had begun to undermine the German home front. Hitler deliberated an occupation of Rome, including the Vatican, drawing on existing plans drawn up months before by the German armed forces, and the arrest of Badoglio's new government and the king. In fact, the German Foreign Ministry requested from the Rome embassy a list of thirty leading Italian officials known as notoriously anti-German in anticipation of planned reprisals.[199]

Yet neither arrests nor occupation went ahead, as these would have further complicated the situation, especially if the Vatican had been invaded by Germany. Instead, Hitler exploited the tricky position of Badoglio, who was unable to turn against Germany, as this would have meant the immediate German occupation of Italy. Thus, the German army, whose presence in Italy had been increased since the summer, began to send reinforcements to Italy. The justification for this step was that they were aiding the new Italian government. They encountered no resistance from the Italian army. At that time, in contrast to Hitler, leading German military officials such as Field Marshal Kesselring believed that Badoglio and the Italian army would honour the alliance with Germany.[200]

In this chaotic situation, now that the masks were off after the inglorious end of the show of unity and friendship with Italy, Hitler gave Goebbels a detailed account of his real views on the alliance with Mussolini. According to Hitler, the German people had never fully supported the alliance with Italy and were 'far too Italophobic', an admission that Nazi propaganda about the alliance with Italy had failed. For Hitler, a coterie of unreliable personalities, above all Ciano, who had allegedly acted in tandem with the Vatican and the despised monarchy, had deposed the Duce. Badoglio's regime was weak and only supported by 'Jews and scum', although Goebbels believed that Badoglio might succeed in establishing an authoritarian dictatorship, backed up by the monarchy. Hitler insisted that a new Fascist government must be established by the Germans, and the Italian government would offer no resistance. He thus ordered preparations for Mussolini's liberation and the arrest of anti-German Italian political and military elites. Himmler even forced astrologists, imprisoned by the Nazis, to locate Mussolini (whose whereabouts were a secret) with pendula, actions bordering on idiocy.[201]

In order to minimise the impact of Mussolini's deposal on German public morale, the German press was instructed to report it soberly as a change in the Italian government, as *The Times* noted.[202] If this strategy had aimed to reassure Germans that the war could still be won after the downfall of Hitler's principal ally, it failed. SD reports covered rumours circulating in Germany that Mussolini's fall would soon bring the war to an end. Some, according to the SD, had even blamed Hitler for devoting too much energy to the friendship with Mussolini, which had led to the disastrous military situation. This was scapegoating Italy for Germany's military misfortunes.[203]

If we shift attention from the Nazis to the Allies, it is clear that Mussolini's dismissal gave a massive momentum to the Allied campaign. On 27 July 1943, Churchill, invoking his 'one man alone' theory and reinforcing the anti-German mood in Italy, suggested that after Mussolini's fall from power, the new Italian government should free itself from the German yoke and join the Allies, lest the Italian peninsula be destroyed completely by brutal warfare.[204]

In the meantime, Mussolini had been taken to the island of Ponza, previously used for the confinement of anti-Fascists. Hitler soon made a public gesture that expressed his sympathy towards the Duce. For Mussolini's sixtieth birthday on 29 July 1943, he sent him Nietzsche's collected works, a gift announced by the German press, as the dissolution of the Fascist party and its organisations was being announced in Italy. An SD report claimed that at least some Nazi party members had been reassured by news of this gift as a demonstration of Hitler's steadfast loyalty, which was implicitly superior to Italian disloyalty.[205] Nevertheless, some in the Nazi leadership, reflecting their ambivalent attitude, wrote off Mussolini. Thus, an article also marking his sixtieth birthday on the front page of the *Völkischer Beobachter* read like an adulatory obituary of the ex-Duce.[206]

After the 1941 Berghof meeting had marked the end of the parallel war, Italy's military fortunes declined even further, and Mussolini's regime soon entered a severe crisis. Italian dependency on the Third Reich increased, but the display of unity and friendship centred upon the Mussolini–Hitler alliance continued to resonate as the strongest symbol of the Axis, although propaganda about the Italo-German alliance changed according to the vicissitudes of the alliance. Until 1942, the German-dominated Axis was on the brink of reaching world domination. As Italy slid from one defeat to another, culminating in the Allied invasion of Sicily, more and more Italians in positions of authority, including Fascist grandees, began to distance themselves from the alliance with Germany. War had been a central tenet of Fascist ideology and practice, and it was not only Mussolini who had cultivated the alliance with Germany, but also a wider group of Italian elites. The Axis was not solid. It lacked a principal strategic and ideological basis and was compromised by the stereotypes against the other nation that loomed large in both Italy and Germany. For Hitler and the Nazi leadership, well informed as they were about the domestic crisis of

Fascism, the figure of Mussolini had been central to the war effort, increasingly so after the turning of the tide in 1942–3 when Germany began to lose momentum in the war. The belief that Italy would only remain in the Axis with Mussolini at the top had been widespread amongst the Nazi leadership. The implications of the toppling of the Fascist dictator for the people of Europe, especially of Italy, would be dramatic.

8

ENDGAME
1943–5

I

Mussolini's fall from power represented one of the most profound legitimacy crises facing the Nazi regime since its inception in 1933, as Nazi propaganda had constantly drummed up the message that Mussolini's Italy was Germany's principal ally. Hitler's attitude towards the new Italian government was characterised by a mix of hostility and contempt. When, a few days after his appointment as Prime Minister, Badoglio sent Hitler a telegram with the promise that Italy would continue to fight on Germany's side, Hitler did not reply, as he was not keen to deal with the man he accused of stabbing Mussolini in the back. Nevertheless, in order to maintain the facade of the Axis, he received General Luigi Efisio Marras, the Italian military attaché. A tense and suspicious Führer warned Marras of the grave consequences for Italy if it were to leave the alliance with the Third Reich. While the talks were inconclusive, it is noteworthy that Hitler asked Marras about Mussolini's condition and whereabouts. He demanded that the ex-Italian dictator be treated well, in an implicit threat to the new Italian government.[1] Furthermore, Hitler instructed Georg von Mackensen to request an audience with the king, who, Hitler hoped, would allow the ambassador to visit Mussolini.[2]

Victor Emmanuel III was afraid of German reprisals. Thus, in a gesture of crocodile politeness, he received Mackensen a few minutes before their official appointment. The king, backing secret negotiations for an armistice with the Allies, feared that the Nazis would liberate Mussolini if they discovered his whereabouts; hence he claimed that he did not know where the ex-Duce was being held.[3] Hitler, while rejecting a meeting with the king in Italy, signalled that he would be prepared to see the king, the crown prince and Badoglio together. His plan was to arrest them in retaliation for bringing down Mussolini but the Italian government wisely decided to postpone indefinitely such a meeting.[4]

German pressure on the new Italian government to honour the alliance with the Third Reich intensified. In late July 1943, as we have seen, German troops had been infiltrating Italy, adding to the German contingents already present on the peninsula. Some had entered Italy via the Brenner Pass, the site of so many Hitler–Mussolini meetings. The Italian *Comando supremo* had mobilised Italian troops at the German border, leading to an extremely tense situation and, in late August 1943, German troops were even posted on the Italian side of the Brenner railway station.[5] In effect, Germany was intent on turning Italy into a complete vassal state during the weeks after Mussolini's downfall, with German divisions moving their way down the peninsula, laying the groundwork for an occupation in the event of an Italian armistice with the Allies. The Italian government was left powerless, but still levelled the accusation that 'from a certain German side' 'a putsch was being prepared against the Badoglio government'. A furious Ribbentrop instructed the German embassy to reject these accusations robustly. The aggressive tone of these diplomatic exchanges did not bode well for the future of Italian–German relations.[6]

After the collapse of his propaganda performance with Mussolini, Hitler no longer had the need to continue the performance of unity and friendship amongst his entourage. In a conversation with Otto Meissner, chief of the Presidential Chancellery (*Chef der Präsidialkanzlei*) and previously head of the Reich president's office under presidents Friedrich Ebert and Paul von Hindenburg, he regretted that, after his return from his first meeting with Mussolini in June 1934, he had not heeded Hindenburg's advice about Mussolini and Italy: 'The old man has unfortunately been right with his experiences and wisdom!'[7] Similarly, Hitler told Goebbels that Mussolini had, after all, been a weak dictator who had only himself to blame for his overthrow. Mussolini had not followed Hitler's suggestion to eliminate the monarchy and to cultivate a loyal following amongst other Fascist leaders. Hitler, repeating a familiar trope, added that Mussolini had fallen victim to a conspiracy of international aristocrats. The Prince of Hesse was a particularly malign traitor for Hitler, and he had him placed under effective house arrest.

Soon, Hitler's aim to reinstall the ex-Duce crystallised. Hitler's priority was to defend Germany at the new front that had opened in southern Europe after the Allied landing in Sicily. It was for this reason that Hitler still articulated, in typical fashion, his admiration for Mussolini and 'praise[d] him as the only Roman of this time who has, unfortunately, not found a worthy people', while at the same time dismissing the Italian populace. Even so, for Hitler, strategic considerations mattered more than the restoration of his supposed friend; he also announced that Germany would annex the South Tyrol, which had been the pawn for an alliance with Mussolini.[8] In this way, the Italian government started to lose control of the German-speaking population as German troops marched through the region, according to a report that had reached Himmler's personal staff in early August. As the South Tyrolese, strongly encouraged by the German authorities, were cheering the troops, expecting them to displace the Italian army, Italian authorities began to crack down on German speakers, increasing the profound tensions within the Italo-German alliance that, without Mussolini, continued but in name.[9]

While the sparse evidence that has survived on German popular opinion had always suggested a widespread scepticism towards the alliance with Italy, SD reports now diagnosed an even stronger anti-Italian sentiment. Although most ordinary Germans were primarily concerned with the continuing Allied bombings of German towns, many believed that Italy was on its knees. Some even compared Badoglio to Prince Max von Baden, the last Imperial Reich chancellor before the November 1918 revolution. Such comparisons were, of course, complete anathema to the Nazis and help explain the radical attitude of the Nazi leadership towards post-Fascist Italy. While Hitler and the Nazis had previously pursued the alliance with Mussolini's Italy regardless of German popular opinion, they were, now that the tide of the war had turned, determined to keep the German people under control more than ever before.[10]

Despite the fact that Italian–German relations were tenser than ever before after the Duce's overthrow, both sides reassured each other formulaically that they would remain allies just as the Italian government's secret negotiations for an armistice with the Allies continued. Yet the show of Italian–German friendship and unity, so closely tied to Mussolini and Hitler, was over. A particularly insightful manifestation of this strange situation was the meeting of Ribbentrop with his new Italian counterpart, Raffaele Guariglia, at Tarvisio on the German–Italian border on 6 August 1943. A closer examination of some details of the meeting reveals the profound transformation of Italian–German relations. Before crossing into Italy, armed SS guards had joined Ribbentrop's train. All secret German documents had been left behind in Germany, as Ribbentrop, subscribing to a conspiracy theory, feared that the new Italian government would kidnap him and leak the documents to the Allies. Unlike at previous meetings, the Italian delegation did not greet the German guests with the Fascist salute. Furthermore, in contrast to the wartime meetings of Mussolini and Hitler, no communiqué was issued. Instead, the atmosphere was tense, bordering on the unfriendly, which did not bode well for the future. For instance, when asked about Mussolini's whereabouts, Guariglia replied that the Italian government had had to arrest him to protect him 'against the hatred of the Italian people'. At the end, the Italian foreign minister snapped at the German delegation that Mussolini's status was '*a matter that did not concern Germany*'.[11]

With the Mussolini–Hitler relationship in tatters, Churchill and Roosevelt, who met in late August 1943 in Quebec to coordinate the Allied war effort, began to symbolise increasing hopes that the Allies would prevail in the war against the Axis.[12] As the Italian government feared that the Germans might abduct Mussolini, he was shipped around Italy. After being held in Rome and Ponza, he was taken in August 1943 to La Maddalena, an island off the northern tip of Sardinia. This was a symbolic location, as some of Fascism's political enemies had been confined there. La Maddalena is also close to Caprera, the island where Garibaldi had spent many years of his life, sometimes withdrawing from politics altogether. It was on La Maddalena that Mussolini had finally received Hitler's Nietzsche volumes. While the war was raging, with further Allied bombings of Italian cities, the former Duce started writing an account of his fall from power and jotted down some philosophical and political musings in order to shape his own political legacy, later published as 'Pontine and Sardinian Thoughts'. Finally, on 28 August 1943, just as representatives of the Badoglio government were negotiating the armistice with the Allies in

Lisbon, Mussolini was transferred to the Campo Imperatore skiing resort on the Gran Sasso mountain massif. In the meantime, the Badoglio government orchestrated a press campaign to demolish the Duce cult. For instance, papers such as the *Corriere della Sera* printed lurid details of Mussolini's affair with Clara Petacci that dented the image of the heroic Duce.[13]

II

As Mussolini was held on the Gran Sasso, General Giuseppe Castellano signed the armistice on 3 September 1943 in Cassibile in Sicily, on the same day as the Allies landed in Calabria on the Italian mainland. On 8 September, despite the previous Italian denials of such negotiations, Guariglia informed the new German envoy, Rudolf Rahn, of the armistice. The latter immediately shouted: 'This is a betrayal of the given word.' Guariglia rejected the term 'betrayal' and insisted that the Italian people had fought to their limits. Rahn, marking the complete breakdown of diplomatic relations, then stormed out of Guariglia's office without pausing to say goodbye. Badoglio justified the armistice in a letter to Hitler as inevitable for Italy, which was no longer capable of fighting. The Nazi leader's reply was not in writing, but in the form of massive military retaliation, as we shall see.[14]

Immediately, Italians reacted with a mix of relief and concern. In Milan, for instance, Magda Ceccarelli De Grada had heard rumours of the armistice in a café and saw Germans and Italians toasting the armistice. But her feelings of joy were accompanied by fear of a German invasion: 'But the Germans? Hitler, the Brenner?' In Maria Carazzolo's small town near Padua, church bells rang in celebration. But, soon, joy gave way to fear of the German reaction.[15]

Let us pause here for a moment and consider the broader significance of the armistice. For some Italian historians, including De Felice and Ernesto Galli Della Loggia, writing in the 1990s, the Italian nation died on 8 September 1943. From the vantage point of the early 1990s, after the collapse of the Italian post-war political consensus, such an interpretation was attractive for Italian right-wing historians as they were trying to delegitimise the anti-Fascist consensus of the Italian Republic; this at the time when the media tycoon Silvio Berlusconi had included, for the first time in post-war Italy, the neo-Fascists in his coalition government. But the interpretation of the armistice as the 'death of the fatherland' misses the point, as Italy had already lost its independence well before 8 September 1943 because of Fascism's fateful alliance with Nazi Germany.[16]

At the time, Churchill and Roosevelt shared the view that Italy had long ceased to be truly independent. In a joint message to Badoglio on 10 September 1943, they warned the Italian government of the expected brutal German reaction:

> Hitler, through his accomplice Mussolini, has brought Italy to the verge of ruin. He has driven the Italians into disastrous campaigns in the sands of Egypt and the snows of Russia. The Germans have always deserted the Italian troops on the battlefield, sacrificing them contemptuously in order to cover their own method of retreat. Now Hitler threatens to subject you all to the cruelties he is perpetrating in so many lands.[17]

After the proclamation of the armistice, German officials and soldiers unleashed the anti-Italian sentiment which they had had to keep under control for as long as Italy had remained an ally. For instance, on Hitler's orders, the Italian military attachés in Germany were arrested on their repatriation train in clear breach of their diplomatic immunity.[18] More significantly, the Wehrmacht, facilitated by their already strong presence on the peninsula, now formally occupied Italy and met relatively little resistance from an exhausted and demoralised Italian army, effectively left without leadership. For, on 9 September 1943, the king, Badoglio and his government abandoned Rome and boarded a ship near Pescara which took them to Brindisi, still held by the Italian army.

The king's flight created a power vacuum, as no clear instructions that the Germans were now the enemy were given to the Italian army until 11 September.[19] Chaos, confusion and uncertainty over the immediate future cast a dark shadow over the lives of all Italians. Except for the southern parts of Italy, already held or soon to be occupied by the Allies, the peninsula, including Rome, the most potent symbol of the Italian nation state, came under German occupation, with only the Vatican and the small Republic of San Marino remaining independent. Elsewhere, in southern France, the Balkans and northern and central Italy, the German army gave Italian soldiers the option of either continuing to fight on Germany's side or being disarmed and interned in Germany. Of the 3,488,000 Italian soldiers, just over a million were disarmed by the Germans. Brutal orders from the Wehrmacht's Supreme Command followed suit, reflecting hatred of the 'Italian traitors'. Altogether, between 7,000 and 12,200 Italian officers, non-commissioned officers and ordinary soldiers were killed by the German army in the wake of the armistice.[20] Only a few Italian troops, in Italy and abroad, followed Badoglio's vague call for resistance against the Germans. On the island of Cephalonia, occupied by Italy since 1940/41, fierce Italian resistance against the Germans in mid-September 1943 led to massive German reprisals that left at least 6,000 Italian soldiers dead.[21]

Following these harsh orders, some 600,000 Italian soldiers were taken to Germany. There, they were denied the status of prisoners of war and came to be known instead as 'military internees'. An SD report of late December 1943 approvingly cited the hostile views of several Germans towards the Italians, dismissed as 'Badoglio swine'. The report also cited a worker who had complained that, until 8 September 1943, any criticism of Italy would have amounted to a 'state slur' (*Staatsbeleidigung*). A Stuttgart shopkeeper, quoted by the SD, went even further in his racist condemnation of the Italians when he likened them to the Jews. Although the degree of knowledge amongst the German people of the mass murder of the Jews is the subject of a controversial debate, the Stuttgart shopkeeper's remarks suggest that Italians had to be treated as subhuman beings that should be killed, if necessary.[22]

While welcomed by the German war economy as additional labourers, the 'military internees' were subjected to appalling treatment by the German authorities and many civilians, reflecting the Nazi belief that Italy had betrayed the Third Reich. In the hierarchy of foreign workers, the Italian military internees were often placed even below the Soviets. A brief analysis of the health conditions of Italian military internees forced to work in the Krupp factory in Rheinhausen illustrates their systematic maltreatment. Here, by March 1944, because of insufficient rations, one-quarter of the internees were unable to work.[23]

But this was not all. Altogether, between the armistice and the end of the war, some 24,000 civilians were arrested and deported to German prisons and concentration camps. Almost half of them died in Germany, where they were placed on the lowest rungs of the prisoner hierarchy. An even more graphic illustration of the abject Nazi treatment of Italians is mortality rates. In the Mauthausen concentration camp in Austria, for example, the general mortality rate was 50.48 per cent, while for Italians, it was 55 per cent.[24]

Hitler's main concern, apart from securing the military occupation of Italy, was to locate Mussolini, who should not be allowed to fall into Allied hands. Instead, the Duce would spearhead a new Italian regime that would legitimise the effective German occupation of the peninsula. On 10 September 1943, Hitler and Goebbels discussed their views on Italy and Mussolini. Their pro-Mussolini masks were off. Goebbels, one of the architects of pro-Italian propaganda since the 1930s, revealingly admitted that the German people, unlike the Nazi leadership, had always been sceptical of an alliance with Italy. Nazi propaganda had failed. For Goebbels the Italians were after all 'a people of gypsies'. The Nazis had made a huge mistake, Goebbels admitted, when they had pursued the alliance with Italy 'for ideological considerations'.[25]

On the same day, after long hesitation, given the simultaneous intensification of Allied area bombings of Germany, Hitler spoke on the wireless to the German people, who had been nervously waiting for their leader's explanation of the 'betrayal' of their principal ally. Goebbels and Göring had had to push Hitler to deliver the speech, not least because the Nazi leader was undecided about his military strategy.[26] In his broadcast, Hitler squarely identified the king, Badoglio and the army leadership as traitors. They had already undermined Mussolini on previous occasions and had allegedly stopped him from entering the war in September 1939. To maintain his credibility, Hitler emphatically excluded Mussolini from blame and called him '[his] friend', before expressing 'understanding . . . for the extraordinarily domestic difficulties of the Duce', 'the greatest son of the Italian soil since the collapse of the ancient world'. Hitler's assertion that 'the breakdown of Italy means little militarily', given the weakness of the Italian army, reflected his strategy to appeal to popular anti-Italian stereotypes amongst his audience. The *Völkischer Beobachter* even accused Badoglio of a 'failed stab in the back', a reference to the powerful legend with which most Germans were familiar. According to an SD report, Hitler's speech resonated well with the German people. Some were overheard by SD agents to say 'The Italians can only be considered in future as chestnut salesmen [*Maroniverkäufer*] or donkey drivers', suggesting that the Italian people would need to be treated severely in the future, given their government's betrayal of Germany.[27]

German revenge against Italy was the order of the day. Vitriolic anti-Italian sentiment prompted Goebbels to declare that 'the Italians have lost any right to a nation state of the modern kind because of their disloyalty and betrayal. They have to be punished severely, as the law of History demands it.' Goebbels' punitive tone was followed by harsh military and political repression of alleged anti-German elements in Italy. In this sense, it was Germany, rather than Italy, which betrayed the other country through brutal repression and revenge.[28] Territories that had been under Habsburg control until the end of the First World War came under German control. Thus, South Tyrol, the Trentino and Belluno became the Alpenvorland Operational Zone and was placed under the control of the *Gauleiter* of the Tyrol, Franz Hofer, while the eastern provinces of upper Italy, including Gorizia, Udine, Trieste and Istria, were put under the de facto rule of Friedrich Rainer, *Gauleiter* of Carinthia, as the Adriatisches Küstenland Operational Zone. This huge humiliation did little to enhance the reputation of the Germans amongst the war-weary population.[29]

Reflecting the often chaotic and competitive decision-making processes in the Third Reich, the Nazi elite was divided over plans for Italy under German occupation. Two broad factions emerged in the Nazi polycracy, the web of party and state institutions and individuals 'working towards the Führer' and competing for his favour.[30] To start with, the Wehrmacht's leadership, reflecting its experiences of military occupation elsewhere in Europe, advocated a formal occupation of Italy, a strategy that would enhance its power and enable the exploitation of the Italian economy for the German war effort, while also facilitating military operations against the Allies. In contrast, the Foreign Ministry was in favour of maintaining Italy's formal independence and running Italy as a satellite state, so that other German institutions would have to filter all their dealings with Italy through the ministry, thus increasing its power in the Nazi regime.[31]

Hitler followed his usual irregular working routine and did not give clear orders, reflecting his belief that the strongest individuals and institutions would eventually prevail. On 10 September 1943, he appointed Rahn 'plenipotentiary of the Great German Reich at the National Fascist Government'. Rahn, a career diplomat who had earned his spurs as a crisis manager in other Nazi-occupied countries and had played a role in deporting Jews from France to Nazi Germany, recommended that Hitler control Italy through 'indirect rule', similar to the way in which he believed the British were running India. Thus, he suggested delegating as much power as possible to Italian institutions, as this would enhance the prestige of the new Italian government and save the Germans a lot of effort, since they would not need to introduce as much repression. However, the Wehrmacht soon obtained a contradicting order from Hitler, giving Field Marshal Kesselring and other military commanders supreme authority in Italy. Predictably, this created frictions amongst the army and other German institutions, with Albert Speer's Organisation Todt, a paramilitary and engineering organisation notorious for its use of forced labour, and Fritz Sauckel, *Gauleiter* of Thuringia and Reich plenipotentiary for labour deployment, both determined ruthlessly to milk the Italian economy and manpower for the German war effort, conflicting with the SS. This constant competition effected a radicalisation of German occupation policies, as competition for Hitler's favour led to a 'cumulative radicalisation' of state, army and party institutions, each trying to dominate Italy – with devastating effects.[32] Nothing illustrates the nature of the German occupation of Italy more drastically than the following sobering statistic compiled by the German military historian Gerhard Schreiber: every day between September 1943 and May 1945, on average 160 Italians of all ages, men and women, died as a direct or indirect result of the German occupation. Casuality rates were even higher if one adds those 2,027 Italians killed in action while fighting alongside the Allies, the partisans killed in action or murdered by the Germans, and Italian civilians killed in air raids.[33]

III

At that time, the ex-Duce's future was unclear. De Felice suggests that he tried, in desperation, to cut his wrists when he heard of the armistice, because he was afraid that the British would arrest and try him, but this has never been conclusively proven.[34] As we have seen, Hitler was determined to free Mussolini. Two considerations guided the Führer. First, while he had lost faith in Mussolini, he had to continue to treat him as his friend in public to avoid losing his own credibility. Second, he believed that only Mussolini, and not other Fascist leaders such as Farinacci, would be able to bring a sense of order to Italy, help Germany exploit the peninsula for manpower and economic resources, and thereby help keep the Allies at bay. Thus, on 12 September 1943, having established his whereabouts in

Campo Imperatore, following the interception of Italian radio messages and tip-offs from Italian officials who had remained loyal to him, German soldiers and SS men, led by Otto Skorzeny, liberated the ex-Duce in a daring raid, using light aeroplanes. For the Italians who had remained faithful to Mussolini, seeing him as the only man able to restore Italy's honour after the shameful betrayal of the king and Badoglio, news of his liberation raised hopes, bordering on delusion, that he would lead Italy to victory alongside its German ally.[35]

The Duce's treatment after his liberation seemed to reflect Hitler's belief in him. Mussolini was flown to Munich, accompanied by Dr Rüther, a German military doctor, who wrote an account of the mission in late September 1943 in order to create a historical record of what the Nazis saw as a heroic mission. The title of the report, 'The Transfer of Mussolini to the Führer Head Quarters', suggests that the former Duce had lost all independent power and that his fate was now at the mercy of the Nazis. Rüther met the fallen dictator at an airfield south of Rome where he had been flown from the Gran Sasso massif. Mussolini's dress, a creased civilian suit with an untidy collar, was a clear demonstration of his lowly status. An insecure Mussolini greeted Rüther and other German officials with a handshake, rather than with the Fascist salute. During their subsequent flight, Rüther conducted a quick diagnosis of his patient, whom he found mentally and physically exhausted with 'wrinkled skin [and] an occasional subtle tremor of the hands'. As the plane flew over German-dominated Italy, Mussolini, in order to divert attention from his failure as a political and military leader, kept chatting. After landing en route in Vienna, he tried to hide his face with his turned-up coat collar and was taken to the Imperial Hotel through the back entrance. This arrangement was a striking and radical contrast to the pomp and glory of Mussolini's previous visits to the Reich.

Whether or not his stopover in Vienna reminded Mussolini of Hitler's promise after the Anschluss that the Nazi leader would never forget his support is not clear, but it must remain a possibility. Immediately after his arrival, Mussolini was summoned to a telephone conversation with Hitler, who later told Goebbels that the ex-Duce had been deeply moved by his loyalty. Whether or not Mussolini had really been emotional is a moot point. What matters more is that the telephone conversation reanimated his belief that his special relationship with Hitler had been restored. The next morning, Mussolini and his German watchers left the hotel through a side entrance. Some pedestrians allegedly recognised the Duce and began to applaud, which raised the mood of the vain ex-dictator.[36]

After a short flight from Vienna, the party landed at Munich. The welcoming ceremony for Mussolini at the airport reinvoked his former status as head of the Italian government. The Nazi regime had organised a rally similar to the ones on the ex-Duce's previous visits to the Bavarian capital to make him feel like a head of government. From Munich, Mussolini was flown across war-torn Germany to Hitler's headquarters in East Prussia. To avoid an early arrival and in order to maintain protocol, the plane had to fly extra rounds before landing on schedule.

German newsreel announced Mussolini's arrival at Hitler's headquarters with great fanfare. It shows how, after he had disembarked, Mussolini, still wearing a civilian suit, greeted the uniformed Hitler with the Fascist salute. Hitler shook Mussolini's hand, rather than then extend the Hitler salute, a gesture that reinforced the message that the failed Italian ex-dictator was no longer Hitler's equal; the scene also evokes the memory of Hitler's first meeting with Mussolini at Venice when the Reich chancellor, wearing civilian clothes, had been denied the Fascist salute by Mussolini. Now their roles were completely reversed. Mussolini, stuck in a foreign country and separated from his political supporters and his family, depended entirely on Hitler's goodwill. While Mussolini had previously wavered between jealousy and admiration for Hitler, the Nazi leader had always manifested a surety of attention and admiration for the Duce.[37]

When Hitler suggested that Mussolini must establish a republican government in the German-held zones of Italy, Mussolini had little option but to comply. Behind the scenes, Hitler, though impressed by the Duce's visit, remained profoundly disappointed with him. As he lamented to Goebbels, Mussolini had failed to draw the 'moral consequences' when he had not purged traitors such as Ciano and Grandi or abolished the monarchy. Furthermore, Hitler denied that the Italian was a true revolutionary, unlike Stalin or himself.[38]

These damning statements reveal that Hitler's admiration for Mussolini, with all its typical sentimental undertones, had always been closely related to his perception of the Duce's power position. This had been a constant from the beginning of their relationship in the wake of the March on Rome, when Hitler had viewed Mussolini as a powerful dictator whose political strategy was worth imitating, through the intensification of their rapport in the late 1930s, and into its decline during Italy's fateful campaigns in the Second World War. Without power, Mussolini was no longer an equal for Hitler. But he was still useful to the Nazi leader in serving as a figurehead for a Nazi satellite state in northern Italy, which is why the display of unity and friendship was revived by the Nazis, although on a smaller scale than before 1943. If Hitler had publicly denounced Mussolini, Nazism's credibility, already severely under pressure because of declining military fortunes and the Allied bombing campaign, would have been further undermined.[39]

Mussolini's living arrangements after his departure from Hitler's headquarters reflected his deep fall from grace. The ex-dictator was reunited with his family in an Upper Bavarian guesthouse of the German Foreign Ministry. SS guards of honour were posted outside. Although the guards added prestige, as they suggested that Mussolini had the rank of a head of government, they were also a clear symbol of German domination. Mussolini's life was mundane, and the ex-dictator and his family regularly suffered from the noise of drunken German officials residing on the floor above.[40] From his Upper Bavarian retreat, Mussolini, using a telephone tapped by the Germans, assembled the personnel to form a new republican government.[41]

Hitler and the Nazis, despite their reservations about Mussolini, hoped that his restoration would undermine the Allied campaign in Italy and give a tremendous boost to the Nazi war effort. Therefore Goebbels initiated a propaganda campaign, giving select details of the daring German rescue mission to the German press. In its coverage of Mussolini's liberation, the *Völkischer Beobachter* contrasted German 'loyalty' against Italian 'betrayal', giving details of the Badoglio government's secret negotiations with the Allies. In an attempt to reactivate the Mussolini–Hitler relationship with which German readers were already familiar, the paper also covered the two men's meeting at Wolf's Lair.[42]

According to an SD report, this strategy resonated with some Germans who welcomed the news of Mussolini's liberation as proof of German loyalty and superiority over the Italians. Yet the SD also cited voices stressing that Italy and Mussolini would never regain their former status as Germany's principal ally. On 18 September 1943, Mussolini proclaimed the new Fascist state in Italy via Radio Munich. A small detail is noteworthy: before leaving the guest house to make the broadcast, Mussolini had to borrow a black shirt in an attempt to restore his dictatorial appeal.[43] In his broadcast, Mussolini outlined the central themes of his restored government and gave an account of his last audience with the king. The Duce insisted that his new government stood in a Mazzinian republican tradition, having overcome the treacherous monarchy. Traitors were to be eliminated, he thundered. In a variation of his previous propaganda on the transformative quality of war, he demanded that Italians make sacrifices to atone for the betrayal of their German ally. But the fact Mussolini made this speech via Radio Munich further revealed his total dependence on Nazi Germany. Indeed, an SD public opinion report noted that Mussolini was practically a 'Reich governor' (*Reichsstatthalter*), a variation of his previous title as *Gauleiter* of Italy.[44] The purpose of Mussolini's restoration did not get lost on Allied observers. For the well-informed diplomatic correspondent of *The Times*, for example, the Nazis had reinstated the Duce so as to legitimise what was effectively their occupation of northern and central Italy.[45]

According to anti-Fascists such as Piero Calamandrei, who, afraid of German reprisals, had left Florence for the Tuscan countryside, many Italians thought that someone had imitated Mussolini on the radio, as the Duce's voice had sounded deeper than usual. But such rumours soon gave way to the dire reality of life under a resurrected Fascism, now backed by a powerful German military presence in Italy.[46] Italy effectively became a divided country, with German domination over the north and the centre, separate from the kingdom of the south, under Allied domination, with the king and Badoglio as figureheads. Here was a country deeply polarised between diehard Fascists, partisans and the vast majority of people concerned only with their own survival.

Despite the Fascist performance of the radio broadcast, Mussolini failed to rehabilitate his reputation amongst the Nazi leadership, including Hitler. Echoing his rant of three months earlier, Hitler railed against the Duce on 20 December 1943 in a conversation with Goebbels and gave a realistic assessment of his true reasons for entering into a pact with Italy. As Germany was increasingly at risk of losing the war, Hitler' anti-Italian feelings had become even more pronounced, amplified by Goebbels in his diaries. According to the propaganda minister, Mussolini had 'remained the old Marxist', a great irony given Hitler's previous flirtations with the Duce. Goebbels concluded dismissively that 'neither with

Italy nor the Fascist movement can anything be done'. Italy had failed and would never become a great power. Hitler went on to expand on his reasons for the alliance with Italy. As a counterweight to Britain, the entanglement with Italy, powerfully reinforced during the triumphant 1937 and 1938 dictatorial visits, had helped the Third Reich seize territories such as Austria and the Sudetenland. Hitler insisted that he had always known about the duplicity of Mussolini and the Italian government; he had long been aware of the great efforts of Mussolini's previous government to fortify the Italian–German border. Hitler thus confirmed once again that his liaison with Mussolini had thus principally been motivated by strategic rather than ideological considerations.[47]

In the meantime, after reaching the Italian mainland, the Allies initially progressed swiftly in the south, landing at the strategically important Salerno on 9 September. After fierce fighting and a popular uprising, later remembered as the 'Four Days of Naples', Naples was liberated on 1 October. Here, German troops, motivated by feelings of revenge against the Italian 'traitors', had burned the contents of the university library, alongside archival documents and paintings.[48] In mid-October 1943, the king declared war on Germany, but the Italian army remained a rump of its former size. The Allies only gave the kingdom of the south 'co-belligerent' status, rather than that of an ally, an interesting variation of the 'non-belligerent' status of late 1939 and early 1940.[49] Hitler had decided that the defence of southern Italy was not a priority so the Germans withdrew to the Gustav defence line south of Rome, which they held amidst heavy fighting. From there, the frontline only moved north after the fall of Monte Cassino Abbey in the spring of 1944, following heavy fighting between the Germans and the Allies.[50]

IV

The new state headed by Mussolini soon came to be known as the Italian Social Republic (*Repubblica sociale italiana* or RSI). Although the name of the state invoked the radical and violent spirit of a 'social' and republican fascism, it was only a shadow of Fascist Italy's former pomp and glory. Writing the history of the RSI is difficult, as it has been shaped in public memory and historiography by the notion of the 'evil German', forming, alongside a small group of Fascist thugs, a gang of 'Nazi-Fascists', supposedly vehemently opposed by the 'good Italian'. But this view is too simplistic. For, in reality, some Italians, due to a combination of ideological fanaticism, extreme patriotism and loyalty towards the alliance with Germany, fought hand in hand with the Germans until the bitter end.[51]

Italians, including women and young people who had grown up under Fascism, continued to cherish Mussolini, sending in adulatory letters to RSI institutions which deemed these letters as expression of popular enthusiasm for the Duce, so they duly archived them. One such letter, written by a young Fascist girl from Venice to Mussolini on 22 November 1944, insisted: 'I wish to express to you my unshakeable faith in the resurrection of the Fatherland. If God has saved you from horrendous infamy, it means that your lofty mission for Italy and for the world has not yet been accomplished.' As with the letters that had been sent to Mussolini's secretariat before his downfall, it is a moot point whether the correspondents really meant what they were writing. Rather, the point of these letters is that they reinforced Mussolini's sense of being on the right mission to rehabilitate Italy's national reputation.[52]

Like his new regime, Mussolini's status depended entirely on German backing. His living and working arrangements illustrated his lowly status. In contrast to the previous pompous office in the centre of Rome, the RSI government offices were located in various small towns on the picturesque shores of Lake Garda, with Mussolini and his entourage residing in the villa of the Feltrinelli industrialist clan, in Gargnano. The Foreign Ministry, the Ministry of Popular Culture and the Stefani news agency were based in Salò (which is why the RSI is often known to this day as the 'Salò Republic'). The presence of SS and Wehrmacht troops was a clear sign that the Germans were in control, as was the fact that they tapped the telephone lines and studied all official correspondence. The location of the RSI's government away from Rome, the most potent symbol of Fascism and its Roman heritage, was a huge loss in prestige for Mussolini, who now truly became little more than the *Gauleiter* of Italy. Still, it was felt that the proximity to Germany would enable Mussolini to escape to the Reich in the eventuality of an Allied advance.

Reunited with his family, Mussolini resumed his personal and work habits. But this routine failed to overcome his sense of profound failure, now that he was at the whim of Hitler and his acolytes who closely supervised the day-to-day business of the RSI. Mussolini's quotidian habits suggested that there was no war. Soon, a number of German journalists developed an interest in Mussolini's private life. Some, like Kurt Eggers, correspondent of the SS journal *Das Schwarze Korps*, drew a sympathetic picture of the Duce while others eviscerated his image as the firm leader of a reborn Italy. Let us consider an October 1944 article by Alexander Boltho von Hohenbach, a correspondent for the Transocean-Europapress news agency. Hohenbach mocked Mussolini's 'buen ritiro on Lake Garda water, rocks and subtropical vegetation'. Allegedly, Mussolini had been telling all the German officials he met that he believed in a German victory. Hohenbach raised doubts about the Duce's determination to win the war when he gave a detailed account of Mussolini's hobbies such as tennis, spending time with his grandchildren and reading. Predictably, Hohenbach's article, even though it did not see his way into the press, deeply irritated RSI diplomats such as Filippo Anfuso, the ambassador to Germany, who dismissed the report as a 'stupidity'.[53]

In the meantime, the full vengeance of the RSI was directed against those accused of having betrayed the Duce at the last meeting of the Fascist Grand Council, including Ciano, who, together with his wife and children, had escaped to Germany in late August 1943, fearing reprisals by the Badoglio government. Soon after the liberation of his father-in-law, Ciano was deported to Italy and arrested. Edda, his wife and Mussolini's daughter, tried to exchange his life for his diaries, full of compromising material on Mussolini and Hitler, but the German government refused. She even wrote letters to Hitler and her father, imploring them to spare Ciano the death penalty, but to no avail. Following a show trial in Verona together with leading Fascists who had voted in favour of Grandi's motion at the Grand Council Meeting, Ciano was executed alongside others, including Emilio De Bono, one of the *quadrumviri* of Fascism, on 11 January 1944 in Verona, after Mussolini had refused to pardon him. According to an SS report, the executions were carried out by Fascist paramilitaries in a particularly brutal manner. In a humiliating arrangement, the prisoners, tied to chairs, had had their backs to the shooting squad. A grisly scene was revealed: since the shots had been so imprecise, the prisoners, lying on the floor, had to be 'finished off with pistols'. Hitler did not have to order the execution. Rather, for Mussolini, this merciless step was morally necessary to rehabilitate Fascism's rule and to reassure Hitler that Republican Fascism would be tough and uncompromising. For Mussolini, the executions, especially that of Ciano, whom he could have easily pardoned, were a powerful instrument to demonstrate to his German masters that he, the Duce, was in control of Italy. In reality, he knew that he had failed as a politician. It scarcely improved his deep depression.[54]

Mussolini's motivation in taking over the Nazi satellite state in German-occupied Italy has caused considerable controversy amongst historians. For De Felice, Mussolini sacrificed himself for Italy in order to spare the peninsula a fate similar to Poland, where the Nazis had systematically repressed, exploited and killed civilians. De Felice insinuated that the Nazis wanted to rule Italy in the same brutal way as they had treated German-occupied eastern Europe with its Slav populations, seen by the Nazis as subhuman. However, while there were some German racist prejudices against Italians, the Nazis did not have a racially motivated plan for the systematic subjugation of Italy's civilian population nor its enslavement. Despite German atrocities against Italian civilians, partisans and Jews, and German exploitation of the Italian economy and the conscription of workers for the war effort, the occupation of Italy more closely resembled the Nazi domination of western European countries such as France. Italy had, of course, a special status as the Third Reich's former principal ally, and German resentment of Italy's supposed betrayal of Germany, coupled with national stereotypes, often hardened German occupation policies.[55] What is also clear is that, like in other Nazi-occupied countries, various German military, state and party officials competed for authority and control in the RSI. Together with the incompetence of the RSI government, this created a chaotic and increasingly violent political situation.[56]

Mussolini's own justification for his decision to take over the RSI is instructive. He later told a confidant that Hitler had left him no choice but to become the head of the RSI for, otherwise, Hitler would have instructed German officials to run the country themselves. Allegedly, the Nazi leader had told him: 'Either you assume the leadership of the Italian state, or I will send German officials to govern Italy.'[57] Although this apologetic interpretation needs to be regarded with some scepticism – Mussolini was far from merely a passive executioner of Hitler's order – his room for manoeuvre was quite limited. In the event, Mussolini and others in the RSI chose to develop violent policies that included a massive crackdown on partisans and suppressed Jews and other 'social outsiders': part and parcel of what Mussolini and the Fascists saw as the radical and pure aims of early Fascism. Likewise, it would be wrong to portray Mussolini as the man who sacrificed himself in order to protect Italy from Hitler and the Nazis. In reality, the Duce and his followers were motivated by feelings of revenge against those who had betrayed him on 25 July 1943, by fear of being held responsible by the Allies, and by a personal ambition to prove to Hitler that Mussolini could still run Italy and restore Italian honour. The latter point becomes clear in letters which Mussolini sent in the autumn of 1943 to Hitler, when he requested Hitler's permission to establish a new Italian army so that 'Italy takes back its post of fighting as soon as possible', on Nazi Germany's side, in order to rehabilitate the Italian nation through war.[58]

What kind of lethal dynamic the Fascist–Nazi relationship unleashed after Mussolini's reinstallation can be seen most clearly in the persecution of the approximately 32,000 Jews who lived in the RSI.[59] Soon after 8 September 1943, they had become the target of the SS, like the Jews in other German-dominated countries in Europe. Already during the 1943 German invasion of Italy, there had been spontaneous outbursts of anti-Jewish violence; for instance, in mid-September, members of the *Leibstandarte Adolf Hitler* had murdered fifty-four Jews as they were trying to escape to Switzerland.[60] Almost immediately after the German occupation of Rome, Herbert Kappler, Rome chief of the SD and the *Sicherheitspolizei*, had received an order from Himmler to deport the city's Jews, Italy's largest Jewish community. Some historians even suggest that Hitler himself gave the order for the deportation of 8,000 Roman Jews as hostages to Mauthausen, but it is more likely that bureaucrats of the German Foreign Ministry, on Ribbentrop's orders, used the notion of a 'Führer decree' (*Führerweisung*) to emphasise that the deportation was the SS's business. On 16 October 1943, the SS and German police units arrested 1,259 Jews in Rome, many of them women, children or elderly people. They could not imagine that they would be deported, although they had been living under the Fascist anti-racial laws since 1938. According to a report by the Italian police, a special train left Rome's Tiburtina station on the night of 19 October with twenty-eight cattle trucks on its way to the Brenner Pass whence the train travelled to Auschwitz. Seventeen people returned after the war.[61] Most of the several thousand Jews who had survived the raid went into hiding in monasteries and the Vatican, but no public protest from Pius XII was forthcoming.[62]

There are sharply different interpretations of the repression of Italy's Jews. Jonathan Steinberg has focused on Italian political and military elites who had undermined Nazi deportations of Jews in Italian-occupied Croatia, France and Greece before Mussolini's fall from power in July 1943. Allegedly, the Italians (*una brava gente*), because of their innate humanity, had been unwilling to hand over Jews to the Germans. In reality, the same Italian officials had been capable of the utmost brutality against civilians. Contrary to their post-war attempts to portray themselves as good-natured compared to the evil and barbarous Nazis, these officials, by refusing to hand over Jews to the Germans, had tried to maintain Italian prestige vis-à-vis German attempts to intervene in Italian-occupied territories. These officials also believed that their refusal to hand over the Jews to the Nazis would stand them in good stead with the Allies, who, they thought, were going to win the war.[63] While the order for the deportations came from Germany, they would not have been possible without the assistance of RSI officials, including the police, and the opportunism of some ordinary Italians who became complicit in the persecution of Jews through denunciations, casting into doubt the powerful post-war stereotype of Italians as incapable of inhumanity and anti-Semitism.[64]

The *italiani, una brava gente* interpretation becomes even less persuasive if we consider that at its November 1943 Verona congress, the Republican Fascist party stigmatised all Italian Jews as foreigners and enemies. This reflected the racist nature of the RSI as well as the racist trajectory of Italian Fascism in its final phase. On 30 November 1943, Guido Buffarini Guidi, interior minister of the RSI, ordered the arrest of all Jews in camps. The Reich Security head office and the Foreign Ministry made the RSI authorities complicit. Altogether, up to 8,000 Jews were deported to Germany. Only 837 survived.[65] Thus, Fascist Italy was not 'outside the Holocaust's shadow' (*fuori dal cono d'ombra dell'Olocausto*), as De Felice has claimed. Rather, the radicalisation of the RSI made the regime closer than ever to Nazi Germany in what would be the final phase of the war.[66]

After Mussolini's failure to turn Italy into a great power, the lives of Italians were now in the hands of foreign powers. Mussolini's abject failure as a political and military leader, now at Hitler's mercy, was matched by his personal behaviour. Goebbels concluded that Mussolini had lost all sense of reality: despite the grave situation, he had surrounded himself 'with a heroic bombast', spending much time communicating with Clara Petacci (who had been reunited with him and became his only friend) instead of dealing with the political and military crises. Mussolini, hitherto a master of performance and oratory, was not even able to deliver a public speech in Milan, as he had wished. The Nazis tried to stop the speech taking place, as they believed that people would either heckle the Duce or even attack him, and insisted that German guards accompany him in public. In order to save face, Mussolini put off his speech.[67]

Mussolini's lowly status was also reflected in his health. Hitler, still believing that Mussolini was essential to German control over Italy, had sent Georg Zachariae, a German doctor, to treat the Duce's ulcer after Theo Morell, Hitler's own physician, had examined him on a previous occasion. Morell had diagnosed problems with the Duce's gut flora, which Goebbels saw as 'the typical ailment of modern, revolutionary politicians'. In a 1948 memoir (highly apologetic of Mussolini), Zachariae gave an alarming diagnosis of his patient. Suffering from low blood pressure, anaemia and constipation, the emaciated Mussolini was constantly in pain and in every way a physical wreck when Zachariae had first met him. The doctor prescribed his patient a vitamin and hormone cure as well as a new diet. This treatment soon restored the Duce's health.[68]

But Mussolini's improving health and Hitler's concerns about the Duce's wellbeing could not hide the fact that their relationship had paled into insignificance, especially if compared to that of Churchill and Roosevelt, which was on the ascendant after the Allies had managed to put the Axis powers into a defensive position. A clear turning point was the Tehran conference, held in late November and early December 1943, where the British and American leaders met Stalin and decided to open a second front against Germany through an invasion of France. Despite strategic disagreements, this was a powerful representation of the personal rapport between Churchill and Roosevelt, as well as of Stalin's role in the war against the Nazis.[69] The reaction of the RSI's Ministry of Popular Culture was not slow in coming. In its officious newsletter *Corrispondenza Repubblicana*, it dismissed the Tehran meeting as a typical manifestation of plutocracy and Communism. It is worth noting that the report made no mention of the Mussolini–Hitler relationship.[70]

V

Behind the scenes, tensions between the German masters and the Italian vassals were higher than ever before. At the end of 1943, the most turbulent year in the Mussolini–Hitler relationship so far, the *Völkischer Beobachter* printed reports from its foreign correspondents on the situation in their host countries. From Milan, Ludwig Alwens filed a report. Thanks to the Führer's rescue of Mussolini, he argued, the Italian Social Republic, a third way between Bolshevism and capitalism, had reanimated the radical zeal of early Fascism. Alwens diagnosed the birth defect of Fascism, namely that it had brought together the bourgeoisie with other elements in the early 1920s to combat the left. There would be no half measures: the Italians had to 'work and fight'. Other German officials in Italy were alarmed at the plans advocated by Fascist intellectuals such as Nicola Bombacci and Carlo Silvestri, both, like Mussolini, from originally left-wing backgrounds, to nationalise key industries, in line with the 'social' revolutionary commitment of the RSI. German observers feared that such experiments would lower industrial outputs needed for the war effort. Hitler himself rebuked German critics of these schemes and let the German plenipotentiary Rahn know that 'we Germans had to get out of the habit of believing that we had to play the "medicine man" in all of Europe'. Clearly, Hitler still felt protective of the Duce; although he had written off Mussolini as a serious political actor, Hitler still believed that offending the Duce would undermine German dominance over Italy.[71]

Yet, the more Germany's war fortunes declined, the more aggressive became Hitler's views on Italy, which he increasingly singled out as a scapegoat. In late January 1944, he discussed his Italian strategy with Goebbels, who was receptive of his leader's growing disillusion. Goebbels ranted against the 'lazy, cowardly' Italians, and claimed that Ciano, shortly before his execution, had confessed to a German official that in 1940 he had revealed the German plans for an invasion of Belgium to the Belgian ambassador, apparently on Mussolini's orders. According to Goebbels, it was this revelation that marked the definite end of Hitler's close relationship with Mussolini. Goebbels rejoiced that his leader had 'no more personal relations and also no more friendship' with Mussolini. As if he had to defend his previous strategy, Hitler had admitted that the real reason for the reinstallation of Mussolini was to enhance German prestige 'in the whole world' and to legitimise what was effectively the German occupation of Italy.[72]

Nevertheless, Hitler had little choice but to continue with the performance of unity and friendship. Thus, in conversations with Italian officials, he still expressed his admiration for the Duce, for example when Anfuso presented his credentials in late 1943 as the RSI's ambassador to Germany. His reception went beyond the usual diplomatic protocol, as Anfuso noted in his report to Mussolini, since he had had lunch with Ribbentrop before having tea with Hitler. Hitler repeated his formula that the Duce was 'the greatest man whom you have had since the fall of the ancient world until today'.[73] Moreover, Axis propaganda continued in the German and RSI press to legitimise the alliance. In early April 1944, for instance, the *Hamburger Fremdenblatt* republished an interview which Mussolini had given to Paul Gentizon, writing for *Le Mois Suisse*. In the interview, Mussolini had delivered an account of his deposition, his subsequent arrest and his rescue from the Gran Sasso. The editorial strategy to republish this interview was to reassure the ever more Italophobic German readership of Mussolini's indefatigable loyalty towards Germany. The *New York Times* summarised the interview, implying that the ranks between Mussolini and Hitler were closed.[74] But nothing could have been further from the truth.

VI

Mussolini and Hitler met at Schloss Klessheim on 22 and 23 April 1944. This springtime meeting followed the routine of the previous springtime meetings that had been held there, and was meant to suggest that the Mussolini–Hitler relationship was as firm as ever, even after the Duce's fall from power. As on previous occasions, the meeting was held in a more or less secretive atmosphere, and, as in previous years, at around the same time as his meeting with Mussolini, Hitler had summoned other Axis leaders to the Berghof and Klessheim in order to maintain the momentum of a German-led coalition against Bolshevism, thus further confirming that the alliance with Mussolini was less and less important for the German war effort.[75]

As during the previous meetings, small details reflected power relations. For example, because of Mussolini's subservient status, he did not travel on his own special train, but on one provided by the German *Reichsbahn*. At the same time, Mussolini's big retinue suggested that the Duce was the head of a sovereign state, even though the presence of SS and German army officials on the train marred the picture of him as a strong leader. Furthermore, Dr Zachariae's presence was a reminder of the Duce's frailty. Gone were the days of Mussolini's triumphant departures from Rome with enthusiastic crowds looking on. Instead, the train departed from a small station near Trento, as it was felt that the Duce, for security reasons, could not appear in public.[76]

Mussolini had requested to meet Hitler, as he had hoped that a personal discussion with the Nazi leader would be the most appropriate way to scale back the growing German interference with the RSI's government. Of particular concern was the fate of the 'military internees' and the squeezing of the Italian economy through the mobilisation of forced workers. While in the first four months of 1944, 23,000 Italian workers had been recruited for labour in the Reich, Hitler himself boasted on 25 April 1944 'that one could take three million out of Italy'. A subsequent agreement between the RSI and the Third Reich to regulate the recruitment did not result in higher numbers of labourers because Rahn and others were concerned that the recruitments would jeopardise the stability of the Italian war theatre as a whole.[77]

Mussolini may have hoped to reanimate his special rapport with Hitler, but his request to have his meals on his own reveals that the dictators' personal relationship was ruined (in the end, for the sake of protocol, he ate with the Nazi leader).[78] The organisation of the meetings followed earlier precedents and included the usual formulaic telegram exchange. Propaganda continued to stress the Italian–German friendship: invoking Axis routine, the *Corriere della Sera* reported on 'the talks in the spirit of old friendship', while the *Völkischer Beobachter* emphasised Hitler and Mussolini's plan to win the war 'against the Bolsheviks of the East and the Jews and plutocrats of the West'. But the failure of such plans cannot have escaped anyone present.[79] Mussolini later told Anfuso that he had not shared Hitler's belief in an Axis victory, but had not contradicted the Nazi leader, as he did not have the power to do so.[80]

For the first time in their relationship, Hitler allowed the defensive Mussolini to talk at length. This was a strategy to expose the Duce's weakness and complete reliance on Germany. It did not help that Mussolini was speaking in German, of which he did not have a perfect command. The Duce had to admit that his 'work [was] subjected to a number of burdens'. In other words, his regime was unable to keep society under control. Furthermore, he confessed to Hitler that the new National Republican Army had not succeeded in conscripting recruits, who feared that they would be taken to Germany (most senior German army officers were not in favour of setting up a new Italian army, reflecting their distrust of Italy). Although the RSI cracked down brutally on dissenters, Mussolini had to tell Hitler that it lacked sufficient police to force the recruits to report to the barracks. Instead, many recruits fled, and some joined the partisans.[81] As the conversation continued, Hitler, returning to his default mode of superiority, lectured Mussolini about the need to stabilise the RSI and recruit more troops, who had to be trained and toughened up in Germany. Hitler left Mussolini under no illusion: Germany was in charge; and he brushed aside Mussolini's carefully worded complaints about German behaviour in the operational zones, citing 'military reasons'. Mussolini and Italy must keep fighting the Allies, otherwise Italy and the Duce, because of their bond with the Third Reich, would be brutally crushed. Hitler, in a further display of superiority, refused to make concessions to the military internees, although he was prepared to 'take out individuals who are good and useful and put them in the army'.[82]

Despite the failure of the Klessheim talks in resolving tensions, Mussolini had no option but to keep declaring his support for the alliance with Hitler. Before his return to Italy, the Duce's inspection of a division of the National Republican Army, training under the Germans at Grafenwöhr in Bavaria's Upper Palatinate, was one of the his first public appearances since his fall from power. Accordingly, his speech was given ample coverage in the RSI and German press.[83] The name of the division he addressed was 'San Marco', a reference to the glorious history of Venice as an Adriatic and Mediterranean power, implying criticism of the revived German thrust to the Adriatic port of Trieste. In his speech to the troops, Mussolini took up a familiar trope and insisted that the new army would fight until victory alongside the Germans and rehabilitate Italy after 'the dreadful shame of betrayal'.[84]

For some favourable foreign observers, such as the Japanese ambassador to the Salò Republic (whose report to Tokyo was intercepted by the British), the Mussolini–Hitler meeting succeeded in projecting the image of a strong and solid rapport.[85] But, more than ever before, both leaders and their propaganda apparatuses had no choice but to drone on with this message. On 30 April, days after Mussolini's return from Germany, Alessandro Pavolini, the secretary of the Republican Fascist party, gave a speech in Milan, broadcast over the radio. Looking back at the months since Mussolini's liberation, he waxed lyrical about Mussolini and Hitler's historic meeting. Pavolini reinforced Mussolini's mantra that the only way for Italy to rehabilitate itself as an honourable nation was war on Nazi Germany's side, and he compared the National Republican Army to Garibaldi's Thousand, who had fought against Bourbon rule in the Kingdom of the Two Sicilies in 1860 to bring about Italian unification. This attempt to legitimise the RSI with the Risorgimento appeared as mere rhetoric for most Italians who were simply concerned about surviving the war, but, for some, it helped encourage a fanatical campaign to purge Italy of those who had betrayed the nation when they had sided with Badoglio and the Allies.[86]

While Mussolini was broadly in agreement with the Wehrmacht's brutal crackdown on partisans, whose activity increased, he occasionally complained to the German authorities about excessive violence against the partisans and civilians, not because he was motivated by humanitarian thinking, but because he believed that German violence against women and children, especially if they were relatives of Fascists, would further increase resistance and delegitimise his regime. At the same time, however, he let the RSI police and Fascist special units crack down on supposed or real enemies.[87]

Increasingly unfettered by diplomatic considerations, many German institutions and officials in Italy showed who was the real boss. Mussolini was well informed about this process, and his secretariat duly filed reports of incidents in which German officials had displayed their superiority. On 12 May 1944, for instance, the Duce received a message on the situation in the South Tyrol. Prior to his meeting with Hitler, the correspondent claimed, all official signs in the region had been bilingual. Yet, after Mussolini's return to Italy, German officials had removed the Italian signs. In an Italian school in the South Tyrol, the German authorities had allegedly even forbidden the singing of Italian songs. While these changes did not happen on Hitler's direct orders, the fact that local Nazi leaders brought in these policies illustrates their anti-Italian feeling and their impunity to articulate it so openly.[88]

Such reports were just the tip of the iceberg. The RSI's Foreign Ministry too, officially headed by Mussolini himself, received a string of complaints from Italian officials about the arrogant behaviour of German soldiers and institutions in Italy who had been ignoring the RSI's authorities. One correspondent from the ministry had written to the Duce in October 1943 to implore him to use his contacts with Hitler to help improve the relationship between the German troops, which the official, not entirely incorrectly, identified as 'occupying troops', and the local population. The belief in the special influence of Mussolini on Hitler was thus still present amongst Italian officials, although, as we have seen, Mussolini had largely lost his leverage with Hitler.[89]

Mussolini's regime soon lost any remaining credibility and legitimacy as Allied troops advanced up the peninsula after the end of heavy fighting at Monte Cassino in May 1944. The clearest symbol of Mussolini's failure was the fall of Rome, which Fascism abandoned on 4 June 1944 when the Allies liberated it. The diary of Corrado Di Pompeo, a young Roman civil servant, gives us a good insight into everyday life in the capital on that momentous day. In the early morning, Corrado was woken up by gunshots. His relief at the end of the German occupation of Rome was palpable: 'All the suffering, anguish, sacrifices are erased with a clean slate. One breathes some free air.'[90]

Needless to say, the fall of Rome resonated more widely. Just before, the National Republican Guard, a radical militia modelled on the SS, following its practice of issuing 'daily news' about popular opinion to Mussolini's offices, had compiled a secret report on public opinion in Italy. The report, for the exclusive attention of Mussolini and Renato Ricci, the Guard's commander, was tainted by a fanatical belief in a Fascist–Nazi victory, but it astutely diagnosed that 'for the masses, Rome is Rome', suggesting that the fall of the capital had dashed the hopes of an Axis victory.[91]

After the fall of Rome, Mussolini ordered state mourning. Petacci, who knew about the importance of the city for Mussolini and Fascism, implored him to prompt Hitler to reconquer it, but this was wishful thinking.[92] For many Fascists, the Italian people had shown themselves unworthy of Fascism. Furthermore, the fall of the Eternal City had damaged the self-understanding of many Fascists for whom Rome had been the founding myth. For some, like the National Republican Guard officials who compiled a report on popular opinion in Genoa on 21 June 1944, the prospect of an almost certain Allied invasion of the rest of Italy raised fears amongst Fascist supporters of Allied reprisals.[93] This feeling prompted some to return to the violent origins of Fascism. Some Fascists, ever more radical facing almost certain defeat, began brutally to eliminate anti-Fascists for whom the liberation of Rome raised high hopes that the RSI and the Nazis would be defeated soon.[94]

As the Allies landed in Normandy in June 1944, followed by their August 1944 landing on the French Mediterranean coast, a German defeat became only a matter of time. Florence, site of two Mussolini–Hitler meetings, fell in August. After these Allied gains, the frontline remained more or less stable until spring 1945. Brutal German reprisals became part of the everyday lives of Italians living in the RSI where, from June 1944, the *Brigate nere*, Fascist terror squads, fought hand in hand with the Germans against the partisans.[95]

For the German army and the SS, partisan activity served as an excuse to brutally repress the civilian population. Long denied after the war by German veterans, German massacres at the Fosse Ardeatine outside Rome on 23–24 March 1944 (the twenty-fifth anniversary of the foundation of the *Fasci di combattimento*), at Sant'Anna di Stazzema in August 1944, at Marzabotto in September and October 1944 and elsewhere were nothing less than war crimes against the civilian population. Altogether, although precise numbers are impossible to obtain, at least 10,000 Italian civilians were killed in the partisan war in reprisal raids, not to mention the more than 30,000 partisans who died (some even suggest that 44,720 partisans were killed in action or murdered). Some have likened these actions to German war atrocities in Poland and the Soviet Union. However, the number of those killed by the Germans in Italy scarcely tally with the number of dead in eastern Europe. Moreover, Italy was different because the war crimes were not always deliberately planned by the Germans to order to create a racially pure living space. Instead, German war crimes in Italy occurred as brutal reactions to purported or real partisan activity, although this does in no way excuse the atrocities.[96]

In essence, the period between 1943 and 1945 saw three different but simultaneous conflicts in Italy, later controversially characterised by the Italian historian Claudio Pavone as a civil war: the first, a patriotic war against the Germans; the second, a civil war between the Fascists and anti-Fascists; the third, a class war of the proletariat against property owners.

Of course, most ordinary people, while inevitably drawn into these conflicts, were primarily concerned with their own survival.[97] Mussolini tried hard to maintain the illusion that he was still in charge of Italy and sometimes posed as Italy's saviour from Nazi oppression. While he backed brutal reprisals by the Wehrmacht, the SS and Fascist terror squads against purported or real partisans, he also complained to Rahn, rather than Hitler, about Wehrmacht atrocities against civilians, including women and children. But the Duce, always prepared to use violence to reach his aims, was not guided by humanitarian concerns, as we have seen; rather, he hoped that his interventions would prevent further partisan activity.[98]

Amidst all the terror and destruction, the Duce found the time and energy to write a great deal. This was a return to his early career as a journalistic agitator when Fascism had emerged as a violent, revolutionary and dynamic force whose momentum, he hoped, the RSI would keep going. A central aim of Mussolini's journalism and his administration's publication strategies was to deny the widespread view that he was Hitler's lackey. For instance, a booklet compiled by his secretariat summarised Italian newspapers' coverage on what Mussolini regarded as the 'coup d'état' of 25 July 1943. A special section was dedicated to the fateful April 1943 meeting at Klessheim where the Nazi leader had read Mussolini the riot act. Mussolini's staff underlined the passages on the document that denied his paladin status. Another folder in the press digest was entitled 'Immaturity and guilt of the Italian people'. This title reflected Mussolini's core belief that the Italian nation had failed him and thus had to be turned into a nation of warriors through war on Nazi Germany's side, sacrifice and repression.[99]

Mussolini's writings were also an attempt to control and influence his memory after his death and defeat. In mid-July 1944, the *Corriere della Sera* published his reflections about his fall from power, which he had written while under arrest. Mussolini's aim was to muster support and to dismiss the fronde around Grandi and, above all, the king and Badoglio as traitors. But Mussolini, tucked away on Lake Garda and listening to classical music such as Beethoven's Pastoral Symphony, also reflected on his rapport with Hitler and proudly announced this to Petacci on 2 July 1944. In his *Drama of Diarchy* (*Il dramma di diarchia*), a lamentation about his inability to eliminate the monarchy, Mussolini gave a bitter account of Hitler's 1938 visit to Italy and resentfully complained that the king as head of state had stolen the show, although it had been 'clear that the Führer intended above all to visit the Duce's Rome'. Despite a frustration that sometimes bordered on delusion, Mussolini was realistic enough to recognise that he would be defeated. Accordingly, he acknowledged to Petacci that the US army had hoisted the Stars and Stripes on the balcony of the Palazzo Venezia, site of some of his most important speeches including the triumphant proclamation of the Italian Empire in 1936 and, of course, the Italian declarations of war in 1940 and 1941.[100]

VII

As plans for their New Order were shattered, Mussolini and Hitler, in an attempt to keep the momentum of their display of unity and friendship going, met at Wolf's Lair in East Prussia on 20 July 1944. The request had come from the German government and was a thinly veiled order to Mussolini to pay homage to Hitler. The Duce had been unwilling to meet Hitler since the liberation of Rome, which had been a massive loss of prestige for him. What is more, on 13 July 1944, as Mussolini reported in a letter to Petacci, Rahn had more or less ordered him to prepare for an immediate departure for Germany.[101] Mussolini's itinerary en route to East Prussia included visits to the National Republican Army, who were training across Germany. The purpose of these tours, given broad coverage in the RSI press, was to reinforce yet again Mussolini's mantra that war as Germany's ally would rehabilitate Italy's reputation after the supposed betrayal of 8 September 1943.[102]

Even at the height of military and political crises, the itineraries of previous Mussolini–Hitler meetings had always been maintained, but this time the Duce's delayed arrival on 20 July 1944 suggested something was wrong. A few hours previously, a bomb had detonated in Wolf's Lair, planted by Count Claus Schenk von Stauffenberg, part of a national-conservative conspiracy to assassinate Hitler. Hitler had survived, and had, by the end of the day, brutally put down the conspiracy.[103] A grotesque scene was revealed. Since his right arm had been injured in the explosion, Hitler had to greet Mussolini with his left; he also showed the scene of the assassination attempt to the Duce and even made him look at his torn uniform. Mussolini's reactions to the assassination attempt can be reconstructed from a pensive love letter he later sent to Petacci. While acknowledging Germany's disastrous military situation, he wrote that he greatly admired Hitler's kindness and, above all, his 'cold blood' when retaliating against the conspirators. Between the lines, however, Mussolini was envious of Hitler who had survived the putsch, while he had fallen from power almost exactly a year previously.[104] At the same time, it is noteworthy that the Duce's secretariat compiled a thick dossier of press reports on the assassination attempt which highlighted fears that Mussolini too might be the subject of such an attack. In fact, given the much stronger resistance in Italy, such fears were astute.[105]

The meeting's setting in the gloomy and mosquito-infested forests of East Prussia contrasted sharply with the pompous surroundings of many of their previous meetings. As the explosion had destroyed parts of Hitler's usual conference venue, the Nazi leader had to perch on a crate and invited Mussolini to sit on a rickety chair. Even in this strange situation, the conversation followed the set pattern. Hitler, who had returned to his previous form, quickly seized the conversation and gave Mussolini a long lecture about 'premonitions of coming dangers'. Unusually for him, he acknowledged that Germany was facing a military crisis, but would prevail eventually. Towards the end of the conversation, Mussolini finally had the chance to share his view. His remarks were defensive. The Duce drew a realistic picture of the increasing lack of popular support for the RSI, exacerbated by the fall of Rome. Finally, a submissive Mussolini asked Hitler to alleviate the fate of the 'war internees', as a generous gesture from the Führer would be 'a particular joy' for the Duce and increase popular support for the RSI. Hitler was in a generous mood, showing off his superiority. Not only did he promise to release Italian naval officers who had been sentenced to death by the Germans to the RSI authorities but, in a calculated gesture which, he hoped, would add to the Duce's prestige within Italy, Hitler also agreed to give the military internees the status of civilian workers.[106]

In truth, many of the military internees opposed this new status, as they feared being drafted into the National Republican Army. Significantly, Mussolini was decisively not interested in a humanitarian intervention on behalf of all Italian military internees, but only asked Hitler to ensure better treatment of those internees working in the war industry, who he knew had mostly refused to declare their allegiance to the RSI. Furthermore, the transformation of the status of the military internees into that of civilian workers was the result not principally of Mussolini's request, but of the demands of the Nazi total war. The Nazis hoped that this change of status would increase their productivity. Thus, while the status change was a symbolic victory for the RSI, the abysmal living and working conditions of the former military internees did not improve significantly, so Mussolini's half-hearted intervention did not yield significant results. Once again his subordinate position was demonstrated.[107]

Still, after the failed assassination attempt of 20 July 1944, the meeting succeeded in keeping the momentum of the Axis friendship going as the most potent symbol of the New Order. The *New York Times* even reprinted Mussolini's usual thank-you telegram to Hitler.[108] Yet, below the surface, war-weariness mounted. In Italy, some were disappointed to hear of Hitler's survival, as they rightly thought that it would prolong the war. In Milan, Magda Ceccarelli De Grada lamented in her diary: 'Two metres, an error of two metres', referring to the fact that Hitler would not have survived if he had stood closer to the bomb planted by Stauffenberg.[109]

Needless to say, the propaganda surrounding Mussolini's visit to Germany did not raise the attitudes of most Italians towards the RSI. Instead, as the war affected the everyday lives of people more and more, defeatist reports on popular opinion reached the RSI's government. For instance, a September 1944 report by the National Republican Guard on popular opinion in Turin, a hotbed of working-class militancy, lamented that the majority of the population, especially the working class, 'openly demonstrates its hostility towards the Social Republican government' and, rather lamely, blamed Allied propaganda for this hostility.[110]

Although initially relieved about Hitler's survival, many Germans too began to despair at the military situation. Hitler's reputation began to decline, as the Allies gradually pushed the German army back into its home territory. In early August 1944, the SD reported from Stuttgart 'that most national comrades, even those who up to now have believed unwaveringly, have now lost all faith in the Leader'.[111]

Military defeat was the order of the day, with the Allies penetrating into Germany from the west and the east. Erstwhile Axis allies, such as Bulgaria and Romania, were invaded by the Soviets in late 1944, leading to the almost total isolation of Nazi Germany. Yet, for Mussolini, the only option was war on Germany's side. A let-up of the Allied advance in Italy, together with General Alexander's call to the partisans to stop large-scale attacks on the Germans, gave him brief hope about regaining the initiative, which is why he penned a letter to Hitler on 14 November 1944. In it, he boasted that Italy would soon launch an attack on the Allies on the peninsula and defend the strategically important Po valley. But this remained wishful thinking, not least since his regime had failed to create an effective Republican Army.[112]

Now that there was almost nothing left to lose, Mussolini, in order to boost his dictatorial reputation and his ego, sometimes risked alienating his German masters. The clearest expression of this tendency was his speech in Milan's Teatro Lirico on 16 December 1944. This was his first major public speech in Italy since his reinstallation. As we have seen, the German authorities in Italy had been trying to dissuade Mussolini from speaking in public, citing security concerns, and it is noteworthy that it took Mussolini so long to have his way.[113] That he chose Milan was not a coincidence. The Lombard capital had been the city of many of Mussolini's political triumphs, including the 1919 foundation of the *Fasci italiani di combattimento*, and the 1936 proclamation of the Axis with Germany. The choice of Milan thus provided the Duce's regime with some historical legitimacy, especially the mantra that the RSI was a return to the 'true' violent fascism of the early years. After such a long absence from the lectern, Mussolini took the opportunity to show off his oratory skills and justify the history of the RSI. As could have been predicted, he railed against the king's supposed betrayal of the Italian people before he praised the alliance with Nazi Germany. He bitterly complained that 'one part of the Italian people ha[d] accepted the capitulation, for unawareness or exhaustion', while, on a more positive note, the other part had 'immediately stood by Germany'. His speech was met with applause by the hand-picked audience. To some in the audience, the Duce, while looking quite thin, was on top form. A female auxiliary in the Decima Mas, a naval cracktroop commanded by Prince Valerio Junio Borghese, later commended Mussolini in her diary, insisting that 'everything that has been done in these tragic days to uplift the honour of Italy, to give our Fatherland a new face and a new way of living in society, can never be lost'. Some Fascists even associated the brief German gains in the Ardennes offensive with the Duce's revitalised energies as shown during his encounter with the people of Milan. (In the event, the so-called 'Battle of the Bulge', which had begun in mid-December 1944 and involved some 200,000 German soldiers with 600 tanks taking on 80,000 American soldiers with 400 tanks, ended in failure for the Germans in January 1945).[114]

The Milan speech was Mussolini's swan song. His fate was completely in the hands of the Germans, who more or less ignored his histrionics. In a carefully scripted choreography, after the performance in the Teatro Lirico, Mussolini appeared in Piazza San Sepolcro, the birthplace of the *Fasci italiani del combattimento*. Finally, on 18 December 1944, the anniversary of the 1935 Day of Faith (*Giornata delle fede*), when the regime had asked Italians to sacrifice their gold, including wedding rings, for the nation in response to the imposition of the League of Nations' sanctions against Italy, he inspected a parade of the various armed forces of the RSI.[115]

Mussolini's determination for Italy to appear as an honourable nation that would redeem itself through war and sacrifice explains why, in late 1944, he suggested to his son Vittorio, general secretary of the Republican Fascist party's German branch, that its 30,000 members should be fighting in the *Volkssturm*. This was the final German contingent consisting of those previously deemed unfit for war service, including the elderly and teenagers. While there is no evidence that Italians fought in the *Volkssturm*, this idea reveals Mussolini's fanaticism and weak grip on reality, oscillating between delusion and fanaticism.[116]

While for Mussolini and Hitler, seconded by their acolytes, war had a transformative value, for the vast majority of people living through this war experience, it was a ghastly period, characterised by fear, hunger, uncertainty about the whereabouts of one's loved ones, and a bitter will to survive. Altogether, the period between the July 1943 Allied landing in Sicily and the German surrender in Italy that became effective on 2 May 1945 was one of intense and brutal warfare for Italians. At least 330,000 Italian men, women and children had died, alongside the 312,000 Allied soldiers and at least 415,615 German troops who had perished on the peninsula's battlegrounds. In Germany as a whole, more soldiers and civilians died in the months between 20 July 1944 and the end of the war in Europe in May 1945 than in all previous years of the war.[117]

After the German offensive in the Ardennes failed in January 1945, pressure on Germany from the west, the east and increasingly from the south gradually brought the war to its end in Europe. The regimes so closely associated with Mussolini and Hitler had reached their aim of bringing total war to the continent, a conflict which now entered their homelands. As the war was lost, both regimes returned to their violent origins in the aftermath of the First World War. The destructive zeal to fight a total war, if necessary until self-annihilation, was on the mind of the Nazis, who turned against anyone, increasingly also the civilian population, thought to stand in the way of 'final victory'.[118] His relationship with Mussolini became insignificant to Hitler, who in January 1945 withdrew to the bunker below the Reich Chancellery in Berlin to command his last battle. News of the chaotic situation in Germany, characterised by mass bombings, the approaching Allies and ever harsher Nazi repression, including the dispensation of death sentences to alleged or real deserters, soon gave a new impetus to the partisans in Italy, who managed to intercept one of Filippo Anfuso's reports to Mussolini which carried this news. Indeed, on 21 February 1945, the neutral *Basler Nachrichten* gave ample coverage to the interception by *Il partigiano*, a clandestine Milanese newspaper, of another report which further unmasked the Duce's rule as a shadow of its former glory.[119]

As Mussolini, less fanatical than Hitler at the eleventh hour, left the Lake Garda area on 18 April 1945 for Milan to negotiate an armistice with the partisans and the Allies, he sent a birthday note to Hitler. In his last official letter, he extended best wishes to the Nazi leader 'for your historic mission' against Judaism and Bolshevism. In his reply, Hitler reinforced his central beliefs in the Judaeo-Bolshevik conspiracy, but refrained from personal or emotional references to his friendship with Mussolini. This was the end of a correspondence which Hitler had initiated with his letters begging for a signed Mussolini photograph, and it was Hitler who terminated it.[120]

The inglorious end of both dictators reveals some striking differences between their personalities and regimes. In late April 1945, Mussolini refused an armistice with the partisans in the house of the Archbishop of Milan after he discovered that the Germans had been holding separate talks with the partisans and the Allies, who had finally penetrated the German frontline in northern Italy. Again, the Germans had left him in the dark – even in the final hour. On 25 April, just before the liberation of Milan, Mussolini left the city and was soon joined by Petacci near the Swiss border. That they travelled in a convoy, assisted by a German military unit, again reflected the Duce's complete dependence on the Germans and his determination not to fall into enemy hands. In the small town of Dongo, on the shores of Lake Como, Mussolini was stopped and identified by partisans on the morning of 27 April. The founder of Italian Fascism, the ultra-national movement that had promised to turn Italy into a great power, was wearing a German army coat. Petacci was reunited with Mussolini. They were both shot on 28 April, and on 29 April, the day of the signing of German surrender to the Allies in Italy, their bodies were hanged upside down in Piazzale Loreto in Milan, site of a 1944 atrocity against the partisans, after an angry mob had attacked and mutilated the corpses of Mussolini and Petacci, alongside those of other Fascist leaders, including Farinacci and Starace. This was the ignominious end to Mussolini's hubris in the city where he had established Fascism in 1919.[121]

Hitler's death also provided a stark contrast to the bombastic propaganda displays. While he was told about Mussolini's execution by the partisans, it is uncertain whether he knew the macabre details of his erstwhile idol's death. In any case, news of the Duce's death confirmed Hitler's plan to commit suicide, always on his mind in the event of defeat, in order to avoid a similarly grisly fate. As Soviet troops were advancing towards the Reich Chancellery, Hitler shot himself, while Eva Braun, whom he had married a few hours previously, took cyanide. This suicide was followed by those of other Nazi leaders, including Goebbels, and thousands of ordinary people who associated the end of the Third Reich and Allied occupation with hopelessness and despair. This brought to an end the fatal relationship of Mussolini and Hitler which had inflicted unprecedented violence, genocide and destruction on Europe.[122] Given the symbolic importance of the Brenner Pass, site of three wartime Mussolini–Hitler meetings, it was perhaps not coincidental that American troops who had previously fought in France and Germany linked up there with their compatriots who had fought their way up through Italy.[123]

Amidst the gradual and eventually rapid build-up to an Allied victory over the Axis powers, Hitler and Mussolini maintained their display of unity and friendship until the bitter end. They had no other option but to continue with the show, although it resonated less and less with domestic and international audiences. Furthermore, the alliance with Italy, a nation that had 'betrayed' its German ally in 1943 after its first 'betrayal' in 1915, became increasingly insignificant for Hitler. After the first three years of Italy's war, which had gone disastrously, Mussolini had finally become *Gauleiter* of the German-dominated parts of Italy. But this is not to say that Mussolini and his RSI acolytes were mere lackeys of Hitler. Instead,

Mussolini's new republican regime did not have to respect the monarchy and thus promised to a minority of Fascist fanatics a return to the origins of squadrist violence and their commitment to establishing a New Order at home and abroad. Accordingly, the RSI brought out the most destructive elements of Fascism, which included the deportation of Jews to the Nazi gas chambers and massive violence and repression against the partisans.

Unlike the other European nations under Nazi domination, the RSI's position was unique, as it always oscillated between that of an occupied country and an allied nation, and keeping the balance between these two categories was an impossible task for Mussolini.[124] There were three reasons for this ambivalent status of the RSI. The first reason was undeniably Hitler's admiration for Mussolini, albeit on the wane since Italy had run into military defeats. The German treatment of Mussolini, at least in public, especially at his final encounters with Hitler in Germany, was designed to add prestige to the Duce as the head of a sovereign state. This was a strategy designed to mobilise popular support in Italy for the alliance with Germany and defend the Italian peninsula against Allied advances. This strategy largely failed in mobilising popular support, but it maintained the frontline until the final stages of the war, adding to the agony of Italians living this war experience. The second reason was the political structure of the Third Reich, where competing Nazi, state and military institutions created a chaotic political situation over which Mussolini could exert little but symbolic control. Third, all of these institutions wanted to maximise their grip on Italy by exploiting the economy and the population for the German war effort. Tucked away on the beautiful Lake Garda, far away from the real centres of political power, Mussolini's final period in office turned Italy into a deeply polarised nation experiencing civil-war-like violence. The New Order, Hitler and Mussolini's aggressive challenge to the culture and politics of liberal internationalism, democracy and Communism, had failed spectacularly. The menace, spearheaded by Mussolini and Hitler, that had emerged out of the ashes of the First World War had finally been defeated, and the unconditional German surrender to the Allies became effective on 8 May 1945 when the weapons fell silent across Europe.

CONCLUSION

On a staircase in the Bardini Museum in Florence, a rare Persian carpet is on prominent display. It is said that in May 1938, the Italian authorities, in their attempt to convey to their Nazi guests a sense of cultural superiority, rolled out this carpet on the platform at Santa Maria Novella station to welcome Hitler. Using carpets to create a special area upon which only rulers are allowed to set foot has evolved over the centuries as a gesture of diplomatic honour. The Führer's foot allegedly made its mark: the Bardini carpet is slightly damaged, apparently because of Hitler's spurs.

Despite his and Mussolini's shared taste in boots and uniforms, Hitler, unlike the Duce, never wore spurs. Moreover, there is no clear evidence that the carpet was used during Hitler's visit that spring. But, after the war, the story of a boorish and destructive Hitler as an invader of Italy served as a powerful myth for many Italians to dissociate themselves from the Axis and to portray Hitler as the 'evil German', in sharp contrast to the 'good Italian'. Despite Italian war crimes in the Balkans and, above all, in the African colonies, it is clear that Germany's genocidal violence during the Second World War, at the heart of the Nazi project, was on an entirely different scale from Italy's atrocities under Fascism.[1]

Yet, comparisons to the Nazi death toll were used to whitewash Italian involvement in the Axis. Almost as soon as Fascism fell, Italian political elites began to distance themselves and the Italian nation from their former German ally. They could rightly refer to German war crimes in Nazi-occupied

Europe and to the fact that the mass murder of Europe's Jews that later came to be known as the Holocaust had been a German project, although, as we have seen, Fascist officials and some ordinary Italians had joined in the ostracism and discrimination of Italy's Jews. Yet the 'good Italians' sought to absolve themselves in many ways. Emblematic in this respect was the view of the distinguished anti-Fascist philosopher Benedetto Croce: Nazism was deeply rooted in German history, while Fascism was merely a parenthesis in Italy's glorious history.[2] Italy, unlike Germany, had seen a large resistance movement against the dictatorship. This was soon elevated into the myth of a popular *resistenza* and, together with the notion of the 'good Italian', provided soothing amnesia for the millions of Italians who had been involved in the Fascist project in one way or another. Such views, while attacked by Italian historians, still resonate today in Italian popular culture, as the vignette about the carpet shows.[3]

In the public memory of the Third Reich, as it has evolved over the decades since 1945, there is now a clear and unmistakable recognition of German responsibility for the war and the Holocaust. Post-war Germany was divided into four zones of occupation and subsequently into two republics, an arrangement that lasted until the end of the Cold War. Those former members of the Reich government and Nazi party elites who had not committed suicide were put on trial by the Allies at Nuremberg. Italy, however, retained its territorial integrity, and after a short wave of brutal reckoning with the Fascists did not pursue them further: there were no Allied war crimes trials, as for strategic reasons the Allies had decided to keep the country, with its strong Communist Party, on the side of the West.[4]

In Communist East Germany, the regime promoted a blunt view of Fascism and Nazism that emphasised close links between fascism and capitalism, but remained awkwardly silent about the racist dimension of these dictatorships, above all of the Third Reich. This interpretation served as a way of attacking liberal-democratic capitalist societies, especially West Germany.[5] In contrast, in post-war West Germany, a popular anti-Italian myth about the Second World War emerged that built on decades of national stereotypes that had pre-dated the rise of the Axis and that were reinforced during the war. Hitler's scapegoating of Mussolini was typical in this regard. Let us consider a February 1945 conversation between Hitler and Martin Bormann, head of the Nazi Party Chancellery. According to a post-war publication of the conversations, the Nazi leader bluntly concluded that his friendship with Mussolini had been a grave mistake: it had served Germany's enemies more than the Third Reich itself. If Germany lost the war, Hitler had added, the alliance with Italy would be an important contributing factor. Despite the dubious provenance of Bormann's notes of these conversations, it is clear that Hitler harboured fiercely anti-Italian racist feelings. A variation on these remarks, building on widespread anti-Italian prejudices, coalesced into a powerful legend in Germany after the war that held that without the Italian entanglement, particularly the bailout in the Balkans, Nazi Germany would have been able to attack the Soviet Union in the spring rather than the summer of 1941, which would have meant in turn a quick German victory before the Russian winter set in. Hitler's scapegoating of Mussolini's Italy to explain Germany's military misfortunes was akin to a new stab-in-the-back myth.[6]

However, the German intervention on Italy's side in the Balkans did not significantly delay the invasion of the Soviet Union; the original German plan to attack Russia in May 1941 had proved too ambitious and unrealistic, not least because of atrocious conditions on the ground which would have put a halt to the German infantry and artillery in the mud. Ultimately, Germany's interventions in Greece and Yugoslavia delayed the Barbarossa campaign by a mere two weeks – a span of time so short that it could hardly be a sufficient explanation for Germany losing the war.[7]

Blaming Mussolini and Hitler for the fateful alliance had its roots during the war, as we have seen, when German and Italian diplomatic and military officials internalised the powerful propaganda that any important decision affecting the Axis would have to be taken by the leaders in their conferences. But this simplistic interpretation was also a convenient way for political and military elites, as well as for the millions of Germans and Italians who had served in the war, to offload responsibility for the Axis alliance onto Mussolini and Hitler.

One of the central contentions of this book has been that the Mussolini–Hitler relationship was much more contingent than many have assumed. I have used their relationship to explore three broader questions: How do we study the personal relationship of dictators? How do dictators represent their power in diplomacy? And how do propaganda, representation and performance gain political momentum? In this book, instead of pursuing a conventional biographical approach, I have approached these questions by deconstructing the personal relationship of Mussolini and Hitler. I have shown how it was continually performed to provide a clearer understanding of the disastrous first half of the twentieth century and two of the men at its heart.[8] I have, through a cultural reading of diplomacy, focused on the ways in which they and their staffs constructed and represented a display of unity and friendship. My emphasis on their relationship has enabled a close reading of their personalities, but also of their political visions and use of propaganda, which ultimately became so convincing that they found themselves stuck with each other until war's bitter end. Yet, from the beginning, Mussolini and Hitler's relationship was functional. It was not simply based on a 'common ideology' but also on strategic interests, interests that were masked by emotional declarations of friendship – especially by Hitler – and displays of unity. There was without doubt a common ideological denominator, including territorial revision and conquest, the use of violence as a means of politics, anti-Communism and a strong appeal to the old elites. However, in sum, there was no clear dichotomy between strategic interest and ideology; rather, both factors influenced each other in different ways in specific situations during the 1930s and early 1940s.

Crucial to the Mussolini–Hitler relationship was the fact that it was set in the era of modern mass media that created national audiences and constantly reinforced ideas of national belonging. In such a context, the personality of individuals such as Mussolini and Hitler became increasingly seductive, particularly given state censorship in Fascist Italy and the Third Reich. The image of the dictatorial friends served as an extension of the Führer and Duce cults and tied them together even more. The use of summits in which 'friendship' was on display has to be seen in this broader context. During the same period there was therefore also a palpable shift amongst democratic leaders to get together at summits, a tendency later amplified by live television. The wartime meetings of Roosevelt and Churchill soon expressed the personalised liberal-democratic alternative to Mussolini and Hitler's dictatorial friendship, but the relationship between president and prime minister was based more on substance and shared interests, less on performance – which was, after all, a central aspect of fascism.[9]

The relationship between Mussolini and Hitler cannot be dismissed as pure propaganda, however. The show of unity, masculinity and friendship was essential to both regimes and soon became a reality for the dictators, their members of staff, and indeed millions of Europeans. Distinctions between style and substance, representation and power, were not so clearly drawn for these two regimes. My close examination of the cultural aspects of the Mussolini–Hitler meetings has therefore opened up a different perspective on this defining political relationship of the early twentieth century, one which has allowed me to focus both on the relationship itself and its wider social and cultural context. Probing the organisation and choreography of the Mussolini–Hitler meetings, they appear, at least to a certain extent, to have followed, especially in their early stages, some of the rituals of state visits. At the same time, both regimes, as part of their attack on the rules of post-1919 international diplomacy, emphasised the personal relationship of Mussolini and Hitler, one which could dispense with established ceremonial patterns and bureaucracy and, instead, create a new style of diplomacy based on friendship which stood in opposition to the other European powers. Nowhere was this more clearly seen than in the substantial 1937 and 1938 encounters, with the former in particular standing for a new era of diplomacy as a direct expression of the Fascist–Nazi quest for a New Order. Like their regimes more generally, the choreography of Hitler and Mussolini's meetings was a mix between old and new, between established diplomatic protocol and an original, even unique relationship of two executive leaders who dispensed with bureaucratic forms of negotiating and representing international relations and replaced it with a powerful, carefully choreographed show. Without advocating a simplistic presentist reading of the story, it is sobering to reflect on how familiar these themes sounded as I was finishing this book in June 2017.

Behind the scenes, private misunderstandings, tensions, rivalry and attempts to display national superiority were always present. Yet the display of friendship and unity succeeded in disguising that discord, in ways that proved fatal to world peace. The propagandistic notion of friendship soon created its own momentum, leading to a situation in which Mussolini and Hitler, despite all their disagreements, felt obliged to believe in their special bond. The notion of friendship became a powerful edifice, the popular and political resonances of which reflected the vicissitudes of Italo-German relations and the war and made the Italo-German alliance look stronger than it was in reality. Here were two dictators, sharing an imperialist, expansionist and violent ideology. This political display was put to its first use during the crucial 1938 Munich conference where Mussolini's and Hitler's aggression outperformed the efforts of France and Britain, countries they had dismissed as decadent, 'plutocratic' and outdated. As the Axis war turned sour, the meetings became more low-key, but still both regimes maintained the display of friendship, even until the end when neither leader could bear the other. As I have shown, the dictators' relationship was overshadowed by their pretensions to world domination and by petty personal jealousies; spite and small-mindedness was equally a characteristic of their ambitions, ambitions that led to war, destruction, death and violence on a scale never hitherto seen. It would be decades before the devastating effects wrought by this lethal relationship were overcome.

ENDNOTES

Abbreviations

ACS	Archivio centrale dello Stato, Rome
ADAP	*Akten zur Deutschen Auswärtigen Politik: Serie C: 1933–1937. Das Dritte Reich: die ersten Jahre,* 6 vols, Göttingen, 1971–81; *Serie D: 1937–1945*, 13 vols, Baden-Baden, 1950–70; *Serie E: 1941–1945*, 8 vols, Göttingen, 1969–79
ASMAE	Archivio storico diplomatico del Ministero degli affari esteri, Rome
BAB	Bundesarchiv, Berlin
BAK	Bundesarchiv, Koblenz
BA-MA	Bundesarchiv-Militärarchiv, Freiburg
DBFP	*Documents on British Foreign Policy: Second Series*, 21 vols, London, 1965–84; *Third Series*, 10 vols, London, 1949–72
DDF	*Documents diplomatiques français 1932–1939, 2e série: 1936–1939*. 15 vols, Paris, 1963–81
DDI	*I documenti diplomatici italiani*, ed. Ministero degli affari esteri: *7. serie: 1922–1935*, 16 vols, Rome, 1953–90; *8. serie: 1935–1939*, 13 vols, Rome, 1952–2006; *9. serie: 1939–1943*, 10 vols, Rome, 1954–90; *10. serie: 1943–1948*, 7 vols, Rome, 1992–2000
DRZW	Militärgeschichtliches Forschungsamt (ed.), *Das Deutsche Reich und der Zweite Weltkrieg*, 10 vols, Stuttgart/Munich, 1979–2008
FRUS	*Foreign Relations of the United States*, available at http://digicoll.library.wisc.edu/cgi-bin/FRUS/FRUS-idx?type=browse&scope=FRUS.FRUS1
IfZ	Institut für Zeitgeschichte, Munich
JCH	*Journal of Contemporary History*
OO	Benito Mussolini, *Opera Omnia di Benito Mussolini*, ed. Edoardo and Duilio Susmel, 44 vols, Florence, 1959–80.
PAAA	Politisches Archiv des Auswärtigen Amts, Berlin
PRO	The National Archives, Public Records Office, Kew
QFIAB	*Quellen und Forschungen aus italienischen Archiven und Bibliotheken*
SD	Sicherheitsdienst
TBJG	Fröhlich, Elke (ed.), *Die Tagebücher von Joseph Goebbels, Teil I: Aufzeichungen 1923–1941*, 9 vols, Munich, 1998–2006; *Teil II: Diktate 1941–1945*, 15 vols, Munich, 1993–6

VB *Völkischer Beobachter*
VfZ *Vierteljahrshefte für Zeitgeschichte*
WL Wiener Library, London

Introduction

1. For the minutes of the meeting, see *ADAP*, E, VIII, doc. 128, note by Schmidt, 21 July 1944.
2. For a study of the origins of Fascism and Nazism, see MacGregor Knox, *To the Threshold of Power, 1922/33: Origins and Dynamics of the Fascist and National Socialist Dictatorships*, I, Cambridge, 2007.
3. Such as in A.J.P. Taylor, *The Origins of the Second World War*, London, 1963, p. 56. Recent work on political leadership includes Archie Brown, *The Myth of the Strong Leader: Political Leadership in the Modern Age*, London, 2014; R.A.W. Rhodes and Paul 't Hart (eds), *The Oxford Handbook of Political Leadership*, Oxford, 2014.
4. For the 'parallel lives' approach, see Alan Bullock, *Hitler and Stalin: Parallel Lives*, London, 1991; Walter Rauscher, *Hitler und Mussolini: Macht, Krieg und Terror*, Graz, 2001; Max Domarus, *Mussolini und Hitler: zwei Wege, gleiches Ende*, Würzburg, 1977; for Hitler's role in the Third Reich, see Ian Kershaw, '"Working towards the Führer": Reflections on the Nature of the Nazi Dictatorship', *Contemporary European History*, 2 (1993), pp. 103–18; for Italy, see R.J.B. Bosworth, *Mussolini*, London, 2002, pp. 7–8.
5. For the nexus between militarism and masculinity, see Christopher Dillon, '"Tolerance Means Weakness": The Dachau Concentration Camp SS, Militarism and Masculinity', *Historical Research*, 86 (2013), pp. 373–89.
6. For context, see MacGregor Knox, 'Conquest, Foreign and Domestic, in Fascist Italy and Nazi Germany', *Journal of Modern History*, 56 (1984), pp. 1–57.
7. Cf. Timothy Snyder, *Bloodlands: Europe between Hitler and Stalin*, New York, 2010; for a review, see Richard J. Evans, 'Who Remembers the Poles?', *London Review of Books*, 32/21 (2010), pp. 21–2.
8. For context, see Wolfgang Schieder, *Faschistische Diktaturen: Studien zu Italien und Deutschland*, Göttingen, 2008; for the traditional approach, see Christopher Duggan, *The Force of Destiny: A History of Italy since 1796*, London, 2007; Denis Mack Smith, *Mussolini*, London, 1981; for the centrality of warfare in Fascist Italy, see Giorgio Rochat, *Le guerre italiane 1935–1943: dall'impero d'Etiopia alla disfatta*, Turin, 2005; Patrick Bernhard, 'Colonial Crossovers: Nazi Germany and its Entanglement with Other Empires', *Journal of Global History*, 12 (2017), pp. 206–27.
9. Christian Goeschel, 'The Cultivation of Mussolini's Image in Weimar and Nazi Germany', in Jan Rüger and Nikolaus Wachsmann (eds), *Rewriting German History: New Perspectives on Modern Germany*, Basingstoke, 2015, pp. 247–66.
10. For context, see R.J.B. Bosworth, 'Italian Foreign Policy and its Historiography', in R.J.B. Bosworth and Gino Rizzo (eds), *Altro Polo: Intellectuals and their Ideas in Contemporary Italy*, Sydney, 1983, pp. 65–86; cf. MacGregor Knox, 'Il fascismo e la politica estera italiana', in R.J.B. Bosworth and Sergio Romano (eds), *La politica estera italiana, 1860–1985*, Bologna, 1991, pp. 287–330; see also R.A. Webster, *Industrial Imperialism in Italy, 1908–1915*, Berkeley, 1975.
11. Cf. Hans Woller, *Mussolini: der erste Faschist – eine Biografie*, Munich, 2016, p. 177.
12. For the traditional approach, Friedrich-Karl von Plehwe, *Als die Achse zerbrach: das Ende des deutsch-italienischen Bündnisses im Zweiten Weltkrieg*, Wiesbaden, 1980, p. 11; Elisabeth Wiskemann, *The Rome–Berlin Axis: A History of the Relations Between Hitler and Mussolini*, Oxford, 1949; D.C. Watt, 'The Rome–Berlin Axis, 1936–1940: Myth and Reality', *Review of Politics*, 22 (1960), pp. 519–43.
13. For this approach, see Jeffrey C. Alexander, 'Cultural Pragmatics: Social Performance between Ritual and Strategy', in Jeffrey C. Alexander, Bernhard Giesen and Jason L. Mast (eds), *Social Performance: Symbolic Action, Cultural Pragmatics, and Ritual*, Cambridge, 2006, pp. 29–90; for the centrality of performance, see Simonetta Falasca-Zamponi, *Fascist Spectacle: The Aesthetics of Power in Mussolini's Italy*, Berkeley, 1997; for comparative studies

of performances, see Christoph Kühberger, *Metaphern der Macht: ein kultureller Vergleich der politischen Feste im faschistischen Italien und im nationalsozialistischen Deutschland*, Berlin, 2006; Wenke Nitz, *Führer und Duce: politische Machtinszenierungen im nationalsozialistischen Deutschland und im faschistischen Italien*, Cologne, 2013; see also Ralph-Miklas Dobler, *Bilder der Achse: Hitlers Empfang in Italien 1938 und die mediale Inszenierung des Staatsbesuches in Fotobüchern*, Munich, 2015.

14. See, among others, Sven Reichardt and Armin Nolzen (eds), *Faschismus in Italien und Deutschland: Studien zu Transfer und Vergleich*, Göttingen, 2005; Thomas Schlemmer and Hans Woller (eds), *Der Faschismus in Europa: Wege der Forschung*, Munich, 2014; Bernhard, 'Colonial Crossovers'.
15. For the wider debate, see Michel Dobry, 'La thèse immunitaire face aux fascismes: pour une critique de la logique classificatoire', in Michel Dobry (ed.), *Le mythe d'allergie française du fascisme*, Paris, 2003, pp. 17–67.
16. See especially Roger Griffin, *The Nature of Fascism*, London, 1993; Roger Eatwell, 'On Defining the "Fascist Minimum": The Centrality of Ideology', *Journal of Political Ideologies*, 1 (1996), pp. 303–19; Roger Griffin, 'Studying Fascism in a Postfascist Age: From New Consensus to New Wave?', *Fascism*, 1 (2012), pp. 1–17; cf. Robert O. Paxton, *The Anatomy of Fascism*, New York, 2004; Adrian Lyttelton, 'What was Fascism?', *New York Review of Books*, 51/16 (2004), pp. 33–6.
17. Work includes Johannes Paulmann, *Pomp und Politik: Monarchenbegegnungen in Europa zwischen Ancien Régime und Erstem Weltkrieg*, Paderborn, 2000; Naoko Shimazu, 'Diplomacy as Theatre: Staging the Bandung Conference of 1955', *Modern Asian Studies*, 48 (2014), pp. 225–52; Brian Vick, *The Congress of Vienna: Power and Politics after Napoleon*, Cambridge, MA, 2014; Todd H. Hall, *Emotional Diplomacy: Official Emotion on the International Stage*, Ithaca, NY, 2015.
18. Cf. David Reynolds, *Summits: Six Meetings that Shaped the Twentieth Century*, London, 2007; Kristina Spohr and David Reynolds (eds), *Transcending the Cold War: Summits, Statecraft, and the Dissolution of Bipolarity in Europe, 1970–1990*, Oxford, 2016.
19. See, e.g., Maria Inácia Rezola, 'The Franco–Salazar Meetings: Foreign Policy and Iberian Relations during the Dictatorships (1942–1963)', *e-journal of Portuguese History*, 6/2 (2008); for a survey of Latin southern European dictatorships, see Giulia Albanese, *Dittature mediterranee: sovversioni fasciste e colpi di Stato in Italia, Spagna e Portogallo*, Bari, 2016.
20. See, e.g., Garrett Mattingly, *Renaissance Diplomacy*, London, 1955; Paulmann, *Pomp und Politik*.
21. James Joll, *Europe since 1870: An International History*, 4th edn, Harmondsworth, 1990, p. 178; for a recent survey of the alliances, see Christopher Clark, *Sleepwalkers: How Europe Went to War in 1914*, London, 2013, pp. 121–67.
22. Recent work includes Patricia Clavin, *Securing the World Economy: The Reinvention of the League of Nations, 1920–1946*, Oxford, 2013; Mark Mazower, *Governing the World: The History of an Idea*, London, 2012; Glenda Sluga, *Internationalism in the Age of Nationalism*, Philadelphia, 2013; Susan Pedersen, *The Guardians: The League of Nations and the Crisis of Empire*, Oxford, 2015.
23. For literature on friendship, see Allan Silver, 'Friendship and Trust as Moral Ideals: An Historical Approach', *Archives européennes de sociologie*, 30 (1989), pp. 274–97; for recent essay collections, see Barbara Caine (ed.), *Friendship: A History*, London, 2009; Bernadette Descharmes, Eric Anton Heuser, Caroline Krüger and Thomas Loy (eds), *Varieties of Friendship: Interdisciplinary Perspectives on Social Relationships*, Göttingen, 2011; William M. Reddy, *The Navigation of Feeling: A Framework for the History of Emotions*, Cambridge, 2001, pp. 63–111; on gestures, see Michael J. Braddick (ed.), 'The Politics of Gesture: Historical Perspectives', *Past & Present*, 203/4 (2009), pp. 9–35; for the Paris Peace Conference, see Margaret MacMillan, *Peacemakers: The Paris Peace Conference and its Attempt to End War*, London, 2001.
24. For the leadership cults, see Ian Kershaw, *The 'Hitler Myth': Image and Reality in the Third Reich*, Oxford, 1987; Stephen Gundle, Christopher Duggan and Giuliana Pieri (eds), *The Cult of the Duce: Mussolini and the Italians*, Manchester, 2013.

25. For institutional histories of 'fascist internationalism', see Michael Ledeen, *Universal Fascism: The Theory and Practice of the Fascist International, 1928–1936*, New York, 1972; Marco Cuzzi, *L'internazionale delle camicie nere: i CAUR, Comitati d'azione per l'universalità di Roma, 1933–1939*, Milan, 2005; Jens Steffek, 'Fascist Internationalism', *Millennium*, 44 (2015), pp. 3–22; Madeleine Herren, 'Fascist Internationalism', in Glenda Sluga and Patricia Clavin (eds), *Internationalisms: A Twentieth-Century History*, Cambridge, 2017, pp. 191–212; for context, see also Mark Mazower, *Hitler's Empire: Nazi Rule in Occupied Europe*, London, 2008; Benjamin G. Martin, *The Nazi-Fascist New Order for European Culture*, Cambridge, MA, 2016.
26. For the Roosevelt–Churchill friendship, see Jon Meacham, *Franklin and Winston: An Intimate Portrait of an Epic Friendship*, New York, 2004; for context, see David Reynolds, *The Creation of the Anglo-American Alliance, 1937–1941: A Study in Competitive Co-operation*, London, 1981.
27. For crowds as participants, see Shimazu, 'Diplomacy as Theatre'.
28. For context, see the essays in Paul Corner (ed.), *Popular Opinion in Totalitarian Regimes: Fascism, Nazism, Communism*, Oxford, 2009; see also Richard J. Evans, 'Coercion and Consent in Nazi Germany', *Proceedings of the British Academy*, 151 (2007), pp. 53–81.
29. For German and Italian perceptions of each other, see, e.g., Gian-Enrico Rusconi, *Deutschland-Italien, Italien-Deutschland: Geschichte einer schwierigen Beziehung von Bismarck bis zu Berlusconi*, Paderborn, 2006, pp. 107–205; see also Christian Goeschel, 'A Parallel History? Rethinking the Relationship between Italy and Germany, ca. 1860–1945', *Journal of Modern History*, 88 (2016), pp. 610–32.
30. For instance, Peter Longerich, *Hitler: Eine Biographie*, Munich, 2015; Volker Ullrich, *Adolf Hitler: Biographie, Band 1: Die Jahre des Aufstiegs, 1889–1939*, Frankfurt am Main, 2013; Wolfram Pyta, *Hitler: Der Künstler als Politiker und Feldherr – eine Herrschaftsanalyse*, Munich, 2015; Wolfgang Schieder, *Mythos Mussolini: Deutsche in Audienz beim Duce*, Munich, 2013; Wolfgang Schieder, *Benito Mussolini*, Munich, 2014; Woller, *Mussolini*; two slight accounts are Santi Corvaja, *Mussolini nella tana del lupo*, Milan, 1983; Pierre Milza, *Conversations Hitler–Mussolini, 1934–1944*, Paris, 2013.
31. F.W. Deakin, *The Brutal Friendship: Mussolini, Hitler and the Fall of Italian Fascism*, London, 1962.
32. See, among others, Reichardt and Nolzen (eds), *Faschismus in Italien und Deutschland*; for a survey of recent work on the Axis, see Christian Goeschel, '*Italia docet*?' The Relationship between Italian Fascism and Nazism Revisited', *European History Quarterly*, 42 (2012), pp. 480–92.
33. For Nazi Germany as a unique form of a racial dictatorship, see Ian Kershaw, 'Hitler and the Uniqueness of Nazism', *JCH*, 39 (2004), pp. 239–54; for comparative work, see Ian Kershaw and Moshe Lewin (eds), *Stalinism and Nazism: Dictatorships in Comparison*, Cambridge, 1997; Michael Geyer and Sheila Fitzpatrick (eds), *Beyond Totalitarianism: Stalinism and Nazism Compared*, Cambridge, 2009.
34. Renzo De Felice, *Intervista sul fascismo*, ed. Michael A. Ledeen, Bari, 1997, pp. 24–5; cf. Gianpasqualc Santomassimo, 'Il ruolo di Renzo De Felice', in Enzo Collotti (ed.), *Fascismo e antifascismo: rimozioni, revisioni, negazioni*, Bari, 2000, pp. 415–29.
35. For memory, see Filippo Focardi, '"Bravo italiano" e "cattivo tedesco": riflessioni sulla genesi di due immagini incrociate', *Storia e Memoria*, 5/1 (1996), pp. 55–83; see also Filippo Focardi, *Il cattivo tedesco e il bravo italiano: la rimozione delle colpe della seconda guerra mondiale*, Bari, 2013.
36. Davide Rodogno, *Fascism's European Empire: Italian Occupation during the Second World War*, Cambridge, 2006; Asfa-Wossen Asserate and Aram Mattioli (eds), *Der erste faschistische Vernichtungskrieg: die italienische Aggression gegen Äthiopien*, Cologne, 2006.
37. For an account that takes a European perspective, see Jens Petersen, *Hitler–Mussolini: die Entstehung der Achse Berlin–Rom 1933–1936*, Tübingen, 1973.
38. *DDI*, 8s, which deals with the crucial years 1935–9, was only completed in 2006; *00*.
39. *TBJG, Teil I; TBJG, Teil II.*
40. Galeazzo Ciano, *Diario 1937–1943*, ed. Renzo De Felice, Milan, 1980; for the authenticity of the diaries, see MacGregor Knox, *Mussolini Unleashed, 1939–1941: Politics and*

Strategy in Fascist Italy's Last War, Cambridge, 1982, pp. 291–2; Tobias Hof, 'Die Tagebücher von Galeazzo Ciano', *VfZ*, 60 (2012), pp. 507–28.

1 In Mussolini's Shadow, 1922–33

1. Kurt G.W. Ludecke, *I Knew Hitler: The Story of a Nazi Who Escaped the Blood Purge*, London, 1938, pp. 71–7.
2. Mack Smith, *Mussolini*, p. 172; for Mussolini's journey to Germany, see Silvana Casmirri, 'Il viaggio di Mussolini in Germania nel marzo del '22', *Storia e politica*, 12 (1973), pp. 86–112, here p. 92, n. 23.
3. IfZ, Fb 32, Foreign Ministry to Bavarian Ministry of the Interior, 2 December 1923; Ian Kershaw, *Hitler, 1889–1936: Hubris*, Harmondsworth, 2001, p. 186.
4. 'Gespräch mit F. C. Holtz am 3.11.1922', printed in Eberhard Jäckel and Alex Kuhn (eds), *Hitler: Sämtliche Aufzeichnungen, 1905–1924*, Stuttgart, 1980, pp. 721–2.
5. Cf. Schieder, *Faschistische Diktaturen*, pp. 265–78.
6. For another example, see Kershaw, *Hitler, 1889–1936*, p. 180.
7. Wiener Library, NSDAP Hauptarchiv, MF 29, reel 26 A: *Fränkische Tagespost*, 17 October 1922; ibid., *Pester Lloyd*, 12 November 1922. *The Times* ran a very short report on the 'German Fascisti' in Bavaria, led by 'Herr Hitler' on 18 October 1922.
8. Printed in Jäckel and Kuhn (eds), *Hitler*, p. 1027; see also Hans-Ulrich Thamer, 'Der Marsch auf Rom: ein Modell für die nationalsozialistische Machtergreifung', in Wolfgang Michalka (ed.), *Die nationalsozialistische Machtergreifung*, Paderborn, 1984, pp. 245–60, here pp. 251–2; for the notion of Hitler as the 'German Mussolini', see Detlev Clemens, 'The "Bavarian Mussolini" and his "Beerhall Putsch": British Images of Adolf Hitler, 1920–24', *English Historical Review*, 114 (1999), pp. 64–84, here p. 68.
9. Walter Werner Pese, 'Hitler und Italien 1920–1926', *VfZ*, 3 (1955), pp. 13–26.
10. Adrian Lyttelton, *The Seizure of Power: Fascism in Italy, 1919–1929*, rev. edn, London, 2009, pp. 100–22.
11. Arthur Moeller van den Bruck, *Das Recht der jungen Völker*, ed. Hans Schwarz, Berlin, 1932, pp. 123–5; for context, see Stefan Breuer, 'Moeller van den Bruck und Italien', *Archiv für Kulturgeschichte*, 84 (2002), pp. 413–38.
12. Tedaldi's report is reprinted in *DDI*, 7s, I, doc. 131; cf. Edgar R. Rosen, 'Mussolini und Deutschland 1922–1923', *VfZ*, 5 (1957), pp. 17–41, here pp. 22–4; for context, see Dennison I. Rusinow, *Italy's Austrian Heritage 1919–1946*, Oxford, 1969, pp. 166–84; Roberta Pergher, 'Staging the Nation in Fascist Italy's "New Provinces"', *Austrian History Yearbook*, 43 (2012), pp. 98–115.
13. Stanley G. Payne, 'Fascist Italy and Spain', *Mediterranean Historical Review*, 13 (1998), pp. 99–115, here pp. 100–1.
14. James Barros, *The Corfu Incident of 1923: Mussolini and the League of Nations*, Princeton, 1965; Sally Marks, 'Mussolini and the Ruhr Crisis', *International History Review*, 8 (1986), pp. 56–69; Mack Smith, *Mussolini*, p. 95; for Italy and the League, see Elisabetta Tollardo, *Fascist Italy and the League of Nations*, Basingstoke, 2016, pp. 1–5.
15. Wolfgang Schieder, 'Das italienische Experiment: der Faschismus als Vorbild in der Weimarer Republik', *Historische Zeitschrift*, 262 (1996), pp. 73–125.
16. *Corriere Italiano*, 16 October 1923, printed in Jäckel and Kuhn (eds), *Hitler*, pp. 1035–7, here p. 1037.
17. *L'Epoca*, 4 November 1923, printed in Jäckel and Kuhn (eds), *Hitler*, p. 1051.
18. See Frank's resignation letter in Klaus-Peter Hoepke, *Die deutsche Rechte und der italienische Faschismus: ein Beitrag zum Selbstverständnis und zur Politik von Gruppen und Verbänden der deutschen Rechten*, Düsseldorf, 1968, p. 327; for context, see Christoph Klessmann, 'Der Generalgouverneur Hans Frank', *VfZ*, 19 (1971), pp. 245–60, here p. 249.
19. Hans Woller, 'Machtpolitisches Kalkül oder ideologische Affinität? Zur Frage des Verhältnisses zwischen Mussolini und Hitler vor 1933', in Wolfgang Benz, Hans Buchheim and Hans Mommsen (eds), *Der Nationalsozialismus: Studien zur Ideologie und Herrschaft*, Frankfurt am Main, 1990, pp. 42–64, here p. 46.
20. For context, see Schieder, 'Das italienische Experiment'.

21. See WL, NSDAP Hauptarchiv, MF 29, reel 26 A; for the March on Rome, see Lyttelton, *The Seizure of Power*, pp. 64–77.
22. For context, see Richard J. Evans, *The Coming of the Third Reich*, London, 2003, pp. 176–94; for Atatürk, see Stefan Ihrig, *Atatürk in the Nazi Imagination*, Princeton, 2014.
23. Quoted in Wolfgang Schieder, 'Fascismo e nazionalsocialismo: profilo d'uno studio comparativo', *Nuova rivista storica*, 54 (1970), pp. 114–24, here p. 117; Rosen, 'Mussolini und Deutschland 1922–1923'; Alan Cassels, 'Mussolini and German Nationalism, 1922–25', *Journal of Modern History*, 35 (1963), pp. 137–57; for an Italian report on the Beer Hall Putsch that reached Mussolini, see *DDI*, 7s, II, doc. 474, Durini di Monza to Mussolini, 10 November 1923.
24. Thamer, 'Der Marsch auf Rom', p. 253; for background, see also Hans Woller, *Rom, 28. Oktober 1922: die faschistische Herausforderung*, Munich, 1999; Schieder, 'Das italienische Experiment'; for the Mussolini cult, see Gundle, Duggan and Pieri (eds), *The Cult of the Duce*; Goeschel, 'The Cultivation of Mussolini's Image in Weimar and Nazi Germany', pp. 247–66.
25. Christian Hartmann, Thomas Vordermeyer, Othmar Plöckinger and Roman Töppel (eds), *Hitler, Mein Kampf: eine kritische Edition*, Munich, 2016, II, p. 1723.
26. Filippo Anfuso, *Roma Berlino Salò*, Milan, 1950, p. 42.
27. For context, see Meir Michaelis, 'I rapporti tra fascismo e nazismo prima dell'avvento di Hitler al potere (1922–1933): parte prima, 1922–1928', *Rivista storica italiana*, 85 (1973), pp. 544–600, here p. 591.
28. Alfred Rosenberg, 'The Folkish Idea of State', in Barbara Miller Lane and Leila J. Rupp (eds), *Nazi Ideology before 1933: A Documentation*, Manchester, 1978, pp. 59–73, here p. 64; for context see Kilian Bartikowski, *Der italienische Antisemitismus im Urteil des Nationalsozialismus 1933–1943*, Berlin, 2013, pp. 36–7.
29. Michael Palumbo, 'Goering's Italian Exile 1924–1925', *Journal of Modern History*, 50 (1978), pp. D1035–D1051; for the articles, see *VB*, 3 March 1926, 6 March 1932.
30. Schieder, 'Das italienische Experiment'; Andrea Hoffend, 'Konrad Adenauer und das faschistische Italien', *QFIAB*, 75 (1995), pp. 481–544.
31. An overview is provided by Federico Scarano, *Mussolini e la Repubblica di Weimar: le relazioni diplomatiche tra Italia e Germania dal 1927 al 1933*, Naples, 1996.
32. André François-Poncet, *The Fateful Years: Memoirs of a French Ambassador in Berlin, 1931–1938*, London, 1949, p. 238; cf. Michael Palumbo, 'Mussolini and the Munich Putsch', *Intellect*, 106/2397 (1978), pp. 490–2.
33. Thamer, 'Der Marsch auf Rom'; Schieder, 'Das italienische Experiment'.
34. Petersen, *Hitler–Mussolini*, pp. 25–6; Tolomei's report is reprinted in Karl Heinz Ritschel, *Diplomatie um Südtirol: politische Hintergründe eines europäischen Versagens*, Stuttgart, 1966, pp. 134–7.
35. The February 1930 trial was the appeal to a May 1929 trial; *VB*, 6 February 1932, 'Der politische Hochstapler als "Kronzeuge" gegen Adolf Hitler', in *Hitler: Reden, Schriften, Anordnungen, Februar 1925 bis Januar 1933*, ed. Christian Hartmann, Munich, 1995, III, p. 70; see also PAAA, Botschaft Rom (Quirinal), Geheim, Bd. 10 for press clippings; for context, see Douglas G. Morris, *Justice Imperilled: The Anti-Nazi Lawyer Max Hirschberg in Weimar Germany*, Ann Arbor, 2005, pp. 254–72.
36. For Graefe, see Jeremy Noakes, 'Conflict and Development in the NSDAP 1924–1927', *JCH*, 1 (1966), pp. 3–36; for the quotation, see Petersen, *Hitler–Mussolini*, p. 26.
37. Petersen, *Hitler–Mussolini*, p. 27.
38. More generally, see Ledeen, *Universal Fascism*; Beate Scholz, 'Italienischer Faschismus als "Exportartikel": ideologische und organisatorische Ansätze zur Verbreitung des Faschismus im Ausland', PhD dissertation, Universität Trier, 2001.
39. Theodor Wolff, 'Bei Mussolini', *Berliner Tageblatt*, 11 May 1930.
40. PRO, GFM 36/263, Capasso Torre to Mussolini, 20 June 1931; also printed in Renzo De Felice, *Mussolini e Hitler: I rapporti segreti, 1922–1933, con documenti inediti*, Rome, 2013, pp. 189–91.
41. Eberhard Kolb, *Die Weimarer Republik*, Munich, 2002, p. 127; for Mussolini's reactions, see Petersen, *Hitler–Mussolini*, pp. 37–41.

42. Printed in De Felice, *Mussolini e Hitler*, p. 138; *VB*, 21/22 September 1930, copy in IfZ, ED 414, Band 187.
43. For Renzetti, see Schieder, *Faschistische Diktaturen*, pp. 223–52.
44. 'La Germania non sopporterà il trattato di Versailles', *Gazzetta del Popolo*, 29 September 1930, printed in *Hitler: Reden, Schriften, Anordnungen*, III/3, pp. 461–8; for context, see Filippo Focardi, 'Journalisten und Korrespondenten der italienischen Presse in Deutschland', in Gustavo Corni and Christof Dipper (eds), *Italiener in Deutschland im 19. und 20. Jahrhundert: Kontakte, Wahrnehmungen, Einflüsse*, Berlin, 2012, pp. 53–78, here pp. 72–3.
45. 'Con Adolfo Hitler alla "Casa Bruna" ', *Popolo d'Italia*, 12 May 1931, printed in *Hitler: Reden, Schriften, Anordnungen, Februar 1925 bis Januar 1933*, ed. Constantin Goschler, Munich, 1994, IV/1, pp. 342–6.
46. ACS, SpD, CR 1922–1943, b. 71, 'Appunto per l'On Gabinetto', 30 June 1931; for details of Göring's visit on 25 April 1931, see Schieder, *Mythos Mussolini*, p. 363.
47. ACS, SpD, CR 1922–1943, b. 71, printed in *Hitler: Reden, Schriften, Anordnungen*, IV/1, pp. 405–6.
48. 'A colloquio con Hitler', *Gazzetta del Popolo*, 7 December 1931, printed in *Hitler: Reden, Schriften, Anordnungen, Februar 1925 bis Januar 1933*, ed. Christian Hartmann, Munich, 1996, IV/2, pp. 240–4; for the greeting, see Tilman Allert, *Der deutsche Gruß: Geschichte einer unheilvollen Geste*, Frankfurt am Main, 2005; see also Schieder, 'Das italienische Experiment', pp. 108–9; for dissonant Nazi voices in the Nazi party's daily newspaper, see Karl Egon Lönne, 'Der "Völkische Beobachter" und der italienische Faschismus', *QFIAB*, 51 (1971), pp. 539–84.
49. De Felice, *Mussolini e Hitler*, p. 190; for the negative role of Germany in the Italian imaginary, see Klaus Heitmann, *Das italienische Deutschlandbild in seiner Geschichte, III: das kurze zwanzigste Jahrhundert*, Heidelberg, 2012, I.
50. Meir Michaelis, 'I nuclei nazisti in Italia e la loro funzione nei rapporti tra fascismo e nazismo nel 1932', *Nuova rivista storica*, 57 (1973), pp. 422–38.
51. *Mussolinis Gespräche mit Emil Ludwig*, Berlin, 1932; for context, see Wolfgang Schieder, 'Von Stalin zu Mussolini: Emil Ludwig bei Diktatoren des 20. Jahrhunderts', in Dan Diner, Gideon Reuveni and Yfaat Weiss (eds), *Deutsche Zeiten: Geschichte und Lebenswelt – Festschrift zur Emeritierung von Moshe Zimmermann*, Göttingen, 2012, pp. 123–31.
52. Adolf Hitler, 'Geleitwort', in Cav. Vincenzo Meletti, *Die Revolution des Faschismus*, Munich, 1931, pp. 7–8, printed in *Hitler: Reden, Schriften, Anordnungen*, IV/1, pp. 340–1.
53. Giorgio Fabre, *Hitler's Contract: How Mussolini Became Hitler's Publisher*, New York, 2006, pp. 8–9.
54. Mack Smith, *Mussolini*, p. 158.
55. Schieder, *Faschistische Diktaturen*, p. 243.
56. For details of the meetings, see Schieder, *Faschistische Diktaturen*, pp. 236–41; Mussolini received Renzetti at least 11 times between 1925 and 1933, while Hitler met Renzetti at least 38 times between 1929 and 1934. Renzetti's reports are available in PRO, GFM 36/54 and GFM 36/263 and in BAK, N 1235; see also De Felice, *Mussolini e Hitler*, pp. 175–214.
57. 'Un colloquio con Hitler alla Casa Bruna', *Il Tevere*, 4/5 October 1932, printed in *Hitler: Reden, Schriften, Anordnungen, Februar 1925 bis Januar 1933*, ed. Christian Hartmann and Klaus A. Lankheit, Munich, 1998, V/2, pp. 9–13, here p. 11; for Interlandi, see Meir Michaelis, 'Mussolini's Unofficial Mouthpiece: Telesio Interlandi, *Il Tevere* and the Evolution of Mussolini's Anti-Semitism', *Journal of Modern Italian Studies*, 3 (1998), pp. 217–40.
58. PRO, GFM 36/263, Renzetti, 20 November 1931; also printed in De Felice, *Mussolini e Hitler*, pp. 192–3; cf. Petersen, *Hitler–Mussolini*, pp. 44–5.
59. Schieder, *Faschistische Diktaturen*, p. 243; for the German government's concerns about a Mussolini–Hitler meeting, see PAAA, Botschaft Rom (Quirinal), Geheim, Bd. 12, secret telegram from State Secretary Bülow to the embassy in Rome, 11 December 1931.

60. Curzio Malaparte, *Der Staatsstreich*, Leipzig, 1932, pp. 219–45; for similar views, see Theodor Heuss, *Hitlers Weg: Eine Schrift aus dem Jahre 1932*, new edn, Tübingen, 1968, p. 127; Hubertus Prinz zu Löwenstein, 'Das Dritte Reich', *Vossische Zeitung*, 12 July 1930.
61. ACS, SpD, CR, b. 71, Mussolini to Italian embassy Berlin, 16 October 1931; cf. Petersen, *Hitler–Mussolini*, p. 103; BAK, N 1235, no. 4, copy of letter from Renzetti to Hitler, 19 October 1931; for Malaparte and Fascism, see Alexander De Grand, 'Curzio Malaparte: The Illusion of the Fascist Revolution', *JCH*, 7 (1972), pp. 73–89.
62. ACS, SpD, CR 1922–1943, b. 71, 'Il Capo del Governo', 12 January 1932.
63. PRO, GFM 36/263, Renzetti, 12 January 1932; also printed in De Felice, *Mussolini e Hitler*, p. 196.
64. PRO, GFM 36/263, Renzetti, 21 June 1932; also printed in De Felice, *Mussolini e Hitler*, pp. 198–9; cf. Petersen, *Hitler–Mussolini*, pp. 104–5.
65. PRO, GFM 36/263, Renzetti to Starace, 12 June 1932; also printed in De Felice, *Mussolini e Hitler*, pp. 196–8.
66. Schieder, 'Das italienische Experiment', pp. 116–17.
67. PRO, GFM 36/263, 'Segreteria particolare del Duce al Barone Ottavio Serena di Lapigio, Gabinetto Esteri', 22 June 1932; cf. Petersen, *Hitler–Mussolini*, p. 105.
68. Petersen, *Hitler–Mussolini*, p. 109; for details of Göring's audience, see Schieder, *Mythos Mussolini*, p. 365.
69. See Renzetti's report of 23 January 1933 in De Felice, *Mussolini e Hitler*, pp. 205–9.
70. PRO, GFM 36/263, report by Renzetti, 31 January 1933; also printed in De Felice, *Mussolini e Hitler*, pp. 207–9; cf. Petersen, *Hitler–Mussolini*, p. 112.
71. PRO, GFM 36/263, report by Renzetti, 31 January 1933; also printed in De Felice, *Mussolini e Hitler*, pp. 209–10; cf. Petersen, *Hitler–Mussolini*, pp. 112–13.
72. For the Fascist rise to power, see Lyttelton, *The Seizure of Power*; for Germany, see Evans, *The Coming of the Third Reich*, pp. 309–90.
73. Fabre, *Hitler's Contract*, pp. 20–8.
74. Petersen, *Hitler–Mussolini*, pp. 123–5.
75. De Felice, *Mussolini e Hitler*, pp. 141, 177; cf. Hans Woller, 'I rapporti tra Mussolini e Hitler prima del 1933: politica del potere o affinità ideologica?', *Italia contemporanea*, 196 (1994), p. 507.

2 First Date, June 1934

1. For context, see Zara Steiner, *The Triumph of the Dark: European International History 1933–1939*, Oxford, 2011, pp. 32–4.
2. For this view, see Renzo De Felice, *Mussolini il Duce. I. Gli anni del consenso, 1929–1936*, Turin, 1974, pp. 447–67; for a critique, see R.J.B. Bosworth, *The Italian Dictatorship: Problems and Perspectives in the Interpretation of Mussolini and Fascism*, London, 1998, p. 95.
3. For context, see MacGregor Knox, *Common Destiny: Dictatorship, Foreign Policy, and War in Fascist Italy and Nazi Germany*, Cambridge, 2000, pp. 113–47.
4. For Cerruti's role, see Renzo De Felice, *Storia degli ebrei italiani sotto il fascismo*, Turin, 1993, p. 127; for Mussolini's instructions to counter anti-German propaganda, see BAB, R 43 II/1447, Bl. 30, Neurath-Hitler, 2 April 1933, also kept in WL, doc. 675, Neurath-Hitler, 2 April 1933; for background, see Bartikowski, *Der italienische Antisemitismus*, pp. 29–30.
5. For anti-Semitism in Italy, see Frauke Wildvang, *Der Feind von nebenan: Judenverfolgung im faschistischen Italien 1936–1944*, Cologne, 2008, pp. 9–16.
6. Petersen, *Hitler–Mussolini*, p. 173; *ADAP*, C, I/2, memorandum by Bülow, dated 1 June 1933; for Fascist foreign policy, see Jens Petersen, 'Die Außenpolitik des faschistischen Italien als historiographisches Problem', *VfZ*, 22 (1974), pp. 417–54; for a more recent account, see MacGregor Knox, 'The Fascist Regime, its Foreign Policy and its Wars: An "Anti-Anti-Fascist" Orthodoxy?', *Contemporary European History*, 4 (1995), pp. 347–65.
7. *Vossische Zeitung*, 30 July 1933, copy in BAB, R 8034 III/323, Bl. 35.

8. *FRUS*, 1933, I, pp. 301–6, Consul-General George Messersmith to Secretary of State Cordell Hull, 3 November 1933; also cited by Petersen, *Hitler–Mussolini*, p. 251, n. 98.
9. Kershaw, *Hitler, 1889–1936*, pp. 490–5; Petersen, *Hitler–Mussolini*, pp. 256–7.
10. ASMAE, Gabinetto del Ministro 1923–1943, Gab. 350, Hitler–Mussolini, 2 November 1933; for Göring's visit, see Petersen, *Hitler–Mussolini*, pp. 262–6.
11. For context, see Günter Wollstein, *Vom Weimarer Revisionismus zu Hitler: das Deutsche Reich und die Großmächte in der Anfangsphase der nationalsozialistischen Herrschaft in Deutschland*, Bonn, 1973.
12. BAB, R 43 II/1448, Bl. 27–8, memorandum by Neurath, 27 February 1934.
13. 'Bilanz einer Studienreise nach Italien', *Der Deutsche*, 23 March 1934, copy in BAB, R 43 II/1448; for background, see Petersen, *Hitler–Mussolini*, p. 340; for wider context, see Daniela Liebscher, *Freude und Arbeit: zur internationalen Freizeit- und Sozialpolitik des faschistischen Italien und des NS-Regimes*, Cologne, 2009, pp. 319–49.
14. BAB, R 43 II/1448, Bl. 47, Renzetti to Reichskanzler Hitler, 28 March 1934.
15. PRO, GFM 36/54, Renzetti to Ciano, 12 April 1934; also printed in *DDI*, 7s, XV, doc. 93.
16. PRO, GFM 36/54, Renzetti to Ciano, 29 May 1934, a copy sent to Mussolini; also printed in *DDI*, 7s, XV, doc. 314; see also Petersen, *Hitler–Mussolini*, pp. 339–40.
17. Printed in Fabre, *Hitler's Contract*, p. 216.
18. Ibid., pp. 95–8; for Dinale's article, see *Il Popolo d'Italia*, 3 April 1934, p. 2, printed in Fabre, *Hitler's Contract*, pp. 220–1; for Dinale's previous attacks, see BAB, R 43 II/1448, Bl. 62–3, Foreign Ministry to Rome Embassy, 17 March 1934.
19. Petersen, *Hitler–Mussolini*, p. 330.
20. Printed in Max Domarus, *Hitler: Reden und Proklamationen*, Munich, 1965, I/1, p. 372; Petersen, *Hitler–Mussolini*, p. 330; Elisabetta Cerruti, *Ambassador's Wife*, New York, 1953, p. 146.
21. *DDI*, 7s, XV, doc. 349, conversation between Hassell and Suvich, 5 June 1934; for background, see Petersen, *Hitler–Mussolini*, pp. 332–9.
22. Petersen, *Hitler–Mussolini*, p. 344; for Mussolini's inviting the world press, see Mack Smith, *Mussolini*, p. 184; *New York Times*, 11 June 1934.
23. For an apologetic study, see Karl Uhlig, *Mussolinis Deutsche Studien*, Jena, 1941.
24. BAK, N 1235/13, Berlin, 7 June 1934, XII; for context, see Patrick Bernhard, 'Italien auf dem Teller: zur Geschichte der italienischen Küche und Gastronomie in Deutschland 1900–2000', in Corni and Dipper (eds), *Italiener in Deutschland*, pp. 217–36.
25. PRO, GFM 33/1163, 'Entzifferung', 15 May 1934.
26. Camilla Poesio, 'Hitler a Venezia: l'immagine del regime e della città nei primi anni trenta', *Memoria e ricerca* 43 (2013), pp. 149–50; for Fascist celebrations, see Falasca-Zamponi, *Fascist Spectacle*, pp. 9–14; for Mussolini's visits to the regions, see Stephen Gundle, 'Mussolini's Appearances in the Regions', in Gundle, Duggan and Pieri (eds), *The Cult of the Duce*, pp. 110–28; for Venice under Fascism, see Kate Ferris, *Everyday Life in Fascist Venice, 1929–1940*, Basingstoke, 2012.
27. PRO, GFM 33/1163, 'Vorläufiges Programm', undated; see also PAAA, Botschaft Rom (Quirinal), 695a, 'Ministero degli Affari Esteri, Programma di visita del cancelliere germanico a Venezia', undated.
28. PRO, GFM 33/1163, 'Entzifferung', 25 May 1934.
29. PRO, GFM 33/1163, telegram, 5 June 1934.
30. PRO, GFM 33/1163, 'Cito', 13 June 1934.
31. *Wall Street Journal*, 14 June 1934.
32. The report is not addressed to anyone, although it is likely that it landed on Mussolini's desk, like Renzetti's other reports. BAK, N 1235/13, Berlin, 13 June 1934; also quoted in De Felice, *Mussolini il Duce*, I, p. 491.
33. *DDI*, 7s, XV, doc. 401, Berlin, 14 June 1934.
34. For context, see Conrad F. Latour, *Südtirol und die Achse Berlin–Rom, 1938–1945*, Stuttgart, 1962; Jens Petersen, 'Deutschland, Italien und Südtirol 1938–1940', in Klaus Eisterer and Rolf Steininger (eds), *Die Option: Südtirol zwischen Faschismus und Nationalsozialismus*, Innsbruck, 1989, pp. 127–50.

35. For a description of the journey, see *VB*, 15 June 1934.
36. *VB*, 15 June 1934; for Mussolini's journey, see also *OO*, XXVI, p. 263.
37. *Il Popolo d'Italia*, 14 June 1934, no. 140.
38. Ibid.
39. For a cursory exploration, see Nina Breitsprecher, 'Die Ankunft des Anderen im interepochalen Vergleich: Heinrich III. von Frankreich und Adolf Hitler in Venedig', in Susann Baller (ed.), *Die Ankunft des Anderen: Repräsentationen sozialer und politischer Ordnungen in Empfangszeremonien*, Frankfurt am Main, 2008, pp. 82–105, esp. pp. 94–101.
40. *New York Times*, 14 June 1934; for Cortesi, see John P. Diggins, *Mussolini and Fascism: The View from America*, Princeton, 1972, pp. 39, 44.
41. André François-Poncet, 'Hitler et Mussolini', in *Les Lettres secrètes échangées par Hitler et Mussolini*, Paris, 1946, pp. 12–13; for François-Poncet, see Claus W. Schäfer, *André François-Poncet als Botschafter in Berlin (1931–1938)*, Munich, 2004, pp. 115–280.
42. *Illustrierter Beobachter*, 30 June 1934; cf. Paxton, *The Anatomy of Fascism*, p. 216.
43. Schieder, *Benito Mussolini*, p. 73.
44. *DBFP*, 2nd series, VI, pp. 762–4, Sir Eric Drummond to Sir John Simon, 20 June 1934; *New York Times*, 14 June 1934.
45. *New York Times*, 14 June 1934.
46. Printed in Domarus, *Hitler*, I/1, p. 387; for the ritual of exchanging telegrams, see Simone Derix, *Bebilderte Politik: Staatsbesuche in der Bundesrepublik*, Göttingen, 2009, p. 37; for the king's views of Hitler, see Denis Mack Smith, *Italy and its Monarchy*, New Haven, 1989, p. 273.
47. PRO, GFM 33/1163, 'Telegramm', 5 June 1934; ibid., 'Entzifferung'; ibid., 'Telegramm', 7 June 1934.
48. PAAA, Botschaft Rom (Quirinal) 695a, undated list of rooms; for Volpi, see Sergio Romano, *Giuseppe Volpi: industria e finanza tra Giolitti e Mussolini*, Milan, 1979.
49. Cerruti, *Ambassador's Wife*, p. 148.
50. For context, see David Laven, *Venice and Venetia under the Habsburgs, 1815–1835*, Oxford, 2002.
51. *VB*, North German edn, 16 June 1934.
52. Anfuso, *Roma Berlino Salò*, p. 42.
53. PRO, GFM 33/1163, 'Zusammenkunft in Venedig', Berlin, 23 June 1934.
54. For the minutes, see *ADAP*, C, III/1, doc. 5, note by Neurath, 15 June 1934; for a summary, see De Felice, *Mussolini il Duce*, I, pp. 494–7.
55. *ADAP*, C, III/1, doc. 5, note by Neurath, 15 June 1934; Petersen, *Hitler–Mussolini*, p. 349.
56. Mack Smith, *Mussolini*, p. 185; cf. *Il Popolo d'Italia*, 16 June 1934; see also Breitsprecher, 'Die Ankunft des Anderen', p. 100; Fritz Wiedemann, *Der Mann, der Feldherr werden wollte: Erlebnisse und Erfahrungen des Vorgesetzten Hitlers im I. Weltkrieg und seines späteren persönlichen Adjutanten*, Velbert, 1964, pp. 62–3.
57. For context, see Ruth Ben-Ghiat, *Fascist Modernities: Italy, 1922–1945*, Berkeley, 2001; see also Martin, *The Nazi-Fascist New Order*, pp. 34–5.
58. *VB*, North German edn, 16 June 1934; Bosworth, *Mussolini*, p. 281
59. Bosworth, *Mussolini*, p. 281.
60. Cerruti, *Ambassador's Wife*, p. 149.
61. *ADAP*, C III/1, doc. 5, note by Neurath, 15 June 1934.
62. For study of Mussolini–Hitler photographs, see Schieder, *Faschistische Diktaturen*, pp. 417–63.
63. For the minutes, see PRO, GFM 33/1163, Abschrift, 15 June 1934, also printed in *ADAP*, C, III/1, doc. 5; PRO, GFM 36/263, Mussolini to De Vecchi, 22 June 1934, also printed in *DDI*, 7s, XV, doc. 430. On De Vecchi, see Frank M. Snowden, 'De Vecchi, Cesare Maria', in Victoria de Grazia and Sergio Luzzatto (eds), *Dizionario del fascismo*, Turin, 2002, I, pp. 425–8.
64. PRO, GFM 33/1163, 'Abschrift', 19 June 1934; also printed in *ADAP*, C, III/1, doc. 19, note by Neurath, 19 June 1934.
65. *VB*, 16 June 1934, p. 2.

66. For the speech, see *OO*, XXVI, pp. 263–5.
67. *Il Popolo d'Italia*, 16 June 1934; on context, see Falasca-Zamponi, *Fascist Spectacle*, pp. 42–88.
68. Jürgen Matthäus und Frank Bajohr (eds), *Alfred Rosenberg: die Tagebücher von 1934 bis 1944*, Frankfurt am Main, 2015, pp. 135–6 (19 June 1934).
69. Ulrich von Hassell, *Römische Tagebücher und Briefe, 1932–1938*, ed. Ulrich Schlie, Munich, 2004, pp. 219–20.
70. PRO, GFM 33/1163, 'Zusammenkunft in Venedig, Berlin', 23 June 1934.
71. Domarus, *Hitler*, I, p. 389; for the Italian version, published in *Il Popolo d'Italia*, 16 June 1934, printed in *OO*, XXVI, p. 442.
72. Cerruti, *Ambassador's Wife*, p. 150.
73. *VB*, 17/18 June 1934.
74. *DBFP*, 2nd series, VI, pp. 762–4, Sir Eric Drummond to Sir John Simon, 20 June 1934.
75. *DDI*, 7s, XV, doc. 419, Renzetti report, 19–20 June 1934; also in BAK, N 1235/13, 'confidenziale', Berlin, 19 June 1934 XII; De Felice, *Mussolini il Duce*, I, p. 496; Rachele Mussolini, *The Real Mussolini as Told to Albert Zarca*, London, 1974, p. 144.
76. ASMAE, Serie Affari Politici Germania 1931–1945, b. 20, telegram Cerruti to Esteri Roma, 22 June 1934, also printed in *DDI*, 7s, XV, doc. 429; Hans Bohrmann (ed.), *NS-Presseanweisungen der Vorkriegszeit*, Munich, 1985, II, p. 238.
77. For the original manuscript of Papen's speech, see http://www.bundesarchiv.de/oeffentlichkeitsarbeit/bilder_dokumente/00634/index.html.de, accessed 31 August 2017.
78. For Papen's telegram, dated 17 June 1934, see BAB, R 43 II/971, Bl. 49; see also Petersen, *Hitler–Mussolini*, p. 352.
79. Quoted in De Felice, *Mussolini il Duce*, I, p. 497.
80. Domarus, *Hitler*, I/1, p. 392; for the quotation, see Otto Meissner, *Staatssekretär unter Ebert-Hindenburg-Hitler*, Hamburg, 1950, p. 354.
81. Kershaw, *Hitler, 1889–1936*, pp. 512–17.
82. *Il Popolo d'Italia*, 3 July 1934, 11 July 1934; *ADAP* C, III/1, Doc. 118, Hassell to Foreign Ministry, 25 July 1934, 243–5.
83. ASMAE, SP Germania 1931–1945, b. 20.
84. PRO, GFM, 36/54, 'confidenziale', Berlin, 14 July 1934; also printed in De Felice, *Mussolini e Hitler*, pp. 245–52.
85. Edvige Mussolini, *Mio fratello Benito*, Florence, 1957, p. 147.
86. *DDI*, 7s, XV, doc. 528, Mussolini to Grazzi, 15 July 1934; cf. Bosworth, *Mussolini*, p. 281.
87. Richard J. Evans, *The Third Reich in Power*, New York, 2005, pp. 619–23.
88. *DDI*, 7s, XV, doc. 458, Dollfuss to Suvich, 27–28 June 1934.
89. Evans, *The Third Reich in Power*, pp. 621–3.
90. De Felice, *Mussolini il Duce*, I, p. 499.
91. PAAA, R 73399, note by Fischer, 25 July 1934.
92. Mack Smith, *Mussolini*, p. 185.
93. *ADAP*, C, III/1, Doc. 122, Note by the State Secretary, 27 July 1934.
94. PAAA, R 73399, 'Deutsche Botschaft Rom, Weitere Entwicklung der italienischen Stellungnahme zu den Ereignissen in Oesterreich', 29 July 1934; see ibid. for a copy of *Il Popolo d'Italia*, 29 July 1934; De Felice, *Mussolini il Duce*, I, pp. 500–1
95. ACS, SpD, CR, b. 71, 'Comm. Pol. Frontiera (Bolzano) al Ministero Interno, PS', 30 July 1934; for general context, see Evans, *The Third Reich in Power*, pp. 619–23.
96. *ADAP*, C, III/1, doc. 152, Hassell to the foreign ministry, 8 August 1934.
97. De Felice, *Mussolini il Duce*, I, pp. 505–6; for the speech, see *OO*, XXVI, pp. 318–20.
98. Breitsprecher, 'Die Ankunft des Anderen', p. 100; Carl Vincent Krogmann, *Es ging um Deutschlands Zukunft 1932–1939: Erlebtes täglich diktiert von dem früheren Regierenden Bürgermeister von Hamburg*, Leoni, 1976, pp. 155–6.
99. Mack Smith, *Mussolini*, p. 186.
100. Louise Diel, *Mussolinis neues Geschlecht: die junge Generation in Italien – unter Mitarbeit von Mussolini*, Dresden, 1934; for context, see Schieder, *Mythos Mussolini*, p. 95.

101. *ADAP*, C, III/2, doc. 376, Hassell to Foreign Ministry, 6 December 1934; IfZ, MA 273, 'Chef T 3, Bericht über das Ergebnis der Besprechungen in Rom v. 3.–8.12.34', 6288–94; for context, see Schieder, *Mythos Mussolini*.
102. *ADAP*, C, III/2, doc. 381, Hassell to Foreign Ministry, 6 December 1934.
103. For context, see Steiner, *The Triumph of the Dark*, pp. 62–161; more specifically, see G. Bruce Strang, 'Imperial Dreams: The Mussolini–Laval Accords of January 1935', *Historical Journal*, 44 (2001), pp. 799–809; see also the essays in Bruce G. Strang (ed.), *Collision of Empires: Italy's Invasion of Ethiopia and its International Impact*, London, 2013; Charles de Chambrun, *Traditions et souvenirs*, Paris, 1952, p. 188.

3 Second Time Around, September 1937

1. For a good survey, see Esmonde Robertson, *Mussolini as Empire Builder: Europe and Africa, 1932–36*, London, 1977, pp. 93–113; Robert Mallett, *Mussolini in Ethiopia, 1919–1935*, Cambridge, 2015, pp. 72–123; Rochat, *Le guerre italiane*, pp. 15–31.
2. For a recent take on Mussolini's foreign policy, see MacGregor Knox, 'Fascism: Ideology, Foreign Policy, and War', in Adrian Lyttelton (ed.), *Liberal and Fascist Italy*, Oxford, 2002, pp. 105–38; John Gooch, *Mussolini and his Generals: The Armed Forces and Fascist Foreign Policy, 1922–1940*, Cambridge, 2007; for Mussolini's showmanship, see Mack Smith, *Mussolini*; for foreign policy and *romanità*, see Denis Mack Smith, *Mussolini's Roman Empire*, London, 1976; Romke Visser, 'Fascist Doctrine and the Cult of Romanità', *JCH*, 27 (1992), pp. 5–22.
3. For context, see Petersen, *Hitler–Mussolini*, pp. 399–401.
4. For context, see Gerhard L. Weinberg, *The Foreign Policy of Hitler's Germany*, I: *Diplomatic Revolution in Europe 1933–36*, Chicago, 1970, pp. 207–8; H. James Burgwyn, *Italian Foreign Policy in the Interwar Period, 1918–1940*, Westport, CT, 1997, pp. 112–15.
5. Weinberg, *The Foreign Policy of Hitler's Germany*, I, p. 208; Petersen, *Hitler–Mussolini*, p. 402.
6. See Rosaria Quartararo, *Roma tra Londra e Berlino: la politca estera fascista dal 1930 al 1940*, Rome, 1980, pp. 271–325, 326–403; for a critique, see Bosworth, *The Italian Dictatorship*, pp. 94–6.
7. Cf. Quartararo, *Roma tra Londra e Berlino*; for global context, see Thomas W. Burkman, *Japan and the League of Nations: Empire and World Order, 1914–1938*, Honolulu, 2008, pp. 165–93.
8. For background, see D.C. Watt, 'The Anglo-German Naval Agreement of 1935: An Interim Judgment', *Journal of Modern History*, 28 (1956), pp. 155–75.
9. Petersen, *Hitler–Mussolini*, pp. 406, 409; Michael Ceadel, 'The First British Referendum: The Peace Ballot, 1934–5', *English Historical Review*, 95 (1980), pp. 810–39.
10. *DDI*, 8s, I, doc. 419, Renzetti to Ciano, 21 June 1935; Petersen, *Hitler–Mussolini*, pp. 415–20; see also De Felice, *Mussolini il Duce*, I, pp. 665–6; Renato Mori, 'Verso il riavvicinamento fra Hitler e Mussolini, ottobre 1935–giugno 1936', *Storia e Politica*, 15 (1976), pp. 70–120.
11. BAB, R 43 II/1448, Bl. 249–53, 'Vertraulicher Bericht. Audienz bei Mussolini', 15 July 1935 (emphasis in the original); see also ibid., Bl. 260, Thomsen to Broschek, 22 July 1935; the report is also reprinted in Schieder, *Mythos Mussolini*, pp. 297–300.
12. BAB, R 43 II/1448, Bl. 270–8; see Manacorda's letter to Mussolini in ACS, SpD, CO 550702, 30 September 1935; for Manacorda's audiences with Mussolini see ibid., Segreteria particolare del Capo del Governo a Prof. Giulio Manacorda, 6 and 8 October 1935; for his March 1937 audience, see ibid., *Il Messaggero*, 11 March 1937; cf. Petersen, *Hitler–Mussolini*, pp. 446, 469; Giuseppe Vedovato, 'Guido Manacorda tra Italia, Germania e Santa Sede', *Rivista di studi politici internazionali*, 301 (2009), pp. 96–131, here p. 105.
13. Angelo Del Boca, *La guerra di Abissinia, 1935–1941*, Milan, 1965; Rochat, *Le guerre italiane*, p. 67.
14. *DBFP*, 2nd series, XV, doc. 84, Sir E. Phipps (Berlin) to Sir S. Hoare, 15 October 1935.

15. *ADAP*, C, IV/2, no. 485, Hassell to Foreign Ministry, 7 January 1936; Manfred Messerschmidt, 'Aussenpolitik und Kriegsvorbereitung', in *DRZW*, I, pp. 535–701, here 620–3; see also Klaus Hildebrand, *Das Dritte Reich*, Munich, 2009, pp. 31–2.
16. *DDI*, 8s, III, doc. 403, conversation between Hassell and Suvich, 8 March 1936; Esmonde R. Robertson, 'Hitler and Sanctions: Mussolini and the Rhineland', *European Studies Review*, 7 (1977), pp. 409–35; Strunk's conversation with Mussolini is reprinted in Schieder, *Mythos Mussolini*, pp. 301–7, and in Robert H. Whealey, 'Mussolini's Ideological Diplomacy: An Unpublished Document', *Journal of Modern History*, 39 (1967), pp. 432–7 (my quotations are based on the Whealey interview); for the use of emotions in diplomacy, see Hall, *Emotional Diplomacy*.
17. For context, see Alexander Wolz, 'Das Auswärtige Amt und die Entscheidung zur Remilitarisierung des Rheinlands', *VfZ*, 63 (2015), pp. 487–511.
18. Cf. Martin, *The Nazi-Fascist New Order*, pp. 12–73.
19. For the Italian reaction, see *DDI*, 8s, III, doc. 395, Attolico to Mussolini, 7 March 1936; on context, see Weinberg, *The Foreign Policy of Hitler's Germany*, I, pp. 250–3.
20. For the birthday telegrams, see ACS, SpD, CR, b. 71.
21. Christopher Duggan, *Fascist Voices: An Intimate History of Mussolini's Italy*, London, 2012, p. 279.
22. Knox, 'Fascism: Ideology, Foreign Policy, and War', pp. 127–8; for Mussolini's proclamation, see *OO*, XXVII, pp. 268–9; for the Spanish Civil War and Italy, see John F. Coverdale, *Italian Intervention in the Spanish Civil War*, Princeton, 1975, pp. 153–204; Paul Preston, 'Mussolini's Spanish Adventure: From Limited Risk to War,' in Paul Preston and Ann L. Mackenzie (eds), *The Republic Besieged: Civil War in Spain, 1936–1939*, Edinburgh, 1996, pp. 21–51; Rochat, *Le guerre italiane*, pp. 98–126; R.J.B. Bosworth, *Mussolini's Italy: Life under the Dictatorship*, London, 2006, pp. 401–2.
23. *DDI*, 8s, III, doc. 736, Suvich–Hassell conversation, 23 April 1936.
24. Meir Michaelis, 'La prima missione del Principe d'Assia presso Mussolini (agosto '36)', *Nuova rivista storica*, 55 (1971), pp. 367–70; see also Jonathan Petropoulos, *Royals and the Reich: The Princes von Hessen in Nazi Germany*, Oxford, 2006, p. 159; for police cooperation, see Renzo De Felice, 'Alle origini del Patto d'acciaio: l'incontro e gli accordi fra Bocchini e Himmler del marzo–aprile 1936', *La cultura*, 1 (1963), pp. 524–38; cf. Patrick Bernhard, 'Konzertierte Gegnerbekämpfung im Achsenbündnis: Die Polizei im Dritten Reich und im faschistischen Italien 1933 bis 1943', *VfZ*, 59 (2011), pp. 229–62; for anti-Bolshevism, see Bosworth, *Mussolini's Italy*, pp. 285–6.
25. Massimo Magistrati, *L'Italia a Berlino (1937–1939)*, Milan, 1956, p. 55.
26. For general context, see Paulmann, *Pomp und Politik*.
27. Sally Marks, 'Mussolini and Locarno: Fascist Foreign Policy in Microcosm', *JCH*, 14 (1979), pp. 423–39.
28. For Mussolini's foreign travel, see Mack Smith, *Mussolini*, pp. 59–61; Burgwyn, *Italian Foreign Policy*, p. 31.
29. For Ciano's appointment, see Mori, 'Verso il riavvicinamento', p. 120; on Frank's April 1936 visits to Rome, see *DDI*, 8s, III, doc. 589, Il Capo di Gabinetto Aloisi al Capo del Governo e Ministero degli Esteri, Mussolini, 4 April 1936; *ADAP*, C, V, doc. 255, telegram, Rome, 4 April 1936; ibid., doc. 553, unsigned notes found amongst Frank's papers, 23 September 1936; for a summary of the September meeting, see *DDI*, 8s, V, doc. 101, conversation between Mussolini and Frank; see also Frank's recollections, written at Nuremberg: Hans Frank, *Im Angesicht des Galgens: Deutung Hitlers und seiner Zeit auf Grund eigener Erlebnisse und Erkenntnisse, geschrieben im Nürnberger Justizgefängnis*, Neuhaus bei Schliersee, 1955, pp. 211–26; cf. Schieder, *Mythos Mussolini*, pp. 177–80.
30. See Adam Tooze, *The Wages of Destruction: The Making and Breaking of the Nazi Economy*, London, 2006, pp. 203–43.
31. *DDI*, 8s, V, doc. 277, conversation between Ciano and Hitler, 24 October 1936; Manfred Funke, 'Die deutsch-italienischen Beziehungen: Antibolschewismus und außenpolitische Interessenkonkurrenz als Strukturprinzip der "Achse"', in Manfred Funke (ed.), *Hitler, Deutschland und die Mächte*, Kronberg, 1978, pp. 823–46, here p. 832.

32. For Ciano's conversation with Neurath, see *DDI*, 8s, doc. 256, 21 October 1936; for his conversation with Hitler, see ibid., doc. 277, 24 October 1936; see *ADAP*, C, V, doc. 624, German–Italian Protocol, 23 October 1936; see also *DDI*, 8s, V, doc. 273; cf. Funke, 'Die deutsch-italienischen Beziehungen', p. 833.
33. Funke, 'Die deutsch-italienischen Beziehungen', p. 836; *VB*, 26 October 1936.
34. *OO*, XXVIII, pp. 69–72; cf. Paul Preston, 'Italy and Spain in Civil War and World War 1936–1943', in Sebastian Balfour and Paul Preston (eds), *Spain and the Great Powers in the Twentieth Century*, London, 1999, pp. 151–84, here p. 161.
35. Schieder, *Benito Mussolini*, pp. 25, 71.
36. For context, see Gerhard L. Weinberg, *The Foreign Policy of Hitler's Germany*, II: *Starting World War II 1937–1939*, Chicago, 1980, p. 1; Funke, 'Die deutsch-italienischen Beziehungen', p. 836.
37. Cf. Watt, 'The Rome–Berlin Axis, 1936–1940', pp. 519–43.
38. For the figures, see Vera Zamagni, *The Economic History of Italy 1860–1990*, Oxford, 1993, pp. 267, 270; for context see Brunello Mantelli, 'Vom "bilateralen Handelsausgleich" zur "Achse Berlin–Rom": der Einfluß wirtschaftlicher Faktoren auf die Entstehung des deutsch-italienischen Bündnisses 1933–1936', in Jens Petersen and Wolfgang Schieder (eds), *Faschismus und Gesellschaft in Italien: Staat – Wirtschaft – Kultur*, Cologne, 1998, pp. 253–79.
39. For propaganda, see *Rurali di Mussolini nella Germania di Hitler*, ed. Ufficio Propaganda della Confederazione Fascista dei Lavatori dell'Agricoltura, Rome, 1939; for context, see Luigi Cajani and Brunello Mantelli, 'In Deutschland arbeiten: die Italiener von der "Achse" bis zur Europäischen Gemeinschaft', *Archiv für Sozialgeschichte*, 32 (1992), pp. 231–46, here pp. 232–3; see also Brunello Mantelli, *'Camerati del lavoro': i lavoratori italiani emigrati nel Terzo Reich nel periodo dell'Asse 1938–1943*, Florence, 1992.
40. *DDI*, 8s, VI, doc. 60, dichiarazioni del Ministro Göring nel colloquio con Mussolini, 15 January 1937; for the itinerary of Göring's visit, see ACS, SpD, CO 532091, 'Programma di soggiorno in Italia del Ministro Presidente Generale Göring'; ibid., 'provvedimento', 17 January 1937; for context, see Preston, 'Italy and Spain', pp. 167–8.
41. BAB, R 43 II/1449, Bl. 34, 'Mitteilung des Italienischen Botschafters', 2 February 1937; for Hitler's speech, see Adolf Hitler, *On National Socialism and World Relations: Speech delivered in the German Reichstag, 30 January 1937*, Berlin, 1937; for context, see Ian Kershaw, *Hitler, 1936–1945: Nemesis*, Harmondsworth, 2001, pp. 27–9.
42. For Italian reprisals, see Angelo Del Boca, *Italiani, brava gente? Un mito duro a morire*, Vicenza, 2005, pp. 223–5; the most recent study is Ian Campbell, *The Addis Ababa Massacre: Italy's National Shame*, London, 2017, pp. 327–9; for German knowledge, see Michael Thöndl, 'Mussolinis ostafrikanisches Imperium in den Aufzeichnungen des deutschen Generalkonsulats in Addis Abeba', *QFIAB*, 88 (2008), pp. 449–87, here pp. 470–86; for the telegrams, see Bartikowski, *Der italienische Antisemitismus im Urteil des Nationalsozialmus*, pp. 47–8; for copies of the telegrams, see PAAA, Botschaft Rom (Quirinal), 717b, Hitler-Mussolini telegrams, 20 February 1937.
43. Jens Petersen, 'Vorspiel zu "Stahlpakt" und Kriegsallianz: das deutsch-italienische Kulturabkommen vom 23. November 1938', *VfZ*, 36 (1988), pp. 41–77, here p. 48; for details of Nazi visits, see ASMAE, SP Germania 1931–1945, b. 49.
44. ASMAE, Rappresentanza italiana a Berlino, 1867–1943, b. 157, Attolico to Ciano, 20 March 1937.
45. For details of visits of Nazi leaders to Italy, see PAAA, Botschaft Rom (Quirinal), 696b.
46. *DDI*, 8s, VI, doc. 425, Grandi to Ciano, 7 April 1937; for a critique, see Knox, 'Fascism: Ideology, Foreign Policy, and War', pp. 112–13.
47. *OO*, XXVIII, p. 242.
48. For basic context, see Michael Meyer, *Symbolarme Republik? Das politische Zeremoniell der Weimarer Republik in den Staatsbesuchen zwischen 1920 und 1933*, Frankfurt am Main, 2014.
49. Fred G. Willis, *Mussolini in Deutschland: eine Volkskundgebung für den Frieden in den Tagen vom 25. bis 29. September 1937*, Berlin, 1937; Claretta Petacci, *Mussolini segreto: diari 1932–1938*, ed. Mauro Suttora, Milan, 2009, p. 75 (27 October 1937).

50. *TBJG, Teil I*, IV, pp. 292–3 (2 and 3 September 1937), 324 (23 September 1937).
51. Wolfgang Benz, 'Die Inszenierung der Akklamation: Mussolini in Berlin 1937', in Michael Grüttner, Rüdiger Hachtmann and Heinz-Gerhard Haupt (eds), *Geschichte und Emanzipation: Festschrift für Reinhard Rürup*, Frankfurt am Main, 1999, pp. 401–17.
52. *DDF*, 2e série, VI, doc. 483, François-Poncet to Delbos, 22 September 1937.
53. In May 1937, amidst a closer coordination of Italo-German policies, German and Italian diplomats met in Rome to coordinate the press coverage of Italy and Germany with each other. ASMAE, SP Germania 1931–1945, b. 40, 'Ministero della Stampa e la Propaganda al R. Ministero degli Affari Esteri', 14 May 1937, 'telespresso Asse Roma Berlino e stampa italiana e tedescha'.
54. ASMAE, SP Germania 1931–1945, b. 40, 'R. Consolato Stoccarda al R. Ministero degli Affari Esteri/R. Ministero della Cultura Popolare', 30 September 1937.
55. *VB*, 25 September 1937.
56. Dr Walther Schmitt, 'Benito Mussolini: Mann und Werk', *VB*, 25 September 1937.
57. *VB*, 25 September 1937.
58. Willis, *Mussolini in Deutschland*, pp. 6–7; for Willis, see Schieder, *Mythos Mussolini*, p. 168; for the Triple Alliance, see Holger Afflerbach, *Der Dreibund: europäische Großmacht- und Allianzpolitik vor dem Ersten Weltkrieg*, Vienna, 2002, pp. 229–89; for Crispi, see Christopher Duggan, *Francesco Crispi, 1818–1901: From Nation to Nationalism*, Oxford, 2002, pp. 495–531; for the cultivation of Bismarck as a precursor to Hitler, see Robert Gerwarth, *The Bismarck Myth: Weimar Germany and the Legacy of the Iron Chancellor*, Oxford, 2005.
59. Heinrich Hoffmann, *Mussolini erlebt Deutschland*, Munich, 1937, p. 7; for context, see Nitz, *Führer und Duce*, pp. 338–43.
60. *Il Popolo d'Italia*, 4 September 1937; ibid., 22 September 1937; for the same tenor, see also Virginio Gayda, 'Duce und Führer', *Europäische Revue*, 13 (1937), pp. 771–7.
61. *Il Popolo d'Italia*, 25 September 1937; for the organisation of the farewell ceremony, see ACS, PCM 1941–1943 20/2/13100, viaggio del Duce in Germania, sf. 1, Il Sottosegretario di stato, 23 September 1937; on context, see Falasca-Zamponi, *Fascist Spectacle*, pp. 84–8.
62. Renzo De Felice, *Mussolini il Duce. II. Lo Stato totalitario, 1936–1940*, Turin, 1981, pp. 414–15; cf. Weinberg, *The Foreign Policy of Hitler's Germany*, II, p. 281; for the importance of rituals, see Peter Reichel, *Der schöne Schein des Dritten Reiches: Faszination und Gewalt des Faschismus*, Munich, 1992; for Italy, see Emilio Gentile, *The Sacralization of Politics in Fascist Italy*, Cambridge, MA, 1996.
63. PAAA, Botschaft Rom (Quirinal), 695B, Programm für den Besuch des italienischen Regierungschefs Benito Mussolini, September 1937.
64. *DBFP*, 2nd series, XIX, doc. 225, Sir George Ogilvie-Forbes to Mr Eden, 6 October 1937; for Ogilvie-Forbes, see Bruce Strang, 'Two Unequal Tempers: Sir George Ogilvie-Forbes, Sir Nevile Henderson and British Foreign Policy, 1938–9', *Diplomacy & Statecraft*, 5 (1994), pp. 107–37.
65. Anfuso, *Roma Berlino Salò*, pp. 47–9; for the seating arrangements on the last leg, see PAAA, R 269004, 'Platzverteilung im italienischen Sonderzug auf der Fahrt Kiefersfelden–München', undated.
66. ACS, MinCulPop, Gabinetto, b. 37, sf. 2, 'Ministero della Cultura Popolare, appunto per l'On Gabinetto di SE Il Ministro', 9 September 1937; see ibid. for a list of instructions 'Alla Delegazione Italiana Servizio Stampa', undated.
67. 'Nel treno del Duce da Roma a Monaco di Baviera', *Il Popolo d'Italia*, 26 September 1937; *New York Times*, 26 September 1937.
68. *VB*, 26 September 1937; *Il Popolo d'Italia*, 26 September 1937; for pictures of cheering Germans, see Hoffmann, *Mussolini erlebt Deutschland*, pp. 12–13; for the Berlin editor, see Hans Bohrmann (ed.), *NS-Presseanweisungen der Vorkriegszeit*, Munich, 1998, V/3, pp. 771–2.
69. *Daily Telegraph*, 25 September 1937, copy in PAAA, R 103300, Bl. 14.
70. *Daily Herald*, 25 September 1937, copy in PAAA, R 103300, Bl. 9.
71. Klaus Behnken (ed.), *Deutschland-Berichte der Sopade*, Frankfurt am Main, 1980, IV, p. 1221, for the Lord Mayor's appeal, see PAAA, R 269004, 'Aufruf!', undated.

72. Behnken (ed.), *Deutschland-Berichte*, IV, pp. 1219–23.
73. *Das Schwarze Korps*, 7 October 1937.
74. For the arrival ceremony, see PAAA, R 103298, Bl. 16, *Berliner Tageblatt*, 25 September 1937; Nicolaus von Below, *Als Hitlers Adjutant 1937–45*, Mainz, 1980, p. 42.
75. For the preparations of the Munich parade, see BAB, NS 22/234, 'Der Aufmarschstab für den Empfang des Italienischen Regierungschefs', 10 September 1937; for Goebbels' views, see *TBJG, Teil I*, IV, pp. 328–9 (26 September 1937); ACS, MinCulPop, Gabinetto, b. 139, sf. 'settembre 1937', Munich, 26 September 1937.
76. Paul Schmidt, *Statist auf diplomatischer Bühne 1923–45: Erlebnisse des Chefdolmetschers im Auswärtigen Amt mit den Staatsmännern Europas*, Bonn, 1949, pp. 365–7.
77. *ADAP*, D, I, doc. 2, memorandum by Bülow-Schwante, 2 October 1937; for a detailed investigation of the Duce's racist remarks, see Kilian Bartikowski and Giorgio Fabre, 'Donna bianca e uomo nero (con una variante): il razzismo anti-nero nei colloqui tra Mussolini e Bülow-Schwante', *Quaderni di storia*, 70 (2009), pp. 181–218.
78. Leonidas E. Hill (ed.), *Die Weizsäcker-Papiere 1933–1950*, Frankfurt am Main, 1974, pp. 117–18.
79. For the text, see Herbert Michaelis and Ernst Schraepler (eds), *Ursachen und Folgen: vom deutschen Zusammenbruch 1918 und 1945 bis zur staatlichen Neuordnung in der Gegenwart*, Berlin, n.d., XI, p. 507; Schmidt, *Statist auf diplomatischer Bühne*, p. 366; *Il Popolo d'Italia*, 26 September 1937; ACS, MinCulPop, Gabinetto, b. 139, sf. 'settembre 1937', Berlin, 27 September 1937.
80. *TBJG, Teil I*, IV, p. 329 (26 September 1937).
81. Hoffmann, *Mussolini erlebt Deutschland*, pp. 40–1.
82. IfZ, MA 329, '7. Befehl für den Vorbeimarsch am 25.9.1937', 22 September 1937.
83. *VB*, 26 September 1937; Domarus, *Hitler*, I/2, p. 734.
84. For the itinerary, see PAAA, Botschaft Rom (Quirinal), 695B, 'Programm für den Besuch des Italienischen Regierungschefs, September 1937'; see also PAAA, R 269004, 'Führerprogramm'; ibid., 'Platzverteilung des italienischen Sonderzug [*sic!*] ab München', undated.
85. *DDF*, 2e série, VI, p. 846, M. François-Poncet to M. Delbos, 22 September 1937.
86. *VB*, 27 September 1937; *Il Popolo d'Italia*, 27 September 1937; see also Below, *Als Hitler's Adjutant*, p. 43.
87. Hoffmann, *Mussolini erlebt Deutschland*, pp. 49, 56–9.
88. Schmidt, *Statist auf diplomatischer Bühne*, p. 367; *DBFP*, 2nd series, XIX, doc. 225, Ogilvie-Forbes to Eden, 6 October 1937.
89. BAB, R 55/512, 'Kostenvoranschlag der dekorativen Ausgestaltung der Stadt Berlin nach Entwürfen des Prof. Benno von Arent', undated; Benz, 'Die Inszenierung der Akklamation'.
90. Erich Ebermayer, '*. . . und morgen die ganze Welt*': *Erinnerungen an Deutschlands dunkle Zeit*, Bayreuth, 1966, p. 198 (2 October 1937).
91. *TBJG, Teil I*, IV, p. 326 (24 September 1937); for the role of audiences, see Shimazu, 'Diplomacy as Theatre', pp. 225–52.
92. See Behnken (ed.), *Deutschland-Berichte*, IV, pp. 1219–20; *DBFP*, 2nd series, XIX, doc. 225, Ogilvie-Forbes to Eden, 6 October 1937.
93. Behnken (ed.), *Deutschland-Berichte*, IV, p. 1220.
94. *DBFP*, 2nd series, XIX, doc. 225, Ogilvie-Forbes to Eden, 6 October 1937; *DDF*, 2e série, VI, doc. 502, François-Poncet to Delbos, 29 September 1937.
95. For the speeches, see ASMAE, Gab. 1923–1943, 681; *OO*, XXVIII, pp. 245–7; Domarus, *Mussolini und Hitler*, pp. 212–13.
96. For Hitler's speech, see Michaelis and Schraepler (eds), *Ursachen und Folgen*, XI, pp. 507–9, here p. 508.
97. *DBFP*, 2nd series, XIX, doc. 225, Ogilvie-Forbes to Eden, 6 October 1937.
98. For the text, see Michaelis and Schraepler (eds), *Ursachen und Folgen*, XI, pp. 509–12, here pp. 510–11; see also *Ausgewählte Reden des Führers und seiner Mitarbeiter 1937: Rede des italienischen Regierungschefs auf dem Maifeld in Berlin – Sonderausgabe für die Wehrmacht*, Munich, 1937, pp. 196–201; for the joke, see Below, *Als Hitlers Adjutant*,

p. 44; see also the memoirs by the unrepentant Nazi Reinhard Spitzy, *So haben wir das Reich verspielt: Bekenntnisse eines Illegalen*, Munich, 1988, pp. 147–7.

99. Benz, 'Die Inszenierung der Akklamation', p. 413.
100. *DBFP*, 2nd series, XIX, doc. 225, Ogilvie-Forbes to Eden, 6 October 1937.
101. *VB*, 30 September 1937.
102. Hoffmann, *Mussolini erlebt Deutschland*, pp. 98–9. For the itinerary, see PAAA, Botschaft Rom (Quirinal), 695b, 'Programm für den Besuch des italienischen Regierungschefs Benito Mussolini', September 1937; *Il Popolo d'Italia*, 30 September 1937.
103. *TBJG, Teil I*, IV, p. 335.
104. Ibid., IV, p. 336.
105. *BZ am Mittag*, 30 September 1937, copy in PAAA, R 103298, Bl. 84.
106. *OO*, XXVIII, p. 275.
107. For the meeting, see John Woodhouse, *Gabriele D'Annunzio: Defiant Archangel*, Oxford, 1998, pp. 378–9; see also the report in *Il Popolo d'Italia*, 1 October 1937.
108. For the reception of Mussolini in Rome, see ACS, PCM 1941–1943, 20/2/13100, sf. 2–2–2–5; see also ACS, MinCulpop, Gabinetto, b. 37, sf. 2, 'Biglietti d'invito per rendere omaggio al Duce al suo rientro', for Mussolini's speech, see *Il Popolo d'Italia*, 1 October 1937.
109. ACS, MinCulPop, Gabinetto, b. 159, sf. 'ottobre 1937', letter of 1 October 1937.
110. ACS, MinCulPop, Gabinetto, b. 159, sf. 'settembre 1937', Appunto per SE il Ministro, 30 September 1937.
111. *ADAP*, D, I, doc. 5, Hassell to Foreign Ministry, 8 October 1937.
112. Galeazzo Ciano, *Diario 1937–1943*, p. 40 (29 September 1937).
113. *DDI*, 8s, VII, doc. 393, Mussolini to King, 4 October 1937.
114. Quoted in Duggan, *Fascist Voices*, p. 282; for the Italian version, see Petacci, *Mussolini segreto*, p. 74 (27 October 1937); for an evaluation of the Petacci diaries, see Giorgio Fabre, 'Mussolini, Claretta e la questione della razza, 1937–38', *Annali della Fondazione Ugo La Malfa*, 24 (2009), pp. 347–70; R.J.B. Bosworth, *Claretta: Mussolini's Last Lover*, New Haven, 2017.
115. Petacci, *Mussolini segreto*, p. 73 (27 October 1937); Filippo Anfuso, *Da Palazzo Venezia al Lago di Garda (1936–1945)*, Bologna, 1957, p. 33.
116. *OO*, XXIX, pp. 1–2.
117. Weinberg, *The Foreign Policy of Hitler's Germany*, II, p. 282; Bosworth, *Mussolini*, p. 329; Kershaw, *Hitler, 1936–1945*, pp. 44–5; *TBJG, Teil I*, IV, p. 334 (29 September 1937).
118. *Il Popolo d'Italia*, 1 October 1937; Bohrmann (ed.), *NS-Presseanweisungen der Vorkriegszeit*, V/3, pp. 774–5.
119. *TBJG, Teil I*, IV, p. 337 (1 October 1937).
120. Behnken (ed.), *Deutschland-Berichte der Sopade*, V, p. 26.
121. *Il Duce in Germania*, with preface by Gherardo Casini, Milan, 1937, p. 8; for Casini, see Guido Bonsaver, *Censorship and Literature in Fascist Italy*, Toronto, 2007, pp. 171, 196; for popular opinion, see Simona Colarizi, *L'opinione degli italiani sotto il regime 1929–1943*, 2nd edn, Rome, 2009, p. 227.
122. Cf. Watt, 'The Rome–Berlin Axis', p. 519; Weinberg, *The Foreign Policy of Hitler's Germany*, II, p. 282; see also Wiskemann, *The Rome–Berlin Axis*, pp. 81–2.

4 Springtime for Hitler, May 1938

1. *ADAP*, D, I, doc. 413, Dieckhoff to Foreign Ministry, 9 October 1937; for context, see David F. Schmitz, *The United States and Fascist Italy, 1922–1940*, Chapel Hill, NC, 1988, pp. 182–3.
2. For context, see Weinberg, *The Foreign Policy of Hitler's Germany*, II, p. 307; for the Hoßbach memorandum, see *ADAP*, D, I, doc. 19; Messerschmidt, 'Außenpolitik und Kriegsvorbereitung', pp. 620–1.
3. For background, see Karl-Heinz Janßen and Fritz Tobias, *Der Sturz der Generäle: Hitler und die Blomberg–Fritsch Krise 1938*, Munich, 1994; for Mussolini's telegram, see Paul Meier-Benneckenstein (ed.), *Dokumente der Deutschen Politik*, Berlin, 1939, VI/1, p. 73; for the Italian version and Hitler's telegram, see *OO*, XXIX, pp. 458–9.

4. For context, see Zachary Shore, *What Hitler Knew: The Battle for Information in Nazi Foreign Policy*, Oxford, 2002, p. 84.
5. Ciano, *Diario*, p. 104 (25 February 1938); for Hassell, see PAAA, Personalakten 5404; Gregor Schöllgen, *Ulrich von Hassell 1881–1944: Ein Konservativer in der Opposition*, Munich, 1990, pp. 91–5; for the German foreign ministry, see Eckart Conze, Norbert Frei, Peter Hayes and Moshe Zimmermann (eds), *Das Amt und die Vergangenheit: Deutsche Diplomaten im Dritten Reich und in der Bundesrepublik*, Munich, 2010; for a critique, see Richard J. Evans, 'The German Foreign Office and the Nazi Past', *Neue Politische Literatur*, 56 (2011), pp. 165–83.
6. Paul Corner, *The Fascist Party and Popular Opinion in Mussolini's Italy*, Oxford, 2012, pp. 226–7.
7. The order is reprinted in Nicola Tranfaglia (ed.), *La stampa del regime 1932–1943: le veline del Minculpop per orientare l'informazione*, Milan, 2005, p. 247; for the pact, see Weinberg, *The Foreign Policy of Hitler's Germany*, II, pp. 170–91.
8. *VB*, 12 December 1937; *Berliner Börsenzeitung*, 19 December 1937; copies of both articles in BAB, R 43 III/324; Claudia Repin, 'Die "Achse Hannover–Cremona"', *QFIAB*, 90 (2010), pp. 373–414, here p. 376; for Italy's departure from the League, see Tollardo, *Fascist Italy and the League of Nations*, p. 1.
9. Corner, *The Fascist Party*, p. 228; for the campaign, see Thomas Buzzegoli, *La polemica antiborghese nel fascismo (1937–1939)*, Rome, 2007.
10. Knox, 'Fascism: Ideology, Foreign Policy, and War', p. 128; for the press instruction, see Tranfaglia (ed.), *La stampa del regime*, p. 246.
11. Mack Smith, *Mussolini*, p. 216; for context, see Silvana Patriarca, *Italian Vices: Nation and Character from the Risorgimento to the Republic*, Cambridge, 2010, pp. 133–60.
12. MacGregor Knox, *Hitler's Italian Allies: Royal Armed Forces, Fascist Regime, and the War of 1940–1943*, Cambridge, 2000, p. 5; Preston, 'Mussolini's Spanish Adventure', pp. 21–51.
13. ACS, PCM 1937–1939, 4.11.3711, b. 2405, sf. 1, letter from Ciano to G Medici del Vascello, 10 November 1937; for a descriptive survey, see Maddalena Vianello, 'La visita di Hitler a Roma nel maggio 1938', in Istituto romano per la storia d'Italia dal fascismo alla Resistenza (ed.), *Roma tra fascismo e liberazione*, Rome, 2006, pp. 67–92, here p. 68; for the railway lines, see ACS, PCM 1937–1939, 4.11.3711, b. 2405, sf. 2, 'Commissione interministeriale', undated; Paul Baxa, 'Capturing the Fascist Moment: Hitler's Visit to Italy in 1938 and the Radicalization of Fascist Italy', *JCH*, 42 (2007), p. 229 wrongly dates the commission's origins to January 1938; see also Arnd Bauerkämper, 'Die Inszenierung transnationaler faschistischer Politik: der Staatsbesuch Hitlers in Italien im Mai 1938', in Stefan Voigt (ed.), *Ideengeschichte als politische Aufklärung: Festschrift für Wolfgang Wippermann zum 65. Geburtstag*, Berlin, 2010, pp. 129–53.
14. The most detailed study, overwhelmingly based on Italian documents, is Dobler, *Bilder der Achse*.
15. ACS, PCM 1937–39, 4.11.3711, b. 2405, sf. 5. Bandiere; cf. Baxa, 'Capturing the Fascist Moment', pp. 230–1.
16. ACS, PCM 1937–39, 4.11.3711, b. 2405, sf. 5, undated and unsigned memorandum.
17. ACS, SpD, CR, b. 71, *Il Lavoro Fascista*, 8 January 1938; PAAA, Botschaft Rom (Quirinal), Bd. 50, 'Postchiffre', 25 February 1938; *Il Popolo d'Italia*, 1 March 1938.
18. PAAA, R 103297, Vermerk, 21 February 1938.
19. *DDI*, 8s, VIII, doc. 461, Pignatti to Ciano, 7 April 1938; see also ibid., docs. 474–476, Pignatti to Ciano, 11 April 1938.
20. *Osservatore Romano*, 2–3 May 1938; for the role of the Vatican in Italian foreign policy, see John Pollard, 'Il Vaticano e la politica estera italiana', in Bosworth and Romano (eds), *La politica estera italiana*, pp. 197–230.
21. Cf. Emma Fattorini, *Hitler, Mussolini, and the Vatican: Pope Pius XI and the Speech that Was Never Made*, Cambridge, 2011, pp. 147–51.
22. PAAA, R 103297, Weizsäcker to von Bergen, 26 February 1938; on context, see Fattorini, *Hitler, Mussolini, and the Vatican*, pp. 144–5; ASMAE, SP Germania 1931–1945, b. 47,

copy of secret letter by Ciano to Magistrati, 1 March 1938; Baxa, 'Capturing the Fascist Moment', p. 238; Archivio Capitolino, Gabinetto del Sindaco Anno 1938, b. 1622, f.1, sf. 1, Ciano to Colonna, 27 March 1938; for Nazism and the Catholic Church, see Richard Steigmann-Gall, 'Religion and the Churches', in Jane Caplan (ed.), *Nazi Germany*, Oxford, 2008, pp. 146–67, here pp. 148–53; *La Civiltà Cattolica*, 21 May 1938; David I. Kertzer, *The Pope and Mussolini: The Secret History of Pius XI and the Rise of Fascism in Europe*, Oxford, 2014, pp. 276–86.

23. For context, see Catherine Brice, 'Riti della Corona, riti del fascio', in Emilio Gentile (ed.), *Modernità italiana: il fascismo italiano*, Rome, 2008, pp. 171–90.
24. Mack Smith, *Italy and its Monarchy*, pp. 158, 275.
25. PAAA, Botschaft Rom (Quirinal), 694a, 'Geheim, Aufzeichnung für den Herrn Deutschen Geschäftsträger'; for context, see Alexander, 'Cultural pragmatics: social performance between ritual and strategy', pp. 29–90.
26. Spitzy, *So haben wir das Reich verspielt*, p. 261; Schmidt, *Statist auf diplomatischer Bühne*, pp. 383–4; for the dress code, see PAAA, Botschaft Rom (Quirinal), 694a, 'Anzugsordnung'; for an official list of the German delegation, see R. Ministero degli Affari Esteri Gabinetto, *Reise des Führers in Italien – Viaggio del Führer in Italia*, Rome, 1938.
27. For context, see Evans, *The Third Reich in Power*, pp. 648–52.
28. Weinberg, *The Foreign Policy of Hitler's Germany*, II, p. 299.
29. *ADAP*, D, I, doc. 352, Hitler to Mussolini, 11 March 1938; see also *DDI*, 8s, VIII, doc. 296; see also the Prince of Hesse's interrogation on 1 March 1948 by Robert Kempner, IfZ, Zs 918; for context, see Georg Christoph Berger Waldenegg, 'Hitler, Göring, Mussolini und der "Anschluß" Österreichs an das Deutsche Reich', *VfZ*, 51 (2003), pp. 147–82, here pp. 171–5; for the Italian communiqué, see *FRUS*, 1938, I, p. 430, The Ambassador in Italy to the Secretary of State, 12 March 1938.
30. *Trial of the Major War Criminals before the International Military Tribunal*, XXXI, pp. 368–70, 2949-PS; see also Petropoulos, *Royals and the Reich*, pp. 183–4.
31. See *Il Popolo d'Italia*, 14 March 1938.
32. ACS, SpD, CR, b. 71, telegram Hitler–Mussolini, 13 March 1938.
33. *Il Popolo d'Italia*, 15 March 1938; for the German version, see Meier-Benneckenstein (ed.), *Dokumente der Deutschen Politik*, VI/1, p. 146, n. 2.
34. *Il Popolo d'Italia*, 16 March 1938; Schmidt, *Statist auf diplomatischer Bühne*, p. 382.
35. Petacci, *Mussolini segreto*, pp. 241–6 (13 March 1938).
36. Tranfaglia (ed.), *La stampa del regime*, pp. 248–9.
37. *FRUS*, 1938, I, pp. 425–6, Wilson to the Secretary of State, 12 March 1938.; ibid, p. 428, Wilson to the Secretary of State, 12 March 1938.
38. For the Fascist Grand Council, see Alberto Aquarone, *L'organizzazione dello Stato totalitario*, Turin, 1965, pp. 159–62; Aldo Cecconi, 'Il Gran Consiglio del fascismo', *Passato e presente*, 19 (1989), pp. 53–81.
39. *Il Popolo d'Italia*, 13 March 1938.
40. For the Grand Council meeting, see *OO*, XXIX, pp. 65–6; Ciano, *Diario*, p. 112 (13 March 1938); for Mussolini's speech, see *OO*, XXIX, pp. 67–71; for the edited publication of Hitler's letter, see Meier-Benneckenstein (ed.), *Dokumente der Deutschen Politik*, VI/1, pp. 135–7.
41. *FRUS*, 1938, I, pp. 450–1, Ambassador Phillips to Secretary of State, 16 March 1938; for intellectuals' views, see Ben-Ghiat, *Fascist Modernities*, pp. 124, 158; for the *Vallo del Littorio*, see Malte König, *Kooperation als Machtkampf: das faschistische Achsenbündnis Berlin–Rom im Krieg 1940/41*, Cologne, 2007, pp. 238–9.
42. Edward R. Tannenbaum, *Fascism in Italy: Society and Culture 1922–1945*, London, 1972, pp. 282–3; for a cursory study of Italian anti-German feeling in an earlier period, see Federico Niglia, *L'antigermanismo tedesco italiano: da Sedan a Versailles*, Florence, 2012, pp. 89–128.
43. ACS, Min. Interno, Pol. Pol. (1928–1944), Materia, p. 5, unsigned memorandum, 1 April 1938; for popular opinion, see Colarizi, *L'opinione degli italiani sotto il regime*, p. 256; see more generally, Paul Corner, 'Fascist Italy in the 1930s: Popular Opinion in the Provinces',

in Paul Corner (ed.), *Popular Opinion in Totalitarian Regimes: Fascism, Nazism, Communism*, Oxford, 2009, pp. 122–48; Alberto Aquarone, 'Public Opinion in Italy before the Outbreak of World War II', in Roland Sarti (ed.), *The Ax Within: Italian Fascism in Action*, New York, 1974, pp. 212–20.

44. Ciano, *Diario*, p. 130 (24 April 1938); Mack Smith, *Mussolini*, p. 218.
45. *OO*, XXIX, p. 72, Ciano, *Diario*, p. 114 (18 March 1938); for the duke, see Hoepke, *Die deutsche Rechte und der italienische Faschismus*, pp. 283–4, 298–303; Karina Urbach, *Go-Betweens for Hitler*, Oxford, 2015, pp.165–216.
46. De Felice, *Mussolini il Duce*, II, p. 465.
47. Mack Smith, *Mussolini*, p. 219; for the speech, see *OO*, XXIX, pp. 74–82.
48. Mack Smith, *Mussolini*, p. 219; cf. De Felice, *Mussolini il Duce*, II, p. 466.
49. For Bocchini and the police, see Mimmo Franzinelli, *I tentacoli dell'Ovra: agenti, collaboratori e vittime della polizia politica fascista*, Turin, 1999.
50. See the various decrees in ACS, MI, DGPS, DAGR, Massime S1, b. 193, sf 1c; scf. 2c; for context, see Michael R. Ebner, *Ordinary Violence in Mussolini's Italy*, Cambridge, 2011, pp. 48–71; for rallies, see Falasca-Zamponi, *Fascist Spectacle*.
51. ACS, MI, DGPS, DAGR, Massime S1, fasc. 48, 'Visita in Italia del Fuhrer del Reich', 4 October 1937; see also Vianello, 'La visita di Hitler a Roma', pp. 72–3; for context, see Bernhard, 'Konzertierte Gegnerbekämpfung', pp. 229–62.
52. ACS, MI, DGPS, DAGR, Massime S1, fasc. 48, Müller to Leto, 23 November 1937.
53. Klaus Voigt, *Zuflucht auf Widerruf: Exil in Italien 1933–1945*, Stuttgart, 1989, I, pp. 17–65, 141–252.
54. For context, see ibid., I, pp. 122–40; see also Klaus Voigt, 'Jewish Refugees and Immigrants in Italy, 1933–1945', in Ivo Herzer (ed.), *The Italian Refuge: Rescue of Jews during the Holocaust*, Washington, DC, 1989, pp. 141–58, here pp. 144–5; Klaus Voigt, 'Refuge and Persecution in Italy, 1933–1945', *Simon Wiesenthal Annual*, 4 (1987), pp. 3–64, here pp. 22–5; ACS, SpD, CO 183298, 'telegramma no. 20821', 27 April 1938.
55. PAAA, Botschaft Rom (Quirinal), 694b, German Consulate Livorno to German Embassy, 30 March 1938; ACS, SpD, CO 183258, telegram by Rabbi Giosuè Gruenwald, 4 May 1938; see also ACS, MI, DGPS, Dagr, 1938, b. 17.
56. *New York Times*, 29 April 1938.
57. See, e.g., ACS, SpD, CO 183298, urgent telegram from Bolzano border police to Bocchini, 3 May 1938.
58. ACS, SpD, CO 183298, Prefetto Passerini (Modena), 1 May 1938; for the threatening letter, see ACS, MI, DGPS, DAGR, PS 1938, b. 17, Il Capo della Compagnia della Morte to Mussolini, 28 March 1938.
59. ACS, SpD, CO 183298, 'telegramma no. 20820', 27 April 1938; for the unpopularity of the alliance with Germany, see Corner, *The Fascist Party*, p. 242.
60. ASMAE, MinCulPop, b. 128, sf C/1, 'Viaggio Führer in Italia, servizi giornalistici, communicati stampa'; for German correspondents, see ibid., sf D, 'tessere'; sf F, 'rapporti riservati'; see also ACS, MinCulPop, Gab. B. 159, Varie, Maggio 1938, 'Appunto per il Sig. Ministro', 9 May 1938.
61. ACS, MinCulPop, Gab., b. 63, 'relazione', 25 April 1938; ibid., Direzione generale per la cinematografia, 'appunto per SE Il Ministro', undated; for a list of foreign correspondents and their distribution to the various points on Hitler's itinerary, see ASMAE, MinCulPop, b. 126.
62. Archivio Capitolino, Gabinetto del Sindaco Anno 1938, b. 1622, f. 1, sf. 1, Ciano to Starace etc., 10 March 1938; ibid., Buffarini Guidi to Colonna, 24 March 1938.
63. See the correspondence in ACS, PCM 1937–39, 4.11.3711, b. 2414. The plans of the commission, which even regulated the distribution of tickets to the events, fill just under twenty thick folders archived by the Presidenza del Consiglio dei Ministri, see ACS, PCM 1937–39, 4.11.3711.
64. Archivio Capitolino, Gabinetto del Sindaco Anno 1938, b. 1621, f. 1, sf. 1, Ettel to Cav. Bertini, 27 April 1938; ibid., memorandum for Colonna's office, 3 May 1938.
65. ACS, Agenzia Stefani, b. 70, 'Riservata per il Sig. Presidente', 28 April 1938.

66. Ibid.
67. *Il Popolo d'Italia*, 29 April 1938; for the decree, see also ACS, PCM, 1937–39, 4.11/3711, b. 2414, sf. 15.
68. ACS, Agenzia Stefani, b. 70, 'riservata per il Sig. Presidente', 29 April 1938; for context, see Duggan, *Fascist Voices*, pp. 206–7.
69. *Il Popolo d'Italia*, 30 April 1938; see also ibid., 1 & 2 May 1938; cf. Schieder, *Faschistische Diktaturen*, pp. 417–63.
70. *VB*, 30 April 1938, copy in BAB, R 901/58672; 'Führerbesuch!', *Italien-Beobachter*, n.d. [1938], p. 2.
71. PAAA, Botschaft Rom (Quirinal), 694a, Cesare S. to German Embassy, 12 April 1938; ibid., Paul H. to German Embassy, 27 April 1938; cf. Duggan, *Fascist Voices*.
72. PAAA, Botschaft Rom (Quirinal), 694c, Kanzler, 3 July 1938; ibid., 'Quittung', 13 June 1938; ibid., Kanzler, 3 July 1938; cf. Duggan, *Fascist Voices*.
73. Deutsches Nachrichtenbüro, No. 120, 2 May 1938, copy in BAB, R 901/58673.
74. For details, see *VB*, 4 May 1938; for context, see Brice, 'Riti della Corona'.
75. PAAA, Botschaft Rom (Quirinal), 694a, 'Anlage 4 Geheim!, Reihenfolge der Züge'; Below, *Als Hitlers Adjutant*, p. 98.
76. For the trains, see PAAA, Botschaft Rom (Quirinal), 694a, 'Anlage 4, Reihenfolge der Züge, Geheim'; for the itinerary, see IfZ, Fk 7181–1, 'Staatsbesuch des Führers und Reichskanzlers in Italien, Mai 1938, Zeitfolge'; for *adunate*, see Mabel Berezin, *Making the Fascist Self: The Political Culture of Interwar Italy*, Ithaca, NY, 1997, p. 165; *Il Popolo d'Italia*, 3 & 4 May 1938, 'Sul Treno Speciale del Führer'; ACS, SpD, CO 183298, Prefetto Mastromattei to MinCulPop and Interior Ministry's Gabinetto, 30 April 1938; ibid., Ispettore Generale Andreani to Bocchini, 3 May 1938.
77. *TBJG, Teil I*, V, pp. 284–5 (3 May 1938), 285–6 (4 May 1938).
78. See Evans, 'Coercion and Consent in Nazi Germany', pp. 53–81; Paul Corner, 'Italian Fascism: Whatever Happened to Dictatorship?', *Journal of Modern History*, 74 (2002), pp. 325–51; see also the essays in Roberta Pergher and Giulia Albanese (eds), *In the Society of Fascists: Acclamation, Acquiescence, and Agency in Fascist Italy*, Basingstoke, 2012; for the masses as participants, see Shimazu, 'Diplomacy as Theatre'.
79. For letters to Mussolini, see Christopher Duggan, 'The Internalisation of the Cult of the Duce: The Evidence of Diaries and Letters', in Gundle, Duggan and Pieri (eds), *The Cult of the Duce*, pp. 129–43.
80. Cf. De Felice, *Mussolini il Duce*, II, p. 531; for Fascist repression, see Ebner, *Ordinary Violence*.
81. ACS, SpD, CO 183258, anonymous letter, 20 May 1938; ibid., undated letter.
82. *VB*, 5 May 1938.
83. *Il Popolo d'Italia*, 4 May 1938.
84. For the king and Hitler, see Petacci, *Mussolini segreto*, p. 318 (10 May 1938).
85. For the order of carriages, see ACS, Ufficio del prefetto di palazzo, anni 1871–1946, Anno 1938, filza 322 bis, Ufficio del Grande Scuderie, Servizio per l'arrivo in Roma del Führer, 3 May 1938; Ciano, *Diario*, p. 134 (7 May 1938); Mack Smith, *Italy and its Monarchy*, pp. 275–6.
86. Ciano, *Diario*, p. 134 (8 May 1938); Anfuso, *Roma Berlino Salò*, p. 68.
87. Hildegard von Kotze (ed.), *Heeresadjutant bei Hitler 1938–1943: Aufzeichnungen des Majors Engel*, Stuttgart, 1974, p. 23 (22 May 1938); Werner Jochmann (ed.), *Adolf Hitler: Monologe im Führerhauptquartier 1941–1944 – die Aufzeichnungen Heinrich Heims*, Hamburg, 1980, pp. 246–8; *TBJG, Teil I*, V, pp. 288–90 (6 May 1938).
88. Eugen Dollmann, *The Interpreter: Memoirs of Doktor Eugen Dollman*, London, 1967, pp. 115–16; for a list of the wives to be received see ACS, Ufficio del prefetto di palazzo, 1871–1946, 1938, filza 322 ter, German Embassy to Primo Maestro delle Cerimonie di Corte, 27 April 1938.
89. Heike B. Görtemaker, *Eva Braun: Leben mit Hitler*, Munich, 2010, pp. 214–15.
90. 'Führerbesuch!', *Italien-Beobachter*, pp. 33–4; for background, see Alex Scobie, *Hitler's State Architecture: The Impact of Classical Antiquity*, University Park, PA, 1990, p. 24.

91. For photographs, see Federico Mastrigli, 'Roma Pavesata', *Capitolium*, 13 (1938), pp. 219–34; for the setup of the illuminations, see Archivio Capitolino, Gabinetto del Sindaco Anno 1938, b. 1623, f., sf.1 (see also in this file Ettore Salani, *Le illuminazioni straordinarie a Roma e a bordo delle navi da Guerra in occasione della visita del Fuehrer: note sui risultati ottenuti da alcuni nuovi tipi di apparecchiature e sugl'insegnamenti che non sono derivati* (May 1938)); Luigi Huetter, 'Gli ingressi trionfali di Roma', *Capitolium*, 13 (1938), pp. 235–45; cf. Scobie, *Hitler's State Architecture*, p. 24; Dobler, *Bilder der Achse*, pp. 176–81; for the wider context of entries, see Paulmann, *Pomp und Politik*, pp. 337–400.
92. *TBJG, Teil I*, V, pp. 285–6 (4 May 1938).
93. Domarus, *Hitler*, I/2, p. 857; BAB, R 2/4509, Bl. 97, Kostenrechnung, 24 August 1938; see also Peter Köhler, 'Das "Mussolini-Observatoriumsprojekt"', *Jenaer Jahrbuch zur Technik- und Industriegeschichte*, 10 (2007), pp. 413–34.
94. Pietro Pastorelli (ed.), *Le carte del Gabinetto del Ministro e della Segreteria generale dal 1923 al 1943*, Rome, 1999, p. 30.
95. *TBJG, Teil I*, V, pp. 285–6 (5 May 1938).
96. Ernst von Weizsäcker, *Memoirs of Ernst von Weizsäcker*, London, 1951, p. 130; Ciano, *Diario*, p. 133 (5 May 1938); see also PAAA, R 29647, memorandum by Weizsäcker, 9 May 1938.
97. D.C. Watt, 'An Earlier Model for the Pact of Steel: The Draft Treaties Exchanged between Germany and Italy during Hitler's Visit to Rome in May 1938', *International Affairs*, 3 (1957), pp. 185–97; see also D.C. Watt, 'Hitler's Visit to Rome and the May Weekend Crisis: A Study in Hitler's Response to External Stimuli', *JCH*, 9 (1974), pp. 23–32; *Il Popolo d'Italia*, 5 May 1938; *TBJG, Teil I*, V, p. 287 (5 May 1938).
98. *TBJG, Teil I*, V, p. 287 (5 May 1938).
99. *VB*, 5 May 1938; PAAA, Botschaft Rom (Quirinal), 694a, note by military attaché, 2 May 1938; see also ACS, ufficio del Primo Aiutante di Campo Generale di Sua Maestà il Re e Imperatore, Quinquennio 1936–1940, b. 664, 'Visita del Führer alle RR. Tombe del Pantheon, Milite Ignoto, Ara Caduti Fascisti', 4 May 1938.
100. Domarus, *Hitler*, I/2, pp. 855–6; for the official German news agency report, see BAB, R 901/58675, Bl. 2–5.
101. *Il Popolo d'Italia*, 5 May 1938.
102. ACS, Min, Interno Direz. Generale di Pubblica Sicurezza, Divisione Affari Generali e Riservati (Dagr), Massime, fasc. S1 (servizi di vigilanza), 'Viaggio in Italia di S.E. Hitler', b. 193, sf. 4c; the R Questura di Napoli also prepared a booklet on 'Disposizioni e servizi per le manifestazioni del 5 Maggio 1938-XVI', 29 April 1938.
103. *Il Popolo d'Italia*, 6 May 1938; *TBJG, Teil I*, V, p. 289 (6 May 1938), *VB*, 7 May 1938; Jens Petersen, 'Die Stunde der Entscheidung: das faschistische Italien zwischen Mittelmeerimperium und neutralistischem Niedergang', in Helmut Altrichter and Josef Becker (eds), *Kriegausbruch 1939: Beteiligte, Betroffene, Neutrale*, Munich, 1989, pp. 131–52, here pp. 145–6; Gerhard Schreiber, *Revisionismus und Weltmachtstreben: Marineführung und deutsch-italienische Beziehungen 1919–1944*, Stuttgart, 1978, pp. 121–34.
104. See the correspondence in ACS, PCM 1937–39, 4/11.3711, b. 2113, sf. 7/1, 7/2.
105. Schmidt, *Statist auf diplomatischer Bühne*, p. 386; for the dress rules, see PAAA, Botschaft Rom (Quirinal), 694a, 'Anzugsordnung'.
106. Below, *Als Hitlers Adjutant*, pp. 99–100; Wiedemann, *Der Mann der Feldherr werden wollte*, p. 137; for the Luftwaffe's view, see Petersen, 'Die Stunde der Entscheidung', p. 146.
107. On the *Mostra*, see Friedemann Scriba, 'Die Mostra Augustea della Romanità in Rom 1937/38', in Petersen and Schieder (eds), *Faschismus und Gesellschaft in Italien*, pp. 133–58; see also Aristotle Kallis, '"Framing" *Romanità*: The Celebrations for the *Bimillenario Augusteo* and the *Augusteo–Ara Pacis* Project', *JCH*, 46 (2011), pp. 809–31.
108. Scobie, *Hitler's State Architecture*, pp. 30–1.
109. Ranuccio Bianchi Bandinelli, *Diario di un borghese*, new edn, Rome, 1996, pp. 122–6.

110. 'Roma nel Mondo: rassegna della stampa germanica', *Capitolium*, 13 (1938), p. 43.
111. Archivio Capitolino, Gabinetto del Sindaco Anno 1938, b. 1621, f. 1, sf. 1, Colonna to Foreign Ministry, 27 April 1938; see also *Bozzetti di addobbo dell'urbe per la visita del Führer / Die Ausschmückungsentwürfe der Stadt Roms für den Besuch des Führers*, Rome, 1938, p. 2.
112. Archivio Capitolino, Gabinetto del Sindaco Anno 1938, b. 1623, f. 1, sf.2, programme, 6 May 1938; see also *VB*, 8 May 1938; Below, *Als Hitlers Adjutant*, p. 99.
113. *Il Popolo d'Italia*, 7 May 1938; Weinberg, *The Foreign Policy of Hitler's Germany*, II, pp. 308–9; *TBJG, Teil I*, V, p. 292 (7 May 1938).
114. Quoted in Paolo Orano (ed.), *L'Asse nel pensiero dei due popoli / Die Achse im Denken der beiden Völker*, Rome, 1938, pp. 11–12; *Gerarchia*, XIII/6, (1938); for context, see Arnold Esch and Jens Petersen (eds), *Deutsches Ottocento: die deutsche Wahrnehmung Italiens im Risorgimento*, Tübingen, 2000.
115. For the speeches, see *VB*, 9 May 1938; *Il Popolo d'Italia*, 8 May 1938; for the toasts, see Orano (ed.), *L'Asse / Die Achse*, pp. 129–30; for Nazi reactions, see *TBJG, Teil I*, V, p. 294 (8 May 1938); for the French reaction, see *DDF*, 2e série, IX, doc. 298, M. Blondel to Georges Bonnet, 8 May 1938.
116. Weinberg, *The Foreign Policy of Hitler's Germany*, II, pp. 308–9.
117. For Mussolini's toast, see *OO*, XXIX, pp. 94–6; Hans Bohrmann and Karen Peter (eds), *NS-Presseanweisungen der Vorkriegszeit*, Munich, 1999, VI/2, pp. 451–2.
118. *VB*, 9 May 1938; *Il Popolo d'Italia*, 9 May 1938; *TBJG, Teil I*, V, p. 296 (9 May 1938); ACS, SpD, CO 183258, anonymous letter to the Duce, 9 May 1938.
119. For general context, see Martin, *The Nazi-Fascist New Order*.
120. For detailed accounts, see D. Medina Lasansky, *The Renaissance Perfected: Architecture, Spectacle, and Tourism in Fascist Italy*, University Park, PA, 2004, pp. 83–98; Roberto Mancini (ed.), *Apparati e feste per la visita di Hitler e Mussolini a Firenze (1938)*, Florence, 2010, pp. 101–56; Roger J. Crum, 'Shaping the Fascist "New Man": Donatello's *St George* and Mussolini's Appropriated Renaissance of the Italian Nation', in Claudia Lazzaro and Roger J. Crum (eds), *Donatello among the Blackshirts: History and Modernity in the Visual Culture of Fascist Italy*, Ithaca, NY, 2005, pp. 133–44, here pp. 136–8; for the preparations, see the files in Archivio storico del Comune di Firenze, Gabinetto del podestà, CF 5173; Visita del Führer a Firenze. Servizi d'Onore Florence, 1938; Archivio Storico (ed.), *Firenze 9 maggio 1938*, Florence, 2012.
121. *La Nazione*, 10 May 1938; for context, see Roberta Suzzi Valli, 'The Myth of Squadrismo in the Fascist Regime', *JCH*, 35 (2000), pp. 131–50.
122. Dollmann, *The Interpreter*, p. 114.
123. Domarus, *Hitler*, I/2, p. 863; *Il Popolo d'Italia*, 10 May 1938.
124. Alexander, 'Cultural Pragmatics', pp. 29–90; cf. Dobler, *Bilder der Achse*, p. 379.
125. IfZ, Fk–7181–1, 'Staatsbesuch des Führers und Reichskanzlers in Italian. Mai 1938. Zeitfolge, 6'.
126. *TBJG, Teil I*, V, p. 297 (10 May 1938).
127. Bohrmann and Peter (eds), *NS-Presseanweisungen*, VI/2, p. 462.
128. Petersen, 'Deutschland, Italien und Südtirol 1938–1940', pp. 127–50.
129. *Il Popolo d'Italia*, 11 May 1938; for the German version, see Domarus, *Hitler*, I/2, p. 862.
130. Domarus, *Hitler*, I/2, p. 862; for the Italian version, see ACS, SpD, CO 183258, Hitler to Mussolini, 10 May 1938.
131. *VB*, 10 May 1938.
132. Cf. Watt, 'The Rome–Berlin Axis'; see now Dobler, *Bilder der Achse*, p. 379.
133. *TBJG, Teil I*, V, pp. 298–9 (11 May 1938); Bohrmann and Peter (eds), *NS-Presseanweisungen*, VI/2, p. 453.
134. *TBJG, Teil I*, V, pp. 300–1 (12 May 1938); Ciano, *Diario*, p. 134.
135. Petacci, *Mussolini segreto*, pp. 313 (7 May 1938), 315–16 (10 May 1938).
136. *Manchester Guardian*, 10 May 1938.
137. *OO*, XXIX, pp. 99–102; PAAA, Botschaft Rom (Quirinal), 693c, 'Politischer Bericht', undated.

138. *DDF*, 2e série, IX, doc. 310, Blondel to Bonnet, 10 May 1938; ibid., doc. 327, François-Poncet to Bonnet, 13 May 1938.
139. *Das Schwarze Korps*, 12 May 1938.
140. PAAA, Botschaft Rom (Quirinal), Geheim, Bd. 50, Braun von Stumm to Aschmann, 11 May 1938; PAAA, R 29647, confidential memorandum by Weizsäcker, undated; for the official German summary, see PAAA, Botschaft Rom (Quirinal), 693c, telegram from Ribbentrop to German Embassy, 12 May 1938; cf. Watt, 'Hitler's Visit to Rome'.
141. Printed in Simona Colarizi, *L'Italia antifascista dal 1922 al 1940*, Rome, 1976, II, p. 449.
142. Cf. De Felice, *Mussolini il Duce*, II, p. 485.

5 On the Road to War, 1938–9

1. Enno von Rintelen, *Mussolini als Bundesgenosse: Erinnerungen des deutschen Militärattachés in Rom 1936–1943*, Tübingen, 1951, pp. 55–6; Petersen, 'Die Stunde der Entscheidung', p. 147.
2. BAB, R 43 II/1449b, Bl. 138–9, Lammers memorandum, 19 December 1938; for details of academic and cultural exchanges, see Andrea Albrecht, Lutz Danneberg and Simone De Angelis (eds), *Die akademische 'Achse Berlin-Rom'? Der wissenschaftlich-kulturelle Austausch zwischen Italien und Deutschland 1920 bis 1945*, Berlin, 2017.
3. Rudy Koshar, *German Travel Cultures*, New York, 2000, p. 129.
4. De Felice, *Mussolini il Duce*, II, p. 487.
5. Ciano, *Diario*, p. 150 (21 June 1938); Giuseppe Bottai, *Diario 1935–1944*, Milan, 2001, p. 121 (23 June 1938).
6. *ADAP*, D, II, doc. 135, memorandum of the eight demands made by Konrad Henlein, 24 April 1938; on context, see Weinberg, *The Foreign Policy of Hitler's Germany*, II, pp. 313–77.
7. Evans, *The Third Reich in Power*, pp. 667–8; for background, see Jürgen Tampke, *Czech–German Relations and the Politics of Central Europe: From Bohemia to the EU*, London, 2003, pp. 25–44; Keith Robbins, *Munich 1938*, London, 1968, pp. 168–74.
8. Cf. De Felice, *Mussolini il Duce*, II, pp. 509–17.
9. Quartararo, *Roma tra Londra e Berlino*, p. 399; cf. Bosworth, *The Italian Dictatorship*, pp. 94–6; G. Bruce Strang, 'War and Peace: Mussolini's Road to Munich', *Diplomacy & Statecraft*, 10 (1999), pp. 160–90; see also Patrizia Dogliani, 'Das faschistische Italien und das Münchner Abkommen', in Jürgen Zarusky and Martin Zückert (eds), *Das Münchener Abkommen in europäischer Perspektive*, Munich, 2013, pp. 53–68; Hans Woller, 'Vom Mythos der Moderation: Mussolini und die Münchener Konferenz 1938', in Zarusky and Zückert (eds), *Das Münchener Abkommen in europäischer Perspektive*, pp. 211–15; Gooch, *Mussolini and his Generals*, pp. 384–449.
10. Strang, 'War and Peace', pp. 160–1; Knox, *Mussolini Unleashed*, pp. 37–8.
11. Maximiliane Rieder, *Deutsch-italienische Wirtschaftsbeziehungen: Kontinuitäten und Brüche 1936–1957*, Frankfurt am Main, 2003, p. 133; Mantelli, 'Vom "bilateralen Handelsausgleich" zur "Achse Berlin–Rom"', pp. 253–79.
12. Cf. Bosworth, *The Italian Dictatorship*, pp. 94–6; for the view that Mussolini was a buffoon, see Mack Smith, *Mussolini's Roman Empire*, pp. 130–1; cf. Strang, 'War and Peace', p. 160.
13. *ADAP*, D, II, doc. 334, note by Ribbentrop, 4 August 1938; cf. Woller, 'Vom Mythos der Moderation', p. 213.
14. Ciano, *Diario*, p. 172 (2 September 1938).
15. Paul Kennedy, 'Appeasement', in Gordon Martel (ed.), *The Origins of the Second World War Reconsidered*, Boston, 1986, pp. 140–61.
16. Heinz Boberach (ed.), *Meldungen aus dem Reich: die geheimen Lageberichte des Sicherheitsdienstes der SS 1938–1945*, Herrsching, 1984, II, p. 73.
17. Behnken (ed.), *Deutschland-Berichte der Sopade*, V (1938), pp. 913–39.
18. Schmidt, *Statist auf diplomatischer Bühne*, p. 382; for context, see Petropoulos, *Royals and the Reich*, p. 188.

19. *ADAP*, D, II, doc. 220, Mackensen to Foreign Ministry, 29 May 1938; cf. Strang, 'War and Peace', p. 163.
20. *ADAP*, D, II, doc. 415, memorandum, September 1938; for the Italian text, translated for Mussolini, see *DDI*, 8s, IX, doc. 495, Ciano to Attolico, 8 September 1938; *DDI*, 8s, X, doc. 14, Attolico to Ciano, 13 September 1938.
21. *ADAP*, D, II, doc. 421, Chargé d'Affaires Washington DC to Foreign Ministry, 2 September 1938.
22. *DBFP*, 3rd series, II, doc. 887, Sir N. Charles to Viscount Halifax, 15 September 1938; for Farinacci at Nuremberg, see Bartikowski, *Der italienische Antisemitismus*, p. 109.
23. *Il Popolo d'Italia*, 10 September 1938.
24. Winston Churchill, 'Dictators on Dynamite', *Collier's*, 3 September 1938; for context, see Hans Woller, 'Churchill und Mussolini: offene Konfrontation und geheime Kooperation?', *VfZ*, 49 (2001), pp. 563–94.
25. *ADAP*, D, II, doc. 488, Woermann to Weizsäcker, 15 September 1938; for the official German translation of the article, see *Deutsche Allgemeine Zeitung*, 15 September 1938 (printed in *Documents on German Foreign Policy*, D, II, doc. 488). My translation is based on the Italian original in *OO*, XXIX, pp. 141–3.
26. See *DBFP*, 3rd series, II, doc. 895, notes of conversation with Herr Hitler, 15 September 1938; ibid., doc. 896, translation of notes made by Herr Schmidt, 15 September 1938.
27. *DBFP*, 3rd series, II, doc. 899, Sir N. Charles to Viscount Halifax, 16 September 1938; for general context, see Gooch, *Mussolini and his Generals*, pp. 384–449.
28. *ADAP*, D, II, doc. 495, 'Aufzeichnung des Leiters der Politischen Abteilung', 16 September 1938; for the German reply to Mussolini, see ibid., doc. 510, unsigned memorandum, presumably by Ribbentrop, 17 September 1938.
29. For the speech, see *OO*, XXIX, pp. 144–7; for the introduction of anti-Semitic legislation in Italy, see, amongst others, Esmonde Robertson, 'Race as a Factor in Mussolini's Policy in Africa and Europe', *JCH*, 23 (1988), pp. 37–58; Michele Sarfatti, *Gli ebrei nell'Italia fascista: vicende, identità, persecuzione*, Turin, 2000; Meir Michaelis, *Mussolini and the Jews: German–Italian relations and the Jewish Question in Italy, 1922–1945*, Oxford, 1978.
30. *DDF*, 2e série, XI, doc. 210, M. Blondel to Georges Bonnet, 18 September 1938; ibid., doc. 214, François-Poncet to Bonnet, 19 September 1938.
31. Paul Baxa, '"*Il nostro Duce*": Mussolini's Visit to Trieste in 1938 and the Workings of the Cult of the Duce', *Modern Italy*, 18 (2013), pp. 117–28; for the Verona speech, see *OO*, XXIX, p. 164.
32. *OO*, XXIX, pp. 144–7; cf. De Felice, *Mussolini il Duce*, II, pp. 516–17; for a perceptive report on the Verona speech of 26 September 1938, see *DDF*, 2e série, doc. 373, Blondel to Bonnet, 26 September 1938; ibid., doc. 399, Blondel to Bonnet, 27 September 1938; on public opinion in Italy, see Colarizi, *L'opinione degli italiani sotto il regime*, pp. 261–5.
33. Ciano, *Diario*, p. 183 (25 September 1938); for the meeting, see *DDI*, 8s, X, doc. 134, n. 1.
34. For the minutes, see *ADAP*, D, II, doc. 562, notes by Schmidt on the Hitler–Chamberlain conversation, 22 September 1938; for the British minutes, see *DBFP*, 3rd series, II, doc. 1033.
35. *DDF*, 2e série, XI, doc. 338, Blondel to Bonnet, 24 September 1938.
36. Evans, *The Third Reich in Power*, p. 674.
37. *TBJG, Teil I*, VI, p. 118 (28 September 1938).
38. Below, *Als Hitlers Adjutant*, p. 127; see also *TGJB, Teil I*, VI, p. 119 (29 September 1938).
39. *ADAP*, D, II, doc. 661, Mackensen to Foreign Ministry, 28 September 1938; Kershaw, *Hitler 1936–1945*, pp. 119–21.
40. *DDF*, 2e série, XI, doc. 417, Blondel to Bonnet, 29 September 1938.
41. Cf. Quartararo, *Roma tra Londra e Berlino*, pp. 399–400.
42. Printed in Tranfaglia (ed.), *La stampa del regime*, pp. 250–1; for Alfieri's press directives, see also ACS, MinCulPop, Gabinetto b. 39, sf. 253; for the selection of journalists, see ibid., Alfieri to General Giuseppe Valle, 28 September 1938.

43. Printed in Piero Melograni, *Rapporti segreti della polizia fascista*, Rome, 1979, pp. 16–17.
44. Domarus, *Mussolini und Hitler*, pp. 248–9; for a photograph of the leaders at Munich, see Dante Maria Tuninetti (ed.), *Incontri di Popoli: Hitler e Mussolini*, Roma, n.d. [1943], pp. 17–20; for uniforms, see Perry Willson, 'The Nation in Uniform? Fascist Italy, 1919–43', *Past & Present*, 221 (2013), pp. 239–72.
45. Ciano, *Diario*, pp. 187–9 (29–30 September 1938); *New York Times*, 30 September 1938; cf. Weinberg, *The Foreign Policy of Hitler's Germany*, II, p. 457.
46. Ciano, *Diario*, pp. 187–9 (29–30 September 1938).
47. *The Times*, 30 September 1938.
48. *Manchester Guardian*, 30 September 1938.
49. *DDF*, 2e série, XII, doc. 19, François-Poncet to Bonnet, 4 October 1938; for an eyewitness account, see Schmidt, *Statist auf diplomatischer Bühne*, pp. 413–19; for the official German minutes, see *ADAP*, D, II, docs. 670 and 674; for Mussolini's claiming of authorship, see *ADAP*, D, II, p. 805, n. 1; Robbins, *Munich 1938*, p. 316.
50. *DDF*, 2e série, XII, doc. 19, François-Poncet to Bonnet, 4 October 1938; cf. Quartararo, *Roma tra Londra e Berlino*, p. 400; De Felice, *Mussolini il Duce*, II, pp. 542–3.
51. *ADAP*, D, II, doc. 675, 'Abkommen zwischen Deutschland, Großbritannien, Frankreich und Italien', 29 September 1938; ibid., 676, 'Deutsch-Englische Erklärung', 30 September 1938; Domarus, *Mussolini und Hitler*, p. 251; for an account of the conference, see Robbins, *Munich 1938*, pp. 315–19; for Hitler's reactions, see Weinberg, *The Foreign Policy of Hitler's Germany*, II, p. 463.
52. François-Poncet, *The Fateful Years*, p. 271.
53. ACS, MinCulPop, Gabinetto b. 39, sf. 253, 'Itinerario del treno presidenziale', undated.
54. *OO*, XXIX, p. 166; cf. De Felice, *Mussolini il Duce*, II, p. 530.
55. Petacci, *Mussolini segreto*, pp. 413–17 (1 October 1938); see also Duggan, *Fascist Voices*, p. 324.
56. *OO*, XXIX, p. 192.
57. Printed in Colarizi, *L'Italia antifascista dal 1922 al 1940*, II, p. 403.
58. Roland Sarti (ed.), *The Ax Within: Italian Fascism in Action*, New York, 1974, p. 210; Aquarone, 'Public Opinion in Italy', pp. 212–20.
59. Colarizi, *L'opinione degli italiani*, p. 264.
60. Printed in De Felice, *Mussolini il Duce*, II, p. 533.
61. ACS, SpD, CO, b. 2815, sf. 37–5, letter of 1 October 1938.
62. For the letters, see ACS, SpD, CO, Sentimenti b. 2815–20; some of these letters are reprinted in De Felice, *Mussolini il Duce*, II, p. 531, n. 176; cf. Duggan, *Fascist Voices*, p. 228.
63. Behnken (ed.), *Deutschland-Berichte*, V (1938), p. 940.
64. Ibid., p. 946.
65. Bernhard, 'Konzertierte Gegnerbekämpfung', pp. 229–62; Andrea Hoffend, *Zwischen Kultur-Achse und Kulturkampf: die Beziehungen zwischen 'Drittem Reich' und faschistischem Italien in den Bereichen Medien, Kunst, Wissenschaft und Rassenfragen*, Frankfurt am Main, 1998; Martin, *The Nazi-Fascist New Order*.
66. For a contemporaneous evaluation, see R.W. Seton-Watson, *Munich and the Dictators: A Sequel to 'Britain and the Dictators'*, London, 1939, p. 105.
67. Robbins, *Munich 1938*, pp. 319–37.
68. Tampke, *German–Czech Relations*, p. 57.
69. For the three meetings of the Grand Council of Fascism, see *OO*, XXIX, pp. 167–77; for the 'Dichiarazione sulla razza', written by Mussolini, see De Felice, *Storia degli ebrei italiani*, pp. 567–75; Mack Smith, *Mussolini*, p. 225; on the racial laws, see Michaelis, *Mussolini and the Jews*, pp. 172, 187; for German reactions, see Bartikowski, *Der italienische Antisemitismus*, pp. 83–103.
70. Wildvang, *Der Feind von nebenan*, pp. 104–11.
71. Above all by De Felice, *Storia degli ebrei italiani*, p. 258.
72. For a survey, see Alan E. Steinweis, *Kristallnacht 1938*, Cambridge, MA, 2009; for the text of the passing of the racial laws, see *OO*, XXIX, p. 210.

73. Ciano, *Diario*, pp. 211–12 (12 & 13 November 1938); for an overstated interpretation of Pius XI's protests, see Fattorini, *Hitler, Mussolini, and the Vatican*, pp. 152–4; see also Kertzer, *The Pope and Mussolini*, pp. 316–31.
74. Wildvang, *Der Feind von nebenan*, pp. 117; the law is printed in De Felice, *Storia degli ebrei italiani*, pp. 576–80.
75. Bartikowski, *Der italienische Antisemitismus*, pp. 100–1.
76. Wildvang, *Der Feind von nebenan*, p. 144; see also Fabrizio De Donno, 'La Razza Ario Mediterranea: Ideas of Race and Citizenship in Colonial and Fascist Italy', *Interventions: International Journal of Postcolonial Studies*, 8 (2006), pp. 394–412.
77. *ADAP*, D, IV, doc. 400, notes by Schmidt on conversation between Ciano and Ribbentrop, 28 October 1938.
78. Ciano, *Diario*, p. 213 (16 November 1938); *ADAP*, D, IV, doc. 413, Mackensen to Foreign Ministry, 7 December 1938.
79. André François-Poncet, *Au Palais Farnèse: souvenirs d'une ambassade à Rome*, Paris, 1961, pp. 7–9; for his reactions to the speech, see ibid., 21–3 and *DDF*, 2e série, XIII, doc. 1, François-Poncet to Bonnet, 1 December 1938; Mack Smith, *Mussolini*, pp. 225–6; cf. De Felice, *Mussolini il Duce*, II, pp. 556–64; Ciano, *Diario*, pp. 218–19 (30 November 1938).
80. *ADAP*, D, IV, doc. 412, Mackensen to Foreign Ministry, 1 December 1938; Mack Smith, *Mussolini*, pp. 226–7.
81. *Manchester Guardian*, 11 January 1939; for anti-French articles, see e.g. Giovanni Selvi, 'Corsica, terra italiana', *Gerarchia*, XVII/1 (1939), pp. 2–8; Carlo Alberto Cremonini, 'La Francia contro l'Italia (1849–1939)', *Gerarchia*, XVII/3, (1939), pp. 181–5; Renato Famea, 'Discorso ai francofili: Italia e Francia dal 1797 ad oggi', *Gerarchia*, XVII/8 (1939), pp. 519–27.
82. See Tranfaglia (ed.), *La stampa del regime*, 251–2; ACS, Agenzia Stefani, b. 71, Riservata per il Sig. Presidente, 10 January and 11 January 1939; see *Il Popolo d'Italia*, 12 and 13 January 1939; for the dress code, see Quinto Navarra, *Memorie del cameriere di Mussolini*, Bracigliano, 2004, pp. 92–3; see also De Felice, *Mussolini il Duce*, II, pp. 574–7; Mack Smith, *Mussolini*, pp. 226–7.
83. *Il Popolo d'Italia*, 12 January 1939. For a photograph, see *Il Popolo d'Italia*, 13 January 1939. *DBFP*, 3rd series, III, doc. 502, Enclosure 1.
84. *DBFP*, 3rd series, III, doc. 500, Conversations between British and Italian Ministers, 11–14 January 1939; *ADAP*, D, IV, doc. 435, Mackensen to Foreign Ministry, 18 January 1939.
85. For the Italian minutes which highlight Mussolini's position, see *DDI*, 8s, XI, doc. 48, conversation Mussolini–Chamberlain, 11 January 1939; ibid., doc. 50, conversation Mussolini–Chamberlain, 12 January 1939.
86. *DBFP*, 3rd series, III, doc. 502, Enclosure 1; *OO*, XXIX, p. 225; Mack Smith, *Mussolini*, pp. 226–7.
87. Mack Smith, *Mussolini*, p. 227.
88. *DDF*, 2e série, XIII, doc. 367, François-Poncet to Bonnet, 14 January 1939; see also François-Poncet, *Au Palais Farnèse*, p. 45.
89. *DDI*, 8s, XI, 80, n. 8; for background, see Paul Stafford, 'The Chamberlain–Halifax Visit to Rome: A Reappraisal', *English Historical Review*, 98 (1983), pp. 61–100; Alan Cassels, 'Deux Empires face à face: la chimère d'un rapprochement Anglo-Italien (1936–1940)', *Guerres mondiales et conflits contemporains*, 161 (1991), pp. 67–96; Burgwyn, *Italian Foreign Policy*, p. 185; *ADAP*, D, IV, doc. 435, Mackensen to Foreign Ministry, 18 January 1939; for the Italian's handing over of the minutes, see ibid., p. 484, n. 1; Ciano, *Diario*, pp. 238–9 (12 January 1939).
90. For the speech, see Domarus, *Hitler*, II/1, pp. 1047–67; for context, see Hans Mommsen, 'Hitler's Reichstag Speech of 30 January 1939', *History and Memory*, 9 (1997), pp. 147–61; *DBFP*, 3rd series, IV, doc. 65, Sir G. Ogilvie Forbes to Viscount Halifax, 31 January 1939; *TBJG, Teil I*, VI, p. 245 (31 January 1939).
91. *OO*, XXIX, pp. 230, 469; *DDI*, 8s, XI, doc. 130, Attolico to Ciano, 31 January 1939 (the document was seen by Mussolini); ibid., doc. 131, Attolico to Ciano, 31 January 1939;

Ciano, *Diario*, p. 245 (31 January 1939; for Nazi propaganda, see *Italien-Beobachter*, 3 (1939), Heft 2, p. 4.

92. Ciano, *Diario*, pp. 264–6 (15 March 1939); *DDI*, 8s, XI, doc. 319, Ciano to Attolico, 17 March 1939; for the meeting between Hitler, Attolico and Ribbentrop, see *ADAP*, D, VI, doc. 52, Memorandum by Schmidt, 20 March 1939 (the note is in English); for Mussolini's fury and concern about public opinion, see *ADAP*, D, VI, doc. 87, Mackensen to Kordt, 24 March 1939; Claretta Petacci, *Verso il disastro: Mussolini in guerra – diari 1939–1940*, ed. Mimmo Franzinelli, Milan, 2011, p. 79; for the Prince of Hesse's meeting with Mussolini, see *ADAP*, D, IV, doc. 463, Mackensen to Foreign Ministry, 15 March 1939; for Ciano's reaction, see *DDI*, 8s, XI, doc. 319, Ciano-Attolico; for the Ciano–Mackensen conversations, see *DDI*, 8s, XI, doc. 325, conversation Ciano–Mackensen, 17 March 1939; see also *ADAP*, D, VI, doc. 15, Mackensen to Foreign Ministry, 17 March 1939; ibid., doc. 45, Mackensen to Foreign Ministry, 20 March 1939; ibid., doc. 55, Ribbentrop to Ciano, 20 March 1939; the report is printed in Colarizi, *L'Italia antifascista*, II, p. 461.
93. Ciano, *Diario*, pp. 272–3 (27 March 1939); Burgwyn, *Italian Foreign Policy*, p. 187.
94. Ciano, *Diario*, pp. 268–9 (19 March 1939); König, *Kooperation als Machtkampf*, pp. 238–40.
95. De Felice, *Mussolini il Duce*, II, pp. 589–90.
96. *OO*, XXIX, pp. 248–9; Bottai, *Diario*, pp. 142–4 (21 March 1939); for popular opinion, see Colarizi, *L'opinione degli italiani*, pp. 295–6.
97. For emotions in diplomacy, see Hall, *Emotional Diplomacy*.
98. *DDI*, 8s, XI, doc. 394, Hitler to Mussolini, 25 March 1939 (the German original has been lost); see also the retranslated version in *ADAP*, D, VI, doc. 100, Hitler to Mussolini, 25 March 1939; cf. De Felice, *Mussolini il Duce*, II, p. 601.
99. Cf. De Felice, *Mussolini il Duce*, II, pp. 594–5.
100. *OO*, XXIX, pp. 249–53.
101. For the king's speech, see Enrico Colombardo, *La monarchia fascista 1922–1940*, Bologna, 2010, pp. 93–4; see also Mack Smith, *Italy and its Monarchy*, pp. 278–9.
102. ACS, PNF, Situazione politica ed economica delle provincie, b. 19, Rome, 30 March 1939; translated in Aquarone, 'Public opinion in Italy', p. 214; on the unpopularity of the Axis in Italy, see also *ADAP*, D, VI, doc. 140, note by Weizsäcker, 31 March 1939.
103. *DDI*, 8s, XI, doc. 472, conversation between Pariani and Keitel, 5 April 1939; G. Bruce Strang, *On the Fiery March: Mussolini Prepares for War*, Westport, CT, 2003, pp. 247–8; Alessandro Massignani, 'Die italienischen Streitkräfte und der Krieg der "Achse"', in Lutz Klinkhammer, Amedeo Osti Guerrazzi and Thomas Schlemmer (eds), *Die 'Achse' im Krieg: Politik, Ideologie und Kriegführung 1939–1945*, Paderborn, 2010, pp. 122–46, here p. 130.
104. *DDF*, 2e série, XV, doc. 362, François-Poncet to Bonnet, 12 April 1939; for Italy and Albania, see Alessandro Roselli, *Italy and Albania: Financial Relations in the Fascist Period*, London, 2006, pp. 97–106.
105. François-Poncet, *The Fateful Years*, pp. 248–9; for context, see Bosworth, *Mussolini's Italy*, pp. 404–5.
106. *TBJG, Teil I*, VI, p. 313 (11 April 1939).
107. Mack Smith, *Mussolini*, p. 230–1; Burgwyn, *Italian Foreign Policy*, pp. 188–91.
108. *ADAP*, D, VI, doc. 205, unsigned memorandum, 15 April 1939; ibid., doc. 211, unsigned memorandum, 18 April 1939; on details of Göring's visit, see Schieder, *Mythos Mussolini*, pp. 186–7, 372; on Roosevelt's appeal, see Günther Moltmann, 'Franklin D. Roosevelts Friedensappell vom 14. April 1939: Ein fehlgeschlagener Versuch zur Friedensicherung', *Jahrbuch für Amerikastudien*, 9 (1964), pp. 91–109.
109. *ADAP*, D, VI, doc. 199, Heydrich to Ribbentrop, 14 April 1939; Domarus, *Hitler*, II/1, p. 1146.
110. Cf. Woller, *Mussolini*, p. 176.
111. Domarus, *Hitler*, II/1, p. 1165; *DDI*, 8s, XI, doc. 610, Attolico to Ciano, 28 April 1939; ibid., doc. 613, Attolico to Ciano, 29 April 1939.

112. *DDI*, 8s, XI, doc. 641, Mussolini to Ciano, 4 May 1939.
113. See for example, *ADAP*, D, VI, doc. 318, Mackensen to Foreign Ministry, 3 May 1939.
114. *DDI*, 8s, XI, doc. 653, Mellini to Ciano, 6 May 1939; ibid., doc. 660, Magistrati to Ciano, 6 May 1939; Burgwyn, *Italian Foreign Policy*, pp. 191–2.
115. Ferdinand Siebert, *Italiens Weg in den Zweiten Weltkrieg*, Frankfurt am Main, 1962, pp. 163–6; Mario Toscano, *The Origins of the Pact of Steel*, Baltimore, 1967.
116. *DDI*, 8s, XI, doc. 666, conversation between Ciano and Ribbentrop, 6–7 May 1939.
117. Melograni, *Rapporti segreti*, pp. 32–4; see also Aquarone, 'Public Opinion in Italy', pp. 214–15; for the anti-coffee-drinking campaign, see ACS, Agenzia Stefani, b. 71, 'Riservata per il Sig. Presidente', 13 May 1939.
118. Melograni, *Rapporti segreti*, p. 32; *DDI*, 8s, XI, doc. 663, nota n. 30 dell'Informazione Diplomatica, 6 May 1939; see also the press instructions in Tranfaglia (ed.), *La stampa del regime*, p. 304.
119. Mack Smith, *Mussolini*, p. 231; Dollmann, *The Interpreter*, p. 155; Ciano, *Diario*, pp. 294–5 (6 & 7 May 1939); for Ciano's minutes, see *DDI*, 8s, XI, doc. 666, conversations between Ciano and Ribbentrop, 6–7 May 1939; for the German minutes, see *ADAP*, D, VI, doc. 341, unsigned memorandum, 18 May 1939; for context, see Toscano, *The Origins of the Pact of Steel*, pp. 307–34.
120. *OO*, XXIX, p. 270; for context, see Hoffend, *Zwischen Kultur-Achse und Kulturkampf*, pp. 221–2, 325–55.
121. Colarizi, *L'opinione degli italiani*, pp. 298–9; see also Paul Corner, *The Fascist Party*, pp. 240–4; for the memory of Mussolini's visit to Turin, see Luisa Passerini, *Fascism in Popular Memory: The Cultural Experience of the Turin Working Class*, Cambridge, 1987, pp. 189–95.
122. Ciano, *Diario*, p. 297 (13 May 1939).
123. *Il patto d'acciaio (Italia e Germania)*, ed. Ministero della cultura popolare, Rome, 1939, pp. 65–7.
124. *Italien-Beobachter*, 3 (1939), Heft 6; *Il Popolo d'Italia*, 23 May 1939; *TBJG, Teil I*, VI, pp. 356–7 (23 May 1939).
125. Weinberg, *The Foreign Policy of Hitler's Germany*, II, pp. 567–8; Knox, 'Fascism: Ideology, Foreign Policy, and War', p. 131.
126. Mack Smith, *Mussolini*, p. 232.
127. *ADAP*, D, VI, pp. 367–72 (unnumbered document).
128. For Cavallero's memorandum, see *DDI*, 8s, XII, doc. 59, Mussolini to Hitler, 30 May 1939; *ADAP*, D, VI, doc. 459, Ciano to Ribbentrop, 31 May 1939; see also Mario Toscano, *The Origins of the Pact of Steel* (first published in Italian in 1948), pp. 376–88; Focardi, *Il cattivo tedesco*, pp. 83–4; for the lack of preparation, see Knox, *Common Destiny*, pp. 148–85.
129. John Gooch, 'Mussolini's Strategy, 1939–1943', in John Ferris and Evan Mawdsley (eds), *The Cambridge History of the Second World War*, Cambridge, 2015, I, pp. 132–58, here p. 135; Mack Smith, *Mussolini*, pp. 233–4; *DDI*, 8s, XII, doc. 662, Mussolini to Magistrati, 24 July 1939.
130. ACS, SpD, CR, b. 71, Hitler to Mussolini, 29 July 1939.
131. Ciano, *Diario*, p. 327 (13 August 1939).
132. *DDI*, 8s, XIII, doc. 1, minutes of the conversation between Ciano and Ribbentrop, 12 August 1939; *ADAP*, D, VII, doc. 43, note by Schmidt, 12 August 1939; Mack Smith, *Mussolini*, p. 234; Ciano, *Diario*, pp. 325–9 (6–15 August 1939); cf. Focardi, *Il cattivo edesco*, pp. 83–4; Hof, 'Die Tagebücher von Galeazzo Ciano', pp. 507–28.
133. *TBJG, Teil I*, VII, p. 85 (31 August 1939).
134. De Felice, *Mussolini il Duce*, II, pp. 664–5; for context, see Focardi, *Il cattivo tedesco*, p. 87.
135. *ADAP*, D, VII, doc. 266, Hitler to Mussolini, 25 August 1939; see also *DDI*, 8s, XIII, doc. 245
136. Mario Toscano, *L'Italia e gli accordi edesco-sovietici dell'agosto 1939*, Florence, 1955.

137. *ADAP*, D, VII, doc. 271, Mussolini to Hitler, 25 August 1939; see also *DDI*, 8s, XIII, doc. 250.
138. *ADAP*, D, VII, doc. 277, Hitler to Mussolini, 25 August 1939; see also *DDI*, 8s, XIII, doc. 262.
139. *ADAP*, D, VII, doc. 301, Mussolini to Hitler, 26 August 1939; see also *DDI*, 8s, XIII, doc. 293.
140. *ADAP*, D, VII, doc. 307, Hitler to Mussolini, 26 August 1939; see also *DDI*, 8s, XIII, doc. 298.
141. The correspondence between the two leaders was preserved in a special file by the cabinet of the Italian Foreign Ministry and found its way to the Italian embassy in Lisbon, where it was transferred before the 1943 armistice to the Allies. See PRO, GFM, 36/605, fol. 13–35; for context, see Howard McGaw Smyth, *Secrets of the Fascist Era: How Uncle Sam Obtained Some of the Top-Level Documents of Mussolini's Period*, Carbondale, IL, 1975, pp. 1–19; for Hitler's insistence on secrecy, see *DDI*, 8s, XIII, doc. 331, Attolico to Ciano, 27 August 1939.
142. *ADAP*, D, VII, doc. 341, Hitler to Mussolini, 27 August 1939; see also *DDI*, 8s, XIII, doc. 329; Ciano, *Diario*, pp. 338–9 (31 August 1939), 340–1 (1–3 September 1939)
143. Helmut Heiber (ed.), *Hitlers Lagebesprechungen: die Protokollfragmente seiner militärischen Konferenzen 1942–1945*, Stuttgart, 1962, p. 227.
144. *ADAP*, D, VII, doc. 417, Mussolini to Hitler, 29 August 1939; see also *DDI*, 8s, XIII, doc. 414.
145. *ADAP*, D, VII, doc. 500, Hitler to Mussolini, 1 September 1939. For the reading out of Hitler's letter see ibid., p. 406; see also *DDI*, 8s, XIII, doc. 530.
146. *DDI*, 8s, XIII, doc. 542, Hitler to Mussolini, 1 September 1939; *ADAP*, D, VII, doc. 504; Jürgen Förster, 'Die Wehrmacht und die Probleme der Koalitionskriegsführung', in Klinkhammer, Osti Guerrazzi and Schlemmer (eds), *Die 'Achse' im Krieg*, pp. 108–21, here p. 111.
147. *ADAP*, D, VII, doc. 559, circular by Ribbentrop, 2 September 1939.
148. *DDI*, 8s, XIII, doc. 639, Hitler to Mussolini, 3 September 1939; *ADAP*, D, VII, doc. 565.
149. Mack Smith, *Mussolini*, pp. 235–7.
150. ACS, Min Int, PS, Div Pol Pol., p. 220, Rome, 30 August 1939.
151. See, e.g., Gen. Ambrogio Bollati, 'Le Forze Armate dell'Italia fascista', *Gerarchia*, XVII/10 (1939), pp. 661–72.
152. For the lack of an Axis strategy, see Massignani, 'Die italienischen Streitkräfte und der Krieg der "Achse"', pp. 122–46.

6 Point of No Return, 1939–41

1. Ciano, *Diario*, p. 357 (7 October 1939).
2. Knox, *Hitler's Italian Allies*, p. 26.
3. Ciano, *Diario*, p. 342 (4 September 1939); Petacci, *Verso il disastro*, pp. 191–2 (13 September 1939); for Mussolini's ambivalence, see Gooch, 'Mussolini's Strategy, 1939–1943', p. 136.
4. For the speech, see Domarus, *Hitler*, II/1, pp. 1377–93; Wiskemann, *The Rome–Berlin Axis*, pp. 178–9.
5. Printed in Claudio Matteini (ed.), *Ordini alla stampa*, Rome, 1945, pp. 68, 77; Gooch, 'Mussolini's Strategy', p. 136.
6. *ADAP*, D, VIII, doc. 493, n. 1; *DDI*, 9s, II, doc. 240, Luppis to Ciano, 16 November 1939; see also Wiskemann, *The Rome–Berlin Axis*, p. 181.
7. Ciano, *Diario*, p. 351 (24 September 1939); *ADAP*, D, VIII, doc. 23, Aufzeichnung des Staatssekretärs, 7 September 1939; *TBJG, Teil I*, VII, p. 78 (26 August 1939).
8. *OO*, XXIX, pp. 336–7.
9. For the speech, see Ciano, *Diario*, pp. 701–24; Gerhard Schreiber, 'Die politische und militärische Entwicklung im Mittelmeerraum 1939/40', in *DRZW*, III, pp. 4–271, here p. 16; *TBJG, Teil I*, VII, p. 234 (17 December 1939).

10. Brian R. Sullivan, '"Where one man, and only one man, led": Italy's Path from Neutrality to Non-belligerency to War, 1937–1940', in Neville Wylie (ed.), *European Neutrals and Non-belligerents during the Second World War*, Cambridge, 2002, pp. 119–49.
11. *ADAP*, D, VIII, doc. 505, 'Bemerkungen zu den deutsch-italienischen Beziehungen aus Anlaß der Jahreswende 1939/1940', 3 January 1940; for context, see Schreiber, 'Die politische und militärische Entwicklung', p. 12; for Italian popular opinion, see Aquarone, 'Public Opinion in Italy', p. 219.
12. ACS, PNF, Situazione economica politica delle provincie, b. 27, sf. Udine, PNF, 7 February 1940; on context, see Corner, *The Fascist Party*, pp. 253–64; Colarizi, *L'opinione degli italiani sotto il regime*, pp. 302–8; for context, see Harry Cliadakis, 'Neutrality and War in Italian Policy 1939–40', *JCH*, 9 (1974), pp. 171–90; see also Gooch, *Mussolini and his Generals*, pp. 450–518.
13. PAAA, Botschaft Rom (Quirinal), Geheim, Bd. 73, German consulate Palermo to German ambassador, 27 February 1940.
14. Mack Smith, *Mussolini*, pp. 238–9; Ciano, *Diario*, p. 357 (7 October 1939).
15. MacGregor Knox, 'The Sources of Italy's Defeat in 1940: Bluff or Institutionalized Incompetence?', in Carole Fink, Isabel V. Hull and MacGregor Knox (eds), *German Nationalism and the European Response, 1890–1945*, Norman, OK, 1985, pp. 247–66, here pp. 248–9.
16. See *DDI*, 9s, III, doc. 1, Mussolini to Hitler, 1 January 1940 (Hitler's telegram of 31 December 1939 is printed ibid. on p. 1, n. 1).
17. PRO, GFM 36/605, fol. 44–55, Mussolini–Hitler, 5 January 1940 (see also *DDI*, 9s, III, doc. 33); for the German version, see *ADAP*, D, VIII, doc. 504 (the latter is dated 3 January; for the dating, see ibid., p. 474, n. 2).
18. Ciano, *Diario*, pp. 371–3 (4 and 9 December 1939); Bosworth, *Mussolini*, pp. 359–60; Siebert, *Italiens Weg in den Zweiten Weltkrieg*, pp. 372–6.
19. *ADAP*, D, VIII, doc. 553, Weizsäcker to Mackensen, 18 January 1940; for Italy's dependency on German resources, see Schreiber, 'Die politische und militärische Entwicklung', pp. 23–33.
20. Schreiber, 'Die politische und militärische Entwicklung', pp. 17–18; cf. Siebert, *Italiens Weg in den Zweiten Weltkrieg*, pp. 394–7; for a critical interpretation, see Knox, *Mussolini*, pp. 68–9.
21. *ADAP*, D, VIII, doc. 599, Mackensen to Foreign Ministry, 8 February 1940; for the prince's mission, see ibid., p. 591, n. 2; for context, see Wiskemann, *The Rome–Berlin Axis*, pp. 192–3.
22. *DDI*, 9s, III, doc. 395, Ciano's notes, 26 February 1940; for Welles' mission, see Stanley E. Hilton, 'The Welles Mission to Europe, February–March 1940: Illusion or Realism?', *Journal of American History*, 57 (1971), pp. 93–120; for the documents, see *FRUS*, 1940, II, pp. 685–716; see also De Felice, *Mussolini il Duce*, II, pp. 754–6; for Mussolini's views, see Ciano, *Diario*, pp. 399–400 (26 & 28 February 1940); for Welles' conversation with Hitler, see *ADAP*, D, VIII, doc. 649, note by Schmidt, 2 March 1940.
23. *ADAP*, D, VIII, doc. 663, Hitler to Mussolini, 8 March 1940; for the Italian version, see *DDI*, 9s, III, doc. 492; for Ribbentrop's delivering the letter, see *ADAP*, D, VIII, doc. 665, note by Schmidt, 10 March 1940; for Ribbentrop's telegram to Hitler, see ibid., doc. 667, 11 March 1940; for the second meeting between the Duce and Ribbentrop, see ibid., doc. 669, note by Schmidt, 11 March 1940; for context, see Wiskemann, *The Rome–Berlin Axis*, pp. 196–9; De Felice, *Mussolini il Duce*, II, pp. 761–5.
24. Burgwyn, *Italian Foreign Policy*, pp. 210–11.
25. *ADAP*, D, VIII, doc. 670, Ribbentrop to Hitler, 12 March 1940.
26. König, *Kooperation als Machtkampf*, pp. 240–1.
27. For the Brenner frontier, see Hans Heiss, 'Die Brennergrenze 1918/19', *Österreich in Geschichte und Literatur mit Geographie*, 52 (2008), pp. 318–35.
28. König, *Kooperation als Machtkampf*, pp. 227–38; Petersen, 'Deutschland, Italien und Südtirol', pp. 145–8; Federico Scarano, *Tra Mussolini e Hitler: le opzioni dei sudtirolesi nella politica estera fascistca*, Milan, 2012, pp. 164–218.

29. Ciano, *Diario*, pp. 405 (12 March 1940), 407 (16 March 1940).
30. Petacci, *Verso il disastro*, p. 311 (17 March 1940).
31. For a British report, see *The Times*, 18 March 1940.
32. See the telegrams in ACS, PCM 1941–1943, 20.2/604, 'Viaggio del Duce al Brennero per incontrarsi col Fuhrer', 17 and 18 March 1940.
33. Schmidt, *Statist auf diplomatischer Bühne*, p. 479.
34. Ciano, *Diario*, p. 408 (18 March 1940).
35. Hill (ed.), *Die Weizsäcker Papiere 1933–1950*, p. 194 (17 March 1940).
36. For the communiqué, see BAB, R 901/58822, Bl. 3–4, report by Deutsches Nachrichtenbüro, 18 March 1940; see also *Il Popolo d'Italia*, 19 March 1940; for Ciano's warning the Belgians, see Ciano, *Diario*, pp. 377 (26 December 1939), 383 (2 January 1940); *ADAP*, D, VIII, doc. 553, Weizsäcker to Mackensen, 18 January 1940; Burgwyn, *Italian Foreign Policy*, p. 209.
37. *TBJG, Teil I*, VII, p. 355–6 (19 March 1940).
38. For the minutes of the meeting, see *ADAP*, D, IX, doc. 1, note by Schmidt, 17 March 1940 (the document is dated incorrectly); *TBJG, Teil I*, VII, pp. 355–6 (19 March 1940).
39. *Berliner Morgenpost*, 19 March 1940, copy in BAB, R 901/58822, Bl. 11.
40. *Il Popolo d'Italia*, 19 March 1940; Nicola Tranfaglia (ed.), *Ministri e giornalisti: la guerra e il Minculpop (1939–43)*, Turin, 2005, pp. 30–2.
41. *Il Popolo d'Italia*, 19 March 1940.
42. Ciano, *Diario*, pp. 408–9 (19 March 1940).
43. For the minutes of the meeting, see *ADAP*, D, IX, doc. 1, note by Schmidt, 17 March 1940 (the document is dated incorrectly); for the Italian translation of the minutes, see ASMAE, Gabinetto, UC–15, fasc. 13, 'Resoconto Sommario', 18 March 1940; also printed in *DDI*, 9s, III, doc. 578. Cf. Burgwyn, *Italian Foreign Policy*, pp. 211–12; De Felice, *Mussolini il Duce*, II, pp. 767–72.
44. *ADAP*, D, IX, doc. 9, 'Runderlaß des Reichsaußenministers', 21 March 1940; Leonardo Simoni (Michele Lanza), *Berlin ambassade d'Italie: journal d'un diplomate italien*, Paris, 1947, p. 103 (18 March 1940).
45. Luca Pietromarchi, *I diari e le agende di Luca Pietromarchi (1938–1940): politica estera del fascismo e vita quotidiana di un diplomatico romano del '900*, ed. Ruth Nattermann, Rome, 2009, p. 413 (20 March 1940).
46. Schmidt, *Statist auf diplomatischer Bühne*, p. 480; for the Italian minutes, see ASMAE, Gabinetto, UC–15, fasc. 13, 'Resoconto Sommario', 18 March 1940; see also *DDI*, 9s, III, doc. 578, Colloquio Mussolini–Hitler verbale, 18 March 1940.
47. *Il Popolo d'Italia*, 20 March 1940; Knox, *Mussolini Unleashed*, pp. 87–91.
48. Ciano, *Diario*, pp. 408–9 (19 March 1940).
49. Bosworth, *Mussolini*, pp. 366–7; for the memorandum, see *DDI*, 9s, III, doc. 669, Mussolini to the King, 31 March 1940; see also De Felice, *Mussolini il Duce*, II, pp. 772–5; for the 'parallel war', see Gooch, 'Mussolini's Strategy', p. 137.
50. *ADAP*, D, IX, doc. 68, Hitler to Mussolini, 9 April 1940; *DDI*, 9s, IV, doc. 16. (The Italian version is dated 9 April 1940, and no record of the German original has been preserved.)
51. Ciano, *Diario*, pp. 417–18 (10 April 1940); *Il Popolo d'Italia*, 10 April 1940.
52. For examples of Italian Axis propaganda, see Roberto Pavese, 'Fatalità dell'Asse', *Gerarchia*, XVIII/5 (1940), pp. 258–9; Giancarlo Moro, 'Come la Germania si è preparata a sostenere la guerra economica', ibid., pp. 260–5.
53. *The Times*, 15 April 1940.
54. Bottai, *Diario 1935–1944*, pp. 183 (2 April 1940), 187 (17 April 1940).
55. Bosworth, *Mussolini*, pp. 368–9; Ciano, *Diario*, pp. 414–18 (2–11 April 1940).
56. See the reports printed in Melograni, *Rapporti segreti della polizia fascista*, pp. 52–4.
57. See the April 1940 reports ibid., pp. 55–8; for 'deep belief', see R.J.B. Bosworth, 'War, Totalitarianism and Deep Belief in Fascist Italy, 1935–43', *European History Quarterly*, 34 (2004), pp. 475–505.
58. See the police reports in Melograni, *Rapporti segreti*, pp. 58–9; for context, see Colarizi, *L'opinione degli italiani*, pp. 324, 329, 333.

59. Petacci, *Verso il disastro*, p. 313 (11 April 1940); for the mounting pressure on the Duce, see Rochat, *Le guerre italiane*, pp. 239–41.
60. Corner, *The Fascist Party*, pp. 253–64; for Fascist propaganda on the anniversary, see *Il Popolo d'Italia*, 23 March 1940.
61. Corner, *The Fascist Party*, pp. 264–5.
62. Wiskemann, *The Rome–Berlin Axis*, p. 211.
63. Knox, *Hitler's Italian Allies*, pp. 53–5.
64. ADAP, D, IX, doc. 138, Hitler to Mussolini, 18 April 1940; DDI, 9s, IV, doc. 130; Ciano, *Diario*, p. 419 (20 April 1940); cf. Hall, *Emotional Diplomacy*.
65. Mark Harrison, 'The Economics of World War II: An Overview', in Mark Harrison (ed.), *The Economics of World War II: Six Great Powers in International Comparison*, Cambridge, 1998, pp. 1–42, here pp. 10, 21; see also Vera Zamagni, 'Italy: How to Lose the War and Win the Peace', ibid., pp. 177–223; Bosworth, *Mussolini*, pp. 371–2.
66. *ADAP*, D, IX, doc. 92, Mussolini to Hitler, 11 April 1940; *DDI*, 9s, IV, doc. 37; *Osservatore Romano*, 10 April 1940; see also Melograni, *Rapporti segreti*, p. 59.
67. For context, see Gianluca Falanga, *Mussolinis Vorposten in Hitlers Reich: Italiens Politik in Berlin 1933–1945*, Berlin, 2008, pp. 143–51, p. 145 for the quotation.
68. *DDI*, 9s, IV, doc. 218; Hitler to Mussolini, 26 April 1940; *ADAP*, D, IX, doc. 168, Hitler to Mussolini, 26 April 1940; ibid., doc. 170, Mackensen to Auswärtiges Amt, 26 April 1940; for Mussolini's reply, see *ADAP*, D, IX, doc. 190, Mussolini to Hitler, 2 May 1940; *DDI*, 9s, IV, doc. 276.
69. *ADAP*, D, IX, doc. 276, Mussolini to Hitler, 19 May 1940 (for the Italian version, see *DDI*, 9s, IV, doc. 493).
70. For context, see Schreiber, 'Die politische und militärische Entwicklung', p. 107; for popular opinion, see Melograni, *Rapporti segreti*, p. 83; Corner, *The Fascist Party*, p. 265; for the quotation, see Colarizi, *L'opinione degli italiani*, p. 337.
71. Cf. Colarizi, *L'opinione degli italiani*, p. 339.
72. ACS, SpD, CO, b. 2821 (sentimenti), sf. 33–2, Arturo S. to Mussolini, 24 May 1940; for context, see Duggan, 'The Internalisation of the Cult of the Duce', pp. 129–43; see also Duggan, *Fascist Voices*, pp. 342–5.
73. ACS, SpD, CO, b. 2821 (sentimenti), sf. 33–5, Rosa S. to Mussolini, 16 May 1940; ibid., anonymous letter to Mussolini, undated; see also the note on the cover of sf. 33–5.
74. ACS, SpD, CO, b. 2825, sf. 34–15.
75. ACS, SpD, CO, b. 2825 (sentimenti), undated letter to Mussolini.
76. PRO, GFM 36/605, fol. 155–7, Mussolini to Hitler, 30 May 1940; for the German version, see *ADAP*, D, IX, doc. 356.
77. *ADAP*, D, IX, doc. 357, Hitler to Mussolini, 31 May 1940; *DDI*, 9s, IV, doc. 680; for context, see König, *Kooperation als Machtkampf*, p. 24; Franz Halder, *Kriegstagebuch. Tägliche Aufzeichnungen des Chefs des Generalstabes des Heeres 1939–1942*, ed. Hans-Adolf Jacobsen, Stuttgart, 1962, I, p. 308 (21 May 1940); Knox, *Mussolini Unleashed*, pp. 117–19.
78. Bosworth, *Mussolini*, p. 369.
79. Ciano, *Diario*, p. 442 (10 June 1940).
80. *OO*, XXIX, pp. 403–5.
81. Maria Carazzolo, *Più forte della paura: diario di guerra e dopoguerra (1938–1947)*, Caselle di Sommacampagna, 2007, p. 48 (11 June 1940).
82. *ADAP*, D, IX, doc. 410, Hitler to Mussolini, 10 June 1940; *DDI*, 9s, IV, doc. 844; *Il Popolo d'Italia*, 11 June 1940.
83. Kotze (ed.), *Heeresadjutant bei Hitler 1938*–1943, pp. 81–2 (10 June 1940).
84. Kershaw, *The 'Hitler Myth'*, pp. 151–68.
85. Boberach (ed.), *Meldungen aus dem Reich*, IV, p. 1236.
86. König, *Kooperation als Machtkampf*, p. 25; Knox, *Mussolini Unleashed*, pp. 125–6; Rochat, *Le guerre italiane*, pp. 249–51; for numbers, see Gooch, 'Mussolini's Strategy', p. 137; for a recent study, see Emanuele Sica, *Mussolini's Army in the French Riviera: Italy's Occupation of France*, Urbana, IL, 2016.
87. *ADAP*, D, IX, doc. 373, Mussolini to Hitler, 2 June 1940; *DDI*, 9s, IV, doc. 706; Mack Smith, *Mussolini's Roman Empire*, p. 216.

88. *ADAP*, D, IX, doc. 406, Hitler to Mussolini, 9 June 1940; *DDI*, 9s, IV, doc. 828.
89. Mack Smith, *Mussolini's Roman Empire*, p. 217.
90. 'To the People of Italy', 23 December 1940, in Robert Rhodes James (ed.), *Winston S. Churchill: His Complete Speeches 1897–1963*, New York, 1974, VI, pp. 6322–5.
91. Knox, *Mussolini Unleashed*, p. 123.
92. See e.g. *Il Popolo d'Italia*, 12 May 1940 (see also the coverage in the following issues in May and early June 1940, esp. 'L'esercito francese in totta su tutto il fronte da Aumale a Nyon', 9 June 1940); Bosworth, *Mussolini*, p. 370.
93. Focardi, *Il cattivo tedesco*, pp. 87–95; for a simplistic interpretation subscribing to Churchill's view, see De Felice, *Mussolini il Duce*, II, pp. 843–4; cf. Rochat, *Le guerre italiane*, pp. 239–41.
94. König, *Kooperation als Machtkampf*, pp. 23–7; Massignani, 'Die italienischen Streitkräfte und der Krieg der "Achse"', pp. 122–46, here p. 132.
95. For the lack of military coordination, see Jürgen Förster, 'Die Wehrmacht und die Probleme der Koalitionskriegsführung', in Klinkhammer, Osti Guerrazzi and Schlemmer (eds), *Die 'Achse' im Krieg*, pp. 108–21 (pp. 118–19 for quotation); on the Italians, see Massignani, 'Die italienischen Streitkräfte'.
96. Ciano, *Diario*, p. 443 (17 June 1940).
97. Schmidt, *Statist auf diplomatischer Bühne*, p. 484; for the dress, see *Il Popolo d'Italia*, 19 June 1940.
98. *Il Popolo d'Italia*, 19 June 1940.
99. Ciano, *Diario*, p. 444 (18 & 19 June 1940).
100. *ADAP*, D, IX, doc. 479, 'Aufzeichnung ohne Unterschrift', undated; for context, see Davide Rodogno, 'Die faschistische Neue Ordnung und die politisch-ökonomische Umgestaltung des Mittelmeerraums 1940 bis 1943', in Klinkhammer, Osti Guerrazzi and Schlemmer (eds), *Die 'Achse' im Krieg*, pp. 211–30.
101. *Il Popolo d'Italia*, 19 June 1940.
102. *VB*, 19 June 1940.
103. *ADAP*, D, X, doc. 166, Hitler to Mussolini, 13 July 1940; ibid., doc. 26, Mussolini to Hitler, 26 June 1940 (Italian versions in *DDI*, 9s, V, docs 109, 242); Richard Overy, *The Bombing War: Europe 1939–1945*, London, 2014, p. 493.
104. Ciano, *Diario*, p. 452 (16 July 1940).
105. *OO*, XXX, pp. 3–5.
106. *ADAP*, D, X, doc. 185, Mussolini to Hitler, 17 July 1940; *DDI*, 9s, V, doc. 264; *OO*, XXX, p. 9; for military context, see Gooch, 'Mussolini's Strategy', p. 138.
107. For the fall of France, see Julian Jackson, *The Fall of France: The Nazi Invasion of 1940*, Oxford, 2003, p. 181; Kershaw, *The 'Hitler Myth'*, pp. 151–68.
108. Ciano, *Diario*, p. 445 (21 June 1940).
109. König, *Kooperation als Machtkampf*, pp. 26–7.
110. BA-MA, RW 4/326, Bl. 44–5, Abschrift, 13 July 1940.
111. *DDI*, 9s, V, doc. 9, Mussolini to Hitler, 12 June 1940; *ADAP*, D, IX, doc. 421, 'Aufzeichnung des Staatssekretärs', 13 June 1940; for the impact of bombing on society, see Claudia Baldoli and Marco Fincardi, 'Italian Society under Anglo-American Bombs: Propaganda, Experience, and Legend, 1940–1945', *Historical Journal*, 52 (2009), pp. 1017–38.
112. Overy, *The Bombing War*, pp. 511–12.
113. Domarus, *Hitler*, II/1, pp. 1540–59, here p. 1553; for Mussolini's reaction, see Ciano, *Diario*, p. 453 (22 July 1940); for the press directive, see Matteini (ed.), *Ordini alla stampa*, p. 113; for context, see Kershaw, *Hitler, 1936–1945*, pp. 303–4.
114. ACS, PNF, Situazione politica per province, b. 6, sf. 2, Milan, 6 August 1940.
115. König, *Kooperation als Machtkampf*, p. 242.
116. Woller, *Mussolini*, pp. 207–8.
117. For the pact, see Jost Dülffer, 'The Tripartite Pact of 27 September 1940: Fascist Alliance or Propaganda Trick?', *Australian Journal of Politics and History*, 32 (1986), pp. 228–37; Jeremy A. Yellen, 'Into the Tiger's Den: Japan and the Tripartite Act, 1940', *JCH*, 51

(2016), pp. 555–76; for context, see Robert Gerwarth, 'The Axis: Germany, Japan and Italy on the Road to War', in R.J.B. Bosworth and Joseph A. Maiolo (eds), *The Cambridge History of the Second World War*, Cambridge, 2015, pp. 21–42.

118. König, *Kooperation als Machtkampf*, pp. 30–1.
119. Stanley G. Payne, *Franco and Hitler: Spain, Germany, and World War II*, New Haven, 2008, pp. 61–86.
120. *TBJG, Teil I*, VIII, pp. 359–62 (4 & 5 October 1940).
121. Ciano, *Diario*, p. 469 (4 October 1940); *New York Herald Tribune*, 5 October 1940, copy in BAB, R 901/59104, Bl. 10; *ADAP*, D, XI/1, doc. 149, note by Schmidt, 4 October 1940; for Ciano's minutes, see *DDI*, 9s, V, doc. 677, 4 October 1940.
122. *Il Popolo d'Italia*, 6 October 1940; for the press directive, see Matteini (ed.), *Ordini alla stampa*, p. 126; for a photograph, see the cover of *Italien-Beobachter*, 4 (1940), Heft 8; for the different audiences, cf. Watt, 'The Rome–Berlin Axis.'
123. *ADAP*, D, XI/1, doc. 84, Oberkommando der Wehrmacht to Foreign Ministry, 21 September 1940; for context, see Rodogno, *Fascism's European Empire*, pp. 17–36.
124. Cf. Renzo De Felice, *Mussolini l'alleato*, Turin, 1990, I/1, pp. 304–8.
125. *ADAP*, D, XI/1, doc. 73, note by Schmidt, 20 September 1940; see also ibid., doc. 209, Weizsäcker to Mackensen, 21 October 1940; cf. Kershaw, *Hitler, 1936–1945*, p. 328.
126. *ADAP*, D, XI/1, doc. 192, Mackensen to Weizsäcker, 18 October 1940; Ciano, *Diario*, p. 470 (12 October 1940).
127. *ADAP*, D, IX, doc. 46, 'Führerweisung', 4 April 1940; Gooch, 'Mussolini's Strategy', pp. 140–1; for the bribes, see Payne, *Franco and Hitler*, p. 70.
128. De Felice, *Mussolini l'alleato*, I/1, p. 190; cf. Knox, *Mussolini Unleashed*, pp. 291–2.
129. *FRUS*, 1940, III, pp. 557–8, The Chargé in France to the Secretary of State, 4 November 1940.
130. For context, see Kershaw, *Hitler, 1936–1945*, pp. 328–31; for the Franco–Hitler meeting, see Paul Preston, 'Franco and Hitler: The Myth of Hendaye 1940', *Contemporary European History*, 1 (1992), pp. 1–16; see also his 'Spain: Betting on a Nazi Victory', in R.J.B. Bosworth and Joseph A. Maiolo (eds), *The Cambridge History of the Second World War*, Cambridge, 2015, pp. 324–48; for Hitler's remarks about Franco, see Malcolm Muggeridge (ed.), *Ciano's Diplomatic Papers*, London, 1948, p. 402; *ADAP*, D, XI/1, doc. 246, note by Schmidt, 28 October 1940.
131. Kershaw, *Hitler, 1936–1945*, p. 331; for Mussolini's letter, see *ADAP*, D, XI/1, doc. 199, Mussolini to Hitler, 19 October 1940 (for the Italian version, see *DDI*, 9s, V, doc. 753); for the scheduling of the visit, see *ADAP*, XI/1, doc. 228, Ribbentrop to German Embassy in Rome, 25 October 1940; cf. the reconstruction of Hitler's journey through southern Europe, see Martin van Creveld, '25 October 1940: A Historical Puzzle', *JCH*, 6 (1971), pp. 87–96; Halder, *Kriegstagebuch*, II, p. 154 (29 October 1940).
132. *VB*, 29 October 1940; see also Prof. M. Werner, 'Die Geburtsstunde des Imperiums: der Marsch auf Rom', *VB*, 28 October 1940.
133. Magda Ceccarelli De Grada, *Giornale del tempo di guerra, 12 giugno 1940–7 maggio 1945*, Bologna, 2011, p. 50 (28 October 1940).
134. *Rheinisch-Westfälische Zeitung*, 28 October 1940, copy in BAB, R 901/58869, Bl. 4.
135. *VB*, 29 October 1940; for the Florence meeting, see De Felice, *Mussolini l'alleato*, I/1, pp. 307–10; Knox, *Mussolini Unleashed*, pp. 226–30; Schmidt, *Statist auf diplomatischer Bühne*, p. 506; *New York Times*, 29 October 1940, copy in BAB, R 901/59108, Bl. 3.
136. For photographs, see Tuninetti (ed.), *Incontri di Popoli*, pp. 34–7, 50, 52.
137. *Il Regime Fascista*, 29 October 1940, copy in BAB, R 901/59108, Bl. 60; *Il Popolo d'Italia*, 29 October 1940.
138. Tranfaglia (ed.), *Ministri e giornalisti*, pp. 89–91.
139. *ADAP*, D, XI/1, doc. 246, note by Schmidt, 28 October 1940; Halder, *Kriegstagebuch*, II, p. 157 (1 November 1940); for the Italian minutes, edited by Ciano, see *DDI*, 9s, V, doc. 807, colloquio tra il capo del governo, Mussolini, ed il cancelliere del Reich, Hitler, 28 October 1940.

140. Percy E. Schramm (ed.), *Kriegstagebuch des Oberkommandos der Wehrmacht (Wehrmachtführungsstab)*, Frankfurt am Main, 1965, I, p. 130 (28 October 1940).
141. Halder, *Kriegstagebuch*, II, pp. 158–9 (1 November 1940); for the Italian campaign, see Gerhard Schreiber, 'Deutschland, Italien und Südosteuropa: von der politischen und wirtschaftlichen Hegemonie zur militärischen Intervention', in *DRZW*, III, pp. 278–414, esp. pp. 368–414; Rochat, *Le guerre italiane*, pp. 259–85.
142. *FRUS*, 1940, III, pp. 560–1, The Chargé in Germany to the Secretary of State, 14 November 1940.
143. Schramm (ed.), *Kriegstagebuch des Oberkommandos*, I, p.144 (1 November 1940); for Hitler's views on Italy at the time, see also *TBJG, Teil I*, VIII, p. 406 (5 November 1940); for context, see König, *Kooperation als Machtkampf*, pp. 35–6.
144. Boberach (ed.), *Meldungen aus dem Reich*, V, p. 1728.
145. *TBJG, Teil I*, VIII, p. 406 (5 November 1940).
146. Schreiber, 'Deutschland, Italien und Südosteuropa', p. 413.
147. Antonello Biagini and Fernando Frattolillo (eds), *Diario storico del comando supremo: raccolta di documenti della seconda guerra mondiale*, Rome, 1986–2002, II/2, doc. 67, 14 & 15 November 1940.
148. Walter Baum and Eberhard Weichold, *Der Krieg der 'Achsenmächte' im Mittelmeer-Raum: die 'Strategie' der Diktatoren*, Zurich, 1973, pp. 58–9, n. 22.
149. Ciano, *Diario*, p. 480 (20 November 1940); König, *Kooperation als Machtkampf*, pp. 37–9.
150. *ADAP*, XI/2, doc. 369, Hitler to Mussolini, 20 November 1940; *DDI*, 9s, VI, doc. 140; Ciano, *Diario*, pp. 480–1 (21 & 22 November 1940).
151. *ADAP*, XI/2, doc. 383, Mussolini to Hitler, 22 November 1940; *DDI*, 9s, VI, doc. 146; Gooch, 'Mussolini's Strategy', pp. 147–8.
152. For the speech, see *OO*, XXX, pp. 30–8.
153. Boberach (ed.), *Meldungen aus dem Reich*, VI, p. 1787.
154. Ibid., pp. 1799, 1834.
155. *DDI*, 9s, VI, doc. 244, Hitler to Mussolini, 5 December 1940.
156. König, *Kooperation als Machtkampf*, pp. 47–8.
157. *DDI*, 9s, VI. doc. 323, Alfieri to Ciano, 20 December 1940; *ADAP*, XI/2, doc. 538, note by Schmidt, 20 December 1940; ibid., doc. 541, Rome Embassy to Foreign Ministry, 20 December 1940; Gooch, 'Mussolini's Strategy', p. 148.
158. Bernd Stegemann, 'Die italienisch-deutsche Kriegführung im Mittelmeer und in Afrika', in *DRZW*, III, pp. 591–682, here p. 595; James J. Sadkovich, 'The Italo-Greek War in Context: Italian Priorities and Axis Diplomacy', *JCH*, 28 (1993), pp. 439–64.
159. Bosworth, *Mussolini*, p. 376.
160. Rochat, *Le guerre italiane*, pp. 302–4; König, *Kooperation als Machtkampf*, pp. 48–9.
161. *ADAP*, XI/2, doc. 583, note by Bismarck, 27 December 1940; *ADAP*, XI/2, doc. 597, Rintelen to OKW, 2 January 1941.
162. Schramm (ed.), *Kriegstagebuch des Oberkommandos*, I, p. 283 (28 January 1941).
163. De Felice, *Mussolini l'alleato*, I/1, pp. 371–8; König, *Kooperation als Machtkampf*, p. 55.
164. Andreas Hillgruber (ed.), *Staatsmänner und Diplomaten bei Hitler: vertrauliche Aufzeichnungen über Unterredungen mit Vertretern des Auslandes 1939–1941*, Frankfurt am Main, 1967, I, p. 435; Gooch, 'Mussolini's Strategy', p. 148.
165. *ADAP*, XI/2, doc. 477, note by Noack, 8 December 1940; *DDI*, 9s, VI, doc. 274, Alfieri to Ciano, 8 December 1940; Dino Alfieri, *Dictators Face to Face*, London, 1954, pp. 86–8.
166. *ADAP*, XI/ 2, doc. 586, Hitler to Mussolini, 31 December 1940 (Italian version in *DDI*, 9s, VI, doc. 385).
167. Alfieri, *Dictators Face to Face*, p. 89.
168. *ADAP*, XI/2, doc. 635, Mackensen to Foreign Ministry, 10 January 1941; Knox, *Mussolini Unleashed*, p. 279.
169. PAAA, Botschaft Rom (Quirinal), Geheim, Bd. 97, telegram by Ribbentrop, 15 January 1941; ibid., 'lista delle precedenze del seguito del Duce', undated.

170. *DDI*, 9s, VI, doc. 470, conversation between Ribbentrop and Ciano, 19 January 1941; Alfieri, *Dictators Face to Face*, pp. 89–98.
171. Alfieri, *Dictators Face to Face*, p. 93.
172. Ibid., pp. 89–98; for the minutes of the afternoon conversation on 19 January 1941, see *ADAP*, XI/2, doc. 672, note by Schmidt, 21 January 1941; *DDI*, 9s, VI, doc. 471; for the minutes of the meeting on 20 January, see *ADAP*, XI/2, doc. 679, note by Schmidt, 21 January 1941; *DDI*, 9s, VI, doc. 473; Ciano, *Diario*, pp. 500–1 (18–21 January 1941); for Mussolini and Franco, see Preston, 'Italy and Spain', p. 175.
173. Stegemann, 'Die italienisch-deutsche Kriegsführung', p. 4; Kershaw, *Hitler, 1936–1945*, pp. 347–8.
174. Gianluca André, 'La politica estera del governo fascista durante la seconda guerra mondiale', in Renzo De Felice (ed.), *L'Italia fra tedeschi e alleati: la politica estera fascista e la seconda guerra mondiale*, Bologna, 1973, pp. 115–26, here p. 126; cf. Knox, *Mussolini Unleashed*, pp. 231–84; Hill (ed.), *Die Weizsäcker-Papiere*, p. 234 (24 January 1941).
175. Tranfaglia (ed.), *La stampa del regime*, p. 308.
176. Boberach (ed.), *Meldungen aus dem Reich*, VI, p. 1924.
177. Ibid., p. 1938 (27 January 1941); *TBJG, Teil I*, IX, pp. 114–15 (29 January 1941).
178. Rochat, *Le guerre italiane*, p. 303.

7 Into the Abyss, 1941–3

1. Domarus, *Hitler*, II/2, p. 1661.
2. Boberach (ed.), *Meldungen aus dem Reich*, VI, p. 1965.
3. *OO*, XXX, pp. 49–59.
4. Boberach (ed.), *Meldungen aus dem Reich*, VI, p. 2045.
5. *ADAP*, D, XII/1, doc. 17, Hitler to Mussolini, 5 February 1941 (the letter is likely a retranslation from Italian into German; cf. ibid., p. 22, n. 1); for the Italian version, see *DDI*, 9s, VI, doc. 540; for Mussolini's comments to the king, see ibid., doc. 556, 9 February 1941.
6. Alfieri, *Dictators Face to Face*, pp. 103–4.
7. *OO*, XXX, p. 50; Gooch, 'Mussolini's Strategy, 1939–1943', pp. 148–9.
8. Printed in Walter Hubatsch (ed.), *Hitlers Weisungen für die Kriegsführung 1939–1945: Dokumente des Oberkommandos der Wehrmacht*, Frankfurt am Main, 1962, pp. 99–100 (February 1941); cf. König, *Kooperation als Machtkampf*, p. 60.
9. BA-MA, RW 4/326, Bl. 904, note by military attaché, 7 April 1941.
10. Stegemann, 'Die italienisch-deutsche Kriegführung im Mittelmeer und in Afrika', pp. 599–682; Richard J. Evans, *The Third Reich at War*, London, 2008, pp. 150–1; see also Patrick Bernhard, 'Behind the Battle Lines: Italian Atrocities and the Persecution of Arabs, Berbers, and Jews in North Africa during World War II', *Holocaust and Genocide Studies*, 26 (2012), pp. 425–46.
11. James J. Sadkovich, 'Of Myths and Men: Rommel and the Italians in North Africa, 1940–1942', *International History Review*, 13 (1991), pp. 284–313.
12. BA-MA, RW 4/326, Bl. 91, note by military attaché, 31 March 1941.
13. PAAA, Botschaft Rom (Quirinal), Bd. 110, anonymous letter, received 15 January 1941.
14. *ADAP*, D, XII/1, doc. 208, note by Schmidt, 25 March 1941; for the Italian minutes, see *DDI*, 9s, VI, doc. 778; *ADAP*, D, XXI/1, doc. 224, Hewel to Rome Embassy, 27 March 1941; for the Italian version of the telegram, see *DDI*, 9s, VI., doc. 792; ibid., doc. 226, Der Botschafter in Rom an das Auswärtige Amt, 28 March 1941; for context, see Stevan K. Pavlowitch, *Hitler's New Disorder: The Second World War in Yugoslavia*, London, 2008, pp. 11–20; Filippo Focardi, 'Italy as Occupier in the Balkans: Remembrance and War Crimes after 1945', in Jörg Echternkamp and Stefan Martens (eds), *Experience and Memory: The Second World War in Europe*, New York, 2010, pp. 135–46.
15. For details, see Antony Beevor, *Crete: The Battle and the Resistance*, London, 1991; for the German occupation of Greece, see Mark Mazower, *Inside Hitler's Greece: The Experience of Occupation, 1941–44*, New Haven, 1993.

16. Domarus, *Hitler*, II/2, pp. 1703–9; *TBJG, Teil I*, IX, pp. 291–3 (5 May 1941).
17. Ciano, *Diario*, pp. 508–9 (3–5 May 1941).
18. Cajani and Mantelli, 'In Deutschland arbeiten', pp. 231–46, here pp. 235–8.
19. *ADAP*, D, XIII/1, doc. 281, Mackensen to Foreign Ministry, 5 September 1941.
20. For Italian protests, see *ADAP*, D, XIII/2, doc. 411, Botschafter Alfieri an Reichsaußenminister von Ribbentrop, 19 October 1941; for the Italian version, see *DDI*, 9s, VII, 665; Ulrich Herbert, *Fremdarbeiter: Politik und Praxis des 'Ausländer-Einsatzes' in der Kriegswirtschaft des Dritten Reiches*, Bonn, 1999, p. 120; Cajani and Mantelli, 'In Deutschland arbeiten'; see also *ADAP*, D, XIII/2, doc. 355, Mackensen to Foreign Ministry, 25 September 1941; ibid., doc. 356, Mackensen to Foreign Ministry, 25 September 1941; see also Alfieri, *Dictators Face to Face*, pp. 107–18.
21. *ADAP*, D, XIII/2, doc. 446, Ribbentrop to Alfieri, 4 November 1941; see also *DDI*, 9s, VII, doc. 737, Alfieri to Ciano, 10 November 1941; ibid., doc. 738, Alfieri to Ciano, 10 November 1941; Alfieri, *Dictators Face to Face*, pp. 116–17; for Hitler's intervention, see Edward L. Homze, *Foreign Labor in Nazi Germany*, Princeton, 1967, pp. 63–4.
22. For Hess's flight, see Kershaw, *Hitler, 1936–1945*, pp. 369–81.
23. Ciano, *Diario*, pp. 511–12 (13 & 14 May 1941); Tranfaglia (ed.), *La stampa del regime*, p. 309.
24. Ciano, *Diario*, p. 512 (14 May 1941); see also the documents in Stato Maggiore dell'Esercito Ufficio Storico (ed.), *Le operazioni delle unità italiane al fronte russo (1941–1943)*, 2nd edn, Rome, 1993, pp. 519–26.
25. *ADAP*, D, XII/2, doc. 511, note by Schmidt, 14 May 1941; ibid., doc. 513, note by Schmidt, 14 May 1941.
26. Ciano, *Diario*, p. 518 (31 May 1941).
27. Ibid., p. 520 (1 June 1941).
28. Boberach (ed.), *Meldungen aus dem Reich*, VII, p. 2367; for Italian press directives, see Matteini (ed.), *Ordini alla stampa*, p. 151.
29. *Il Popolo d'Italia*, 3 June 1941.
30. *New York Times*, 3 June 1941.
31. Ciano, *Diario*, p. 520 (2 June 1941); Schmidt, *Statist auf diplomatischer Bühne*, p. 537.
32. *ADAP*, XII/2, doc. 584, note by Schmidt, 3 June 1941; for the encounter, see also Kershaw, *Hitler, 1936–1945*, pp. 382–3; for minutes of the Ciano–Ribbentrop talks, see *DDI*, 9s, VII, doc. 200, conversation Ciano–Ribbentrop; see also Muggeridge (ed.), *Ciano's Diplomatic Papers*, pp. 441–3; for minutes of the Ribbentrop–Cavallero meeting, see Lucio Ceva, *La condotta italiana della guerra: Cavallero e il Comando supremo 1941/1942*, Milan, 1975, pp. 144–51.
33. *ADAP*, XII/2, doc. 584; *TBJG, Teil I*, IX, p. 395 (22 June 1941); Thomas Schlemmer, *Die Italiener an der Ostfront 1942/43: Dokumente zu Mussolinis Krieg gegen die Sowjetunion*, Munich, 2005, p. 7; for context, see Magnus Brechtken, *'Madagaskar für die Juden': antisemitische Idee und politische Praxis 1885–1945*, Munich, 1997, esp. pp. 81–283; for the Nazi persecution of the Jews in 1941, see Christopher R. Browning, *The Origins of the Final Solution: The Evolution of Nazi Jewish Policy, September 1939–March 1942*, Lincoln, NE, 2004, pp. 36–234.
34. For context, see Ian Kershaw, *Fateful Choices: Ten Decisions that Changed the World 1940–1941*, London, 2007, pp. 54–90; Omer Bartov, *The Eastern Front, 1941–45: German Troops and the Barbarisation of Warfare*, 2nd edn, Basingstoke, 2001, pp. 2–6.
35. For plans for the conquest of the Soviet Union, see Jürgen Förster, 'Hitlers Entscheidung für den Krieg gegen die Sowjetunion', in *DRZW*, IV, pp. 3–97; Ernst Klink, 'Die militärische Konzeption des Krieges gegen die Sowjetunion, 1: die Landkriegführung', ibid., pp. 190–326; Jürgen Förster, 'Das Unternehmen "Barbarossa" als Eroberungs- und Vernichtungskrieg', ibid., pp. 413–47; for the New Order, see Monica Fioravanzo, 'Die Europakonzeption von Faschismus und Nationalsozialismus (1939–1943)', *VfZ*, 58 (2010), pp. 509–41; Martin, *The Nazi-Fascist New Order*.
36. *ADAP*, D, XII/2, doc. 660, Hitler–Mussolini, 21 June 1941; for the Italian offer of military support, see ibid., p. 769; ibid., Der Geschäftsträger in Rom an das Auswärtige Amt,

22 June 1941; Ciano, *Diario*, p. 526 (22 June 1941); Ceva, *La condotta italiana della guerra*, p. 84; Schlemmer, *Die Italiener an der Ostfront*, pp. 7–9; see also Gerhard Schreiber, 'La partecipazione italiana alla guerra contro l'Urss: motivi fatti conseguenze', *Italia contemporanea*, 191 (1993), pp. 245–75.

37. For anti-Bolshevism in Italy, see Marla Stone, 'Italian Fascism's Wartime Enemy and the Politics of Fear', in Michael Laffan and Max Weiss (eds), *Facing Fear: The History of an Emotion in Global Perspective*, Princeton, 2012, pp. 114–32.
38. For quote in Mussolini's reply to Hitler, see *ADAP*, D, XIII/1, doc. 7, Mussolini to Hitler, 23 June 1941; for the Italian version, see *DDI*, 9s, VII, doc. 299; cf. Woller, *Mussolini*, p. 224.
39. *Il Popolo d'Italia*, 23 June 1941; for context, see Schlemmer, *Die Italiener an der Ostfront*, pp. 6–10.
40. Ciano, *Diario*, pp. 528–9 (29–30 June 1941); for the South Tyrol, see Petersen, 'Deutschland, Italien und Südtirol 1938–1940'.
41. Boberach (ed.), *Meldungen aus dem Reich*, VII, pp. 2426–7; for context, see Ian Kershaw, *Popular Opinion and Political Dissent in the Third Reich: Bavaria 1933–1945*, Oxford, 1983, p. 290.
42. Boberach (ed.), *Meldungen aus dem Reich*, VII, p. 2487.
43. For an example of such propaganda, see Historicus, 'Basi antirusse dell'unità Europea', *Civiltà Fascista*, 8 (1941), pp. 494–506; for context, see Stone, 'Italian Fascism's Wartime Enemy'.
44. ACS, SpD, CO, b. 2824, Vincenzo da P. to Mussolini, 22 June 1941.
45. Duggan, *Fascist Voices*, p. 372; Corner, *The Fascist Party*, pp. 264–74.
46. BA-MA, RW 4/326, Bl. 156, note by military attaché, 25 June 1941.
47. *La Svastica*, 1/17 (1941), pp. 4–6.
48. Ciano, *Diario*, p. 534 (15 July 1941); for Ansaldo, see Ugo Berti Arnoaldi, 'Ansaldo, Giovanni', in de Grazia and Luzzatto (eds), *Dizionario del fascismo*, I, pp. 57–9.
49. Ciano, *Diario*, p. 535 (20 July 1941).
50. H. James Burgwyn, *Mussolini Warlord: Failed Dreams of Empire 1940–43*, New York, 2012, p. 119; for context, see also Thomas Schlemmer, '"Gefühlsmäßige Verwandtschaft"? Zivilisten, Kriegsgefangene und das könglich-italienische Heer im Krieg gegen die Sowjetunion 1941 bis 1943', in Klinkhammer, Osti Guerrazzi and Schlemmer (eds), *Die 'Achse' im Krieg*, pp. 368–97; Schlemmer, *Die Italiener an der Ostfront*, pp. 6–32; Andrea Romano, 'Russia, campagna di', in de Grazia and Luzzatto (eds), *Dizionario del fascismo*, II, pp. 562–7; for numbers, see Rochat, *Le guerre italiane 1935–1943*, p. 378.
51. For war crimes, see Schlemmer, *Die Italiener an der Ostfront*, pp. 44–6; Renzo De Felice, *Mussolini l'alleato*, Turin, 1990–7, I/2, pp. 749–60; for the press directive, see Matteini (ed.), *Ordini alla stampa*, p. 155.
52. Boberach (ed.), *Meldungen aus dem Reich*, VII, p. 2560.
53. *ADAP*, D, XIII/1, doc. 50, Hitler to Mussolini, 30 June 1941; ibid., doc. 62, Mussolini to Hitler, 2 July 1941; *DDI*, 9s, VII, doc. 346; for the Italian version, see *OO*, XXX, p. 206.
54. *New York Times*, 8 August 1941.
55. For context, see Reynolds, *The Creation of the Anglo-American Alliance*, pp. 213–15; Richard Overy, *Why the Allies Won*, London, 1995, p. 248.
56. *Il Popolo d'Italia*, 30 August 1941.
57. For Mussolini's itinerary, see *OO*, XXX, pp. 115–17, n.*; for Hitler's itinerary, see BA-MA, RW 47/9, Bl. 117–40, 'Arbeitsprogramm'.
58. For the Italian minutes, see *ADAP*, D, XIII/1, doc. 242, 'Aufzeichnung über zwei Unterredungen des Duce mit dem Führer', 25 August 1941 (the German minutes have not been preserved); cf. Ceva, *La condotta italiana della guerra*, pp. 86–8.
59. *Il Popolo d'Italia*, 30 August 1941; for the minutes of the Keitel–Cavallero conversation, see Ceva, *La condotta italiana della guerra*, pp. 178–81.
60. See e.g. BA-MA, RW 47/9, Bl. 127, 'Anlage 8, Frontflug Brest am 26.8.1941'.
61. Schmidt, *Statist auf diplomatischer Bühne*, pp. 545–8.
62. Jochmann (ed.), *Adolf Hitler*, pp. 42–4 (21–22 July 1941).

63. Schmidt, *Statist auf diplomatischer Bühne*, pp. 545–8.
64. For the equipment, see Schlemmer, *Die Italiener an der Ostfront*, pp. 14–17.
65. Domarus, *Mussolini und Hitler*, p. 347; Alfieri, *Dictators Face to Face*, p. 154; for the passenger list, see BA-MA, RW 47/9, Bl. 137, 'Frontflug Krosno-Uman am 28.8.1941'; for the myth of aviation, see Fernando Esposito, *Mythische Moderne: Aviatik, Faschismus und die Sehnsucht nach Ordnung in Deutschland und Italien*, Munich, 2011; *La Svastica*, 1/27 (1941), p. 8.
66. The Stefani report is reprinted in Tuninetti (ed.), *Incontri di popoli*, p. 61; on Fascist propaganda, see CV, 'Contro la Russia sovietica', *Almanacco fascista del Popolo d'Italia*, 21 (1942), pp. 109–60.
67. *TBJG, Teil II*, I, p. 336 (31 August 1941); *VB*, 30 August 1941.
68. *New York Times*, 30 August 1941; Domarus, *Hitler*, II/2, pp. 1749–50; Royal Institute of International Affairs (ed.), *Review of the Foreign Press*, V, p. 703 (15 September 1941); Reynolds, *The Creation of the Anglo-American Alliance*.
69. Boberach (ed.), *Meldungen aus dem Reich*, VIII, p. 2712; see also ibid., p. 2825.
70. Ciano, *Diario*, p. 544–5 (13 October 1941).
71. Boberach (ed.), *Meldungen aus dem Reich*, VIII, p. 2949; Mack Smith, *Mussolini*, pp. 271–2; for details on rationing, see Zamagni, 'Italy: How to Lose the War and Win the Peace', p. 191.
72. Corner, *The Fascist Party*, pp. 273–4.
73. Schlemmer, *Die Italiener an der Ostfront*, p. 49; Ciano, *Diario*, p. 540 (30 September 1941).
74. Domarus, *Hitler*, II/2, pp. 1758–67, here p. 1763; Boberach (ed.), *Meldungen aus dem Reich*, VIII, p. 2836; *DDI*, 9s, VII, doc. 620, Alfieri to Ciano, 4 October 1941.
75. Ciano, *Diario*, pp. 541–2 (3–6 October 1941).
76. König, *Kooperation als Machtkampf*, pp. 245–7.
77. For context, see ibid., pp. 89–148.
78. Cesare Bermani, 'Odysse in Deutschland: die alltägliche Erfahrung der italienischen "Fremdarbeiter" im "Dritten Reich", in Cesare Bermani, Sergio Bologna and Brunello Mantelli (eds), *Proletarier der 'Achse': Sozialgeschichte der italienischen Fremdarbeit in NS-Deutschland 1937–1943*, Berlin, 1997, pp. 37–252, here pp. 236–8; Brunello Mantelli, 'Zwischen Strukturwandel auf dem Arbeitsmarkt und Kriegswirtschaft: die Anwerbung der italienischen Arbeiter für das "Dritte Reich" und die "Achse Berlin–Rom" 1938–1943', ibid., pp. 253–391, here pp. 385–91; Josef Schröder, *Italiens Kriegsaustritt 1943: die deutschen Gegenmaßnahmen im italienischen Raum – Fall 'Alarich' und 'Achse'*, Göttingen, 1969, pp. 73–9.
79. Domarus, *Hitler*, II/2, pp. 1771–81, here p. 1780.
80. Stegemann, 'Die italienisch-deutsche Kriegsführung', p. 677.
81. Ernst Klink, 'Die Operationsführung, 1: Heer und Kriegsmarine', in *DRZW*, IV, pp. 451–652, here pp. 568–600; Ciano, *Diario*, pp. 547–8 (18 & 22 October 1941).
82. Schlemmer, *Die Italiener an der Ostfront*, p. 28; Rintelen, *Mussolini als Bundesgenosse*, p. 151.
83. Printed in Schlemmer, *Die Italiener an der Ostfront*, pp. 82–6.
84. For the treaty, see *ADAP*, D, XIII/2, doc. 498, 'Protokoll zur Verlängerung der Gültigkeitsdauer des Abkommens gegen die Kommunistische Internationale', 25 November 1941; for Ciano's observations, see *DDI*, 9s, VII, doc. 786, Ciano to Mussolini, 24–27 November 1941; for the German minutes, see *ADAP*, D, XIII/2, doc. 522, note by Schmidt, 30 November 1941; for military context, see Klink, 'Die Operationsführung', pp. 593–600.
85. Muggeridge (ed.), *Ciano's Diplomatic Papers*, pp. 465–7; for context, see Gerhard L. Weinberg, *A World at Arms: A Global History of World War II*, Cambridge, 1994, pp. 245–63.
86. Kershaw, *Fateful Choices*, pp. 382–430; Weinberg, *A World at Arms*, p. 262.
87. Mack Smith, *Mussolini*, p. 273.
88. *ADAP*, E, I, doc. 53, telegram by Rintelen, 22 December 1941.

89. For a pithy account of the Holocaust, see Evans, *The Third Reich at War*, pp. 217–318; Kershaw, *Fateful Choices*, pp. 431–70; for Hitler's role in the Holocaust, see Ian Kershaw, *The Nazi Dictatorship: Problems and Perspectives of Interpretation*, London, 2000, pp. 93–133.
90. *La Svastica*, 1/35 (1941), pp. 3–5; Ciano, *Diario*, p. 569 (20 December 1941); Schlemmer, *Die Italiener an der Ostfront*, pp. 24–9.
91. Srdjan Trifković, 'Rivalry between Germany and Italy in Croatia, 1942–1943', *Historical Journal*, 36 (1993), pp. 879–904; Klaus Schmider, 'Das Versagen der "Achse" im besetzten Kroatien: ein politisch-militärischer Erklärungsversuch', in Klinkhammer, Osti Guerrazzi and Schlemmer (eds), *Die 'Achse' im Krieg*, pp. 305–18; for the pact, see Reinhard Stumpf, 'Von der Achse Berlin–Rom zum Militärabkommen des Dreierpakts: die Abfolge der Verträge 1936 bis 1942', in *DRZW*, VI, pp. 127–43, here p. 141; for the text, see *ADAP*, E, I, doc. 145, 'Militärische Vereinbarung zwischen Deutschland, Italien und Japan', 18 January 1942.
92. Bosworth, *Mussolini*, pp. 382–4; De Felice, *Mussolini l'alleato*, I, p. 1011; Ciano, *Diario*, p. 572 (29 December 1941); Rintelen, *Mussolini als Bundesgenosse*, pp. 164–5.
93. Bosworth, *Mussolini*, pp. 387–9.
94. *ADAP*, E, I, doc. 62, Hitler to Mussolini, 29 December 1941; ibid., doc. 63, Hitler to Marschall Antonescu, 29 December 1941; ibid., doc. 64, Hitler to Horthy, 29 December 1941.
95. *Hitler e Mussolini: lettere e documenti*, Milan, 1946, pp. 116–18.
96. Ciano, *Diario*, p. 577 (1 January 1942).
97. Ibid., p. 580 (12 January 1942); *ADAP*, E, I, doc. 164, Mussolini an Hitler, 23 January 1942.
98. Ciano, *Diario*, pp. 584 (29 January 1942), 587 (4 February 1942).
99. *ADAP*, E, I, doc. 181, note by Schmidt, 29 January 1942; see also ACS, SpD, CO, 532.091, sf. 3, 'Spese inerenti alla permanenza in Italia dell'Ecc. il Maresciallo del Reich Ermanno Goering', undated; ibid., de Cesare to Direzione della Pubblica Sicurezza, 26 February 1942.
100. Jochmann (ed.), *Adolf Hitler*, pp. 246–7 (31 January 1941).
101. See e.g. the letter by the soldier Ferruccio C., from a Florentine regiment, sent to Mussolini on 29 March 1942, in ACS, SpD, CO, b. 2777.
102. Domarus, *Hitler*, II/2, p. 1893; Ciano, *Diario*, pp. 633–4 (26 June 1942), 635 (4 July 1942).
103. Rintelen, *Mussolini als Bundesgenosse*, pp. 171–3; Ciano, *Diario*, p. 637 (21 July 1942); for context, see John L. Wright, 'Mussolini, Libya, and the Sword of Islam', in Ruth Ben-Ghiat and Mia Fuller (eds), *Italian Colonialism*, Basingstoke, 2005, pp. 121–30, here p. 128.
104. Bernd Wegner, 'Der Krieg gegen die Sowjetunion 1942–43', in *DRZW*, VI, pp. 761–1102, here p. 778.
105. Cf. Hillgruber (ed.), *Staatsmänner und Diplomaten bei Hitler*, II, p. 64.
106. On the choice of location, see *TBJG, Teil II*, IV, p. 176 (26 April 1942); ibid., pp. 223–4 (2 May 1942); Domarus, *Mussolini und Hitler*, p. 357.
107. *ADAP*, E, II, doc. 165, Ribbentrop to Mackensen, 24 April 1942; for Alfieri's statement, see ibid., p. 272, n. 2; for the scheduling, see ibid., p. 273, n. 4; Ciano, *Diario*, p. 612 (24 April 1942); ibid., p. 613 (28 April 1942); for Hitler's Reichstag speech, see Domarus, *Hitler*, II/2, p. 1868.
108. For Mussolini's instructions to the prefects, see *OO*, XXXI, pp. 52–4.
109. *ADAP*, E, II, doc. 178, note by Schmidt, 1 May 1942.
110. *ADAP*, E, II, doc. 182, note by Schmidt, 2 May 1942; Schmidt, *Statist auf Diplomatischer Bühne*, pp. 550–1; *TBJG, Teil II*, IV, pp. 223–4 (2 May 1942).
111. For the Italian minutes, found in Mussolini's suitcase in 1945, see *DDI*, 9s, VIII, doc. 492, conversation Mussolini–Hitler, 29 April 1942; Ciano, *Diario*, pp. 613–16 (29 April–2 May 1942).
112. *DDI*, 9s, VIII, doc. 493, conversation Cavallero–Keitel, 29 April 1942.

113. BA-MA, RW 4/879, 'Besprechung am 30.4.42'; see also *ADAP*, E, II, doc. 183, note by Schmidt, 2 May 1942; for Mussolini's reaction see ibid., p. 316, n. 3; Ciano, *Diario*, pp. 613–15 (29 April–2 May 1942); for the Italian army's minutes, see *DDI*, 9s, VIII, doc. 495, conversation Mussolini–Hitler, 30 April 1942; for context, see Pier Luigi Bertinaria, 'Hitler Mussolini: lo stato dell'alleanza', in R. H. Rainero and A. Biagini (eds), *L'Italia in guerra*, Gaeta, 1992, II, pp. 57–84.
114. *Il Popolo d'Italia*, 2 May 1942; Royal Institute of International Affairs (ed.), *Review of the Foreign Press*, VI, p. 357 (18 May 1942).
115. *The Times*, 2 May 1942; for the communiqué, see *VB*, 2/3 May 1942.
116. König, *Kooperation als Machtkampf*, p. 59.
117. *ADAP*, E, III, doc. 306, note by Weizsäcker, 23 September 1942; for context, see Wegner, 'Der Krieg gegen die Sowjetunion', pp. 962–1063; Richard Overy, *Russia's War*, London, 1998, pp. 154–85.
118. ACS, SpD, CO, b. 50, Vidussoni to Mussolini, 24 October 1942; also printed in Schlemmer (ed.), *Die Italiener an der Ostfront*, pp. 168–79; *ADAP*, D, IV, doc. 22, note by Hewel, 8 October 1942; for propaganda on Italo-German comradeship on the eastern front, see *La Svastica*, 1/34 (1941), p. 11; De Felice, *Mussolini l'alleato*, I/1, p. 454.
119. BAB, NS 19/2410, Reichsführer SS Himmler an Reichsaußenminister von Ribbentrop, 22 October 1942; on context, see Helmut Krausnick, 'Himmler über seinen Besuch bei Mussolini vom 11.–14. Oktober 1942', *VfZ*, 4 (1956), pp. 423–6; Giovanni Preziosi, 'Per la soluzione del problema ebraico', *Vita italiana*, 30 (1942), pp. 221–4.
120. MacGregor Knox, 'Das faschistische Italien und die Endlösung', *VfZ*, 55 (2007), pp. 53–92, here pp. 53–4, 82.
121. Harrison, 'The Economics of World War II: An Overview', pp. 10, 14; for context, see Overy, *Why the Allies Won*, pp. 180–207.
122. For military context, see Reinhard Stumpf, 'Der Krieg im Mittelmeerraum 1942/43: die Operationen in Nordafrika und im mittleren Mittelmeer', in *DRZW*, VI, pp. 569–757.
123. *ADAP*, E, IV, doc. 82, Hitler an Mussolini, 21 October 1942; for the Italian version, see *DDI*, 9s, IX, doc. 249.
124. Stumpf, 'Der Krieg im Mittelmeerraum', pp. 688–709, 715; Evans, *The Third Reich at War*, p. 467.
125. Overy, *The Bombing War*, pp. 512–13.
126. Marco Cuzzi, 'I bombardamenti delle città italiane e l'UNPA', in R. H. Rainero and A. Biagini (eds), *L'Italia in guerra*, Gaeta, 1992, II, pp. 173–84; see also Gabriella Gribaudi, 'The True Cause of the "Moral Collapse": People, Fascists and Authorities under the Bombs – Naples and the Countryside, 1940–1944', in Richard Overy, Claudia Baldoli and Andrew Knapp (eds), *Bombing, States and Peoples in Western Europe 1940–1945*, London, 2011, pp. 219–38; Overy, *The Bombing War*, p. 513.
127. For copies of the leaflets, see PAAA, Botschaft Rom (Quirinal), Geheim, Bd. 132, German Consulate-General to German Embassy, 24 November 1942 and 9 December 1942.
128. For a succinct survey, see Elena Agarossi, *A Nation Collapses: The Italian Surrender of September 1943*, Cambridge, 2000, pp. 32–7; cf. De Felice, *Mussolini l'alleato*, I/2, pp. 1155–73.
129. See for instance the industrialist Alberto Pirelli's audience with Mussolini: Alberto Pirelli, *Taccuini 1922/1943*, ed. Donato Barbone, Bologna, 1984, pp. 364–70; cf. De Felice, *Mussolini l'alleato*, I/1, pp. 454–5.
130. *ADAP*, D, IV, doc. 165, note by Schmidt, 12 November 1942; ibid., doc. 146, Rome Embassy to Foreign Ministry, 7 November 1942.
131. *ADAP*, D, IV, doc. 301, Bismarck to Weizsäcker, 19 December 1942.
132. *OO*, XXXI, pp. 134–45.
133. *TBJG, Teil II*, VI, p. 431 (12 December 1942).
134. Ciano, *Diario*, pp. 677 (16 December 1942), 678 (18 December 1942).

135. *ADAP*, E, IV, doc. 315, note by Schmidt, 24 December 1942; Simoni, *Berlin ambassade d'Italie*, p. 346 (18 December 1942); for context, see Jürgen Förster, *Stalingrad: Risse im Bündnis 1942/43*, Freiburg, 1975, p. 55.
136. ACS, MI, DGPS, Pol. Pol. Materia, b. 215, f. 2, 'voci', Rome, 23 February 1943.
137. Ciano, *Diario*, p. 687 (8 January 1943); for context, see Rochat, *Le guerre italiane*, p. 358.
138. Wegner, 'Der Krieg gegen die Sowjetunion', pp. 962–1063.
139. Jeremy Noakes (ed.), *Nazism: A Documentary Reader*, Exeter, 1998, IV, pp. 490–4; Claudia Baldoli, 'Spring 1943: The Fiat Strikes and the Collapse of the Italian Home Front', *History Workshop Journal*, 72 (2011), pp. 181–9; Timothy W. Mason, 'The Turin Strikes of March 1943', in *Nazism, Fascism, and the Working Class: Essays by Tim Mason*, ed. Jane Caplan, Cambridge, 1995, pp. 274–94.
140. Deakin, *The Brutal Friendship*, p. 231.
141. Ibid., pp. 316–34.
142. *Rom Berlin Tokio*, 5 (1943), pp. 9–11; Bosworth, *Mussolini*, pp. 395–7.
143. *DDI*, 9s. X, doc. 71, Alfieri to Bastianini, 15 February 1943.
144. *ADAP*, E, V, doc. 108, Mackensen to Foreign Ministry, 8 February 1943; *TBJG, Teil II*, VII, p. 319 (11 February 1943); *ADAP*, V, doc. 131, Rome Embassy to Foreign Ministry, 13 February 1943; ibid., doc. 1939; for context, see Lutz Klinkhammer, *Zwischen Bündnis und Besatzung: das nationalsozialistische Deutschland und die Republik von Salò 1943–1945*, Tübingen, 1993, pp. 29–31.
145. *TBJG, Teil II*, VII, p. 208 (28 January 1942); Weinberg, *A World at Arms*, pp. 437–42.
146. ACS, Ambasciata tedesca in Roma, busta unica, 1-C, memorandum, 25 March 1943.
147. *ADAP*, E, V doc. 207, Hitler to Mussolini, 14 March 1943; Deakin, *The Brutal Friendship*, p. 217.
148. *DDI*, 9s, X, doc. 71, Alfieri-Bastianini, 3 March 1943; ibid., doc. 117, Alfieri-Bastianini, 14 March 1943.
149. *ADAP*, E, V, doc. 135, Hitler an Mussolini, 16 February 1943; *DDI*, 9s, X, doc. 31.
150. *ADAP*, E, V, doc. 192, Mussolini to Hitler, 9 March 1943; see also *DDI*, 9s, X, doc. 95.
151. *ADAP*, E, V, doc. 152, Mackensen to Auswärtiges Amt, 23 February 1943; ibid., doc. 184, note by Schmidt, 8 March 1943; for context, see Gerhard Schreiber, *Deutsche Kriegsverbrechen in Italien: Täter, Opfer, Strafverfolgung*, Munich, 1996, pp. 16–17.
152. *ADAP*, E, V, doc. 214, Sonnleithner to Rome Embassy, 17 March 1943; ibid., doc. 228, memo by Mackensen, 21 March 1943; ibid., doc. 252, Mussolini to Hitler, 26 March 1943; Weinberg, *A World at Arms*, pp. 443–7.
153. Plehwe, *Als die Achse zerbrach*, pp. 14, 27.
154. Ibid., pp. 14, 27.
155. *TBJG, Teil II*, VIII, p. 93 (11 April 1943).
156. Deakin, *The Brutal Friendship*, pp. 273–4.
157. Alfieri, *Dictators Face to Face*, pp. 203–4, 225–6.
158. Deakin, *The Brutal Friendship*, pp. 259–60; Giuseppe Bastianini, *Volevo fermare Mussolini: memorie di un diplomatico fascista*, Milan, 2005, pp. 104–18; for the Duce's itinerary, see *OO*, XXXI, n.*, pp. 172–4.
159. Deakin, *The Brutal Friendship*, pp. 259–75; PRO, HW 1/1637, Hitler–Mussolini Talks: Reports from Japanese Chargé Rome, 26 April 1943; for an inaccurate account of Bastianini, see Owen Chadwick, 'Bastianini and the Weakening of the Fascist Will to Fight the Second World War', in T.C.W. Blanning and David Cannadine (eds), *History and Biography: Essays in Honour of Derek Beales*, Cambridge, 1996, pp. 243–65.
160. De Felice, *Mussolini l'alleato*, I/1, pp. 464–9; *ADAP*, E, V., doc. 286, note by Schmidt, 10 April 1943; ibid., doc. 291, note by Schmidt, 11 April 1943; Heiber (ed.), *Hitlers Lagebesprechungen*, p. 229.
161. *TBJG, Teil II*, VIII, p. 94–5 (12 April 1943); cf. *ADAP*, E, V, doc. 285, note by Mackensen, 9 April 1943; for the communiqué, see *VB*, 12 April 1943; *Il Popolo d'Italia*, 12 April 1943; for Italo-German disagreement, see *DDI*, 9s, X, doc. 202, Suster–Megerle conversation, 7 April 1943.

162. *New York Times*, 12 April 1943; Royal Institute of International Affairs (ed.), *Review of the Foreign Press*, VIII, pp. 165–6 (3 May 1943).
163. *TBJG, Teil II*, VIII, p. 126 (18 April 1943); Boberach (ed.), *Meldungen aus dem Reich*, XIII, p. 5125.
164. Domarus, *Mussolini und Hitler*, p. 379.
165. For details, see Hillgruber (ed.), *Staatsmänner und Diplomaten bei Hitler*, II, pp. 214–85.
166. *TBJG, Teil II*, VIII, p. 220 (7 May 1943); for the speech, see *OO*, XXXI, p. 178; *DDI*, 9s, X, doc. 316, Alfieri-Mussolini, 12 May 1943.
167. For the telegrams, see Domarus, *Mussolini und Hitler*, pp. 379–80.
168. Owen Chadwick, *Britain and the Vatican during the Second World War*, Cambridge, 1986, p. 254; Weinberg, *A World at Arms*, p. 446.
169. *ADAP*, E, VI, doc. 44, Sonnleithner to Rome Embassy, 18 May 1943.
170. Klinkhammer, *Zwischen Bündnis und Besatzung*, pp. 30–1.
171. PRO, GFM 36/608, fol. 108–122, Hitler to Mussolini, 19 May 1943; Deakin, *The Brutal Friendship*, pp. 353–6.
172. This plan was later found by the Allies in the German embassy in Rome. ACS, Ambasciata tedesca in Roma (1925–1943), busta unica, sf. 3, 'Presidenza del Consiglio dei Ministri, Direzione dei servizi di P.S.', 1 July 1943.
173. For details, see Gerhard Schreiber, 'Das Ende des nordafrikanischen Feldzugs und der Krieg in Italien 1943 bis 1945', in *DRZW*, VIII, pp. 1100–62, here pp. 1113–14; Deakin, *The Brutal Friendship*, pp. 376–7.
174. Rochat, *Le guerre italiane*, pp. 305–6, 312–13.
175. Deakin, *The Brutal Friendship*, pp. 371–7; for the invasion of Sicily, see Sandro Attanasio, *Sicilia senza Italia: luglio–agosto 1943*, Milan, 1976.
176. *Il Popolo d'Italia*, 25 July 1943; Mack Smith, *Mussolini*, p. 291.
177. Paolo Puntoni, *Parla Vittorio Emanuele III*, Bologna, 1993, pp. 133–4 (1–3 June 1943), 136 (18 June 1943), 137 (5 July 1943).
178. De Felice, *Mussolini l'alleato*, I/2, pp. 1184–6; Woller, *Mussolini*, pp. 264–6.
179. Bosworth, *Mussolini*, p. 399.
180. Alfieri, *Dictators Face to Face*, pp. 235–7.
181. Bernd Wegner, 'Von Stalingrad nach Kursk', in *DRZW*, VIII, pp. 3–79; Karl-Heinz Frieser, 'Die Schlacht im Kursker Bogen', in *DRZW*, VIII, pp. 83–208.
182. Schröder, *Italiens Kriegsaustritt*, pp. 193–5.
183. Alfieri, *Dictators Face to Face*, p. 238.
184. Benito Mussolini, *My Rise and Fall*, New York, 1998, II, pp. 49–50.
185. Plehwe, *Als die Achse zerbrach*, pp. 62–5.
186. *ADAP*, E, VI, doc. 159, note by Schmidt, 20 July 1943; Bastianini, *Volevo fermare Mussolini*, 139–41; see also *DDI*, 9s, X, doc. 531; Mussolini kept a copy in one of his suitcases as he fled Milan in April 1945; see ACS, SpD, Carte della valigia di Benito Mussolini, b. 2, sf. 13–2.
187. Alfieri, *Dictators Face to Face*, pp. 246–9; for an exhaustive, but unpersuasive, account, see De Felice, *Mussolini l'alleato*, I/2, pp. 1325–38.
188. PRO, HW 1/1895, Most secret, 29 July 1943; for Italian press instructions, see Matteini (ed.), *Ordini alla stampa*, p. 253; on the bombing, see Overy, *The Bombing War*, p. 527; *TBJG, Teil II*, VIII, pp. 133–4 (21 July 1943); for the German communiqué, see *VB*, 21 July 1943; for the Italian one, see *Il Messaggero*, 22 July 1943, copy in PRO, GFM 36/7.
189. Klinkhammer, *Zwischen Bündnis und Besatzung*, pp. 32–3.
190. See Grandi's memoirs, written after the war: Dino Grandi, *25 luglio: quarant'anni dopo*, ed. Renzo De Felice, Bologna, 1983, pp. 249–303; for his motion, see Dino Grandi, *Il mio paese: ricordi autobiografici*, ed. Renzo De Felice, Bologna, 1985, pp. 637–8; for an overview of other memoirs, see De Felice, *Mussolini l'alleato*, I/2, pp. 1362–83.
191. Hill (ed.), *Die Weizsäcker-Papiere 1933–1950*, p. 344 (26 & 29 July 1943).
192. Piero Calamandrei, *Diario 1939–1945*, ed. Giorgi Agosti, Florence, 1982, II, pp. 153–4 (26 July 1943).

193. *Corriere della Sera*, 26 July 1943.
194. Giorgio Bocca, *La repubblica di Mussolini*, Milan, 1995, p. 5; Aurelio Lepre, *La storia della repubblica di Mussolini: Salò – il tempo dell'odia e della violenza*, Milan, 2000, p. 70; for details, see also the account by the ex-Fascist historian Attilio Tamaro, *Due anni di storia 1943–45*, Rome, 1948, I, pp. 55–8, 63–4.
195. Carazzolo, *Più forte della paura*, p. 836 (26 July 1943); Ceccarelli De Grada, *Giornale del tempo di guerra*, pp. 217–18 (25–26 July 1943).
196. Bosworth, *Mussolini*, pp. 400–2; Paul Ginsborg, *A History of Contemporary Italy: Society and Politics 1943–1988*, London, 1990, p. 12.
197. Schröder, *Italiens Kriegsaustritt*, p. 203.
198. *TBJG, Teil II*, VIII, pp. 165–6 (26 July 1943).
199. Heiber (ed.), *Hitlers Lagebesprechungen*, pp. 312–25; pp. 328–31; *ADAP*, E, VI, doc. 174, Steengracht–Rome Embassy, 26 July 1943; Marlis G. Steinert, *Hitlers Krieg und die Deutschen: Stimmung und Haltung der deutschen Bevölkerung im Zweiten Weltkrieg*, Düsseldorf, 1970, p. 392; for the Hamburg raids, see Overy, *The Bombing War*, pp. 435–6.
200. Klinkhammer, *Zwischen Bündnis und Besatzung*, pp. 34–7; Plehwe, *Als die Achse zerbrach*, pp. 76–92; Schramm (ed.), *Kriegstagebuch des Oberkommandos der Wehrmacht (Wehrmachtführungsstab)*, III/2, p. 834.
201. Heiber (ed.), *Hitlers Lagebesprechungen*, pp. 369–70; *TBJG, Teil II*, VIII, pp. 169–80 (27 July 1943); for military background, see Schröder, *Italiens Kriegsaustritt*, pp. 217–32; Deakin, *The Brutal Friendship*, p. 544.
202. *VB*, 27 July 1943; *The Times*, 27 July 1943.
203. Boberach (ed.), *Meldungen aus dem Reich*, XIV, pp. 5540–3.
204. *The Times*, 28 July 1943.
205. *VB*, 31 July 1943; Boberach (ed.), *Meldungen aus dem Reich*, XIV, pp. 5560–1.
206. *VB*, 30 July 1943, copy in BAB, R 8034 II/325, Bl. 15.

8 Endgame, 1943–5

1. *ADAP*, E, VI, doc. 189, Mackensen to Foreign Ministry, 28 July 1943; ibid., doc. 204, Rome Embassy to Foreign Ministry, 1 August 1943; for the Italian version of Badoglio's letter, see *DDI*, 9s, X, doc. 565, 28 July 1943; for Marras's audience with Hitler, see *DDI*, 9s, X, doc. 579, Marras to Guariglia, 30 July 1943.
2. *ADAP*, E, VI, doc. 190, Ribbentrop to Mackensen, 28 July 1943.
3. Ibid., doc. 192, Mackensen to Foreign Ministry, 29 July 1943.
4. Ibid., doc. 200, Ribbentrop to Rome Embassy, 31 July 1943; Klinkhammer, *Zwischen Bündnis und Besatzung*, pp. 34–5, n. 34.
5. Michael Wiedekind, *Nationalsozialistische Besatzungs- und Annexionspolitik in Norditalien 1943 bis 1945: die Operationszonen 'Alpenvorland' und 'Adriatisches Küstenland'*, Munich, 2003, pp. 49–50; Klinkhammer, *Zwischen Bündnis und Besatzung*, pp. 35–40.
6. *ADAP*, E, VI, doc. 244, Bismarck to Foreign Ministry, 24 August 1943 (for quotation); ibid., doc. 246, Rome Embassy to Foreign Ministry, 25 August 1943; ibid., doc. 247, Ribbentrop to Rome Embassy, 26 August 1943.
7. Meissner, *Staatssekretär unter Ebert-Hindenburg-Hitler*, p. 354.
8. *TBJG, Teil II*, VIII, pp. 251–5; 263–5 (10 August 1943); for the Prince, see Petropoulos, *Royals and the Reich*, pp. 290–1.
9. BAB, NS 19/1880, Bl. 53–5, Abschrift, 4 August 1943; Wiedekind, *Nationalsozialistische Besatzungs- und Annexionspolitik*, p. 51.
10. Boberach (ed.), *Meldungen aus dem Reich*, XIV, p. 5574.
11. *ADAP*, E, VI, doc. 217, note by Schmidt, 6 August 1943; for the Italian minutes, see *DDI*, 9s, X, docs. 611–613, all dated 6 August; for the conversation between Mackensen and Guariglia, see doc. 614, Guariglia to Badoglio, 6 August 1943 (italics in the original); Schmidt, *Statist auf diplomatischer Bühne*, p. 568; for context, see Klinkhammer, *Zwischen Bündnis und Besatzung*, p. 37.

12. Weinberg, *A World at Arms*, pp. 612–16.
13. For the writings, see *OO*, XXXIV, pp. 273–99; for their dubious provenance, see Toni Bernhart, 'Benito Mussolini als Schriftsteller und seine Übersetzungen ins Deutsche', in Albrecht, Danneberg and De Angelis (eds), *Die akademische 'Achse Berlin-Rom?'*, pp. 345–99, here 382–7; De Felice, *Mussolini l'alleato*, II, pp. 17–21; Mimmo Franzinelli, *Il prigioniero di Salò: Mussolini e la tragedia italiana del 1943–1945*, Milan, 2012, pp. 7–18; Domarus, *Mussolini und Hitler*, p. 407–8; for the reports, see *Corriere della Sera*, 29 & 30 August 1943; Bosworth, *Claretta*, pp. 174–5.
14. *ADAP*, E, VI, doc. 290, Rahn to Foreign Ministry, 8 September 1943; ibid., doc. 291, Badoglio to Hitler, 8 September 1943; Halder, *Kriegstagebuch*, III, pp. 1076–80; for the Italian version of Badoglio's letter, see *DDI*, 9s, X, doc. 773.
15. Ceccarelli De Grada, *Giornale del tempo di guerra*, p. 226 (8 September 1943); Carazzolo, *Più forte della paura*, p. 97–9 (8–9 September 1943).
16. Renzo De Felice, *Rosso e nero*, Milan, 1996; Ernesto Galli Della Loggia, *La morte della patria*, 4th edn, Rome/Bari, 2008.
17. *DDI*, 10s, I, doc. 3, Churchill and Roosevelt to Badoglio, 10 September 1943.
18. Plehwe, *Als die Achse zerbrach*, pp. 256–7.
19. Gerhard Schreiber, *Die italienischen Militärinternierten im deutschen Machtbereich 1943 bis 1945: verraten – verachtet – vergessen*, Munich, 1990, p. 91.
20. Schreiber, 'Das Ende des nordafrikanischen Feldzugs', p. 1123; Amedeo Osti Guerrazzi, *Storia della Repubblica sociale italiana*, Rome, 2012, p. 54; Enzo Collotti, *L'amministrazione tedesca dell'Italia occupata 1943–1945*, Milan, 1963, pp. 413–15.
21. The best study is Elena Aga Rossi, *Cefalonia: la resistenza, l'eccidio, il mito*, Bologna, 2016; see also Giorgio Rochat, *Le guerre italiane*, pp. 434–6.
22. Boberach (ed.), *Meldungen aus dem Reich*, XV, pp. 6179–80; on context, see Schreiber, *Die italienischen Militärinternierten im deutschen Machtbereich*, pp. 377–8; on knowledge of the Final Solution, see Peter Longerich, *'Davon haben wir nichts gewußt': die Deutschen und die Judenverfolgung 1933–1945*, Munich, 2006.
23. Herbert, *Fremdarbeiter*, p. 301; see also 'Bericht der von den Außenministern der Bundesrepublik Deutschland und Republik Italien am 28.3.2009 eingesetzten Deutsch-Italienischen Historikerkommission', July 2012, available at http://www.villavigoni.it/contents/files/Abschlussbericht.pdf, accessed 14 December 2017; Oreste Foppiani, 'La "Croix-Rouge de Mussolini" et les internés militaires italiens (1943–1945)', *Relations internationales*, 142 (2010), pp. 23–36.
24. Brunello Mantelli and Nicola Tranfaglia (eds), *Il libro dei deportati*, Turin, 2009, I/1, p. 47.
25. *TBJG, Teil II*, VIII, pp. 455–77 (10 September 1943).
26. Kershaw, *Hitler, 1936–1945*, p. 601.
27. Domarus, *Hitler*, II/2, pp. 2035–9; *VB*, 11 September 1943; Boberach (ed.), *Meldungen aus dem Reich*, XV, pp. 5753–5; Kershaw, *The 'Hitler Myth'*, p. 211.
28. *TBJG, Teil II*, VIII, pp. 479–87 (11 September 1943); cf. Erich Kuby, *Verrat auf deutsch: wie das Dritte Reich Italien ruinierte*, Frankfurt am Main, 1987.
29. For context, see Wiedekind, *Nationalsozialistische Besatzungs- und Annexionspolitik*.
30. Kershaw, '"Working towards the Führer"', pp. 103–18.
31. Klinkhammer, *Zwischen Bündnis und Besatzung*, pp. 559–61.
32. Osti Guerrazzi, *Storia della Repubblica sociale italiana*, pp. 55–7; Klinkhammer, *Zwischen Bündnis und Besatzung*, pp. 63–95.
33. Schreiber, 'Das Ende des nordafrikanischen Feldzugs', p. 1125.
34. De Felice, *Mussolini l'alleato*, II, p. 26.
35. For details of the liberation, see Deakin, *The Brutal Friendship*, pp. 543–7; see also Skorzeny's post-war testimony in IfZ, ZS 1517; Maria Fraddosio, 'The Fallen Hero: The Myth of Mussolini and Fascist Women in the Italian Social Republic (1943–5)', *JCH*, 31 (1996), pp. 99–124, here p. 106.
36. *TBJG, Teil II*, VIII, pp. 496–501 (13 September 1943); IfZ, Fd 44, Bl. 71–9, 'Erlebnisbericht über die Überführung des Duce zum Führerhauptquartier', 26 September 1943; Domarus, *Mussolini und Hitler*, p. 413.

37. IfZ, Fd 44, Bl. 79; Deakin, *The Brutal Friendship*, p. 555; for the picture, see the cover of *Illustrierter Beobachter*, 30 September 1943.
38. *TBJG, Teil II*, VIII, pp. 557–92 (23 September 1943).
39. Deakin, *The Brutal Friendship*, pp. 559–60.
40. Anfuso, *Roma Berlino Salò*, p. 391.
41. Deakin, *The Brutal Friendship*, p. 561.
42. *VB*, 13 September 1943, 14 September 1943, 16 September 1943, 20 September 1943; see also the press agency report in *Deutschlanddienst*, 16 September 1943, copy in BAB, R 8034 II/325, Bl. 10; on context, see Bettina Goetzinger, 'Italien zwischen dem Sturz Mussolinis und der Errichtung der faschistischen Politik in der NS-Propaganda', in Rudolf Lill (ed.), *Deutschland–Italien 1943–1945: Aspekte einer Entzweiung*, Tübingen, 1992, pp. 151–76.
43. Anfuso, *Roma Berlino Salò*, p. 412; for context, see Fraddosio, 'The Fallen Hero', pp. 99–124.
44. Boberach (ed.), *Meldungen aus dem Reich*, pp. 5773, 5778; for the speech, see *OO*, XXXII, pp. 1–5.
45. *The Times*, 15 September 1943.
46. Calamandrei, *Diario 1939–1945*, II, p. 199 (20 September 1943).
47. *TBJG, Teil II*, VIII, pp. 517–19 (20 December 1943).
48. For the landing at Salerno, see Schreiber, 'Das Ende des nordafrikanischen Feldzugs', pp. 1126–31; for German behaviour in Naples, see Lynn H. Nicholas, *The Rape of Europa: The Fate of Europe's Treasures in the Third Reich and the Second World War*, New York, 1995, pp. 232–3.
49. Agarossi, *A Nation Collapses*, p. 130.
50. Weinberg, *A World at Arms*, p. 661.
51. For a simplistic account, see Richard Lamb, *War in Italy 1943–1945: A Brutal Story*, New York, 1994; cf. Focardi, *Il cattivo tedesco*, pp. 15–32.
52. Quoted in Fraddosio, 'The Fallen Hero', p. 111.
53. ASMAE, RSI, b. 34, sf. 8, Anfuso to Mazzolini, 11 October 1944; ibid., 'Wie Mussolini lebt', *Trans-Ocean Express*, 9 October 1944; ibid., translation of Kurt Eggers's article 'Dove sta oggi l'Italia', *Das Schwarze Korps*, 4 October 1944.
54. Pasquale Chessa and Barbara Raggi, *L'ultima lettera di Benito: Mussolini e Petacci – amore e politica a Salò, 1943–45*, Milan, 2010, p. 8; Deakin, *The Brutal Friendship*, pp. 642–3, 645 (for the German report on the executions); Hof, 'Die Tagebücher von Galeazzo Ciano', pp. 513–14; Bosworth, *Mussolini*, pp. 16–17.
55. Lutz Klinkhammer, 'Grundlinien nationalsozialistischer Besatzungspolitik in Frankreich, Jugoslawien und Italien', in Dipper, Hudemann and Petersen (eds), *Faschismus und Faschismen im Vergleich*, pp. 183–216.
56. Bosworth, *Mussolini*, p. 406; Klinkhammer, *Zwischen Bündnis und Besatzung*, pp. 96–137; see also Francesca Romana Scardaccione, 'La Repubblica sociale italiana: aspetti istituzionali e archivistici', in Archivio centrale dello stato (ed.), *Verbali del consiglio dei ministri della Repubblica sociale italiana*, Rome, 2002, I, pp. xvii–xxxvi.
57. *OO*, XXXII, p. 189.
58. De Felice, *Mussolini l'alleato*, II, p. 66; Renzo De Felice, 'Mussolinis Motive für seine Rückkehr in die Politik und die Übernahme der Führung der RSI (September 1943)', in Lill (ed.), *Deutschland–Italien 1943–1945*, pp. 38–50, here p. 48; for a sharp critique, see Monica Fioravanzo, *Mussolini e Hitler: la Repubblica sociale sotto il Terzo Reich*, Rome, 2009, pp. 3–56; for the letters, see OO, XXXII, pp. 205–8, p. 206 for quotation (4 October 1943).
59. Liliana Picciotto, 'The Shoah in Italy: Its History and Characteristics', in Joshua D. Zimmerman (ed.), *Jews in Italy under Fascist and Nazi Rule, 1922–1945*, Cambridge, 2005, pp. 209–23.
60. Wildvang, *Der Feind von nebenan*, p. 232.
61. Ibid., pp. 230–66, pp. 265–6 for numbers; for the alleged Hitler order, see Michaelis, *Mussolini and the Jews*, pp. 363–4; Kershaw, *Hitler, 1936–1945*, p. 604; for the text of the telegram, see Wildvang, *Der Feind von nebenan*, p. 255; Sara Berger, 'I persecutori del

16 ottobre 1943', in Martin Baumeister, Amedeo Osti Guerrazzi and Claudio Procaccia (eds), *16 ottobre 1943: la deportazione degli ebrei romani tra storia e memoria*, Rome, 2016, pp. 21–40; Lutz Klinkhammer, 'Diplomatici e militari tedeschi a Roma di fronte alla politica di sterminio nazionalsocialista', ibid., pp. 41–62.

62. Wildvang, *Der Feind von nebenan*, pp. 277–9; Susan Zuccotti, 'Pius XII and the Rescue of Jews in Italy: Evidence of a Papal Directive', in Joshua D. Zimmerman (ed.), *Jews in Italy under Fascist and Nazi Rule, 1922–1945*, Cambridge, 2005, pp. 287–307.
63. Jonathan Steinberg, *All or Nothing: The Axis and the Holocaust 1941–43*, London, 1990; for a critique, see Carlo Moos, *Ausgrenzung, Internierung, Deportation: Antisemitismus und Gewalt im späten italienischen Faschismus 1938–1945*, Zurich, 2004, pp. 19–22; Knox, 'Das faschistische Italien und die Endlösung', pp. 53–92; Thomas Schlemmer and Hans Woller, 'Der italienische Faschismus und die Juden', VfZ, 53 (2005), pp. 164–201.
64. Wildvang, *Der Feind von nebenan*, pp. 361–2.
65. Liliana Picciotto, *Il libro della memoria: gli ebrei deportati dall'Italia (1943–1945)*, Milan, 2002, p. 28; for the manifesto, see De Felice, *Mussolini l'alleato*, II, pp. 610–13.
66. Liliana Picciotto Fargion, 'Italien', in Wolfgang Benz (ed.), *Dimension des Völkermords: Die Zahl der jüdischen Opfer des Nationalsozialismus*, Munich, 1996, pp. 219–228, here pp. 215–16; see De Felice's interview in *Corriere della Sera*, 27 December 1987, printed in Jader Jacobelli (ed.), *Il fascismo e gli storici oggi*, Rome, 1988, pp. 3–6, here p. 6.
67. *TBJG, Teil II*, VIII, p. 263 (9 November 1943).
68. *TBJG, Teil II*, IX, p. 569 (23 September 1943); Georg Zachariae, *Mussolini si confessa: rivelazioni del medico tedesco inviato da Hitler al Duce*, Milan, 1948, pp. 9–28; Bosworth, *Mussolini*, pp. 404–6; Giovanni Dolfin, *Con Mussolini nella tragedia: diario del capo della segreteria particulare del Duce 1943–1944*, Milan, 1949, p. 47.
69. Weinberg, *A World at Arms*, pp. 628–31.
70. *OO*, XXXII, p. 274.
71. *VB*, 31 December 1943; for context, see Osti Guerrazzi, *Storia della Repubblica sociale italiana*, p. 139; Klinkhammer, *Zwischen Bündnis und Besatzung*, pp. 334–42.
72. *TBJG, Teil II*, IX, pp. 158–9 (25 January 1944).
73. ASMAE, RSI, b. 31, Anfuso to Mussolini, 9 November 1943.
74. *New York Times*, 9 April 1944; *Hamburger Fremdenblatt*, 1 April 1944.
75. For details, see Hillgruber (ed.), *Staatsmänner und Diplomaten bei Hitler*, II, pp. 345–406.
76. Zachariae, *Mussolini si confessa*, pp. 123–4.
77. For the labourers, see Herbert, *Fremdarbeiter*, pp. 303–4 (p. 304 for quotation); Deakin, *The Brutal Friendship*, pp. 678–81.
78. Deakin, *The Brutal Friendship*, pp. 681–9.
79. Matteini (ed.), *Ordini alla stampa*, p. 341; *Corriere della Sera*, 26 April 1944; for a photograph, see *Corriere della Sera*, 1 May 1944; *VB*, 26 April 1944; see also *Deutsche Allgemeine Zeitung*, 26 April 1944, copy in BAB, R 8034 II/325; for the telegrams, see *OO*, XXXII, pp. 218–19; ASMAE, RSI, b. 31.
80. Deakin, *The Brutal Friendship*, p. 689; Anfuso, *Roma Berlino Salò*, p. 478.
81. Hillgruber (ed.), *Staatsmänner und Diplomaten bei Hitler*, II, pp. 406–14; Deakin, *The Brutal Friendship*, pp. 678–89; for context, see Fioravanzo, *Mussolini e Hitler*, pp. 135–44; Klinkhammer, *Zwischen Bündnis und Besatzung*, pp. 368–91; on the new army, see Adolfo Scalpelli, 'La formazione delle forze armate di Salò attraverso i documenti dello stato magg. Della RSI', *Movimento di liberazione in Italia*, 72 (1963), pp. 19–70; Giampaolo Pansa, *L'esercito di Salò*, Milan, 1970.
82. Hillgruber (ed.), *Staatsmänner und Diplomaten bei Hitler*, II, pp. 424–33; see also ibid., pp. 414–24, for the minutes of the afternoon meeting on 22 April 1944, and ibid., pp. 434–8, for the minutes of the afternoon meeting on 23 April 1944.
83. *Corriere della Sera*, 26 April 1944; *VB*, 26 April 1944; see also *Deutsche Allgemeine Zeitung*, 26 April 1944, copy in BAB, R 8034 II/325.
84. Matteini (ed.), *Ordini alla stampa*, pp. 341–2; *OO*, XXXII, pp. 84–5.
85. PRO, HW 1/2888, Hitler–Mussolini conversations, 3 June 1944; for newspaper reports, see PRO, GFM 36/451; *OO*, XXXII, p. 218.

86. *Corriere della Sera*, 1 May 1944.
87. Klinkhammer, *Zwischen Bündnis und Besatzung*, p. 485; Woller, *Mussolini*, pp. 296–7.
88. ACS, SpD, RSI, c.r., b. 16, sf. 6, appunto per il Duce, 12 May 1944.
89. ASMAE, RSI, b. 31, segreto appunto per il Duce, 10 October 1943.
90. Corrado Di Pompeo, *Più della fame e più dei bombardamenti: diario dell'occupazione di Roma*, Bologna, 2009, pp. 151–2 (4 June 1944).
91. Printed in Natale Verdina, *Riservato a Mussolini: notiziari giornalieri della Guardia nazionale repubblicana novembre 1943/giugno 1944*, Milan, 1974, p. 10.
92. Printed in Benito Mussolini, *A Clara: tutte le lettere a Clara Petacci 1943–1945*, ed. Luisa Montevecchi, Milan, 2011, p. 19.
93. Istituto storico della Resistenza in Toscana, fondo Repubblica sociale italiana, b. 1, fol. 38, Notiziario politico interno, 21 June 1944.
94. For context, see Dianella Gagliani, *Brigate nere: Mussolini e la militarizzazione del Partito fascista repubblicano*, Turin, 1999, pp. 82–3.
95. Maria Ferretti, 'Mémoires divisées: résistance et guerre aux civils en Italie', *Annales. Histoire, sciences sociales*, 60 (2005), 627–51; for an account by a leading historian and partisan, see Federico Chabod, *A History of Italian Fascism*, London, 1963, pp. 101–16.
96. Steffen Prauser, 'Mord in Rom? Der Anschlag in der via Rasella und die deutsche Vergeltung in den Fosse Ardeatine', *VfZ*, 50 (2002), pp. 269–310; Carlo Gentile, *Wehrmacht und Waffen-SS im Partisanenkrieg: Italien 1943–1945*, Paderborn, 2012, pp. 14–15; see also Lutz Klinkhammer, *Stragi naziste in Italia: la guerra contro i civili (1943–44)*, Rome, 1997, p. 21; Schreiber, *Deutsche Kriegsverbrechen in Italien*; for the higher figure, see Schreiber, 'Das Ende des nordafrikanischen Feldzugs', p. 1125; Paolo Pezzino, *Memory and Massacre: Revisiting Sant'Anna di Stazzema*, New York, 2012.
97. Claudio Pavone, *Una guerra civile: saggio sulla moralità nella Resistenza*, Turin, 1991; for a recent appraisal of Pavone, see Guri Schwarz, 'The Moral Conundrums of the Historian: Claudio Pavone's *A Civil War* and its Legacy', *Modern Italy*, 20 (2015), pp. 427–37.
98. Dianella Gagliani, 'Diktat oder Konsens? Die Republik von Salò und das Dritte Reich', in Klinkhammer, Osti Guerrazzi and Schlemmer (eds), *Die 'Achse' im Krieg*, pp. 456–71, here pp. 467–70; Klinkhammer, *Zwischen Bündnis und Besatzung*, p. 485.
99. ACS, SpD, RSI, CR, b. 60, fasc. 628, sf. 1, 'Il Colpo di Stato', p. 54; ibid., sf. 2, 'Immaturità e colpa del popolo italiano'.
100. Mussolini, *A Clara*, pp. 229–30 (2 July 1944); *OO*, XXXIV, pp. 303–444; for the article on Grandi, see 'Uno dei tanti: il conte di Mordano', in *OO*, XXXIV, pp. 399–405, and 'Il dramma della diarchia', ibid., pp. 406–16 (p. 413 for quotation).
101. Chessa and Raggi, *L'ultima lettera*, p. 121; Mussolini, *A Clara*, p. 149 (13 July 1944).
102. *OO*, XXXII, pp. 94–105; for Mussolini's itinerary, see *OO*, XXXV, pp. 438–9.
103. Hillgruber (ed.), *Staatsmänner und Diplomaten bei Hitler*, II, p. 468; Anfuso, *Roma Berlino Salò*, p. 541; for the assassination attempt, see Kershaw, *Hitler, 1936–1945*, pp. 658–84.
104. Mussolini, *A Clara*, pp. 239–40 (22 July 1944).
105. For the dossier, see ACS, SpD, RSI, CR, b. 60, sf. 629.
106. *ADAP*, E, VIII, doc. 128, note by Schmidt, 21 July 1944; Schmidt, *Statist auf diplomatischer Bühne*, p. 582.
107. For the military internees, see 'Bericht der von den Außenministern der Bundesrepublik Deutschland und Republik Italien am 28.3.2009 eingesetzten Deutsch-Italienischen Historikerkommission,' July 2012, p. 134, available at http://www.villavigoni.it/contents/files/Abschlussbericht.pdf, accessed 14 December 2017; Schmidt, *Statist auf diplomatischer Bühne*, pp. 580–3; Anfuso, *Roma Berlino Salò*, pp. 546–7; Gabriele Hammermann, *Zwangsarbeit für den 'Verbündeten': die Arbeits- und Lebensbedingungen der italienischen Militärinternierten in Deutschland 1943–1945*, Tübingen, 2002, pp. 461–73; Schreiber, *Die italienischen Militärinternierten*, pp. 409–43.
108. *New York Times*, 24 July 1944; see also *Corriere della Sera*, 21, 22 & 23 July 1944.
109. Ceccarelli De Grada, *Giornale del tempo di guerra*, p. 270 (20 July 1944).

110. Istituto Storico della Resistenza in Toscana, fondo RSI, b. 1, n. 71, notiziario politico interno, 26 September 1944.
111. Quoted in Kershaw, *The 'Hitler Myth'*, p. 220.
112. Printed in Deakin, *The Brutal Friendship*, pp. 735–6. There is no evidence that the letter was sent.
113. Ibid., p. 742.
114. For the speech, see *OO*, XXXII, pp. 126–39; quoted in Fraddosio, 'The Fallen Hero', p. 115; see also ibid., p. 116; for the speech, see *Corriere della Sera*, 17 December 1944; on context, see Franzinelli, *Il prigioniero di Salò*, pp. 113–32; on the mobilisation of women for the RSI, see Roberta Cairoli, *Dalla parte del nemico: ausiliare, delatrici e spie nella Repubblica sociale italiana (1943–1945)*, Milan, 2013; for their post-war treatment, see Cecilia Nubola, *Fasciste di Salò*, Rome, 2016; for details of the Ardennes offensive, see Weinberg, *A World at Arms*, pp. 765–71.
115. For details, see *OO*, XXIII, pp. 139–42; for press reports, see *Corriere della Sera*, 18 & 19 December 1944; Mussolini, *A Clara*, p. 333; for context, see Deakin, *The Brutal Friendship*, pp. 744–5; Fraddosio, 'The Fallen Hero', p. 117; for the *Giornata delle fede*, see Petra Terhoeven, *Liebespfand fürs Vaterland: Krieg, Geschlecht und faschistische Nation in der italienischen Gold- und Eheringsammlung 1935/36*, Tübingen, 2003; for German reactions, see *TBJG, Teil II*, IX, p. 500 (31 December 1944); ASMAE, RSI, b. 34, sf. 8, Anfuso to Ministero degli affari esteri, 19 December 1944; ASMAE, RSI, b. 31, Anfuso-Mussolini, 4 January 1945.
116. ASMAE, RSI, b. 34, sf. 6, Anfuso to Vittorio Mussolini and Ministero degli affari esteri, 23 November 1944; on the *Volkssturm*, see David K. Yelton, *Hitler's Volkssturm: The Nazi Militia and the Fall of Germany, 1944–1945*, Lawrence, KS, 2002.
117. Schreiber, 'Das Ende des nordafrikanischen Feldzugs', p. 1161; Christian Goeschel, *Suicide in Nazi Germany*, Oxford, 2009, p. 149.
118. Hans Mommsen, 'Die Rückkehr zu den Ursprüngen: Betrachtungen zur inneren Auflösung des Dritten Reiches nach der Niederlage von Stalingrad', in Michael Grüttner, Rüdiger Hachtmann and Heinz-Gerhard Haupt (eds), *Geschichte und Emanzipation: Festschrift für Reinhard Rürup*, Frankfurt am Main, 1999, pp. 418–34.
119. ASMAE, RSI, b. 33, Ministero degli affari esteri, il capo del gabinetto to Anfuso, 16 March 1945; for the translated article and broadcast, see ibid., *Basler Nachrichten*, 21 February 1945; ibid., Foreign Ministry to Italian Embassy Berlin, undated.
120. ASMAE, RSI, b. 33, Mussolini to Hitler, 18 April 1945; *OO*, XLIII, p. 221.
121. For details, see Sergio Luzzatto, *Il corpo del Duce*, Turin, 1998; for the last days of Mussolini, see Bosworth, *Claretta*, pp. 221–31.
122. Kershaw, *Hitler, 1936–1945*, p. 826; Goeschel, *Suicide in Nazi Germany*, pp. 150–5.
123. Weinberg, *A World at Arms*, pp. 823, 827.
124. Klinkhammer, *Zwischen Bündnis und Besatzung*.

Conclusion

1. Costanza Caraffa and Avinoam Shalem, '"Hitler's Carpet": A Tale of One City', *Mitteilungen des Kunsthistorischen Instituts in Florenz*, 55 (2013), pp. 119–43; Focardi, *Il cattivo tedesco*.
2. Benedetto Croce, *Il dissidio spirituale della Germania con l'Europa*, Bari, 1944, p. 21.
3. Focardi, *Il cattivo tedesco*, pp. 77–106, 179–93; see also Michele Battini, *The Missing Italian Nuremberg: Cultural Amnesia and Postwar Politics*, Basingstoke, 2007.
4. Hans Woller, *Die Abrechnung mit dem Faschismus in Italien 1943 bis 1948*, Munich, 1996, esp. pp. 257–307; for Germany, see Konrad H. Jarausch, *After Hitler: Recivilizing Germans, 1945–1995*, Oxford, 2006.
5. For an overview, see Kershaw, *The Nazi Dictatorship*, pp. 40–1.
6. François Genoud (ed.), *The Testament of Adolf Hitler: The Hitler–Bormann Documents February–April 1945*, London, 1961, pp. 69–75; Deakin, *The Brutal Friendship*, p. 800; for the accuracy of the testament, see Kershaw, *Hitler, 1936–1945*, pp. 1024–5.

7. Schreiber, *Deutsche Kriegsverbrechen in Italien*, pp. 16–17.
8. For a stimulating approach, see Lucy Riall, 'The Shallow End of History? The Substance and Future of Political Biography', *Journal of Interdisciplinary History*, 40 (2010), pp. 375–93.
9. For context, see Lucy Riall, *Garibaldi: Invention of a Hero*, New Haven and London, 2007, pp. 390–2; for summits, see Reynolds, *Summits.*

BIBLIOGRAPHY

ARCHIVAL SOURCES

Archivio Storico Capitolino, Rome

Gabinetto del sindaco

Archivio centrale dello Stato, Rome

Agenzia Stefani
Ambasciata tedesca in Roma (1925–1943)
Ministero della cultura popolare
Ministero dell'interno
Presidenza del consiglio dei ministri
Partito nazionale fascista, Situazione politica ed economica delle provincie
Segreteria particolare del Duce
Ufficio del prefetto di palazzo, anni 1871–1946
Ufficio del primo aiutante di campo generale di Sua Maestà il Re e Imperatore

Archivio storico del Comune di Firenze

Gabinetto del podestà

Archivio storico diplomatico del Ministero degli affari esteri, Rome

Gabinetto del Ministro, 1923–1943
Ministero della cultura popolare
Rappresentanza italiana a Berlino, 1867–1943
Repubblica Sociale Italiana
Serie affari politici, 1931–1945, Germania

Bundesarchiv, Berlin-Lichterfelde

NS 19 Persönlicher Stab Reichsführer SS

NS 22 Reichsorganisationsleiter der NSDAP
R 2 Reichsfinanzministerium
R 43 II Reichskanzlei
R 55 Reichsministerium für Volksaufklärung und Propaganda
R 901 Auswärtiges Amt
R 8034 II Reichslandbund-Pressearchiv

Bundesarchiv, Koblenz

N 1235 Nachlaß Giuseppe Renzetti

Bundesarchiv-Militärarchiv, Freiburg

RW 4 Wehrmachtführungsstab

Institut für Zeitgeschichte, Munich

Istituto storico della Resistenza in Toscana

Fondo Repubblica sociale italiana

The National Archives, Public Record Office, Kew

GFM German Foreign Ministry and Italian documents captured by the British
HW Records created or inherited by Government Communications Headquarters (GCHQ)

Politisches Archiv des Auswärtigen Amts, Berlin

Botschaft Rom (Quirinal)
Botschaft Rom (Quirinal) Geheimakten
Büro des Staatssekretärs
Nachlaß Mackensen
Personalakten
Politische Abteilung

Wiener Library, London

NSDAP Hauptarchiv

NEWSPAPERS AND MAGAZINES

Basler Nachrichten
Berlin Rom Tokio
Berliner Börsenzeitung
Berliner Morgenpost
Berliner Tageblatt
Capitolium
La Civiltà Cattolica
Civiltà Fascista
Collier's
Corriere della Sera
Corriere Italiano
Daily Herald
Daily Telegraph

Der Deutsche
Deutsche Allgemeine Zeitung
L'Epoca
Gazzetta del Popolo
Gerarchia
Hamburger Fremdenblatt
Illustrierter Beobachter
Italien-Beobachter
Il Lavoro fascista
Manchester Guardian
Il Messaggero
La Nazione
New York Herald Tribune
New York Times
Observer
L'Osservatore Romano
Il Popolo d'Italia
Il Regime Fascista
Rheinisch-Westfälische Zeitung
Das Schwarze Korps
La Svastica
Il Tevere
The Times
Völkischer Beobachter
Vossische Zeitung
Wall Street Journal

OFFICIAL PUBLICATIONS

Akten zur Deutschen Auswärtigen Politik, Serie C: 1933–1937. Das Dritte Reich: die ersten Jahre, 6 vols, Göttingen, 1971–81.
Akten zur Deutschen Auswärtigen Politik, Serie D: 1937–1945, 13 vols, Baden-Baden, 1950–70.
Akten zur Deutschen Auswärtigen Politik, Serie E: 1941–1945, 8 vols, Göttingen, 1969–79.
Ausgewählte Reden des Führers und seiner Mitarbeiter 1937: Rede des italienischen Regierungschefs auf dem Maifeld in Berlin – Sonderausgabe für die Wehrmacht, Munich, 1937.
Bozzetti di addobbo dell'urbe per la visita del Führer / Die Ausschmückungsentwürfe der Stadt Roms für den Besuch des Führers, Rome, 1938.
I documenti diplomatici italiani, 7. serie: 1922–1935, ed. Ministero degli affari esteri, 16 vols, Rome, 1953–90.
I documenti diplomatici italiani, 8. serie: 1935–1939, ed. Ministero degli affari esteri, 13 vols, Rome, 1952–2006.
I documenti diplomatici italiani, 9. serie: 1939–1943, ed. Ministero degli affari esteri, 10 vols, Rome, 1954–90.
I documenti diplomatici italiani, 10. serie: 1943–1948, ed. Ministero degli affari esteri, 7 vols, Rome, 1992–2000.
Documents diplomatiques français 1932–1939, 2e série: 1936–1939. 15 vols, Paris, 1963–81.
Documents on British Foreign Policy, Second Series, 21 vols, London, 1965–84.
Documents on British Foreign Policy, Third Series, 10 vols, London, 1949–72.
Documents on German Foreign Policy, Series D, 13 vols, London, 1949–64.
Militärgeschichtliches Forschungsamt (ed.), *Das Deutsche Reich und der Zweite Weltkrieg*, 10 vols, Stuttgart/Munich, 1979–2008.
Pastorelli, Pietro (ed.), *Le carte del Gabinetto del Ministro e della Segreteria generale dal 1923 al 1943*, Rome, 1999.
Il patto d'acciaio (Italia e Germania), ed. Ministero della cultura popolare, Rome, 1939.
R. Ministero degli Affari Esteri Gabinetto, *Reise des Führers in Italien / Viaggio del Führer in Italia*, Rome, 1938.

Royal Institute of International Affairs (ed.), *Review of the Foreign Press 1939–1945, Series A*, 9 vols, Munich, 1980.
Stato Maggiore dell'Esercito Ufficio Storico (ed.), *Le operazioni delle unità italiane al fronte russo (1941–1943)*, 2nd edn, Rome, 1993.
Trial of the Major War Criminals before the International Military Tribunal, 42 vols, Nuremberg, 1948.

ELECTRONIC SOURCES

'Bericht der von den Außenministern der Bundesrepublik Deutschland und Republik Italien am 28.3.2009 eingesetzten Deutsch-Italienischen Historikerkommission', July 2012, available at http://www.villavigoni.it/contents/files/Abschlussbericht.pdf, accessed 14 December 2017.
'Die Rede des Reichsvizekanzlers von Papen am 17. Juni 1934', available at http://www.bundesarchiv.de/oeffentlichkeitsarbeit/bilder_dokumente/00634/index.html.de, accessed 31 August 2017.
Foreign Relations of the United States, available at http://digicoll.library.wisc.edu/cgi-bin/FRUS/FRUS-idx?type=browse&scope=FRUS.FRUS1, accessed 1 September 2017.

UNPUBLISHED SOURCES

Scholz, Beate, 'Italienischer Faschismus als "Exportartikel": ideologische und organisatorische Ansätze zur Verbreitung des Faschismus im Ausland', PhD dissertation, Universität Trier, 2001.

PUBLISHED SOURCES

Afflerbach, Holger, *Der Dreibund: europäische Großmacht- und Allianzpolitik vor dem Ersten Weltkrieg*, Vienna, 2002.
Aga Rossi, Elena, *Cefalonia: la resistenza, l'eccidio, il mito*, Bologna, 2016.
Agarossi, Elena, *A Nation Collapses: The Italian Surrender of September 1943*, Cambridge, 2000.
Albanese, Giulia, *Dittature mediterranee: sovversioni fasciste e colpi di Stato in Italia, Spagna e Portogallo*, Rome, 2016.
Albrecht, Andrea, Lutz Danneberg and Simone De Angelis (eds), *Die akademische 'Achse Berlin-Rom'? Der wissenschaftlich-kulturelle Austausch zwischen Italien und Deutschland 1920 bis 1945*, Berlin, 2017.
Alexander, Jeffrey C., 'Cultural Pragmatics: Social Performance between Ritual and Strategy', in Jeffrey C. Alexander, Bernhard Giesen and Jason L. Mast (eds), *Social Performance: Symbolic Action, Cultural Pragmatics, and Ritual*, Cambridge, 2006, pp. 29–90.
Alfieri, Dino, *Dictators Face to Face*, London, 1954.
Allert, Tilman, *Der deutsche Gruß: Geschichte einer unheilvollen Geste*, Frankfurt am Main, 2005.
André, Gianluca, 'La politica estera del governo fascista durante la seconda guerra mondiale', in Renzo De Felice (ed.), *L'Italia fra tedeschi e alleati: la politica estera fascista e la seconda guerra mondiale*, Bologna, 1973, pp. 115–26.
Anfuso, Filippo, *Da Palazzo Venezia al Lago di Garda (1936–1945)*, Bologna, 1957.
Anfuso, Filippo, *Roma Berlino Salò*, Milan, 1950.
Aquarone, Alberto, *L'organizzazione dello Stato totalitario*, Turin, 1965.
Aquarone, Alberto, 'Public Opinion in Italy before the Outbreak of World War II', in Roland Sarti (ed.), *The Ax Within: Italian Fascism in Action*, New York, 1974, pp. 212–20.
Archivio Storico (ed.), *Firenze 9 Maggio 1938*, Florence, 2012.
Asserate, Asfa-Wossen and Aram Mattioli (eds), *Der erste faschistische Vernichtungskrieg: die italienische Aggression gegen Äthiopien*, Cologne, 2006.
Attanasio, Sandro, *Sicilia senza Italia: luglio–agosto 1943*, Milan, 1976.
Baldoli, Claudia, 'Spring 1943: The Fiat Strikes and the Collapse of the Italian Home Front', *History Workshop Journal*, 72 (2011), pp. 181–9.

Baldoli, Claudia and Marco Fincardi, 'Italian Society under Anglo-American Bombs: Propaganda, Experience, and Legend, 1940–1945', *Historical Journal*, 52 (2009), pp. 1017–38.

Barros, James, *The Corfu Incident of 1923: Mussolini and the League of Nations*, Princeton, 1965.

Bartikowski, Kilian, *Der italienische Antisemitismus im Urteil des Nationalsozialismus 1933–1943*, Berlin, 2013.

Bartikowski, Kilian and Giorgio Fabre, 'Donna bianca e uomo nero (con una variante): il razzismo anti-nero nei colloqui tra Mussolini e Bülow-Schwante', *Quaderni di storia*, 70 (2009), pp. 181–218.

Bartov, Omer, *The Eastern Front, 1941–45: German Troops and the Barbarisation of Warfare*, 2nd edn, Basingstoke, 2001.

Bastianini, Giuseppe, *Volevo fermare Mussolini: memorie di un diplomatico fascista*, Milan, 2005.

Battini, Michele, *The Missing Italian Nuremberg: Cultural Amnesia and Postwar Politics*, Basingstoke, 2007.

Bauerkämper, Arnd, 'Die Inszenierung transnationaler faschistischer Politik: der Staatsbesuch Hitlers in Italien im Mai 1938', in Stefan Voigt (ed.), *Ideengeschichte als politische Aufklärung: Festschrift für Wolfgang Wippermann zum 65. Geburtstag*, Berlin, 2010, pp. 129–53.

Baum, Walter and Eberhard Weichold, *Der Krieg der 'Achsenmächte' im Mittelmeer-Raum: die 'Strategie' der Diktatoren*, Zurich, 1973.

Baxa, Paul, 'Capturing the Fascist Moment: Hitler's Visit to Italy in 1938 and the Radicalization of Fascist Italy', *JCH*, 42 (2007), pp. 227–43.

Baxa, Paul, '"Il nostro Duce": Mussolini's Visit to Trieste in 1938 and the Workings of the Cult of the Duce', *Modern Italy*, 18 (2013), pp. 117–28.

Beevor, Antony, *Crete: The Battle and the Resistance*, London, 1991.

Behnken, Klaus (ed.), *Deutschland-Berichte der Sopade*, 7 vols, Frankfurt am Main, 1980.

Below, Nicolaus von, *Als Hitlers Adjutant 1937–45*, Mainz, 1980.

Ben-Ghiat, Ruth, *Fascist Modernities: Italy, 1922–1945*, Berkeley, 2001.

Benz, Wolfgang, 'Die Inszenierung der Akklamation: Mussolini in Berlin 1937', in Michael Grüttner, Rüdiger Hachtmann and Heinz-Gerhard Haupt (eds), *Geschichte und Emanzipation: Festschrift für Reinhard Rürup*, Frankfurt am Main, 1999, pp. 401–17.

Berezin, Mabel, *Making the Fascist Self: The Political Culture of Interwar Italy*, Ithaca, NY, 1997.

Berger, Sara, 'I persecutori del 16 ottobre 1943', in Martin Baumeister, Amedeo Osti Guerrazzi and Claudio Procaccia (eds), *16 ottobre 1943: la deportazione degli ebrei romani tra storia e memoria*, Rome, 2016, pp. 21–40.

Berger Waldenegg, Georg Christoph, 'Hitler, Göring, Mussolini und der "Anschluß" Österreichs an das Deutsche Reich', *VfZ*, 51 (2003), pp. 147–82.

Bermani, Cesare, 'Odysse in Deutschland: die alltägliche Erfahrung der italienischen "Fremdarbeiter" im "Dritten Reich"', in Cesare Bermani, Sergio Bologna and Brunello Mantelli (eds), *Proletarier der 'Achse': Sozialgeschichte der italienischen Fremdarbeit in NS-Deutschland 1937–1943*, Berlin, 1997, pp. 37–252.

Bernasconi, Paola, 'A Fairy Tale Dictator: Children's Letters to the Duce', *Modern Italy*, 18 (2013), pp. 129–40.

Bernhard, Patrick, 'Behind the Battle Lines: Italian Atrocities and the Persecution of Arabs, Berbers, and Jews in North Africa during World War II', *Holocaust and Genocide Studies*, 26 (2012), pp. 425–46.

Bernhard, Patrick, 'Colonial Crossovers: Nazi Germany and its Entanglement with Other Empires', *Journal of Global History*, 12 (2017), pp. 206–27.

Bernhard, Patrick, 'Italien auf dem Teller: zur Geschichte der italienischen Küche und Gastronomie in Deutschland 1900–2000', in Gustavo Corni and Christof Dipper (eds), *Italiener in Deutschland im 19. und 20. Jahrhundert: Kontakte, Wahrnehmungen, Einflüsse*, Berlin, 2012, pp. 217–36.

Bernhard, Patrick, 'Konzertierte Gegnerbekämpfung im Achsenbündnis: die Polizei im Dritten Reich und im faschistischen Italien 1933 bis 1943', *VfZ*, 59 (2011), pp. 229–62.

Bernhart, Toni, 'Benito Mussolini als Schriftsteller und seine Übersetzungen ins Deutsche', in Albrecht, Danneberg and De Angelis (eds), *Die akademische 'Achse Berlin-Rom?'*, pp. 345–99.

Berti Arnoaldi, Ugo, 'Ansaldo, Giovanni', in Victoria de Grazia and Sergio Luzzatto (eds), *Dizionario del fascismo*, Turin, 2002, I, pp. 57–9.
Bertinaria, Pier Luigi, 'Hitler Mussolini: lo stato dell'alleanza', in R. H. Rainero and A. Biagini (eds), *L'Italia in guerra*, Gaeta, 1992, II, pp. 57–84.
Bessel, Richard, 'The Nazi Capture of Power', *JCH*, 39 (2004), pp. 169–88.
Biagini, Antonello and Fernando Frattolillo (eds), *Diario storico del comando supremo: raccolta di documenti della seconda guerra mondiale*, 9 vols, Rome, 1986–2002.
Bianchi Bandinelli, Ranuccio, *Diario di un borghese*, new edn, Rome, 1996.
Boberach, Heinz (ed.), *Meldungen aus dem Reich: die geheimen Lageberichte des Sicherheitsdienstes der SS 1938–1945*, 17 vols, Herrsching, 1984.
Bocca, Giorgio, *La repubblica di Mussolini*, Milan, 1995.
Bohrmann, Hans (ed.), *NS-Presseanweisungen der Vorkriegszeit*, 7 vols, Munich, 1984–2001.
Bollati, General Ambrogio, 'Le Forze Armate dell'Italia fascista', *Gerarchia*, XVII/10 (1939), pp. 661–72.
Bonsaver, Guido, *Censorship and Literature in Fascist Italy*, Toronto, 2007.
Bosworth, R.J.B., *Claretta: Mussolini's Last Lover*, New Haven, 2017.
Bosworth, R.J.B., *The Italian Dictatorship: Problems and Perspectives in the Interpretation of Mussolini and Fascism*, London, 1998.
Bosworth, R.J.B., 'Italian Foreign Policy and its Historiography', in R.J.B. Bosworth and Gino Rizzo (eds), *Altro Polo: Intellectuals and their Ideas in Contemporary Italy*, Sydney, 1983, pp. 65–86.
Bosworth, R.J.B., *Mussolini*, London, 2002.
Bosworth, R.J.B., *Mussolini's Italy: Life under the Dictatorship*, London, 2006.
Bosworth, R.J.B., 'War, Totalitarianism and Deep Belief in Fascist Italy, 1935–43', *European History Quarterly*, 34 (2004), pp. 475–505.
Bosworth, R.J.B. and Sergio Romano (eds), *La politica estera italiana, 1860–1985*, Bologna, 1991.
Bottai, Giuseppe, *Diario 1935–1944*, Milan, 2001.
Braddick, Michael J. (ed.), 'The Politics of Gesture: Historical Perspectives', *Past & Present*, 203/4 (2009), pp. 9–35.
Brechtken, Magnus, *'Madagaskar für die Juden': antisemitische Idee und politische Praxis 1885–1945*, Munich, 1997.
Breitsprecher, Nina, 'Die Ankunft des Anderen im interepochalen Vergleich: Heinrich III. von Frankreich und Adolf Hitler in Venedig', in Susann Baller (ed.), *Die Ankunft des Anderen: Repräsentationen sozialer und politischer Ordnungen in Empfangszeremonien*, Frankfurt am Main, 2008, pp. 82–105.
Breuer, Stefan, 'Moeller van den Bruck und Italien', *Archiv für Kulturgeschichte*, 84 (2002), pp. 413–38.
Brice, Catherine, 'Riti della Corona, riti del fascio', in Emilio Gentile (ed.), *Modernità italiana: il fascismo italiano*, Rome, 2008, pp. 171–90.
Brown, Archie, *The Myth of the Strong Leader: Political Leadership in the Modern Age*, London, 2014.
Browning, Christopher R., *The Origins of the Final Solution: The Evolution of Nazi Jewish Policy, September 1939–March 1942*, Lincoln, NE, 2004.
Bullock, Alan, *Hitler and Stalin: Parallel Lives*, London, 1991.
Burgwyn, H. James, *Italian Foreign Policy in the Interwar Period, 1918–1940*, Westport, CT, 1997.
Burgwyn, H. James, *Mussolini Warlord: Failed Dreams of Empire 1940–43*, New York, 2012.
Burkman, Thomas W., *Japan and the League of Nations: Empire and World Order, 1914–1938*, Honolulu, 2008.
Buzzegoli, Thomas, *La polemica antiborghese nel fascismo (1937–1939)*, Rome, 2007.
Caine, Barbara (ed.), *Friendship: A History*, London, 2009.
Cairoli, Roberta, *Dalla parte del nemico: ausiliare, delatrici e spie nella Repubblica sociale italiana (1943–1945)*, Milan, 2013.
Cajani, Luigi and Brunello Mantelli, 'In Deutschland arbeiten: die Italiener von der "Achse" bis zur Europäischen Gemeinschaft', *Archiv für Sozialgeschichte*, 32 (1992), pp. 231–46.

Calamandrei, Piero, *Diario 1939–1945*, ed. Giorgi Agosti, 2 vols, Florence, 1982.
Campbell, Ian, *The Addis Ababa Massacre: Italy's National Shame*, London, 2017.
Caraffa, Costanza and Avinoam Shalem, '"Hitler's Carpet": A Tale of One City', *Mitteilungen des Kunsthistorischen Instituts in Florenz*, 55 (2013), pp. 119–43.
Carazzolo, Maria, *Più forte della paura: diario di guerra e dopoguerra (1938–1947)*, Caselle di Sommacampagna, 2007.
Casmirri, Silvana, 'Il viaggio di Mussolini in Germania nel marzo del '22', *Storia e politica*, 12 (1973), pp. 86–112.
Cassels, Alan, 'Deux Empires face à face: la chimère d'un rapprochement Anglo-Italien (1936–1940)', *Guerres mondiales et conflits contemporains*, 161 (1991), pp. 67–96.
Cassels, Alan, 'Mussolini and German Nationalism, 1922–25', *Journal of Modern History*, 35 (1963), pp. 137–57.
Ceadel, Michael, 'The First British Referendum: The Peace Ballot, 1934–5', *English Historical Review*, 95 (1980), pp. 810–39.
Ceccarelli De Grada, Magda, *Giornale del tempo di guerra: 12 giugno 1940–7 maggio 1945*, Bologna, 2011.
Cecconi, Aldo, 'Il Gran Consiglio del fascismo', *Passato e presente*, 19 (1989), pp. 53–81.
Cerruti, Elisabetta, *Ambassador's Wife*, New York, 1953.
Ceva, Lucio, *La condotta italiana della guerra: Cavallero e il Comando supremo 1941/1942*, Milan, 1975, pp. 144–51.
Chabod, Federico, *A History of Italian Fascism*, London, 1963.
Chadwick, Owen, 'Bastianini and the Weakening of the Fascist Will to Fight the Second World War', in T.C.W. Blanning and David Cannadine (eds), *History and Biography: Essays in Honour of Derek Beales*, Cambridge, 1996, pp. 243–65.
Chadwick, Owen, *Britain and the Vatican during the Second World War*, Cambridge, 1986.
Chambrun, Charles de, *Traditions et souvenirs*, Paris, 1952.
Chessa, Pasquale and Barbara Raggi, *L'ultima lettera di Benito: Mussolini e Petacci – amore e politica a Salò, 1943–45*, Milan, 2010.
Churchill, Winston, 'Dictators on Dynamite', *Collier's*, 3 September 1938.
Ciano, Galeazzo, *Diario 1937–1943*, ed. Renzo De Felice, Milan, 1980.
Clark, Christopher, *Sleepwalkers: How Europe Went to War in 1914*, London, 2013.
Clavin, Patricia, *Securing the World Economy: The Reinvention of the League of Nations, 1920–1946*, Oxford, 2013.
Clemens, Detlev, 'The "Bavarian Mussolini" and his "Beerhall Putsch": British Images of Adolf Hitler, 1920–24', *English Historical Review*, 114 (1999), pp. 64–84.
Cliadakis, Harry, 'Neutrality and War in Italian Policy 1939–40', *JCH*, 9 (1974), pp. 171–90.
Colarizi, Simona, *L'Italia antifascista dal 1922 al 1940*, 2 vols, Rome, 1976.
Colarizi, Simona, *L'opinione degli italiani sotto il regime 1929–1943*, 2nd edn, Rome, 2009.
Collotti, Enzo, *L'amministrazione tedesca dell'Italia occupata 1943–1945*, Milan, 1963.
Collotti, Enzo, *Fascismo, fascismi*, Milan, 1994.
Colombardo, Enrico, *La monarchia fascista 1922–1940*, Bologna, 2010.
Conze, Eckart, Norbert Frei, Peter Hayes and Moshe Zimmermann (eds), *Das Amt und die Vergangenheit: Deutsche Diplomaten im Dritten Reich und in der Bundesrepublik*, Munich, 2010.
Corner, Paul, 'Fascist Italy in the 1930s: Popular Opinion in the Provinces', in Paul Corner (ed.), *Popular Opinion in Totalitarian Regimes: Fascism, Nazism, Communism*, pp. 122–48.
Corner, Paul, *The Fascist Party and Popular Opinion in Mussolini's Italy*, Oxford, 2012.
Corner, Paul, 'Italian Fascism: Whatever Happened to Dictatorship?', *Journal of Modern History*, 74 (2002), pp. 325–51.
Corner, Paul (ed.), *Popular Opinion in Totalitarian Regimes: Fascism, Nazism, Communism*, Oxford, 2009.
Corvaja, Santi, *Mussolini nella tana del lupo*, Milan, 1983.
Coverdale, John F., *Italian Intervention in the Spanish Civil War*, Princeton, 1975.
Cremonini, Carlo Alberto, 'La Francia contro l'Italia (1849–1939)', *Gerarchia*, XVII/3, (1939), pp. 181–5.
Creveld, Martin van, '25 October 1940: A Historical Puzzle', *JCH*, 6 (1971), pp. 87–96.

Croce, Benedetto, *Il dissidio spirituale della Germania con l'Europa*, Bari, 1944.
Crum, Roger J., 'Shaping the Fascist "New Man": Donatello's St George and Mussolini's Appropriated Renaissance of the Italian Nation', in Claudia Lazzaro and Roger J. Crum (eds), *Donatello among the Blackshirts: History and Modernity in the Visual Culture of Fascist Italy*, Ithaca, NY, 2005, pp. 133–44.
Cuzzi, Marco, 'I bombardamenti delle città italiane e l'UNPA', in Rainero and Biagini (eds), *L'Italia in guerra*, II, pp. 173–84.
Cuzzi, Marco, *L'internazionale delle camicie nere: i CAUR, Comitati d'azione per l'universalità di Roma*, 1933–1939, Milan, 2005.
CV, 'Contro la Russia sovietica', *Almanacco fascista del Popolo d'Italia*, 21 (1942), pp. 109–60.
De Donno, Fabrizio, 'La Razza Ario Mediterranea: Ideas of Race and Citizenship in Colonial and Fascist Italy', *Interventions: International Journal of Postcolonial Studies*, 8 (2006), pp. 394–412.
De Felice, Renzo, 'Alle origini del Patto d'acciaio: l'incontro e gli accordi fra Bocchini e Himmler del marzo–aprile 1936', *La cultura*, 1 (1963), pp. 524–38.
De Felice, Renzo, *Intervista sul fascismo*, ed. Michael A. Ledeen, Bari, 1997.
De Felice, Renzo, *Mussolini*, 8 vols, Turin, 1965–97.
Mussolini il Duce. I. Gli anni del consenso, 1929–1936, 1974.
Mussolini il Duce. II. Lo Stato totalitario, 1936–1940, 1981.
Mussolini l'alleato, 2 vols, 1990–6.
De Felice, Renzo, *Mussolini e Hitler. I rapporti segreti, 1922–1933, con documenti inediti*, Rome, 2013.
De Felice, Renzo, 'Mussolinis Motive für seine Rückkehr in die Politik und die Übernahme der Führung der RSI (September 1943)', in Rudolf Lill (ed.), *Deutschland-Italien 1943–1945: Aspekte einer Entzweiung*, Tübingen, 1992, pp. 38–50.
De Felice, Renzo, *Rosso e nero*, Milan, 1996.
De Felice, Renzo, *Storia degli ebrei italiani sotto il fascismo*, Turin, 1993.
De Grand, Alexander, 'Curzio Malaparte: The Illusion of the Fascist Revolution', *JCH*, 7 (1972), pp. 73–89.
de Grazia, Victoria, *How Fascism Ruled Women: Italy, 1922–1945*, Berkeley, 1992.
Deakin, F.W., *The Brutal Friendship: Mussolini, Hitler and the Fall of Italian Fascism*, London, 1962.
Del Boca, Angelo, *La guerra di Abissinia*, 1935–1941, Milan, 1965.
Del Boca, Angelo, *Italiani, brava gente? Un mito duro a morire*, Vicenza, 2005.
Derix, Simone, *Bebilderte Politik: Staatsbesuche in der Bundesrepublik Deutschland 1949–1990*, Göttingen, 2009.
Descharmes, Bernadette, Eric Anton Heuser, Caroline Krüger and Thomas Loy (eds), *Varieties of Friendship: Interdisciplinary Perspectives on Social Relationships*, Göttingen, 2011.
Di Pompeo, Corrado, *Più della fame e più dei bombardamenti: diario dell'occupazione di Roma*, Bologna, 2009.
Diel, Louise, *Mussolinis neues Geschlecht: die junge Generation in Italien – unter Mitarbeit von Mussolini*, Dresden, 1934.
Diggins, John P., *Mussolini and Fascism: The View from America*, Princeton, 1972.
Dillon, Christopher, '"Tolerance Means Weakness": The Dachau Concentration Camp SS, Militarism and Masculinity', *Historical Research*, 86 (2013), pp. 373–89.
Dobler, Ralph-Miklas, *Bilder der Achse: Hitlers Empfang in Italien 1938 und die mediale Inszenierung des Staatsbesuches in Fotobüchern*, Munich, 2015.
Dobry, Michel, 'La thèse immunitaire face aux fascismes: pour une critique de la logique classificatoire,' in Michel Dobry (ed.), *Le mythe d'allergie française du fascisme*, Paris, 2003, pp. 17–67.
Dogliani, Patrizia, 'Das faschistische Italien und das Münchner Abkommen', in Jürgen Zarusky and Martin Zückert (eds), *Das Münchener Abkommen in europäischer Perspektive*, Munich, 2013, pp. 53–68.
Dolfin, Giovanni, *Con Mussolini nella tragedia: diario del capo della segreteria particulare del Duce 1943–1944*, Milan, 1949.
Dollmann, Eugen, *The Interpreter: Memoirs of Doktor Eugen Dollmann*, London, 1967.

Domarus, Max, *Hitler: Reden und Proklamationen*, 2 vols, Munich, 1965.
Domarus, Max, *Mussolini und Hitler: zwei Wege, gleiches Ende*, Würzburg, 1977.
Il Duce in Germania, with preface by Gherardo Casini, Milan, 1937.
Duggan, Christopher, *Fascist Voices: An Intimate History of Mussolini's Italy*, London, 2012.
Duggan, Christopher, *The Force of Destiny: A History of Italy since 1796*, London, 2007.
Duggan, Christopher, *Francesco Crispi, 1818–1901: From Nation to Nationalism*, Oxford, 2002.
Duggan, Christopher, 'The Internalisation of the Cult of the Duce: The Evidence of Diaries and Letters', in Stephen Gundle, Christoper Duggan and Giuliana Pieri (eds), *The Cult of the Duce: Mussolini and the Italians*, Manchester, 2013, pp. 129–43.
Dülffer, Jost, 'The Tripartite Pact of 27 September 1940: Fascist Alliance or Propaganda Trick?', *Australian Journal of Politics and History*, 32 (1986), pp. 228–37.
Eatwell, Roger, 'On Defining the "Fascist Minimum": The Centrality of Ideology', *Journal of Political Ideologies*, 1 (1996), pp. 303–19.
Ebermayer, Erich, *'. . . und morgen die ganze Welt': Erinnerungen an Deutschlands dunkle Zeit*, Bayreuth, 1966.
Ebner, Michael R., *Ordinary Violence in Mussolini's Italy*, Cambridge, 2011.
Esch, Arnold and Jens Petersen (eds), *Deutsches Ottocento: die deutsche Wahrnehmung Italiens im Risorgimento*, Tübingen, 2000.
Esposito, Fernando, *Mythische Moderne: Aviatik, Faschismus und die Sehnsucht nach Ordnung in Deutschland und Italien*, Munich, 2011.
Evans, Richard J., 'Coercion and Consent in Nazi Germany', *Proceedings of the British Academy*, 151 (2007), pp. 53–81.
Evans, Richard J., *The Coming of the Third Reich*, London, 2003.
Evans, Richard J., 'The German Foreign Office and the Nazi Past', *Neue Politische Literatur*, 56 (2011), pp. 165–83.
Evans, Richard J., *The Third Reich at War*, London, 2008.
Evans, Richard J., *The Third Reich in Power*, New York, 2005.
Evans, Richard J., 'Who Remembers the Poles?', *London Review of Books*, 32/21 (2010), pp. 21–2.
Fabre, Giorgio, *Hitler's Contract: How Mussolini Became Hitler's Publisher*, New York, 2006.
Fabre, Giorgio, 'Mussolini, Claretta e la questione della razza, 1937–38', *Annali della Fondazione Ugo La Malfa*, 24 (2009), pp. 347–70.
Falanga, Gianluca, *Mussolinis Vorposten in Hitlers Reich: Italiens Politik in Berlin 1933–1945*, Berlin, 2008.
Falasca-Zamponi, Simonetta, *Fascist Spectacle: The Aesthetics of Power in Mussolini's Italy*, Berkeley, 1997.
Famea, Renato, 'Discorso ai francofili: Italia e Francia dal 1797 ad oggi', *Gerarchia*, XVII/8 (1939), pp. 519–27.
Fattorini, Emma, *Hitler, Mussolini, and the Vatican: Pope Pius XI and the Speech that Was Never Made*, Cambridge, 2011.
Favagrossa, Carlo, *Perché perdemmo la guerra: Mussolini e la produzione bellica*, Milan, 1946.
Ferretti, Maria, 'Mémoires divisées: résistance et guerre aux civils en Italie', *Annales. Histoire, sciences sociales*, 60 (2005), pp. 627–51.
Ferris, Kate, *Everyday Life in Fascist Venice, 1929–1940*, Basingstoke, 2012.
Fioravanzo, Monica, 'Die Europakonzeption von Faschismus und Nationalsozialismus (1939–1943)', *VfZ*, 58 (2010), pp. 509–41.
Fioravanzo, Monica, *Mussolini e Hitler: la Repubblica sociale sotto il Terzo Reich*, Rome, 2009.
Focardi, Filippo, '"Bravo italiano" e "cattivo tedesco": riflessioni sulla genesi di due immagini incrociate', *Storia e Memoria*, 5/1 (1996), pp. 55–83.
Focardi, Filippo, *Il cattivo tedesco e il bravo italiano: la rimozione delle colpe della seconda guerra mondiale*, Bari, 2013.
Focardi, Filippo, 'Italy as Occupier in the Balkans: Remembrance and War Crimes after 1945', in Jörg Echternkamp and Stefan Martens (eds), *Experience and Memory: The Second World War in Europe*, New York, 2010.

Focardi, Filippo, 'Journalisten und Korrespondenten der italienischen Presse in Deutschland', in Gustavo Corni and Christof Dipper (eds), *Italiener in Deutschland im 19. und 20. Jahrhundert: Kontakte, Wahrnehmungen, Einflüsse*, Berlin, 2012, pp. 53–78.

Foppiani, Oreste, 'La "Croix-Rouge de Mussolini" et les internés militaires italiens (1943–1945)', *Relations internationales*, 142 (2010), pp. 23–36.

Förster, Jürgen, 'Hitlers Entscheidung für den Krieg gegen die Sowjetunion', in *DRZW*, IV, pp. 3–97.

Förster, Jürgen, *Stalingrad: Risse im Bündnis 1942/43*, Freiburg, 1975.

Förster, Jürgen, 'Das Unternehmen "Barbarossa" als Eroberungs- und Vernichtungskrieg', in *DRZW*, IV, pp. 413–47.

Förster, Jürgen, 'Die Wehrmacht und die Probleme der Koalitionskriegsführung', in Lutz Klinkhammer, Amedeo Osti Guerrazzi and Thomas Schlemmer (eds), *Die 'Achse' im Krieg: Politik, Ideologie und Kriegführung 1939–1945*, Paderborn, 2010, pp. 108–21.

Fraddosio, Maria, 'The Fallen Hero: The Myth of Mussolini and Fascist Women in the Italian Social Republic (1943–5)', *JCH*, 31 (1996), pp. 99–124.

François-Poncet, André, *Au Palais Farnèse: souvenirs d'une ambassade à Rome*, Paris, 1961.

François-Poncet, André, *The Fateful Years: Memoirs of a French Ambassador in Berlin, 1931–1938*, London, 1949.

Frank, Hans, *Im Angesicht des Galgens: Deutung Hitlers und seiner Zeit auf Grund eigener Erlebnisse und Erkenntnisse, geschrieben im Nürnberger Justizgefängnis*, Neuhaus bei Schliersee, Bavaria, 1955.

Franzinelli, Mimmo, *Il prigioniero di Salò: Mussolini e la tragedia italiana del 1943–1945*, Milan, 2012.

Franzinelli, Mimmo, *I tentacoli dell'Ovra: agenti, collaboratori e vittime della polizia politica fascista*, Turin, 1999.

Frieser, Karl-Heinz, 'Die Schlacht im Kursker Bogen', in *DRZW*, VIII, pp. 83–208.

Fröhlich, Elke (ed.), *Die Tagebücher von Joseph Goebbels, Teil I: Aufzeichungen 1923–1941*, 9 vols, Munich, 1998–2006.

Fröhlich, Elke (ed.), *Die Tagebücher von Joseph Goebbels, Teil II: Diktate 1941–1945*, 15 vols, Munich, 1993–6.

Funke, Manfred, 'Die deutsch-italienischen Beziehungen: Antibolschewismus und außenpolitische Interessenkonkurrenz als Strukturprinzip der "Achse"', in Manfred Funke (ed.), *Hitler, Deutschland und die Mächte*, Kronberg, 1978, pp. 823–46.

Gagliani, Dianella, *Brigate nere: Mussolini e la militarizzazione del Partito fascista repubblicano*, Turin, 1999.

Gagliani, Dianella, 'Diktat oder Konsens? Die Republik von Salò und das Dritte Reich', in Klinkhammer, Osti Guerrazzi and Schlemmer (eds), *Die 'Achse' im Krieg*, pp. 456–71.

Galli Della Loggia, Ernesto, *La morte della patria*, 4th edn, Rome/Bari, 2008.

Gayda, Virginio, 'Duce und Führer', *Europäische Revue*, 13 (1937), pp. 771–7.

Genoud, François (ed.), *The Testament of Adolf Hitler: The Hitler–Bormann Documents February–April 1945*, London 1961.

Gentile, Carlo, *Wehrmacht und Waffen-SS im Partisanenkrieg: Italien 1943–1945*, Paderborn, 2012.

Gentile, Emilio, *The Sacralization of Politics in Fascist Italy*, Cambridge, MA, 1996.

Gerwarth, Robert, 'The Axis: Germany, Japan and Italy on the Road to War', in R.J.B. Bosworth and Joseph A. Maiolo (eds), *The Cambridge History of the Second World War*, Cambridge, 2015, II, pp. 21–42.

Gerwarth, Robert, *The Bismarck Myth: Weimar Germany and the Legacy of the Iron Chancellor*, Oxford, 2005.

Geyer, Michael and Sheila Fitzpatrick (eds), *Beyond Totalitarianism: Stalinism and Nazism Compared*, Cambridge, 2009.

Ginsborg, Paul, *A History of Contemporary Italy: Society and Politics 1943–1988*, London, 1990.

Goeschel, Christian, 'The Cultivation of Mussolini's Image in Weimar and Nazi Germany', in Jan Rüger and Nikolaus Wachsmann (eds), *Rewriting German History: New Perspectives on Modern Germany*, Basingstoke, 2015, pp. 247–66.

Goeschel, Christian, '*Italia docet*? The Relationship between Italian Fascism and Nazism Revisited', *European History Quarterly*, 42 (2012), pp. 480–92.
Goeschel, Christian, 'A Parallel History? Rethinking the Relationship between Italy and Germany, ca. 1860–1945', *Journal of Modern History*, 88 (2016), pp. 610–32.
Goeschel, Christian, *Suicide in Nazi Germany*, Oxford, 2009.
Goetzinger, Bettina, 'Italien zwischen dem Sturz Mussolinis und der Errichtung der faschistischen Politik in der NS-Propaganda', in Rudolf Lill (ed.), *Deutschland–Italien 1943–1945: Aspekte einer Entzweiung*, Tübingen, 1992, pp. 151–76.
Gooch, John, *Mussolini and his Generals: The Armed Forces and Fascist Foreign Policy, 1922–1940*, Cambridge, 2007.
Gooch, John, 'Mussolini's Strategy, 1939–1943', in John Ferris and Evan Mawdsley (eds), *The Cambridge History of the Second World War*, Cambridge, 2015, I, pp. 132–58.
Görtemaker, Heike B., *Eva Braun: Leben mit Hitler*, Munich, 2010.
Grandi, Dino, *25 luglio: quarant'anni dopo*, ed. Renzo De Felice, Bologna, 1983.
Grandi, Dino, *Il mio paese: ricordi autobiografici*, ed. Renzo De Felice, Bologna, 1985.
Gribaudi, Gabriella, 'The True Cause of the "Moral Collapse": People, Fascists and Authorities under the Bombs – Naples and the Countryside, 1940–1944', in Richard Overy, Claudia Baldoli and Andrew Knapp (eds), *Bombing, States and Peoples in Western Europe 1940–1945*, London, 2011, pp. 219–38.
Griffin, Roger, *The Nature of Fascism*, London, 1993.
Griffin, Roger, 'Studying Fascism in a Postfascist Age: From New Consensus to New Wave?', *Fascism*, 1 (2012), pp. 1–17.
Gundle, Stephen, 'Mussolini's Appearances in the Regions', in Gundle, Duggan and Pieri (eds), *The Cult of the Duce*, pp. 110–28.
Halder, Franz, *Kriegstagebuch. Tägliche Aufzeichnungen des Chefs des Generalstabes des Heeres 1939–1942*, ed. Hans-Adolf Jacobsen, 3 vols, Stuttgart, 1962–4.
Hall, Todd M., *Emotional Diplomacy: Official Emotion on the International Stage*, Ithaca, NY, 2015.
Hammermann, Gabriele, *Zwangsarbeit für den 'Verbündeten': die Arbeits- und Lebensbedingungen der italienischen Militärinternierten in Deutschland 1943–1945*, Tübingen, 2002.
Harrison, Mark, 'The Economics of World War II: An Overview', in Mark Harrison (ed.), *The Economics of World War II: Six Great Powers in International Comparison*, Cambridge, 1998, pp. 1–42.
Hartmann, Christian, Thomas Vordermeyer, Othmar Plöckinger and Roman Töppel (eds), *Hitler, Mein Kampf: eine kritische Edition*, 2 vols, Munich, 2016.
Hassell, Ulrich von, *Römische Tagebücher und Briefe, 1932–1938*, ed. Ulrich Schlie, Munich, 2004.
Heiber, Helmut (ed.), *Hitlers Lagebesprechungen: die Protokollfragmente seiner militärischen Konferenzen 1942–1945*, Stuttgart, 1962.
Heiss, Hans, 'Die Brennergrenze 1918/19', *Österreich in Geschichte und Literatur mit Geographie*, 52 (2008), pp. 318–35.
Heitmann, Klaus, *Das italienische Deutschlandbild in seiner Geschichte, III: Das kurze zwanzigste Jahrhundert*, Heidelberg, 2012.
Herbert, Ulrich, *Fremdarbeiter: Politik und Praxis des 'Ausländer-Einsatzes' in der Kriegswirtschaft des Dritten Reiches*, Bonn, 1999.
Herren, Madeleine, 'Fascist Internationalism', in Glenda Sluga and Patricia Clavin (eds), *Internationalisms: A Twentieth-Century History*, Cambridge, 2017, pp. 191–212.
Heuss, Theodor, *Hitlers Weg: Eine Schrift aus dem Jahre 1932*, new edn, Tübingen, 1968.
Hildebrand, Klaus, *Das Dritte Reich*, Munich, 2009.
Hill, Leonidas E. (ed.), *Die Weizsäcker-Papiere 1933–1950*, Frankfurt am Main, 1974.
Hillgruber, Andreas (ed.), *Staatsmänner und Diplomaten bei Hitler: vertrauliche Aufzeichnungen über Unterredungen mit Vertretern des Auslandes 1939–1941*, 2 vols, Frankfurt am Main, 1967.
Hilton, Stanley E., 'The Welles Mission to Europe, February–March 1940: Illusion or Realism?', *Journal of American History*, 57 (1971), pp. 93–120.

Historicus, 'Basi antirusse dell'unità Europea', *Civiltà fascista*, 8 (1941), pp. 494–506.
Hitler, Adolf, *On National Socialism and World Relations: Speech Delivered in the German Reichstag, 30 January 1937*, Berlin, 1937.
Hitler: Reden, Schriften, Anordnungen: Februar 1925 bis Januar 1933, 6 vols, Munich, 1992–2003.
Hitler e Mussolini: lettere e documenti, Milan, 1946.
Hoepke, Klaus-Peter, *Die deutsche Rechte und der italienische Faschismus: ein Beitrag zum Selbstverständnis und zur Politik von Gruppen und Verbänden der deutschen Rechten*, Düsseldorf, 1968.
Hof, Tobias, 'Die Tagebücher von Galeazzo Ciano', *VfZ*, 60 (2012), pp. 507–28.
Hoffend, Andrea, 'Konrad Adenauer und das faschistische Italien', *QFIAB*, 75 (1995), pp. 481–544.
Hoffend, Andrea, *Zwischen Kultur-Achse und Kulturkampf: die Beziehungen zwischen 'Drittem Reich' und faschistischem Italien in den Bereichen Medien, Kunst, Wissenschaft und Rassenfragen*, Frankfurt am Main, 1998.
Hoffmann, Heinrich, *Mussolini erlebt Deutschland*, Munich, 1937.
Homze, Edward L., *Foreign Labor in Nazi Germany*, Princeton, 1967.
Hubatsch, Walter (ed.), *Hitlers Weisungen für die Kriegsführung 1939–1945: Dokumente des Oberkommandos der Wehrmacht*, Frankfurt am Main, 1962.
Huetter, Luigi, 'Gli ingressi trionfali di Roma', *Capitolium*, 13 (1938), pp. 235–45.
Ihrig, Stefan, *Atatürk in the Nazi Imagination*, Princeton, 2014.
Jäckel, Eberhard and Alex Kuhn (eds), *Hitler: Sämtliche Aufzeichnungen 1905–1924*, Stuttgart, 1980.
Jackson, Julian, *The Fall of France: The Nazi Invasion of 1940*, Oxford, 2003.
Jacobelli, Jader (ed.), *Il fascismo e gli storici oggi*, Rome, 1988.
James, Robert Rhodes (ed.), *Winston S. Churchill: His Complete Speeches 1897–1963*, 8 vols, New York, 1974.
Janßen, Karl-Heinz and Fritz Tobias, *Der Sturz der Generäle: Hitler und die Blomberg–Fritsch Krise 1938*, Munich, 1994.
Jarausch, Konrad H., *After Hitler: Recivilizing Germans, 1945–1995*, Oxford, 2006.
Jochmann, Werner (ed.), *Adolf Hitler: Monologe im Führerhauptquartier 1941–1944 – die Aufzeichnungen Heinrich Heims*, Hamburg, 1980.
Joll, James, *Europe since 1870: An International History*, 4th edn, Harmondsworth, 1990.
Kallis, Aristotle, '"Framing" *Romanità*: The Celebrations for the Bimillenario Augusteo and the *Augusteo–Ara Pacis* Project', *JCH*, 46 (2011), pp. 809–31.
Kennedy, Paul, 'Appeasement', in Gordon Martel (ed.), *The Origins of the Second World War Reconsidered*, Boston, 1986, pp. 140–61.
Kershaw, Ian, *Fateful Choices: Ten Decisions that Changed the World 1940–1941*, London, 2007.
Kershaw, Ian, *Hitler, 1889–1936: Hubris*, London, 2001.
Kershaw, Ian, *Hitler, 1936–1945: Nemesis*, London, 2001.
Kershaw, Ian, 'Hitler and the Uniqueness of Nazism', *JCH*, 39 (2004), pp. 239–54.
Kershaw, Ian, *The 'Hitler Myth': Image and Reality in the Third Reich*, Oxford, 1987.
Kershaw, Ian, *The Nazi Dictatorship: Problems and Perspectives of Interpretation*, London, 2000.
Kershaw, Ian, *Popular Opinion and Political Dissent in the Third Reich: Bavaria 1933–1945*, Oxford, 1983.
Kershaw, Ian, '"Working Towards the Führer": Reflections on the Nature of the Nazi Dictatorship', *Contemporary European History*, 2 (1993), pp. 103–18.
Kershaw, Ian and Moshe Lewin (eds), *Stalinism and Nazism: Dictatorships in Comparison*, Cambridge, 1997.
Kertzer, David I., *The Pope and Mussolini: The Secret History of Pius XI and the Rise of Fascism in Europe*, Oxford, 2014.
Klein, Adolf, *Von nordischer Art: das Ringen um die Weltanschauung*, Leipzig, 1934.
Klessmann, Christoph, 'Der Generalgouverneur Hans Frank', *VfZ*, 19 (1971), pp. 245–60.

Klink, Ernst, 'Die militärische Konzeption des Krieges gegen die Sowjetunion, 1: die Landkriegführung', in *DRZW*, IV, pp. 190–326.
Klink, Ernst, 'Die Operationsführung, 1: Heer und Kriegsmarine', in *DRZW*, IV, pp. 451–652.
Klinkhammer, Lutz, 'Diplomatici e militari tedeschi a Roma di fronte alla politica di sterminio nazionalsocialista', in Baumeister, Osti Guerrazzi and Procaccia (eds), *16 ottobre 1943*, pp. 41–62.
Klinkhammer, Lutz, 'Grundlinien nationalsozialistischer Besatzungspolitik in Frankreich, Jugoslawien und Italien', in Christof Dipper, Rainer Hudemann and Jens Petersen (eds), *Faschismus und Faschismen im Vergleich: Wolfgang Schieder zum 60. Geburtstag*, Cologne, 1998, pp. 183–216.
Klinkhammer, Lutz, *Stragi naziste in Italia: la guerra contro i civili (1943–44)*, Rome, 1997.
Klinkhammer, Lutz, *Zwischen Bündnis und Besatzung: das nationalsozialistische Deutschland und die Republik von Salò 1943–1945*, Tübingen, 1993.
Knox, MacGregor, *Common Destiny: Dictatorship, Foreign Policy, and War in Fascist Italy and Nazi Germany*, Cambridge, 2000.
Knox, MacGregor, 'Conquest, Foreign and Domestic, in Fascist Italy and Nazi Germany', *Journal of Modern History*, 56 (1984), pp. 1–57.
Knox, MacGregor, 'Das faschistische Italien und die Endlösung', *VfZ*, 55 (2007), pp. 53–92.
Knox, MacGregor, 'Fascism: Ideology, Foreign Policy, and War', in Adrian Lyttelton (ed.), *Liberal and Fascist Italy*, Oxford, 2002, pp. 105–38.
Knox, MacGregor, 'Il fascismo e la politica estera italiana', in Bosworth and Romano (eds), *La politica estera italiana*, pp. 287–330.
Knox, MacGregor, 'The Fascist Regime, its Foreign Policy and its Wars: An 'Anti-Anti-Fascist' orthodoxy?', *Contemporary European History*, 4 (1995), pp. 347–65.
Knox, MacGregor, *Hitler's Italian Allies: Royal Armed Forces, Fascist Regime, and the War of 1940–1943*, Cambridge, 2000.
Knox, MacGregor, *Mussolini Unleashed 1939–1941: Politics and Strategy in Fascist Italy's Last War*, Cambridge, 1982.
Knox, MacGregor, 'The Sources of Italy's Defeat in 1940: Bluff or Institutionalized Incompetence?', in Carole Fink, Isabel V. Hull and MacGregor Knox (eds), *German Nationalism and the European Response, 1890–1945*, Norman, OK, 1985, pp. 247–66.
Knox, MacGregor, *To the Threshold of Power, 1922/33: Origins and Dynamics of the Fascist and National Socialist Dictatorships*, I, Cambridge, 2007.
Köhler, Peter, 'Das "Mussolini-Observatoriumsprojekt"', *Jenaer Jahrbuch zur Technik- und Industriegeschichte*, 10 (2007), pp. 413–34.
Kolb, Eberhard, *Die Weimarer Republik*, Munich, 2002.
König, Malte, *Kooperation als Machtkampf: das faschistische Achsenbündnis Berlin–Rom im Krieg 1940/41*, Cologne, 2007.
Koshar, Rudy, *German Travel Cultures*, New York, 2000.
Kotze, Hildegard von (ed.), *Heeresadjutant bei Hitler 1938–1943: Aufzeichnungen des Majors Engel*, Stuttgart, 1974.
Krausnick, Helmut, 'Himmler über seinen Besuch bei Mussolini vom 11.–14. Oktober 1942', *VfZ*, 4 (1956), pp. 423–6.
Krogmann, Carl Vincent, *Es ging um Deutschlands Zukunft 1932–1939: Erlebtes täglich diktiert von dem früheren Regierenden Bürgermeister von Hamburg*, Leoni, 1976.
Kuby, Erich, *Verrat auf deutsch: wie das Dritte Reich Italien ruinierte*, Frankfurt am Main, 1987.
Kühberger, Christoph, *Metaphern der Macht: ein kultureller Vergleich der politischen Feste im faschistischen Italien und im nationalsozialistischen Deutschland*, Berlin, 2006.
Lamb, Richard, *War in Italy 1943–1945: A Brutal Story*, New York, 1994.
Lasansky, D. Medina, *The Renaissance Perfected: Architecture, Spectacle, and Tourism in Fascist Italy*, University Park, PA, 2004.
Latour, Conrad F., *Südtirol und die Achse Berlin–Rom, 1938–1945*, Stuttgart, 1962.
Laven, David, *Venice and Venetia under the Habsburgs, 1815–1835*, Oxford, 2002.
Ledeen, Michael A., *Universal Fascism: The Theory and Practice of the Fascist International*, New York, 1972.

Lepre, Aurelio, *La storia della repubblica di Mussolini: Salò – il tempo dell'odia e della violenza*, Milan, 2000.
Les Lettres secrètes échangées par Hitler et Mussolini, Paris, 1946.
Liebscher, Daniela, *Freude und Arbeit: zur internationalen Freizeit- und Sozialpolitik des faschistischen Italien und des NS-Regimes*, Cologne, 2009.
Longerich, Peter, *'Davon haben wir nichts gewußt': die Deutschen und die Judenverfolgung 1933–1945*, Munich, 2006.
Longerich, Peter, *Hitler: eine Biographie*, Munich, 2015.
Longo, Gisella, 'Pellizzi, Camillo', in de Grazia and Luzzatto (eds), *Dizionario del fascismo*, II, pp. 356–7.
Lönne, Karl Egon, 'Der "Völkische Beobachter" und der italienische Faschismus', *QFIAB*, 51 (1971), pp. 539–84.
Ludecke, Kurt G. W., *I Knew Hitler: The Story of a Nazi who Escaped the Blood Purge*, London, 1938.
Luzzatto, Sergio, *Il corpo del Duce*, Turin, 1998.
Lyttelton, Adrian, *The Seizure of Power: Fascism in Italy, 1919–1929*, rev. edn, London, 2009.
Lyttelton, Adrian, 'What was Fascism?', *New York Review of Books*, 51 (2004), pp. 33–6.
McGaw Smyth, Howard, *Secrets of the Fascist Era: How Uncle Sam Obtained Some of the Top-Level Documents of Mussolini's Period*, Carbondale, IL, 1975.
Mack Smith, Denis, *Italy and its Monarchy*, New Haven, 1989.
Mack Smith, Denis, *Mussolini*, London, 1981.
Mack Smith, Denis, *Mussolini's Roman Empire*, London, 1976.
MacMillan, Margaret, *Peacemakers: The Paris Peace Conference and its Attempt to End War*, London, 2001.
Magistrati, Massimo, *L'Italia a Berlino (1937–1939)*, Milan, 1956.
Malaparte, Curzio, *Der Staatsstreich*, Leipzig, 1932.
Mallett, Robert, *Mussolini in Ethiopia, 1919–1935*, Cambridge, 2015.
Mancini, Roberto (ed.), *Apparati e feste per la visita di Hitler e Mussolini a Firenze (1938)*, Florence, 2010.
Mantelli, Brunello, *'Camerati del lavoro': i lavoratori italiani emigrati nel Terzo Reich nel periodo dell'Asse 1938–1943*, Florence, 1992.
Mantelli, Brunello, 'Vom "bilateralen Handelsausgleich" zur "Achse Berlin–Rom": der Einfluß wirtschaftlicher Faktoren auf die Entstehung des deutsch-italienischen Bündnisses 1933–1936', in Jens Petersen and Wolfgang Schieder (eds), *Faschismus und Gesellschaft in Italien: Staat – Wirtschaft – Kultur*, Cologne, 1998, pp. 253–79.
Mantelli, Brunello, 'Zwischen Strukturwandel auf dem Arbeitsmarkt und Kriegswirtschaft: die Anwerbung der italienischen Arbeiter für das "Dritte Reich" und die "Achse Berlin–Rom" 1938–1943', in Bermani, Bologna and Mantelli (eds), *Proletarier der 'Achse'*, pp. 253–391.
Mantelli, Brunello and Nicola Tranfaglia (eds), *Il libro dei deportati*, 4 vols, Turin, 2009.
Marks, Sally, 'Mussolini and Locarno: Fascist Foreign Policy in Microcosm', *JCH*, 14 (1979), pp. 423–39.
Marks, Sally, 'Mussolini and the Ruhr Crisis', *International History Review*, 8 (1986), pp. 56–69.
Martin, Benjamin G., *The Nazi-Fascist New Order for European Culture*, Cambridge, MA, 2016.
Mason, Timothy W., 'The Turin Strikes of March 1943', in *Nazism, Fascism, and the Working Class: Essays by Tim Mason*, ed. Jane Caplan, Cambridge, 1995, pp. 274–94.
Mason, Timothy W., 'Whatever Happened to "Fascism"?', in *Nazism, Fascism and the Working Class*, pp. 323–31.
Massignani, Alessandro, 'Die italienischen Streitkräfte und der Krieg der "Achse"', in Klinkhammer, Osti Guerrazzi and Schlemmer (eds), *Die 'Achse' im Krieg*, pp. 122–46.
Mastrigli, Federico, 'Roma Pavesata', *Capitolium*, 13 (1938), pp. 219–34.
Matteini, Claudio (ed.), *Ordini alla stampa*, Rome, 1945.
Matthäus, Jürgen and Frank Bajohr (eds), *Alfred Rosenberg: die Tagebücher von 1934 bis 1944*, Frankfurt am Main, 2015.

Mattingly, Garrett, *Renaissance Diplomacy*, London, 1955.
Mazower, Mark, *Governing the World: The History of an Idea*, London, 2012.
Mazower, Mark, *Hitler's Empire: Nazi Rule in Occupied Europe*, London, 2008.
Mazower, Mark, *Inside Hitler's Greece: The Experience of Occupation, 1941–44*, New Haven, 1993.
Meacham, Jon, *Franklin and Winston: An Intimate Portrait of an Epic Friendship*, New York, 2004.
Meier-Benneckenstein, Paul (ed.), *Dokumente der Deutschen Politik*, 9 vols, Berlin, 1935–44.
Meissner, Otto, *Staatssekretär unter Ebert-Hindenburg-Hitler*, Hamburg, 1950.
Melograni, Piero, *Rapporti segreti della polizia fascista*, Rome, 1979.
Messerschmidt, Manfred, 'Aussenpolitik und Kriegsvorbereitung', in *DRZW*, I, pp. 535–701.
Meyer, Michael, *Symbolarme Republik? Das politische Zeremoniell der Weimarer Republik in den Staatsbesuchen zwischen 1920 und 1933*, Frankfurt am Main, 2014.
Michaelis, Herbert and Ernst Schraepler (eds), *Ursachen und Folgen: vom deutschen Zusammenbruch 1918 und 1945 bis zur staatlichen Neuordnung in der Gegenwart*, 26 vols, Berlin, n.d.
Michaelis, Meir, *Mussolini and the Jews: German–Italian Relations and the Jewish Question in Italy, 1922–1945*, Oxford, 1978.
Michaelis, Meir, 'Mussolini's Unofficial Mouthpiece: Telesio Interlandi, *Il Tevere* and the Evolution of Mussolini's Anti-Semitism', *Journal of Modern Italian Studies*, 3 (1998), pp. 217–40.
Michaelis, Meir, 'I nuclei nazisti in Italia e la loro funzione nei rapporti tra fascismo e nazismo nel 1932', *Nuova rivista storica*, 57 (1973), pp. 422–38.
Michaelis, Meir, 'La prima missione del Principe d'Assia presso Mussolini (agosto '36)', *Nuova rivista storica*, 55 (1971), pp. 367–70.
Michaelis, Meir, 'I rapporti tra fascismo e nazismo prima dell'avvento di Hitler al potere (1922–1933): parte prima, 1922–1928', *Rivista storica italiana*, 85 (1973), pp. 544–600.
Milza, Pierre, *Conversations Hitler–Mussolini, 1934–1944*, Paris, 2013.
Moeller van den Bruck, Arthur, *Das Recht der jungen Völker*, ed. Hans Schwarz, Berlin, 1932.
Moltmann, Günther, 'Franklin D. Roosevelts Friedensappell vom 14. April 1939: ein fehlgeschlagener Versuch zur Friedensicherung', *Jahrbuch für Amerikastudien*, 9 (1964), pp. 91–109.
Mommsen, Hans, 'Die Rückkehr zu den Ursprüngen: Betrachtungen zur inneren Auflösung des Dritten Reiches nach der Niederlage von Stalingrad', in Grüttner, Hachtmann and Haupt (eds), *Geschichte und Emanzipation*, pp. 418–34.
Mommsen, Hans, 'Hitler's Reichstag Speech of 30 January 1939', *History and Memory*, 9 (1997), pp. 147–61.
Moos, Carlo, *Ausgrenzung, Internierung, Deportation: Antisemitismus und Gewalt im späten italienischen Faschismus 1938–1945*, Zurich, 2004.
Mori, Renato, 'Verso il riavvicinamento fra Hitler e Mussolini, ottobre 1935–giugno 1936', *Storia e politica*, 15 (1976), pp. 70–120.
Moro, Giancarlo, 'Come la Germania si è preparata a sostenere la guerra economica', *Gerarchia*, XVIII/5 (1940), pp. 260–5.
Morris, Douglas G., *Justice Imperilled: The Anti-Nazi Lawyer Max Hirschberg in Weimar Germany*, Ann Arbor, 2005.
Muggeridge, Malcolm (ed.), *Ciano's Diplomatic Papers*, London, 1948.
Mussolini, Benito, *A Clara: tutte le lettere a Clara Petacci 1943–1945*, ed. Luisa Montevecchi, Milan, 2011.
Mussolini, Benito, *My Rise and Fall*, 2 vols, New York, 1998.
Mussolini, Benito, *Opera Omnia di Benito Mussolini*, ed. Edoardo and Duilio Susmel, 44 vols, Florence, 1959–80.
Mussolini, Edvige, *Mio fratello Benito*, Florence, 1957.
Mussolini, Rachele, *The Real Mussolini as Told to Albert Zarca*, London, 1974.
Mussolinis Gespräche mit Emil Ludwig, Berlin, 1932.
Navarra, Quinto, *Memorie del cameriere di Mussolini*, Bracigliano, 2004.

Nicholas, Lynn H., *The Rape of Europa: The Fate of Europe's Treasures in the Third Reich and the Second World War*, New York, 1995.
Niglia, Federico, *L'antigermanismo tedesco italiano: da Sedan a Versailles*, Florence, 2012.
Nitz, Wenke, *Führer und Duce: politische Machtinszenierungen im nationalsozialistischen Deutschland und im faschistischen Italien*, Cologne, 2013.
Noakes, Jeremy, 'Conflict and Development in the NSDAP 1924–1927', *JCH*, 1 (1966), pp. 3–36.
Noakes, Jeremy (ed.), *Nazism: A Documentary Reader*, 4 vols, Exeter, 1998.
Nolte, Ernst, *Three Faces of Fascism: Action Française, Italian Fascism, National Socialism*, New York, 1969.
Nubola, Cecilia, *Fasciste di Salò*, Rome, 2016.
Orano, Paolo (ed.), *L'Asse nel pensiero dei due popoli / Die Achse im Denken der beiden Völker*, Rome, 1938.
Osti Guerrazzi, Amedeo, *Storia della Repubblica sociale italiana*, Rome, 2012.
Overy, Richard, *The Bombing War: Europe 1939–1945*, London, 2014.
Overy, Richard, *Russia's War: A History of the Soviet Union, 1941–1945*, London, 1998.
Overy, Richard, *Why the Allies Won*, London, 1995.
Palumbo, Michael, 'Goering's Italian Exile 1924–1925', *Journal of Modern History*, 50 (1978), pp. D1035–D1051.
Palumbo, Michael, 'Mussolini and the Munich Putsch', *Intellect*, 106/2397 (1978), pp. 490–2.
Pansa, Giampaolo, *L'esercito di Salò*, Milan, 1970.
Passerini, Luisa, *Fascism in Popular Memory: The Cultural Experience of the Turin Working Class*, Cambridge, 1987.
Patriarca, Silvana, *Italian Vices: Nation and Character from the Risorgimento to the Republic*, Cambridge, 2010.
Paulmann, Johannes, *Pomp und Politik: Monarchenbegegnungen in Europa zwischen Ancien Régime und Erstem Weltkrieg*, Paderborn, 2000.
Pavese, Roberto, 'Fatalità dell'Asse', *Gerarchia*, XVIII/5 (1940), pp. 258–9.
Pavlowitch, Stevan K., *Hitler's New Disorder: The Second World War in Yugoslavia*, London, 2008.
Pavone, Claudio, *Una guerra civile: saggio sulla moralità nella Resistenza*, Turin, 1991.
Paxton, Robert O., *The Anatomy of Fascism*, New York, 2004.
Payne, Stanley G., 'Fascist Italy and Spain', *Mediterranean Historical Review*, 13 (1998), pp. 99–115.
Payne, Stanley G., *Franco and Hitler: Spain, Germany, and World War II*, New Haven, 2008.
Pedersen, Susan, *The Guardians: The League of Nations and the Crisis of Empire*, Oxford, 2015.
Pergher, Roberta, 'Staging the Nation in Fascist Italy's "New Provinces"', *Austrian History Yearbook*, 43 (2012), pp. 98–115.
Pergher, Roberta and Giulia Albanese (eds), *In the Society of Fascists: Acclamation, Acquiescence, and Agency in Fascist Italy*, Basingstoke, 2012.
Pese, Walter Werner, 'Hitler und Italien 1920–1926', *VfZ*, 3 (1955), pp. 13–26.
Petacci, Claretta, *Mussolini segreto: diari 1932–1938*, ed. Mauro Suttora, Milan, 2009.
Petacci, Claretta, *Verso il disastro: Mussolini in guerra – diari 1939–1940*, ed. Mimmo Franzinelli, Milan, 2011.
Petersen, Jens, 'Die Außenpolitik des faschistischen Italien als historiographisches Problem', *VfZ*, 22 (1974), pp. 417–54.
Petersen, Jens, 'Deutschland, Italien und Südtirol 1938–1940', in Klaus Eisterer and Rolf Steininger (eds), *Die Option: Südtirol zwischen Faschismus und Nationalsozialismus*, Innsbruck, 1989, pp. 127–50.
Petersen, Jens, *Hitler–Mussolini: Die Entstehung der Achse Berlin–Rom 1933–1936*, Tübingen, 1973.
Petersen, Jens, 'Die Stunde der Entscheidung: das faschistische Italien zwischen Mittelmeerimperium und neutralistischem Niedergang', in Helmut Altrichter and Josef Becker (eds), *Kriegausbruch 1939: Beteiligte, Betroffene, Neutrale*, Munich, 1989, pp. 131–52.
Petersen, Jens, 'Vorspiel zu "Stahlpakt" und Kriegsallianz: das deutsch-italienische Kulturabkommen vom 23. November 1938', *VfZ*, 36 (1988), pp. 41–77.

Petropoulos, Jonathan, *Royals and the Reich: The Princes von Hessen in Nazi Germany*, Oxford, 2006.

Pezzino, Paolo, *Memory and Massacre: Revisiting Sant'Anna di Stazzema*, New York, 2012.

Picciotto, Liliana, *Il libro della memoria: gli ebrei deportati dall'Italia (1943–1945)*, Milan, 2002.

Picciotto, Liliana, 'The Shoah in Italy: Its History and Characteristics', in Joshua D. Zimmerman (ed.), *Jews in Italy under Fascist and Nazi Rule, 1922–1945*, Cambridge, 2005, pp. 209–23.

Picciotto Fargion, Liliana, 'Italien', in Wolfgang Benz (ed.), *Dimension des Völkermords: die Zahl der jüdischen Opfer des Nationalsozialismus*, Munich, 1996, pp. 219–228.

Pietromarchi, Luca, *I diari e le agende di Luca Pietromarchi (1938–1940): politica estera del fascismo e vita quotidiana di un diplomatico romano del '900*, ed. Ruth Nattermann, Rome, 2009.

Pirelli, Alberto, *Taccuini 1922/1943*, ed. Donato Barbone, Bologna, 1984.

Plehwe, Friedrich-Karl von, *Als die Achse zerbrach: das Ende des deutsch-italienischen Bündnisses im Zweiten Weltkrieg*, Wiesbaden, 1980.

Poesio, Camilla, 'Hitler a Venezia: l'immagine del regime e della città nei primi anni trenta', *Memoria e ricerca*, 43 (2013), pp. 149–50.

Pollard, John, 'Il Vaticano e la politica estera italiana', in Bosworth and Romano (eds), *La politica estera italiana, 1860–1985*, pp. 197–230.

Prauser, Steffen, 'Mord in Rom? Der Anschlag in der via Rasella und die deutsche Vergeltung in den Fosse Ardeatine', *VfZ*, 50 (2002), pp. 269–310.

Preston, Paul, 'Franco and Hitler: The Myth of Hendaye 1940', *Contemporary European History*, 1 (1992), pp. 1–16.

Preston, Paul, 'Italy and Spain in Civil War and World War 1936–1943', in Sebastian Balfour and Paul Preston (eds), *Spain and the Great Powers in the Twentieth Century*, London, 1999, pp. 151–84.

Preston, Paul, 'Mussolini's Spanish Adventure: From Limited Risk to War,' in Paul Preston and Ann L. Mackenzie (eds), *The Republic Besieged: Civil War in Spain, 1936–1939*, Edinburgh, 1996, pp. 21–51.

Preston, Paul, 'Spain: Betting on a Nazi Victory', in Bosworth and Maiolo (eds), *The Cambridge History of the Second World War*, II, pp. 324–48.

Preziosi, Giovanni, 'Per la soluzione del problema ebraico', *Vita italiana*, 30 (1942), pp. 221–4.

Puntoni, Paolo, *Parla Vittorio Emanuele III*, Bologna, 1993.

Pyta, Wolfram, *Hitler: der Künstler als Politiker und Feldherr – eine Herrschaftsanalyse*, Munich, 2015.

Quartararo, Rosaria, *Roma tra Londra e Berlino: la politca estera fascista dal 1930 al 1940*, Rome, 1980.

Rauscher, Walter, *Hitler und Mussolini: Macht, Krieg und Terror*, Graz, 2001.

Reddy, William M., *The Navigation of Feeling: A Framework for the History of Emotions*, Cambridge, 2001.

Reichardt, Sven and Armin Nolzen (eds), *Faschismus in Italien und Deutschland: Studien zu Transfer und Vergleich*, Göttingen, 2005.

Reichel, Peter, *Der schöne Schein des Dritten Reiches: Faszination und Gewalt des Faschismus*, Munich, 1992.

Repin, Claudia, 'Die "Achse Hannover–Cremona" ', *QFIAB*, 90 (2010), pp. 373–414.

Reynolds, David, *The Creation of the Anglo-American Alliance, 1937–1941: A Study in Competitive Co-operation*, London, 1981.

Reynolds, David, *Summits: Six Meetings that Shaped the Twentieth Century*, London, 2007.

Rezola, Maria Inácia, 'The Franco–Salazar Meetings: Foreign Policy and Iberian Relations during the Dictatorships (1942–1963)', *e-journal of Portuguese History*, 6/2 (2008).

Rhodes, R.A.W. and Paul 't Hart (eds), *The Oxford Handbook of Political Leadership*, Oxford, 2014.

Riall, Lucy, *Garibaldi: Invention of a Hero*, New Haven and London, 2007.

Riall, Lucy, 'The Shallow End of History? The Substance and Future of Political Biography', *Journal of Interdisciplinary History*, 40 (2010), pp. 375–93.

Rieder, Maximiliane, *Deutsch-italienische Wirtschaftsbeziehungen: Kontinuitäten und Brüche 1936–1957*, Frankfurt am Main, 2003.
Rintelen, Enno von, *Mussolini als Bundesgenosse: Erinnerungen des deutschen Militärattachés in Rom 1936–1943*, Tübingen, 1951.
Ritschel, Karl Heinz, *Diplomatie um Südtirol: politische Hintergründe eines europäischen Versagens*, Stuttgart, 1966.
Robbins, Keith, *Munich 1938*, London, 1968.
Robertson, Esmonde, 'Hitler and Sanctions: Mussolini and the Rhineland', *European Studies Review*, 7 (1977), pp. 409–35.
Robertson, Esmonde, *Mussolini as Empire Builder: Europe and Africa, 1932–36*, London, 1977.
Robertson, Esmonde, 'Race as a Factor in Mussolini's Policy in Africa and Europe', *JCH*, 23 (1988), pp. 37–58.
Rochat, Giorgio, *Le guerre italiane 1935–1943: dall'impero d'Etiopia alla disfatta*, Turin, 2005.
Rodogno, Davide, 'Die faschistische Neue Ordnung und die politisch-ökonomische Umgestaltung des Mittelmeerraums 1940 bis 1943', in Klinkhammer, Osti Guerrazzi and Schlemmer (eds), *Die 'Achse' im Krieg*, pp. 211–30.
Rodogno, Davide, *Fascism's European Empire: Italian Occupation during the Second World War*, Cambridge, 2006.
'Roma nel Mondo: rassegna della stampa germanica', *Capitolium*, 13 (1938), p. 43.
Romano, Andrea, 'Russia, campagna di', in de Grazia and Luzzatto (eds), *Dizionario del fascismo*, II, pp. 562–7.
Romano, Sergio, *Giuseppe Volpi: industria e finanza tra Giolitti e Mussolini*, Milan, 1979.
Roselli, Alessandro, *Italy and Albania: Financial Relations in the Fascist Period*, London, 2006.
Rosen, Edgar R., 'Mussolini und Deutschland 1922–1923', *VfZ*, 5 (1957), pp. 17–41.
Rosenberg, Alfred, 'The Folkish Idea of State', in Barbara Miller Lane and Leila J. Rupp (eds), *Nazi Ideology before 1933: A Documentation*, Manchester, 1978, pp. 59–73.
Rurali di Mussolini nella Germania di Hitler, ed. Ufficio Propaganda della Confederazione Fascista dei Lavatori dell'Agricoltura, Rome, 1939.
Rusconi, Gian-Enrico, *Deutschland-Italien, Italien-Deutschland: Geschichte einer schwierigen Beziehung von Bismarck bis zu Berlusconi*, Paderborn, 2006.
Rusinow, Dennison I., *Italy's Austrian Heritage 1919–1946*, Oxford, 1969.
Sadkovich, James J., 'Anglo-American Bias and the Italo-Greek War of 1940–1941', *Journal of Military History*, 58 (1994), pp. 617–42.
Sadkovich, James J., 'The Italo-Greek War in Context: Italian Priorities and Axis diplomacy', *JCH*, 28 (1993), pp. 439–64.
Sadkovich, James J., 'Of Myths and Men: Rommel and the Italians in North Africa, 1940–1942', *International History Review*, 13 (1991), pp. 284–313.
Santomassimo, Gianpasquale, 'Il ruolo di Renzo De Felice', in Enzo Collotti (ed.), *Fascismo e antifascismo: rimozioni, revisioni, negazioni*, Bari, 2000, pp. 415–29.
Sarfatti, Michele, *Gli ebrei nell'Italia fascista: vicende, identità, persecuzione*, Turin, 2000.
Sarti, Roland (ed.), *The Ax Within: Italian Fascism in Action*, New York, 1974.
Scalpelli, Adolfo, 'La formazione delle forze armate di Salò attraverso i documenti dello stato magg. della RSI', *Movimento di Liberazione in Italia*, 72 (1963), pp. 19–70.
Scarano, Federico, *Mussolini e la Repubblica di Weimar: le relazioni diplomatiche tra Italia e Germania dal 1927 al 1933*, Naples, 1996.
Scarano, Federico, *Tra Mussolini e Hitler: le opzioni dei sudtirolesi nella politica estera fascistca*, Milan, 2012.
Scardaccione, Francesca Romana, 'La Repubblica sociale italiana: aspetti istituzionali e archivistici', in Archivio centrale dello stato (ed.), *Verbali del consiglio dei ministri della Repubblica sociale italiana*, Rome, 2002, I, pp. xvii–xxxvi.
Schäfer, Claus W., *André François-Poncet als Botschafter in Berlin (1931–1938)*, Munich, 2004.
Schieder, Wolfgang, *Benito Mussolini*, Munich, 2014.
Schieder, Wolfgang, *Faschistische Diktaturen: Studien zu Italien und Deutschland*, Göttingen, 2008.

Schieder, Wolfgang, 'Fascismo e nazionalsocialismo: profilo d'uno studio comparativo', *Nuova rivista storica*, 54 (1970), pp. 114–24.
Schieder, Wolfgang, 'Das italienische Experiment: der Faschismus als Vorbild in der Weimarer Republik', *Historische Zeitschrift*, 262 (1996), pp. 73–125.
Schieder, Wolfgang, *Mythos Mussolini: Deutsche in Audienz beim Duce*, Munich, 2013.
Schieder, Wolfgang, 'Von Stalin zu Mussolini: Emil Ludwig bei Diktatoren des 20. Jahrhunderts', in Dan Diner, Gideon Reuveni and Yfaat Weiss (eds), *Deutsche Zeiten: Geschichte und Lebenswelt – Festschrift zur Emeritierung von Moshe Zimmermann*, Göttingen, 2012, pp. 123–31.
Schlemmer, Thomas, '"Gefühlsmäßige Verwandtschaft"? Zivilisten, Kriegsgefangene und das könglich-italienische Heer im Krieg gegen die Sowjetunion 1941 bis 1943', in Klinkhammer, Osti Guerrazzi and Schlemmer (eds), *Die 'Achse' im Krieg*, pp. 368–397.
Schlemmer, Thomas (ed.), *Die Italiener an der Ostfront 1942/43: Dokumente zu Mussolinis Krieg gegen die Sowjetunion*, Munich, 2005.
Schlemmer, Thomas and Hans Woller (eds), *Der Faschismus in Europa: Wege der Forschung*, Munich, 2014.
Schlemmer, Thomas and Hans Woller, 'Der italienische Faschismus und die Juden', *VfZ*, 53 (2005), pp. 164–201.
Schmider, Klaus, 'Das Versagen der "Achse" im besetzten Kroatien: ein politisch-militärischer Erklärungsversuch', in Klinkhammer, Osti Guerrazzi and Schlemmer (eds), *Die 'Achse' im Krieg*, pp. 305–18.
Schmidt, Paul, *Statist auf diplomatischer Bühne 1923–45: Erlebnisse des Chefdolmetschers im Auswärtigen Amt mit den Staatsmännern Europas*, Bonn, 1949.
Schmitz, David F., *The United States and Fascist Italy, 1922–1940*, Chapel Hill, NC, 1988.
Schöllgen, Gregor, *Ulrich von Hassell 1881–1944: ein Konservativer in der Opposition*, Munich, 1990.
Schramm, Percy E. (ed.), *Kriegstagebuch des Oberkommandos der Wehrmacht (Wehrmachtführungsstab)*, 4 vols, Frankfurt am Main, 1963.
Schreiber, Gerhard, 'Das Ende des nordafrikanischen Feldzugs und der Krieg in Italien 1943 bis 1945', in *DRZW*, VIII, pp. 1100–62.
Schreiber, Gerhard, *Deutsche Kriegsverbrechen in Italien: Täter, Opfer, Strafverfolgung*, Munich, 1996.
Schreiber, Gerhard, 'Deutschland, Italien und Südosteuropa: von der politischen und wirtschaftlichen Hegemonie zur militärischen Intervention', in *DRZW*, III, pp. 278–414.
Schreiber, Gerhard, *Die italienischen Militärinternierten im deutschen Machtbereich 1943 bis 1945: verraten – verachtet – vergessen*, Munich, 1990.
Schreiber, Gerhard, 'La partecipazione italiana alla guerra contro l'Urss: motivi fatti conseguenze', *Italia contemporanea*, 191 (1993), pp. 245–75.
Schreiber, Gerhard, 'Die politische und militärische Entwicklung im Mittelmeerraum 1939/40', in *DRZW*, III, pp. 4–271.
Schreiber, Gerhard, *Revisionismus und Weltmachtstreben: Marineführung und deutsch-italienische Beziehungen 1919–1944*, Stuttgart, 1978.
Schröder, Josef, *Italiens Kriegsaustritt 1943: die deutschen Gegenmaßnahmen im italienischen Raum – Fall 'Alarich' und 'Achse'*, Göttingen, 1969.
Schwarz, Guri, 'The Moral Conundrums of the Historian: Claudio Pavone's *A Civil War* and its Legacy', *Modern Italy*, 20 (2015), pp. 427–37.
Scobie, Alex, *Hitler's State Architecture: The Impact of Classical Antiquity*, University Park, PA, 1990.
Scriba, Friedemann, 'Die Mostra Augustea della Romanità in Rom 1937/38', in Petersen and Schieder (eds), *Faschismus und Gesellschaft in Italien*, pp. 133–58.
Seton-Watson, R. W., *Munich and the Dictators: A Sequel to 'Britain and the Dictators'*, London, 1939.
Shimazu, Naoko, 'Diplomacy as Theatre: Staging the Bandung Conference of 1955,' *Modern Asian Studies*, 48 (2014), pp. 225–52.
Shore, Zachary, *What Hitler Knew: The Battle for Information in Nazi Foreign Policy*, Oxford, 2002.

Sica, Emanuele, *Mussolini's Army in the French Riviera: Italy's Occupation of France*, Urbana, IL, 2016.
Siebert, Ferdinand, *Italiens Weg in den Zweiten Weltkrieg*, Bonn, 1962.
Silver, Allan, 'Friendship and Trust as Moral Ideals: An Historical Approach', *Archives européennes de sociologie*, 30 (1989), pp. 274–97.
Simoni, Leonardo (d.i. Michele Lanza), *Berlin ambassade d'Italie: journal d'un diplomate italien*, Paris, 1947.
Sluga, Glenda, *Internationalism in the Age of Nationalism*, Philadelphia, 2013.
Snowden, Frank M., 'De Vecchi, Cesare Maria', in de Grazia and Luzzatto (eds), *Dizionario del fascismo*, I, pp. 425–8.
Snyder, Timothy, *Bloodlands: Europe between Hitler and Stalin*, New York, 2010.
Spitzy, Reinhard, *So haben wir das Reich verspielt: Bekenntnisse eines Illegalen*, Munich, 1988.
Spohr, Kristina and David Reynolds (eds), *Transcending the Cold War: Summits, Statecraft, and the Dissolution of Bipolarity in Europe, 1970–1990*, Oxford, 2016.
Stafford, Paul, 'The Chamberlain–Halifax Visit to Rome: A Reappraisal', *English Historical Review*, 98 (1983), pp. 61–100.
Steffek, Jens, 'Fascist Internationalism', *Millennium*, 44 (2015), pp. 3–22.
Stegemann, Bernd, 'Die italienisch-deutsche Kriegführung im Mittelmeer und in Afrika', in *DRZW*, III, pp. 591–682.
Steigmann-Gall, Richard, 'Religion and the Churches', in Jane Caplan (ed.), *Nazi Germany*, Oxford, 2008, pp. 146–67.
Steinberg, Jonathan, *All or Nothing: The Axis and the Holocaust 1941–43*, London, 1990.
Steiner, Zara, *The Triumph of the Dark: European International History 1933–1939*, Oxford, 2011.
Steinert, Marlis G., *Hitlers Krieg und die Deutschen: Stimmung und Haltung der deutschen Bevölkerung im Zweiten Weltkrieg*, Düsseldorf, 1970.
Steinweis, Alan E., *Kristallnacht 1938*, Cambridge, MA, 2009.
Stone, Marla, 'Italian Fascism's Wartime Enemy and the Politics of Fear', in Michael Laffan and Max Weiss (eds), *Facing Fear: The History of an Emotion in Global Perspective*, Princeton, 2012, pp. 114–32.
Strang, Bruce G. (ed.), *Collision of Empires: Italy's Invasion of Ethiopia and its International Impact*, London, 2013.
Strang, G. Bruce, 'Imperial Dreams: The Mussolini–Laval Accords of January 1935', *Historical Journal*, 44 (2001), pp. 799–809.
Strang, G. Bruce, *On the Fiery March: Mussolini Prepares for War*, Westport, CT, 2003.
Strang, G. Bruce, 'Two Unequal Tempers: Sir George Ogilvie-Forbes, Sir Nevile Henderson and British Foreign Policy, 1938–9', *Diplomacy & Statecraft*, 5 (1994), pp. 107–37.
Strang, G. Bruce, 'War and Peace: Mussolini's Road to Munich', *Diplomacy & Statecraft*, 10 (1999), pp. 160–90.
Streit, Christian, *Keine Kameraden: die Wehrmacht und die sowjetischen Kriegsgefangenen, 1941–1945*, Stuttgart, 1978.
Stumpf, Reinhard, 'Der Krieg im Mittelmeerraum 1942/43: die Operationen in Nordafrika und im mittleren Mittelmeer', in *DRZW*, VI, pp. 569–757.
Stumpf, Reinhard, 'Von der Achse Berlin–Rom zum Militärabkommen des Dreierpakts: die Abfolge der Verträge 1936 bis 1942', in *DRZW*, VI, pp. 127–43.
Sullivan, Brian R., '"Where one man, and only one man, led": Italy's Path from Neutrality to Non-belligerency to War, 1937–1940', in Neville Wylie (ed.), *European Neutrals and Non-belligerents during the Second World War*, Cambridge, 2002, pp. 119–49.
Suzzi Valli, Roberta, 'The Myth of Squadrismo in the Fascist Regime', *JCH*, 35 (2000), pp. 131–50.
Tamaro, Attilio, *Due anni di storia 1943–45*, 3 vols, Rome, 1948.
Tampke, Jürgen, *Czech–German Relations and the Politics of Central Europe: From Bohemia to the EU*, London, 2003.
Tannenbaum, Edward R., *Fascism in Italy: Society and Culture 1922–1945*, London, 1972.
Taylor, A.J.P., *The Origins of the Second World War*, London, 1963.

Terhoeven, Petra, *Liebespfand fürs Vaterland: Krieg, Geschlecht und faschistische Nation in der italienischen Gold- und Eheringsammlung 1935/36*, Tübingen, 2003.
Thamer, Hans-Ulrich, 'Der Marsch auf Rom: ein Modell für die nationalsozialistische Machtergreifung', in Wolfgang Michalka (ed.), *Die nationalsozialistische Machtergreifung*, Paderborn, 1984, pp. 245–60,
Thöndl, Michael, 'Mussolinis ostafrikanisches Imperium in den Aufzeichnungen des deutschen Generalkonsulats in Addis Abeba', *QFIAB*, 88 (2008), pp. 449–87.
Tiedtke, Per, *Germany, Italy, and the International Economy 1929–1936: Co-operation or Rivalries at Times of Crisis?*, Marburg, 2016.
Tollardo, Elisabetta, *Fascist Italy and the League of Nations*, Basingstoke, 2016.
Tooze, Adam, *The Wages of Destruction: The Making and Breaking of the Nazi Economy*, London, 2006.
Toscano, Mario, *L'Italia e gli accordi tedesco-sovietici dell'agosto 1939*, Florence, 1955.
Toscano, Mario, *The Origins of the Pact of Steel*, Baltimore, 1967.
Tranfaglia, Nicola (ed.), *Ministri e giornalisti: la guerra e il Minculpop (1939–43)*, Turin, 2005.
Tranfaglia, Nicola (ed.), *La stampa del regime 1932–1943: le veline del Minculpop per orientare l'informazione*, Milan, 2005.
Trifković, Srdjan, 'Rivalry between Germany and Italy in Croatia, 1942–1943', *Historical Journal*, 36 (1993), pp. 879–904.
Tuninetti, Dante Maria (ed.), *Incontri di Popoli: Hitler e Mussolini*, Rome, n.d. [1943].
Uhlig, Karl, *Mussolinis Deutsche Studien*, Jena, 1941.
Ullrich, Volker, *Adolf Hitler: Biographie, Band 1: Die Jahre des Aufstiegs, 1889–1939*, Frankfurt am Main, 2013.
Urbach, Karina, *Go-Betweens for Hitler*, Oxford, 2015.
Vedovato, Giuseppe, 'Guido Manacorda tra Italia, Germania e Santa Sede', *Rivista di studi politici internazionali*, 301 (2009), pp. 96–131.
Verdina, Natale, *Riservato a Mussolini: notiziari giornalieri della Guardia nazionale repubblicana novembre 1943/giugno 1944*, Milan, 1974.
Vianello, Maddalena, 'La visita di Hitler a Roma nel maggio 1938', in Istituto romano per la storia d'Italia dal fascismo alla Resistenza (ed.), *Roma tra fascismo e liberazione*, Rome, 2006, pp. 67–92.
Vick, Brian, *The Congress of Vienna: Power and Politics after Napoleon*, Cambridge, MA, 2014.
Visser, Romke, 'Fascist Doctrine and the Cult of Romanità', *JCH*, 27 (1992), pp. 5–22.
Voigt, Klaus, 'Jewish Refugees and Immigrants in Italy, 1933–1945', in Ivo Herzer (ed.), *The Italian Refuge: Rescue of Jews during the Holocaust*, Washington, DC, 1989, pp. 141–58.
Voigt, Klaus, 'Refuge and Persecution in Italy, 1933–1945', *Simon Wiesenthal Annual*, 4 (1987), pp. 3–64.
Voigt, Klaus, *Zuflucht auf Widerruf: Exil in Italien 1933–1945*, 2 vols, Stuttgart, 1989–1993.
Watt, D.C., 'The Anglo-German Naval Agreement of 1935: An Interim Judgment', *Journal of Modern History*, 28 (1956), pp. 155–75.
Watt, D.C., 'An Earlier Model for the Pact of Steel: The Draft Treaties Exchanged between Germany and Italy during Hitler's Visit to Rome in May 1938', *International Affairs*, 3 (1957), pp. 185–97.
Watt, D.C., 'Hitler's Visit to Rome and the May Weekend Crisis: A Study in Hitler's Response to External Stimuli', *JCH*, 9 (1974), pp. 23–32.
Watt, D.C., 'The Rome–Berlin Axis, 1936–1940: Myth and Reality', *Review of Politics*, 22 (1960), pp. 519–43.
Webster, R.A., *Industrial Imperialism in Italy, 1908–1915*, Berkeley, 1975.
Wegner, Bernd, 'Der Krieg gegen die Sowjetunion 1942–43', in *DRZW*, VI, pp. 761–1102.
Wegner, Bernd, 'Von Stalingrad nach Kursk', in *DRZW*, VIII, pp. 3–79.
Weinberg, Gerhard L., *The Foreign Policy of Hitler's Germany: Diplomatic Revolution in Europe 1933–36*, Chicago, 1970.
Weinberg, Gerhard L., *The Foreign Policy of Hitler's Germany*, I: *Starting World War II 1937–1939*, Chicago, 1980.
Weinberg, Gerhard L., *A World at Arms*, II: *A Global History of World War II*, Cambridge, 1994.

Weizsäcker, Ernst von, *Memoirs of Ernst von Weizsäcker*, London, 1951.

Whealey, Robert H., 'Mussolini's Ideological Diplomacy: An Unpublished Document', *Journal of Modern History*, 39 (1967), pp. 432–7.

Wiedekind, Michael, *Nationalsozialistische Besatzungs- und Annexionspolitik in Norditalien 1943 bis 1945: die Operationszonen 'Alpenvorland' und 'Adriatisches Küstenland'*, Munich, 2003.

Wiedemann, Fritz, *Der Mann, der Feldherr werden wollte: Erlebnisse und Erfahrungen des Vorgesetzten Hitlers im I. Weltkrieg und seines späteren persönlichen Adjutanten*, Velbert, 1964.

Wildvang, Frauke, *Der Feind von nebenan: Judenverfolgung im faschistischen Italien 1936–1944*, Cologne, 2008.

Willis, Fred G., *Mussolini in Deutschland: eine Volkskundgebung für den Frieden in den Tagen vom 25. bis 29. September 1937*, Berlin, 1937.

Willson, Perry, 'The Nation in Uniform? Fascist Italy, 1919–43', *Past & Present*, 221 (2013), pp. 239–72.

Wiskemann, Elizabeth, *The Rome–Berlin Axis: A History of the Relations between Hitler and Mussolini*, London, 1949.

Woller, Hans, *Die Abrechnung mit dem Faschismus in Italien 1943 bis 1948*, Munich, 1996.

Woller, Hans, 'Churchill und Mussolini: offene Konfrontation und geheime Kooperation?', *VfZ*, 49 (2001), pp. 563–94.

Woller, Hans, 'Machtpolitisches Kalkül oder ideologische Affinität? Zur Frage des Verhältnisses zwischen Mussolini und Hitler vor 1933', in Wolfgang Benz, Hans Buchheim and Hans Mommsen (eds), *Der Nationalsozialismus: Studien zur Ideologie und Herrschaft*, Frankfurt am Main, 1990, pp. 42–64.

Woller, Hans, *Mussolini: der erste Faschist – eine Biografie*, Munich, 2016.

Woller, Hans, 'I rapporti tra Mussolini e Hitler prima del 1933: politica del potere o affinità ideologica?', *Italia contemporanea*, 196 (1994), pp. 491–508.

Woller, Hans, *Rom, 28. Oktober 1922: die faschistische Herausforderung*, Munich, 1999.

Woller, Hans, 'Vom Mythos der Moderation: Mussolini und die Münchener Konferenz 1938', in Zarusky and Zückert (eds), *Das Münchener Abkommen in europäischer Perspektive*, pp. 211–15.

Wollstein, Günter, *Vom Weimarer Revisionismus zu Hitler: das Deutsche Reich und die Großmächte in der Anfangsphase der nationalsozialistischen Herrschaft in Deutschland*, Bonn, 1973.

Wolz, Alexander, 'Das Auswärtige Amt und die Entscheidung zur Remilitarisierung des Rheinlands', *VfZ*, 63 (2015), pp. 487–511.

Woodhouse, John, *Gabriele D'Annunzio: Defiant Archangel*, Oxford, 1998.

Wright, John L., 'Mussolini, Libya, and the Sword of Islam', in Ruth Ben-Ghiat and Mia Fuller (eds), *Italian Colonialism*, Basingstoke, 2005, pp. 121–30.

Yellen, Jeremy A. 'Into the Tiger's Den: Japan and the Tripartite Act, 1940', *JCH*, 51 (2016), pp. 555–76.

Yelton, David K., *Hitler's Volkssturm: The Nazi Militia and the Fall of Germany, 1944–1945*, Lawrence, KS, 2002.

Zachariae, Georg, *Mussolini si confessa: rivelazioni del medico tedesco inviato da Hitler al Duce*, Milan, 1948.

Zamagni, Vera, *The Economic History of Italy 1860–1990*, Oxford, 1993.

Zamagni, Vera, 'Italy: how to lose the war and win the peace' in Harrison (ed.), *The Economics of World War II*, pp. 177–223.

Zuccotti, Susan, 'Pius XII and the rescue of Jews in Italy: evidence of a papal directive', in Zimmerman (ed.), *Jews in Italy under Fascist and Nazi Rule*, pp. 287–307.

INDEX

Abel, Werner, 27
Addis Ababa: falls (May 1936), 67
Adenauer, Konrad, 25
Adowa (Ethiopia): Italian defeat (1896), 57
Adriatisches Küstenland Operational Zone, 262
Africa Corps (German), 208, 228
Agenzia Stefani *see* Stefani
Alamein, El, Battle of (October 1942), 234
Albania: BM invades, 152–3
Alexander, General Sir Harold, 285
Alexander, Jeffrey C.: on 'social performance', 6
Alfa ('boss of death squad'), 108
Alfieri, Dino: accompanies BM on meetings with AH, 76, 116; heads Ministry of Popular Culture, 89, 108; on inadequate planning for AH–BM meeting, 109; forbids coverage of demonstrations at BM's departure, 139; succeeds Attolico as ambassador to Germany, 180; AH attacks over Italian military performance, 202; and BM's reaction to AH's patronising manner, 203; post-war memoirs justifying views, 207; letter to Weizsäcker querying value of wartime meetings, 229; and German advance on Stalingrad, 231; Ribbentrop complains to of inadequacy of Italian officers, 241; and AH–BM's July 1943 meeting, 246
Alfonso XIII, King of Spain: visits Rome, 21
Allies: strength, 233; north African landings (1942), 234; invade and occupy Sicily, 244; advance in Italy, 280, 285; invade France (June and August 1944), 281
Alpenvorland Operational Zone, 262
Alto Adige *see* South Tyrol
Alwens, Ludwig, 275
Ambrosio, General Vittorio, 238, 247
Anfuso, Filippo, 276–7, 288
Anglo-Italian declaration (16 November 1938), 147
Ansaldo, Giovanni, 217
Anschluss: BM attempts to delay, 57; AH carries out, 100–3; *see also* Austria
Anti-Comintern Pact (1936), 70, 95, 155, 224
anti-Semitism: in AH's ideology, 3, 149; increase in Italy, 96, 106, 145–6; BM's, 136, 145–6, 225, 232; *see also* Jews
Antonescu, Marshal Ion, 227
Appelius, Mario, 77
Ardennes: Battle of the Bulge (1944–5), 286–7
Arent, Benno von, 84, 100
Atlantic Charter (1941), 218–19, 242
Attolico, Bernardo, 72, 132, 179
Austria: AH's wish to control, 4, 55, 93; Nazi party legalised, 10; Italo-German differences over independence of, 15; AH seeks unification with Germany, 26; AH's unpopularity in, 33; and AH's travel to 1934 Venice meeting, 43–4; difficult relations with Germany, 43–5; discussed at 1934 Venice meeting,

49–50; prospective annexation by Germany (Anschluss), 52, 57; political situation, 55–6; Nazi putsch (1934), 56, 59, 65, 101; BM admits German claim to, 63, 65, 100; Italy surrenders guarantee of independence, 66; as German state, 67; Italy maintains guarantee of independence, 78; AH invades and annexes, 100–3; war with Prussia (1866), 155
Axis (Germany–Italy): BM on, 70–1, 73; Grandi on, 73; function in uniting Italo-German bureaucracies, 82; Pini on, 83; Nazi doubts about Italy honouring, 91; Vatican opposition to, 98; unpopularity in Italy, 104, 146; reservations about strength of, 126; develops and strengthens, 128–9, 134–5; Italy's commitment to, 151; Italy emphasises power of, 155; and joint strategy, 174; upheld by AH–BM relationship, 201–2, 207; German dominance in, 231, 252; strength of forces, 233; and impending defeat, 240; defeat in north Africa, 244; condition after BM's downfall, 252

Badoglio, Marshal Pietro: AH meets, 83; war strategy, 185; meeting with Keitel, 198; replaced by Cavallero, 199; peace overtures, 235; succeeds BM as head of government, 246, 249, 251; authoritarian regime, 250; letter to AH promising continuing alliance with Germany, 254; justifies armistice with Allies, 258; evacuates to Brindisi, 259; German attitude to, 261; BM criticises circle, 282
Balbo, Italo, 103
Balkans: Axis campaign in, 193, 201, 210, 293
Ballila (Fascist youth organisation), 118
Barbarossa, Operation (German invasion of Soviet Union), 214, 216–17
Basler Nachrichten, 288
Bastianini, Giuseppe, 240, 242, 247
Battle of Britain (1940), 190
Bavaria: separatist forces in, 20
Bayreuth: Wagner festival, 56
Belgium: Germans invade (1940), 172, 180, 182, 186, 275
Belluno, 262
Below, Nicolaus von, 80, 120
Berghof: AH–BM meeting at (January 1941), 202–4, 206, 252
Berlin: BM visits with AH (1937), 84, 86–7; Olympic Games (1936), 86
Berliner Morgenpost, 173
Berlusconi, Silvio, 258
Bianchi Bandinelli, Ranuccio, 120
Bismarck, Prince Otto von, 75
Bismarck, Otto von (German envoy in Rome), 200, 213, 215, 236, 239
Bizerta, 243
Blomberg, Field Marshal Werner von, 39, 94
Blondel, Jules, 122, 126, 136–7
Bocchini, Arturo, 105–7
Bojano, Filippo, 46, 110
Bologna, 112
Bolshevism: Italo-German hostility to, 67, 69, 105, 168, 216–17, 222; Church's hostility to, 216–17
Bolzano, South Tyrol, 97, 112
Bombacci, Nicola, 275
Borghese, Prince Valerio Junio, 286
Bormann, Martin, 292–3
Bottai, Giuseppe, 129, 151, 215, 237–8, 238, 248
Braun, Eva: accompanies AH on state visit to Italy, 115; suicide, 289
Brenner Pass: 72, 101, 103; AH–BM's first meeting at (March 1940), 170–5, 181; second meeting (October 1940), 191–2; third meeting (June 1941), 213–14
Brigate Nere (Fascist terror squads), 281
Britain: AH hopes for alliance with, 5, 94; accused of hypocrisy over colonialism, 62; naval agreement with Germany (1935), 62; concern over German–Italian relations, 64; Grandi hopes for alliance with Italy, 73; and BM's 1937 visit to Germany, 74; Gentleman's Agreement with Italy (1937), 96, 105; condescending view of Italy, 135; and BM's readiness to go to war on Germany's side, 137; dominance in Mediterranean, 147; joint declaration with Italy (November 1938), 147; BM maintains friendship with, 154; Mutual Assistance agreement with Poland, 161; declares war on Germany (3 September 1939), 162; refuses to buy off BM, 162; Italy ceases arms exports to, 169; naval blockade of Italy, 169–70; Italians attack in north Africa, 188, 190, 192–3, 200; AH makes peace offer to (July 1940), 189–90; bombs Italian cities, 189; German invasion postponed, 192; supports Greece, 197; victory over Italian navy at Taranto,

Britain (contd):
197; victories against Italy in East Africa, 200; under threat of defeat, 205; evacuates Greece and Crete, 210; offensive in north Africa, 224; area bombings of Italy, 234; aircraft production, 245
Brüning, Heinrich, 27
Bulgaria, 242, 285
Bülow-Schwante, Vicco von, 81
Busch, Karl, 40–1

C., Ferruccio, 228
Calamandrei, Piero, 249, 267
Campo Imperatore, 264
Capasso Torre di Caprara, Giovanni, 27
Caporetto, Battle of (1917), 208
Carazzolo, Maria, 183, 249, 258
Casablanca conference (January 1943), 239–40, 242
Casini, Gherardo, 92
Cassibile, Sicily, 258
Castellano, General Giuseppe, 258
Catholic Church: relations with Fascism in Italy, 25; opposes Italian entry into war, 179, 181; supports campaign against Bolshevism, 216–17
Cavallero, General Ugo, 158, 199, 201, 219, 230, 238
Cavour (Italian battleship), 118, 126
Ceccarelli De Grada, Magda, 195, 239, 250, 258, 285
Cephalonia: Italian resistance and German reprisals, 260
Cerruti, Elisabetta, 48–9
Cerruti, Vittorio, 38–40, 53–4, 63, 94
Chamberlain, Neville: plans closer alliance with Italy, 105; meets AH over Czech crisis, 132, 135, 137; sends Runciman to Czechoslovakia, 135; at Munich conference, 140–1; disbelieves AH's further territorial claims, 144; official visit to Italy, 147–9; applauded in Milan cinema, 177
Chaplin, Charlie, 2
Churchill, Winston S.: meetings with Roosevelt, 10–11, 228, 239, 257; admiration for BM, 134; warnings on BM–AH alliance, 134, 144; and BM's declaration of war, 185; relations with Roosevelt, 206, 218–19, 221, 274, 294; AH mocks, 224; on BM's downfall, 252; believes Italy dependent on Germany, 259
Ciano, Edda (*née* Mussolini), 270
Ciano, Count Galeazzo: diaries, 14, 176, 193, 270; attends 1934 Venice meeting of AH and BM, 45, 49; appointed foreign minister, 68; visits AH in Bavaria, 69; Attolico complains to about excessive Italian delegations to Germany, 72; accompanies BM on 1937 visit to Germany, 76, 82; dislikes Ribbentrop, 94; welcomes Mackensen's appointment as German ambassador, 94; ambiguous foreign policy, 96; and AH's state visit to Italy, 97, 109, 114, 116, 121; and Vatican opposition to Axis, 98; and AH's invasion of Austria, 103; and BM's reaction to German invasion of South Tyrol, 104; ridicules Duke of Saxe-Coburg-Gotha, 104; presents counter-treaty to Ribbentrop, 117; on Fascist recognition of change in foreign policy, 129; expresses moderation over proposed military alliance with Germany, 134; and BM's readiness to go to war on Germany's side, 137; meetings with Perth, 137–8; on Sudeten crisis, 137; at Munich conference (1938), 139; and BM's increasing anti-Semitism, 145; anti-French speech (November 1938), 147; and Chamberlain's visit to Italy, 147–9; appreciates AH's speech on cooperation with Italy, 149; and AH's occupation of Czechoslovakia, 150; and BM's frustration at reporting to king, 150–1; urges invasion of Albania, 153; negotiates alliance with Ribbentrop, 154, 156–8; and BM's wish to postpone war, 159; anti-German views, 165; reluctance to go to war, 166, 180; supports Finns against Soviet Russia, 168; and Welles' peace mission (1940), 169; attends March 1940 Brenner Pass meeting, 171, 175; warns Belgian ambassador of impending German attack, 172; BM complains to of AH's dominant role, 173; BM declares intention to go to war, 175; on BM's belief in AH, 176; appoints Alfieri ambassador to Germany, 180; announces declaration of war, 183; and BM's June 1940 Munich meeting with AH, 187; at second Brenner Pass meeting (October 1940), 191–2; on German troops in Romania, 193; responsibility for attack on Greece, 193; at Florence meeting (October 1940), 195–6; Vienna meeting with AH

(November 1940), 198; at Berghof meeting (January 1941), 203; complains of German treatment of Italian workers, 211; at third Brenner Pass meeting (June 1941), 213–14; reads out AH's letter announcing Soviet invasion to BM, 215; on BM's not understanding AH's declining respect, 227; at Salzburg meeting (April 1942), 230; visits AH (November and December 1942), 235, 237; dismissed and appointed ambassador to Holy See, 238–9; plots BM's downfall, 248; AH blames for BM's downfall, 251; BM fails to purge, 265; escapes to Germany, deported to Italy and executed, 270
Clemenceau, Georges, 9
Colonna, Prince Piero, 121
Communists *see* Bolshevism
Compiègne, 189
Corfu: Italy occupies, 21–2
Corner, Paul, 177
Corriere della Sera (newspaper), 258, 277, 282
Corrispondenza Repubblicana (RSI newsletter), 274
Corsica, 236
Cortesi, Arnaldo, 46
Crete: AH offers paratroopers for campaign in, 196; falls to Germans, 210
Crispi, Francesco, 75
Croatia, 209, 226, 233
Croce, Benedetto, 292
Cultural Treaty (Italy–Germany, November 1938), 156
Czechoslovak–Soviet Treaty of Alliance (1935), 61
Czechoslovakia: AH's aim to annex, 93, 127, 129; AH delays attack on, 138; dismantled at Munich conference, 141, 144; Germany occupies, 150; *see also* Sudetenland

Daily Mail, 19
Daily Telegraph, 78
Daladier, Édouard, 140
D'Annunzio, Gabriele, 88
Dante Alighieri Cultural Association, 46
Danube basin: Italy hopes to dominate, 150, 193
Danzig, 144
Deakin, F.W., 12, 242
De Bono, General Emilio, 248, 270
De Felice, Renzo, 13, 36, 73, 258, 263, 271, 273
De Grada, Magda Ceccarelli *see* Ceccarelli De Grada, Magda
Denmark: Germany attacks, 169, 175, 179; joins Anti-Comintern Pact, 224
Deutsche, Der (journal), 40
De Vecchi, General Cesare Maria, 50, 248
Diel, Louise, 57
Dietrich, Otto, 50, 53, 76
Dinale, Ottavio ('Farinata'), 41
diplomacy: AH/BM style of, 8, 295
Di Pompeo, Corrado, 280
disarmament conference: Germany walks out on, 39
DNVP (German national conservatives), 34
Dollfuss, Engelbert: BM finances, 35; Austrian Nazis undermine, 44; authoritarianism, 55; killed, 56
Dollmann, Eugen, 156
Drummond, Sir Eric, 52
Duce in Germania, Il (commemorative book), 92
Dunkirk evacuation (May 1940), 182

East Africa: Italian expansion in, 61–2; Italian Empire ended, 200
East Germany: view of Fascism and Nazism, 292
Eatwell, Roger, 7
Ebermayer, Erich, 84
Ebert, Friedrich, 255
Eden, Anthony, 77, 235
Eggers, Kurt, 270
Egypt: Italian advance on, 188, 190, 192–3
Eher Verlag (Nazi publishing house), 31, 35
Elena, Queen of Victor Emmanuel, 115, 119
Engel, Major Gerhard, 184
Epoca, l' (newspaper), 22
Eritrea, 61, 190
Essen, 84
Ethiopia: Italy invades and campaigns in, 4–5, 15, 57, 59, 61–4, 131; Italian atrocities in, 72; Italians defeated by African-British force (1941), 200
Ettel, Erwin, 109

Farinacci, Roberto, 54, 134, 180, 210, 248, 263
Fasci italiani di combattimento, 36, 151, 176
Fascism: regime in Italy, 2, 5; and German Nazism, 3, 10, 14, 16, 17, 23, 24–5, 30, 63, 108, 125, 151–2; and AH–BM relationship, 11; public view of, 13, 155; and anti-Semitism, 25, 106; BM declares not for export, 30; *Mein Kampf*

Fascism (contd):
on, 41; belief in Jewish–Bolshevik–freemason world conspiracy, 107; and mass support, 112–13; unpopular aggressive stance, 143–4; AH praises, 151; decline, 227; disintegrates in face of defeat, 238, 244; terror squads and atrocities in Italy, 282; transient appeal in Italy, 291
Fascist Grand Council, 102, 145, 151, 165, 246, 249
Fascist party (Italy): established (March 1919), 17; March on Rome (1922), 18–20, 23; relations with established Italian institutions, 25; rise to power, 25–6; radicalisation following BM's German visit, 95; organisation impresses Germans on 1938 state visit, 118; ambivalence over alliance with Germany, 126; foreign policy, 131; unpopularity in Italy, 176; and growing popular discontent, 222
Federzoni, Luigi, 31
Fiat: Turin strikes (1943), 238
Finland: as Nazi ally, 217, 219, 223; joins Anti-Comintern Pact, 224
Finnish–Soviet War (Winter War, 1939–40), 168
Florence: AH visits, 122–3; AH–BM meeting (October 1940), 195–6; falls to Allies, 281
Focardi, Filippo, 13
four-power pact (France–Britain–Italy–Germany): BM proposes, 37, 39
France: AH perceives as arch-enemy, 5; AH and BM criticise, 50; BM consents to agreement with, 56, 59; Popular Front, 67; alliance with Czechoslovakia, 130–1; potential war with Italy, 147, 150; declares war on Germany (3 September 1939), 162; Germany invades, 180; Italian campaign against, 184–5; armistice negotiations with AH, 187; signs armistice with Germany (June 1940), 189; *see also* Vichy France
Franco, General Francisco: dictatorship, 8; coup (1936), 67; captures Madrid, 152; prospective joining with Axis in war against Britain, 191, 203; AH meets at Hendaye, 194
Franco-Soviet Treaty of Mutual Assistance (1935), 61
François-Poncet, André: ridicules AH's dress, 46; on Italy and Germany wishing to avoid alienating Britain, 74; on German military manoeuvres, 83; on popular German reaction to BM's visit, 85; on BM's subservience to Germany, 102; on AH–BM relationship, 126, 136, 141; transferred to Rome, 147; on Italian invasion of Albania, 153
Frank, Brigitte, 112
Frank, Hans, 26, 29, 53, 68–9, 128
Fricke, Counter-Admiral Kurt, 201
Fritsch, General Werner von, 94

Gaggia, Villa, near San Fermo, 246–7
Galli Della Loggia, Ernesto, 258
Garibaldi, Giuseppe, 121, 147, 257
Gazzetta del Popolo (newspaper), 29
Genoa: BM's 1938 speech in, 126; British air attacks on, 234
Gentizon, Paul, 276
Gentleman's Agreement (Italy–Britain, 1937), 96, 105
Gerarchia (Fascist journal), 28, 121, 176
German Labour Front, 40
German Sixth Army, 238
Germany (Third Reich): pre-war foreign policy successes, 4; remilitarises Rhineland, 4, 65; Axis with Italy, 5, 13, 15, 126; BM visits (September 1937), 5–6, 74–87; relations with Italy, 5–7, 9, 15; popular attitudes to regime, 11–12; military support for Italy, 15; occupies north and Central Italy, 16, 259, 262–3; popular unfavourable view of Italy, 18, 35, 64, 79, 91, 199, 201, 205, 256, 261; Italian popular view of, 30; demands relaxation of rearmament restrictions, 39; rivalry with Italy over leading fascist power, 39; walks out on disarmament conference and League of Nations, 39; declining relations with Italy (1933), 40–1; Law for the Order of National Labour (1934), 40; prospective annexation of Austria, 52; naval agreement with Britain (1935), 62; closer relations with Italy, 64, 70–3; developing networks with Italy, 65–6; offers to re-join League of Nations, 66; recognises Italian Empire, 66; anti-Bolshevik policy with Italy, 67, 69; Police Accords with Italy, 67, 106, 129; supports Franco in Spanish Civil War, 67; Four-Year Plan (1936), 69, 71; in Anti-Comintern Pact, 70, 95; Italian labour in, 71, 210–12, 223, 239, 277; trade with Italy, 71, 210; crowds mustered to cheer BM, 84–5; military parade at conclusion of BM's 1937

visit, 87; effect of BM's visit on popular opinion in, 91–2; expansionist foreign policy, 93; military strength, 93; popular Italian wariness of, 103–4; unpopularity in Italy for alliance, 127; mutual restriction with Italy on medal awards, 129; exports coal to Italy, 131; ambiguity over military alliance with Italy, 133–4; popular apprehension about forthcoming war, 133; popular opposition to warmongering, 144; alliance with Italy (1939), 154–6; formal alliance with Italy (May 1939), 157–8; non-aggression pact with Soviet Russia (1939), 160, 168, 174; invades and occupies Poland, 161, 164; mistrust of Italy, 166; Britain blocks German deliveries to Italy, 169; invades Denmark and Norway, 169; advance in west (1940), 175–6; military spending and war economy, 179; invades France, Belgium, Netherlands and Luxembourg, 180; early military victories, 184; scepticism over Italian declaration of war, 184; lacks military coordination with Italy, 186, 191; scorn for Italian military resolve, 186; armistice with France (June 1940), 189; designs on Romanian oilfields, 192–3; plans invasion of Soviet Union, 192, 194, 212; intervention in Balkans and Greece, 199–200, 293; supports Italy in north Africa, 207; invades Greece, 209–10; invades Yugoslavia, 209; invades Soviet Union (June 1941), 215–16; Italy imports goods from, 223; declares war on USA, 224–5; secret military convention with Japan and Italy, 226; casualties on eastern front, 229; dominance over Italy, 231; June 1942 offensive on eastern front, 231; Allied bombing campaign against, 235, 250, 261; and prospective Italian defeat, 236; determination in facing defeat, 238; Sixth Army surrenders at Stalingrad, 238; Allies demand unconditional surrender, 239, 242; blames Italy for military misfortunes, 240; plans for eventuality of putsch against BM, 244; armaments production, 245; reaction to BM's downfall, 251; strengthens forces in Italy, 251, 254; anti-Italian acts after armistice (1943), 259–60, 262; Italian military internees in, 260, 278, 284–5; takes control of former Habsburg territories, 262; treatment of occupied Italy, 271; tensions with RSI government, 275; brutal repression in Italy, 281; increasing defeatism, 285; defeat in Battle of the Bulge, 286; casualties in Italy, 287; final defeat and surrender, 287–8, 290; surrenders in Italy (2 May 1945), 287; political structure, 290; wartime atrocities, 291; post-war divisions, 292; responsibility for war and Holocaust, 292; state censorship, 294; *see also* East Germany; West Germany

Gestapo: lists German citizens in Italy, 106

Giolitti, Giovanni, 238

Giornale d'Italia, 32

Goebbels, Joseph: diaries, 14, 165, 214; AH feels comfortable with, 51; and BM's 1937 visit to Germany, 74, 80, 82, 88; scepticism over Italy's honouring Axis, 91; accompanies AH on state visit to Italy, 108–9, 112, 114, 116–17; AH confides to on sealing friendship with BM, 121; sends telegram on leaving Italy, 124; on status of South Tyrol, 124; on BM's assurance to AH of bond, 125; confidence in AH over Sudeten crisis, 137; on potential alliance with Italy, 149; on BM's invasion of Albania, 153; organises German book fair in Rome (May 1939), 156; doubts of formal Italo-German pact (1939), 158; accuses Italy of betrayal in commitment to war, 159; and Italian anti-German views, 165; reports on first Brenner Pass meeting, 172; doubts on Italian reliability, 191; AH praises BM to, 197; recognises failing Fascist regime in Italy, 205; on AH's outlining Soviet invasion plan to BM, 214; bans report of BM piloting AH's aircraft, 221; on Salzburg meeting (April 1942), 230; impressed by BM's December 1942 speech to Fascist party, 236; on total war in face of defeat, 238; and BM's cabinet reshuffle, 239; on impact of Churchill–Roosevelt meeting at Casablanca, 239; and AH–BM March 1943 Klessheim meeting, 241–2; on BM's May 1943 speech, 243; insists on communique from July 1943 meeting, 247–8; on effect of BM's downfall in Germany, 250; AH gives true view of alliance with BM, 251; AH tells of BM being

Goebbels (contd):
weak dictator, 255; reveals anti-Italian sentiments, 261–2, 275; and BM's liberation and flight to Germany, 264–6; and AH's growing anti-Italian feelings, 267; on BM's losing sense of reality, 273–4; on BM's health problems, 274; AH discusses Italian strategy with, 275; suicide, 289
Gömbös, Gyula, 70
Gonella, Guido, 179
Göring, Hermann: asylum in Italy, 24–5; BM gives signed photograph for AH, 29; visits Royal Italian Academy congress, 34; hands AH letter to BM, 40; and AH's 1934 Venice meeting with BM, 44; January 1937 visit to Italy, 72; and German annexation of Austria, 101; admires Italian air force, 120; urges AH to accept Chamberlain's offer on Sudetenland, 137–8; drafts Munich Agreement, 141; visit to Rome (April 1939), 153; urges close military coordination with Italy, 186; diminishing influence on AH, 213; visit to Italy (January 1942), 227; persuades AH to broadcast after Italian armistice, 261
Graefe, Albrecht von, 26
Grandi, Dino: supports proposed four-power pact, 37; on Axis, 73; peace overtures, 235; dismissed, 238; calls for BM's downfall, 248; BM fails to purge, 265; BM criticises, 282
Graziani, Marshal Rodolfo: assassination attempt on, 72
Great Dictator, The (film), 2
Greece: Italy attacks, 192–4, 196; Italy repelled, 196–7, 199; German intervention in, 199–200; Germans invade, 210
Griffin, Roger, 7
Guadalajara, Battle of (1937), 104
Guariglia, Raffaele, 257–8
Guidi, Guido Buffarini, 109, 273
Gustav defence line, Italy (German), 268
Guzzoni, General Alfredo, 203

H., Paul (ex-hussar), 111
Habicht, Theodor, 53
Halder, General Franz, 183, 197
Halifax, Edward Frederick Lindley Wood, 1st Earl of, 134–5, 148
Hamburg: bombed by British, 250
Hamburger Fremdenblatt (newspaper), 276
Harzburg Front, 31
Hassell, Ulrich von: and AH's proposed meeting with BM, 42; on AH's view of BM, 51; on Dollfuss assassination, 56; replaced as ambassador, 94
Henderson, Nevile, 102
Henlein, Konrad, 129–30
Hess, Ilse, 112
Hess, Rudolf: on origins of Nazi salute, 29–30; Renzetti meets after 1934 Venice meeting, 53; meets BM on 1937 visit to Germany, 78, 82; accompanies AH on state visit to Italy, 114; on status of South Tyrol, 124; welcomes BM to Munich conference, 139; flies to Scotland, 212
Hesse, Prince of *see* Philip, Prince of Hesse
Himmler, Heinrich: in Munich for BM's 1937 visit, 80, 82; and arrest of German refugees in Italy, 106; accompanies AH on state visit to Italy, 109, 114; plans annexation of Sudetenland, 130; and resettlement of South Tyrolese, 160; focuses on war with Soviet Union, 216; BM receives (October 1942), 232; employs astrologers to locate BM, 251; orders deportation of Rome's Jews, 272
Hindenburg, Paul Ludwig Hans Anton von Beneckendorff und von, 54, 255
Hitler, Adolf: assassination attempt on (July 1944), 1, 283–5; nature of relationship with BM, 1–3, 6–12, 14–16, 293–6; political status, 2; background and aims, 3–4; pre-war foreign policy successes, 4–5; sees BM as model leader, 4; wish to take over Austria, 4, 55; state visit to Italy (1938), 6, 96–8, 105, 109–12, 114–18, 121–4; value of meetings with BM, 6; style of diplomacy, 8–9, 42, 294–5; correspondence with BM, 14–15, 29, 160–1, 167, 180, 182, 207; first meeting with BM (Venice, June 1934), 15, 42–53; early years in Munich, 17; on early Fascist government in Italy, 18–20; admiration and praise for BM, 19, 22, 24, 27–8, 41, 51, 53, 165, 206, 227, 230, 233, 256, 261, 276, 290; seeks anti-French alliance with Italy, 19; seen as German BM, 19; and Italian claims to South Tyrol, 21–2, 28, 45; stresses Nazi similarity to Fascism, 22; in Beer Hall Putsch, 23; tried and imprisoned, 23; and Fascist rise to power, 25; denies

receiving Italian funding, 26–7; BM's ambiguous attitude to, 28, 31, 35; interviewed in Italian newspapers, 28–9; and *Heil Hitler* salute, 29, 82; praises Italian history, 30; contributes to Meletti book, 31; influenced by Renzetti, 31; keeps bust of BM in Munich HQ, 32; Malaparte belittles, 32; proposes visits to BM in Rome, 32–3, 36; as vegetarian and teetotaller, 33, 43, 48, 99; appointed Reich chancellor, 34; courts BM as Reich chancellor, 34; and BM's opposition to Nazi anti-Semitism, 38; accuses BM of jealousy of National Socialism, 39; fiftieth birthday, 39, 154; and German abandonment of disarmament conference and League of Nations, 40; Italian criticisms of, 41; views Italians as inferior, 41, 57; travels by air, 43, 45; dress, 46, 49, 99–100, 119, 140; taste in modern art, 49, 83, 123; invites BM to Germany, 50, 68, 73; demands copy of von Papen's Marburg speech, 54; and elimination of SA and Röhm, 54–5; visits dying Hindenburg, 54; BM signs Diel biography for, 57–8; and Italian ridicule of Nazi race theories, 57; signs non-aggression pact with Poland, 58; expansionist policy, 59, 149, 151; increasing rivalry with BM, 59; aims to revise Versailles Treaty, 60, 66; and Italian invasion of Ethiopia, 64; meeting with Manacorda, 64; BM's indirect communication with, 66; march into Rhineland, 66; hostility to Bolshevism, 67; proposes joint Italo-German intervention in Spain, 67; Ciano visits (October 1936), 69; courts BM in January 1937 Reichstag speech, 72; and BM's September 1937 visit to Germany, 74–7, 80–6; appointed honorary corporal of Fascist militia, 81–2; awards honour to BM, 82–3; in Berlin with BM, 84; and BM's departure from 1937 visit, 88; invited to second visit to Italy, 90–1; belief in bond with BM, 92; designs on Czechoslovakia, 93, 127; throat polyp, 93; becomes supreme commander of army, 94, 105; BM's ideological attachment to, 96; wish for war, 96; Vatican opposition to, 98; avoids churches on state visit to Italy, 99; diet, 99; claims on Austria, 100; invades and annexes Austria, 100–2; security measures for state visit to Italy, 107–9; travels by train to Italy, 111; discomfort in presence of Victor Emmanuel, 114–15; presents telescope and funds observatory for Italy, 117; impressed by Fascist organisation, 118; Bianchi Bandinelli claims dislikes BM, 120; on unpopularity in Germany of alliance with Italy, 120; speech at state visit to Italy, 122; states admiration for Italy, 123; sends telegrams on leaving Italy, 124–5; welcome on return from state visit, 125; effect of state visit, 126–7; international comments on state visit to Italy, 126; believes fate linked with BM, 128; overestimates Italy's military capabilities, 128; at Nuremberg party rallies, 130; demands on Sudetenland, 130, 133–8; receives Chamberlain in Berchtesgaden and Bad Godesberg, 135, 137; welcomes BM's Trieste speech, 136; delays invasion of Czechoslovakia, 138; at Munich conference (1938), 139–41, 296; successful cooperation with BM at Munich, 144; speech on friendship with Italy (January 1939), 149–50; threatens extermination of Jews, 149; occupies Czechoslovakia, 150; plans invasion of Poland, 153–4, 158–60; declines Pius XII's proposal for multilateral conference, 154; negotiations for formal alliance with Italy, 154; Reichstag speech (28 April 1939), 154; repeated messages of friendship with BM, 154; and formal alliance with Italy (1939), 157–8; and BM's lack of support over invasion of Poland, 159; exasperated by BM's reluctance to enter war, 160–1; celebrates triumph in Poland, 165; and BM's non-belligerency, 169; suggests further meeting with BM, 169–70; Brenner Pass meeting with BM (March 1940), 170–4; declines to send minutes of Brenner Pass meeting to BM, 174–5; booed in Milan cinema, 177; brags to BM about German victories, 178, 182; reaction to Italian declaration of war, 184; calls Munich meeting with BM (June 1940), 186–8; declines Italian military assistance, 188; gives two railway anti-aircraft guns to BM, 188; peace offer to Britain, 189; second Brenner Pass meeting with BM (October 1940), 191–2; attempts to

Hitler (contd):
recruit European far right regimes, 194; dislike of Franco, 194; plans to invade Soviet Russia, 194, 212; told of BM's attack on Greece, 194, 196; Florence meeting with BM (October 1940), 195; delays intervention in Greece, 197; dominance over BM, 198, 202–5, 219–20, 233–4; refuses to put Italian armed forces under German control, 201; Berghof meeting with BM (January 1941), 202–4; disappointment with BM, 202; concern about Italian conduct of war, 207; orders invasion of Yugoslavia, 209; gives credit to Italy for Balkan campaign, 210; third Brenner Pass meeting (June 1941), 213–14; proposes sending Jews to Madagascar, 214; secrecy over plans to invade Soviet Union, 214; accepts Italian troops in war against Soviet Union, 218; Wolf's Lair meeting with BM (August 1941), 219–20; flies to eastern front with BM, 220–1; believes in victory over USA, 224–5; justifies attack on Soviet Union as crusade, 224; assumes supreme command of German army, 225; on extermination of Jews, 225; concern over Italy becoming liability, 226; disparages Italian nobility, 227; concedes German setbacks in Soviet Russia, 229–30; Salzburg meeting with BM (April 1942), 230; Ciano meets (November–December 1942), 235, 237; orders BM to East Prussian HQ (December 1942), 237; forbids retreat at Stalingrad, 238; and BM's cabinet reshuffle (1943), 239; and breakdown of relations with BM, 239–40; on historic origins of Nazism, 240; Klessheim meeting with BM (March 1943), 240–3; exhaustion, 241; aggressive letters to BM, 244; anger at Italian generals, 244; and Allied invasion of Sicily, 245; meets BM in Italy (July 1943), 246–8; and BM's dismissal and arrest, 249–50, 252; exploits Badoglio, 251; gives Goebbels true views on alliance with BM, 251; attitude to Badoglio government, 254; plans to arrest king and Badoglio, 254; admits BM weak dictator, 255; plans to reinstall BM, 256, 265, 275–6; attempts to locate BM, 261, 263; broadcast on Italian armistice, 261; and BM's liberation and flight to Germany, 263–5; growing anti-Italian feelings, 267–8, 275, 293; maintains regard for BM, 275–6; Klessheim meeting with BM (April 1944), 276–9; BM writes on 1938 visit, 282–3; Wolf's Lair meeting with BM (July 1944), 283–5; loses popular support, 285; final correspondence with BM, 288; takes refuge in Berlin bunker, 288; maintains display of unity and friendship with BM, 289; suicide, 289; image as boorish and destructive, 291; blames BM and Italy for German failures, 292–3; declares friendship with BM a mistake, 293; *Mein Kampf*, 24, 35, 41; *Second Book*, 22
Hoare, Sir Samuel, 64
Hoffmann, Heinrich: photographs of AH and BM, 50, 82, 87–8
Hohenbach, Alexander Boltho von, 270
Holocaust: and AH's ideology, 3; study of, 13; and Italian Jews, 273; German responsibility for, 292; *see also* Jews
Horthy, Admiral Miklós, 226
Hoßbach, Colonel Friedrich, 93
Hull, Cordell, 193, 197
Hungary: disputes with Romania, 192; joins Tripartite Pact, 198; as wartime ally of Germany, 223, 242–3

Illustrierter Beobachter (magazine), 50
Innsbruck: BM stops at on way to Germany, 78; Italo-German meeting (5 April 1939), 152
Inter-Allied Rhineland High Commission, 20
Interlandi, Telesio, 31
Italian Communist Party, 142
Italian Eighth Army, 237
Italian Expedition Corps (in Soviet Union), 217
Italian Social Republic (RSI): established, 268–70; regime, 271–3, 275, 278, 290; agreement with Germany over Italian workers, 277; Pavolini praises, 279; and German arrogant behaviour in Italy, 280; loses popular support, 284–5; ambivalent status, 290
Italien-Beobachter (magazine), 110, 115, 157
Italo-German congress of law, Rome (June 1938), 129
Italy (Fascist): Fascist regime, 2; anti-Semitism, 3, 96, 107, 136, 145–6, 232, 292; racialism and colonial rule, 3–4,

13, 96; invades Ethiopia, 4–5, 15, 57, 59, 61–3; as theatre of war (1943–5), 4; forms Axis with Germany, 5, 13, 15, 126; relations with Germany, 5–7, 9, 15, 40–1; enters war (June 1940), 6; military setbacks, 11, 15; popular attitudes to regime as benign, 11–14; Germany occupies north and centre, 16, 259, 262–3; effect of First World War on, 17; popular German unfavourable view of, 18, 35, 64, 199, 201, 205, 256, 261; failed campaign in north Africa, 19, 192–3, 200, 204–5; occupies Corfu, 21; AH describes as Germany's natural ally, 22; view of Germans, 30; BM seeks to make great power, 37–8, 60, 131; Labour Charter (*carta del lavoro*), 40; AH's disparaging view of, 41; criticisms of AH, 41; reaction to 1934 Nazi putsch in Austria, 56; expansionism in East Africa and Mediterranean, 61–2; closer relations with Germany, 64–6, 70–3; anti-Bolshevik policy with Germany, 67, 69, 216; Police Accords with Germany, 67, 106, 129; supports Franco in Spanish Civil War, 67, 95–6, 131; in Anti-Comintern Pact, 70, 95; trade with Germany, 71, 210; workers in Germany, 71, 210–12, 223, 239, 277; welcomes BM's return from 1937 meeting, 89; Nazis believe inferior to Germany, 91; military weakness, 94, 200–3; anti-bourgeois campaign, 95–6; expansionist policy, 95; quits League of Nations, 95; AH's state visit (1938), 96–9, 105–24; Gentleman's Agreement with Britain, 96, 105; flags prepared for AH's state visit, 97; popular suspicion of Germany, 103–4; readiness for war on German side, 105; tightens security for AH's state visit, 105–6; anti-German and anti-Fascist attitudes, 107–8, 113, 176–7, 209; protests against AH's state visit, 113; status of monarchy, 115; navy, 118–19; armed forces demonstrate on AH's state visit, 119–20, 122, 128; effect of AH's state visit to, 126–7; unpopularity of alliance with Germany, 127, 142; mutual restriction with Germany on medal awards, 129; coal imports from Germany, 131; doubts on alliance with Germany, 133; racial legislation, 136, 145–6; popular resistance to Fascist warmongering, 143; Jews repressed and deported, 145, 273; move to totalitarianism, 145; Chamberlain visits, 147–9; Anglo-Italian declaration (November 1938), 147; formal alliance with Germany (May 1939), 154–8; coffee shortage, 155; denies blame for Second World War, 158–9; and Franco-British declaration of war on Germany, 162; non-belligerency period, 162, 165–7, 169, 184; popular desire for peace, 162; delay in entering war, 165–6, 180–1, 190; German view of as unreliable, 165; mistrust of Germany, 166; British naval blockade of, 169–70; expects territorial gains from war, 175; unpreparedness for war, 178–9, 183; Church opposes war, 179, 181; economic weakness, 179; popular letters supporting entry into war, 181; declares war on France and Britain, 183; attack on France, 184–5; lacks military coordination with Germany, 186, 191; support for short war, 186; attack on British in north Africa, 188, 190, 192–3; armistice with France (1940), 189; attack on Greece, 192–4; repelled in Greece, 196–7, 199; military strategies fail, 200; popular shame over military setbacks, 208–9; joins Germany in war against Soviet Union, 215–18, 220, 222, 224, 225, 232, 237; growing discontent and war weariness, 222, 237, 285; rationing, 222; imports goods from Germany, 223; declares war on USA, 224–5; secret military convention with Germany and Japan (January 1942), 226; and German superiority, 231; area bombing by British, 234, 245; early peace overtures, 235; faces defeat, 236, 238–9; Germany blames for military misfortunes, 240, 275; Allied invasion, 244; armaments production and mobilisation, 245; reaction to downfall of BM, 249–50; Germany strengthens forces in, 251, 255; withdraws from German alliance after BM's fall, 252; position in Axis after BM's fall, 253; negotiates with Allies for armistice, 256–7, 258; Allied landings in Calabria, 258; armistice with Allies (3 September 1943), 258–9; under German occupation, 259, 262–3; civilian deportees in Germany, 260–1;

Italy (contd):
military internees in Germany, 260, 278, 284–5; soldiers disarmed and killed by Germans, 260; deaths under German occupation, 263; German defensive strategy in, 268; partisan activity in, 279, 281, 285; Allied advance in, 280, 285; German reprisals in, 281; three conflicts in, 281; German surrender in (May 1945), 287; wartime casualties, 287; atrocities under Fascism, 291; post-war position and image, 292; state censorship, 294

Japan: invades Manchuria (1931), 62; signs Anti-Comintern Pact (1936), 70, 95, 155; warned in Roosevelt's 'quarantine speech', 93; AH seeks closer relations with, 154; Ribbentrop hopes for pact with, 155; Tripartite Pact with Germany and Italy (1940), 190; as ally of Germany, 224; attack on Pearl Harbor, 224; neutrality in war against Soviet Union, 225; secret military convention with Italy and Germany (January 1942), 226
Jews: Nazi hostility and repression, 9, 17, 24, 38, 145; BM's attitude to, 81, 136, 145–6, 225, 232–3; German refugees in Italy, 106–7; and Italian racial legislation, 136, 146; growing Italian attacks on, 145; AH's extermination policy, 149, 225; German repression in Poland, 164; AH believes in world conspiracy, 206; Nazi persecution increases in war, 214, 225, 232; suppressed and deported under BM's RSI regime, 271–3, 290; Italian discrimination against, 292; *see also* anti-Semitism
Jung, Edgar Ernst, 53–4

Kappler, Herbert, 272
Keitel, General Wilhelm, 152–3, 187, 192, 203, 219, 230
Kesselring, Field Marshal Albert: command and authority in Italy, 245, 251, 263
Klessheim *see* Schloss Klessheim
Klinkhammer, Lutz, 271
Kristallnacht (9 November 1938), 145
Krogmann, Carl Vincent, 57
Kursk, Battle of (1943), 246

L., Giacomo (anti-German Italian), 108
Lanza, Michele, 174
Lateran Treaties (1929), 19, 98
Lausanne conference on German reparations, 33
Laval, Pierre, 59–60, 194, 236
League of Nations: sanctions against Italy, 5, 71, 131, 287; and international order, 6, 10; Council, 19; BM despises, 21, 37, 50; and Corfu crisis, 21; Italy maintains membership, 21; AH's low opinion of, 24, 50; Germany walks out on, 39; and Italian invasion of Ethiopia, 62, 64, 66–7; Germany offers to rejoin, 66; Germany refuses to support sanctions against Italy, 86; Italy leaves, 95
Leto, Guido, 106
Libya: campaign in, 228–9, 237–8
Little Entente (Czechoslovakia–Romania–Yugoslavia), 131
Lloyd George, David, 9
Locarno conference and Treaty (1925), 65, 68
Lochner, Louis P., 42
Lüdecke, Kurt, 17–18
Ludendorff, General Erich: supports AH, 17
Ludwig, Emil, 30
Lufthansa: number of passengers between Rome and Berlin, 129
Luxembourg: Germany invades, 180

M., Gherardo, 107
MacDonald, Ramsay, 60
Mackensen, Hans Georg von: appointed ambassador to Rome, 94; and AH's July 1943 meeting with BM, 246; AH instructs to request audience with king, 254
Mackensen, Winifred von, 115
Mack Smith, Denis, 61
Maddalena, La (island), 257
Maifeld (Berlin), 86–7
Malaparte, Curzio, 32
Malta: Italian attack on, 189; AH plans attack on, 231
Manacorda, Guido, 64
Manchester Guardian, 126
Manchuria: Japan invades (1931), 62
Manifesto of Racial Scientists, 136
Marras, General Luigi Efisio, 254
Martin, Benjamin G., 65
Mastromattei, Giuseppe, 112
Matteotti, Giacomo: assassinated, 183, 236
Mauthausen concentration camp, Austria, 261
Max von Baden, Prince, 256
Mecklenburg, 83

Meissner, Otto, 255
Meletti, Vincenzo, 31
Messersmith, George, 39
Metaxas, General Ioannis, 196–7
Milan: BM's speech in (November 1936), 70; popular discontent with Fascist policies, 155, 195; opposition to war on German side, 176–7; bombed by British, 189; BM's December 1944 speech in, 286–7; BM's and Petacci's bodies hanged upside down in, 289
Mit brennende Sorge (papal encyclical), 98
Moeller van den Bruck, Arthur, 20
Mois Suisse, Le, 276
Molotov–Ribbentrop Pact (1939), 160
Monte Cassino Abbey: battle for, 268, 280
Montgomery, General Bernard Law, 234
Morell, Dr Theo, 240, 274
Morris, Leland B., 197
Moscow: German attack on, 223, 225
Mostra Augustea della Romanità (exhibition), 120
Müller, Heinrich, 106
Müller, Sven von, 63, 65
Munich: early Nazi activities, 17; Beer Hall Putsch (1923), 23; architecture inspired by Italy, 46; BM visits, 78–9; AH–BM meeting in (June 1940), 186–8; BM flown to after liberation, 264–5
Munich conference (1938): AH and BM challenge European order at, 15; BM attends with AH, 139–40; negotiations and agreement, 139, 141–2, 150, 296
Mussolini, Arnaldo (BM's brother): death, 33
Mussolini, Benito: nature of relationship with AH, 1–3, 6–12, 14–16, 293–6; visits AH after July 1944 assassination plot, 1; background and aims, 3–4; visits AH in Germany (September 1937), 5–6, 68, 74–86; fall from power (July 1943), 6, 249; style of diplomacy, 8–9, 294–5; maintains visits to Germany, 11; correspondence with AH, 14–15, 29, 161, 167, 180, 182, 207; forms Fascist party (1919), 17; meets Lüdecke in Milan, 17; early relations with German politicians and groups, 18; AH admires and praises, 19, 22, 24, 27–8, 41, 51, 53, 206, 227, 233, 256, 261, 290; asserts role as doyen of European fascism, 19; and occupation of Corfu, 21; and Ruhr crisis, 22; proclaims dictatorship (1925), 23; cult, 24, 177; influence on German right, 24; postpones meeting with AH, 24, 26; and promotion of Fascism in Weimar Republic, 27; ambivalent attitude to AH, 28, 31, 35; foreign policy, 28, 60; denies Fascism anti-Semitic, 30; AH keeps bust of in Munich, 32; AH requests visits (1931–3), 32–3, 36; AH courts as Reich chancellor, 34; funds Italian edition of *Mein Kampf*, 35; proposes four-power pact (France–Britain–Italy–Germany), 37, 39; resists Nazi anti-Jewish action, 38; congratulates AH on fiftieth birthday, 39, 154; and German abandonment of disarmament conference and League of Nations, 40; and Dinale's poor review of *Mein Kampf*, 41; first (Venice) meeting with AH (June 1934), 42–52; speaks German, 43, 48, 86, 120, 278; dress, 46, 49, 219, 249, 264; AH invites to Germany, 50, 68, 73; closing speech at Venice meeting, 50–1; less ruthless than AH, 54; aware of AH's wish to take over Austria, 55–6; on assassination of Dollfuss, 56; consents to agreement with France, 56; cult in Germany, 57; ridicules Nazi race theories, 57; envies AH, 58; hostile attitude to Germany, 58; signs Diel biography with dedication to AH, 58; expansionist aims, 59–61, 151; increasing rivalry with AH, 59; aims to revise Versailles Treaty, 60, 66; wishes to revise Versailles Treaty, 60; and invasion of Ethiopia, 61–3; showmanship, 61; uncertainty over making alliances, 61; on German claim to annex Austria, 63; gives audience to Sven von Müller, 63; shifts closer to AH, 63; accepts German claim to control Austria, 65; receives Roland Strunk, 65; pursues closer cooperation with Germany, 66; threatens to quit League of Nations, 66; anti-Bolshevik policy with Germany, 67; popularity after conquest of Ethiopia, 67; declares admiration for AH (1936), 69; on Berlin–Rome Axis, 70–1, 73; unwillingness to sign formal alliance with Germany, 74, 146–7; stops in Austria on way to 1937 meeting in Germany, 78; appoints AH honorary corporal in Fascist militia, 81–2; on racial question, 81; AH awards honour to, 82–3; introduces goose-step (as *passo romano*), 82; in Berlin with AH, 84;

Mussolini (contd):
speech in pouring rain at close of 1937 German visit, 86–7, 91; meets D'Annunzio, 88; welcomed on return from 1937 meeting, 88–9; confesses admiration for Germany, 89; reaction to visit to Germany, 89–90; popular German reaction to, 91–2; belief in bond with AH, 92; and AH's assuming command of army, 94; receives gift of horse from Hanover, 95; ideological attachment to AH, 96; wish for war, 96; and AH's invasion of Austria, 100–3, 105; ambiguous view of AH, 104; boasts of readiness for war, 104–5; made marshal of the Empire, 105; plans alliance with Germany, 105; anti-Semitism, 106, 136, 145–6, 225, 232; approves arrest of German Jewish refugees, 106; receives protests about AH's state visit, 113; and AH's state visit to Italy, 114, 116–19, 121, 123–4; Bianchi Bandinelli claims dislikes AH, 120; speech at AH's state visit, 122; telegram from AH on leaving Italy, 124–5; believes fate linked with AH, 128; on prospective war with Western powers, 130–2; role in Sudeten crisis, 130–3, 135–6; on alliance with Germany against West, 131, 134; Churchill on, 134–5; Trieste speech, 136–7; anxious to delay war, 138; welcomes AH's suggestion of four-power conference, 138; at Munich conference (1938), 139–41, 296; wears Hitler-style cap, 139; prestige after Munich, 142; popular opposition to extremist behaviour, 143; successful cooperation with AH at Munich, 144; growing aggression, 145; and Chamberlain's visit to Italy, 147–9; relations with Britain, 147; not consulted over AH's occupation of Czechoslovakia, 150; jealousy of AH's territorial successes, 151; and invasion of Albania, 152–3; speech on affinity with Nazi ideology, 152; and formal alliance with Germany ('Pact of Steel' 1939), 154, 157–8; maintains friendship with Britain, 154; repeated messages of friendship with AH, 154; proclaims Axis (November 1936), 156; Turin speech (May 1939), 156; visits German book fair (Rome, May 1939), 156; reluctance to support German attack on Poland, 158–60; not consulted over German–Soviet non-aggression pact, 160; requests war materials from AH, 160; 'non-belligerency' policy, 162, 165, 167, 168; lacks consistent policy, 163; delays entry into war, 164, 167, 180; increases defence spending, 164; believes in Italy as negotiator between Germany and Allies, 165; dismisses senior army and party leaders, 167; claims superior political experience, 168; letter to AH on Finnish–Soviet war, 168; on Nazi–Soviet pact, 168; sees France and Britain as primary enemies, 168–9; AH suggests further meeting with, 169–70; Brenner Pass meeting with AH (March 1940), 170–5; praises German advance in west, 175; praises AH to Council of Ministers, 176; eagerness to enter war, 176, 181–2; uncertain authority, 177; AH brags to about Germany victories, 178; receives letters supporting and opposing entry into war, 181–2; declares war on France and Britain, 183; offers Italian *bersaglieri* troops to AH, 185; Munich meeting with AH (June 1940), 186–7; scorn for soft Italians, 186; hopes for booty from French collapse frustrated, 187–8; AH declines offer of military assistance, 188; AH gives anti-aircraft guns to, 188; prepares attack on British in Egypt, 188; second Brenner Pass meeting with AH (October 1940), 191–2; orders attack on Greece, 193–4; Florence meeting with AH (October 1940), 195–6; AH dominates, 198, 202–5, 219–20, 233–4; Berghof meeting with AH (January 1941), 204; Mediterranean policy fails, 204, 209–10; Teatro Adriano speech (23 February 1941), 206–7; and AH's demands to secure Yugoslav–Albanian border, 209; on ill-treatment of Italian workers in Germany, 211; and Hess's flight to Scotland, 212; questions Ribbentrop over planned invasion of Soviet Union, 212; third Brenner Pass meeting (June 1941), 213–14; letter from AH on invasion of Soviet Union, 215; promises to side with Germany to end, 215; and Italy's role in war against Soviet Union, 216–17; Wolf's Lair meeting with AH (August 1941), 218–20; pilots AH's

aircraft, 220–1; visits eastern front with AH, 220–1; assessment of relations with AH, 222, 294–5; irritated by AH's speech on fighting against Russians, 223; announces declaration of war against USA, 225; increases troop numbers on eastern front, 225; health problems, 226, 236–7, 241–3, 274; relations with Clara Petacci publicised, 226, 258; maintains belief in victory, 228, 232; and recapture of Tobruk, 228; receives letters of support and congratulations, 228; wartime visit to Libya, 228–9; Salzburg meeting with AH (April 1942), 230–1; Himmler visits, 232; caricatured in British leaflets, 234–5; power declines, 235; and prospective Italian defeat, 236; urges peace with Soviet Russia, 236–7, 242; reshuffles ministers (1943), 238; and breakdown of relationship with AH, 239–40; Klessheim meeting with AH (March 1943), 240–3; speech of 5 May 1943, 243; personal security increased, 244; refuses Vatican plea for peace, 244; leading Fascists call for dismissal, 246, 248–9; meeting with AH in Italy (July 1943), 246–8; dismissed and arrested, 249; movements after dismissal, 252, 257; AH plans to reinstall, 256, 266, 275–6; writes account of fall from power, 257; press campaign to discredit, 258; liberated by Skorzeny and flown to Munich, 264; living arrangements under German protection, 266; proclaims new Fascist state (September 1943), 266–7; heads RSI government, 269–72; popularity as head of RSI, 269; and execution of Ciano, 270–1; decline in status and understanding, 273–4; Klessheim meeting with AH (April 1944), 276–9; speech to troops of National Republican Army in Germany, 278; agrees on suppression of partisans, 279; reaction to fall of Rome, 280; and German reprisals in Italy, 282; writings, 282; Wolf's Lair meeting with AH (July 1944), 283–5; boasts of prospective attack on Allies, 286; speech in Milan (December 1944), 286–7; sends final birthday note to AH, 288; shot together with Petacci and body hanged upside down in Milan, 288–9; maintains display of unity and friendship with AH, 289; AH scapegoats, 292–3; relationship with AH analysed, 293–6; *Drama of Diarchy* (*Il dramma di diarchia*), 282; *Opera Omnia*, 14
Mussolini, Bruno (BM's son): killed, 218
Mussolini, Vittorio (BM's son), 287
Mutschmann, Martin, 165

Naples: and AH's state visit, 97, 118–19; falls to Allies, 268
Narvik, 169, 175
National Republican Army (Italian), 278, 283
National Republican Guard (Italian), 280, 285
Nazi party: anti-Semitism, 17, 24, 94, 145–6, 149, 214, 225, 232; in Munich, 17, 23; influenced by Fascist rise to power, 25–6; poor results in 1928 Reichstag elections, 26; success in 1930 Reichstag elections, 27–8; Roman greeting (salute), 29; losses in second 1932 Reichstag elections, 34; consolidates rule (1933), 35, 36; announces boycott of Jewish businesses, 38; gains majority in November 1933 election, 40; condemned in Italy as dangerous, 56; and racial question, 75; and BM's 1937 visit to Germany, 76; hostility to Church, 127, 146; leaders criticise BM, 239; AH on origins, 240; demands total war before defeat, 288
Nazism: and Italian Fascism, 3, 10, 14, 16, 17, 24–5, 30, 63, 108, 125, 151–2; and AH–BM relationship, 11; accepted by non-party Germans, 20; ideology, 24, 292; and mass support, 113
Negrelli, Leo, 22
Netherlands: Germany invades, 180, 186
Neurath, Konstantin von: and foreign views of Nazi anti-Jewish boycott, 38; and German walk-out from League of Nations, 39; Cerutti complains to of deteriorating Italo-German reactions, 40; on first (Venice) meeting between AH and BM, 48, 50, 51; replaced as foreign minister by Ribbentrop, 94; drafts Munich Agreement, 141
New Order: quest for, in Europe, 4, 6, 8, 10, 86, 92, 95, 110, 112, 127, 182, 202, 204, 214–15, 219, 229, 242–3, 283, 290; Japan joins, 190
New York Herald Tribune, 191
New York Times, 42, 46, 78, 196, 213, 218, 221, 276, 285

Nietzsche, Friedrich, 252, 257
Night of the Long Knives (30 June 1934), 54–5
Normandy: Allied landings (June 1944), 281
North Africa: failed Italian campaign against British, 190, 192–3, 200, 204–5; German military support for Italy in, 207–8; British offensive campaign, 224; Axis supply lines, 226; Rommel's advance in, 228; Allied landings (November 1942), 234; Allied victories in, 234; Axis defeat in, 244
Norway: Germany attacks, 169, 175, 179
Nuremberg: Nazi party rallies, 130, 134
Nuremberg laws (racial), 146

Ogilvie-Forbes, George, 77, 84–7
Orano, Paolo: *L'Asse nel pensiero dei due popoli*, 121
Organisation Todt, 263
Orlando, Vittorio: at Paris Peace Conference, 9
Osservatore Romano (newspaper), 54, 98, 179

Pact of Steel (1939), 6, 157–9, 162, 197
Palermo: BM's speech in (20 August 1937), 73
Palmeri, Ruggiero, 106
Papen, Franz von: and AH's proposed meeting with BM, 42; speech criticising Nazi terror, 53–4; under house arrest, 54; appointed ambassador to Vienna, 56
Pariani, General Alberto, 152–3, 167
Paris Peace Conference (1919), 9
Partigiano, Il (Milanese clandestine newspaper), 288
Paul, Prince Regent of Yugoslavia, 209
Paulmann, Johannes, 7
Paulus, General Friedrich, 231, 238
Pavelić, Ante, 209
Pavolini, Alessandro, 217, 279
Pavone, Claudio, 281
Pearl Harbor (7 December 1941), 224–5
Perth, James Eric Drummond, 16th Earl of, 137–8
Petacci, Clara: and BM's 1937 visit to Germany, 74; BM confesses admiration for Germany to, 89; and BM's abandonment of British and French ties, 90; bourgeois lifestyle, 96; and AH's reception in Austria, 102; and result of AH's state visit, 125; BM boasts to of effect on AH, 142; and BM's reaction to AH's occupation of Czechoslovakia, 150; BM's relations with, 164; and BM's attendance at Brenner Pass meeting, 171; and BM's scorn for Italian people, 177; relationship with BM publicised, 226, 258; reunited with BM, 274; pleads for reconquest of Rome, 280; and BM's expectation of defeat, 283; and BM's reaction to AH assassination attempt, 283–4; and BM's summons to Wolf's Lair (July 1944), 283; shot with BM and body hanged in Milan, 288–9
Pétain, Marshal Philippe, 194
Philip, Prince of Hesse: as contact between AH and BM, 28, 82, 133, 137; visits BM in Italy (August 1936), 67; delivers AH messages to BM, 100–1, 103, 150; AH sends to Rome, 169; AH places under house arrest, 256
Phillips, William, 103
Phipps, Sir Eric, 64
Pietromarchi, Luca, 174
Pini, Giorgio, 83
Pistoia, Prince Filiberto, Duke of, 111, 115
Pius XI, Pope, 98, 127, 146
Pius XII, Pope: position, 2; suggests conference on Danzig and Italian claims on France, 154; condemns Soviet attack on Finland, 168; visits bomb victims in Rome, 247; silence on deportation of Jews, 272
Plessen, Johannes von, 166
Poland: non-aggression pact with Germany, 58; German plans to invade, 153–4, 158–60; Germans invade and occupy, 161, 164; Mutual Assistance agreement with Britain, 161; Jews repressed by Germans, 164
Police Treaty (Germany–Italy, 1936), 67, 106, 129
Popolo d'Italia, Il (newspaper): interviews AH (spring 1931), 29; Arnaldo Mussolini runs, 30; reviews *Mein Kampf*, 41; and BM's 1934 journey to Venice, 45; reports on Dante Association visit to Munich, 46; on BM's Venice speech, 51; justifies Night of Long Knives, 54; on second AH–BM meeting (September 1937), 76, 78, 88; on BM's belief in superiority of Fascism, 90; publishes protocol of 1938 meeting, 103; reports on AH's April 1938 visit, 109–10; obscures picture of

Victor Emmanuel, 114; on power of Italian navy, 118; pictures parade of troops, 119; on strength of Rome–Berlin axis, 134, 173, 175; BM article translated by German press, 135; on Italian military strength, 157; and Italian declaration of war, 184; reports June 1940 Munich meeting, 188; on AH–BM agreement on war with Britain, 192; on BM's welcome in South Tyrol, 213; on BM's military dress at Wolf's Lair meeting, 219; warns of British aim to exterminate Italians, 245; condemns Nazism, 565
Popular Culture, Ministry of (Italian): on AH–BM meetings, 77, 80, 89, 108–10, 139; reports on public opinion of AH's visit, 80; dismissive comment on AH, 82; on Chamberlain's visit to Rome, 148; on coffee shortage, 155; on German–Italian alliance, 157; instructs press to support Germany, 165, 173, 190, 192
Popular Front: in France and Spain, 67, 147, 152
Preziosi, Giovanni, 232
Primo de Rivera, General Miguel: admires BM, 21
Prussia: war with Austria (1866), 155
Puccini, Giacomo: 'Hymn to Rome', 80
Puntoni, Paolo, 246

Quartararo, Rosaria, 61
Quebec: Churchill–Roosevelt meeting (August 1943), 257

Raeder, Admiral Erich, 119
Rahn, Rudolf, 258, 262, 277, 283
Rainer, Friedrich, 262
Rastenburg *see* Wolf's Lair
Rathenau, Walther, 18
Reich Commissar for the Strengthening of German Volkssturm (Himmler), 216
Reichstag:
  elections: (1928), 26; (1930), 27–8; (1932), 33–4; (March 1933), 35; (November 1933), 40
  fire, 35
Renzetti, Major Giuseppe: influence, 28, 57; and AH's visits to BM, 31–4, 44; relations with AH, 34; on Italian support for Nazis, 35; complains to AH about offensive claims on Italy, 41; reports on 1934 Venice meeting, 52–3; on Röhm purge, 55; and AH's request for withdrawal of Cerruti, 63; attends lunch for BM's 1937 visit to Germany, 82
Republican Fascist party: Verona Congress (November 1943), 273
Reynolds, David, 7
Rhineland: Germany remilitarises (1936), 4, 65–6; Allied supervision of, 20
Ribbentrop, Anneliese von, 112, 115
Ribbentrop, Joachim von: as ambassador to London, 69; appointed foreign minister, 94; mutual dislike with Ciano, 94; and AH's state visit to Italy, 98–9, 116; Ciano presents counter-treaty to, 117; Attolico predicts Italy–Germany military alliance, 132; at Munich conference (1938), 141; report from Heydrich on distrust of Italy, 153; negotiates alliance with Ciano, 154–7; on invasion of Poland, 158; on prospective Italian territorial gains in war, 159; signs non-aggression pact with Molotov (1939), 160; telegram claiming strong Italo-German policy, 162; delivers AH's reply to BM, 169; asserts Italian commitment to supporting Germany, 174; at Munich meeting (June 1940), 187; at second Brenner Pass meeting (October 1940), 191; informs Italians of German designs on Romanian oilfields, 193; at Berghof meeting (January 1941), 203; confers with BM after Hess's flight to Scotland, 212; reassures Alfieri of positive German attitude towards Italians, 212; hopes to improve alliance with Italy, 227; prescribes further AH–BM meeting, 229; dismisses rumours of Italian–Allied peace negotiations, 235; on AH's private letter to BM on origins of Nazism, 240; Bastianini reassures of continuing alliance, 240; blames Italy for military misfortunes, 241; and rumour of ban on Germans wearing uniform in Rome, 244; refutes rumours of German putsch against Badoglio government, 255; meeting with Guariglia, 257; and deportation of Italian Jews, 272
Ricci, Renato, 280
Rintelen, Enno von, 128, 189, 200, 208, 229, 244, 248
Roatta, Mario, 187, 192
Robison, Carson: musical hits, 2
Rochat, Giorgio, 200

Rodogno, Davide, 14
Röhm, Ernst, 44, 54–5
Romania: German designs on oil, 192–3; joins Tripartite Pact, 198, 217; as wartime ally of Germany, 223, 243; joins Anti-Comintern Pact, 224; invaded by Soviet Union, 285
Rom Berlin Tokio (journal), 238
Rome: Fascist March on (1922), 18–20, 23, 265–6; BM stays in on return from 1937 German visit, 89; and AH's state visit, 97, 113, 116, 120–1; Germany sponsors archaeological work in, 120–1; Chamberlain invited for official visit, 147; bombed by Allies, 247; Jews deported, 272; falls to Allies, 280–1
Rommel, Field Marshal Erwin, 207–8, 210, 228, 244
Roosevelt, Franklin D.: meetings with Churchill, 10–11, 228, 230, 257; 'quarantine speech' (October 1937), 95; pleads for peace in Europe, 153–4; sends Sumner Welles on peace mission, 169; third election (1940), 195; relations with Churchill, 206, 218–19, 221, 274, 294; believes Italy dependent on Germany, 259
Rosenberg, Alfred: criticises lack of Fascist anti-Semitism, 24; visits Royal Italian Academy congress, 34; on AH's admiration for BM, 51; attends lunch for BM's 1937 visit to Germany, 82
Royal Institute of International Affairs (Chatham House, London), 221, 243
Royal Italian Academy: congress (1932), 34
RSI *see* Italian Social Republic
Ruhr: Franco-Belgian occupation (1923), 21–2
Runciman, Walter, 1st Viscount, 135

S., Cesare (of Calabria), 110
S., Rosa, 181
SA (*Sturm Abteilung*), 54
Salazar, António de Oliveira, 8
Salerno: Allied landings (September 1943), 268
Salò, 269, 278
Salzburg *see* Schloss Klessheim
San Marino, 259
Sauckel, Fritz, 263
Savoy, 236
Saxe-Coburg-Gotha, Carl-Eduard, Duke of, 104
Schieder, Wolfgang, 4, 70
Schleicher, General Kurt von, 54
Schloss Klessheim, near Salzburg, 229–30, 241–3, 276–9, 282
Schmidt, Paul, 81, 174, 196
Schreiber, Gerhard, 263
Schuschnigg, Kurt von, 100
Schwarze Korps, Das (SS newspaper), 79, 126, 270
SD (*Sicherheitsdienst*): on German anxiety about impending war, 133; public opinion reports, 199; on popular welcome of AH's 1941 speech, 206; on reception of BM's speeches, 207, 236; on German lack of interest in 1941 Brenner Pass meeting, 213; on hostile German view of Italian assistance in Russia, 216, 218; on AH's praise of Finns and Romanians as snub to Italy, 223; on German anti-Italian views, 243, 256, 261, 266; on effect of BM's fall, 251; and AH's speech on Italian capitulation, 261; describes BM as 'practically Reich governor', 267; on Germany losing faith in AH, 285
Sebastiani, Osvaldo, 76
Sei mesi di guerra (film), 177
Seldte, Franz, 34
Senise, Carmine, 238
Serena, Adelchi, 226
Shimazu, Naoko, 7
Sicily: Italy fails to control, 167; Allied invasion, 235, 244, 256
Sidi Barrani (Libya), 199
Silvestri, Carlo, 275
Skorzeny, Otto, 264
Slovakia: joins Tripartite Pact, 198; joins Anti-Comintern Pact, 224
Slovenia: Italy occupies and persecutes, 209
Social Democratic Party (Germany; *Sopade*), 79, 85, 133, 144
Solari, Pietro, 29
Somaliland, 61, 200
Sopade see Social Democratic Party
South Tyrol (Alto Adige): Italian claims to, 20–2, 26–8, 45, 103, 122, 124, 127, 154, 213; Germany prepared to recognise as Italian, 72, 78; BM's train travels through for 1937 visit to Germany, 77; and AH's state visit to Italy, 97; BM's reaction to German threat to invade, 104; AH crosses by train, 112; popular German attitude to, 144; resettlement proposals (1940), 170–1, 216, 226; AH announces plans to annex, 256; Germany controls, 262, 279

Soviet Russia: treaties of alliance and mutual assistance, 61; and Anti-Comintern Pact, 95, 155; non-aggression pact with Germany (1939), 160, 168, 174; partitions Poland with Germany, 164; Winter War with Finland (1939–40), 168; German plans to invade, 192, 194, 212; AH keeps BM uninformed of invasion, 204, 214; Germans invade (June 1941), 215–17; Italian troops fight in, 216–18, 232, 237; German casualties in, 229; strength, 233; BM proposes separate peace treaty with, 242; aircraft production, 245; German delay in invading, 293
Spain: Popular Front, 67; *see also* Franco, General Francisco
Spanish Civil War: and Italo-German relations, 5, 15, 81; Italy and Germany intervene in, 67; Italian volunteers in, 95–9, 131; Italian casualties in, 104
spazio vitale, 61, 95, 204, 210, 232
Speer, Albert, 84, 263
SS: eliminates SA, 54; protects AH and BM on visit to Berlin, 85
Stahlhelm: BM's relations with, 18, 28; allies with Nazis in Harzburg Front, 31
Stalin, Joseph V.: regime, 4, 10; at Tehran conference, 274
Stalingrad, 231, 237–8
Starace, Achille, 76, 82, 95, 111, 139, 167
Stauffenberg, Count Claus Schenk von, 283
Stefani (Italian news agency), 123, 221
Steinberg, Jonathan, 273
Stresa: 1935 meeting and front, 60–2, 95, 194
Stresemann, Gustav, 18
Strunk, Roland, 65
Sudetenland: BM promises to support AH over, 121; Germans in, 129–30; AH plans to annex, 130, 134–6; BM's role in crisis, 130–3, 135; popular Italian moderate views on, 143; seized by Germany, 144; *see also* Czechoslovakia
Suñer, Ramón Serrano, 191
Susmel brothers, 14
Suvich, Fulvio: attends 1934 Venice meeting, 45, 47, 52; demoted, 68
Svastic, La (journal), 217

Tacchi-Venturi, Pietro, SJ, 98
Taranto: British attack Italian navy at, 197
Teatro Adriano: BM gives speech on parallel war (1941), 206–7
Tedaldi, Adolfo, 20–1
Tehran conference (November–December 1943), 274
Tevere, Il (newspaper), 31
'Third Reich': coined as term by Bruck, 20
Times, The (newspaper), 26, 176, 231, 251
Tobruk, 204, 228–9
Tolomei, Ettore, 26
Toscano, Mario, 159
Trentino, 262
Trieste: BM speech in, 136; German advance on, 278
Tripartite Pact (Germany–Italy–Japan, 1940), 190, 198
Triple Alliance (Germany–Italy–Austria-Hungary), 75–6
Tripoli (Libya), 237–8
Tunis: falls to Allies, 243
Turin: BM's speech in (May 1939), 156; bombed by British, 189; industrial strikes, 238; hostility to Social Republican government, 285
Turkey: dictatorship under Atatürk, 23

Ukraine: war in, 222
Umberto I, King of Italy: AH visits grave, 118
United States of America: threatened by 1940 Tripartite Pact, 190; Germany and Italy declare war on, 224–5; Japanese attack at Pearl Harbor, 224–5; aircraft production, 245
Ustaše (Croatia), 209, 233

Valle, General Giuseppe, 167
Vallo del Littorio (alpine border defences), 103, 151, 170, 223
Vansittart, Sir Robert, 62
Vatican: AH avoids on state visit, 98; supports short war, 186; and prospective end to war, 235–6; suggests separate peace for Italy, 244; retains independence after German occupation of Italy, 259
Venice: AH and BM first meet in (14 June 1934), 43–52, 85, 90
Verdi, Giuseppe: *Aida*, 119
Versailles Treaty (1919): AH and BM aim to revise, 60, 66; and German rearmament, 62
Vichy France: AH attempts to persuade to cooperate against British, 194; Germans occupy, 236
Victor Emmanuel II, King of Italy: monument, 116, 118

Victor Emmanuel III, King of Italy: position as monarch, 2, 224; appoints BM prime minister, 18; Alfonso III visits, 21; receives telegram from AH on 1934 Venice meeting, 47; Germanophobia, 89; hosts AH state visit, 96, 99, 116, 118–19; welcomes AH on arrival for state visit, 113–14; telegram from AH on leaving Italy, 124; welcomes BM from Munich conference, 142; signs racial laws, 146; humiliates BM over AH's occupation of Prague, 150; speech emphasising peace, 152; congratulates AH on 50th birthday, 154; endorses Pact of Steel (1939), 157; reluctance to go to war, 166; hands over supreme command to BM, 167; telegram from BM about Brenner Pass meeting, 175; supports short war on Germany's side, 176; telegram from AH on Italian declaration of war, 184; importance of role increases, 235; supports BM, 236; asked to dismiss BM, 246, 248–9; fears German reprisals after BM's departure, 254–5; supports secret peace negotiations with Allies, 255; evacuates to Brindisi, 259; declares war on Germany, 268; BM criticises, 282, 286
Vidussoni, Aldo: appointed party secretary, 226; believes in military victory, 231–2; sacked, 238
Vienna: Ciano meets AH in (November 1940), 198; BM stops at on final flight to Germany, 264–5
Vienna Award, Second (August 1940), 192
Vita italiana (journal), 232
Vittorio Veneto, Battle of (1918), 51
Völkischer Beobachter: Göring contributes to, 25; on BM's endorsement of Nazi election successes, 28; on AH's flying to Italy, 45, 52; on AH's Venice visit, 45, 48; Strunk writes on Ethiopian campaign for, 65; on Ciano's 1936 mission to Germany, 69; on BM's 1937 visit, 74; on review of Italian troops in Rome, 119; on German victory in France, 188; on BM piloting AH's plane, 221; reports BM's 60th birthday, 252; accuses Badoglio of betrayal, 261, 266; on BM's rescue and liberation, 266, 275; on AH–BM plan to win war, 277
Volkssturm (German military contingent), 287
Volpi, Giuseppe, 47, 48

W., Ekkehard (stage painter), 107
Wagner, Richard, 48, 56
Wall Street Journal, 44
Watt, Donald Cameron, 71
Weimar Republic: established, 17; weakness, 25, 27, 30
Weiß, Wilhelm, 74
Weizsäcker, Ernst von, 81, 98, 117, 141, 171, 205, 229, 249
Welles, Sumner: peace mission (1940), 169, 171, 175
West Germany: anti-Italian myth, 292
Wiedemann, Fritz, 49
Willis, Fred, 75–6
Wilson, Woodrow, 9
Wirth, Joseph, 18
Wolff, Theodor, 27
Wolf's Lair (Rastenburg): assassination attempt on AH at, 1, 283–5; AH–BM meeting (August 1941), 219–20; AH–BM meeting (July 1944), 283–5

Yugoslavia: Germans invade and dismember, 209, 293

Zachariae, Dr Georg, 274, 277